Financial Accounting

Financial Accounting

THIRD EDITION

WALTER B. MEIGS, Ph.D., C.P.A.
Professor of Accounting
University of Southern California

ROBERT F. MEIGS, D.B.A.
Professor of Accounting
School of Accountancy
San Diego State University

McGRAW-HILL BOOK COMPANY

New York   St. Louis   San Francisco   Auckland   Bogotá   Düsseldorf
Johannesburg   London   Madrid   Mexico   Montreal   New Delhi   Panama
Paris   São Paulo   Singapore   Sydney   Tokyo   Toronto

Financial Accounting

67890 KPKP 8321

Library of Congress Cataloging in Publication Data

Meigs, Walter B.
    Financial accounting.

    1. Accounting. I. Meigs, Robert F., joint author.
II. Title.
HF5635.M492   1979   657   78-17818
ISBN 0-07-041220-0

This book was set in Vega by York Graphic Services, Inc.
The editors were Donald E. Chatham, Jr., Marjorie Singer,
Annette Hall, and M. Susan Norton;
the designer was Anne Canevari Green;
the cover painting was done by Glen Heller;
the production supervisor was Dennis J. Conroy.
Kingsport Press, Inc., was printer and binder.

Contents

The purpose and nature of accounting. A system for creating accounting information. Communicating accounting information—who uses accounting reports? Public accounting. Private accounting. Governmental accounting. Development of accounting standards—the FASB. Two primary business objectives. Accounting as the basis for business decisions. Internal control. Forms of business organization. Financial statements: the starting point in the study of accounting. The balance sheet. Assets. Accounting for inflation. Liabilities. Owners' equity. What is capital stock? The accounting equation. Effects of business transactions upon the balance sheet. Effects of business transactions upon the accounting equation. Use of financial statements by outsiders.

The use of "accounts" for recording transactions. The ledger. Debit and credit entries. Recording transactions in ledger accounts: illustration. Running balance form of ledger account. The normal balance of an account. Sequence and numbering of ledger accounts. Flow of information through the accounting system. The journal. Posting. The trial balance. Uses and limitations of the trial balance. Locating errors. Accounting records in perspective.

Profits: public image versus economic function. Retained earnings. Net income. Revenue. Expenses. Dividends. Matching revenue and expenses. Relating revenue and expenses to time periods. Rules of debit and credit for revenue and expenses. Ledger accounts for Greenhill Real Estate Company: illustration. Recording depreciation at the end of the period. The adjusted trial balance. Financial statements. The income statement. Statement of retained earnings. The balance sheet. Closing the accounts. After-closing trial balance. Sequence of accounting procedures. Dividends—declaration and payment. Accrual basis of accounting versus cash basis of accounting.

journal. The general journal. Subsidiary ledger accounts. Variations in special journals. Direct posting from invoices.

MECHANICAL ACCOUNTING SYSTEMS

Unit record for each transaction. Simultaneous preparation of documents, journals, and ledgers. Accounting machines. Punched cards and tabulating equipment.

EDP ACCOUNTING SYSTEMS

Elements of an EDP system. Hardware and software. Input devices. Output devices. Processing operations in the computer. Programs. Reliability of EDP systems. Accounting applications of the computer. Computer service centers and time-sharing. Do computers make decisions? Information systems.

SINGLE PROPRIETORSHIPS

Accounting for the owner's equity in a single proprietorship. Closing the accounts. Financial statements for a single proprietorship.

PARTNERSHIPS

Significant features of a partnership. Partnership accounting. Partnership profits and income taxes. Alternative methods of dividing partnership income.

CORPORATIONS

Advantages and disadvantages of the corporate form of organization. Formation of a corporation. Functions of the board of directors. Functions of corporate officers. Authorization and issuance of capital stock. Par value. No-par value stock. Preferred and common stock. Characteristics of preferred stock. The underwriting of stock issues. Market price of common stock. Stock issued for assets other than cash. Subscriptions to capital stock. Retained earnings or deficit. Special records of corporations. Income taxes in corporate financial statements. Balance sheet for a corporation illustrated.

Developing predictive information. Discontinued operations of a segment of a business. Extraordinary items. Other nonoperating gains and losses. Earnings per share (EPS). Primary and fully diluted earnings per share. Income statement for a corporation illustrated. Cash dividends. Dividend dates. Property and liquidating dividends. Stock dividends. Stock splits. Retained earnings. Prior period adjustments to the Retained Earnings account. Appropriations and restrictions of retained earnings. Statement of retained earnings. Treasury stock. Book value per share of common stock. Illustration of stockholders' equity section.

CASH
Balance sheet presentation. Management responsibilities relating to cash. Basic requirements for internal control over cash. Cash receipts. Cash disbursements. The voucher system. Petty cash. Bank checking accounts. The bank statement. Reconciling the bank account. Electronic funds transfer system (EFTS).

INVESTMENTS IN MARKETABLE SECURITIES
Reasons for investing in marketable securities. Securities exchanges. Determining the cost of investments in stocks and bonds. Gains and losses from sale of investments in securities. Balance sheet valuation of marketable securities. Lower of cost or market. The argument for valuation at market value. Presentation of marketable securities in financial statements. Investments for purposes of control. The equity method.

Accounts receivable. Uncollectible accounts. Reflecting uncollectible accounts in the financial statements. The allowance for doubtful accounts. Estimating uncollectible accounts expense. Writing off an uncollectible account receivable. Recovery of an account previously written off. Direct charge-off method of recognizing uncollectible accounts expense. Credit card sales. Analysis of accounts receivable. Notes receivable. Nature of interest. Accounting for notes receivable. Discounting notes receivable. Classification of receivables in the balance sheet. Current liabilities. Notes payable. Notes payable with interest included in the face amount. Discounts on notes payable. Comparison of the two forms of notes payable. The concept of present value applied to long-term notes. Installment receivables. Income tax aspects of installment sales.

Some basic questions relating to inventory. Inventory defined. Inventory valuation and the measurement of income. Importance of an accurate valuation of inventory. Taking a physical inventory. Pricing the inventory. Cost basis of inventory valuation. Inventory valuation methods. Consistency in the valuation

Preface

The environment of accounting is changing fast, and these environmental changes, such as continued inflation and the critical financial problems of many cities, affect the goals and the content of an introductory text in accounting. In order to function intelligently as a citizen, as well as in a business of any size or type, every individual needs more than ever before a clear understanding of basic accounting concepts. In this third edition, we have tried to reflect the impact of inflation on accounting measurements and to suggest the direction of needed changes in accounting concepts and methods. The importance of adequate disclosure in the system of financial reporting is stressed, and attention is drawn to the need for improved accounting controls in all sectors of society. We have emphasized the responsibility of the modern corporation to do an adequate job of financial reporting to investors and others outside the corporate entity. However, management's internal use of accounting data is by no means neglected.

This third edition of *Financial Accounting* is designed as a one-semester introduction to accounting. It is suitable for courses of three to four semester-hours' credit; or in the case of schools on the quarter system, for courses of four to six quarter-hours' credit. In these courses, instructors often recognize three general groups of students: those who stand at the threshold of preparation for a career in accounting, students of business administration who need a good understanding of accounting as an important element of the total business information system, and students from a variety of other disciplines who will find the ability to use and interpret accounting information a valuable accomplishment. During the process of revision we have tried to keep in mind the needs and interests of all three groups.

A new edition provides authors with an opportunity to add new material, to condense the coverage of topics that have declined in relative importance, to reorganize portions of the book to improve instructional efficiency, and to refine and polish the treatment of basic subject matter. We have tried to do all these things in this third edition.

New features of this edition

Among the many new features of this edition are:

1 A glossary at the end of each chapter, with concise explanations of key terms introduced or emphasized in that chapter.

2 An increase of over 30% in the number of questions, exercises, and problems throughout the book.

3 A discussion of the impact of inflation on the measurement of profits, on inventories, and on plant and equipment.

4 The concept of present value, presented in clear understandable terms, integrated into discussions of the valuation of assets and liabilities.

5 People-oriented problems which depict the hard decisions that must be made by men and women acting as managers, investors, and in other roles.

6 Increased attention to perpetual inventory systems.

7 Increased emphasis on internal control—how a business can strengthen its system of internal control.

8 Evaluation of corporate profits. Are they adequate? Are they reasonable? What are the appropriate yardsticks?

9 New emphasis on replacement cost and the implied move from historical cost to current-value accounting.

10 Careful integration into the text and problems of the pronouncements of the Financial Accounting Standards Board.

11 Attention to the increased activity of the SEC in establishing accounting standards.

12 An examination booklet, with test material arranged chapter by chapter for the entire text.

13 Improved format for supplementary materials. Partially filled-in working papers and practice sets appear in a new improved format, with wider rulings and printed in color.

Features carried forward from prior editions

Special qualities that are carried forward from prior editions include:

1 The only introductory accounting book that is part of an integrated series of introductory, intermediate, and advanced accounting textbooks with continuity of authorship. This established series concept provides assurance that students finishing the introductory course will be prepared to move readily into intermediate accounting without gaps or unnecessary overlaps.

2 Respect for the needs of the student. Topics are covered in a depth which will qualify the student for subsequent course work in accounting.

3 Provocative problems that raise a variety of interesting questions and carry the student far beyond routine drill.

4 Problem material developed and tested firsthand by the authors in their own classes for introductory accounting students.

5 A good blend of *(a)* the theoretical and conceptual aspects of accounting and *(b)* the realities of applying these concepts to everyday practical business situations.

New and extensively revised chapters

Chapter 5, "Merchandising Transactions and Internal Control," contains much new material. It explains the purpose and nature of internal control and illustrates the methods of achieving good internal control. Also discussed is the Foreign Corrupt Practices Act of 1977, which makes an adequate system of internal control legally mandatory. Chapter 8, dealing with such topics as earnings per share, extraordinary items, and discontinued operations, is extensively revised to emphasize the interpretation of this information by users of financial statements. The concepts of primary and fully diluted earnings per share are illustrated and discussed in clear understandable terms. Chapter 9 is updated to reflect the new position of the FASB with respect to the valuation of marketable equity securities. Alternative valuation models, including the use of market prices and the equity method, also are illustrated and discussed. Chapter 10, "Receivables and Payables," includes a discussion of the concept of present value in terms that students will find readily understandable. Chapter 11, on the subject of inventories, contains much new material on the impact of inflation upon the measurement of cost of goods sold and the valuation of inventories. The topic of inventory profits is related to recent official pronouncements pointing to the need for considering replacement costs when measuring the profit realized on sales transactions. Chapter 12, covering plant assets, presents the problems arising from an environment of inflation. Attention is focused on the rules issued by the SEC requiring large corporations to disclose the replacement cost of plant and equipment and to show what depreciation would amount to computed on a replacement cost basis. Chapter 13, on the subject of long-term liabilities, includes new up-to-date coverage of leases. Amortization of bond premium and discount is illustrated using both the straight-line and effective interest methods, and problem material is supplied covering both methods. Chapter 14, "Accounting Principles," pulls together the theoretical concepts covered in preceding chapters and gives further attention to the problems created by rising prices. The dramatic change in the position of many of the large international CPA firms which are now advocating current-value accounting as the wave of the future is related to the increasingly active role of the SEC. Chapter 16, "Analysis and Interpretation of Financial Statements," invites students to use the accounting expertise they have acquired to evaluate the adequacy or inadequacy of corporate profits in relation to sales volume, to total assets of the firm, to invested capital, and to other yardsticks. The last chapter, "Income Taxes and Business Decisions," is extensively revised to include the many recent changes in tax law affecting both individuals and corporations. Increased emphasis is given to tax planning and the impact of taxes upon business decisions.

Supplementary materials

A full assortment of supplementary materials accompanies this text:
1 A set of four *Achievement Tests* and a *Comprehensive Examination.* Each test covers three or four chapters; the Comprehensive Examination covers the entire text, and may be used as a final examination.

2 *An examination booklet.* With an abundance of test questions and exercises arranged chapter by chapter for the entire text, this examination booklet will be a most useful source for instructors who prefer to assemble their own examinations. The questions in this book are

printed in an $8\frac{1}{2}$ x 11 format on one side of a page. They can be torn out and copied to prepare individual examinations.

3 *A self-study guide.* Written by the authors of the textbook, the **Study Guide** enables students to measure their progress by immediate feedback. This self-study guide includes an outline of the most important points in each chapter, an abundance of objective questions, and several short exercises for each chapter. In the back of the self-study guide are answers to questions and solutions to exercises to help students evaluate their understanding of the subject. The self-study guide will also be useful in classroom discussions and for review by students before examinations.

4 *Working papers.* A soft-cover book of *partially filled-in working papers* for the problem material is published separately from the text. On these work sheets, the problem headings and some preliminary data have been entered to save students much of the mechanical pencil-pushing inherent in problem assignments. All the working papers are in a new improved format featuring wider money columns and the use of color

5 *Practice set.* The practice set available with the preceding edition has been completely revised and appears in convenient bound form with improved format. It is designed for use after covering the first six chapters of the book.

6 *Checklist of key figures for problems.* This list appears on the front and back inside covers of this book. The purpose of the checklist is to aid students in verifying their problem solutions and in discovering their own errors.

7 *Transparencies of problem solutions.* This is a visual aid prepared by the publisher for the instructor who wishes to display in a classroom the complete solutions to problems.

   In the development of problem material for this book, special attention has been given to the inclusion of problems of varying length and difficulty. By referring to the time estimates, difficulty ratings, and problem descriptions in the *Solutions Manual,* instructors can choose problems that best fit the level, scope, and emphasis of the course they are offering.

8 *Additional transparencies for classroom illustrations.* Sixteen special transparencies have been produced for use in the classroom to illustrate such concepts as closing entries, the preparation of a work sheet, and the use of special journals, subsidiary ledgers, and controlling accounts. These transparencies contain original material and do not duplicate illustrations contained in the text.

9 *A booklet of learning objectives.* This brief statement of learning objectives for each chapter is designed to focus the student's attention on key principles and procedures. A clear understanding of these points will be especially helpful in directing attention to the most fundamental concepts in each chapter.

Contributions by others

We want to express our sincere thanks to the many users of preceding editions who offered helpful suggestions for this edition. Especially helpful was the advice received from Professors Larry P. Bailey, Temple University; Francis A. Bird, University of Richmond; Harold L. Cannon, State University of New York; Victoria L. Carvey, Indiana University; Harold Cook, Central Michigan University; Larry Godwin, Oregon State University; William C. Lins, Rutgers University; Frank C. Lordi, Widener College; Lawrence H. Malchman, Northeastern University; G. Kenneth Nelson, Pennsylvania State University; Richard A. Samuelson, San Diego State University; R. W. Schneider, Winona State University; and Edwin E. Thele, University of Wisconsin.

Special thanks go to Professors Robert K. Eskew, Purdue University and Ira E. Steele, George Mason University for assisting us in the proof stages of this edition by reviewing the end-of-chapter problem material and text examples for accuracy.

The assistance of Richard Fell, Barbara Freeman, Robert Graziano, and Paul Kidman was most helpful in preparation of the manuscript.

We acknowledge with appreciation permission from the American Institute of Certified Public Accountants to quote from many of its pronouncements. All quotations are copyrighted by the American Institute of Certified Public Accountants.

We also are grateful to the Financial Accounting Standards Board which granted us permission to quote from FASB Statements, Discussion Memoranda, Interpretations, and Exposure Drafts. All quotations are copyrighted © by the Financial Accounting Standards Board, High Ridge Park, Stamford, Connecticut 06905, U.S.A., and are reprinted with permission. Copies of the complete documents are available from the FASB.

WALTER B. MEIGS
ROBERT F. MEIGS

1 Accounting: The Language of Business

What is accounting? Many people think of accounting as a highly technical field which can be understood only by professional accountants. Actually, nearly everyone practices accounting in one form or another on an almost daily basis. Accounting is the art of measuring, communicating, and interpreting financial activity. Whether you are preparing a household budget, balancing your checkbook, preparing your income tax return, or running General Motors, you are working with accounting concepts and accounting information.

Accounting has often been called the "language of business." In recent years, corporate profits have become a topic of considerable public interest. What are "corporate profits"? What levels of corporate profits are necessary to finance the development of new products, new jobs, and economic growth? One cannot hope to answer such questions without understanding the accounting concepts and terms involved in the measurement of income.

Since a language is a means of social communication, it is logical that a language should change to meet the changing needs of society. In accounting, too, changes and improvements are continually being made. For example, as society has become increasingly interested in measuring the profitability of business organizations, accounting concepts and techniques have been changing to make such measurements more meaningful and more reliable.

We live in an era of accountability. Although accounting has made its most dramatic progress in the field of business, the accounting function is vital to every unit of our society. Individuals must account for their income. Large corporations are accountable to their stockholders, to governmental agencies, and to the public. The federal government, the states, the cities, the school districts: all must use accounting as a basis for controlling their resources and measuring their accomplishments. Accounting is equally essential to the successful operation of a business, a university, a fraternity, a social program, or a city.

In every election the voters must make decisions at the ballot box on issues involving accounting concepts; therefore, some knowledge of accounting is needed by all citizens if they are to act intelligently in meeting the challenges of our society. The objective of this text is to help you develop your knowledge of accounting and your ability to use accounting information in making economic decisions.

THE PURPOSE AND NATURE OF ACCOUNTING

The underlying purpose of accounting is to provide financial information about an economic entity. In this book the economic entity which we shall be concentrating upon is a business enterprise. The financial information provided by an accounting system is needed by managerial decision makers to help them plan and control the activities of the economic entity. Financial information is also needed by *outsiders*—owners, creditors, potential investors, the government, and the public—who have supplied money to the business or who have some other interest in the business that will be served by information about its financial position and operating results.

A system for creating accounting information

In order to provide useful financial information about a business enterprise, we need some means of keeping track of the daily business activities and then summarizing the results in accounting reports. The methods used by a business to keep records of its financial activities and to summarize these activities in periodic accounting reports comprise the *accounting system.*

The first function of an accounting system is to create a systematic record of the daily business activity, in terms of money. For example, goods and services are purchased and sold, credit is extended to customers, debts are incurred, and cash is received and paid out. These *transactions* are typical of business events which can be expressed *in monetary terms,* and must be entered in accounting records. The *recording* process may be performed in many ways: that is, by writing with pen or pencil, by printing with mechanical or electronic equipment, or by punching holes or making magnetic impressions on cards or tape.

Of course, not all business events can be measured and described in monetary terms. Therefore, we do not show in the accounting records the appointment of a new chief executive or the signing of a labor contract, except as these happenings in turn affect future business transactions.

In addition to compiling a narrative record of events as they occur, we *classify* transactions and events into related groups or categories. Classification enables us to reduce a mass of detail into compact and usable form. For example, grouping all transactions in which cash is received or paid out is a logical step in developing useful information about the cash position of a business enterprise.

To organize accounting information in a useful form, we *summarize* the classified information into accounting reports designed to meet the information needs of business decision makers.

These three steps we have described—recording, classifying, and summarizing—are the means of creating accounting information. It is important, however, to recognize that the accounting process is not limited to the function of *creating* information. It also involves *communicating* this information to interested parties and *interpreting* accounting information as it relates to specific business decisions.

Communicating accounting information—
Who uses accounting reports?

An accounting system must provide information to managers and also to a number of outsiders who have an interest in the financial activities of the business enterprise. The major types of accounting reports which are developed by the accounting system of a business enterprise and the parties receiving this information are illustrated in the following diagram:

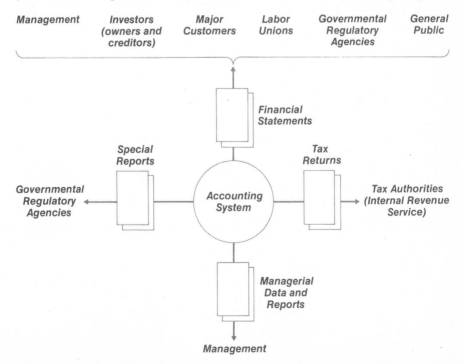

Accounting information is user-oriented

The parties receiving accounting reports are termed the *users* of accounting information. The type of information that a specific user will require depends upon the kinds of decisions that information user must make. For example, managers need detailed information about daily operating costs for the purpose of controlling the operations of the business and setting reasonable selling prices. Outsiders, on the other hand, usually require summarized information concerning resources on hand and information on operating results to use in making investment decisions, levying income taxes, or making regulatory decisions.

Since the information needs of various users differ, it follows that the accounting system of a business entity must be able to provide various types of accounting reports. The information in these reports must be presented in accordance with certain "ground rules" and assumptions, so that users of the reports will be able to interpret the information properly. For example, if a report indicates that a business owns land with an accounting value of $90,000, what does this dollar amount represent? Is it the original cost of the land to the business, the current market value of the land, or the assessed value for purposes of levying property taxes? Obviously the user of any accounting report needs to understand the standards and assumptions which have been used in preparing that report. In turn, the standards employed in the preparation of an accounting report must relate to the information needs of the user.

FINANCIAL STATEMENTS Among the most important types of accounting reports are financial statements. Financial statements are useful to management and also are the main source of financial information to parties outside the business enterprise. These statements are concise, perhaps only three or four pages for a large business. They summarize the business transactions of a specific time period such as a month or a year. Financial statements show the *financial position* of the business at the time of the report and the *operating results* by which it arrived at this position.

The basic purpose of financial statements is to assist decision makers in evaluating the financial strength, profitability, and future prospects of the business entity. Thus, managers, investors, major customers, and labor all have a direct interest in these reports. Every large corporation prepares annual financial statements which are distributed to all owners of the business. In addition, these statements may be filed with various governmental agencies.

One governmental agency with a particular interest in corporate financial statements is the *Securities and Exchange Commission* (SEC). The SEC establishes requirements regarding the content and reporting standards used in financial statements, and all large corporations must file with the SEC annual financial statements meeting these requirements. Financial statements filed with the SEC are available to the general public. Thus, the

SEC is the governmental agency which regulates the extent and the fairness of accounting disclosures made by large corporations to the public.

The accounting concepts, measurement techniques, and standards of presentation used in the preparation of financial statements are called *generally accepted accounting principles.* These principles continually change and evolve in response to changes in the business environment.

Developing accounting information in conformity with generally accepted accounting principles is called *financial accounting,* because this information is designed to summarize the financial position and operating results of a business entity. In this text we shall emphasize financial accounting concepts rather than income tax rules, reports to regulatory agencies, or internal reports to management. As we shall see, financial accounting concepts apply to all types and sizes of business organizations. These concepts are useful to decision makers in both business and government in evaluating a wide range of economic issues.

TAX RETURNS The Internal Revenue Service, as well as certain state and local tax authorities, requires businesses and individuals to file annual tax returns designed to measure taxable income. *Taxable income* is a legal concept defined by laws originating in Congress (or in state legislatures). Since Congress uses the income tax laws to achieve various social objectives as well as to finance the government, income tax laws are frequently modified or changed. Thus the rules used in preparing income tax returns may vary from one year to the next. In general, however, there is a close parallel between income tax laws and financial accounting concepts.

Businesses also must file tax returns for state and federal payroll taxes, federal excise taxes, and state sales taxes. The form and content of these reports is determined by the rules of the specific tax agency involved.

MANAGERIAL DATA AND REPORTS In addition to financial statements, management needs much detailed accounting data to assist it in planning and controlling the daily operations of the business. Management also needs specialized information for long-range planning and for major decisions such as the introduction of a new product or the closing of an older plant.

Determining the types of information most relevant to specific managerial decisions, and interpreting that information, is called *managerial accounting.* Although we shall discuss many uses of accounting information by managers, a more detailed study of managerial accounting is often the subject of a second course in accounting.

REPORTS TO REGULATORY AGENCIES The activities of many business enterprises are regulated by various governmental agencies. For example, the Civil Aeronautics Board regulates the fares charged by most airlines, as well as specifying the areas to be serviced and the frequency of flights. The rates charged by companies which provide electricity, gas, water, and other public utilities usually are regulated by state utilities commissions.

Regulatory agencies often require special types of accounting information specifically tailored to their needs. For example, a state utilities commission making a decision as to whether to allow a rate increase by an electric company might request information about the cost to that company of producing electricity, the company's need to accumulate funds to provide service to outlying areas, and trends in population growth. In large part, however, reports to regulatory agencies are based upon generally accepted accounting principles.

Using accounting information

Accounting extends beyond the process of creating records and reports. The ultimate objective of accounting is the *use* of this information, its analysis and interpretation. Accountants are always concerned with the significance of the figures they have produced. They look for meaningful relationships between events and financial results; they study the effect of various alternatives; and they search for significant trends that may throw some light on what will happen in the future.

Interpretation and analysis are not the sole province of the accountant. If managers, investors, and creditors are to make effective use of accounting information, they too must have some understanding of how the figures were put together and what they mean. An important part of this understanding is to recognize clearly the limitations of accounting reports. A business manager, an investor, or a creditor who lacks an understanding of accounting may fail to appreciate the extent to which accounting information is based upon *estimates* rather than upon precisely accurate measurements.

THE DISTINCTION BETWEEN ACCOUNTING AND BOOKKEEPING Persons with little knowledge of accounting may also fail to understand the difference between accounting and bookkeeping. *Bookkeeping* means the recording of transactions, the record-making phase of accounting. The recording of transactions tends to be mechanical and repetitive; it is only a small part of the field of accounting and probably the simplest part. *Accounting* includes the design of accounting systems, preparation of financial statements, audits, cost studies, development of forecasts, income tax work, computer applications to accounting processes, and the analysis and interpretation of accounting information as an aid to making business decisions. A person might become a reasonably proficient bookkeeper in a few weeks or months; to become a professional accountant, however, requires several years of study and experience.

The work of accountants

Accountants tend to specialize in a given subarea of the discipline just as do attorneys and members of other professions. In terms of career opportunities, the field of accounting may be divided into three broad areas: (*1*) the public accounting profession, (*2*) private accounting, and (*3*) governmental accounting.

Public accounting

Certified public accountants are independent professional persons comparable to attorneys or physicians, who offer accounting services to clients for a fee. The *CPA certificate* is a license to practice granted by the state on the basis of a rigorous examination and evidence of practical experience. All states require that candidates pass an examination prepared and administered on a national basis twice each year by the American Institute of Certified Public Accountants. Requirements as to education and practical experience differ somewhat among the various states.

AUDITING The principal function of CPAs is auditing. How do people outside a business entity—owners, creditors, government officials, and other interested parties—know that the financial statements prepared by a company's management are reliable and complete? In large part, these outsiders rely upon *audits* performed by a CPA firm which is *independent* of the company issuing the financial statements.

   To perform an audit of a business, a firm of certified public accountants makes a careful review of the accounting system and gathers evidence both from within the business and from outside sources. This evidence enables the CPA firm to express its professional *opinion* as to the fairness and reliability of the financial statements. Persons outside the business, such as bankers and investors who rely upon financial statements for information, attach great importance to the annual *audit report* by the CPA firm. The *independent* status of a CPA firm retained to make an annual audit is just as important as its technical competence in assuring outsiders that the financial statements prepared by management disclose all relevant information and provide a fair picture of the company's financial position and operating results.

TAX SERVICES An important element of decision making by business executives is consideration of the income tax consequences of each alternative course of action. The CPA is often called upon for "tax planning," which will show how a future transaction such as the acquisition of new equipment may be arranged in a manner that will hold income taxes to a minimum amount. The CPA is also frequently retained to prepare the federal and state income tax returns. To render tax services, the CPA must have extensive knowledge of tax statutes, regulations, and court decisions, as well as a thorough knowledge of accounting.

MANAGEMENT ADVISORY SERVICES Auditing and income tax work have been the traditional areas of expertise for CPA firms, but the field of management advisory services has recently become a rapidly growing new area. When a CPA firm during the course of an audit discovers problems in a client's business, it is natural for the CPAs to make suggestions for corrective action. In response, the client often engages the CPAs to make a thorough investigation of the problem and to recommend new policies and precedures needed for a solution.

Public accounting firms gradually found themselves becoming more involved in management consulting work. Although this work often concerned accounting and financial matters, sometimes it dealt with organizational structure, statistical research, and a wide variety of problems not closely related to accounting. In recent years many CPA firms have created separate management advisory service departments which are staffed with mathematicians, industrial engineers, and other specialists as well as accountants. The experience, reputation, and independence of the CPA firms have placed them in an advantageous position to render advisory services to management over a broad range of administrative and operating problems. For example, these services might include study of the desirability of a merger with another company, the creation of a pension plan for employees, or the researching of a foreign market for the company's products.

Private accounting

In contrast to the CPA in public practice who serves many clients, an accountant in private industry is employed by a single enterprise. The chief accounting officer of a medium-sized or large business is usually called the *controller,* in recognition of the fact that one of the primary uses of accounting data is to aid in controlling business operations. The controller manages the work of the accounting staff. He or she is also a part of the top management team charged with the task of running the business, setting its objectives, and seeing that these objectives are met.

The accountants in a private business, large or small, must record transactions and prepare periodic financial statements from accounting records. Within this area of general accounting, a number of specialized phases of accounting have developed. Among the more important of these are:

DESIGN OF ACCOUNTING SYSTEMS Although the same basic accounting principles are applicable to all types of businesses, each enterprise requires an individually tailored *financial information system.* This system includes accounting forms, records, instruction manuals, flow charts, and reports to fit the particular needs of the business. Designing an accounting system and putting it into operation are thus specialized phases of accounting. With the advent of electronic data processing equipment, the problems that arise in creating an effective financial information system have become increasingly complex. However, computers compile information that would be too costly to gather by hand methods and also increase the speed with which reports can be made available to management.

COST ACCOUNTING Knowing the cost of a particular product, a manufacturing process, or any business operation is vital to the efficient management of a business. The phase of accounting particularly concerned with collecting and interpreting cost data is called *cost accounting.* Determining the cost of anything is not as simple as it appears at first glance, because the term *cost* has many meanings and different kinds of costs are useful for different purposes.

FINANCIAL FORECASTING A financial forecast (or budget) is a plan of financial operations for some future period, expressed in monetary terms. By using a forecast, management is able to make comparisons between *planned operations* and the *actual results achieved.* A forecast is thus an attempt to preview operating results before the actual transactions have taken place. A forecast is a particularly valuable tool for the controller because it provides each division of the business with a specific goal, and because it gives management a means of measuring the efficiency of performance throughout the company.

TAX ACCOUNTING As income tax rates have gone up and the determination of taxable income has become more complex, both internal accountants and independent public accountants have devoted more time to problems of taxation. Although many companies rely largely on CPA firms for tax planning and the preparation of income tax returns, larger companies also maintain their own tax departments.

INTERNAL AUDITING Most large corporations maintain staffs of *internal auditors* with the responsibility of evaluating the efficiency of operations and determining whether company policies are being followed consistently in all divisions of the corporation. The internal auditor, in contrast to the independent auditor or CPA, is not responsible for determining the overall fairness of the company's annual financial statements.

Governmental accounting

Government officials rely on financial information to help them direct the affairs of their agencies just as do the executives of private corporations. Many governmental accounting problems are similar to those applicable to private industry. In other respects, however, accounting for governmental affairs requires a somewhat different approach because the objective of earning a profit is absent from public affairs. Universities, hospitals, churches, and other not-for-profit institutions also follow a pattern of accounting that is similar to governmental accounting.

INTERNAL REVENUE SERVICE One of the governmental agencies which perform extensive accounting work is the Internal Revenue Service (IRS). The IRS handles the millions of income tax returns filed by individuals and corporations, and frequently performs auditing functions relating to these income tax returns and the accounting records on which they are based. Also, the IRS has been called upon to administer certain temporary economic controls, such as wage and price controls. These temporary controls have involved extensive and complex financial reporting by businesses, followed by review and audit by the IRS.

SECURITIES AND EXCHANGE COMMISSION Another governmental agency greatly involved in accounting is the Securities and Exchange Commission. The SEC reviews the financial statements of corporations which offer securities for sale to the public. In addition, the SEC has the legal power to require specific accounting methods and standards of financial disclosure for these companies.

Other governmental agencies employ accountants to prepare budgets and to audit the accounting records of various governmental departments and of private businesses which hold government contracts. Every agency of government at every level (federal, state, and local) must have accountants to carry out its responsibilities.

Development of accounting standards—the FASB

Research to develop accounting principles and practices which will keep pace with changes in the economic and political environment is a major activity of professional accountants and accounting educators. In the United States four groups which have been influential in the improvement of financial reporting and accounting practices are the American Institute of Certified Public Accountants, the Financial Accounting Standards Board, the Securities and Exchange Commission, and the American Accounting Association. Of special importance in establishing generally accepted accounting principles is the Financial Accounting Standards Board, known as the FASB. The FASB consists of seven full-time members, including representatives from public accounting, industry, and accounting education. In addition to conducting extensive research, the FASB issues Statements of Financial Accounting Standards, which represent authoritative expressions of generally accepted accounting principles.

Note that the FASB is part of the private sector of the economy and not a government agency. The development of accounting standards in the United States has traditionally been carried on in the private sector although the government, acting through the SEC, has exercised great influence on the FASB and other groups concerned with accounting research and standards of financial reporting.

The contribution of the FASB and the other groups mentioned above will be considered in later chapters. At this point we merely want to emphasize that accounting is not a closed system or a fixed set of rules, but a constantly evolving body of knowledge. As we explore accounting principles and related practices in this book, you will become aware of certain problems and conflicts for which fully satisfactory answers are yet to be developed. The need for further research is apparent despite the fact that present-day American accounting practices and standards of financial reporting are by far the best achieved anywhere at any time.

Two primary business objectives

The management of every business must keep foremost in its thinking two primary objectives. The first is to earn a profit. The second is to stay solvent, that is, to have on hand sufficient funds to pay debts as they fall due. Profits and solvency are of course not the only objectives of business managers. There are many others, such as providing jobs for people, protecting the environment, creating new and improved products, and providing more goods and services at a lower cost. It is clear, however, that a business cannot hope to accomplish these things unless it meets the two basic tests of survival—operating profitably and staying solvent.

A business is a collection of resources committed by an individual or group of individuals, who hope that the investment will increase in value. Investment in any given business, however, is only one of a number of alternative investments available. If a business does not earn as great a profit as might be obtained from alternative investments, its owners will be well-advised to sell or terminate the business and invest elsewhere. A business that continually operates at a loss will eventually exhaust its resources and be forced out of existence. Therefore, in order to operate successfully and to survive, the owners or managers of an enterprise must direct the business in such a way that it will earn a reasonable profit.

Business concerns that have sufficient funds to pay their debts promptly are said to be *solvent.* In contrast, a company that finds itself unable to meet its obligations as they fall due is called *insolvent.* Solvency must also be ranked as a primary objective of any enterprise, because a business that becomes insolvent may be forced by its creditors to stop operations and end its existence.

Accounting as the basis for business decisions

How do business executives know whether a company is earning profits or incurring losses? How do they know whether the company is solvent or insolvent, and whether it will probably be solvent, say, a month from today? The answer to both these questions in one word is *accounting.*

Accounting is the process by which the profitability and solvency of a company can be measured. Accounting also provides information needed as a basis for making business decisions that will enable management to guide the company on a profitable and solvent course.

Stated simply, managing a business is a matter of deciding what should be done, seeing to it that the means are available, and getting people employed in the business to do it. At every step in this process management is faced with alternatives, and every decision to do something or to refrain from doing something involves a choice. Successful managers must make the right choice when "the chips are down." In most cases the probability that a good decision will be made depends on the amount and validity of the information that the manager has about the alternatives and their consequences. However, it is seldom that all the information needed is either available or obtainable. Often a crystal ball in good working order would be helpful. As a practical matter, however, information which flows from the accounting records, or which can be developed by special analysis of accounting data, constitutes the basis on which a wide variety of business decisions should be made.

For specific examples of these decisions, consider the following questions. What price should the firm set on its products? If production is increased, what effect will this have on the cost of each unit produced? Will it be necessary to borrow from the bank? How much will costs increase if a pension plan is established for employees? Is it more profitable to produce and sell product A or product B? Shall a given part be made or be bought from suppliers? Should an investment be made in new equipment? All these issues call for decisions that should depend, in part at least, upon accounting information. It might be reasonable to turn the question around and ask: What business decisions could be intelligently made without the use of accounting information? Examples would be hard to find.

In large-scale business undertakings such as the manufacture of automobiles or the operation of nationwide chains of retail stores, and even in enterprises much smaller than these, the top executives cannot possibly have close physical contact with and knowledge of the details of operations. Consequently, these executives must depend to an even greater extent than the small business owner upon information provided by the accounting system.

We have already stressed that accounting is a means of measuring the results of business transactions and of communicating financial information. In addition, the accounting system must provide the decision maker with *predictive information* for making important business decisions in a changing world.

Internal control

Throughout this book, the fact that business decisions of all types are based at least in part on accounting data is emphasized. Management, therefore, needs assurance that the accounting data it receives are accurate and dependable. This assurance is provided in large part by developing a strong system of *internal control.* A basic principle of internal control is that no one person should handle all phases of a transaction from beginning to end. When business operations are so organized that two or more employees are required to participate in every transaction, the possibility of fraud is reduced and the work of one employee gives assurance of the accuracy of the work of another.

A system of internal control comprises all the measures taken by an organization for the purpose of (*1*) protecting its resources against waste, fraud, and inefficiency; (*2*) ensuring accuracy and reliability in accounting and operating data; (*3*) securing compliance with company policies; and (*4*) evaluating the level of performance in all divisions of the company.

A CPA firm in conducting an audit of a company will evaluate the adequacy of internal control in each area of the company's operations. The stronger the system of internal control, the more confidence the CPA can place in the integrity of the company's financial statements and accounting records. Consequently, the audit work can be performed more rapidly, with less detailed investigation of transactions, when internal controls are strong. The internal auditors also regard the study of internal control as a major part of their work. If internal controls are weak, the usual consequences are waste, fraud, inefficiency, and unprofitable operations.

Forms of business organization

A business enterprise may be organized as a *single proprietorship,* a *partnership,* or a *corporation.*

SINGLE PROPRIETORSHIP   A business owned by one person is called a single proprietorship. Often the owner also acts as the manager. This form of business organization is common for small retail stores and service enterprises, for farms, and for professional practices in law, medicine, and public accounting. From a legal viewpoint the business and its owner are not separate entities. From an accounting viewpoint, however, the business is an entity separate from the proprietor.

PARTNERSHIP   A business owned by two or more persons voluntarily associated as partners is called a partnership. Partnerships, like single proprietorships, are widely used for small businesses and professional practices. As in the case of a single proprietorship, a partnership is not legally an entity separate from its owners; consequently, a partner is personally responsible for the debts of the partnership. From an accounting standpoint, however, a partnership is a business entity separate from the personal activities of the partners.

CORPORATION A business incorporated under the laws of one of the 50 states is called a corporation, and its owners are identified as *stockholders.* Ownership of a corporation is evidenced by shares of *capital stock* which can be sold by one investor to another. Persons wanting to form a corporation must file an application with state officials for a corporate charter. When the application for a charter has been approved, it is referred to as the *articles of incorporation.* After payment of an incorporation fee to the state and approval of the articles of incorporation by the designated state official, the corporation comes into existence as a *legal entity separate from its owners.* The owners (who are now called stockholders) hold a meeting to elect a board of directors. The directors in turn appoint the officers of the corporation who serve as the active managers of the business. Capital stock certificates are issued to the owners (stockholders), and the formation of the corporation is complete.

Nearly all large businesses and many small ones are organized as corporations. The dominant role of the corporation in our economy is based on such advantages as the ease of gathering large amounts of money for use in the business, transferability of shares of ownership, limited liability of owners, and continuity of existence. Because the corporation is legally an entity separate from its owners, the stockholders are not personally liable for the debts of the business. Thus, the stockholders' liability for any losses incurred by an unsuccessful corporation is limited to the amount they have invested in acquiring shares of capital stock.

Accounting principles apply to all three forms of business organization, but are most carefully defined to aid corporations in making satisfactory financial reports to public investors. In this book we shall use the corporate form of organization as our basic model, along with some specific references to single proprietorships and partnerships.

FINANCIAL STATEMENTS: THE STARTING POINT IN THE STUDY OF ACCOUNTING

The preparation of financial statements is not the first step in the accounting process, but it is a convenient point to begin the study of accounting. The financial statements are the means of conveying to management and to interested outsiders a concise picture of the profitability and financial position of the business. Since these financial statements are in a sense the end product of the accounting process, the student who acquires a clear understanding of the content and meaning of financial statements will be in an excellent position to appreciate the purpose of the earlier steps of recording and classifying business transactions.

The two most widely used financial statements are the **balance sheet** and the **income statement**.[1] Together, these two statements (perhaps a page each in length) summarize all the information contained in the hundreds or thousands of pages comprising the detailed accounting records of a business. In this introductory chapter and in Chapter 2, we shall explore the nature of the balance sheet, or statement of financial position, as it is sometimes called. Once we have become familiar with the form and arrangement of the balance sheet and with the meaning of technical terms such as **assets, liabilities,** and **owners' equity,** it will be as easy to read and understand a report on the financial position of a business as it is for an architect to read the blueprint of a proposed building. (We shall discuss the income statement in Chapter 3.)

The balance sheet

The purpose of a balance sheet is to show the financial position of a business **at a particular date.** Every business prepares a balance sheet at the end of the year, and most companies prepare one at the end of each month. A balance sheet consists of a listing of the assets and liabilities of a business and of the owners' equity. The following balance sheet portrays the financial position of the Westside Cleaning Company at December 31.

WESTSIDE CLEANING COMPANY
Balance Sheet
December 31, 19___

	Assets		*Liabilities & Stockholders' Equity*		
	Cash	$ 19,500	Liabilities:		
	Accounts receivable	9,000	Notes payable		$ 22,000
	Supplies	500	Accounts payable		12,000
	Land	21,000	Income taxes payable		6,000
	Building	44,500	Total liabilities		$ 40,000
	Cleaning equipment	13,000	Stockholders' equity:		
	Delivery equipment	7,500	Capital stock	$60,000	
			Retained earnings	15,000	75,000
		$115,000			$115,000

Balance sheet shows financial position at a specific date

Note that the balance sheet sets forth in its heading three items: (1) the name of the business, (2) the name of the financial statement "Balance Sheet," and (3) the date of the balance sheet. Below the heading is the body of the balance sheet, which consists of three distinct sections: assets, liabilities, and stockholders' equity. The remainder of this chapter is largely devoted to making clear the nature of these three sections.

[1] A third financial statement, called a *statement of changes in financial position,* will be discussed in Chapter 15.

We can tell from the illustrated balance sheet that Westside Cleaning Company is a corporation, because the ownership section is listed as *stockholders' equity* and shows that capital stock of $60,000 has been issued. A corporation is the only form of business organization which issues capital stock, or in which the owners are called stockholders.

THE BUSINESS ENTITY The illustrated balance sheet refers only to the financial affairs of the business entity known as Westside Cleaning Company and not to the personal financial affairs of the owners. Individual stockholders may have personal bank accounts, homes, automobiles, and investments in other businesses; but since these personal belongings are not part of the cleaning company business, they are not included in the balance sheet of this business unit.

In brief, *a business entity is an economic unit which enters into business transactions that must be recorded, summarized, and reported.* The entity is regarded as separate from its owner or owners; the entity owns its own property and has its own debts. Consequently, for each business entity, there should be a separate set of accounting records. A balance sheet and an income statement are intended to portray the financial position and the operating results of a single business entity. If the owners were to intermingle their personal affairs with the transactions of the business, the resulting financial statements would be misleading and would fail to describe clearly the activities of the business entity.

Assets

Assets are economic resources which are owned by a business and are expected to benefit future operations. Assets may have definite physical form such as buildings, machinery, or merchandise. On the other hand, some assets exist not in physical or tangible form but in the form of valuable legal claims or rights; examples are amounts due from customers, investments in government bonds, and patent rights.

One of the most basic, and at the same time most controversial, problems in accounting is the assignment of dollar values to the assets of a business. Two kinds of assets cause little difficulty. Cash and amounts due from customers represent assets that either are available for expenditure or will be in the near future (when the customers pay their accounts). The amount of cash on hand is a clear statement of the dollars that are available for expenditure. The amount that customers owe the business (after taking into account that some receivables may prove uncollectible) represents the dollars that will be received in the near future.

THE COST PRINCIPLE Assets such as land, buildings, merchandise, and equipment represent economic resources that will be used in producing income for the business. The prevailing accounting view is that such assets should be accounted for on the basis of the dollars that have been invested in these resources, that is, the **historical cost** incurred in acquiring such property or property rights. In recording a business transaction, it is the transaction price that establishes the accounting value for the property or service received. In accounting terms, therefore, the "value" or "valuation" of an asset ordinarily means the cost of that asset to the entity owning it.

For example, let us assume that a business buys a tract of land for use as a building site, paying $40,000 in cash. The amount to be entered in the accounting records as the value of the asset will be the cost of $40,000. If we assume a booming real estate market, a fair estimate of the market value of the land 10 years later might be $100,000. Although the market price or economic value of the land has risen greatly, the accounting value as shown in the accounting records and on the balance sheet would continue unchanged at the cost of $40,000. This policy of accounting for assets at their original cost is often referred to as the **cost principle** of accounting.

In reading a balance sheet, it is important to bear in mind that the dollar amounts listed **do not** indicate the prices at which the assets could be sold, nor the prices at which they could be replaced. One useful generalization to be drawn from this discussion is that a balance sheet does **not** show "how much a business is worth."

THE GOING-CONCERN ASSUMPTION It is appropriate to ask **why** accountants do not change the recorded values of assets to correspond with changing market prices for these properties. One reason is that the land and building used to house the business are acquired for **use** and not for resale; in fact, these assets cannot be sold without disrupting the business. The balance sheet of a business is prepared on the assumption that the business is a continuing enterprise, a "going concern." Consequently, the present estimated prices at which the land and buildings could be sold are of less importance than if these properties were intended for sale.

THE OBJECTIVITY PRINCIPLE Another reason for using cost rather than current market values in accounting for assets is the need for a definite, factual basis for valuation. The cost for land, buildings, and many other assets purchased for cash can be rather definitely determined. Accountants use the term **objective** to describe asset valuations that are factual and can be verified by independent experts. For example, if land is shown on the balance sheet at cost, any CPA who performed an audit of the business would be able to find objective evidence that the land was actually valued at the cost incurred in acquiring it. Estimated market values, on the other hand, for assets such as buildings and specialized machinery are not factual and objective. Market values are constantly changing and estimates of what prices assets could be sold for are largely a matter of personal opinion. Of course at the date an asset is acquired, the cost and market value are usually the same because the buyer would not pay more than the asset was worth and the seller would not take less than current market value. The bargaining process which results in the sale of an asset serves to establish both the current market value of the property and the cost to the buyer. With the passage of time, however, the current market value of assets is likely to differ considerably from the cost recorded in the owner's accounting records.

ACCOUNTING FOR INFLATION   Severe worldwide inflation in recent years has raised serious doubts as to the adequacy of the conventional cost basis in accounting for assets. When inflation becomes very severe, historical cost values for assets simply lose their relevance as a basis for making business decisions. Proposals for adjusting recorded dollar amounts to reflect changes in the value of the dollar, as shown by a price index, have been considered for many years.[2] However, stronger interest is being shown at present in balance sheets which would show assets at *current appraised values* or *replacement costs* rather than at historical cost. The British government recently gave basic approval to the concept of revising corporate accounting to reflect inflation. The British plan requires that year-end balance sheets show assets at their current value rather than at historical or original cost. Many companies in the Netherlands are now using some form of current-value accounting. In the United States, the Securities and Exchange Commission requires that large corporations disclose the *current replacement cost* of certain assets as *supplementary information* to conventional cost-based financial statements.

Accounting concepts are not as exact and unchanging as many persons assume. To serve the needs of a fast-changing economy, accounting concepts and methods must also undergo continuous evolutionary change. As of today, however, the cost basis of valuing assets is still in almost universal use.

The problem of valuation of assets is one of the most complex in the entire field of accounting. It is merely being introduced at this point; in later chapters we shall explore carefully some of the valuation principles applicable to the major types of assets.

Liabilities

Liabilities are debts. All business concerns have liabilities; even the largest and most successful companies find it convenient to purchase merchandise and supplies on credit rather than to pay cash at the time of each purchase. The liability arising from the purchase of goods or services on credit (on time) is called an *account payable,* and the person or company to whom the account payable is owed is called a *creditor.*

[2] See *Financial Statements Restated for General Price-Level Changes,* Statement No. 3 of the Accounting Principles Board, American Institute of Certified Public Accountants (New York: 1969).

A business concern frequently finds it desirable to borrow money as a means of supplementing the funds invested by the owner, thus enabling the business to expand more rapidly. The borrowed funds may, for example, be used to buy merchandise which can be sold at a profit to the firm's customers. Or, the borrowed money might be used to buy new and more efficient machinery, thus enabling the company to turn out a larger volume of products at lower cost. When a business borrows money for any reason, a liability is incurred and the lender becomes a creditor of the business. The form of the liability when money is borrowed is usually a *note payable,* a formal written promise to pay a certain amount of money, plus interest, at a definite future time.

An *account payable,* as contrasted with a *note payable,* does not involve the issuance of a formal written promise to the creditor, and it does not call for payment of interest. When a business has both notes payable and accounts payable, the two types of liabilities are shown separately in the balance sheet.

Another important form of liability for corporations is *income taxes payable.* This type of liability does not appear in the balance sheet of a single proprietorship or a partnership because an unincorporated business is not a taxable entity. The sequence in which these liabilities are listed is not important, although notes payable are usually shown as the first item among the liabilities. A figure showing the total of the liabilities should also be inserted, as shown by the illustrated balance sheet on page 15.

Owners' equity

The owners' equity in a corporation is called *stockholders' equity.* In the following discussion, we will use the broader term "owners' equity" because the concepts being presented are equally applicable to the ownership equity in corporations, partnerships, and single proprietorships.

The owners' equity in a business represents the resources invested by the owners. The equity of the owners is a *residual claim* because the claims of the creditors legally come first. If you are the owner of a business, you are entitled to whatever remains after the claims of the creditors are fully satisfied. Thus, owners' equity is equal to the total assets minus the liabilities. For example:

The Westside Cleaning Company has total assets of	*$115,000*
And total liabilities amounting to	*40,000*
Therefore, the owners' equity must equal	*$ 75,000*

Suppose that the Westside Cleaning Company borrows $3,000 from a bank. After recording the additional asset of $3,000 in cash and recording the new liability of $3,000 owed to the bank, we would have the following:

The Westside Cleaning Company now has total assets of	*$118,000*
And total liabilities are now	*43,000*
Therefore, the owners' equity still is equal to	*$ 75,000*

It is apparent that the total assets of the business were increased by the act of borrowing money from a bank, but the increase in total assets was exactly offset by an increase in liabilities, and the owners' equity remained unchanged. The owners' equity in a business is not increased by the incurring of liabilities of any kind.

INCREASES IN OWNERS' EQUITY The owners' equity in a business comes from two sources:

1 Investment by the owners
2 Earnings from profitable operation of the business

Only the first of these two sources of owners' equity is considered in this chapter. The second source, an increase in owners' equity through earnings of the business, will be discussed in Chapter 3.

DECREASES IN OWNERS' EQUITY Decreases in owners' equity also are caused in two ways:

1 Distribution of cash or other assets by the business to its owners
2 Losses from unprofitable operation of the business

Both causes of decreases in owners' equity will be considered in Chapter 3.

Owners' equity in corporations, partnerships, and single proprietorships

Westside Cleaning Company is a corporation. If the business had been organized as a partnership, we would use the caption Partners' Equity instead of Stockholders' Equity, and would list under that caption the amount of each partner's equity. If the form of the business were a single proprietorship, the owner's equity section would consist of only one item, the equity of the proprietor. These three methods of showing the ownership equity in the balance sheet may be illustrated as follows:

For a Corporation

Equity of stockholders . . .

Stockholders' equity:	
Capital stock	*$1,000,000*
Retained earnings	*278,000*
Total stockholders' equity	*$1,278,000*

For a Partnership

... equity of partners ...

Partners' equity:

William Abbott, capital $30,000

Linda Barnes, capital 35,000

Total partners' equity $65,000

For a Single Proprietorship

... equity of a single proprietor

Owner's equity:

John Smith, capital $30,000

The preceding illustration shows that the ownership equity of a corporation consists of two elements: capital stock and retained earnings. The $1,000,000 shown under the caption *capital stock* represents the amount invested in the business by its owners. The $278,000 of *retained earnings* represents the portion of owners' equity which has been accumulated through profitable operation of the business. The corporation has chosen to retain this $278,000 in the business rather than to distribute these earnings to the stockholders as *dividends.* The total earnings of the corporation may have been considerably more than $278,000, because any earnings which were paid to stockholders as dividends would not appear on the balance sheet. The term *retained earnings* describes only the earnings which were *not* paid out in the form of dividends.

Corporations are required by state laws to maintain a distinction between capital stock and retained earnings. In a single proprietorship, capital earned through profitable operations and retained in the business is merely added to the amount of the original invested capital and a single figure is shown for the owner's equity. A similar procedure is followed in a partnership, each partner's capital being increased by his or her share of the net income. There is no theoretical reason why the balance sheet for a single proprietorship or a partnership should not show each owner's equity divided into two portions: the amount originally invested and the earnings retained in the business, but customarily this separation is not made for an unincorporated business.

What is capital stock?

As previously mentioned, the caption *capital stock* in the balance sheet of a corporation represents the amount of money invested by the owners of the business. When the owners of a corporation invest cash or other assets in the business, the corporation issues in exchange shares of capital stock as evidence of the investor's ownership equity. Thus, the owners of a corporation are termed *stockholders.*

The basic unit of capital stock is called a *share,* but a corporation may issue capital stock certificates in denominations of 1 share, 100 shares, or any other number. The total number of shares of capital stock outstanding at any given time represents 100% ownership of the corporation. Out-standing shares are those in the hands of stockholders. The number of shares owned by an individual investor determines the extent of his or her ownership of the corporation.

Assume, for example, that Draper Corporation issues a total of 5,000 shares of capital stock to investors in exchange for cash. If we assume further that Thomas Draper acquires 500 shares of the 5,000 shares outstanding, we may say that he has a 10% interest in the corporation. Suppose that Draper now sells 200 shares to Evans. The total number of shares outstanding remains unchanged at 5,000, although Draper's percentage of ownership has declined to 6% and a new stockholder, Evans, has acquired a 4% interest in the corporation. The transfer of 200 shares from Draper to Evans had *no effect* upon the corporation's assets, liabilities, or amount of stock outstanding. The only way in which this transfer of stock affects the corporation is that the list of stockholders must be revised to show the number of shares held by each owner.

The accounting equation

One of the fundamental characteristics of every balance sheet is that the total figure for assets always equals the total figure for liabilities (creditors' equity) and owners' equity. This agreement or balance of total assets with total equities is one reason for calling this financial statement a *balance sheet.* But *why* do total assets equal total equities? The answer can be given in one short paragraph, as follows:

The dollar totals on the two sides of the balance sheet are always equal because these two sides are *merely two views of the same business property.* The listing of assets shows us what things the business owns; the listing of liabilities and owners' equity tells us who supplied these resources to the business and how much each group supplied. Everything that a business owns has been supplied to it by the creditors or by the owners. Therefore, the total claims of the creditors plus the claims of the owners equal the total assets of the business.

The equality of assets on the one hand and of the claims of the creditors and the owners on the other hand is expressed in the equation:

Fundamental accounting equation

Assets = Liabilities + Owners' Equity
$115,000 = $40,000 + $75,000

The amounts listed in the equation were taken from the balance sheet illustrated on page 15. A balance sheet is nothing more than a detailed statement of this equation. To emphasize this relationship, compare the balance sheet of the Westside Cleaning Company with the above equation.

To emphasize that the owners' equity is a residual element, secondary to the claims of creditors, it is often helpful to transpose the terms of the equation, as follows:

Alternative
form of
accounting
equation

Assets — Liabilities = Owners' Equity
$115,000 — $40,000 = $75,000

Every business transaction, no matter how simple or how complex, can be expressed in terms of its effect on the accounting equation. A thorough understanding of the equation and some practice in using it are essential to the student of accounting.

Regardless of whether a business grows or contracts, this equality between the assets and the claims against the assets is always maintained. Any increase in the amount of total assets is necessarily accompanied by an equal increase on the other side of the equation, that is, by an increase in either the liabilities or the owners' equity. Any decrease in total assets is necessarily accompanied by a corresponding decrease in liabilities or owners' equity. The continuing equality of the two sides of the balance sheet can best be illustrated by taking a brand-new business as an example and observing the effects of various transactions upon its balance sheet.

Effects of business transactions upon the balance sheet

Assume that John Green, Susan Green, and R. J. Hill organized a corporation called Greenhill Real Estate Company. A charter was obtained from the state authorizing the new corporation to issue 6,000 shares of capital stock with a par value of $10 a share.[3] John and Susan Green each invested $24,000 cash and R. J. Hill invested $12,000. The entire authorized capital stock of $60,000 was therefore issued as follows: 2,400 shares to John Green, 2,400 shares to Susan Green, and 1,200 shares to R. J. Hill. The three stockholders each received a stock certificate as evidence of his or her ownership equity in the corporation.

The planned operations of the new business call for obtaining listings of houses and commercial property being offered for sale by property owners, advertising these properties, and showing them to prospective buyers. The listing agreement signed with each property owner provides that Greenhill Real Estate Company shall receive at the time of sale a commission equal to 6% of the sales price of the property.

The new business was begun on September 1 with the deposit of $60,000 in a bank account in the name of the business, Greenhill Real Estate Company. The initial balance sheet of the new business then appeared as follows:

[3] Par value is the amount assigned to each share of stock in accordance with legal requirements. The concept of par value is more fully explained in Chapter 7.

GREENHILL REAL ESTATE COMPANY

Balance Sheet

September 1, 19___

Assets		Stockholders' Equity	
Cash	$60,000	Capital stock	$60,000

PURCHASE OF AN ASSET FOR CASH The next transaction entered into by Greenhill Real Estate Company was the purchase of land suitable as a site for an office. The price for the land was $21,000, and payment was made in cash on September 3. The effect of this transaction on the balance sheet was twofold: first, cash was decreased by the amount paid out; and second, a new asset, Land, was acquired. After this exchange of cash for land, the balance sheet appeared as follows:

GREENHILL REAL ESTATE COMPANY

Balance Sheet

September 3, 19___

Assets		Stockholders' Equity	
Cash	$39,000	Capital stock	$60,000
Land	21,000		
	$60,000		$60,000

PURCHASE OF AN ASSET AND INCURRING OF A LIABILITY On September 5 an opportunity arose to buy a complete office building which had to be moved to permit the construction of a freeway. A price of $36,000 was agreed upon, which included the cost of moving the building and installing it upon Greenhill Real Estate's lot. As the building was in excellent condition and would have cost approximately $60,000 to build, it was considered as a very fortunate purchase.

The terms provided for an immediate cash payment of $15,000 and payment of the balance of $21,000 within 90 days. Cash was decreased $15,000, but a new asset, Building, was recorded at cost in the amount of $36,000. Total assets were thus increased by $21,000, but the total of liabilities and owners' equity was also increased as a result of recording the $21,000 account payable as a liability. After this transaction had been recorded, the balance sheet appeared as follows:

GREENHILL REAL ESTATE COMPANY
Balance Sheet
September 5, 19___

Assets			Liabilities & Stockholders' Equity		
Totals *Cash*	....	$24,000	Liabilities:		
increased *Land*	....	21,000	Accounts payable	....	$21,000
equally by **purchase of** *Building*	....	36,000	Stockholders' equity:		
building on			Capital stock	....	60,000
credit		$81,000			$81,000

(Margin note: Totals increased equally by purchase of building on credit)

Note that the building appears in the balance sheet at $36,000, its cost to Greenhill Real Estate Company. The estimate of $60,000 as the probable cost to construct such a building is irrelevant. Even if someone should offer to buy the building from Greenhill Real Estate Company for $60,000 or more, this offer, if refused, would have no bearing on the balance sheet. Accounting records are intended to provide a historical record of *costs actually incurred;* therefore, the $36,000 price at which the building was purchased in the amount to be recorded.

SALE OF AN ASSET After the office building had been moved to Greenhill Real Estate Company's lot, the company decided that the lot was much larger than was needed. The adjoining business, Carter's Drugstore, wanted more room for a parking area; so, on September 10, Greenhill Real Estate Company sold the unused part of the lot to Carter's Drugstore for a price of $6,000. Since the selling price was computed at the same amount per foot as the corporation had paid for the land, there was neither a profit nor a loss on the sale. No down payment was required, but it was agreed that the full price would be paid within three months. By this transaction a new asset in the form of an account receivable was acquired, but the asset Land was decreased by the same amount; consequently, there was no change in the amount of total assets. After this transaction, the balance sheet appeared as shown below:

GREENHILL REAL ESTATE COMPANY
Balance Sheet
September 10, 19___

Assets			Liabilities & Stockholders' Equity		
No change *Cash*	....	$24,000	Liabilities:		
in totals by *Accounts receivable*	....	6,000	Accounts payable	....	$21,000
sale of land **at cost** *Land*	....	15,000	Stockholders' equity:		
Building	....	36,000	Capital stock	....	60,000
		$81,000			$81,000

(Margin note: No change in totals by sale of land at cost)

In the illustration thus far, Greenhill Real Estate Company has an account receivable from only one debtor and an account payable to only one creditor. As the business grows, the number of debtors and creditors will increase, but the Accounts Receivable and Accounts Payable accounts will continue to be used. The additional records necessary to show the amount receivable from each debtor and the amount owing to each creditor will be explained in Chapter 6.

PURCHASE OF AN ASSET ON CREDIT A complete set of office furniture and equipment was purchased on credit from General Equipment, Inc., on September 14. The amount of the transaction was $5,400, and it was agreed that payment should be made later. As the result of this transaction the business owned a new asset, Office Equipment, but it had also incurred a new liability. The increase in total assets was exactly offset by the increase in liabilities. After this transaction the balance sheet appeared as follows:

GREENHILL REAL ESTATE COMPANY
Balance Sheet
September 14, 19___

	Assets		**Liabilities & Stockholders' Equity**	
Totals	Cash	*$24,000*	*Liabilities:*	
increased by	Accounts receivable	*6,000*	Accounts payable	*$26,400*
acquiring	Land	*15,000*	*Stockholders' equity:*	
asset on credit	Building	*36,000*	Capital stock	*60,000*
	Office equipment	*5,400*		
		$86,400		*$86,400*

COLLECTION OF AN ACCOUNT RECEIVABLE On September 20, cash in the amount of $1,500 was received as partial settlement of the account receivable from Carter's Drugstore. This transaction caused cash to increase and the accounts receivable to decrease by an equal amount. In essence, this transaction was merely the exchange of one asset for another of equal value. Consequently, there was no change in the amount of total assets. After this transaction was completed the balance sheet appeared as follows:

GREENHILL REAL ESTATE COMPANY
Balance Sheet
September 20, 19___

	Assets		Liabilities & Stockholders' Equity	
Totals	Cash	$25,500	Liabilities:	
unchanged	Accounts receivable	4,500	Accounts payable	$26,400
by				
collection	Land	15,000	Stockholders' equity:	
of a	Building	36,000	Capital stock	60,000
receivable				
	Office equipment	5,400		
		$86,400		$86,400

PAYMENT OF A LIABILITY   On September 30 Greenhill paid $3,000 in cash to General Equipment, Inc. This payment caused a decrease in cash and an equal decrease in liabilities. Therefore the totals of assets and equities were still in balance. After this transaction, the balance sheet appeared as follows:

GREENHILL REAL ESTATE COMPANY
Balance Sheet
September 30, 19___

	Assets		Liabilities & Stockholders' Equity	
Totals	Cash	$22,500	Liabilities:	
decreased	Accounts receivable	4,500	Accounts payable	$23,400
by paying a				
liability	Land	15,000	Stockholders' equity:	
	Building	36,000	Capital stock	60,000
	Office equipment	5.400		
		$83,400		$83,400

The transactions which have been illustrated for the month of September were merely preliminary to the formal opening for business of Greenhill Real Estate Company on October 1. During September no sales were arranged by the company and no commissions were earned. Consequently, the stockholders' equity at September 30 is shown in the above balance sheet at $60,000, unchanged from the original investment on September 1. September was a month devoted exclusively to organizing the business and not to regular operations. In succeeding chapters we shall continue the example of Greenhill Real Estate Company by illustrating operating transactions and considering how the net income of the business can be determined.

Effect of business transactions upon the accounting equation

A balance sheet is merely a detailed expression of the accounting equation, Assets = Liabilities + Owners' Equity. To emphasize the relationship between the accounting equation and the balance sheet, let us now repeat the September transactions of Greenhill Real Estate Company to show the effect of each transaction upon the accounting equation. Briefly restated, the seven transactions were as follows:

Sept. **1** Issued capital stock in exchange for $60,000 cash invested in the business by the stockholders.

3 Purchased land for $21,000 cash.

5 Purchased a building for $36,000, paying $15,000 cash and incurring a liability of $21,000.

10 Sold part of the land at a price equal to cost of $6,000, collectible within three months.

14 Purchased office equipment on credit for $5,400.

20 Received $1,500 cash as partial collection of the $6,000 account receivable.

30 Paid $3,000 on accounts payable.

In the table below, each transaction is identified by date; the effect of each transaction on the accounting equation is shown, and also the new dollar balance of each item is listed. Each of the lines labeled Balances contains the same items as the balance sheet previously illustrated for the particular date. The final line in the table corresponds to the amounts in the balance sheet at the end of September. Note that the equality of the two sides of the equation was maintained throughout the recording of the transactions.

	Cash	+ Accounts + Receivable	Land	+ Building +	Office Equipment	= Accounts + Payable	Capital Stock
			Assets			*= Liabilities +*	*Owners' Equity*
Sept. 1	+$60,000						+$60,000
Sept. 3	−21,000		+$21,000				
Balances	$39,000		$21,000				$60,000
Sept. 5	−15,000			+$36,000		+$21,000	
Balances	$24,000		$21,000	$36,000		$21,000	$60,000
Sept. 10		+$6,000	−6,000				
Balances	$24,000	$6,000	$15,000	$36,000		$21,000	$60,000
Sept. 14					+$5,400	+5,400	
Balances	$24,000	$6,000	$15,000	$36,000	$5,400	$26,400	$60,000
Sept. 20	+1,500	−1,500					
Balances	$25,500	$4,500	$15,000	$36,000	$5,400	$26,400	$60,000
Sept. 30	−3,000					−3,000	
Balances	$22,500 +	$4,500 +	$15,000 +	$36,000 +	$5,400 =	$23,400 +	$60,000

USE OF FINANCIAL STATEMENTS BY OUTSIDERS

Through careful study of the financial statements of a company, it is possible for an outsider with a knowledge of accounting to obtain a fairly complete understanding of the financial position of the business and to become aware of significant changes that have occurred since the date of the preceding balance sheet. Bear in mind, however, that financial statements have limitations. As stated earlier, only those factors which can be reduced to monetary terms appear in the balance sheet. Let us consider for a moment some important business factors which are not set forth in financial statements. Perhaps a new competing store has just opened for business across the street; the prospect of intensified competition in the future will not be described in the balance sheet. As another example, the health, experience, and managerial skills of the key people in the management group are extremely important in the success of a business, but these qualities cannot be measured and expressed in dollars in the balance sheet. Efforts to develop methods of accounting for the human resources of an organization presently constitute an important area of accounting research.

Bankers and other creditors

Bankers who have loaned money to a business or who are considering making such a loan will be vitally interested in the balance sheet of the business. By studying the amount and kinds of assets in relation to the amount and payment dates of the liabilities, a banker can form an opinion as to the ability of the business to pay its debts promptly. The banker gives particular attention to the amount of cash and of other assets (such as accounts receivable) which will soon be converted into cash, and then compares the amount of these assets with the amount of liabilities falling due in the near future. The banker is also interested in the amount of the owners' equity, as this ownership capital serves as a protecting buffer between the banker and any losses which may befall the business. Bankers seldom are willing to make a loan unless the balance sheet and other information concerning the prospective borrower offer reasonable assurance that the loan can and will be repaid promptly at the maturity date.

Another important group making constant use of balance sheets consists of the credit managers of manufacturing and wholesaling firms, who must decide whether prospective customers are to be allowed to buy merchandise on credit. The credit manager, like the banker, studies the balance sheets of customers and prospective customers for the purpose of appraising their debt-paying ability. Credit agencies such as Dun & Bradstreet, Inc., make a business of obtaining financial statements from virtually all business concerns and appraising their debt-paying ability. The conclusions reached by these credit agencies are available to business managers willing to pay for credit reports about prospective customers.

Owners

The financial statements of corporations listed on the stock exchanges are eagerly awaited by millions of stockholders. A favorable set of financial statements may cause the market price of the company's stock to rise dramatically; an unfavorable set of financial statements may cause the "bottom to fall out" of the market price. Current dependable financial statements are one of the essential ingredients for successful investment in securities. Of course, financial statements are equally important in single proprietorships and partnerships. The financial statements tell the owners just how successful their business has been and summarize in concise form its present financial position.

Others interested in accounting information

In addition to owners, managers, bankers, and merchandise creditors, other groups making use of accounting data include financial analysts, governmental agencies, employees, potential investors, and writers for business periodicals. Some very large corporations have more than a million stockholders; these giant corporations send copies of their annual financial statements to each of these many owners. In recent years there has been a definite trend toward wider distribution of financial statements to all interested persons, in contrast to the attitude of a few decades ago when many companies regarded their financial statements as a confidential matter. This trend reflects an increasing awareness of the impact of corporate activities on all aspects of our lives and of the need for greater disclosure of information about the activities of business corporations.

The purpose of this discussion is to show the extent to which a modern industrial society depends upon accounting. Even more important, however, is a clear understanding at the outset of your study that accounting does not exist just for the sake of keeping a record or in order to fill out income tax returns and various other regulatory reports. These are but auxiliary functions. If you gain an understanding of accounting concepts, you will have acquired an analytical skill essential to the field of professional management. *The prime and vital purpose of accounting is to aid decision makers in choosing among alternative courses of action.*

KEY TERMS INTRODUCED IN CHAPTER 1

Accounting equation   Assets equal liabilities plus owners' equity. **A = L + OE.**

Accounting system   A financial information system which includes accounting forms, records, reports, employee work assignments, and internal control procedures designed to fit the particular needs of the business.

Accounts payable   Amounts which a company owes its creditors for goods and services purchased on credit.

Accounts receivable   Amounts which a company expects to collect from its customers for goods and services sold to them on credit.

American Institute of Certified Public Accountants (AICPA)   The national professional association of certified public accountants (CPAs). Carries on extensive research and is influential in improving accounting standards and practices.

Assets   Economic resources owned by a business which are expected to benefit future operations.

Auditing   The principal activity of a CPA. Consists of an independent examination of the accounting records and other evidence relating to a business to support the expression of an impartial expert opinion about the reliability of the financial statements.

Audit report   A report issued by the CPA firm expressing an independent professional opinion on the fairness and reliability of the financial statements of a business.

Balance sheet   A financial statement which shows the financial position of a business entity by summarizing the assets, liabilities, and owners' equity at a specific date.

Business entity   An economic unit that enters into business transactions. For accounting purposes, the activities of the entity are regarded as separate from those of its owners.

Certified public accountant (CPA)   An independent professional accountant licensed by a state to offer auditing and accounting services to clients for a fee.

Controller   The chief accounting officer of a business.

Corporation   A business organized as a separate legal entity and chartered by a state, with ownership divided into transferable shares of capital stock.

Cost principle   The widely used concept of valuing assets for accounting purposes at their original cost to the business.

Creditor   The person or company to whom a liability is owed.

Dividend   A distribution of cash by a corporation to its stockholders.

Financial accounting   The area of accounting which emphasizes measuring and reporting in conformity with generally accepted accounting principles the financial position and operating results of a business entity.

Financial Accounting Standards Board (FASB)   An independent group which conducts research in accounting and issues authoritative statements as to proper accounting principles and methods for reporting financial information.

Financial statements   Reports which summarize the financial position and operating results of a business (balance sheet and income statement).

Generally accepted accounting principles   The accounting concepts, measurement techniques, and standards of presentation used in financial statements. Examples include the cost principle, the going-concern assumption, and the objectivity principle.

Going-concern assumption   An assumption by accountants that a business will continue to operate indefinitely unless specific evidence to the contrary exists, as, for example, impending bankruptcy.

Income taxes payable   A liability to government computed as a percentage of profits earned by a corporation.

Internal control   All measures used by a business to guard against errors, waste, and fraud; to assure the reliability of accounting data; and to promote compliance with all company policies.

Internal Revenue Service A governmental agency charged with responsibility for collecting federal income taxes from individuals and corporations.

Liabilities Debts or obligations of a business. The claims of creditors against the assets of a business.

Managerial accounting The area of accounting which emphasizes developing and interpreting accounting information relevant to specific managerial decisions.

Notes payable Liabilities evidenced by a formal written promise to pay a certain amount of money plus interest at a future date. Usually arise from borrowing.

Owners' equity The excess of assets over liabilities. The amount of the owners' investment in a business plus profits from successful operations which have been retained in the business.

Partnership A business owned by two or more persons voluntarily associated as partners.

Retained earnings That portion of stockholders' equity resulting from profits which have been retained in the business rather than distributed as dividends.

Securities and Exchange Commission (SEC) A governmental agency which reviews the financial statements and other reports of corporations which offer securities for sale to the public. Works closely with the FASB and the AICPA to improve financial reporting practices.

Single proprietorship An unincorporated business owned by one person.

Solvency Having enough money to pay debts as they fall due.

Stockholders' equity The owners' equity in a corporation.

Transactions Business events which can be measured in money and which are entered in accounting records.

DEMONSTRATION PROBLEM FOR YOUR REVIEW

The accounting data (listed alphabetically) for the Crystal Auto Wash as of August 31, 19___, are shown below. The figure for Cash is not given but it can be determined when all the available information is assembled in the form of a balance sheet.

Accounts payable	$ 9,000		Land	$40,000
Accounts receivable	800		Machinery & equipment	85,000
Buildings	60,000		Notes payable	29,000
Capital stock	50,000		Retained earnings	99,400
Cash	?		Supplies	400
Income taxes payable	3,000			

On September 1, the following transactions occurred:
(1) Additional capital stock was issued for $15,000 cash.
(2) The accounts payable of $9,000 were paid in full. (No payment was made on the notes payable.)
(3) One-quarter of the land was sold at cost. The buyer gave a promissory note for $10,000. (Interest applicable to the note may be ignored.)
(4) Washing supplies were purchased at a cost of $2,000, to be paid for within 10 days. Washing supplies were also purchased for $600 cash from another car-washing concern which was going out of business. These supplies would have cost $1,000 if purchased through regular channels.

Instructions
a Prepare a balance sheet at August 31, 19____.
b Prepare a balance sheet at September 1, 19____.

SOLUTION TO DEMONSTRATION PROBLEM

a

CRYSTAL AUTO WASH
Balance Sheet
August 31, 19____

Assets		Liabilities & Stockholders' Equity		
Cash	$ 4,200	Liabilities:		
Accounts receivable	800	Notes payable		$ 29,000
Supplies	400	Accounts payable		9,000
Land	40,000	Income taxes payable . . .		3,000
Buildings	60,000	Total liabilities		$ 41,000
Machinery & equipment	85,000	Stockholders' equity:		
		Capital stock . . . $50,000		
		Retained earnings 99,400		149,400
	$190,400			$190,400

b

CRYSTAL AUTO WASH
Balance Sheet
September 1, 19____

Assets		Liabilities & Stockholders' Equity		
Cash	$ 9,600	Liabilities:		
Notes receivable	10,000	Notes payable		$ 29,000
Accounts receivable	800	Accounts payable		2,000
Supplies	3,000	Income taxes payable . . .		3,000
Land	30,000	Total liabilities		$ 34,000
Buildings	60,000	Stockholders' equity:		
Machinery & equipment	85,000	Capital stock . . . $65,000		
		Retained earnings 99,400		164,400
	$198,400			$198,400

REVIEW QUESTIONS

1 In broad general terms, what is the purpose of accounting?

2 Why is a knowledge of accounting terms and concepts useful to persons other than professional accountants?

3 What is meant by the term *business transaction?*

4 What are financial statements and how do they relate to the accounting system?

5 Explain briefly why each of the following groups is interested in the financial statements of a business:

   a Creditors

   b Potential investors

   c Labor unions

6 Distinguish between *accounting* and *bookkeeping.*

7 What is the principal function of certified public accountants? What other services are commonly rendered by CPA firms?

8 Private accounting includes a number of subfields or specialized phases, of which cost accounting is one. Name four other such specialized phases of private accounting.

9 One primary objective of every business is to operate profitably. What other primary objective must be met for a business to survive? Explain.

10 Not all the significant happenings in the life of a business can be expressed in monetary terms and entered in the accounting records. Identify two or more significant events affecting a business which could not be satisfactorily measured and entered in its accounting records.

11 Information available from the accounting records provides a basis for making many business decisions. List five examples of business decisions requiring the use of accounting information.

12 State briefly the purpose of a balance sheet.

13 Define assets. List five examples.

14 State briefly two proposals which have been made to enable accounting to function better during a period of inflation.

15 Define liabilities. List two examples.

16 Mint Corporation was offered $500,000 cash for the land and buildings occupied by the business. These assets had been acquired five years ago at a price of $300,000. Mint Corporation refused the offer, but is inclined to increase the land and buildings to a total valuation of $500,000 in the balance sheet in order to show more accurately "how much the business is worth." Do you agree? Explain.

17 Explain briefly the concept of the *business entity.*

18 State the accounting equation in two alternative forms.

19 The owners' equity in a business arises from what two sources?

20 Why are the total assets shown on a balance sheet always equal to the total of the liabilities and the owners' equity?

21 Can a business transaction cause one asset to increase or decrease without affecting any other asset, liability, or the owners' equity?

22 If a transaction causes total liabilities to decrease but does not affect the owners' equity, what change, if any, will occur in total assets?

23 Give examples of transactions that would:

   a Cause one asset to increase and another asset to decrease without any effect on the liabilities or owners' equity.

   b Cause both total assets and total liabilities to increase without any effect on the owners' equity.

EXERCISES

Ex. 1-1 a Timber Co. has total assets of $227,000 and stockholders' equity of $72,000. What is the amount of the liabilities?

   b The balance sheet of Hazard Corporation shows retained earnings of $70,000.

The assets amount to $360,000 and are twice as large as the liabilities. What is the dollar amount of capital stock?

c The assets of Rivers Company amounted to $90,000 on December 31 of Year 1 but increased to $126,000 by December 31 of Year 2. During the same period, liabilities increased by $20,000. The stockholders' equity at December 31 of Year 1 amounted to $50,000. What was the amount of stockholders' equity at December 31 of Year 2? Explain the basis for your answer.

Ex. 1-2 The balance sheet items of the Perez Corporation as of December 31, 19 ____ , are shown below in random order. You are to prepare a balance sheet for the company, using a similar sequence for assets as in the illustrated balance sheet on page 15. You must compute the amount for retained earnings.

Land	$30,000	Office equipment	$ 3,400
Accounts payable	14,600	Building	70,000
Accounts receivable	18,900	Capital stock	25,000
Retained earnings	?	Notes payable	71,200
Cash	12,100	Income taxes payable	3,800

Ex. 1-3 Indicate the effect of each of the following transactions upon the total assets of a business by use of the appropriate phrase: "increase total assets," "decrease total assets," "no change in total assets."
(a) Issued capital stock in exchange for land.
(b) Collected an account receivable.
(c) Made payment of a liability.
(d) Purchased an office desk on account (on credit).
(e) Borrowed money from a bank.
(f) Sold land on account (on credit) for a price equal to its cost.
(g) Sold land for cash at a price equal to its cost.
(h) Sold land for cash at a price below its cost.
(i) Sold land for cash at a price above its cost.
(j) Purchased a delivery truck at a price of $7,000, terms $1,000 cash and the balance to be paid in 30 equal monthly installments.

Ex. 1-4 For each of the following, describe a transaction that will have the required effect on elements of the accounting equation.
a Increase an asset and increase owners' equity.
b Increase an asset and increase a liability.
c Increase one asset and decrease another asset.
d Decrease an asset and decrease a liability.
e Increase one asset, decrease another asset, and increase a liability.

Ex. 1-5 List the following four column headings on a sheet of notebook paper as follows:

Transaction	Total Assets	Liabilities	Owners' Equity

Next, you are to identify each of the following transactions by number on a separate line in the first column. Then indicate the effect of each transaction on the total assets, liabilities, and owners' equity by placing a plus sign (+) for an increase, a minus sign (−) for a decrease, or the letters (NC) for no change in the appropriate column.
(1) Purchased a typewriter on credit.
(2) Issued capital stock to a creditor in settlement of a liability.
(3) Purchased office equipment for cash.
(4) Collected an account receivable.
(5) Distributed cash as a dividend to stockholders.
(6) Paid a liability.
(7) Returned for credit some of the office equipment previously purchased on credit but not yet paid for.
(8) Sold land for a price in excess of cost.

As an example, transaction (1) would be shown as follows:

Transaction	Total Assets	Liabilities	Owners' Equity
(1)	+	+	NC

Ex. 1-6 The total assets of Automated Products, Inc., amount to $1.4 million and its total liabilities to $600,000. During the five years of its existence, the corporation has been quite successful and has earned total profits equal to exactly one-half of the original capital invested by stockholders. Of the profits earned, one-half has been distributed as dividends to stockholders; the other half has been retained in the business. Prepare the stockholders' equity section of the balance sheet, including dollar amounts. Explain how you determined the amounts.

Ex. 1-7 Certain transactions relating to Crest Corporation are listed below. For each transaction you are to determine the effect on the total assets, total liabilities, and owners' equity of Crest Corporation. Prepare your answer in tabular form, identifying each transaction by letter and using the symbols (+) for increase, (−) for decrease, and (NC) for no change. An answer is provided for the first transaction to serve as an example. Note that some of the transactions concern the personal affairs of the owner of the business, John Crest, rather than being strictly transactions of the corporation.

	Total Assets	Liabilities	Owners' Equity
a Issued capital stock to John Crest in exchange for cash	+	NC	+
b Purchased office equipment on credit			
c Purchased a delivery truck for cash			
d Distributed cash as dividend to John Crest, the only stockholder			
e Paid a liability of the business			
f Returned for credit some defective office equipment which had been purchased on credit but not yet paid for			
g Obtained a loan from the bank for business use			
h John Crest obtained a personal bank loan and used the money to buy additional shares of capital stock in Crest Corporation			
i John Crest sold some shares of stock in Crest Corporation to another investor at a price in excess of cost			

Ex. 1-8 The following balance sheet of Solar Corporation is incorrect because of improper headings and the misplacement of several accounts. Prepare a corrected balance sheet.

SOLAR CORPORATION

March 31, 19____

Assets		Owners' Equity	
Retained earnings	$ 26,200	Accounts receivable	$ 37,800
Cash	10,900	Notes payable	68,800
Building	48,000	Supplies	1,400
Capital stock	40,000	Land	27,000
Automobiles	16,500	Income taxes payable	6,600
	$141,600		$141,600

PROBLEMS

1-1 A list of balance sheet items in random order appears below for Sugarloaf Chalet at October 31, 19____. You are to prepare a balance sheet at October 31 using a sequence for assets similar to that in the balance sheet on page 15. Include a figure for total liabilities. The figure for notes payable must be computed.

Accounts payable	$16,750	Snowmobiles	$12,300
Capital stock	80,000	Notes payable	?
Buildings	78,000	Equipment	37,500
Accounts receivable	16,875	Land	37,500
Cash	14,625	Retained earnings	68,050
Income taxes payable	7,620		

1-2 Five transactions of Gibraltar Corporation are summarized below in equation form, with each of the five transactions identified by a letter. For each of the transactions (a) through (e), you are to write a separate sentence explaining the nature of the transaction.

	Assets					=	Liabilities	+	Owners' Equity
	Cash +	Accounts Receivable +	Land +	Building +	Office Equipment	=	Accounts Payable +		Capital Stock
Balances	$3,100	$6,400	$21,000	$57,100			$ 9,100		$78,500
	+500	−500							
Balances	$3,600	$5,900	$21,000	$57,100			$ 9,100		$78,500
	−1,200				+$1,200				
Balances	$2,400	$5,900	$21,000	$57,100	$1,200		$ 9,100		$78,500
	+6,000								+6,000
Balances	$8,400	$5,900	$21,000	$57,100	$1,200		$ 9,100		$84,500
					+1,600		+1,600		
Balances	$8,400	$5,900	$21,000	$57,100	$2,800		$10,700		$84,500
	−400				+2,400		+2,000		
Balances	$8,000 +	$5,900 +	$21,000 +	$57,100 +	$5,200	=	$12,700	+	$84,500

1-3 Shown below is a list of balance sheet items in random order for Valencia Farms at September 30, 19____. You are to prepare a balance sheet by using these items and computing the amount of retained earnings. Use a similar sequence of assets as in the illustrated balance sheet on page 15. Include a figure for total liabilities.

Land	$225,000	Fences & gates	$18,650
Buildings	43,500	Irrigation system	32,180
Notes payable	295,000	Income taxes payable	5,640
Accounts receivable	12,425	Cash	7,015
Retained earnings	?	Livestock	67,100
Notes receivable	6,029	Farm machinery	23,872
Accounts payable	42,830	Capital stock	50,000
Property taxes payable	4,675	Wages payable	1,010

1-4 During the period of organizing World Health Spas, Inc., a balance sheet was prepared after each transaction. By studying these successive balance sheets, you can determine what transactions have occurred. You are to prepare a list of these transactions by date of occurrence. For example, the transaction leading to the balance sheet of July 1, 19____, could be described as follows: "On July 1, 19____, issued $120,000 par value capital stock for cash."

(1)

WORLD HEALTH SPAS, INC.

Balance Sheet

July 1, 19____

Assets		**Stockholders' Equity**	
Cash	$120,000	Capital stock	$120,000

(2)

WORLD HEALTH SPAS, INC.

Balance Sheet

July 5, 19____

Assets		**Liabilities & Stockholders' Equity**	
Cash	$ 69,600	Liabilities:	
Land	80,000	Notes payable	$195,000
Building	165,400	Stockholders' equity:	
		Capital stock	120,000
	$315,000		$315,000

(3)

WORLD HEALTH SPAS, INC.

Balance Sheet

July 18, 19____

Assets		**Liabilities & Stockholders' Equity**	
Cash	$ 57,000	Liabilities:	
Land	80,000	Notes payable	$195,000
Building	165,400	Stockholders' equity:	
Equipment	12,600	Capital stock	120,000
	$315,000		$315,000

(4)

WORLD HEALTH SPAS, INC.

Balance Sheet

July 31, 19____

Assets		**Liabilities & Stockholders' Equity**	
Cash	$ 33,200	Liabilities:	
Land	80,000	Notes payable	$192,500
Building	165,400	Stockholders' equity:	
Equipment	33,900	Capital stock	120,000
	$312,500		$312,500

1-5 The balance sheet items for Hernando's Hideaway (arranged in alphabetical order) were as follows at August 1, 19____:

Accounts payable	$ 7,800	Income taxes payable	$ 3,400
Accounts receivable	630	Land	77,000
Building	42,000	Notes payable	75,800
Capital stock	55,000	Retained earnings	22,300
Cash	?	Supplies	6,100
Furniture	35,400		

During the next two days, the following transactions occurred:

Aug. 2 Additional capital stock was issued for $25,000 cash. The accounts payable were paid in full. (No payment was made on the notes payable or income taxes payable.)

Aug. 3 Furniture was purchased at a cost of $8,900 to be paid within 10 days. Supplies were purchased for $1,250 cash from a restaurant supply center which was going out of business. These supplies would have cost $1,890 if purchased through normal channels.

Instructions
a Prepare a balance sheet at August 1, 19____.
b Prepare a balance sheet at August 3, 19____.

1-6 From the accounts listed below, prepare a balance sheet as of June 1, 19____, for Blueline Printers, Inc. Also prepare a new balance sheet after the transaction on June 2 and a third balance sheet after the transactions on June 10.

Capital stock	$140,000	Printing equipment	$139,500
Retained earnings	134,000	Notes payable	25,000
Cash	18,000	Supplies	4,900
Income taxes payable	?	Accounts payable	14,500
Land	114,000	Building	68,500

June 2 One-half the land was sold to a contractor at a price of $57,000. A down payment of $14,250 was received and the buyer signed a note agreeing to pay the balance within 10 days. (The note did not bear interest.)

June 10 Cash in the amount of $42,750 was received from the buyer of the land in final settlement of the June 2 transaction. Also on this date, all the accounts payable were paid in cash.

1-7 Hollywood Scripts is a service-type enterprise in the entertainment field. It was organized as a single proprietorship by Bradford Jones, who operates the business but has only a limited knowledge of accounting. Jones prepared the following balance sheet, which, although arranged satisfactorily, contains certain errors with respect to the concepts of business entity and asset valuation.

HOLLYWOOD SCRIPTS
Balance Sheet
November 30, 19___

Assets		Liabilities & Owners' Equity	
Cash	$ 1,150	Notes payable	$ 75,000
Notes receivable	1,000	Accounts payable	21,000
Accounts receivable	7,565	Total liabilities	$ 96,000
Land	45,000		
Building	61,025	Owners' equity:	
Office furniture	6,953	Bradford Jones, capital . .	35,958
Other assets	9,265		
	$131,958		$131,958

In discussion with Jones and by inspection of the accounting records, you discover the following facts.

(1) One of the accounts receivable amounting to $3,000 is an IOU which Jones received in a poker game about ten years ago. The IOU bears only the initials B.K. and Jones does not know the name or address of the maker.

(2) Office furniture includes an antique desk purchased November 29 of the current year at a cost of $1,800. Jones explains that he is not required to pay for the desk until January and therefore he has not included this debt among the liabilities.

(3) Also included in the amount for office furniture is a typewriter which cost $425 but is not on hand, because Jones gave it to his son as a birthday present.

(4) The "Other assets" of $9,265 represents the total amount of income taxes Jones has paid the federal government over a period of years. Jones explains that he considers the income tax law to be unconstitutional and that a friend who attends law school will help Jones recover the taxes paid as soon as he completes his legal education.

(5) The asset land was acquired at a cost of $25,000, but was increased to a valuation of $45,000 when a friend of Jones offered to pay that much for it if Jones would move the building off the lot.

Instructions

a Prepare a corrected balance sheet at November 30, 19___. (Since the business is organized as a single proprietorship, the owner's equity section of the balance sheet should contain only one account, entitled Bradford Jones, capital.)

b For each of the five numbered items above, use a separate numbered paragraph to explain whether the treatment followed by Jones is in accord with generally accepted accounting principles.

1-8 Linda Shields and Mark Ryan own all the capital stock of Citywide Apartment Service, Inc. Both stockholders also work full time in the business. The company performs management services for apartment house owners, including finding tenants, collecting rents, and doing maintenance and repair work.

When the business was organized, Shields and Ryan invested a total of $50,000 to acquire the capital stock. At December 31, Year 1, a partial list of the corporation's balance sheet items included cash of $14,900, office equipment of $5,300, and accounts payable of $15,300, and income taxes payable of $2,100. The following information concerning the corporation's financial position is also available:

(1) Earlier in Year 1, the corporation purchased an office building from Shields at a price of $37,000 for the land and $62,000 for the building. Shields had

acquired the property several years ago at a cost of $20,000 for the land and $45,000 for the building. At December 31, Year 1, Shields and Ryan estimated that the land was worth $42,000 and the building was worth $65,000. The corporation owes Shields a $44,000 note payable in connection with the purchase of the property.

(2) While working, Shields drives her own automobile, which cost $7,600. Ryan uses a car owned by the corporation, which cost $5,200.

(3) One of the apartment houses managed by the company is owned by Ryan. Ryan acquired the property at a cost of $90,000 for the land and $180,000 for the building.

(4) Company records show a $400 account receivable from Ryan and $9,400 in accounts receivable from other clients.

(5) Shields has a $10,000 bank account in the same bank used by the corporation. She explains that if the corporation should run out of cash, it may use that $10,000 and repay her later.

(6) Company records have not been properly maintained, and the amount of retained earnings is not known.

Instructions

a Prepare a balance sheet for the business entity Citywide Apartment Service, Inc., at December 31, Year 1.

b For each of the notes numbered (1) through (5) above, explain your reasoning in deciding whether or not to include the items on the balance sheet and in determining the proper dollar valuation.

BUSINESS DECISION PROBLEM 1

Sun Company and Terra Corporation are in the same line of business and both were recently organized, so it may be assumed that the recorded costs for assets are close to current market values. The balance sheets for the two companies are as follows at July 31, 19____.

SUN COMPANY
Balance Sheet
July 31, 19____

Assets		Liabilities & Stockholders' Equity		
Cash	$ 4,800	Liabilities:		
Accounts receivable	9,600	Notes payable (due in		
Land	96,000	60 days)		$ 62,400
Building	60,000	Accounts payable		43,200
Office equipment	12,000	Total liabilities		$105,600
		Stockholders' equity:		
		Capital stock	$72,000	
		Retained earnings	4,800	76,800
	$182,400			$182,400

TERRA CORPORATION
Balance Sheet
July 31, 19____

Assets		Liabilities & Stockholders' Equity		
Cash	$24,000	Liabilities:		
Accounts receivable	48,000	Notes payable (due in		
Land	7,200	60 days)		$14,400
Building	12,000	Accounts payable		9,600
Office equipment	1,200	Total liabilities		$24,000
		Stockholders' equity:		
		Capital stock . . .	$60,000	
		Retained earnings	8,400	68,400
	$92,400			$92,400

Instructions

a Assume that you are a banker and that each company has applied to you for a 90-day loan of $12,000. Which would you consider to be the more favorable prospect? Explain your answer fully.

b Assume that you are an investor considering purchasing all the capital stock of one or both of the companies. For which business would you be willing to pay the higher price? Do you see any indication of a financial crisis which you might face shortly after buying either company? Explain your answer fully. (It is recognized that for either decision, additional information would be useful, but you are to reach your decision on the basis of the information available.)

2

Recording Changes in Financial Position

Many business concerns have several hundred or even several thousand business transactions each day. It would obviously be impracticable to prepare a balance sheet after each transaction, and it is quite unnecessary to do so. Instead, the many individual transactions are recorded in the accounting records; and, at the end of the month or other accounting period, a balance sheet is prepared from these records. The purpose of this chapter is to demonstrate how business transactions are analyzed, entered in the accounting records, and stored for use in preparing balance sheets and other financial reports.

The use of "accounts" for recording transactions

An accounting system includes a separate record for each item that appears in the balance sheet. For example, a separate record is kept for the asset Cash, showing all the increases and decreases in cash which result from the many transactions in which cash is received or paid. A similar record is kept for every other asset, for every liability, and for every element of owners' equity. The form of record used to record increases and decreases in a single balance sheet item is called an *account,* or sometimes a *ledger account.* All these separate accounts are usually kept in a loose-leaf binder, and the entire group of accounts is called a *ledger.*

Today many businesses use computers for maintaining accounting records, and data may be stored on magnetic tapes rather than in ledgers. However, an understanding of accounting concepts is most easily acquired by study of a manual accounting system. The knowledge gained by working with manual accounting records is readily transferable to any type of automated accounting system. For these reasons, we shall use standard written accounting records such as ledger accounts as the model for our study of basic accounting concepts. These written records continue to be used by a great many businesses, but for our purposes they should be viewed as conceptual devices rather than as fixed and unchanging structural components of an accounting system.

THE LEDGER

Ledger accounts are a means of accumulating in one place all the information about changes in specific assets, liabilities, and elements of owners' equity. For example, a ledger account for the asset cash provides a record of the amount of cash receipts, cash payments, and the current cash balance. By maintaining a Cash account, management can keep track of the amount of cash available for meeting payrolls and for making current purchases of assets or services. This record of cash is also useful in planning future operations and in advance planning of applications for bank loans. The development of the annual budget requires estimating in advance the expected receipts and payments of cash; these estimates of cash flow are naturally based to some extent on the ledger accounts showing past cash receipts and payments.

In its simplest form, an account has only three elements: (1) a title, consisting of the name of the particular asset, liability, or owners' equity; (2) a left side, which is called the *debit* side; and (3) a right side, which is called the *credit* side. This form of account, illustrated below, is called a *T account* because of its resemblance to the letter T. More complete forms of accounts will be illustrated later.

Title of Account

T account: *a ledger account in simplified form*	*Left or debit side*	*Right or credit side*

Debit and credit entries

An amount recorded on the left or debit side of an account is called a *debit,* or a *debit entry;* an amount entered on the right or credit side is called a *credit,* or a *credit entry.* Accountants also use the words debit and credit as verbs. The act of recording a debit in an account is called *debiting* the account; the recording of a credit is called *crediting* the account. A debit to an account is also sometimes called a *charge* to the account; an account is debited or *charged* when an amount is entered on the left side of the account.

Students beginning a course in accounting often have preconceived but erroneous notions about the meanings of the terms debit and credit. For example, to some people unacquainted with accounting, the word credit may carry a more favorable connotation than does the word debit. Such connotations have no validity in the field of accounting, Accountants use *debit* to mean an entry on the left-hand side of an account, and *credit* to mean an entry on the right-hand side. The student should therefore regard debit and credit as simple equivalents of left and right, without any hidden or subtle implications.

To illustrate the recording of debits and credits in an account, let us go back to the cash transactions of the Greenhill Real Estate Company as illustrated in Chapter 1. When these cash transactions are recorded in an account, the receipts are listed in vertical order on the debit side of the account and the payments are listed on the credit side. The dates of the transactions may also be listed, as shown in the following illustration:

			Cash			
Cash trans- actions entered in ledger account	9/1 9/20	22,500	60,000 1,500 61,500	9/3 9/5 9/30		21,000 15,000 3,000 39,000

Note that the total of the cash receipts, $61,500, is in small-size figures so that it will not be mistaken for a debit entry. The total of the cash payments (credits), amounting to $39,000, is also in small-size figures to distinguish it from the credit entries. These *footings,* or memorandum totals, are merely a convenient step in determining the amount of cash on hand at the end of the month. The difference in dollars between the total debits and the total credits in an account is called the *balance.* If the debits exceed the credits the account has a *debit balance;* if the credits exceed the debits the account has a *credit balance.* In the illustrated Cash account, the debit total of $61,500 is larger than the credit total of $39,000; therefore, the account has a debit balance. By subtracting the credits from the debits ($61,500 − $39,000), we determine that the balance of the Cash account is $22,500. This debit balance is noted on the debit (left) side of the account. The balance of the Cash account represents the amount of cash owned by the business on September 30; in a balance sheet prepared at this date, Cash in the amount of $22,500 would be listed as an asset.

DEBIT BALANCES IN ASSET ACCOUNTS   In the preceding illustration of a cash account, increases were recorded on the left or debit side of the account and decreases were recorded on the right or credit side. The increases were greater than the decreases and the result was a debit balance in the account.

All asset accounts normally have debit balances; as a matter of fact, the ownership by a business of cash, land, or any other asset indicates that the increases (debits) to that asset have been greater than the decreases (credits). It is hard to imagine an account for an asset such as land having a credit balance, as this would indicate that the business had disposed of more land than it had acquired and had reached the impossible position of having a negative amount of land.

The balance sheets previously illustrated in Chapter 1 showed all the assets on the left side of the balance sheet. The fact that assets are located on the *left* side of the balance sheet is a convenient means of remembering the rule that an increase in an asset is recorded on the *left* (debit) side of the account, and also that an asset account normally has a debit (*left-hand*) balance.

<table>
<tr><td></td><td colspan="2" align="center">*Any Asset Account*</td></tr>
<tr><td>*Asset accounts normally have debit balances*</td><td align="center">*(Debit)*

Increase</td><td align="center">*(Credit)*

Decrease</td></tr>
</table>

CREDIT BALANCES IN LIABILITY AND OWNERS' EQUITY ACCOUNTS Increases in liability and owners' equity accounts are recorded by credit entries, and decreases in these accounts are recorded by debits. The relationship between entries in these accounts and their position on the balance sheet may be summed up as follows: (1) Liabilities and owners' equity belong on the *right* side of the balance sheet; (2) an increase in a liability or an owners' equity account is recorded on the *right* side of the account; and (3) liability and owners' equity accounts normally have credit (*right-hand*) balances.

<table>
<tr><td></td><td colspan="2" align="center">*Any Liability Account*
or Owners' Equity Account</td></tr>
<tr><td>*Liability accounts and owners' equity accounts normally have credit balances*</td><td align="center">*(Debit)*

Decrease</td><td align="center">*(Credit)*

Increase</td></tr>
</table>

The diagram on page 47 emphasizes again the relationship between the position of an account in the balance sheet and the method of recording an increase or decrease in the account. The accounts used are those previously shown in the balance sheet (page 26) prepared for the Greenhill Real Estate Company.

Diagram
of balance
sheet
accounts

Balance Sheet Accounts

(Left side of balance sheet)		=	(Right side of balance sheet)	
Assets			**Liabilities + Owners' Equity**	

Cash		**Accounts Payable**	
(Debit)	*(Credit)*	*(Debit)*	*(Credit)*
Increase	Decrease	Decrease	Increase

Accounts Receivable		**Capital Stock**	
(Debit)	*(Credit)*	*(Debit)*	*(Credit)*
Increase	Decrease	Decrease	Increase

Land	
(Debit)	*(Credit)*
Increase	Decrease

Building	
(Debit)	*(Credit)*
Increase	Decrease

Office Equipment	
(Debit)	*(Credit)*
Increase	Decrease

CONCISE STATEMENT OF THE RULES OF DEBIT AND CREDIT The rules of debit and credit, which have been explained and illustrated in the preceding sections, may be concisely summarized as follows:

Mechanics
of debit and
credit

Asset Accounts	*Liability & Owners' Equity Accounts*
Increases are recorded by debits	*Increases are recorded by credits*
Decreases are recorded by credits	*Decreases are recorded by debits*

EQUALITY OF DEBITS AND CREDITS Every business transaction affects two or more accounts. The *double-entry system,* which is the system in almost universal use, takes its name from the fact that *equal debit and credit entries are made for every transaction.* If only two accounts are affected (as in the purchase of land for cash), one account, Land, is debited and the other account, Cash, is credited for the same amount. If more than two accounts are affected by a transaction, the sum of the debit entries must be equal to the sum of the credit entries. This situation was illustrated when the Greenhill Real Estate Company purchased a building for a price of $36,000. The $36,000 debit to the asset account, Building, was exactly equal to the total of the $15,000 credit to the Cash account plus the $21,000 credit to the liability account, Accounts Payable. Since every transaction results in an equal amount of debits and credits in the ledger, it follows that the total of all debit entries in the ledger is equal to the total of all the credit entries.

Recording transactions in ledger accounts: illustration

The procedure for recording transactions in ledger accounts will be illustrated by using the September transactions of Greenhill Real Estate Company. Each transaction will first be analyzed in terms of increases and decreases in assets, liabilities, and stockholders' equity. Then we shall follow the rules of debit and credit in entering these increases and decreases in T accounts. Asset accounts will be shown on the left side of the page, liability and stockholders' equity accounts on the right side. For convenience in following the transactions into the ledger accounts, the letter used to identify a given transaction will also appear opposite the debit and credit entries for that transaction. This use of identifying letters is for illustrative purposes only and is not used in actual accounting practice.

Transaction (a) The sum of $60,000 cash was invested in the business on September 1, and 6,000 shares of capital stock were issued.

	Analysis	Rule	Entry
Recording an investment in the business	The asset Cash was increased	Increases in assets are recorded by debits	Debit: Cash, $60,000
	The stockholders' equity was increased	Increases in stock-holders' equity are re-corded by credits	Credit: Capital Stock, $60,000

Cash	Capital Stock
9/1 (a) 60,000	9/1 (a) 60,000

Transaction (b) On September 3, Greenhill Real Estate Company purchased land for cash in the amount of $21,000.

	Analysis	Rule	Entry
Purchase of land for cash	The asset Land was increased	Increases in assets are recorded by debits	Debit: Land, $21,000
	The asset Cash was decreased	Decreases in assets are recorded by credits	Credit: Cash, $21,000

Cash

9/1	60,000	9/3	(b) 21,000

Land

9/3 (b) 21,000	

Transaction (c)   On September 5, the Greenhill Real Estate Company purchased a building from OK Company at a total price of $36,000. The terms of the purchase required a cash payment of $15,000 with the remainder of $21,000 payable within 90 days.

	Analysis	Rule	Entry
Purchase of an asset, with partial payment	A new asset, Building, was acquired	Increases in assets are recorded by debits	Debit: Building, $36,000
	The asset Cash was decreased	Decreases in assets are recorded by credits	Credit: Cash, $15,000
	A new liability, Accounts Payable, was incurred	Increases in liabilities are recorded by credits	Credit: Accounts Payable, $21,000

Cash				**Accounts Payable**	
9/1	60,000	9/3	21,000	9/5	(c) 21,000
		9/5	(c) 15,000		

Building

9/5 (c) 36,000	

Transaction (d)   On September 10, the Greenhill Real Estate Company sold a portion of its land on credit to Carter's Drugstore for a price of $6,000. The land was sold at its cost, so there was no gain or loss on the transaction.

	Analysis	Rule	Entry
Sale of land on credit	A new asset, Accounts Receivable, was acquired	Increases in assets are recorded by debits	Debit: Accounts Receivable, $6,000
	The asset Land was decreased	Decreases in assets are recorded by credits	Credit: Land, $6,000

Accounts Receivable

9/10	(d) 6,000	

Land

9/3	21,000	9/10	(d) 6,000

Transaction (e) On September 14, the Greenhill Real Estate Company purchased office equipment on credit from General Equipment, Inc., in the amount of $5,400.

	Analysis	Rule	Entry
Purchase of an asset on credit	A new asset, Office Equipment, was acquired	Increases in assets are recorded by debits	Debit: Office Equipment, $5,400
	A new liability, Accounts Payable, was incurred	Increases in liabilities are recorded by credits	Credit: Accounts Payable, $5,400

Office Equipment

9/14	(e) 5,400	

Accounts Payable

9/5		21,000
9/14	(e)	5,400

Transaction (f) On September 20, cash of $1,500 was received as partial collection of the account receivable from Carter's Drugstore.

	Analysis	Rule	Entry
Collection of an account receivable	The asset Cash was increased	Increases in assets are recorded by debits	Debit: Cash, $1,500
	The asset Accounts Receivable was decreased	Decreases in assets are recorded by credits	Credit: Accounts Receivable, $1,500

Cash

9/1	60,000	9/3	21,000
9/20	(f) 1,500	9/5	15,000

Accounts Receivable

9/10	6,000	9/20	(f) 1,500

Transaction (g) A cash payment of $3,000 was made on September 30 in partial settlement of the amount owing to General Equipment, Inc.

	Analysis	Rule	Entry
Payment of a liability	The liability Accounts Payable was decreased	Decreases in liabilities are recorded by debits	Debit: Accounts Payable, $3,000
	The asset Cash was decreased	Decreases in assets are recorded by credits	Credit: Cash, $3,000

Cash

9/1	60,000	9/3	21,000
9/20	1,500	9/5	15,000
		9/30	(g) 3,000

Accounts Payable

9/30	(g) 3,000	9/5	21,000
		9/14	5,400

Running balance form of ledger account

The T form of account used thus far is very convenient for illustrative purposes. Details are avoided and we can concentrate on basic ideas. T accounts are also often used in advanced accounting courses and by professional accountants for preliminary analysis of a transaction. In other words, the simplicity of the T account provides a concise conceptual picture of the elements of a business transaction. In formal accounting records, however, more information is needed, and the T account is replaced in many manual accounting systems by a ledger account with special rulings, such as the following illustration of the Cash account for the Greenhill Real Estate Company.

Ledger account with a balance column

Date	Explanation	Ref	Debit	Credit	Cash — Account No. / Balance
19— Sept. 1			60000 00		60000 00
3				21000 00	39000 00
5				15000 00	24000 00
20			1500 00		25500 00
30				3000 00	22500 00

The *Date* column shows the date of the transaction—which is not necessarily the same as the date the entry is made in the account. The *Explanation* column is needed only for unusual items, and in many companies it is seldom used. The *Ref* (Reference) column is used to list the page number of the journal in which the transaction is recorded, thus making it possible to trace ledger entries back to their source (a journal). The use of a *journal* is explained later in this chapter. In the *Balance* column of the account, the new balance is entered each time the account is debited or credited. Thus the current balance of the account can always be observed at a glance.

Although we shall make extensive use of this three-column running balance form of account in later chapters, there will also be many situations in which we shall continue to use T accounts to achieve simplicity in illustrating accounting principles and procedures.

The normal balance of an account

The running balance form of ledger account does not indicate specifically whether the balance of the account is a debit or credit balance. However, this causes no difficulty because we know that asset accounts normally have debit balances and that accounts for liabilities and owners' equity normally have credit balances.

The balance of any account normally results from recording more increases than decreases. In asset accounts, increases are recorded as debits, so asset accounts normally have debit balances. In liability and owners' equity accounts, increases are recorded as credits, so these accounts normally have credit balances.

Occasionally an asset account may temporarily acquire a credit balance, either as the result of an accounting error or because of an unusual transaction. For example, an account receivable may acquire a credit balance because a customer overpays his account. However, a credit balance in the Building account could be created only by an accounting error.

Sequence and numbering of ledger accounts

Accounts are usually arranged in the ledger in *financial statement order;* that is, assets first, followed by liabilities, owners' equity, revenue, and expenses. The number of accounts needed by a business will depend upon its size, the nature of its operations, and the extent to which management and regulatory agencies want detailed classification of information. An identification number is assigned to each account. A *chart of accounts* is a listing of the account titles and account numbers being used by a given business.

In the following list of accounts, certain numbers have not been assigned; these numbers are held in reserve so that additional accounts can be inserted in the ledger in proper sequence whenever such accounts become necessary. In this illustration, the numbers from 1 to 29 are used exclusively for asset accounts; numbers from 30 to 49 are used for liabilities; numbers in the 50s signify owners' equity accounts; numbers in the 60s represent revenue accounts; and numbers from 70 to 99 designate expense accounts. Revenue and expense accounts are discussed in Chapter 3. The balance sheet accounts with which we are concerned in this chapter are numbered as shown in the following brief chart of accounts.

	Account Title	Account Number
System for numbering ledger accounts	*Assets:*	
	Cash	*1*
	Accounts Receivable	*2*
	Land	*20*
	Building	*22*
	Office Equipment	*25*
	Liabilities:	
	Accounts Payable	*30*
	Stockholders' Equity:	
	Capital Stock	*50*
	Retained Earnings	*51*

In large businesses with many more accounts, a more elaborate numbering system would be needed. Some companies use a four-digit number for each account; each of the four digits carries special significance as to the classification of the account.

Flow of information through the accounting system

The term *transaction* was explained in Chapter 1, but a concise definition at this point may be a helpful reminder. *A transaction is a business event which can be expressed in money and must be recorded in the accounting records.* Common examples are the payment or collection of cash, a purchase or sale on credit, and the payment of dividends to stockholders. Note that a transaction has an accounting value and has an influence on the financial statements. Events such as the opening of a competing business or the retirement of an employee, although possibly of importance to the business, are not considered to be transactions and are not entered in the accounts.

Business transactions are evidenced by **source documents** such as a check, a sales ticket, or a cash register tape. These source documents are the starting point for the flow of accounting information through the accounting system into the financial statements. In our description of the accounting process thus far, emphasis has been placed on the analysis of transactions in terms of debits and credits to ledger accounts. Although transactions **could** be entered directly in ledger accounts, it is much more convenient and efficient in a manual accounting system to record the information shown on source documents first in a *journal* and later to transfer the debits and credits to ledger accounts.

Occurrence of a business trans- action

Prepa- ration of a business document

Infor- mation entered in journal

Debits and credits posted from journal to ledger

Financial statements prepared from ledger

THE JOURNAL

The journal, or book of original entry, is a chronological (day-by-day) record, showing for each transaction the debit and credit changes caused in specific ledger accounts. A brief explanation is also included for each transaction. At convenient intervals, the debit and credit entries recorded in the journal are transferred to the accounts in the ledger. The updated ledger accounts, in turn, serve as the basis from which the balance sheet and other financial statements are prepared. The flow chart on the left side of this page illustrates the sequence of steps by which information flows through an accounting system.

The unit of organization for the journal is the *transaction,* whereas the unit of organization for the ledger is the *account.* By making use of both a journal and a ledger, we can achieve several advantages which are not possible if transactions are recorded directly in ledger accounts:

1 *The journal shows all information about a transaction in one place and also provides an explanation of the transaction.* In a journal entry, the debits and credits for a given transaction are recorded together, but when the transaction is recorded in the ledger, the debits and credits are entered in different accounts. Since a ledger may contain hundreds of accounts, it would be very difficult to locate all the facts about a particular transaction by looking in the ledger. The journal is the record which shows the complete story of a transaction in one entry.

2 *The journal provides a chronological record of all the events in the life of a business.* If we want to look up the facts about a transaction of some months or years back, all we need is the date of the transaction in order to locate it in the journal.

3 *The use of a journal helps to prevent errors.* If transactions were recorded directly in the ledger, it would be very easy to make errors such as omitting the debit or the credit, or entering the debit twice or the credit twice. Such errors are not likely to be made in the journal, since the offsetting debits and credits appear together for each transaction.

The general journal: illustration of entries

Many businesses maintain several types of journals. The nature of operations and the volume of transactions in the particular business determine the number and type of journals needed. The simplest type of journal is called a *general journal* and is illustrated below:

General Journal   Page 1

September journal entries for Greenhill Real Estate Company

Date		Account Titles and Explanations	LP	Debit	Credit
Sept. 19___					
Sept.	1	Cash	1	60,000	
		Capital Stock	50		60,000
		Issued 6,000 shares of capital stock in exchange for cash invested in the business.			
	3	Land	20	21,000	
		Cash	1		21,000
		Purchased land for office site.			
	5	Building	22	36,000	
		Cash	1		15,000
		Accounts Payable	30		21,000
		Purchased building to be moved to our lot. Paid part cash; balance payable within 90 days to OK Company.			
	10	Accounts Receivable	2	6,000	
		Land	20		6,000
		Sold the unused part of our lot at cost to Carter's Drugstore. Due within three months.			
	14	Office Equipment	25	5,400	
		Accounts Payable	30		5,400
		Purchased office equipment on credit from General Equipment, Inc.			
	20	Cash	1	1,500	
		Accounts Receivable	2		1,500
		Collected part of receivable from Carter's Drugstore.			
	30	Accounts Payable	30	3,000	
		Cash	1		3,000
		Made partial payment of the liability to General Equipment, Inc.			

A general journal has only two money columns, one for debits and the other for credits; it may be used for all types of transactions. The process of recording a transaction in a journal is called *journalizing* the transaction. On page 55 we have illustrated the use of the general journal to journalize the transactions of the Greenhill Real Estate Company which have previously been discussed.

Efficient use of a general journal requires two things: (1) ability to analyze the effect of a transaction upon assets, liabilities, and owners' equity and (2) familiarity with the standard form and arrangement of journal entries. Our primary interest is in the analytical phase of journalizing; the procedural steps can be learned quickly by observing the following points in the illustrated journal entries.

1 The year, month, and day of the first entry on the page are written in the date column. The year and month need not be repeated for subsequent entries until a new page or a new month is begun.

2 The name of the account to be debited is written on the first line of the entry and is customarily placed at the extreme left next to the date column. The amount of the debit is entered on the same line in the left-hand money column.

3 The name of the account to be credited is entered on the line below the debit entry and is indented, that is, placed about 1 inch to the right of the date column. The amount credited is entered on the same line in the right-hand money column.

4 A brief explanation of the transaction is usually begun on the line immediately below the title of the account. The explanation need not be indented.

5 A blank line is left after each entry. This spacing causes each journal entry to stand out clearly as a separate unit and makes the general journal easier to read.

6 An entry which includes more than one debit or more than one credit (such as the entry on September 5) is called a *compound journal entry.* Regardless of how many debits or credits are contained in a compound journal entry, all the debits are entered before any credits are listed.

7 The LP (ledger page) column just to the left of the debit money column is left blank at the time of making the journal entry. When the debits and credits are later transferred to ledger accounts, the numbers of the ledger accounts are listed in this column to provide a convenient cross reference with the ledger.

In journalizing transactions, remember that the exact title of the ledger accounts to be debited and credited should be used. For example, in recording the purchase of office equipment for cash, *do not* make a journal entry debiting "Office Equipment Purchased" and crediting "Cash Paid Out." There are no ledger accounts with such titles. The proper journal entry would consist of a debit to *Office Equipment* and a credit to *Cash.*

A familiarity with the general journal form of describing transactions is just as essential to the study of accounting as a familiarity with plus and minus signs is to the study of mathematics. The journal entry is a *tool* for *analyzing* and *describing* the impact of various transactions upon a business entity. The ability to describe a transaction in journal entry form requires a complete understanding of the nature of the transaction and its effects upon the financial position of the business.

Posting

The process of transferring the debits and credits from the general journal to the proper ledger accounts is called *posting.* Each amount listed in the debit column of the journal is posted by entering it on the debit side of an account in the ledger, and each amount listed in the credit column of the journal is posted to the credit side of a ledger account.

The mechanics of posting may vary somewhat with the preferences of the individual. The following sequence is commonly used:

1 Locate in the ledger the first account named in the journal entry.

2 Enter in the debit column of the ledger account the amount of the debit as shown in the journal.

3 Enter the date of the transaction in the ledger account.

4 Enter in the reference column of the ledger account the number of the journal page from which the entry is being posted.

5 The recording of the debit in the ledger account is now complete; as evidence of this fact, return to the journal and enter in the LP (ledger page) column the number of the ledger account or page to which the debit was posted.

6 Repeat the posting process described in the preceding five steps for the credit side of the journal entry.

ILLUSTRATION OF POSTING   To illustrate the posting process, the journal entry for the first transaction of the Greenhill Real Estate Company is now repeated on page 58, along with the two ledger accounts affected by this entry.

Note that the Ref (Reference) column of each of the two ledger accounts illustrated contains the number 1, indicating that the posting was made from page 1 of the general journal. Entering the journal page number in the ledger account and listing the ledger page in the journal provide a cross reference between these two records. The audit of accounting records always requires looking up some journal entries to obtain more information about the amounts listed in ledger accounts. A cross reference between the ledger and journal is therefore essential to efficient audit of the records. Another advantage gained from entering in the journal the number of the account to which a posting has been made is to provide evidence throughout the posting work as to which items have been posted. Otherwise, any interruption in the posting might leave some doubt as to what had been posted.

Journalizing and posting by hand is a useful method for the study of accounting, both for problem assignments and for examinations. The manual approach is also followed in many small businesses. One shortcoming is the opportunity for error that exists whenever information is being copied from one record to another. In businesses having a large volume of transactions, the posting of ledger accounts is performed by accounting machines or by a computer, which speeds up the work and reduces errors. In these more sophisticated systems, transactions may be recorded simultaneously in both the journal and the ledger.

General Journal				Page /
Date	Account Titles and Explanation	LP	Debit	Credit
19— Sept. 1	Cash	1	60000 00	
	Capital Stock	50		60000 00
	Issued 6,000 shares of			
	capital stock in exchange			
	for cash.			

General Ledger

			Cash		Account No. /
Date	Explanation	Ref	Debit	Credit	Balance
19— Sept. 1		1	60000 00		60000 00

			Capital Stock		Account No. 50
Date	Explanation	Ref	Debit	Credit	Balance
19— Sept. 1		1		60000 00	60000 00

Ledger accounts after posting

After all the September transactions have been posted, the ledger of the Greenhill Real Estate Company appears as shown on pages 59 and 60. The accounts are arranged in the ledger in balance sheet order, that is, assets first, followed by liabilities and stockholders' equity.

To conserve space in this illustration, several ledger accounts appear on a single page. In actual practice, however, each account occupies a separate page in the ledger.

Since equal dollar amounts of debits and credits are entered in the accounts for every transaction recorded, the sum of all the debits in the ledger must be equal to the sum of all the credits. If the computation of account balances has been accurate, it follows that the total of the accounts with debit balances must be equal to the total of the accounts with credit balances.

Ledger showing September transactions

Cash — Account No. 1

Date	Explanation	Ref	Debit	Credit	Balance
19— Sept. 1		1	6000000		6000000
3		1		2100000	3900000
5		1		1500000	2400000
20		1	150000		2550000
30		1		300000	2250000

Accounts Receivable — Account No. 2

Date	Explanation	Ref	Debit	Credit	Balance
19— Sept. 10		1	600000		600000
20		1		150000	450000

Land — Account No. 20

Date	Explanation	Ref	Debit	Credit	Balance
19— Sept. 3		1	2100000		2100000
10		1		600000	1500000

Building — Account No. 22

Date	Explanation	Ref	Debit	Credit	Balance
19— Sept. 5		1	3600000		3600000

Office Equipment — Account No. 25

Date	Explanation	Ref	Debit	Credit	Balance
19— Sept. 14		1	540000		540000

		Accounts Payable					Account No. 30
Date	Explanation	Ref	Debit		Credit		Balance
19— Sept. 5		/			21000 00		21000 00
14		/			5400 00		26400 00
30		/	3000 00				23400 00

		Capital Stock					Account No. 50
Date	Explanation	Ref	Debit		Credit		Balance
19— Sept. 1					60000 00		60000 00

THE TRIAL BALANCE

Before using the account balances to prepare financial statements, it is desirable to **prove** that the total of accounts with debit balances is in fact equal to the total of accounts with credit balances. This proof of the equality of debit and credit balances is called a **trial balance.** A trial balance is a two-column schedule listing the names and balances of all the accounts **in the order in which they appear in the ledger;** the debit balances are listed in the left-hand column and the credit balances in the right-hand column. The totals of the two columns should agree. A trial balance taken from the ledger of the Greenhill Real Estate Company appears below.

GREENHILL REAL ESTATE COMPANY
Trial Balance
September 30, 19____

Trial balance at month-end proves ledger is in balance

Cash	$22,500	
Accounts receivable	4,500	
Land	15,000	
Building	36,000	
Office equipment	5,400	
Accounts payable		$23,400
Capital stock		60,000
	$83,400	$83,400

Uses and limitations of the trial balance

The trial balance provides proof that the ledger is in balance. The agreement of the debit and credit totals of the trial balance gives assurance that:

1 Equal debits and credits have been recorded for all transactions.
2 The debit or credit balance of each account has been correctly computed.
3 The addition of the account balances in the trial balance has been correctly performed.

Suppose that the debit and credit totals of the trial balance do not agree. This situation indicates that one or more errors have been made. Typical of such errors are (1) the entering of a debit as a credit, or vice versa; (2) arithmetic mistakes in balancing accounts; (3) clerical errors in copying account balances into the trial balance; (4) listing a debit balance in the credit column of the trial balance, or vice versa; and (5) errors in addition of the trial balance.

The preparation of a trial balance does not prove that transactions have been correctly analyzed and recorded in the proper accounts. If, for example, a receipt of cash were erroneously recorded by debiting the Land account instead of the Cash account, the trial balance would still balance. Also, if a transaction were completely omitted from the ledger, the error would not be disclosed by the trial balance. In brief, *the trial balance proves only one aspect of the ledger, and that is the equality of debits and credits.*

Despite these limitations, the trial balance is a useful device. It not only provides assurance that the ledger is in balance, but it also serves as a convenient steppingstone for the preparation of financial statements. As explained in Chapter 1, the balance sheet is a formal statement showing the financial position of the business, intended for distribution to managers, owners, bankers, and various outsiders. The trial balance, on the other hand, is merely a working paper, useful to the accountant but not intended for distribution to others. The balance sheet and other financial statements can be prepared more conveniently from the trial balance than directly from the ledger, especially if there are a great many ledger accounts.

Locating errors

In the illustrations given thus far, the trial balances have all been in balance. Every accounting student soon discovers in working problems, however, that errors are easily made which prevent trial balances from balancing. The lack of balance may be the result of a single error or a combination of several errors. An error may have been made in adding the trial balance columns or in copying the balances from the ledger accounts. If the preparation of the trial balance has been accurate, then the error may lie in the accounting records, either in the journal or in the ledger accounts. What is the most efficient approach to locating the error or errors? There is no single technique which will give the best results every time, but the following procedures, done in sequence, will often save considerable time and effort in locating errors.

1 Prove the addition of the trial balance columns by adding these columns in the opposite direction from that previously followed.

2 If the error does not lie in addition, next determine the exact amount by which the schedule is out of balance. The amount of the discrepancy is often a clue to the source of the error. If the discrepancy is *divisible by 9,* this suggests either a *transposition* error or a *slide.* For example, assume that the Cash account has a balance of $2,175, but in copying the balance into the trial balance the figures are *transposed* and written as $2,157. The resulting error is $18, and like all transposition errors is divisible by 9. Another common error is the slide, or incorrect placement of the decimal point, as when $2,175.00 is copied as $21.75. The resulting discrepancy in the trial balance will also be an amount divisible by 9.

To illustrate another method of using the amount of a discrepancy as a clue to locating the error, assume that the Office Equipment account has a *debit* balance of $420 but that it is erroneously listed in the *credit* column of the trial balance. This will cause a discrepancy of two times $420, or $840, in the trial balance totals. Since such errors as recording a debit in a credit column are not uncommon, it is advisable, after determining the discrepancy in the trial balance totals, to scan the columns for an amount equal to exactly *one-half* of the discrepancy. It is also advisable to look over the transactions for an item of the *exact amount* of the discrepancy. An error may have been made by recording the debit side of the transaction and forgetting to enter the credit side.

3 Compare the amounts in the trial balance with the balances in the ledger. Make sure that each ledger account balance has been included in the correct column of the trial balance.

4 Recompute the balance of each ledger account.

5 Trace all postings from the journal to the ledger accounts. As this is done, place a check mark in the journal and in the ledger after each figure verified. When the operation is completed, look through the journal and the ledger for un-checked amounts. In tracing postings, be alert not only for errors in amount but for debits entered as credits, or vice versa.

Dollar signs

Dollar signs are not used in journals or ledgers. Some accountants use dollar signs in trial balances; some do not. In this book, dollar signs are used in trial balances. Dollar signs should always be used in the balance sheet, the income statement, and other formal financial reports. In the balance sheet, for example, a dollar sign is placed by the first amount in each column and also by the final amount or total. Many accountants also place a dollar sign by each subtotal or other amount listed below an underlining. In the published financial statements of large corporations, such as those illustrated in the appendix of this book, the use of dollar signs is often limited to the first and last figures in a column.

When dollar amounts are being entered in the columnar paper used in journals and ledgers, commas and decimal points are not needed. On unruled paper, commas and decimal points should be used. Most of the problems and illustrations in this book are in even dollar amounts. In such cases the cents column can be left blank, or if desired, zeros or dashes may be used.

Accounting records in perspective

We have emphasized in this chapter the purpose of the journal and ledger and have explained how these accounting records are used. Now we need to consider how these records fit into the accounting process as a whole. It is important to keep in mind that accounting records are not an end in themselves. Just as the physician uses symbols and cryptic notation to write a prescription in the course of providing medical services, the accountant uses symbols and concise notations to interpret business transactions and to classify information about them. Although the prescription order written by the physician and the records created by the accountant are important and must be accurate and complete, they are only a means to an end. The goal of the physician is to restore the health of the patient. The goal of the accountant is to communicate accounting information to persons who will use this information as a basis for business decisions. These persons include managers, owners, potential investors, creditors, financial analysts, labor unions, and governmental agencies. They want to know the financial position of the business as shown by the balance sheet. What resources (assets) does the business have and what debts (liabilities) does it owe? These persons also want to know how profitable the business has been, as shown by the income statement. Finally, they would like to know about the future prospects of the business. Looking into the future of a business involves much uncertainty, but the accumulating and interpreting of accounting information are vitally important elements of financial forecasting.

The use of journals and ledgers, along with the double-entry system and the various symbols and technical terms, has developed over a long period of time because these devices constitute an efficient information system. On a daily basis, this information system absorbs the economic essence of many business transactions. After classifying and summarizing this mass of data, the accounting process produces concise financial statements for the use of decision makers. Remember that your study of the accounting model in the early chapters of this book will equip you to read financial statements with understanding and to make better decisions because you will be familiar with the underlying accounting concepts and processes.

KEY TERMS INTRODUCED IN CHAPTER 2

Account A record used to summarize all increases and decreases in a particular asset, such as Cash, or any other type of asset, liability, owners' equity, revenue, or expense.

Account balance The difference in dollars between the total debits and total credits in an account.

Credit An amount entered on the right-hand side of an account. A credit is used to record a decrease in an asset and an increase in a liability or owners' equity.

Credit balance The balance of an account in which the total amount of credits exceeds the total amount of debits.

Debit An amount entered on the left-hand side of an account. A debit is used to record an increase in an asset and a decrease in a liability or in owners' equity.

Debit balance The balance of an account in which the total amount of debits exceeds the total amount of credits.

Double-entry method In recording transactions, the total dollar amount of debits must equal the total dollar amount of credits.

Financial statement order The usual sequence of accounts in a ledger; that is, assets first, followed by liabilities, owners' equity, revenue, and expenses.

Footing The total of amounts in a column.

Journal A chronological record of transactions, showing for each transaction the debits and credits to be entered in specific ledger accounts.

Ledger A loose-leaf book, file, or other record containing all the separate accounts of a business.

Posting The process of transferring information from the journal to individual accounts in the ledger.

Source documents Original evidence of transactions as, for example, checks, sales tickets, and cash register tapes.

Trial balance A two-column schedule listing the names and the debit or credit balances of all accounts in the ledger.

DEMONSTRATION PROBLEM FOR YOUR REVIEW

Auto Parks, Inc., was organized on July 1 to operate a parking lot near a new metropolitan sports arena. The following transactions occurred during July prior to the corporation beginning its regular business operations.

July 1 Issued 5,000 shares of $10 par value capital stock to the owners of the corporation in exchange for their investment of $50,000 cash.

July 2 Purchased land to be used as the parking lot for a total price of $60,000. A cash down payment of $20,000 was made and a note payable was issued for the balance of the purchase price.

July 5 Purchased a small portable building for $12,000 cash. The purchase price included installation of the building on the parking lot.

July 12 Purchased office equipment on credit from Suzuki & Co. for $2,500.

July 28 Paid $1,000 of the amount owed to Suzuki & Co.

The account titles and account numbers used by Auto Parks, Inc., to record these transactions are

Cash	1	Notes payable	30
Land	20	Accounts payable	32
Building	22	Capital stock	50
Office equipment	25		

Instructions

a Prepare journal entries for the month of July.

b Post to ledger accounts of the three-column running balance form.

c Prepare a trial balance at July 31.

SOLUTION TO DEMONSTRATION PROBLEM

a

General Journal

Date		Account Titles and Explanations	LP	Debit	Credit
19____					
July	1	Cash	1	50,000	
		Capital Stock	50		50,000
		Issued 5,000 shares of $10 par value capital stock for cash.			
	2	Land	20	60,000	
		Cash	1		20,000
		Notes Payable	30		40,000
		Purchased land. Paid one-third cash and issued a note payable for the balance.			
	5	Building	22	12,000	
		Cash	1		12,000
		Purchased a small portable building for cash. The price included installation on the company's lot.			
	12	Office Equipment	25	2,500	
		Accounts Payable	32		2,500
		Purchased office equipment on credit from Suzuki & Co.			
	28	Accounts Payable	32	1,000	
		Cash	1		1,000
		Paid part of account payable to Suzuki & Co.			

b

				Cash				Account No.	
Date		Explanation	Ref	Debit		Credit		Balance	
19—July	1		/	50000 00				50000 00	
	2		/			20000 00		30000 00	
	5		/			12000 00		18000 00	
	28		/			1000 00		17000 00	

				Land				Account No. 20	
Date		Explanation	Ref	Debit		Credit		Balance	
19—July	2		/	60000 00				60000 00	

	Date		Explanation	Ref	**Building** Debit		Credit	**Account No.** 22 Balance
19—	July	5		1	12000 00			12000 00

	Date		Explanation	Ref	**Office Equipment** Debit		Credit	**Account No.** 25 Balance
19—	July	12		1	2500 00			2500 00

	Date		Explanation	Ref	**Notes Payable** Debit		Credit	**Account No.** 30 Balance
19—	July	2		1			40000 00	40000 00

	Date		Explanation	Ref	**Accounts Payable** Debit		Credit	**Account No.** 32 Balance
19—	July	12		1			2500 00	2500 00
		28		1	1000 00			1500 00

	Date		Explanation	Ref	**Capital Stock** Debit		Credit	**Account No.** 50 Balance
19—	July	1		1			50000 00	50000 00

c

AUTO PARKS, INC.
Trial Balance
July 31, 19____

Cash	$17,000	
Land	60,000	
Building	12,000	
Office equipment	2,500	
Notes payable		$40,000
Accounts payable		1,500
Capital stock		50,000
	$91,500	$91,500

REVIEW QUESTIONS

1 What requirement is imposed by the double-entry method in the recording of any business transaction?

2 In its simplest form, an account has only three elements or basic parts. What are these three elements?

3 Is it true that favorable events are recorded by credits and unfavorable events by debits? Explain.

4 How does a T account differ from a three-column running balance form of ledger account?

5 Does the term *debit* mean increase and the term *credit* mean decrease? Explain.

6 State briefly the rules of debit and credit as applied to asset, liability, and owners' equity accounts.

7 What relationship exists between the position of an account on the balance sheet and the rules for recording increases in that account?

8 For each of the following accounts, state whether it is an asset, a liability, or owners' equity; also state whether it would normally have a debit or a credit balance: (*a*) Office Equipment, (*b*) Capital Stock, (*c*) Accounts Receivable, (*d*) Accounts Payable, (*e*) Cash, (*f*) Notes Payable, (*g*) Retained Earnings.

9 A student beginning the study of accounting prepared a trial balance in which two unusual features appeared. The Buildings account showed a credit balance of $20,000, and the Accounts Payable account a debit balance of $100. Considering each of these two abnormal balances separately, state whether the condition was the result of an error in the records or could have resulted from proper recording of an unusual transaction.

10 Explain precisely what is meant by each of the phrases listed below. Whenever appropriate, indicate whether the left or right side of an account is affected and whether an increase or decrease is indicated.
   a A debit of $200 to the Cash account
   b Credit balance
   c Credit side of an account
   d A debit of $600 to Accounts Payable
   e Debit balance
   f A credit of $50 to Accounts Receivable
   g A debit to the Land account

11 For each of the following transactions, indicate whether the account in parentheses should be debited or credited, and give the reason for your answer.

a Purchased a typewriter on credit, promising to make payment in full within 30 days. (Accounts Payable)

b Purchased land for cash. (Cash)

c Sold an old, unneeded typewriter on 30-day credit. (Office Equipment)

d Obtained a loan of $5,000 from a bank. (Cash)

e Issued 1,000 shares of $25 par value capital stock for cash of $25,000. (Capital Stock)

12 Compare and contrast a *journal* and a *ledger.*

13 What is the primary purpose of journal entries from the point of view of *(a)* a business entity and *(b)* an accounting student?

14 During the first week of an accounting course, one student expressed the opinion that a great deal of time could be saved if a business would record transactions directly in ledger accounts rather than entering transactions first in a journal and then posting the debit and credit amounts from the journal to the ledger. Student B agreed with this view but added that such a system should not be called double-entry bookkeeping since each transaction would be entered only once. Student C disagreed with both A and B. He argued that the use of a journal and a ledger was more efficient than entering transactions directly in ledger accounts. Furthermore, he argued that the meaning of double-entry bookkeeping did not refer to the practice of maintaining both a journal and a ledger. Evaluate the statements made by all three students.

15 Which step in the recording of transactions requires greater understanding of accounting principles: *(a)* the entering of transactions in the journal or *(b)* the posting of entries to ledger accounts?

16 What is a *compound* journal entry?

17 State two facts about the sequence of accounts in a journal entry and the use of indentation which make it easy to distinguish between a debit and a credit.

18 What purposes are served by the preparation of a trial balance?

19 List the following five items in a logical sequence to illustrate the flow of accounting information through the accounting system:

a Information entered in journal

b Preparation of a business document

c Financial statements prepared from ledger

d Occurrence of a business transaction

e Debits and credits posted from journal to ledger

EXERCISES

Ex. 2-1 Analyze separately each of the following transactions, using the format illustrated at the end of the exercise. In each situation, explain the debit portion of the transaction before the credit portion.

a On February 1, Ginger Denton organized a corporation to conduct business under the name of Flair Decorating Services, Inc. The corporation issued 30,000 shares of $2 par value capital stock to Denton in exchange for $60,000 cash which she invested in the business.

b On February 23, the corporation purchased an office building in an industrial park for a total price of $114,000, of which $68,000 was applicable to the land and $46,000 to the building. A cash down payment of $28,500 was made and a note payable was issued for the balance of the purchase price.

c On February 25, office equipment was purchased on credit from ADR Company at a price of $4,600. The account payable was to be paid on March 25.

d On February 28, a portion of the office equipment purchased on February 25 was found to be defective and was returned to ADR Company. ADR Company agreed that Flair Decorating Services would not be charged for the defective equipment, which had cost $750.

e On March 25, the remaining liability to ADR Company was paid in full.

Note: The type of analysis to be made is shown by the following illustration, using transaction (**a**) as an example.

a (1) The asset Cash was increased. Increases in assets are recorded by debits. Debit Cash, $60,000.

    (2) The owners' equity was increased. Increases in owners' equity are re-corded by credits. Credit Capital Stock, $60,000.

Ex. 2-2 The first six transactions of a newly organized company appear in the following T accounts.

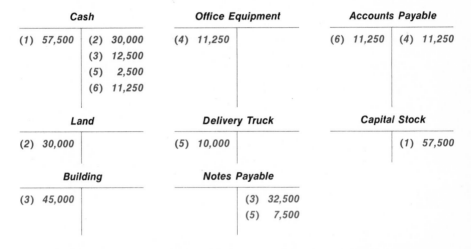

Cash			Office Equipment		Accounts Payable	
(1) 57,500	(2) 30,000		(4) 11,250		(6) 11,250	(4) 11,250
	(3) 12,500					
	(5) 2,500					
	(6) 11,250					

Land		Delivery Truck		Capital Stock	
(2) 30,000		(5) 10,000			(1) 57,500

Building		Notes Payable	
(3) 45,000			(3) 32,500
			(5) 7,500

For each of the six transactions in turn, indicate the type of accounts affected (asset, liability, or owners' equity) and whether the account was increased or decreased. Arrange your answers in the form illustrated for transaction (1), shown here as an example.

	Account Debited		Account Credited	
Transaction	**Type of Account**	**Increase or Decrease**	**Type of Account**	**Increase or Decrease**
(1)	Asset	Increase	Owners' equity	Increase

Ex. 2-3 Enter the following transactions in T accounts drawn on ordinary notebook paper. Label each debit and credit with the letter identifying the transaction. Prepare a trial balance at May 31.

a On May 10, the Bluegrass Corporation was organized and issued 6,400 shares of $10 par value capital stock in exchange for $64,000 cash.

b On May 13, land was acquired for $32,000 cash.

c On May 18, a prefabricated building was purchased from E-Z Built Corporation at a cost of $38,400. A cash payment of $9,600 was made and a note payable was issued for the balance.

d On May 20, office equipment was purchased at a cost of $8,200. A cash down payment of $2,050 was made, and it was agreed that the balance should be paid within 30 days.

e On May 30, $3,200 of the amount due E-Z Built Corporation was paid.

Ex. 2-4 Enter the following transactions in the two-column general journal of World Tours, Inc. Include a brief explanation of the transaction as part of each journal entry. Do not include in the explanation any amounts or account titles since these are shown in the debit-credit portion of the entry.

Aug. 1 Issued an additional 2,600 shares of $5 par value capital stock in exchange for $13,000 cash.

Aug. 3 Purchased an adjacent vacant lot for use as parking space. The price was $31,200, of which $5,200 was paid in cash; a note payable was issued for the balance.

Aug. 12 Collected an account receivable of $4,800 from a customer, Mary Lee Ridgeway.

Aug. 17 Acquired office equipment from DataMax Corp. for $2,210, paying cash.

Aug. 21 Issued a check for $936 in full payment of an account payable to Hampton Supply Co.

Aug. 28 Borrowed $19,000 cash from the bank by signing a 90-day note payable.

Ex. 2-5 The following accounts show the first six transactions of the Greenbriar Corporation. Prepare a journal entry (including written explanation) for each transaction.

Cash					Accounts Payable				
Jan. 1	120,000	Jan. 12	33,600		Jan. 25	480	Jan. 20	3,600	
		Feb. 5	3,120		Feb. 5	3,120			

Land			Notes Payable		
Jan. 12	96,000		Feb. 10	24,000	Jan. 12	116,400

Building			Capital Stock, $10 par value		
Jan. 12	54,000			Jan. 1	120,000
				Feb. 10	24,000

Office Equipment			
Jan. 20	3,600	Jan. 25	480

Ex. 2-6 Some of the following errors would cause the debit and credit columns of the trial balance to have unequal totals. For each of the four paragraphs, write a statement explaining with reasons whether the error would cause unequal totals in the trial balance. Include in your explanations the dollar amounts of errors in trial balance totals or ledger account balances. Each paragraph is to be considered independently of the others.

a An account receivable in the amount of $1,200 was collected in full. The collection was recorded by a *debit* to Cash for $1,200 and a *debit* to Capital Stock for $1,200.

b An account payable was paid by issuing a check for $525. The payment was recorded by debiting Accounts Payable $525 and crediting Accounts Receivable $525.

c A $810 payment for a new typewriter was recorded by a debit to Office Equipment of $81 and a credit to Cash of $81.

d A payment of $600 to a creditor was recorded by a debit to Accounts Payable of $600 and a credit to Cash of $60.

Ex. 2-7 The trial balance prepared by Discount Plumbing Service at June 30 was not in balance. In searching for the error, an employee discovered that a transaction for the purchase of a calculator on credit for $380 had been recorded by a ***debit*** of $380 to the Office Equipment account and a ***debit*** of $380 to Accounts Payable. The credit column of the incorrect trial balance has a total of $129,640.

In answering each of the following five questions, explain fully the reasons underlying your answer and state the dollar amount of the error if any.

a Was the Office Equipment account overstated, understated, or correctly stated in the trial balance?

b Was the total of the debit column of the trial balance overstated, understated, or correctly stated?

c Was the Accounts Payable account overstated, understated, or correctly stated in the trial balance?

d Was the total of the credit column of the trial balance overstated, understated or correctly stated?

e How much was the total of the debit column of the trial balance before correction of the error?

PROBLEMS

2-1 The ledger accounts of Rolling Hills Golf Club at September 30 are shown below in an alphabetical listing.

Accounts payable	$ 5,340	Lighting equipment	$ 52,900
Accounts receivable	1,300	Maintenance equipment	36,500
Building	64,200	Notes payable	340,000
Capital stock	200,000	Notes receivable	24,000
Cash	14,960	Office equipment	1,420
Fences	23,600	Office supplies	490
Golf carts	28,000	Retained earnings	64,060
Land	375,000	Taxes payable	12,970

Instructions

a Prepare a trial balance with the ledger accounts arranged in the usual financial statement order.

b Prepare a balance sheet at September 30, 19___.

c Assume that immediately after the September 30 balance sheet was prepared, a tornado struck the golf course and destroyed the fences, which were not insured against this type of disaster. If the balance sheet were revised to reflect the loss of the fences, explain briefly what other change in the balance sheet would be required.

2-2 After several seasons of World Team tennis competition, Anne Peckham had saved enough money to start her own tennis school, to be known as Winners' Tennis College, Inc. During June, while organizing the business, Peckham kept only an informal record of transactions in the form of T accounts which she maintained on a large blackboard. Peckham asks you to develop from the T accounts a ledger using the standard three-column running balance form of accounts. She says that she will prepare journal entries for June from some rough notes she has kept but that she will need some assistance in establishing the running balance form of ledger accounts. The T accounts reflecting all June transactions are as follows:

Cash			1
6/2	35,000	6/4	21,600
		6/8	212
		6/23	650

Tennis Equipment			25
6/7	1,240		
6/13	650		

Office Supplies			9
6/8	212		

Notes Payable			30
		6/4	75,600

Land			20
6/4	25,200		

Accounts Payable			31
6/18	212	6/7	1,240
6/23	650	6/8	212
		6/13	650

Tennis Courts			22
6/4	72,000		

Capital Stock			50
		6/2	35,000

Instructions

a Transfer the information shown by the T accounts to ledger accounts of the three-column running balance form.

b Prepare a trial balance at June 30 from the ledger accounts completed in part (*a*).

2-3 North County Construction Co. was organized in February to perform remodeling work on homes and office buildings and to act as general contractor on larger jobs. As of February 28, the ledger accounts contained entries as follows:

Cash			
Feb. 3	25,000	Feb. 5	11,700
28	540	15	2,480

Construction Equipment			
Feb. 5	12,960	Feb. 16	1,080

Accounts Receivable			
Feb. 16	1,080	Feb. 28	540

Notes Payable			
Feb. 15	1,500	Feb. 5	4,500

Office Supplies			
Feb. 4	980	Feb. 24	55
22	240		

Accounts Payable			
Feb. 15	980	Feb. 4	980
24	55	22	240

Office Equipment			
Feb. 5	3,240		

Capital Stock, $10 par value			
		Feb. 3	25,000

Instructions

a Reconstruct the journal entries as they were probably made by the company's accountant, giving a full explanation for each transaction.

b Determine account balances and prepare a trial balance at February 28.

c Prepare a balance sheet at February 28.

2-4 Freedom Rider, Inc., was organized on October 1 to rent motorcycles to the public. The clerk who maintained the accounting records of the company did not understand the double-entry system or the proper use of the journal and ledger. The clerk believed that all increases in account balances should be recorded only in the ledger, while all decreases should be recorded only by a written explanation in the journal. He also believed that credit entries should be used to increase all ledger accounts, regardless of whether the accounts were assets, liabilities, or owners' equity. For example, on October 1, the company issued 4,000 shares of $10 par capital stock for cash, which should have been recorded by a debit to Cash and a credit to Capital Stock. Instead, the clerk recorded the increase in the asset cash by crediting the Cash account. (He also credited Capital Stock, which was correct.) During October the clerk made the following entries.

General Journal

Oct. 2 Paid $16,500 cash as part of the purchase price of land and building.
Oct. 6 Sold a part of the land which cost $7,500 to an adjacent business, Community Medical Center, which is expanding its facilities.
Oct. 15 Paid $8,750 cash as part of the purchase price of 25 motorcycles from United Imports.
Oct. 17 Returned two defective motorcycles (cost $750 each) to United Imports, reducing the amount owed on account.
Oct. 27 Community Medical Center paid off $3,150 of the note originating from the sale of land on October 6.
Oct. 31 Paid $8,500 account payable to United Imports.

Ledger

Cash		*1*		*Motorcycles*		*25*
Oct. 1	40,000			Oct. 15	18,750	
Oct. 27	3,150					

Notes Receivable		*5*		*Notes Payable*		*30*
Oct. 6	7,500			Oct. 2	37,500	

Land		*20*		*Accounts Payable*		*31*
Oct. 2	22,500			Oct. 15	10,000	

Building		*23*		*Capital Stock*		*50*
Oct. 2	31,500			Oct. 1	40,000	

Instructions
a Prepare proper journal entries for the month of October.
b Post to ledger accounts of the three-column running balance form.
c Prepare a trial balance at October 31.

2-5 Property Management Corporation was started on November 1 by Chris Evans to provide managerial services for the owners of apartment buildings. The organizational period extended throughout the month of November and included the transactions listed below.

The account titles and account numbers to be used are

Cash	11	Office equipment	25
Accounts receivable	15	Notes payable	31
Land	21	Accounts payable	32
Building	23	Capital stock	51

Nov. 1 The corporation issued 5,000 shares of capital stock to its owner, Chris Evans, in exchange for her investing $56,000 cash in the business.

Nov. 4 Purchased land and an office building for a price of $80,000, of which $38,400 was considered applicable to the land and $41,600 attributable to the building. A cash down payment of $24,000 was made and a note payable for $56,000 was issued for the balance of the purchase price.

Nov. 7 Purchased office equipment on credit from Harvard Office Equipment, $4,400.

Nov. 9 A typewriter (cost $560), which was part of the November 7 purchase of office equipment, proved defective and was returned for credit to Harvard Office Equipment.

Nov. 11 Sold to Regent Pharmacy at cost one-third of the land acquired on November 4. No down payment was required. The buyer promised to pay one-half the purchase price of $12,800 within 10 days and the remainder by December 12.

Nov. 18 Paid $1,600 in partial settlement of the liability to Harvard Office Equipment.

Nov. 21 Received cash of $6,400 as partial collection of the account receivable from Regent Pharmacy.

Instructions
a Prepare journal entries for the month of November.
b Post to ledger accounts of the three-column running balance form.
c Prepare a trial balance at November 30.

2-6 George Harris, after several seasons of professional football, had saved enough money to start his own business, to be known as Number One Auto Rentals, Inc. The business transactions during March while the new corporation was being organized are listed below:

Mar. 1 George Harris invested $140,000 cash in the business, in exchange for which the corporation issued 14,000 shares of its $10 par value capital stock.

Mar. 3 The new company purchased land and a building at a cost of $120,000, of which $72,000 was regarded as applicable to the land and $48,000 to the building. The transaction involved a cash payment of $41,500 and the issuance of a note payable for $78,500.

Mar. 5 Purchased 20 new automobiles at $5,600 each from Fleet Sales Company. Paid $32,000 cash, and agreed to pay another $32,000 by March 26 and the remaining balance by April 15.

Mar. 7 Sold an automobile at cost to Harris's father-in-law, Howard Facey, who paid $2,400 in cash and agreed to pay the balance within 30 days.

Mar. 8 One of the automobiles was found to be defective and was returned to Fleet Sales Company. The amount payable to this creditor was thereby reduced by $5,600.

Mar. 20 Purchased office equipment at a cost of $4,480 cash.

Mar. 26 Issued a check for $32,000 in partial payment of the liability to Fleet Sales Company.

Instructions
a Journalize the above transactions, then post to ledger accounts. Use the running balance form of ledger account rather than T accounts. The account titles and the account numbers to be used are as follows:

Cash	10	Automobiles	22
Accounts receivable	11	Notes payable	31
Land	16	Accounts payable	32
Buildings	17	Capital stock	50
Office equipment	20		

b Prepare a trial balance at March 31, 19____.

2-7 Educational TV, Inc., was organized in February, 19____, to operate as a local television station. The account titles and numbers used by the corporation are listed below:

Cash	11	Telecasting equipment	24
Accounts receivable	15	Film library	25
Supplies	19	Notes payable	31
Land	21	Accounts payable	32
Building	22	Capital stock	51
Transmitter	23		

The transactions for February, 19____, were as follows:

Feb. 1 A charter was granted to Paul and Alice Marshal for the organization of Educational TV, Inc. The Marshals invested $288,000 cash and received 30,000 shares of stock in exchange.

Feb. 3 The new corporation purchased the land, buildings, and telecasting equipment previously used by a local television station which had gone bankrupt. The total purchase price was $249,000, of which $90,000 was attributable to the land, $75,000 to the building, and the remainder to the telecasting equipment. The terms of the purchase required a cash payment of $179,000 and the issuance of a note payable for the balance.

Feb. 5 Purchased a transmitter at a cost of $195,000 from AC Mfg. Co., making a cash down payment of $60,000. The balance, in the form of a note payable, was to be paid in monthly installments of $11,250, beginning February 15. (Interest expense is to be ignored.)

Feb. 9 Purchased a film library at a cost of $31,995 from Modern Film Productions, making a down payment of $14,000 cash, with the balance on account payable in 30 days.

Feb. 12 Bought supplies costing $2,925, paying cash.

Feb. 15 Paid $11,250 to AC Mfg. Co. as the first monthly payment on the note payable created on February 5. (Interest expense is to be ignored.)

Feb. 25 Sold part of the film library to City College; cost was $8,000 and the selling price also was $8,000. City College agreed to pay the full amount in 30 days.

Instructions
a Prepare journal entries for the month of February.
b Post to ledger accounts of the three-column running balance form.
c Prepare a trial balance at February 28, 19____.
d Prepare a balance sheet at February 28, 19____.

2-8 Julie Austin and Tom Miller have operated as independent real estate agents in Portland, Oregon, for many years. Early in January they agree to combine their separate businesses into a corporation. The balance sheets for Austin and Miller before they combine their businesses follow:

	Austin	Miller
Cash	$ 2,400	$ 6,100
Accounts receivable	17,200	23,600
Land	47,000	26,000
Buildings	35,000	57,400
Office equipment	10,400	16,100
	$112,000	$129,200
Notes payable	$ 58,000	$ 49,500
Accounts payable	14,000	19,700
Owners' capital	40,000	60,000
	$112,000	$129,200

The A & M Realty Corporation was organized on January 20, with authority to issue 20,000 shares of capital stock with a total par value of $100,000. Asset values stated on the records of each realtor are to be retained by the corporation. Miller's books will be used to record all transactions of the corporation. Accordingly, assets and liabilities shown in Austin's records are transferred to the corporation and $40,000 of capital stock is issued to Austin. Miller's capital account is closed out; and capital stock is issued to him. Thus, capital stock is received by Austin and Miller in proportion to the capital (assets less liabilities) each has invested.

During the remainder of January the following transactions are completed by the A & M Realty Corporation:

Jan. 21 Sold surplus office equipment on account for $3,800. The equipment is carried in the accounting records at $3,800.

Jan. 24 Purchased a vacant lot for $24,500. Paid $2,450 down; balance is due on February 28 of the current year.

Jar 26 Collected $6,900 on accounts receivable.

Jan. 29 Paid $6,600 on accounts payable and $5,600 on notes payable.

Jan. 31 Issued an additional 2,400 shares of stock to employees for a total consideration of $12,000 in cash.

Instructions

a Prepare journal entries to record the issuance of capital stock to Austin and Miller on Miller's books (which are retained by the corporation).

b Prepare journal entries to record the transactions from January 21 through January 31.

c Post to ledger accounts of the three-column running balance form and determine the account balances on January 31. Account numbers need not be assigned to the ledger accounts.

d Prepare a balance sheet at January 31.

BUSINESS DECISION PROBLEM 2

Richard Fell, a college student with several summers' experience as a guide on canoe camping trips, decided to go into business for himself. He considered incorporating, but decided instead to operate as a single proprietorship for the first year. On June 1, 19___, Fell organized Backcountry Guide Service by depositing $1,600 of personal savings in a bank account in the name of the business. Also on June 1, the business borrowed an additional $3,200 cash from John Fell (Richard's father) by issuing a three-year note payable. To help the business get started, John Fell agreed that no interest would be charged on the loan. The following transactions were also carried out by the business on June 1:

(1) Bought a number of canoes at a total cost of $6,200; paid $1,700 cash and agreed to pay the balance within 60 days.

(2) Bought camping equipment at a cost of $3,400 payable in 60 days.

(3) Bought supplies for cash, $800.

After the close of the season on September 10, Fell asked another student, Sharon Lee, who had taken a course in accounting, to help determine the financial position of the business.

The only record Fell had maintained was a checkbook with memorandum notes written on the check stubs. From this source Lee discovered that Fell had invested an additional $1,200 of savings in the business on July 1, and also that the accounts payable arising from the purchase of the canoes and camping equipment had been paid in full. A bank statement received from the bank on September 10 showed a balance on deposit of $2,840.

Fell informed Lee that all cash received by the business had been deposited in the bank and all bills had been paid by check immediately upon receipt; consequently, as of September 10 all bills for the season had been paid.

The canoes and camping equipment were all in excellent condition at the end of the season and Fell planned to resume operations the following summer. In fact he had already accepted reservations from many customers who wished to return.

Lee felt that some consideration should be given to the wear and tear on the canoes and equipment but she agreed with Fell that for the present purpose the canoes and equipment should be listed in the balance sheet at the original cost. The supplies remaining on hand had cost $40 and Fell felt that a refund for this amount could be obtained if they were returned to the supplier.

Lee suggested that two balance sheets be prepared, one to show the condition of the business on June 1 and the other showing the condition on September 10. She also recommended to Fell that a complete set of accounting records be established.

Instructions

a Use the information in the first paragraph (including the three numbered transactions) as a basis for preparing a balance sheet dated June 1. (As illustrated in Chapter 1, the owner's equity section of the balance sheet for this unincorporated business should consist of only one account, entitled **Richard Fell, Capital.**)

b Prepare a balance sheet at September 10. (Because of the incomplete information available, it is not possible to determine the amount of cash at September 10 by adding cash receipts and deducting cash payments throughout the season. The amount on deposit as reported by the bank at September 10 is to be regarded as the total cash belonging to the business at that date.)

c By comparing the two balance sheets, compute the change in owner's equity. Explain the sources of this change in owner's equity and state whether you consider the business to be successful. Also comment on the cash position at the beginning and end of the season. Has the cash position improved significantly? Explain.

3

Measuring Business Income

The earning of net income, or profits, is a major goal of almost every business enterprise, large or small. Profit is the *increase in the owners' equity resulting from operation of the business.* The opposite of profit, a decrease in owners' equity resulting from operation of the business, is termed a *loss.* If you were to organize a small business of your own, you would do so with the hope and expectation that the business would operate at a profit, thereby increasing your ownership equity. Individuals who invest in the capital stock of large corporations also expect the business to earn a profit which will increase the value of their investment.

Operating profitably usually leads to an increase in total assets as well as in owners' equity. From the fundamental accounting equation (A = L + OE), we know that any transaction which changes total assets must also change either total liabilities or owners' equity. For example, borrowing money from a bank increases both total assets and total liabilities. Operating profitably increases owners' equity and this increase is usually accompanied by an increase in total assets. It is possible that the increase in owners' equity from profitable operations could be accompanied by a decrease in liabilities, but in the great majority of cases, operating profitably increases total assets along with the increase in owners' equity.

The resources generated by profitable operations may be retained in the business to finance expansion, or they may be distributed as dividends to the stockholders. Some of the largest corporations have become large by retaining their profits in the business and using these profits for purposes of growth. Retained profits may be used, for example, to acquire new plant and equipment, to carry on research leading to new and better products, and to extend sales operations into new territories.

Profits: public image versus economic function

In recent years, business profits have become a controversial issue. Critics often call corporate profits "excessive" and charge that profits are a major cause of rising prices. Such charges have received considerable publicity, and as a result many people have come to believe that business profits are something harmful to society. Actually, business profits perform a vital economic function in our economy, and a satisfactory level of business profits is generally associated with high employment, an improving standard of living, and an expanding national economy.

In a free market economy, profits assist in the efficient allocation of resources. When the demand for a particular product is much greater than the supply, the price consumers will pay for the product tends to rise. As the price rises, investors are attracted to that industry by the opportunity to earn greater than normal profits. The inflow of capital into the industry results in greater productive capacity and supply of the product increases to meet demand.

Corporate profits may be viewed as the "return" to stockholders for having invested their resources in a particular company. When creditors lend money to a company, they expect to earn a reasonable rate of interest. When employees invest their time and labor, they expect to earn a reasonable wage. It is equally logical that stockholders, who supply financial resources to a business, should expect to earn a satisfactory return on their investment.

If business profits were reduced to insignificant levels, prices probably would rise rather than fall. Investors would stop providing capital to those industries in which profit opportunities were unsatisfactory. The resulting capital shortages would leave businesses unable to produce enough goods, causing production shortages, higher prices, and unemployment. Thus, a satisfactory level of business profits is essential to maintaining high levels of production and to financing economic growth.

When competition is restricted, profits may become "excessive." Excessive profits, just as excessive wages or excessive materials costs, can be harmful to the economy. Profits are excessive when they become unreasonably large in relation to the amounts of money invested and the degree of risk being taken by the owners of a business. The risk taken by owners of a business is the chance that future losses may decrease or even wipe out their investment. Once we have completed our study of how business profits are measured, we shall discuss some ways of appraising their adequacy.

Retained earnings

The increase in owners' equity resulting from profitable operations is presented in a balance sheet account entitled *Retained Earnings,* which appears in the stockholders' equity section of the balance sheet. If a business has sufficient cash, a distribution of profits may be made to the stockholders. Distributions of this nature are termed *dividends* and decrease both total assets and total stockholders' equity. The decrease in stockholders' equity is reflected by a decrease in the Retained Earnings account. Thus, the balance of the Retained Earnings account represents only the earnings which have *not* been distributed as dividends.

Some people mistakenly believe that retained earnings represent a fund of cash available to a corporation. *Retained earnings are not assets; they are an element of stockholders' equity.* Although the amount of retained earnings indicates the portion of total assets which were *financed* by earning and retaining net income, it does *not* indicate the *form* in which these resources are currently held. The resources generated by retaining profits may have been invested in land, buildings, equipment, or any other kind of asset. The total amount of cash owned by a corporation is shown by the balance of the Cash account, which appears in the asset section of the balance sheet.

Net income

Since the drive for profits underlies the very existence of business organizations, it follows that a most important function of an accounting system is to provide information about the profitability of a business. Before we can measure the profits of a business, we need to establish a sharp, clear meaning for *profits.* Economists often define profits as the amount by which an entity becomes *better off* during a period of time. Unfortunately, how much "better off" an entity has become is largely a matter of personal opinion and cannot be measured *objectively* enough to provide a useful definition for accountants.

For this reason, accountants usually look to actual business transactions to provide objective evidence that a business has been profitable or unprofitable. For example, if an item which cost a business $60 is sold for $100 cash, we have objective evidence that the business has earned a profit of $40. Since business managers and economists use the word *profits* in somewhat different senses, accountants prefer to use the alternative term *net income,* and to define this term very carefully. *Net income is the excess of the price of goods sold and services rendered over the cost of goods and services used up during a given time period.* At this point, we shall adopt the technical accounting term *net income* in preference to the less precise term *profits.*

To determine net income, it is necessary to measure for a given time period (1) the price of goods sold and services rendered and (2) the cost of goods and services used up. The technical accounting terms for these items comprising net income are *revenue* and *expenses.* Therefore, we may state that *net income equals revenue minus expenses.* To understand why this is true and how the measurements are made, let us begin with the meaning of revenue.

Revenue

Revenue is the price of goods sold and services rendered during a given time period. When a business renders services to its customers or delivers merchandise to them, it either receives immediate payment in cash or acquires an account receivable which will be collected and thereby become cash within a short time. The revenue for a given period is equal to the inflow of cash and receivables from sales made in that period. For any single transaction, the amount of revenue is a measurement of the asset values received from the customer.

Not all receipts of cash represent revenue; for example, as shown in Chapter 1, a business may obtain cash by borrowing from a bank. This increase in cash is offset by an increase in liabilities in the form of a note payable to the bank. The owners' equity is not changed by the borrowing transaction.

Collection of an account receivable is another example of a cash receipt that does not represent revenue. The act of collection causes an increase in the asset, Cash, and a corresponding decrease in another asset, Accounts Receivable. The amount of total assets remains unchanged, and, of course, there is no change in liabilities or owners' equity.

As another example of the distinction between revenue and cash receipts, let us assume that a business begins operations in March and makes sales of merchandise and/or services to its customers in that month as follows: sales for cash, $25,000; sales on credit (to be collected in April), $15,000. The revenue for March is $40,000, an amount equal to the cash received or to be received from the month's sales. When the accounts receivable of $15,000 are collected during April, they must not be counted a second time in measuring revenue for April.

Revenue causes an increase in owners' equity. The inflow of cash and receivables from customers increases the total assets of the company; on the other side of the accounting equation, the liabilities do not change, but owners' equity is increased to match the increase in total assets. Thus revenue is the gross increase in owners' equity resulting from business activities. Bear in mind, however, that not every increase in owners' equity comes from revenue. As illustrated in Chapter 1, the owners' equity is also increased by the investment of assets in the business by the owners.

Various terms are used to describe different types of revenue; for example, the revenue earned by a real estate broker may be called *Commissions Earned;* in the professional practice of lawyers, physicians, dentists, and CPAs, the revenue is called *Fees Earned;* a person owning property and leasing it to others has revenue called *Rent Earned;* and businesses selling merchandise rather than services generally use the term *Sales* to describe the revenue earned.

Expenses

Expenses are the cost of the goods and services used up in the process of obtaining revenue. Examples include salaries paid employees, charges for newspaper advertising and for telephone service, and the wearing out (depreciation) of the building and office equipment. All these items are necessary to attract and serve customers and thereby to obtain revenue. Expenses are sometimes referred to as the "cost of doing business," that is, the cost of the various activities necessary to carry on a business. Since expenses are the cost of goods and services used up, they are also called *expired costs.*

Expenses cause the owners' equity to decrease. Revenue may be regarded as the positive factor in creating net income, expenses as the negative factor. The relationship between expenses and revenue is a significant one; the expenses of a given month or other period are incurred in order to generate revenue *in that same period.* The salaries earned by sales employees waiting on customers during July are applicable to July revenue and should be treated as July expenses, even though these salaries may not actually be paid to the employees until sometime in August.

As previously explained, revenue and cash receipts are not one and the same thing; similarly, expenses and cash payments are not identical. Examples of cash payments which are not expenses of the current period include the purchase of an office building for cash, the purchase of merchandise for later sale to customers, the repayment of a bank loan, and the distribution of cash dividends by the business to the stockholders. In deciding whether a given item should be regarded as an expense of the current period, it is often helpful to pose the following questions:

1 Was the alleged "expense" incurred in order to produce revenue of the current period?

2 Does the item in question reduce owners' equity?

If the answer to both questions is Yes, the transaction does represent an expense.

Dividends

A dividend is a distribution of assets (usually cash) by a corporation to its stockholders. Although the payment of a dividend reduces the owners' equity in the corporation, a dividend is not an expense. Unlike payments for advertising, rent, and salaries, the payment of dividends does not serve to generate revenue.

Although withdrawals by the owner of an unincorporated business are somewhat similar to dividends paid by a corporation, significant differences exist. Dividends are paid only when the corporation's board of directors takes formal action to declare a dividend, and dividend payments ordinarily cannot be greater than the retained earnings. The dividend is always a specific amount, such as $1 per share.

Since the declaration and payment of a dividend reduces the stockholders' equity, it could be recorded by debiting the Retained Earnings account. However, a clearer record is created if a separate **Dividends** account is debited for all amounts distributed as dividends to stockholders. The disposition of the Dividends account when financial statements are prepared will be illustrated later in this chapter.

Matching revenue and expenses

To prepare an income statement and determine the net income of a business for any particular time period, we use the **matching principle.** Revenue must be matched with the related expenses incurred in obtaining that revenue. In matching revenue and expenses in the income statement, we show first all the revenue earned during the period and then deduct from the revenue all the expenses incurred in producing that revenue.

Relating revenue and expenses to time periods

A balance sheet shows the financial position of the business at a given date. An income statement, on the other hand, shows the results of operations over *a period of time.* In fact, the concept of income is meaningless unless it is related to a period of time. For example, if a business executive says, "My business produces net income of $5,000," the meaning is not at all clear; it could be made clear, however, by relating the income to a time period, such as "$5,000 a week," "$5,000 a month," or "$5,000 a year."

THE ACCOUNTING PERIOD   Every business concern prepares a yearly income statement, and most businesses prepare quarterly and monthly income statements as well. Management needs to know from month to month whether revenue is rising or falling, whether expenses are being held to the level anticipated, and how net income compares with the net income of the preceding month and with the net income of the corresponding month of the preceding year. The term *accounting period* means *the span of time covered by an income statement.* It may consist of a month, a quarter of a year, a half year, or a year.

Many income statements cover the calendar year ended December 31, but an increasing number of companies are adopting an annual accounting period ending with a month other than December. Generally a business finds it more convenient to end its annual accounting period during a slack season rather than during a time of peak activity. Any

12-month accounting period adopted by a business is called its *fiscal year.* A fiscal year ending at the annual low point of seasonal activity is said to be a *natural business year.* The fiscal year selected by the federal government for its accounting purposes begins on October 1 and ends 12 months later on September 30.

TRANSACTIONS AFFECTING TWO OR MORE ACCOUNTING PERIODS The operation of a business entails an endless stream of transactions, many of which begin in one accounting period but affect several succeeding periods. Fire insurance policies, for example, are commonly issued to cover a period of three years. In this case, the apportionment of the cost of the policy by months is an easy matter. If the policy covers three years (36 months) and costs, for example, $360, the expense each month of maintaining insurance is $10.

Not all transactions can be so precisely divided by accounting periods. The purchase of a building, furniture and fixtures, machinery, a typewriter, or an automobile provides benefits to the business over all the years in which such an asset is used. No one can determine in advance exactly how many years of service will be received from such long-lived assets. Nevertheless, in measuring the net income of a business for a period of one year or less, the accountant must estimate what portion of the cost of the building and similar long-lived assets is applicable to the current year. Since the apportionments for these and many other transactions which overlap two or more accounting periods are in the nature of estimates rather than precise measurements, it follows that income statements should be regarded as *useful approximations* of annual income rather than as absolutely accurate determinations.

If we assume a stable price level, the time period for which the measurement of net income can be most accurate is the entire life span of the business. When a business sells all its assets, pays its debts, and ends its existence, it would then theoretically be possible to determine with precision the net income for the time period from the date of organization to the date of dissolution. Such a theoretically precise measurement of net income would be too late, however, to be of much use to the owners or managers of the business. The practical needs of business enterprise are well served by income statements of reasonable accuracy that tell managers and owners each month, each quarter, and each year the results of business operation.

Rules of debit and credit for revenue and expenses

Our approach to revenue and expenses has stressed the fact that revenue increases the owners' equity and that expenses decrease the owners' equity. The rules of debit and credit for recording revenue and expenses follow this relationship, and therefore the recording of revenue and expenses in ledger accounts requires only a slight extension of the rules of debit and credit presented in Chapter 2. The rule previously stated for recording increases and decreases in owners' equity was as follows:

Increases in owners' equity are recorded by credits.

Decreases in owners' equity are recorded by debits.

This rule is now extended to cover revenue and expense accounts:

Revenue increases owners' equity; therefore revenue is recorded by a credit.

Expenses decrease owners' equity; therefore expenses are recorded by debits.

Ledger accounts for revenue and expenses

During the course of an accounting period, a great many revenue and expense transactions occur in the average business. To classify and summarize these numerous transactions, a separate ledger account is maintained for each major type of revenue and expense. For example, almost every business maintains accounts for Advertising Expense, Telephone Expense, and Salaries Expense. At the end of the period, all the advertising expenses appear as debits in the Advertising Expense account. The debit balance of this account represents the total advertising expense of the period and is listed as one of the expense items in the income statement.

Revenue accounts are usually much less numerous than expense accounts. A small business such as the Greenhill Real Estate Company in our continuing illustration may have only one or two types of revenue, such as commissions earned from arranging sales of real estate and commissions earned from the rental of properties in behalf of clients. In a business of this type, the revenue accounts might be called *Sales Commissions Earned* and *Rental Commissions Earned.*

RECORDING REVENUE AND EXPENSE TRANSACTIONS: ILLUSTRATION
The organization of the Greenhill Real Estate Company during September has already been described in Chapters 1 and 2. The illustration is now continued for October, during which month the company earned commissions by selling several residences for its clients. Bear in mind that the company does not own any residential property; it merely acts as a broker or agent for clients wishing to sell their houses. A commission of 6% of the selling price of the house is charged for this service. During October the company not only earned commissions but incurred a number of expenses.

Note that each illustrated transaction which affects an income statement account also affects a balance sheet account. This pattern is consistent with our previous discussion of revenue and expenses. In recording revenue transactions, we shall debit the assets received and credit a revenue account. In recording expense transactions, we shall debit an expense account and credit the asset Cash, or perhaps a liability account if payment is to be made later. The transactions for October were as follows:

Oct. 1 Paid $360 for publication of newspaper advertising describing various houses offered for sale.

	Analysis	Rule	Entry
Advertising expense incurred and paid	The cost of advertising is an expense	Expenses decrease the owners' equity and are recorded by debits	Debit: Advertising Expense, $360
	The asset Cash was decreased	Decreases in assets are recorded by credits	Credit: Cash, $360

Oct. 6 Earned and collected a commission of $2,250 by selling a residence previously listed by a client.

	Analysis	Rule	Entry
Revenue earned and collected	The asset Cash was increased	Increases in assets are recorded by debits	Debit: Cash, $2,250
	Revenue was earned	Revenue increases the owners' equity and is recorded by a credit	Credit: Sales Commissions Earned, $2,250

Oct. 16 Newspaper advertising was ordered at a price of $270, payment to be made within 30 days.

	Analysis	Rule	Entry
Advertising expense incurred but not paid	The cost of advertising is an expense	Expenses decrease the owners' equity and are recorded by debits	Debit: Advertising Expense, $270
	An account payable, a liability, was incurred	Increases in liabilities are recorded by credits	Credit: Accounts Payable, $270

Oct. 20 A commission of $3,390 was earned by selling a client's residence. The sales agreement provided that the commission would be paid in 60 days.

	Analysis	Rule	Entry
Revenue earned, to be collected later	An asset in the form of an account receivable was acquired	Increases in assets are recorded by debits	Debit: Accounts Receivable, $3,390
	Revenue was earned	Revenue increases the owners' equity and is recorded by a credit	Credit: Sales Commissions Earned, $3,390

Oct. 30 Paid salaries of $2,100 to office employees for services rendered during October.

	Analysis	Rule	Entry
Salaries expense incurred and paid	Salaries of employees are an expense	Expenses decrease the owners' equity and are recorded by debits	Debit: Office Salaries Expense, $2,100
	The asset Cash was decreased	Decreases in assets are recorded by credits	Credit: Cash, $2,100

Oct. 30 A telephone bill for October amounting to $144 was received. Payment was required by November 10.

	Analysis	Rule	Entry
Telephone expense incurred, to be paid later	The cost of telephone service is an expense	Expenses decrease the owners' equity and are recorded by debits	Debit: Telephone Expense, $144
	An account payable, a liability, was incurred	Increases in liabilities are recorded by credits	Credit: Accounts Payable, $144

Oct. 30 A dividend was declared and paid to the owners of the 6,000 shares of capital stock. The amount of the dividend was 30 cents per share, or a total of $1,800. (As explained on page 82, a dividend is not an expense.)

	Analysis	Rule	Entry
Payment of a dividend	Payment of a dividend decreases the owners' equity	Decreases in owners' equity are recorded by debits	Debit: Dividends, $1,800
	The asset Cash was decreased	Decreases in assets are recorded by credits	Credit: Cash, $1,800

The journal entries to record the October transactions are illustrated on page 88. The column headings at the top of the illustrated journal page (**Date, Account Titles and Explanation, LP, Debit,** and **Credit**) are seldom used in practice. They are included here as an instructional guide but will be omitted from some of the later illustrations of journal entries.

General Journal   Page 2

October
journal
entries for
Greenhill
Real Estate
Company

Date		Account Titles and Explanation	LP	Debit	Credit
19___					
Oct.	1	Advertising Expense	70	360	
		Cash	1		360
		Paid for newspaper advertising.			
	6	Cash	1	2,250	
		Sales Commissions Earned	61		2,250
		Earned and collected commission by selling residence for client.			
	16	Advertising Expense	70	270	
		Accounts Payable	30		270
		Ordered newspaper advertising; payable in 30 days.			
	20	Accounts Receivable	2	3,390	
		Sales Commissions Earned	61		3,390
		Earned commission by selling residence for client; commission to be received in 60 days.			
	30	Office Salaries Expense	72	2,100	
		Cash	1		2,100
		Paid office salaries for October.			
	30	Telephone Expense	74	144	
		Accounts Payable	30		144
		To record liability for October telephone service.			
	30	Dividends	51	1,800	
		Cash	1		1,800
		Paid dividend to stockholders (6,000 shares at 30 cents per share).			

Ledger accounts for Greenhill Real Estate Company: illustration

The ledger of the Greenhill Real Estate Company after the October transactions have been posted is now illustrated. The accounts appear in the ledger in financial statement order as follows:

Balance sheet accounts
  Assets
  Liabilities
  Owners' equity
Income statement accounts
  Revenue
  Expenses

Date	Explanation	Ref	Cash Debit	Credit	Account No. 1 Balance
Sept. 1		1	60000 00		60000 00
3		1		21000 00	39000 00
5		1		15000 00	24000 00
20		1	1500 00		25500 00
30		1		3000 00	22500 00
Oct. 1		2		360 00	22140 00
6		2	2250 00		24390 00
30		2		2100 00	22290 00
30		2		1800 00	20490 00

Date	Explanation	Ref	Accounts Receivable Debit	Credit	Account No. 2 Balance
Sept. 10		1	6000 00		6000 00
20		1		1500 00	4500 00
Oct. 20		2	3390 00		7890 00

Date	Explanation	Ref	Land Debit	Credit	Account No. 20 Balance
Sept. 3		1	21000 00		21000 00
10		1		6000 00	15000 00

Date	Explanation	Ref	Building Debit	Credit	Account No. 22 Balance
Sept. 5		1	36000 00		36000 00

			Office Equipment			Account No. 25
Date	Explanation	Ref	Debit	Credit		Balance
19— Sept. 14		1	5400 00			5400 00

			Accounts Payable			Account No. 30
Date	Explanation	Ref	Debit	Credit		Balance
19— Sept. 5		1		21000 00		21000 00
14		1		5400 00		26400 00
30		1	3000 00			23400 00
Oct. 16		2		270 00		23670 00
30		2		144 00		23814 00

			Capital Stock			Account No. 50
Date	Explanation	Ref	Debit	Credit		Balance
19— Sept. 1		1		60000 00		60000 00

			Dividends			Account No. 51
Date	Explanation	Ref	Debit	Credit		Balance
19— Oct. 30		2	1800 00			1800 00

		Sales	Commissions Earned			Account No. 61
Date	Explanation	Ref	Debit	Credit		Balance
19— Oct. 6		2		2250 00		2250 00
20		2		3390 00		5640 00

			Advertising Expense			Account No. 70
Date	Explanation	Ref	Debit	Credit		Balance
19— Oct. 1		2	360 00			360 00
16		2	270 00			630 00

			Office Salaries Expense			Account No. 72
Date	Explanation	Ref	Debit	Credit		Balance
19— Oct. 30		2	2 1 0 0 00			2 1 0 0 00

			Telephone Expense			Account No. 74
Date	Explanation	Ref	Debit	Credit		Balance
19— Oct. 30		2	1 4 4 00			1 4 4 00

Trial balance

The following trial balance was prepared from the preceding ledger accounts.

GREENHILL REAL ESTATE COMPANY
Trial Balance
October 31, 19____

Proving the equality of debits and credits

Cash	$20,490	
Accounts receivable	7,890	
Land	15,000	
Building	36,000	
Office equipment	5,400	
Accounts payable		$23,814
Capital stock		60,000
Dividends	1,800	
Sales commissions earned		5,640
Advertising expense	630	
Office salaries expense	2,100	
Telephone expense	144	
	$89,454	$89,454

Recording depreciation at the end of the period

This trial balance includes all the October expenses requiring cash payments such as salaries, advertising, and telephone service, but it does not include any depreciation expense. Our definition of expense is *the cost of goods and services used up in the process of obtaining revenue.* Some of the goods used up are purchased in advance and used up gradually over a long period of time. Buildings and office equipment, for example, are used up over a period of years. Each year, a portion of these assets *expires,* and a portion of their total cost should be recognized as *depreciation expense.*

Depreciation expense does not require monthly cash outlays; in effect, it is *paid in advance* when the related asset is originally acquired. Nevertheless, depreciation is an inevitable and continuing expense. Failure to record depreciation would result in *understating* total expenses of the period and consequently *overstating* the net income.

BUILDING   The office building purchased by the Greenhill Real Estate Company at a cost of $36,000 is estimated to have a useful life of 20 years. The purpose of the $36,000 expenditure was to provide a place in which to carry on the business and thereby to obtain revenue. After 20 years of use the building will be worthless and the original cost of $36,000 will have been entirely consumed. In effect, the company has purchased 20 years of "housing services" at a total cost of $36,000. A portion of this cost expires during each year of use of the building. If we assume that each year's operations should bear an equal share of the total cost (straight-line depreciation), the annual depreciation expense will amount to $\frac{1}{20}$ of $36,000, or $1,800. On a monthly basis, depreciation expense is $150 ($36,000 cost ÷ 240 months). There are alternative methods of spreading the cost of a depreciable asset over its useful life, some of which will be considered in Chapter 12.

The journal entry to record depreciation of the building during October follows:

General Journal

Page 2

	Date		Account Titles and Explanation	LP	Debit	Credit
Recording depreciation of the building	19___					
	Oct.	31	Depreciation Expense: Building.	76	150	
			Accumulated Depreciation: Building .	23		150
			To record depreciation for October.			

The depreciation expense account will appear in the income statement for October along with the other expenses of salaries, advertising, and telephone expense. The Accumulated Depreciation: Building account will appear in the balance sheet as a deduction from the Building account, as shown by the following illustration of a *partial* balance sheet:

Showing accumulated depreciation in the balance sheet

GREENHILL REAL ESTATE COMPANY

Partial Balance Sheet

October 31, 19___

Building (at cost). $36,000

Less: Accumulated depreciation 150 $35,850

The end result of crediting the Accumulated Depreciation: Building account is much the same as if the credit had been made to the Building account; that is, the net amount shown on the balance sheet for the building is reduced from $36,000 to $35,850. Although the credit side of a depreciation entry *could* be made directly to the asset account, it is customary and more efficient to record such credits in a separate account entitled Accumulated Depreciation. The original cost of the asset and the total amount of depreciation recorded over the years can more easily be determined from the ledger when separate accounts are maintained for the asset and for the accumulated depreciation.

Accumulated Depreciation: Building is an example of a ***contra-asset account,*** because it has a credit balance and is offset against an asset account (Building) to produce the proper balance sheet valuation for the asset.

OFFICE EQUIPMENT Depreciation on the office equipment of the Greenhill Real Estate Company must also be recorded at the end of October. This equipment cost $5,400 and is assumed to have a useful life of 10 years. Monthly depreciation expense on the straight-line basis is, therefore, $45, computed by dividing the cost of $5,400 by the useful life of 120 months. The journal entry is as follows:

General Journal   *Page 2*

	Date		Account Titles and Explanation	LP	Debit	Credit
Recording depreciation of office equipment	*19—* *Oct.*	*31*	*Depreciation Expense: Office Equipment* . .	*78*	*45*	
			Accumulated Depreciation: Office			
			Equipment	*26*		*45*
			To record depreciation for October.			

No depreciation was recorded on the building and office equipment for September, the month in which these assets were acquired, because regular operations did not begin until October. Generally, depreciation is not recognized until the business begins active operation and the assets are placed in use. Accountants often use the expression *matching costs and revenue* to convey the idea of writing off the cost of an asset to expense during the time periods in which the business uses the asset to generate revenue.

The journal entry by which depreciation is recorded at the end of the month is called an *adjusting entry.* The adjustment of certain asset accounts and related expense accounts is a necessary step at the end of each accounting period so that the information presented in the financial statements will be as accurate and complete as possible. In the next chapter, adjusting entries will be shown for some other items in addition to depreciation.

The adjusted trial balance

After all the necessary adjusting entries have been journalized and posted, an *adjusted trial balance* is prepared to prove that the ledger is still in balance. It also provides a complete listing of the account balances to be used in preparing the financial statements. The following adjusted trial balance differs from the trial balance shown on page 91 because it includes accounts for depreciation expense and accumulated depreciation.

GREENHILL REAL ESTATE COMPANY
Adjusted Trial Balance
October 31, 19___

Adjusted Cash	$20,490	
trial balance Accounts receivable	7,890	
Land	15,000	
Building	36,000	
Accumulated depreciation: building		$ 150
Office equipment	5,400	
Accumulated depreciation: office equipment		45
Accounts payable		23,814
Capital stock		60,000
Dividends	1,800	
Sales commissions earned		5,640
Advertising expense	630	
Office salaries expense	2,100	
Telephone expense	144	
Depreciation expense: building	150	
Depreciation expense: office equipment	45	
	$89,649	$89,649

FINANCIAL STATEMENTS

Now that Greenhill Real Estate Company has been operating for a month, managers and outside parties will want to know more about the company than just its financial position. They will want to know the results of Greenhill's operations—whether the company's activities have been profitable or unprofitable. To provide this additional information, we will prepare a more complete set of financial statements, including an income statement, a statement of retained earnings, and a balance sheet.[1]

---

[1] A complete set of financial statements would also include a statement of changes in financial position, which will be discussed in Chapter 15.

The income statement

When we measure the net income earned by a business we are measuring its economic performance—its success or failure as a business enterprise. Stockholders, prospective investors, managers, bankers, and other creditors are anxious to see the latest available income statement and thereby to judge how well the company is doing. The October income statement for Greenhill Real Estate Company appears as follows:

GREENHILL REAL ESTATE COMPANY
Income Statement
For the Month Ended October 31, 19___

Income statement for October

Sales commissions earned		$5,640
Expenses:		
Advertising expense	$ 630	
Office salaries expense	2,100	
Telephone expense	144	
Depreciation expense: building.	150	
Depreciation expense: office equipment	45	3,069
Net income		$2,571

This income statement shows that the revenue during October exceeded the expenses of the month, thus producing a net income of $2,571. Bear in mind, however, that our measurement of net income is not absolutely accurate or precise, because of the assumptions and estimates involved in the accounting process. We have recorded only those economic events which are *evidenced by accounting transactions.* Perhaps during October the Greenhill Real Estate Company has developed a strong interest on the part of many clients who are on the verge of buying or selling homes. This accumulation of client interest is an important step toward profitable operation, but is not reflected in the October 31 income statement because it is not subject to objective measurement. Remember also that in determining the amount of depreciation expense we had to estimate the useful life of the building and office equipment. Any error in our estimates is reflected in the net income reported for October. Despite these limitations, the income statement is of vital importance and indicates that the new business has been profitable during the first month of its operation.

At this point we are purposely ignoring income taxes on corporations. Corporate income taxes will be introduced in Chapter 5 and considered more fully in Chapters 7 and 17.

Alternative titles for the income statement include *earnings statement, statement of operations,* and *profit and loss statement.* However, *income statement* is by far the most popular term for this important financial statement. In brief, we can say that an income statement is used to summarize the **operating results** of a business by matching the revenue earned during a given time period with the expenses incurred in obtaining that revenue.

Statement of retained earnings

Retained earnings is that portion of the stockholders' equity created by earning and retaining net income. The **statement of retained earnings,** which covers the same time period as the related income statement, shows the sources of increase and decrease in retained earnings for that period.

GREENHILL REAL ESTATE COMPANY
Statement of Retained Earnings
For the Month Ended October 31, 19____

<table>
<tr><td rowspan="5">*Statement of retained earnings for October*</td><td>Retained earnings, Sept. 30, 19____ . . . .</td><td>$ –0–</td></tr>
<tr><td>Net income for October. . . . .</td><td>2,571</td></tr>
<tr><td> Subtotal . . . .</td><td>$2,571</td></tr>
<tr><td>Dividends . . . .</td><td>1,800</td></tr>
<tr><td>Retained earnings, Oct. 31, 19____ . . . .</td><td>$ 771</td></tr>
</table>

In this example the company had no retained earnings at the beginning of the period. The statement for the following month would show a beginning balance of $771.

The balance sheet

In preparing a balance sheet for Greenhill Real Estate Company at October 31, we can obtain the current balances of the asset, liability, and capital stock accounts from the adjusted trial balance on page 94. The amount of retained earnings at October 31 does not appear in the adjusted trial balance, but has been determined in the statement of retained earnings.

Previous illustrations of balance sheets have been arranged in the **account form,** that is, with the assets on the left side of the page and the liabilities and stockholders' equity on the right side. The following balance sheet is presented in **report form,** that is, with the liabilities and stockholders' equity sections listed below rather than to the right of the asset section. Both the account form and the report form are widely used.

GREENHILL REAL ESTATE COMPANY
Balance Sheet
October 31, 19___

Assets

Balance
sheet at
October 31:
report
form

Cash			$20,490
Accounts receivable			7,890
Land			15,000
Building		$36,000	
Less: Accumulated depreciation		150	35,850
Office equipment		$ 5,400	
Less: Accumulated depreciation		45	5,355
Total assets			$84,585

Liabilities & Stockholders' Equity

Liabilities:			
Accounts payable			$23,814
Stockholders' equity:			
Capital stock		$60,000	
Retained earnings		771	60,771
Total liabilities & stockholders' equity			$84,585

If we compare the October 31 balance sheet to the one prepared at September 30 (page 27), we see that the stockholders' original investment of $60,000 appears unchanged under the caption of Capital Stock. The amount of retained earnings, however, has changed between the two balance sheet dates. The Retained Earnings account had a zero balance at September 30, but as explained in the statement of retained earnings, it was increased by the $2,571 net income earned during October and decreased by the $1,800 dividend paid, leaving a balance of $771 at October 31.

The amount of the Retained Earnings account at any balance sheet date represents the accumulated earnings of the company since the date of incorporation, minus any losses and minus all dividends distributed to stockholders. One reason for maintaining a distinction between capital stock and retained earnings is that a corporation usually cannot legally pay dividends greater than the amount of retained earnings. The separation of these two elements of ownership may also be informative because it shows how much of the total stockholders' equity resulted from the investment of funds by stockholders and how much was derived from earning and retaining net income.

In the Greenhill Real Estate Company illustration, we have shown the two common ways in which the stockholders' equity may be increased: (1) investment of cash or other assets by the owners and (2) operating the business at a profit. There are also two common ways in which the stockholders' equity may be decreased: (1) payment of dividends and (2) operating the business at a loss.

**The income statement and retained earnings statement
provide a "link" between two balance sheets**

A set of financial statements becomes easier to understand if we recognize that the balance sheet, income statement, and statement of retained earnings are all related to one another. The balance sheet prepared at the end of the last accounting period and the one prepared at the end of the current period each show the amount of retained earnings at the respective balance sheet dates. The statement of retained earnings summarizes the factors (net income and dividends) which have caused the amount of retained earnings to change between these balance sheet dates. The income statement explains in greater detail the change in retained earnings resulting from profitable operation of the business. Thus, the income statement and the retained earnings statement provide an informative link between successive balance sheets.

CLOSING THE ACCOUNTS

The accounts for revenue, expenses, and dividends are *temporary owners' equity accounts* used during the accounting period to classify changes affecting the owners' equity. At the end of the period, we want to transfer the net effect of these various increases and decreases into retained earnings, which is a permanent owners' equity account. We also want to reduce the balances of the temporary owners' equity accounts to zero, so that these accounts will again be ready for use in accumulating information during the next accounting period. These objectives are accomplished by the use of *closing entries.*

Revenue and expense accounts are closed at the end of each accounting period by transferring their balances to a summary account called *Income Summary.* When the credit balances of the revenue accounts and the debit balances of the expense accounts have been transferred into one summary account, the balance of this Income Summary will be the net income or net loss for the period. If the revenue (credit balances) exceeds the expenses (debit balances), the Income Summary account will have a credit balance representing net income. Conversely, if expenses exceed revenue, the Income Summary will have a debit balance representing net loss. This is consistent with the rule that increases in owners' equity are recorded by credits and decreases are recorded by debits.

A journal entry made for the purpose of closing a revenue or expense account is called a *closing entry.* This term is also applied to the journal entries (to be explained later) used in closing the Income Summary account and the Dividends account into the Retained Earnings account.

A principal purpose of the year-end process of closing the revenue and expense accounts is to reduce their balances to zero. Since the revenue and expense accounts provide the information for the income statement of *a given accounting period,* it is essential that these accounts have zero balances at the beginning of each new period. The closing of the accounts has the effect of "wiping the slate clean" and preparing the accounts for the recording of revenue and expenses during the succeeding accounting period.

It is common practice to close the accounts only once a year, but for illustration, we shall now demonstrate the closing of the accounts of the Greenhill Real Estate Company at October 31 after one month's operation.

CLOSING ENTRIES FOR REVENUE ACCOUNTS Revenue accounts have credit balances. Closing a revenue account, therefore, means transferring its credit balance to the Income Summary account. This transfer is accomplished by a journal entry debiting the revenue account in an amount equal to its credit balance, with an offsetting credit to the Income Summary account. The only revenue account of the Greenhill Real Estate Company is Sales Commissions Earned, which had a credit balance of $5,640 at October 31. The journal entry necessary to close this account is as follows:

General Journal Page 3

	Date		Account Titles and Explanation	LP	Debit	Credit
Closing a revenue account	19___ Oct.	31	Sales Commissions Earned	61	5,640	
			Income Summary	53		5,640
			To close the Sales Commissions Earned account.			

After this closing entry has been posted, the two accounts affected will appear as shown below. Arrows have been added to indicate the debit and credit parts of the closing entry.

Sales Commissions Earned 61   **Income Summary** 53

Date		Expla- nation	Ref	Debit	Credit	Balance	Date		Expla- nation	Ref	Debit	Credit	Balance
Oct.	6		2		2,250	2,250	Oct.	31	Revenue	3		5,640	5,640
	20		2		3,390	5,640							
	31	To close	3	5,640		–0–							

Postings

CLOSING ENTRIES FOR EXPENSE ACCOUNTS Expense accounts have debit balances. Closing an expense account means transferring its debit balance to the Income Summary account. The journal entry to close an expense account, therefore, consists of a credit to the expense account in an amount equal to its debit balance, with an offsetting debit to the Income Summary account.

There are five expense accounts in the ledger of the Greenhill Real Estate Company. Five separate journal entries could be made to close these five expense accounts, but the use of one *compound journal entry* is an easier, more efficient, timesaving method of closing all five expense accounts. A compound journal entry is an entry that includes debits to more than one account or credits to more than one account.

General Journal

Page 3

	Date		Account Titles and Explanation	LP	Debit	Credit
Closing	19___					
the	Oct.	31	Income Summary	53	3,069	
various			Advertising Expense	70		630
expense			Office Salaries Expense	72		2,100
accounts			Telephone Expense	74		144
by use			Depreciation Expense: Building. . . .	76		150
of a			Depreciation Expense: Office			
compound			Equipment	78		45
journal			To close the expense accounts.			
entry						

After this closing entry has been posted, the Income Summary account has a credit balance of $2,571, and the five expense accounts have zero balances, as shown on page 101.

CLOSING THE INCOME SUMMARY ACCOUNT The five expense accounts have now been closed and the total amount of $3,069 formerly contained in these accounts appears in the debit column of the Income Summary account. The commissions of $5,640 earned during October appear in the credit column of the Income Summary account. Since the credit entry of $5,640 representing October revenue is larger than the debit of $3,069 representing October expenses, the account has a credit balance of $2,571—the net income for October.

The net income of $2,571 earned during October causes the owner's equity to increase. The *credit* balance of the Income Summary account is, therefore, transferred to the Retained Earnings account by the following closing entry:

General Journal

Page 3

	Date		Account Titles and Explanation	LP	Debit	Credit
Net income	19___					
earned	Oct.	31	Income Summary	53	2,571	
increases			Retained Earnings	51		2,571
the			To close the Income Summary account for			
owners'			October by transferring the net income to the			
equity			Retained Earnings account.			

Advertising Expense   70

Date	Expla-nation	Ref	Debit	Credit	Balance
19__					
Oct. 2		2	360		360
16		2	270		630
31	To close	3		630	–0–

Office Salaries Expense   72

Date	Expla-nation	Ref	Debit	Credit	Balance
19__					
Oct. 30		2	2,100		2,100
31	To close	3		2,100	–0–

Telephone Expense   74

Date	Expla-nation	Ref	Debit	Credit	Balance
19__					
Oct. 30		2	144		144
31	To close	3		144	–0–

Depreciation Expense: Building   76

Date	Expla-nation	Ref	Debit	Credit	Balance
19__					
Oct. 31		2	150		150
31	To close	3		150	–0–

Depreciation Expense: Office Equipment   78

Date	Expla-nation	Ref	Debit	Credit	Balance
19__					
Oct. 31		2	45		45
31	To close	3		45	–0–

Income Summary   53

Date	Expla-nation	Ref	Debit	Credit	Balance
19__					
Oct. 31	Revenue	3		5,640	5,640
31	Expenses	3	3,069		2,571

Postings

After this closing entry has been posted, the Income Summary account has a zero balance, and the net income earned during October appears in the Retained Earnings account as shown below:

						Income Summary	53

Date		Expla-nation	Ref	Debit	Credit	Balance
19__						
Oct.	31	Revenue	3		5,640	5,640
	31	Expense	3	3,069		2,571
	31	To close	3	2,571		–0–

Date		Expla-nation	Ref	Debit	Credit	Balance
19__						
Oct.	31	Net				
		income	3		2,571	2,571

Retained Earnings 51

———— Postings ————

In our illustration the business has operated profitably with revenue in excess of expenses. Not every business is so fortunate; if the expenses of a business are larger than its revenue, the Income Summary account will have a debit balance. In this case, the closing of the Income Summary account would require a debit to the Retained Earnings account and an offsetting credit to the Income Summary account. A debit balance in the Retained Earnings account is referred to as a *deficit;* it would be shown as a deduction from Capital Stock in the balance sheet.

Note that the Income Summary account is used only at the end of the period when the accounts are being closed. The Income Summary account has no entries and no balance except during the process of closing the accounts at the end of the accounting period.

CLOSING THE DIVIDENDS ACCOUNTS As explained earlier in this chapter, the payment of dividends to the owners is not considered as an expense of the business and, therefore, is not taken into account in determining the net income for the period. Since dividends do not constitute an expense, the Dividends account is closed not into the Income Summary account but directly to the Retained Earnings account, as shown by the following entry:

		General Journal			Page 3

Date		Account Titles and Explanation	LP	Debit	Credit
19__					
Oct.	31	Retained Earnings	51	1,800	
		Dividends	52		1,800
		To close the dividends account.			

Dividends account is closed to Retained Earnings account

After this closing entry has been posted, the Dividends account will have a zero balance, and the dividends distributed during October will appear as a deduction or debit entry in the Retained Earnings account, as follows:

Dividends					52
Date	Expla- nation	Ref	Debit	Credit	Balance
19__					
Oct. 30		2	1,800		1,800
31	To close	3		1,800	–0–

Retained Earnings					51
Date	Expla- nation	Ref	Debit	Credit	Balance
19__					
Oct. 31	Net				
	income	3		2,571	2,571
31	Dividends	3	1,800		771

Postings

THE CLOSING PROCESS—IN SUMMARY Let us now summarize the process of closing the accounts.

1 Close the various revenue accounts by transferring their balances into the Income Summary account.

2 Close the various expense accounts by transferring their balances into the Income Summary account.

3 Close the Income Summary account by transferring its balance into the Retained Earnings account.

4 Close the Dividends account into the Retained Earnings account.

The closing of the accounts may be illustrated graphically by the use of T accounts as shown below:

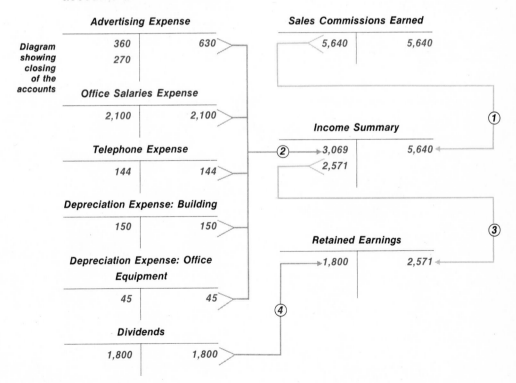

Diagram showing closing of the accounts

After-Closing trial balance

After the revenue and expense accounts have been closed, it is desirable to prepare an *after-closing trial balance,* which of course will consist solely of balance sheet accounts. There is always the possibility that an error in posting the closing entries may have upset the equality of debits and credits in the ledger. The after-closing trial balance, or *post-closing trial balance* as it is often called, is prepared from the ledger. It gives assurance that the accounts are in balance and ready for the recording of the transactions of the new accounting period. The after-closing trial balance of the Greenhill Real Estate Company follows:

GREENHILL REAL ESTATE COMPANY
After-Closing Trial Balance
October 31, 19___

Cash	$20,490	
Accounts receivable	7,890	
Land	15,000	
Building	36,000	
Accumulated depreciation: building		$ 150
Office equipment	5,400	
Accumulated depreciation: office equipment		45
Accounts payable		23,814
Capital stock		60,000
Retained earnings, Oct. 31		771
	$84,780	$84,780

Only the balance sheet accounts remain open

Sequence of accounting procedures

The accounting procedures described to this point may be summarized in eight steps, as follows:

1 Journalize transactions Enter all transactions in the journal, thus creating a chronological record of events.

2 Post to ledger accounts Post debits and credits from the journal to the proper ledger accounts, thus creating a record classified by accounts.

3 Prepare a trial balance Prove the equality of debits and credits in the ledger.

4 Prepare end-of-period adjustments Enter adjusting entries in the general journal, and post to ledger accounts.

5 Prepare an adjusted trial balance Prove again the equality of debits and credits in the ledger.

6 Prepare financial statements An income statement is needed to show the results of operation for the period. A statement of retained earnings is needed to show the changes in retained earnings during the period and the closing balance. A balance sheet is needed to show the financial position of the business at the end of the period.

7 Journalize and post the closing entries The closing entries clear the revenue, expense, and dividends accounts, making them ready for recording the events of the next accounting period, and also bring the Retained Earnings account up-to-date.

8 Prepare an after-closing trial balance This step ensures that the ledger remains in balance after posting of the closing entries.

Dividends—declaration and payment

Earlier in this chapter the declaration and the payment of a cash dividend were treated as a single event recorded by one journal entry. A small corporation with only a few stockholders may choose to declare and pay a dividend on the same day. In large corporations with thousands of stockholders and constant transfers of shares, an interval of a month or more will separate the date of declaration from the later date of payment.

Assume for example that on April 1 the board of directors of Universal Corporation declares the regular quarterly dividend of $1 per share on the 1 million shares of outstanding capital stock. The board's resolution specifies that the dividend will be payable on May 10 to stockholders of record on April 25. To be eligible to receive the dividend, an individual must be listed on the corporation's records as a stockholder on April 25, the date of record. Two entries are required: one on April 1 for the declaration of the dividend and one on May 10 for its payment, as shown below.

Dividends declared and . . .	Apr. 1	Dividends	1,000,000	
		Dividends Payable		1,000,000
		Declared dividend of $1 per share payable May 10 to stockholders of record Apr. 25.		
. . . Dividends paid	May 10	Dividends Payable	1,000,000	
		Cash		1,000,000
		Paid the dividend declared on Apr. 1.		

The Dividends Payable account is a liability which comes into existence when the dividend is declared and is discharged when the dividend is paid.

Accrual basis of accounting versus cash basis of accounting

A business which recognizes revenue in the period in which it is earned and deducts the expenses incurred in generating this revenue is using the *accrual basis of accounting.* To be meaningful, net income must relate to a specified period of time. Since net income is determined by offsetting expenses against revenue, both the expenses and the revenue used in the calculation must relate to the same time period. This *matching* or offsetting of related revenue and expenses gives a realistic picture of the profit performance of the business each period. The accrual basis is thus essential to income determination, which is a major objective of the whole accounting process.

The alternative to the accrual basis of accounting is the *cash basis.* Under cash basis accounting, revenue is not recorded until received in cash; expenses are assigned to the period in which cash payment is made. Most business concerns use the accrual basis of accounting, but individuals and professionals (such as physicians and lawyers) usually maintain their accounting records on a cash basis.

The cash basis of accounting does not give a good picture of profitability. For example, it ignores uncollected revenue which has been earned and expenses which have been incurred but not paid. Throughout this book we shall be working with the accrual basis of accounting, except for that portion of Chapter 17 dealing with the income tax returns of individuals.

KEY TERMS INTRODUCED OR EMPHASIZED IN CHAPTER 3

Accounting period   The span of time covered by an income statement. One year is the accounting period for much financial reporting, but financial statements are also prepared by most companies for each quarter of the year and also for each month.

Accrual basis of accounting   Calls for recording revenue in the period in which it is earned and recording expenses in the period in which they are incurred. The effect of events on the business is recognized as services are rendered or consumed rather than when cash is received or paid.

Accumulated depreciation   A contra-asset account shown as a deduction from the related asset account in the balance sheet. Depreciation taken throughout the useful life of an asset is accumulated in this account.

Adjusted trial balance   A listing of all ledger account balances after the amounts have been changed to include the adjusting entries made at the end of the period.

Adjusting entries   Entries required at the end of the period to update the accounts before financial statements are prepared. Adjusting entries serve to apportion transactions properly between the accounting periods affected and to record any revenue earned or expenses incurred which have not been recorded prior to the end of the period.

After-closing trial balance   A trial balance prepared after all closing entries have been made. Consists only of accounts for assets, liabilities, and owners' equity.

Cash basis of accounting   Revenue is recorded when received in cash and expenses are recorded in the period in which cash payment is made. Fails to match revenue with related expenses and therefore does not lead to a logical measurement of income. Use is limited mostly to individual income tax returns and to accounting records of physicians and other professional firms.

Closing entries Journal entries made at the end of the period for the purpose of closing temporary accounts (revenue, expense, and dividends accounts) and bringing the Retained Earnings account up to date.

Contra-asset account An account with a credit balance which is offset against or deducted from an asset account to produce the proper balance sheet valuation for the asset.

Depreciation The systematic allocation to expense of the cost of an asset (such as a building) during the periods of its useful life.

Dividend A distribution of cash by a corporation to its stockholders.

Dividends payable The ledger account which is credited at the date of declaring a dividend. Classified in the balance sheet as a liability.

Expenses The cost of the goods and services used up in the process of obtaining revenue. Sometimes referred to as **expired costs.**

Financial statement order Sequence of accounts in the ledger; balance sheet accounts first (assets, liabilities and owners' equity), followed by income statement accounts (revenue and expenses).

Fiscal year Any 12-month accounting period adopted by a business.

Income statement A report used to evaluate the performance of a business by matching its revenue and related expenses for a particular accounting period. Shows the net income or net loss.

Income Summary account The summary account in the ledger to which revenue and expense accounts are closed at the end of the period. The balance (credit balance for a net income, debit balance for a net loss) is transferred to the Retained Earnings account.

Matching principle The revenue earned during an accounting period is matched with the expenses incurred in generating this revenue.

Net income The excess of revenue earned over the related expenses for a given period.

Report form balance sheet A balance sheet in which the sections for liabilities and owners' equity are listed below the section for assets.

Retained earnings That portion of stockholders' equity resulting from profits earned and retained in the business.

Revenue The price of goods sold and services rendered by a business. Equal to the inflow of cash and receivables in exchange for services rendered or goods delivered during the period.

Temporary owners' equity accounts The accounts for revenue, expenses, and dividends used during the accounting period to classify changes affecting the owners' equity.

DEMONSTRATION PROBLEM FOR YOUR REVIEW

Key Insurance Company was organized on September 1, 19___. Assume that the accounts are closed and financial statements prepared each month. The company occupies rented office space but owns office equipment estimated to have a useful life of 10 years from date of acquisition, September 1. The trial balance for Key Insurance Company at November 30, 19___ is shown on page 108.

Cash	$ 3,750	
Accounts receivable	1,210	
Office equipment	4,800	
Accumulated depreciation: office equipment		$ 80
Accounts payable		1,640
Capital stock		6,000
Retained earnings		1,490
Dividends	500	
Commissions earned		4,720
Advertising expense	800	
Salaries expense	2,600	
Rent expense	270	
	$13,930	$13,930

Instructions

a Prepare the adjusting journal entry to record depreciation of the office equipment for the month of November.

b Prepare an adjusted trial balance at November 30, 19___.

c Prepare an income statement and a statement of retained earnings for the month ended November 30, 19___, and a balance sheet in report form at November 30, 19___.

SOLUTION TO DEMONSTRATION PROBLEM

a Adjusting journal entry:

Depreciation Expense: Office Equipment	40	
Accumulated Depreciation: Office Equipment		40

To record depreciation for November ($4,800 ÷ 120 months).

b

KEY INSURANCE COMPANY
Adjusted Trial Balance
November 30, 19___

Cash	$ 3,750	
Accounts receivable	1,210	
Office equipment	4,800	
Accumulated depreciation: office equipment		$ 120
Accounts payable		1,640
Capital stock		6,000
Retained earnings		1,490
Dividends	500	
Commissions earned		4,720
Advertising expense	800	
Salaries expense	2,600	
Rent expense	270	
Depreciation expense: office equipment	40	
	$13,970	$13,970

c

KEY INSURANCE COMPANY
Income Statement
For the Month Ended November 30, 19___

Commissions earned		$4,720
Expenses:		
Advertising expense	$ 800	
Salaries expense	2,600	
Rent expense	270	
Depreciation expense: office equipment	40	3,710
Net income		$1,010

KEY INSURANCE COMPANY
Statement of Retained Earnings
For the Month Ended November 30, 19___

Retained earnings, Oct. 31, 19___	$1,490
Net income for the month	1,010
Subtotal	$2,500
Dividends	500
Retained earnings, Nov. 30, 19___	$2,000

KEY INSURANCE COMPANY
Balance Sheet
November 30, 19___

Assets

Cash		$3,750
Accounts receivable		1,210
Office equipment	$4,800	
Less: Accumulated depreciation	120	4,680
Total assets		$9,640

Liabilities & Stockholders' Equity

Liabilities:		
Accounts payable		$1,640
Stockholders' equity:		
Capital stock	$6,000	
Retained earnings	2,000	8,000
Total liabilities & stockholders' equity		$9,640

REVIEW QUESTIONS

1 Explain the effect of operating profitably upon the balance sheet of a business entity.

2 Does the Retained Earnings account represent a supply of cash which could be distributed to stockholders? Explain.

3 Does a well-prepared income statement provide an exact and precise measurement of net income for the period or does it represent merely an approximation of net income? Explain.

4 For each of the following financial statements, indicate whether the statement relates to a single date or to a period of time:
a Balance sheet
b Income statement
c Statement of retained earnings

5 What is the meaning of the term **revenue?** Does the receipt of cash by a business always indicate that revenue has been earned? Explain.

6 What is the meaning of the term **expenses?** Does the payment of cash by a business always indicate that an expense has been incurred? Explain.

7 Explain the rules of debit and credit with respect to transactions recorded in revenue and expense accounts.

8 Supply the appropriate term (debit or credit) to complete the following statements.
a The Capital Stock account, Retained Earnings account, and revenue accounts are increased by _____ entries.
b Asset accounts and expense accounts are increased by _____ entries.
c Liability accounts and owners' equity accounts are decreased by _____ entries.

9 Supply the appropriate term (debit or credit) to complete the following statements.
a When a business is operating profitably, the journal entry to close the Income Summary account will consist of a _____ to that account and a _____ to Retained Earnings.
b When a business is operating at a loss, the journal entry to close the Income Summary account will consist of a _____ to that account and a _____ to Retained Earnings.
c The journal entry to close the Dividends account consists of a _____ to that account and a _____ to Retained Earnings.

10 How does depreciation expense differ from other operating expenses?

11 Assume that a business acquires a delivery truck at a cost of $3,600. Estimated life of the truck is four years. State the amount of depreciation expense per year and per month. Give the adjusting entry to record depreciation on the truck at the end of the first month, and explain where the accounts involved would appear in the financial statements.

12 All ledger accounts belong in one of the following five groups: asset, liability, owners' equity, revenue, and expense. For each of the following accounts, state the group in which it belongs. Also indicate whether the normal balance would be a debit or a credit.
a Fees Earned   **e** Building
b Notes Payable   **f** Depreciation Expense
c Telephone Expense   **g** Accumulated Depreciation: Building
d Retained Earnings

13 A service enterprise performs services in the amount of $500 for a customer in May and receives payment in June. In which month is the $500 of revenue recognized? What is the journal entry to be made in May and the entry to be made in June?

14 Which of the following accounts should be closed by a debit to Income Summary and a credit to the account listed?

Dividends	Salaries Expense
Fees Earned	Accounts Payable
Advertising Expense	Depreciation Expense
Accounts Receivable	Accumulated Depreciation

15 Supply the appropriate terms to complete the following statements. _____ and _____ accounts are closed at the end of each accounting period by transferring their balances to a summary account called _____ _____ . A _____ balance in this summary account represents net income for the period; a _____ balance represents a net loss for the period.

16 Which of the ten accounts listed below are affected by closing entries at the end of the accounting period?

Cash	Capital Stock
Fees Earned	Dividends
Income Summary	Accumulated Depreciation
Accounts Payable	Accounts Receivable
Telephone Expense	Depreciation Expense

17 How does the accrual basis of accounting differ from the cash basis of accounting? Which gives a more accurate picture of the profitability of a business? Explain.

EXERCISES

Ex. 3-1 The following transactions were carried out during the month of August by Rancho Corporation, a firm of real estate brokers. Which of these transactions represented revenue to the firm during the month of August? Explain.
a Borrowed $12,800 from Century Bank to be repaid in three months.
b Collected cash of $2,400 from an account receivable. The receivable originated in July from services rendered to a client.
c Arranged a sale of an apartment building owned by a client, Stephen Roberts. The commission for making the sale was $14,400, but this amount would not be received until October 20.
d Collected $480 rent for August from a dentist to whom Rancho Corporation rented part of its building.
e Rancho Corporation received $25,000 cash from the issuance of additional shares of its capital stock.

Ex. 3-2 During July the Columbus Company carried out the following transactions. Which of these transactions represented expenses for July? Explain.
a Paid a garage $640 for automobile repair work performed in May.
b Declared and paid a $1,000 dividend to shareholders.
c Paid $6,400 in settlement of a loan obtained three months earlier.
d Purchased a typewriter for $960 cash.
e Paid $192 for gasoline purchases for the delivery truck during July.
f Paid $960 salary to an employee for time worked during July.

Ex. 3-3 Label each of the following statements as true or false. Explain the reasoning underlying your answer and give an example of a transaction which supports your position.
a Every transaction that affects a balance sheet account also affects an income statement account.
b Every transaction that affects an income statement account also affects a balance sheet account.

c Every transaction that affects an expense account also affects an asset account.

d Every transaction that affects a revenue account also affects another income statement account.

e Every transaction that affects an expense account also affects a revenue account.

Ex. 3-4 Total assets and total liabilities of Mannix Corporation as shown by the balance sheets at the beginning and end of the year were as follows:

	Beginning of Year	End of Year
Assets	$155,000	$200,000
Liabilities	95,000	110,000

Compute the net income or net loss from operations for the year in each of the following independent cases:

a No dividends were declared or paid during the year and no additional capital stock was issued.

b No dividends were declared or paid during the year, but additional capital stock was issued at par in the amount of $25,000.

c Dividends of $10,000 were declared and paid during the year. No change occurred in capital stock.

d Dividends of $3,000 were declared and paid during the year, and additional capital stock was issued at par in the amount of $18,000.

Ex. 3-5 Supply the missing figures in the following independent cases:

a Capital stock (no change during year)	$ 50,000
Dividends for the year	6,000
Retained earnings at beginning of year	24,000
Net income for the year	17,500
Total stockholders' equity at end of year	_____
b Retained earnings at end of year	$ 83,700
Dividends for the year	12,400
Net income for the year	31,200
Retained earnings at beginning of year	_____
c Net income for the year	$_____
Retained earnings at end of year	47,800
Retained earnings at beginning of year	42,600
Dividends for the year	12,400
d Dividends for the year	$_____
Retained earnings at end of year	99,700
Net income for the year	28,500
Retained earnings at beginning of year	91,200
e Total stockholders' equity at beginning of year	$ 71,300
Total stockholders' equity at end of year	88,400
Amount received from additional capital stock issued during year	7,000
Net income for for the year	_____
Dividends for the year	7,600

Ex. 3-6 Martin Corporation's income statement showed net income of $25,380 for the month of October. In recording October transactions, however, certain transac-

tions were incorrectly recorded. Study the following list of selected October transactions, and identify any which were incorrectly recorded. Also give the journal entry as it should have been made, and compute the correct amount of net income for October.

a Made an error in computing depreciation on the building for October. Recorded as $25. The correct amount of depreciation was $250.

b Recorded the payment on October 31 of a $4,000 dividend by debiting Salaries Expense and crediting Cash. The dividend had been declared on October 2.

c Earned a commission of $2,500 by selling a residence for a client. Commission to be received in 60 days. Recorded by debiting Commissions Earned and crediting Accounts Receivable.

d A payment of $250 for newspaper advertising was recorded by debiting Advertising Expense and crediting Accounts Receivable.

e Received but did not pay a bill of $285 for October telephone service. Recorded by debiting Telephone Expense and crediting Commissions Earned.

Ex. 3-7 Madison Company maintains a ledger with accounts arranged in *financial statement order,* so that a trial balance prepared from the ledger will show the accounts in a convenient sequence for preparing the financial statements. Rearrange the following random list of account titles in the order in which they are located in the ledger of Madison Company. For example, the first account should be (1) Cash.

(1) Notes Payable	*(12) Advertising Expense*
(2) Capital Stock	*(13) Accounts Payable*
(3) Depreciation Expense: Buildings	*(14) Interest Payable*
(4) Rent Expense	*(15) Marketable Securities*
(5) Buildings	*(16) Depreciation Expense:*
(6) Accounts Receivable	*Office Equipment*
(7) Land	*(17) Electricity Expense*
(8) Notes Receivable	*(18) Commissions Earned*
(9) Interest Expense	*(19) Retained Earnings*
(10) Accumulated Depreciation: Buildings	*(20) Salaries Expense*
(11) Accumulated Depreciation:	*(21) Office Equipment*
Office Equipment	*(22) Cash*

Ex. 3-8 An employee of Lawn Care Corporation prepared the following closing entries at the year-end. (a) Identify any errors which the employee made and (b) prepare correct closing entries for the business.

Entry 1

Lawn Service Revenue	*78,000*	
Accumulated Depreciation	*8,000*	
Retained Earnings	*27,000*	
Income Summary		*113,000*
To close accounts with credit balances.		

Entry 2

Income Summary	*73,000*	
Salaries Expense		*56,000*
Dividends		*11,000*
Advertising Expense		*4,000*
Depreciation Expense		*2,000*
To close accounts with debit balances.		

Entry 3

Income Summary *40,000*

    Capital Stock *40,000*

To close Income Summary account.

PROBLEMS

3-1 The transactions during October for Pacific Plumbing Company included the following:

(1) On October 1, paid $640 cash for the month's rent.

(2) On October 3, made repairs for First National Bank and collected in full the charge of $1,014.

(3) On October 8, performed repair work for American Home Builders. Sent bill for $1,332 for services rendered.

(4) On October 15, placed an advertisement in the *Tribune* at a cost of $310 payment to be made within 30 days.

(5) On October 21, purchased equipment for $4,000 cash.

(6) On October 30, received a check for $1,332 from American Home Builders.

(7) On October 31, sent check to the *Tribune* in payment of liability incurred on October 15.

(8) On October 31, declared a cash dividend of $5,000 payable on November 30.

Instructions

a Write an analysis of each transaction. An example of the type of analysis desired is as follows:

(1) **(a)** Rent is an operating expense. Expenses are recorded by debits. Debit Rent Expense, $640.

    (b) The asset Cash was decreased. Decreases in assets are recorded by credits. Credit cash, $640.

b Prepare a journal entry (including explanation) for each of the above transactions.

3-2 Shown below in alphabetical order are the ledger accounts and dollar balances required to prepare an adjusted trial balance for Redmond Insurance Agency at November 30, 19____. Assume that the company closes its accounts at the end of each month.

Accounts payable	$ 3,726	Depreciation expense:		
Accounts receivable	3,033	buildings	$	495
Accumulated depreciation:		Depreciation expense:		
buildings	1,485	office equipment		450
Accumulated depreciation:		Land		111,375
office equipment	1,350	Lighting expense		602
Advertising expense	1,782	Notes payable		90,900
Buildings	237,600	Office equipment		54,000
Capital stock	100,000	Retained earnings		233,000
Cash	42,300	Salaries expense		11,386
Commissions earned	33,462	Telephone expense		900

Instructions

a Prepare an adjusted trial balance with the accounts arranged in the *customary sequence* of ledger accounts.

b Prepare an income statement for the month ended November 30, 19____.

c Prepare a statement of retained earnings for the month ended November 30, 19____, and a balance sheet in report form.

3-3 Mountain Air Service, Inc., was organized on January 1 for the purpose of flying skiers among neighboring ski areas and to remote mountaintops. The following transactions were completed during January.

Jan. 1 Issued 6,000 shares of $10 par value capital stock for cash of $60,000.

Jan. 2 Purchased a helicopter for $51,120 and spare parts for $4,800, paying cash.

Jan. 3 Paid $720 cash to rent a building for January.

Jan. 15 Cash receipts from passengers for the first half of January amounted to $4,560.

Jan. 16 Paid $2,970 to employees for services rendered during the first half of January.

Jan. 24 Placed advertising in local newspapers for publication during January. The agreed price of $270 was payable within ten days after the end of the month.

Jan. 28 Paid $936 to J. J. Motors for maintenance and repair service during January.

Jan. 29 Received a gasoline bill from Indian Oil Co. amounting to $732 and payable by February 10.

Jan. 31 Paid $2,970 to employees for services rendered during the last half of January.

Jan. 31 Cash receipts from passengers during the last half of January amounted to $4,992.

The useful life of the helicopter for depreciation purposes was estimated to be 10 years. Depreciation should not be recorded on the spare parts; these are allocated to expense when they are used. The account titles and account numbers used by the company included the following:

Cash	11		Fees earned	51
Spare parts	14		Advertising expense	61
Helicopter	21		Depreciation expense: helicopter	63
Accumulated depreciation:			Gasoline expense	65
helicopter	23		Rent expense	67
Accounts payable	31		Repair & maintenance expense	69
Capital stock	41		Salaries expense	71

Instructions

a Prepare journal entries for the operating transactions in January and also the month-end adjusting entry for depreciation of the helicopter. Number the general journal pages as Page 1 and Page 2.

b Post to ledger accounts.

c Prepare an adjusted trial balance at January 31.

3-4 Ryan Radio Repair was organized on May 1, 19____. The accounts were closed and financial statements prepared each month. An adjusted trial balance as of the succeeding July 31, 19____, is shown on page 116.

RYAN RADIO REPAIR
Adjusted Trial Balance
July 31, 19___

Cash	$ 8,820	
Accounts receivable	3,640	
Land	73,500	
Building	126,000	
Accumulated depreciation: building		$ 1,260
Repair equipment	16,800	
Accumulated depreciation: repair equipment		840
Notes payable		70,000
Accounts payable		2,100
Capital stock		140,000
Retained earnings		14,000
Dividends	10,500	
Repair service revenue		23,800
Advertising expense	420	
Depreciation expense: building	420	
Depreciation expense: repair equipment	280	
Repair parts expense	1,820	
Utilities expense	350	
Wages expense	9,450	
	$252,000	$252,000

Instructions
a Prepare the closing entries necessary at July 31, 19___.
b Prepare financial statements (income statement, statement of retained earnings, and a balance sheet in report form).
c What were the estimated lives of the building and equipment as assumed by the company in setting the depreciation rates?

3-5 Service Corporation provides public relations services to clients in the entertainment industry. Its offices are rented from a life insurance company on a 10-year lease which expires in three years.

Condensed balance sheet data for the corporation at the end of the last two calendar years are presented below:

	Year 1	Year 2
Cash	$ 28,000	$ 7,000
Receivables from clients	154,000	224,000
Supplies	1,400	1,400
Office equipment	23,100	46,900
Less: Accumulated depreciation	(4,200)	(8,050)
Total assets	$202,300	$271,250
Accounts payable	$ 14,000	$ 14,000
Capital stock	70,000	112,000
Retained earnings	118,300	145,250
Total liabilities & stockholders equity	$202,300	$271,250

In order to be in a position to carry the expanded amount of receivables from clients and to acquire badly needed office equipment, the owners of Service Corporation invested additional cash in the business early in Year 2. At the end of Year 2, the corporation declared and paid a cash dividend. The net income for the corporation for Year 2 follows:

Fees billed to clients		$175,000
Expenses (excluding depreciation).	$116,200	
Depreciation expense: office equipment	3,850	120,050
Net income		$ 54,950

Instructions
a Prepare a statement of retained earnings for Year 2.
b Prepare closing entries required at the end of Year 2.
c The owners are concerned over the fact that cash decreased by $21,000 during Year 2 despite a profit of $54,950. Prepare a schedule of cash receipts and payments to explain the reasons for the decrease in cash. (*Hint:* List the amount of cash receipts from each source and compute the total cash receipts. Next, list the cash payments for various purposes such as purchase of office equipment. Compute the total cash payments and compare with total cash receipts).

3-6 Given below are the balance sheet accounts on September 1, 19＿＿, and the adjusted trial balance as of September 30, 19＿＿, for Del Monte Boat Yard, Inc.

	September 1		September 30	
Cash	$ 24,800		$ 28,640	
Accounts receivable	53,360		44,800	
Supplies on hand	4,240		3,520	
Equipment	27,680		30,400	
Accumulated depreciation: equipment		$ 5,760		$ 6,080
Notes payable		25,600		5,600
Accounts payable (trade).		3,440		880
Capital stock		40,000		40,000
Retained earnings		35,280		35,280
Dividends			12,800	
Revenue				70,400
Operating expenses			37,600	
Depreciation expense: equipment			320	
Interest expense			160	
	$110,080	$110,080	$158,240	$158,240

The new equipment acquired during September was purchased for cash. The company extends credit to all its customers; consequently all revenue transactions are recorded by debits to Accounts Receivable and credits to Revenue.

Instructions
a Prepare the journal entries that were recorded during the month of September. Use one entry for all transactions of a particular type; for example, one entry should be used to summarize all revenue earned during the month. This entry

will consist of a debit to Accounts Receivable and a credit to Revenue for $70,400. This entry will account in full for the increase in the balance of the Revenue account during September and in part for the change in Accounts Receivable during the month. In a similar manner, one entry can be prepared to record all cash collections of accounts receivable during September.

b Prepare an *after-closing* trial balance at September 30, 19___.

3-7 Trusty Investment, Inc., offers investment counseling and brokerage services to its clients and earns revenue in the form of commissions, dividends on securities owned, and interest on loans made to customers for the purchase of securities. The adjusted trial balance of the corporation was as follows at August 31, 19___, the end of the fiscal year:

TRUSTY INVESTMENTS, INC.
Adjusted Trial Balance
August 31, 19___

Cash	$ 82,080	
Marketable securities	288,600	
Accounts receivable	204,000	
Land	36,000	
Building	96,000	
Accumulated depreciation: building		$ 14,640
Furniture & equipment	144,000	
Accumulated depreciation: furniture & equipment		37,800
Notes payable		276,000
Miscellaneous payables		25,680
Capital stock		300,000
Retained earnings, Sept. 1, prior year		230,100
Dividends	12,000	
Commissions earned		219,600
Dividends earned		9,600
Interest earned		13,500
Advertising expense	26,700	
Office expense	50,520	
Interest expense	26,280	
Depreciation expense	21,900	
Salaries and bonuses expense	126,600	
Miscellaneous expense	12,240	
	$1,126,920	$1,126,920

Instructions From the trial balance and supplementary data given, prepare the following at August 31:

a Closing entries
b After-closing trial balance
c Income statement for year 19___
d Statement of retained earnings for the year 19___
e Balance sheet in report form

3-8 On November 1, 19____, Continental Moving Co. was organized to provide transportation of household furniture. During November the following transactions occurred:

Nov. 1 Cash of $1,000,000 was received in exchange for 100,000 shares of $10 par value capital stock.

Nov. 2 Purchased land for $250,000 and building for $360,000, paying $210,000 cash and signing a $400,000 mortgage payable bearing interest at 9%.

Nov. 3 Purchased six trucks from Willis Motors at a total cost of $432,000. A cash down payment of $200,000 was made, the balance to be paid by January 12.

Nov. 6 Purchased office equipment for cash, $24,000.

Nov. 6 Moved furniture for Mr. and Mrs. Don Fitch from New York to Los Angeles for $16,850. Collected $4,850 in cash, balance to be paid within 30 days (credit Moving Service Revenue).

Nov. 9 Moved furniture for various clients for $32,350. Collected $18,350 in cash, balance to be paid within 30 days.

Nov. 15 Paid salaries to employees for the first half of the month, $15,100.

Nov. 25 Moved furniture for various clients for a total of $27,000. Cash collected in full.

Nov. 30 Salaries expense for the second half of November amounted to $13,250.

Nov. 30 Received a gasoline bill for the month of November from Lucier Oil Company in the amount of $17,500, to be paid by December 10.

Nov. 30 Received bill of $1,250 for repair work on trucks during November by Newport Repair Company.

Nov. 30 Paid $5,000 to the holder of the mortgage payable. This $5,000 payment included $3,000 interest expense for November and $2,000 reduction in the liability.

Nov. 30 Declared a $10,000 cash dividend, payable December 15.

Estimated useful life of the building was 20 years, trucks 4 years, and office equipment 10 years.

The account titles to be used and the account numbers are as follows:

Cash	1	*Retained earnings*	41
Accounts receivable	3	*Dividends*	45
Land	11	*Income summary*	50
Building	12	*Moving service revenue*	60
Accumulated depreciation:		*Salaries expense*	70
building	13	*Gasoline expense*	71
Trucks	15	*Repairs & maintenance*	
Accumulated depreciation:		*expense*	72
trucks	16	*Interest expense*	73
Office equipment	18	*Depreciation expense:*	
Accumulated depreciation:		*building*	74
office equipment	19	*Depreciation expense:*	
Accounts payable	30	*trucks*	75
Dividends payable	31	*Depreciation expense*	
Mortgage payable, 9%	32	*office equipment*	76
Capital stock	40		

Instructions

a Prepare journal entries. (Number journal pages to permit cross reference to ledger.)

b Post to ledger accounts. (Number ledger accounts to permit cross reference to journal.)

c Prepare a trial balance at November 30, 19____.
d Prepare adjusting entries and post to ledger accounts.
e Prepare an adjusted trial balance.
f Prepare an income statement for November, and a balance sheet at November 30, 19____, in report form. (A statement of retained earnings is not required.)
g Prepare closing entries and post to ledger accounts.
h Prepare an after-closing trial balance.

BUSINESS DECISION PROBLEM 3

John Bell, owner of a small business called Top-Notch Company, has accepted a salaried position overseas and is trying to interest you in buying his business. He describes the operating results of the business as follows: "The business has been in existence for only 18 months, but the growth trend is very impressive. Just look at these figures."

	Cash Collections from Customers
First six-month period	*$60,000*
Second six-month period	*80,000*
Third six-month period	*90,000*

"I think you'll agree those figures show real growth," Bell concluded.

You then asked Bell whether sales were made only for cash or on both a cash and credit basis. He replied as follows:

"At first we sold both for cash and on open account. In the first six months we made total sales of $100,000 and 70% of those sales were made on credit. We had $40,000 of accounts receivable at the end of the first six-month period.

"During the second six-month period, we tried to discourage selling on credit because of the extra paper work involved and the time required to follow up on slow-paying customers. Our sales on credit in that second six-month period amounted to $35,000, and our total accounts receivable were down to $30,000 at the end of that period.

"During the third six-month period we made sales only for cash. Although we prefer to operate on a cash basis only, we did very well at collecting receivables. We collected in full from every customer to whom we ever sold on credit and we don't have a dollar of accounts receivable at this time."

Instructions

a To facilitate your reaching a decision, prepare a schedule comparing cash collections and sales data for each of the three 6-month periods under review. Use the following column headings:

(1) Sales on Credit	*(2)* Collections on Accounts Receivable	*(3)* Ending Balance of Accounts Receivable	*(4)* Total Cash Collections from Customers	*(5)* Sales for Cash	*(6)* (1) + (5) Total Sales
First six months					
Second six months . .					
Third six months . . .					

b Based upon your analysis in part *a*, do you consider Bell's explanation of the "growth trend" of cash collections to be a well-founded portrayal of the progress of his business? Explain fully any criticism you may have of Bell's line of reasoning.

4

Completion of the Accounting Cycle

Accounting periods and financial statements

For the purpose of making accounting measurements and preparing financial statements, the life of a business is divided into accounting periods of equal length. Since accounting periods are equal in length, we can fairly compare the revenue and expenses of the current period with the revenue and expenses of prior periods and determine whether our operating results are improving or declining. Accounting thus provides a scorekeeping service. If this year's operations set a new record, the accounting system will tell us so.

As explained in Chapter 3, the term *accounting period* means the span of time covered by an income statement. The usual accounting period for which complete financial statements are prepared and distributed to public investors, bankers, and government agencies is one year. The measurement and reporting of taxable income to the Internal Revenue Service by corporations and individuals is also on an annual basis. However, most businesses also prepare quarterly and monthly financial statements so that management will be currently informed on the profitability of the business.

At the end of an accounting period, adjustments of some of the account balances in the ledger must be made before financial statements are prepared. Adjusting entries are necessary, for example, because the recorded costs of buildings and office equipment are gradually expiring with the passage of time. Before financial statements are prepared, the accounts must be brought up to date with respect to depreciation and several other items.

To serve the needs of management, investors, bankers, and other groups, financial statements must be as complete and accurate as possible. The balance sheet must contain all the assets and liabilities at the close of business on the last day of the period. The income statement must contain all the revenue and expenses applicable to the period covered but must not contain any revenue or expenses relating to the following period. In other words, a precise *cutoff* of transactions at the end of the period is essential to the preparation of accurate financial statements.

Apportioning transactions between accounting periods

Some business transactions are begun and completed within a single accounting period, but many other transactions are begun in one accounting period and concluded in a later period. For example, a building purchased this year may last for 25 years; during each of those 25 years a fair share of the cost of the building should be recognized as expense. The making of *adjusting entries* to record the depreciation expense applicable to a given accounting period was illustrated in the preceding chapter. Let us now consider all types of transactions which overlap two or more accounting periods and therefore require adjusting entries.

PRINCIPAL TYPES OF TRANSACTIONS REQUIRING ADJUSTING ENTRIES

The various kinds of transactions requiring adjusting entries at the end of the period may be classified into the following groups:

1 Recorded costs which must be apportioned between two or more accounting periods. Example: the cost of a building.

2 Recorded revenue which must be apportioned between two or more accounting periods. Example: commissions collected in advance for services to be rendered in future periods.

3 Unrecorded expenses. Example: wages earned by employees after the last payday in an accounting period.

4 Unrecorded revenue. Example: commissions earned but not yet collected or billed to customers.

All these adjusting entries involve the recognition of either revenue or expense and, therefore, represent a change in owners' equity. Owners' equity, however, cannot change by itself; there must also be a corresponding change in either assets or liabilities. Thus, every adjusting entry must involve both an income statement account (either a revenue or an expense) *and* a balance sheet account (either an asset or a liability).

To demonstrate these various types of adjusting entries, the illustration of the Greenhill Real Estate Company will be continued for November. We shall consider in detail those November transactions relating to adjusting entries. The routine operating transactions during November such as the earning of sales commissions and payment of expenses are not considered individually, but their overall effect is shown in the November 30 trial balance included in the work sheet on page 133.

Recorded costs apportioned between accounting periods

When a business concern makes an expenditure that will benefit more than one period, the amount is usually debited to an asset account. At the end of each period which benefits from the expenditure, an appropriate portion of the cost is transferred from the asset account to an expense account.

PREPAID EXPENSES Payments in advance are often made for such items as insurance, rent, and office supplies. At the end of the accounting period, a portion of the services or supplies probably will have expired or will have been consumed, but another portion will be unexpired or unused. That portion of the economic benefits from the expenditure which *has expired or has been consumed is an expense of the current period.* However, the *unexpired or unused portion of the economic benefits from the expenditure represents an asset* at the balance sheet date which will not become expense (expired cost) until a later accounting period.

INSURANCE On November 1, the Greenhill Real Estate Company paid $540 for a three-year fire insurance policy covering the building. This expenditure was debited to an asset account by the following journal entry:

Expendi- *Unexpired Insurance* *540*
ture for   *Cash* *540*
insurance
policy *Purchased three-year fire insurance policy.*
recorded
as asset

Since this expenditure of $540 will protect the company against fire loss for three years, the cost of protection each year is $\frac{1}{3}$ of $540, or $180. The insurance expense applicable to each month's operations is $\frac{1}{12}$ of the annual expense, or $15. In order that the accounting records for November show insurance expense of $15, the following adjusting entry is required at November 30:

Portion *Insurance Expense* *15*
of asset   *Unexpired Insurance* *15*
expires
(becomes *To record insurance expense for November.*
expense)

This adjusting entry serves two purposes: (*1*) it apportions the proper amount of insurance expense to November operations and (*2*) it reduces the asset account to $525 so that the correct amount of unexpired insurance will appear in the balance sheet at November 30. What would be the effect on the income statement for November if the above adjustment were not made? The expenses would be understated by $15 and consequently the net income would be overstated by $15. The balance sheet would also be affected by failure to make the adjustment: the assets would be overstated by $15 and so would the owners' equity. The overstatement of the owners' equity would result from the overstated amount of net income transferred to the Retained Earnings account when the accounts were closed at November 30.

OFFICE SUPPLIES On November 2, the Greenhill Real Estate Company purchased a sufficient quantity of stationery and other office supplies to last for several months. The cost of the supplies was $720, and this amount was debited to an asset account by the following journal entry:

Expenditure for office supplies recorded as asset

Office Supplies	720	
Cash		720
Purchased office supplies.		

No entries were made during November to record the day-to-day usage of office supplies, but on November 30 a careful count was made of the supplies still on hand. This count, or physical inventory, showed unused supplies with a cost of $600. It is apparent, therefore, that supplies costing $120 were used during November. An adjusting entry is made on the basis of the November 30 count, debiting an expense account $120 (the cost of supplies consumed during November), and reducing the asset account by $120 to show that only $600 worth of office supplies remained on hand at November 30.

Portion of supplies used represents expense

Office Supplies Expense	120	
Office Supplies		120
To record consumption of office supplies in November.		

The Office Supplies account will appear in the balance sheet as an asset; the Office Supplies Expense account will be shown in the income statement. How would failure to make this adjustment affect the financial statements? In the income statement for November, the expenses would be understated by $120 and the net income overstated by the same amount. Since the overstated amount for net income in November would be transferred into the Retained Earnings account in the process of closing the accounts, the owners' equity section of the balance sheet would be overstated by $120. Assets would also be overstated because Office Supplies would be listed at $120 too much.

When payments for insurance, office supplies, and rent are expected to provide economic benefits for more than one accounting period, the advance payment is usually recorded by a debit to an asset account such as Unexpired Insurance or Office Supplies, as shown in the preceding examples. However, the advance payment *could* be recorded by debiting an expense account such as Insurance Expense. At the end of the period, the adjusting entry would then consist of a debit to Unexpired Insurance and a credit to Insurance Expense. This alternative method would lead to the same amounts in the balance sheet and income statement as the method previously illustrated. Under both procedures, we would be treating as an expense of the current period the cost of the economic benefits consumed, and carrying forward as an asset the cost of the economic benefits applicable to future periods.

DEPRECIATION OF BUILDING   The November 30 journal entry to record depreciation of the building used by the Greenhill Real Estate Company is exactly the same as the October 31 entry explained in Chapter 3.

Cost of building is gradually converted to expense

Depreciation Expense: Building	150	
Accumulated Depreciation: Building		150
To record depreciation for November.		

This allocation of depreciation expense to November operations is based on the following facts: the building cost $36,000 and is estimated to have a useful life of 20 years (240 months). Using the straight-line method of depreciation, the portion of the original cost which expires each month is $\frac{1}{240}$ of $36,000, or $150.

The Accumulated Depreciation: Building account now has a credit balance of $300 as a result of the October and November credits of $150 each. The book value of the building is $35,700, that is, the original cost of $36,000 minus the accumulated depreciation of $300. The term *book value* means the net amount at which an asset is shown in the accounting records, as distinguished from its market value. *Carrying value* is an alternative term, with the same meaning as book value.

DEPRECIATION OF OFFICE EQUIPMENT   The November 30 adjusting entry to record depreciation of the office equipment is the same as the entry for depreciation a month earlier, as shown in Chapter 3.

Cost of office equipment gradually converted to expense

Depreciation Expense: Office Equipment	45	
Accumulated Depreciation: Office Equipment		45
To record depreciation for November.		

Original cost of the office equipment was $5,400, and the estimated useful life was 10 years (120 months). Depreciation each month under the straight-line method is therefore $\frac{1}{120}$ of $5,400, or $45. What is the book value of the office equipment at this point? Original cost of $5,400 minus accumulated depreciation of $90 for two months leaves a book value of $5,310.

What would be the effect on the financial statements if the adjusting entries for depreciation of the building and office equipment were omitted at November 30? In the income statement the expenses would be understated by $195 ($150 depreciation of building and $45 depreciation of office equipment), and net income for the month would be overstated by $195. In the balance sheet the assets would be overstated by $195; the owners' equity would be overstated the same amount because of the $195 overstatement of the net income added to the Retained Earnings account. If depreciation had not been recorded in either October or November, the overstatement in the balance sheet at November 30 would, of course, amount to $390 with respect both to assets and to owners' equity.

Recorded revenue apportioned between accounting periods

On November 1, James Fortune, a client of Greenhill Real Estate Company, asked the company to accept the responsibility of managing a number of rental properties. The duties consisted of keeping the buildings rented, arranging for repairs, and collecting rents which were to be deposited in Fortune's bank account. It was agreed that $300 a month would be a reasonable fee to the Greenhill Real Estate Company for its services. Since Fortune was leaving the country on an extended trip, he paid the company for six months' service in advance at the time of signing the agreement. The journal entry to record the transaction on November 1 was as follows:

Commission collected but not yet earned	Cash 1,800	
	Unearned Rental Commissions	1,800
	Collected in advance six months' commissions for management of Fortune properties.	

Note that no service had been performed for the customer at the time the $1,800 was received. As emphasized in Chapter 3, not every receipt of cash represents revenue. In this case the receipt of cash represented an advance payment by the customer which obligated Greenhill Real Estate Company to render services in the future. Revenue is earned only by the **rendering** of services to customers, or the **delivering** of goods to them. A portion of the agreed services (one-sixth, to be exact) will be rendered during November, but it would be unreasonable to regard the entire $1,800 as revenue in that month. The commission is earned gradually over a period of six months as Greenhill Real Estate Company performs the required services. The $1,800 collected in advance is therefore credited to an **unearned revenue** account at the time of its receipt. Some accountants prefer the alternative term **deferred revenue.** At the end of each month, an amount of $300 will be transferred from unearned revenue to an earned revenue account by means of an adjusting entry. The first in this series of transfers will be made at November 30 as follows:

Entry to recognize earning of a part of commission	Unearned Rental Commissions 300	
	Rental Commissions Earned.	300
	Commission earned from Fortune property management in November.	

The $1,500 credit balance remaining in the Unearned Rental Commissions account represents an obligation to render $1,500 worth of services in future months; therefore, it belongs on the balance sheet in the liability section. An unearned revenue account differs from other liabilities since it will ordinarily be settled by the rendering of services rather than by making a cash payment, but it is nevertheless a liability. The Rental Commissions Earned account is shown in the income statement as revenue for the month of November.

Unrecorded expenses

Adjusting entries are necessary at the end of each accounting period to record any expenses which have been incurred but not recognized in the accounts. Salaries of employees and interest on borrowed money are common examples of expenses which accumulate day by day but which may not be recorded until the end of the period. These expenses are said to *accrue,* that is, to grow or accumulate.

ACCRUAL OF INTEREST On November 1, Greenhill Real Estate Company borrowed the sum of $3,000 from a bank. Banks require every borrower to sign a *promissory note,* that is, a formal, written promise to repay the amount borrowed plus interest at an agreed future date. (Various forms of notes in common use and the accounting problems involved will be discussed more fully in Chapter 10.) The note signed by Greenhill, with certain details omitted, is shown below. A 6% annual interest rate is used in this illustration to make the calculations simple. Banks are currently charging interest rates considerably above 6%.

Note payable issued to bank

$3,000 Los Angeles, California	November 1, 19--

Three months **after date** Greenhill Real Estate Company **promises to pay**

to the order of American National Bank

-------Three thousand and no/100------- **dollars**

for value received, with interest at 6 percent

Greenhill Real Estate Company

By John Green

President

The note payable is a liability of the Greenhill Real Estate Company, similar to an account payable but different in that a formal written promise to pay is required and interest is charged on the amount borrowed. A Notes Payable account is credited when the note is issued; the Notes Payable account will be debited three months later when the note is paid. Interest accrues throughout the life of the note payable, but it is not payable until the note matures on January 31. To the bank making the loan, the note signed by Greenhill is an asset, a note receivable. The revenue earned by banks consists largely of interest charged borrowers. To a borrower, interest is an expense, but to a lender, interest represents revenue.

The journal entry made on November 1 to record the borrowing of $3,000 from the bank was as follows:

Entry when bank loan is obtained

Cash	3,000	
Notes Payable		3,000
Obtained from bank three-month loan with interest at 6% a year.		

On January 31, Greenhill Real Estate Company must pay the bank $3,045, representing repayment of the $3,000 note payable plus $45 interest ($3,000 × 0.06 × $\frac{3}{12}$). The $45 is the total interest expense for the three months. Although no payment will be made until January 31, a portion of the interest expense ($15) is *incurred* each month, as shown below.

Accrual of interest

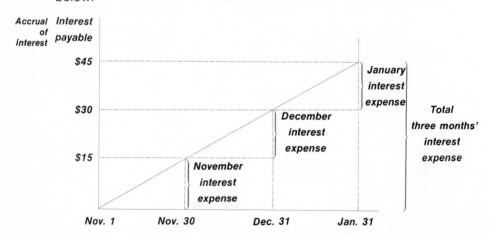

The following adjusting entry is made at November 30 to charge November operations with one month's interest expense and also to record the amount of interest owed to the bank at the end of November.

Entry for interest expense incurred in November

Interest Expense	15	
Interest Payable		15
To record interest expense applicable to November.		

The debit balance in the Interest Expense account will appear in the November income statement; the credit balances in the Interest Payable and Notes Payable accounts will be shown in the balance sheet as liabilities. These two liability accounts will remain in the records until the maturity date of the loan, at which time a cash payment to the bank will wipe out both the Notes Payable account and the Interest Payable account.

ACCRUAL OF SALARY   On November 20, Greenhill hired Carl Nelson as a part-time salesman whose duties were to work evenings calling on property owners to secure listings of property for sale or rent. The agreed salary was $225 for a five-evening week, payable each Friday; payment for the first week was made on Friday, November 24.

Assume that the last day of the accounting period, November 30, fell on Thursday. Nelson had worked four evenings since being paid the preceding Friday and therefore had earned $180 ($\frac{4}{5}$ × $225). In order that this $180 of November salary expense be reflected in the accounts before the financial statements are prepared, an adjusting entry is necessary at November 30. Personal income taxes and other taxes relating to payroll are ignored in this illustration.

Salaries	*Sales Salaries Expense*......................................	*180*
expense	*Sales Salaries Payable*	*180*
incurred but unpaid at November 30	*To record salary expense and related liability to salesman for last four evenings' work in November.*	

The adjusted balance of $405 ($225 + $180) in the Sales Salaries Expense account will appear as an expense in the November income statement; the credit balance of $180 in the Sales Salaries Payable account is the amount owing to the salesman for work performed during the last four days of November and will appear among the liabilities on the balance sheet at November 30.

The next regular payday for Nelson will be Friday, December 1, which is the first day of the new accounting period. Since the accounts were adjusted and closed on November 30, all the revenue and expense accounts have zero balances at the beginning of business on December 1. The payment of a week's salary to the salesman will be recorded by the following entry on December 1:

Payment	*Sales Salaries Payable*	*180*
of salaries	*Sales Salaries Expense*........................	*45*
incurred in two	*Cash*	*225*
accounting periods	*Paid weekly salary to salesman.*	

Note that the net result of the November 30 accrual entry has been to split the salesman's weekly salary expense between November and December. Four days of the work week fell in November, so four days' pay, or $180, was recognized as November expense. One day of the work week fell in December so $45 was recorded as December expense.

No accrual entry is necessary for office salaries in the Greenhill Real Estate Company because the office employees are paid on the last working day of the month.

Unrecorded revenue

The treatment of unrecorded revenue is similar to that of unrecorded expenses. Any revenue which has been earned but not recorded during the accounting period should be recognized in the accounts by means of an adjusting entry, debiting an asset account and crediting a revenue account. *Accrued revenue* is a term often used to describe revenue which has been accumulating during the period but which has not been recorded prior to the closing date.

On November 16, Greenhill Real Estate Company entered into a management agreement with Henry Clayton, the owner of several office buildings. The company agreed to manage the Clayton properties for a commission of $240 a month, payable on the fifteenth of each month. No entry is made in the accounting records at the time of signing the contract, because no services have yet been rendered and no change has occurred in assets or liabilities. The managerial duties were to begin immediately, but the first monthly commission would not be received until December 15. The following adjusting entry is therefore necessary at November 30:

Entry for commissions earned but uncollected

Rental Commissions Receivable	*120*	
Rental Commissions Earned.		*120*
To record revenue accrued from services rendered Henry Clayton during November.		

The debit balance in the Rental Commissions Receivable account will be shown in the balance sheet as an asset. The credit balance of the Rental Commissions Earned account, including earnings from both the Fortune and Clayton contracts, will appear in the November income statement.

The collection of the first monthly commission from Clayton will occur in the next accounting period (December 15, to be exact). Of this $240 cash receipt, half represents collection of the asset account, Rental Commissions Receivable, created at November 30 by the adjusting entry. The other half of the $240 cash receipt represents revenue earned during December; this should be credited to the December revenue account for Rental Commissions Earned. The entry on December 15 is as follows:

Commission applicable to two accounting periods

Cash	*240*	
Rental Commissions Receivable		*120*
Rental Commissions Earned.		*120*
Collected commission for month ended December 15.		

The net result of the November 30 accrual entry has been to divide the revenue from managing the Clayton properties between November and December in accordance with the timing of the services rendered.

Adjusting entries and the accrual basis of accounting

Adjusting entries help make accrual basis accounting work successfully. By preparing adjusting entries, we can recognize revenue in the accounting period in which it is earned and also bring into the accounts any unrecorded expenses which helped to produce that revenue. Adjusting entries cause expenses to be recorded in the accounting period in which the benefits from the expenditures are received, even though cash payment is made in an earlier or later period.

THE WORK SHEET

The work necessary at the end of an accounting period includes construction of a trial balance, journalizing and posting of adjusting entries, preparation of financial statements, and journalizing and posting of closing entries. So many details are involved in these end-of-period procedures that it is easy to make errors. If these errors are recorded in the journal and the ledger accounts, considerable time and effort can be wasted in correcting them. Both the journal and the ledger are formal, permanent records. They may be prepared manually in ink, produced on accounting machines, or created by a computer in a company utilizing electronic data processing equipment. One way of avoiding errors in the permanent accounting records and also of simplifying the work to be done at the end of the period is to use a *work sheet.*

A work sheet is a large columnar sheet of paper, especially designed to arrange in a convenient systematic form all the accounting data required at the end of the period. The work sheet is not a part of the permanent accounting records; it is prepared in pencil by accountants for their own convenience. If an error is made on the work sheet, it may be erased and corrected much more easily than an error in the formal accounting records. Furthermore, the work sheet is so designed as to minimize errors by automatically bringing to light many types of discrepancies which might otherwise be entered in the journal and posted to the ledger accounts. Dollar signs, decimal points, and commas are not used with the amounts entered on work sheets.

The work sheet may be thought of as a testing ground on which the ledger accounts are adjusted, balanced, and arranged in the general form of financial statements. The satisfactory completion of a work sheet provides considerable assurance that all the details of the end-of-period accounting procedures have been properly brought together. After this point has been established, the work sheet then serves as the source from which the formal financial statements are prepared and the adjusting and closing entries are made in the journal.

Preparing the work sheet

A commonly used form of work sheet with the appropriate headings for Greenhill Real Estate Company is illustrated on page 133. Note that the heading of the work sheet consists of three parts: (*1*) the name of the business, (*2*) the title Work Sheet, and (*3*) the period of time covered. The body of the work sheet contains five pairs of money columns, each pair consisting of a debit and a credit column. The procedures to be followed in preparing a work sheet will now be illustrated in five simple steps.

1 Enter the ledger account balances in the Trial Balance columns The titles and balances of the ledger accounts at November 30 are copied into the Trial Balance columns of the work sheet, as illustrated on page 133. It would be a duplication of work to prepare a trial balance as a separate schedule and then to copy this information into the work sheet. As soon as the account balances have been listed on the work sheet, these two columns should be added and the totals entered.

2 Enter the adjustments in the Adjustments columns The required adjustments for Greenhill Real Estate Company have been explained earlier in this chapter; these same adjustments are now entered in the Adjustments columns of the work sheet. (See page 134.) As a cross reference, the debit and credit parts of each adjustment are keyed together by placing a key letter to the left of each amount. For example, the adjustment debiting Insurance Expense and crediting Unexpired Insurance is identified by the key letter (*a*). The use of the key letters makes it easy to match a debit entry in the Adjustments columns with its related credit. The identifying letters also key the debit and credit entries in the Adjustments columns to the brief explanations which appear at the bottom of the work sheet.

  The titles of any accounts debited or credited in the adjusting entries but *not listed* in the trial balance are written on the work sheet *below* the trial balance. For example, Insurance Expense does not appear in the trial balance; it is written on the first available line below the trial balance totals. After all the adjustments have been entered in the Adjustments columns, this pair of columns must be totaled. Proving the equality of debit and credit totals tends to prevent arithmetical errors from being carried over into other columns of the work sheet.

3 Enter the account balances as adjusted in the Adjusted Trial Balance columns The work sheet as it appears after completion of the Adjusted Trial Balance columns is illustrated on page 135. Each account balance in the first pair of columns is combined with the adjustment, if any, in the second pair of columns, and the combined amount is entered in the Adjusted Trial Balance columns. This process of combining the items on each line throughout the first four columns of the work sheet requires horizontal addition or subtraction. It is called *cross footing,* in contrast to the addition of items in a vertical column, which is called *footing* the column.

  For example, the Office Supplies account has an *unadjusted* debit

GREENHILL REAL ESTATE COMPANY
Work Sheet
For the Month Ended November 30, 19___

	Trial Balance		Adjustments		Adjusted Trial Balance		Income Statement		Balance Sheet	
	Dr	Cr	Dr	Cr	Dr	Cr	Dr	Cr	Dr	Cr
Cash	25,800									
Accounts receivable	6,990									
Unexpired insurance	540									
Office supplies	720									
Land	15,000									
Building	36,000									
Accumulated depreciation: building		150								
Office equipment	5,400									
Accumulated depreciation: office equipment		45								
Notes payable		3,000								
Accounts payable		23,595								
Unearned rental commissions		1,800								
Capital stock		60,000								
Retained earnings, Oct. 31, 19		771								
Dividends	1,500									
Sales commissions earned		5,484								
Advertising expense	1,275									
Office salaries expense	1,200									
Sales salaries expense	225									
Telephone expense	195									
	94,845	94,845								

1. Enter ledger account balances before adjustments in Trial Balance columns on work sheet

GREENHILL REAL ESTATE COMPANY
Work Sheet
For the Month Ended November 30, 19___

	Trial Balance Dr	Trial Balance Cr	Adjustments* Dr	Adjustments* Cr	Adjusted Trial Balance Dr	Adjusted Trial Balance Cr	Income Statement Dr	Income Statement Cr	Balance Sheet Dr	Balance Sheet Cr
Cash	25,800									
Accounts receivable	6,990									
Unexpired insurance	540			(a) 15						
Office supplies	720			(b) 120						
Land	15,000									
Building	36,000									
Accumulated depreciation: building		150		(c) 150						
Office equipment	5,400									
Accumulated depreciation: office equipment		45		(d) 45						
Notes payable		3,000								
Accounts payable		23,595								
Unearned rental commissions		1,800	(e) 300							
Capital stock		60,000								
Retained earnings, Oct. 31, 19___		771								
Dividends	1,500									
Sales commissions earned		5,484								
Advertising expense	1,275									
Office salaries expense	1,200									
Sales salaries expense	225		(g) 180							
Telephone expense	195									
	94,845	94,845								
Insurance expense			(a) 15							
Office supplies expense			(b) 120							
Depreciation expense: building			(c) 150							
Depreciation expense: office equipment			(d) 45							
Rental commissions earned				(e) 300						
				(h) 120						
Interest expense			(f) 15							
Interest payable				(f) 15						
Sales salaries payable				(g) 180						
Rental commissions receivable			(h) 120							
			945	945						

Explanatory footnotes keyed to adjustments

* Adjustments:
(a) Portion of insurance cost which expired during November
(b) Office supplies used during November
(c) Depreciation of building during November
(d) Depreciation of office equipment during November
(e) Earned one-sixth of the commission collected in advance on the Fortune properties
(f) Interest expense accrued during November on note payable
(g) Salesman's salary for last four days of November
(h) Rental commission accrued on Clayton contract in November

GREENHILL REAL ESTATE COMPANY
Work Sheet
For the Month Ended November 30, 19___

	Trial Balance Dr	Trial Balance Cr	Adjustments* Dr	Adjustments* Cr	Adjusted Trial Balance Dr	Adjusted Trial Balance Cr	Income Statement Dr	Income Statement Cr	Balance Sheet Dr	Balance Sheet Cr
Cash	25,800				25,800					
Accounts receivable	6,990				6,990					
Unexpired insurance	540			(a) 15	525					
Office supplies	720			(b) 120	600					
Land	15,000				15,000					
Building	36,000				36,000					
Accumulated depreciation: building		150		(c) 150		300				
Office equipment	5,400				5,400					
Accumulated depreciation: office equipment		45		(d) 45		90				
Notes payable		3,000				3,000				
Accounts payable		23,595				23,595				
Unearned rental commissions		1,800	(e) 300			1,500				
Capital stock		60,000				60,000				
Retained earnings, Oct. 31, 19___		771				771				
Dividends	1,500				1,500					
Sales commissions earned		5,484				5,484				
Advertising expense	1,275				1,275					
Office salaries expense	1,200				1,200					
Sales salaries expense	225		(g) 180		405					
Telephone expense	195				195					
	94,845	94,845								
Insurance expense			(a) 15		15					
Office supplies expense			(b) 120		120					
Depreciation expense: building			(c) 150		150					
Depreciation expense: office equipment			(d) 45		45					
Rental commissions earned				(e) 300 (h) 120		420				
Interest expense			(f) 15		15					
Interest payable				(f) 15		15				
Sales salaries payable				(g) 180		180				
Rental commissions receivable			(h) 120		120					
			945	945	95,355	95,355				

Enter the adjusted amounts in columns 5 and 6 of work sheet

*Explanatory notes relating to adjustments are the same as on page 134.

balance of $720 in the Trial Balance columns. This $720 debit amount is combined with the $120 credit appearing on the same line in the Adjustments column; the combination of a $720 debit with a $120 credit produces an *adjusted* debit amount of $600 in the Adjusted Trial Balance debit column. As another example, consider the Office Supplies Expense account. This account had no balance in the Trial Balance columns but shows a $120 debit in the Adjustments debit column. The combination of a zero starting balance and $120 debit adjustment produces a $120 debit amount in the Adjusted Trial Balance.

Many of the accounts in the trial balance are not affected by the adjustments made at the end of the month; the balances of these accounts (such as Cash, Land, Building, or Notes Payable in the illustrated work sheet) are entered in the Adjusted Trial Balance columns in exactly the same amounts as shown in the Trial Balance columns. After all the accounts have been extended into the Adjusted Trial Balance columns, this pair of columns is totaled to prove that no arithmetical errors have been made up to this point.

4 Extend each amount in the Adjusted Trial Balance columns horizontally across the work sheet into one of the four remaining columns Assets and liabilities are entered in the Balance Sheet columns. The owners' equity accounts (Capital Stock, Retained Earnings, and Dividends) are also entered in the Balance Sheet columns. The revenue and expense accounts are entered in the Income Statement columns.

The process of extending amounts horizontally across the work sheet should begin with the account at the top of the work sheet, which is usually Cash. The cash figure is extended to the Balance Sheet debit column. Then the accountant goes down the work sheet line by line, extending each account balance to the appropriate column. The work sheet as it appears after completion of this sorting process is illustrated on page 137. Note that each amount in the Adjusted Trial Balance columns is extended to one *and only one* of the four remaining columns.

5 Total the Income Statement columns and the Balance Sheet columns. Enter the net income or net loss as a balancing figure in both pairs of columns, and again compute column totals The work sheet as it appears after this final step is shown on page 138.

The net income or net loss for the period is determined by computing the difference between the totals of the two Income Statement columns. In the illustrated work sheet, the credit column total is the larger and the excess represents net income:

Income Statement credit column total (revenue)	*$5,904*
Income Statement debit column total (expenses)	*3,420*
Difference: net income for period	*$2,484*

GREENHILL REAL ESTATE COMPANY
Work Sheet
For the Month Ended November 30, 19____

	Trial Balance		Adjustments*		Adjusted Trial Balance		Income Statement		Balance Sheet	
	Dr	Cr	Dr	Cr	Dr	Cr	Dr	Cr	Dr	Cr
Cash	25,800				25,800				25,800	
Accounts receivable	6,990				6,990				6,990	
Unexpired insurance	540			(a) 15	525				525	
Office supplies	720			(b) 120	600				600	
Land	15,000				15,000				15,000	
Building	36,000				36,000				36,000	
Accumulated depreciation: building		150		(c) 150		300				300
Office equipment	5,400				5,400				5,400	
Accumulated depreciation: office equipment		45		(d) 45		90				90
Notes payable		3,000				3,000				3,000
Accounts payable		23,595				23,595				23,595
Unearned rental commissions		1,800	(e) 300			1,500				1,500
Capital stock		60,000				60,000				60,000
Retained earnings, Oct. 31, 19___		771				771				771
Dividends	1,500				1,500				1,500	
Sales commissions earned		5,484				5,484		5,484		
Advertising expense	1,275				1,275		1,275			
Office salaries expense	1,200				1,200		1,200			
Sales salaries expense	225		(g) 180		405		405			
Telephone expense	195				195		195			
	94,845	94,845								
Insurance expense			(a) 15		15		15			
Office supplies expense			(b) 120		120		120			
Depreciation expense: building			(c) 150		150		150			
Depreciation expense: office equipment			(d) 45		45		45			
Rental commissions earned				(e) 300 (h) 120		420		420		
Interest expense			(f) 15		15		15			
Interest payable				(f) 15		15				15
Sales salaries payable				(g) 180		180				180
Rental commissions receivable			(h) 120		120				120	
			945	945	95,355	95,355				

Left margin note: Extend each adjusted amount to columns for income statement or balance sheet

*Explanatory notes relating to adjustments are the same as on page 134.

Completed work sheet

GREENHILL REAL ESTATE COMPANY
Work Sheet
For the Month Ended November 30, 19___

	Trial Balance Dr	Trial Balance Cr	Adjustments* Dr	Adjustments* Cr	Adjusted Trial Balance Dr	Adjusted Trial Balance Cr	Income Statement Dr	Income Statement Cr	Balance Sheet Dr	Balance Sheet Cr
Cash	25,800				25,800				25,800	
Accounts receivable	6,990				6,990				6,990	
Unexpired insurance	540			(a) 15	525				525	
Office supplies	720			(b) 120	600				600	
Land	15,000				15,000				15,000	
Building	36,000				36,000				36,000	
Accumulated depreciation: building		150		(c) 150		300				300
Office equipment	5,400				5,400				5,400	
Accumulated depreciation: office equipment		45		(d) 45		90				90
Notes payable		3,000				3,000				3,000
Accounts payable		23,595				23,595				23,595
Unearned rental commissions		1,800	(e) 300			1,500				1,500
Capital stock		60,000				60,000				60,000
Retained earnings, Oct. 31, 19___		771				771				771
Dividends	1,500				1,500				1,500	
Sales commissions earned		5,484				5,484		5,484		
Advertising expense	1,275				1,275		1,275			
Office salaries expense	1,200				1,200		1,200			
Sales salaries expense	225		(g) 180		405		405			
Telephone expense	195				195		195			
	94,845	94,845								
Insurance expense			(a) 15		15		15			
Office supplies expense			(b) 120		120		120			
Depreciation expense: building			(c) 150		150		150			
Depreciation expense: office equipment			(d) 45		45		45			
Rental commissions earned				(e) 300 (h) 120		420		420		
Interest expense			(f) 15		15		15			
Interest payable				(f) 15		15				15
Sales salaries payable				(g) 180		180				180
Rental commissions receivable			(h) 120		120				120	
			945	945	95,355	95,355	3,420	5,904	91,935	89,451
Net income							2,484			2,484
							5,904	5,904	91,935	91,935

*Explanatory notes relating to adjustments are the same as on page 134.

Note that the net income of $2,484 is entered in the Income Statement *debit* column as a balancing figure and also on the same line as a balancing figure in the Balance Sheet *credit* column. The caption Net Income is written in the space for account titles to identify and explain this item. New totals are then computed for both the Income Statement columns and the Balance Sheet columns. Each pair of columns is now in balance.

The reason for entering the net income of $2,484 in the Balance Sheet *credit column* is that the net income accumulated during the period in the revenue and expense accounts causes an increase in the owners' equity. If the balance sheet columns did not have equal totals after the net income had been recorded in the credit column, the lack of agreement would indicate that an error had been made in the work sheet.

Let us assume for a moment that the month's operations had produced a loss rather than a profit. In that case the Income Statement debit column would exceed the credit column. The excess of the debits (expenses) over the credits (revenue) would have to be entered in the *credit column* in order to bring the two Income Statement columns into balance. The incurring of a loss would decrease the owners' equity; therefore, the loss would be entered as a balancing figure in the Balance Sheet *debit column.* The Balance Sheet columns would then have equal totals.

SELF-BALANCING NATURE OF THE WORK SHEET Why does the entering of the net income or net loss in one of the Balance Sheet columns bring this pair of columns into balance? The answer is short and simple. All the accounts in the Balance Sheet columns have November 30 balances with the exception of the Retained Earnings account, which still shows the October 31 balance of $771. By bringing in the current month's net income of $2,484 and the Dividends of $1,500, the total owners' equity is brought up to date as of November 30. The Balance Sheet columns now prove the familiar proposition that assets are equal to the total of liabilities and owners' equity.

PREPARING FINANCIAL STATEMENTS FROM THE WORK SHEET Preparing the formal financial statements from the work sheet is an easy step. All the information needed for the income statement, the statement of retained earnings, and the balance sheet has already been sorted and arranged in convenient form in the work sheet.

Income statement The following income statement contains the amounts listed in the Income Statement columns of the completed work sheet on page 138.

GREENHILL REAL ESTATE COMPANY
Income Statement
For the Month Ended November 30, 19___

Data
taken Revenue:
from   Sales commissions earned $5,484
Income   Rental commissions earned. 420
Statement
columns   Total revenue $5,904
of work Expenses:
sheet   Advertising $1,275
           Office supplies 120
           Office salaries 1,200
           Sales salaries 405
           Telephone 195
           Insurance 15
           Depreciation: building 150
           Depreciation: office equipment 45
           Interest 15
               Total expenses 3,420
           Net income $2,484

As noted in Chapter 3, we are purposely ignoring income taxes on corporations at this stage of our study. Corporate income taxes are introduced in Chapter 5 and considered more fully in Chapters 7 and 17.

Statement of retained earnings The following statement of retained earnings shows amounts taken from the work sheet for November. The October 31 balance of $771 in retained earnings plus the $2,484 of net income earned in November and minus the $1,500 of dividends paid lead to a new balance of $1,755 in retained earnings at November 30.

GREENHILL REAL ESTATE COMPANY
Statement of Retained Earnings
For the Month Ended November 30, 19___

Net in- Retained earnings, Oct. 31, 19___ . . . . $ 771
come   Net income for November 2,484
exceeded
dividends   Subtotal $3,255
         Less: Dividends 1,500
         Retained earnings, Nov. 30, 19___ $1,755

Balance sheet The balance sheet illustrated on page 141 contains the amounts for assets, liabilities, and capital stock listed in the Balance Sheet columns of the work sheet, along with the new balance of retained earnings.

GREENHILL REAL ESTATE COMPANY
Balance Sheet
November 30, 19___

Assets

Compare these amounts with figures in Balance Sheet columns of work sheet	Cash		$25,800
	Accounts receivable		6,990
	Rental commissions receivable		120
	Unexpired insurance		525
	Office supplies		600
	Land		15,000
	Building	$36,000	
	Less: Accumulated depreciation	300	35,700
	Office equipment	$ 5,400	
	Less: Accumulated depreciation	90	5,310
	Total assets		$90,045

Liabilities & Stockholders' Equity

Liabilities:

Notes payable		$ 3,000
Accounts payable		23,595
Interest payable		15
Sales salaries payable		180
Unearned rental commissions		1,500
Total liabilities		$28,290

Stockholders' equity:

Capital stock	$60,000	
Retained earnings	1,755	61,755
Total liabilities & stockholders' equity		$90,045

RECORDING ADJUSTING ENTRIES IN THE ACCOUNTING RECORDS After the financial statements have been prepared from the work sheet at the end of the period, the ledger accounts are adjusted to bring them into agreement with the statements. This is an easy step because the adjustments have already been computed on the work sheet. The amounts appearing in the Adjustments columns of the work sheet and the related explanations at the bottom of the work sheet provide all the necessary information for the adjusting entries, as shown on page 142, which are first entered in the journal and then posted to the ledger accounts.

RECORDING CLOSING ENTRIES When the financial statements have been prepared from the work sheet, the revenue and expense accounts have served their purpose for the current period and should be closed. These accounts will then have zero balances and will be ready for the recording of revenue and expenses during the next fiscal period.

General Journal   Page 5

Date		Account Titles and Explanation	LP	Debit	Credit
Adjust-ments on work sheet are entered in general journal	19___				
Nov.	30	Insurance Expense		15	
		Unexpired Insurance			15
		Insurance expense for November.			
	30	Office Supplies Expense		120	
		Office Supplies			120
		Office supplies used during November.			
	30	Depreciation Expense: Building		150	
		Accumulated Depreciation: Building .			150
		Depreciation for November.			
	30	Depreciation Expense: Office Equipment . .		45	
		Accumulated Depreciation: Office			
		Equipment			45
		Depreciation for November.			
	30	Unearned Rental Commissions		300	
		Rental Commissions Earned			300
		Earned one-sixth of commission collected in advance for managing the properties owned by James Fortune.			
	30	Interest Expense		15	
		Interest Payable			15
		Interest expense accrued during November on note payable.			
	30	Sales Salaries Expense		180	
		Sales Salaries Payable			180
		To record expense and related liability to salesman for last four evenings' work in November.			
	30	Rental Commissions Receivable		120	
		Rental Commissions Earned			120
		To record the receivable and related revenue earned for managing properties owned by Henry Clayton.			

The journalizing and posting of closing entries were illustrated in Chapter 3. The point to be emphasized now is that the completed work sheet provides in convenient form all the information needed to make the closing entries. The preparation of closing entries from the work sheet may be summarized as follows:

1 To close the accounts listed in the Income Statement credit column, debit the revenue accounts and credit Income Summary.

2 To close the accounts listed in the Income Statement debit column, debit Income Summary and credit the expense accounts.

3 To close the Income Summary account, transfer the balancing figure in the Income Statement columns of the work sheet ($2,484 in the illustration) to the Retained Earnings account. A profit is transferred by debiting Income Summary and crediting the Retained Earnings account; a loss is transferred by debiting the Retained Earnings account and crediting Income Summary.

4 To close the Dividends account, debit the Retained Earnings account and credit the Dividends account.

The entries to close the revenue and expense accounts, as well as the Dividends account, at November 30 are shown below.

General Journal *Page 6*

	Date		Account Titles and Explanation	LP	Debit	Credit
Closing entries derived from work sheet	19___ Nov.	30	Sales Commissions Earned		5,484	
			Rental Commissions Earned		420	
			Income Summary			5,904
			To close the revenue accounts.			
		30	Income Summary		3,420	
			Advertising Expense			1,275
			Office Salaries Expense			1,200
			Sales Salaries Expense			405
			Telephone Expense			195
			Insurance Expense			15
			Office Supplies Expense			120
			Depreciation Expense: Building			150
			Depreciation Expense: Office Equip-			
			ment			45
			Interest Expense			15
			To close the expense accounts.			
		30	Income Summary		2,484	
			Retained Earnings			2,484
			To close the Income Summary account.			
		30	Retained Earnings		1,500	
			Dividends			1,500
			To close the Dividents account.			

Sequence of accounting procedures when work sheet is used

In any business which maintains a considerable number of accounts or makes numerous adjusting entries, the use of a work sheet will save much time and labor. Since the work sheet includes a trial balance, adjusting entries in preliminary form, and an adjusted trial balance, the use of the work sheet will modify the sequence of accounting procedures given in Chapter 3 as follows:

1 Record all transactions in the journal as they occur.

2 Post debits and credits from the journal entries to the proper ledger accounts.

3 Prepare the work sheet. (The work sheet includes a trial balance of the ledger and all necessary adjustments.)

4 Prepare financial statements, consisting of an income statement, a statement of owners' equity, and a balance sheet.

5 Using the information shown on the work sheet as a guide, enter the adjusting and closing entries in the journal. Post these entries to ledger accounts.

6 Prepare an after-closing trial balance to prove that the ledger is still in balance.

Note that the first two procedures, consisting of the journalizing and posting of transactions during the period, are the same regardless of whether a work sheet is to be used at the end of the period.

The accounting cycle

The above sequence of accounting procedures constitutes a complete accounting process, which is repeated in the same order in each accounting period. The regular repetition of this standardized set of procedures is often referred to as the *accounting cycle.* The procedures of a complete accounting cycle are illustrated below:

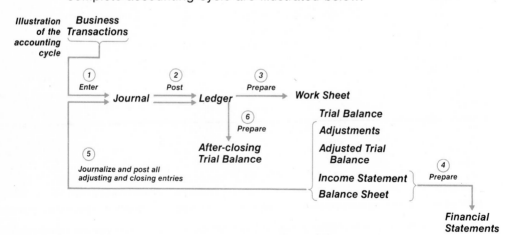

Illustration of the accounting cycle

In most business concerns the accounts are closed only once a year; for these companies the accounting cycle is one year in length. For purposes of illustration in a textbook, it is convenient to assume that the entire accounting cycle is performed within the time period of one month. The completion of the accounting cycle is the occasion for preparing financial statements and closing the revenue and expense accounts.

Preparing monthly financial statements without closing the accounts

Many companies which close their accounts only once a year neverthe-less prepare *monthly* financial statements for managerial use. These monthly statements are prepared from work sheets, but the adjustments indicated on the work sheets are not entered in the accounting records and no closing entries are made. Under this plan, the time-consuming operation of journalizing and posting adjustments and closing entries is performed only at the end of the fiscal year, but the company has the advantage of monthly financial statements. Monthly and quarterly finan-cial statements are often referred to as *interim statements,* because they are in between the year-end statements.

KEY TERMS INTRODUCED OR EMPHASIZED IN CHAPTER 4

Accounting cycle The sequence of accounting procedures performed during an accounting period. The procedures include journalizing transactions, posting, preparation of a work sheet and financial statements, adjusting and closing the accounts, and preparation of an after-closing trial balance.

Accrued expenses Expenses such as salaries of employees and interest on notes payable which have accumulated but are unpaid and unrecorded at the end of the period.

Accrued revenue Revenue which has been earned during the accounting period but has not been collected or recorded prior to the closing date. Also called *unrecorded revenue.*

Book value The net amount at which an asset is shown in accounting records. For depreciable assets, book value equals cost minus accumulated depreciation. Also called *carrying value.*

Carrying value See book value.

Deferred revenue An obligation to render services or deliver goods in the future because of advance receipt of payment.

Interim statements Financial statements prepared at intervals of less than one year. Usually quarterly and monthly statements.

Prepaid expenses Advance payments for such expenses as rent and insurance. The portion which has not been used up at the end of the accounting period is included in the balance sheet as an asset.

Promissory note A formal written promise to repay an amount of a debt plus interest at a future date.

Unearned revenue See deferred revenue.

Unrecorded expenses See accrued expenses.

Work sheet A large columnar sheet designed to arrange in convenient form all the accounting data required at the end of the period. Facilitates preparation of financial statements.

DEMONSTRATION PROBLEM FOR YOUR REVIEW

Reed Geophysical Company adjusts and closes its accounts at the end of the calendar year. At December 31, 1980, the following trial balance was prepared from the ledger:

REED GEOPHYSICAL COMPANY
Trial Balance
December 31, 1980

Cash	$12,540	
Prepaid office rent	8,400	
Prepaid dues and subscriptions	960	
Supplies on hand	1,300	
Equipment	20,000	
Accumulated depreciation: equipment		$ 1,200
Notes payable		5,000
Unearned consulting fees		35,650
Capital stock		10,000
Retained earnings, Jan. 1, 1980		12,950
Dividends	7,000	
Consulting fees earned		15,200
Salaries expense	26,900	
Telephone expense	550	
Miscellaneous expenses	2,350	
	$80,000	$80,000

Other data
(a) On January 1, 1980, the Prepaid Office Rent account had a balance of $2,400, representing the prepaid rent for the months from January to June 1980 inclusive. On July 1, 1980, the lease was renewed and office rent for one year at $500 per month was paid in advance.
(b) Dues and subscriptions expired during the year in the total amount of $710.
(c) A count of supplies on hand was made at December 31; the cost of the unused supplies was $450.
(d) The useful life of the equipment has been estimated at 10 years from date of acquisition.
(e) Accrued interest on notes payable amounted to $100 at year-end. Set up a separate Interest Expense account.
(f) Consulting services valued at $32,550 were rendered during the year for clients who had made payment in advance.
It is the custom of the firm to bill clients only when consulting work is completed or, in the case of prolonged engagement, at six-month intervals. At
(g) December 31, engineering services valued at $3,000 had been rendered to clients but not yet billed. No advance payments had been received from these clients.
(h) Salaries earned by staff engineers but not yet paid amounted to $200 at December 31.

Instructions
a Prepare a work sheet for the year ended December 31, 1980.
b Prepare an income statement, a balance sheet, and a statement of retained earnings.
c Prepare adjusting and closing journal entries.

SOLUTION TO DEMONSTRATION PROBLEM

a

REED GEOPHYSICAL COMPANY
Work Sheet
For the Year Ended December 31, 1980

	Trial Balance Dr	Trial Balance Cr	Adjustments* Dr	Adjustments* Cr	Adjusted Trial Balance Dr	Adjusted Trial Balance Cr	Income Statement Dr	Income Statement Cr	Balance Sheet Dr	Balance Sheet Cr
Cash	12,540				12,540				12,540	
Prepaid office rent	8,400			(a) 5,400	3,000				3,000	
Prepaid dues and subscriptions	960			(b) 710	250				250	
Supplies on hand	1,300			(c) 850	450				450	
Equipment	20,000				20,000				20,000	
Accumulated depreciation: equipment		1,200		(d) 2,000		3,200				3,200
Notes payable		5,000				5,000				5,000
Unearned consulting fees		35,650	(f) 32,550			3,100				3,100
Capital stock		10,000				10,000				10,000
Retained earnings, Jan. 1, 1980		12,950				12,950				12,950
Dividends	7,000				7,000				7,000	
Consulting fees earned		15,200		(f) 32,550 (g) 3,000		50,750		50,750		
Salaries expense	26,900		(h) 200		27,100		27,100			
Telephone expense	550				550		550			
Miscellaneous expenses	2,350				2,350		2,350			
	80,000	80,000								
Rent expense			(a) 5,400		5,400		5,400			
Dues and subscriptions expense			(b) 710		710		710			
Supplies expense			(c) 850		850		850			
Depreciation expense: equipment			(d) 2,000		2,000		2,000			
Interest expense			(e) 100		100		100			
Interest payable				(e) 100		100				100
Consulting fees receivable			(g) 3,000		3,000				3,000	
Salaries payable				(h) 200		200				200
			44,810	44,810	85,300	85,300	39,060	50,750	46,240	34,550
Net income							11,690			11,690
							50,750	50,750	46,240	46,240

*Adjustments:
(a) Rent expense for year
(b) Dues and subscriptions expense for year
(c) Drafting supplies used for year
(d) Depreciation expense for year
(e) Accrued interest on notes payable
(f) Consulting services performed for clients who paid in advance
(g) Services rendered but not billed
(h) Salaries earned but not paid

b

REED GEOPHYSICAL COMPANY
Income Statement
For the Year Ended December 31, 1980

Consulting fees earned		$50,750
Expenses:		
Salaries expense	$27,100	
Telephone expense	550	
Miscellaneous expenses	2,350	
Rent expense	5,400	
Dues and subscriptions expense	710	
Supplies expense	850	
Depreciation expense: equipment	2,000	
Interest expense	100	
Total expenses		39,060
Net income		$11,690

REED GEOPHYSICAL COMPANY
Balance Sheet
December 31, 1980

Assets

Cash		$12,540
Consulting fees receivable		3,000
Prepaid office rent		3,000
Prepaid dues and subscriptions		250
Supplies on hand		450
Equipment	$20,000	
Less: Accumulated depreciation	3,200	16,800
Total assets		$36,040

Liabilities & Stockholders' Equity

Liabilities:		
Notes payable		$ 5,000
Interest payable		100
Salaries payable		200
Unearned consulting fees		3,100
Total liabilities		$ 8,400
Stockholders' equity:		
Capital stock	$10,000	
Retained earnings	17,640	27,640
Total liabilities & stockholders' equity		$36,040

REED GEOPHYSICAL COMPANY
Statement of Retained Earnings
For the Year Ended December 31, 1980

Retained earnings at beginning of year	$12,950
Net income for year	11,690
Subtotal	$24,640
Dividends	7,000
Retained earnings at end of year	$17,640

c **Adjusting Entries**

1980					
Dec.	31	*(a)*			
		Rent Expense		5,400	
		Prepaid Office Rent			5,400
		Rent expense for 1980; $2,400 for first six months and $3,000 for last six months.			
		(b)			
	31	Dues and Subscriptions Expense		710	
		Prepaid Dues and Subscriptions . . .			710
		Dues and subscriptions expired during year.			
		(c)			
	31	Supplies Expense		850	
		Supplies on Hand			850
		Drafting supplies used during year.			
		(d)			
	31	Depreciation Expense: Equipment		2,000	
		Accumulated Depreciation: Equipment			2,000
		Depreciation on equipment for year.			
		(e)			
	31	Interest Expense		100	
		Interest Payable			100
		Accrued interest on notes payable.			
		(f)			
	31	Unearned Consulting Fees		32,550	
		Consulting Fees Earned			32,550
		Consulting services performed for clients who paid in advance.			

c

Adjusting Entries

	31	*(g)*		
	31	Consulting Fees Receivable	3,000	
		Consulting Fees Earned		3,000
		Consulting services rendered but not yet billed.		
		(h)		
	31	Salaries Expense	200	
		Salaries Payable		200
		Salaries earned by employees, but not paid.		

Closing Entries

Dec.	31	Consulting Fees Earned	50,750	
		Income Summary		50,750
		To close revenue account.		
	31	Income Summary	39,060	
		Salaries Expense		27,100
		Telephone Expense		550
		Miscellaneous Expenses		2,350
		Rent Expense		5,400
		Dues and Subscriptions Expense . .		710
		Supplies Expense		850
		Depreciation Expense: Equipment . .		2,000
		Interest Expense		100
		To close expense accounts.		
	31	Income Summary	11,690	
		Retained Earnings		11,690
		To close Income Summary Account.		
	31	Retained Earnings	7,000	
		Dividends		7,000
		To close Dividends account.		

REVIEW QUESTIONS

1 Which of the following statements do you consider most acceptable?
  a Adjusting entries affect balance sheet accounts only.
  b Adjusting entries affect income statement accounts only.
  c An adjusting entry may affect two or more balance sheet accounts or two or more income statement accounts, but cannot affect both a balance sheet account and an income statement account.
  d Every adjusting entry affects both a balance sheet account and an income statement account.

2 The recording of depreciation involves two ledger accounts: Depreciation Expense and Accumulated Depreciation. Explain the purpose of each account; indicate whether it normally has a debit balance or a credit balance; and state where it appears in the financial statements.

3 At the end of this year, the adjusted trial balance of the Black Company showed the following account balances, among others: Depreciation Expense; Building, $1,610; Building, $32,200; Accumulated Depreciation: Building, $14,490. Assuming that straight-line depreciation has been used, what length of time do these facts suggest that the Black Company has owned the building?

4 The weekly payroll for salespeople of the Ryan Company amounts to $1,250. All salespeople are paid up to date at the close of business each Friday. If December 31 falls on Wednesday, what year-end adjusting entry is needed?

5 The Marvin Company purchased a three-year fire insurance policy on August 1 and debited the entire cost of $540 to Unexpired Insurance. The accounts were not adjusted or closed until the end of the year. Give the adjusting entry at December 31.

6 The net income reported by the Haskell Company for Year 2 was $21,400, and the Retained Earnings account stood at $36,000. However, the company had failed to recognize that interest amounting to $375 had accrued on a note payable to the bank. State the corrected figures for net income and retained earnings. In what other respect was the balance sheet of the company in error?

7 Office supplies on hand in the Melville Company amounted to $642 at the beginning of the year. During the year additional office supplies were purchased at a cost of $1,561 and charged to the asset account. At the end of the year a physical count showed that supplies on hand amounted to $812. Give the adjusting entry needed at December 31.

8 The X Company at December 31 recognized the existence of certain unexpired costs which would provide benefits to the company in future periods. Give examples of such unexpired costs and state where they would be shown in the financial statements.

9 In performing the regular end-of-period accounting procedures, does the preparation of the work sheet precede or follow the posting of adjusting entries to ledger accounts? Why?

10 List in order the procedures comprising the accounting cycle when a work sheet is used.

11 Explain why the amount of net income is entered in the Income Statement debit column on a work sheet.

12 Do the totals of the balance sheet ordinarily agree with the totals of the Balance Sheet columns of the work sheet?

13 Is a work sheet ever prepared when there is no intention of closing the accounts? Explain.

14 The Adjustments columns of the work sheet for Davis Company contained only three adjustments, as follows: depreciation of building, $3,600; expiration of insurance, $500; and salaries accrued at year-end, $4,100. If the Trial Balance columns showed totals of $600,000, what would be the totals of the Adjusted Trial Balance columns?

15 Should the Adjusted Trial Balance columns be totaled before or after the adjusted amounts are carried to the Income Statement and Balance Sheet columns? Explain.

16 In extending adjusted account balances from the Adjusted Trial Balance columns to the Income Statement and Balance Sheet columns, is there any particular sequence to be followed in order to minimize the possibility of errors? Explain.

EXERCISES

Ex. 4-1 On Friday of each week, Lake Company pays its sales personnel weekly salaries amounting to $45,000 for a five-day work week.
  a Draft the necessary adjusting entry at year-end, assuming that December 31 falls on Tuesday.
  b Also draft the journal entry for the payment by Lake Company of a week's salaries to its sales personnel on Friday, January 3, the first payday of the new year.

Ex. 4-2 Stone Company adjusts and closes its accounts at the end of the calendar year. Prepare the adjusting entries required at December 31, based on the following information:
  a A six-month bank loan in the amount of $160,000 had been obtained on October 1 at an annual interest rate of 9%. No interest has been paid as yet and no interest expense has been recorded.
  b Depreciation on office equipment is based on the assumption of a 10-year life and no scrap value. The balance in the Office Equipment account is $26,400; no changes have occurred in this account during the current year.
  c Interest receivable on U.S. government bonds owned is $1,920.
  d On December 31, an agreement was signed to lease a truck for 12 months beginning January 1 at a rate of 24 cents a mile. Usage is expected to be 1,500 miles per month and the contract specifies a minimum payment equivalent to 10,000 miles a year.

Ex. 4-3 On September 1, Key Company purchased a three-year fire insurance policy and recorded the payment of the full three-year premium of $4,320 by debiting Unexpired Insurance. The accounts were not adjusted or closed until the end of the calendar year. Give the necessary adjusting entry at December 31.

Ex. 4-4 For each of the following items relating to Glenwood Speedway, write first the journal entry (if one is required) to record the external transaction and secondly, the adjusting entry, if any, required on March 31, the end of the fiscal period.
  a On March 1, paid rent for the next four months at $22,500 per month.
  b On March 2, sold season tickets for a total of $600,000. The season includes 60 racing days: 15 in March, 25 in April, and 20 in May.
  c On March 3, an agreement was reached with Snack-Bars, Inc., allowing that company to sell refreshments at the track in return for 10% of the gross receipts from refreshment sales.
  d On March 5, schedules for the 15 racing days in March and the first 10 racing days in April were printed at a cost of $10,000.
  e On March 31, Snack-Bars, Inc., reported that the gross receipts from refreshment sales in March had been $135,000 and that the 10% owed to Glenwood Speedway would be remitted on April 10.

Ex. 4-5 The Property Management Company manages office buildings and apartment buildings for various owners who wish to be relieved of this responsibility. The revenue earned for this service is credited to Management Fees Earned. On December 1, the company received a check for $10,800 from a client, David Howell, who was leaving for a six-month stay abroad. This check represented payment in advance for management of Howell's real estate properties during the six months of his absence. Explain how this transaction would be recorded, the adjustment, if any, to be made at December 31, and the presentation of this information in the year-end financial statements.

Ex. 4-6 The following amounts are taken from consecutive balance sheets of Raymond Company.

	Year 1	Year 2
Unexpired insurance	$ –0–	$ 900
Unearned rental revenue	3,000	1,500
Interest payable	100	875

The income statement for Year 2 of the Raymond Company shows the following items:

Insurance expense.	$ 700
Rental revenue	18,000
Interest expense	1,000

Instructions Determine the following amounts of cash:
a Paid during Year 2 on insurance policies.
b Received during Year 2 as rental revenue.
c Paid during Year 2 for interest.

Ex. 4-7 The trial balances of Fisher Insurance Agency, as of September 30, 19____, before and after the posting of adjusting entries, are shown below:

	Before Adjustments		After Adjustments	
	Dr	Cr	Dr	Cr
Cash	$ 6,180		$ 6,180	
Commissions receivable			800	
Office supplies on hand	600		360	
Office equipment.	6,220		6,220	
Accumulated depreciation: office equip-				
ment.		$ 2,150		$ 2,240
Accounts payable		1,550		1,550
Salaries payable				450
Unearned commissions.		400		140
Capital stock		4,500		4,500
Retained earnings		2,500		2,500
Commissions earned		3,900		4,960
Salaries expense.	2,000		2,450	
Office supplies expense			240	
Depreciation expense: office equipment . .			90	
	$15,000	$15,000	$16,340	$16,340

Instructions By comparing the two trial balances shown above, it is possible to determine which accounts have been adjusted. You are to prepare the adjusting journal entries which must have been made to cause these changes in account balances. Include an explanation as part of each adjusting journal entry.

PROBLEMS

4-1 The accounting records of Blue Mountain Resort are maintained on the basis of a fiscal year ending April 30. The following facts are to be used for making adjusting entries before the accounts are closed and financial statements prepared at April 30.

(1) Depreciation expense on the buildings for the year ended April 30 amounted to $42,375.

(2) A 36-month fire insurance policy had been purchased on April 1. The premium of $4,320 for the entire life of the policy had been paid on April 1 and recorded as Unexpired Insurance.

(3) A portion of the land owned had been leased on April 16 of the current year to a service station operator at a yearly rental rate of $14,400. One year's rent was collected in advance at the date of the lease and credited to Unearned Rental Revenue.

(4) A bus to carry guests to and from the airport had been rented beginning early on April 19 from Truck Rentals, Inc., at a daily rate of $63. No rental payment had yet been made.

(5) Among the assets owned by Blue Mountain Resort were government bonds in the face amount of $75,000. Accrued interest receivable on the bonds at April 30 was computed to be $2,925.

(6) A three-month bank loan in the amount of $300,000 had been obtained on April 1 at an annual interest rate of 9%. No interest expense has been recorded.

(7) The company signed an agreement on April 30 to lease a truck from Ace Motors for a period of one year beginning May 1 at a rate of 30 cents a mile and with a clause providing for a minimum monthly charge of $900.

(8) Salaries earned by employees but not yet paid amounted to $9,900.

Instructions For each of the above paragraphs which warrants adjustment of the accounts, you are to prepare an adjusting journal entry. Include an explanation as part of each entry.

4-2 White Water Taxi was organized late last year to transport tourists to a nearby resort island. The company adjusts and closes its accounts at the end of each month. Selected account balances appearing on the June 30 *adjusted* trial balance are as follows:

Prepaid rent	$ 2,700	
Unexpired insurance	720	
Boats	28,800	
Accumulated depreciation: boats		$2,100
Unearned passenger revenue		750

Other data

(1) Four months rent had been prepaid on June 1.

(2) The unexpired insurance is a 36-month fire insurance policy purchased on January 1.

(3) The boats are being depreciated over an 8-year estimated useful life, with no residual value.

(4) The unearned passenger revenue represents tickets good for future rides sold to a resort hotel for $6 per ticket on June 1. During June, 175 of the tickets were used.

Instructions

a Determine:

    (1) The monthly rent expense

    (2) The original cost of the 36-month fire insurance policy

    (3) The age in months of the boats

    (4) How many $6 tickets for future rides were sold to the resort hotel on June 1

b Prepare the adjusting entries which were made on June 30.

4-3 Kingspoint Motel maintains its accounting records on the basis of a calendar year. The following information is available as a source for adjusting entries at December 31.

(1) Salaries earned by employees but not yet paid amount to $10,860.

(2) As of December 31 the motel has earned $5,040 rental revenue from current guests who will not be billed until they are ready to check out.

(3) On December 16, a suite of rooms was rented to a guest for six months at a monthly rental of $1,500. Rent for the first three months was collected in advance and credited to Unearned Rental Revenue.

(4) A one-year bank loan in the amount of $90,000 had been obtained on November 1 at an annual interest rate of 9%. No interest has been paid and no interest expense has been recorded.
(5) Depreciation on the motel for the year ended December 31 was $43,800.
(6) Depreciation on a station wagon owned by the motel was based on a four-year life. The station wagon had been purchased new on September 1 of the current year at a cost of $10,800.
(7) On December 31, Kingsport Motel entered into an agreement to host the National Building Suppliers Convention in June of next year. The motel expects to earn rental revenue of at least $15,000 from the convention.

Instructions
a From the information given above, draft the adjusting entries (including explanations) required at December 31.
b Assume that all necessary adjusting entries at December 31 have been recorded and that net income for the year is determined to be $300,000. How much net income would have been indicated by the accounting records if the company had failed to make the above adjusting entries? Show computations.

4-4 Holiday Theater began operations on May 1 of the current year. The company's accounting policy is to adjust and close the accounts each month. Before adjustments at July 31, the account balances were as follows:

Cash	$ 17,250	
Unexpired insurance	5,100	
Prepaid film rental	18,500	
Projection equipment	63,000	
Accumulated depreciation: projection equipment		$ 1,500
Notes payable		30,000
Unearned concessions revenue		7,000
Capital stock		50,000
Retained earnings		6,050
Dividends	7,500	
Admissions revenue		37,350
Salaries expense	17,050	
Building rent expense	3,500	
	$131,900	$131,900

Other data
(1) A three-year fire insurance policy was purchased on May 2 of the current year for $5,400.
(2) Film rental expense for the month of July amounted to $10,950, all of which had been prepaid.
(3) The projection equipment, with an estimated useful life of 7 years, was purchased on May 1 of the current year.
(4) Interest expense on notes payable amounted to $200 for the month of July.
(5) Jeff Wright, concessionaire, reported that net income from concessions for July amounted to $21,000. Holiday Theater's share was 10%, as per agreement. This agreement also provided for semiannual advance payments by Wright based on estimates of future sales. These advance payments were credited to Unearned Concessions Revenue when received.
(6) Salaries earned by employees but not yet paid were $2,875 at July 31.

Instructions
a Prepare an adjusting entry at July 31 for each of the six numbered items. Remember that the accounts were adjusted and closed at May 31 and again on June 30.

b Prepare an adjusted trial balance. (*Note:* You may find the use of T accounts helpful in computing the account balances after adjustments.)

c Prepare closing entries.

4-5 Solar Pools, Inc., was organized on April 1, 1980, and is engaged in the business of building custom swimming pools. All the $150,000 of capital stock in the corporation is owned by Bob Edmonston and his wife, Dianne. Mrs. Edmonston has been maintaining the accounting records on a somewhat "hit and miss" basis. Early in 1981, Mrs. Edmonston prepared the financial statements shown below, which Mr. Edmonston presented to the First National Bank in support of an application for a $75,000 bank loan.

SOLAR POOLS, INC.

Balance Sheet

December 31, 1980

Cash	$ 9,750	Accounts payable	$ 73,350
Receivables	89,400	Capital	158,100
Supplies on hand	17,100		
Equipment	115,200		
	$231,450		$231,450

SOLAR POOLS, INC.

Income Statement

Period: March–December 1980

Contract fees		$252,600
Expenses:		
Building supplies used	$ 84,000	
Dividends paid	25,500	
Labor	108,900	
Rent	10,800	
Other	15,300	244,500
Net income		$ 8,100

After reviewing the financial statements of Solar Pools, Inc., a bank officer asked Edmonston "to restate the financial statements in conformity with generally accepted accounting principles." The banker specifically mentioned the need (1) to record depreciation for nine months, (2) to recognize expenses of the year 1980 which had not been paid as of December 31, 1980, (3) to report the amount of retained earnings on the balance sheet, and (4) to correct the expense total as reported in the income statement.

Mrs. Edmonston comes to you for assistance, and with her help, you ascertain the following:

(*1*) The equipment was acquired on April 1, 1980, and has an estimated useful life of eight years.

(2) Salaries payable on December 31, 1980, are estimated at $14,100.

(3) Building supplies costing $10,200 were erroneously included as an expense on the income statement. These supplies are still in storage and should be reported as an asset.

(4) On December 31, all work was completed on a $11,400 contract; however, the revenue was not recorded until January 4 when a bill was mailed to the customer.

(5) Other expenses reported above as $15,300 consist of oil and gas, $3,300; advertising, $6,600; and office expense, $5,400. (Should be listed separately in the income statement.)

Instructions

a Prepare revised financial statements for Solar Pools, Inc., including a statement of retained earnings.

b Reconcile the corrected net income with the net income of $8,100 as determined by Mrs. Edmonston.

4-6 Green Valley Golf Club began operations on March 1 of the current year on a site rented from the county. The company's accounting policy is to adjust and close its accounts each month. Before adjustments on October 31, the account balances were as follows:

Cash	$ 54,530	
Unexpired insurance	4,060	
Prepaid rent	105,000	
Equipment	336,000	
Accumulated depreciation: equipment		$ 24,500
Accounts payable		56,000
Dividends payable		14,000
Unearned greens fees		28,000
Capital stock		350,000
Retained earnings		28,630
Dividends	14,000	
Greens fees earned		89,600
Salaries expense	54,600	
Repairs and maintenance expense	13,440	
Water expense	9,100	
	$590,730	$590,730

Other data

(a) The unexpired insurance represents a three-year fire insurance policy purchased on March 1 for $5,040.

(b) Monthly rent expense amounted to $35,000.

(c) The equipment was being depreciated over an eight-year life.

(d) On October 10, a local corporation purchased 7,000 special price tickets for $28,000. Each ticket was good for one round of golf. During October, 2,170 of the tickets were used.

(e) The Elks' Club reserved the entire golf course on the last two days of October and the first day of November for a golf tournament, agreeing to pay greens fees of a flat $7,000 per day at the conclusion of the tournament.

(f) Salaries earned by employees but not paid were $4,900 at October 31.

Instructions

Based on the trial balance and other data, prepare a 10-column work sheet for the month ended October 31, 19___. Use a pair of columns for each of the following: Trial Balance, Adjustments, Adjusted Trial Balance, Income Statement, and Balance Sheet.

4-7 Metro Lines, Inc., is a bus company in a major metropolitan area. The company adjusts and closes its accounts each month. At December 31, 19___, the following trial balance was prepared from the ledger.

Cash	$ 200,625	
Prepaid rent	27,000	
Unexpired insurance	31,200	
Spare parts on hand	85,500	
Buses	1,215,000	
Accumulated depreciation: buses		$ 232,875
Unearned passenger revenue		90,000
Capital stock, $10 par value		1,050,000
Retained earnings		171,900
Dividends	18,000	
Passenger revenue		284,700
Fuel expense	38,700	
Repairs & maintenance expense	3,300	
Salaries expense	202,050	
Advertising expense	8,100	
	$1,829,475	$1,829,475

Other data
(a) Monthly rent amounted to $4,500.
(b) Insurance expense for December was $6,300.
(c) Maintenance work costing $7,800 was done on the buses by City Garage in late December. No bill has yet been received, and the expense has not been recorded.
(d) Spare parts used in connection with maintenance work during December amounted to $5,550.
(e) The buses are being depreciated over a useful life of 10 years.
(f) Early in December 15,000 special books of bus tickets were sold to the public for $6 per book. Each ticket book contained 10 bus tickets. As of December 31, 45,000 tickets had been used.
(g) Salaries earned by employees but not paid were $4,950 at December 31.

Instructions
a Prepare a 10-column work sheet for the month ended December 31, 19____ .
b Prepare an income statement, a statement of retained earnings, and a balance sheet (in report form).
c Prepare adjusting and closing entries at December 31.

4-8 Blue Lagoon Airline provides passenger and freight service among some Pacific islands. The accounts are adjusted and closed each month. At June 30, 19____ , the trial balance on page 159 was prepared from the ledger.

Other data
(a) Monthly rent amounted to $3,000.
(b) Insurance expense for June was $3,900.
(c) All necessary maintenance work was provided by Reese Air Service at a fixed charge of $7,500 a month. Service for three months had been paid for in advance on June 1.
(d) Spare parts used in connection with maintenance work amounted to $3,750 during the month.
(e) At the time of purchase, the remaining useful life of the airplanes, which were several years old, was estimated at 5,000 hours of flying time. During June, total flying time amounted to 160 hours.
(f) The Chamber of Commerce purchased 2,000 special tickets for $60,000. Each ticket allowed the holder one flight normally priced at $45. During the month 400 tickets has been used by the holders.
(g) Salaries earned by employees but not paid amounted to $3,300 at June 30.

BLUE LAGOON AIRLINE
Trial Balance
June 30, 19___

Cash	$ 190,500	
Prepaid rent expense	54,000	
Unexpired insurance	46,800	
Prepaid maintenance expense	22,500	
Spare parts	57,000	
Airplanes.	810,000	
Accumulated depreciation: airplanes		$ 76,950
Unearned passenger revenue		60,000
Capital stock		200,000
Retained earnings		777,760
Dividends	12,000	
Passenger revenue earned.		183,990
Gasoline expense	13,800	
Salaries expense.	86,700	
Advertising expense	5,400	
	$1,298,700	$1,298,700

Instructions
a Prepare a 10-column work sheet for the month ended June 30, 19___.
b Prepare an income statement and a statement of retained earnings for the
month of June and a balance sheet at June 30, 19___.
c Prepare adjusting and closing entries.

4-9 Financial Consultants, Inc., is in the business of performing research and preparing financial analyses for business organizations and government agencies.
Much of its work is done through a computer service center for which payment is
made on an hourly basis. The company adjusts and closes its accounts monthly.
At October 31, 19___, the account balances were as follows *before* adjustments
were made.

Cash	$ 71,760
Research fees receivable.	–0–
Prepaid office rent	28,800
Prepaid computer rental expense	42,960
Office supplies	4,200
Office equipment	25,200
Accumulated depreciation: office equipment	600
Notes payable	24,000
Accounts payable	8,760
Interest payable	–0–
Salaries payable	–0–
Unearned research fees	114,600
Capital stock	50,000
Retained earnings	33,820
Dividends	2,400
Research fees earned.	16,200
Office salaries expense.	5,040

Research salaries expense	*$58,320*
Telephone expense	*2,640*
Travel expense	*6,660*
Office rent expense	*–0–*
Computer rental expense	*–0–*
Office supplies expense	*–0–*
Depreciation expense: office equipment	*–0–*
Interest expense	*–0–*

Other data
(a) The amount in the Prepaid Office Rent account represented office rent for eight months paid in advance on October 1, 19____ when the lease was renewed.
(b) During October, 220 hours of computer time were used at a cost of $180 an hour.
(c) Office supplies on hand October 31 were determined by count to amount to $840.
(d) Office equipment was estimated to have a useful life of 7 years from date of purchase.
(e) Accrued interest on notes payable amounted to $96 on October 31.
(f) Services to clients amounting to $76,440 performed during October were chargeable against the Unearned Research Fees account.
(g) Services to clients who had not made advance payments and had not been billed amounted to $35,280 at October 31.
(h) Salaries earned by research staff but not paid amounted to $5,160 on October 31.

Instructions
a Prepare a 10-column work sheet for the month of October.
b Prepare financial statements consisting of an income statement and statement of retained earnings for the month of October and a balance sheet at October 31, 19____.

BUSINESS DECISION PROBLEM 4

Seven Souls Marina rents 50 slips in a large floating dock to owners of pleasure boats in the area. The marina also performs repair services on small craft.

Bob Mathews, a friend of yours, is convinced that recreational boating will become increasingly popular in the area and has entered into negotiations to buy Seven Souls Marina.

Bob does not have quite enough cash to purchase the business at the price the owner has demanded. However, the owner of the marina has suggested that Bob might purchase the marina with what cash he does have, and turn the net income of the business over to the retiring owner until the balance of the purchase price has been paid. A typical month's income for Seven Souls Marina is determined as follows:

Revenue:

Slip rentals		*$2,520*
Repairs		*3,180*
Total revenue		*$5,700*
Operating expenses:		
Wages	*$1,920*	
Insurance	*36*	
Depreciation expense: docks	*960*	
Depreciation expense: equipment	*180*	
Other expenses	*240*	*3,336*
Net income		*$2,364*

Bob is concerned about turning the whole net income of the business over to the former owner for the next several months, because he estimates that he and his family will need to keep at least $960 a month to meet their living expenses. In coming to you for advice, Bob explains that all revenue of Seven Souls Marina is collected when earned and that both wages and "other" expenses are paid when incurred. Bob does not understand, however, when depreciation expense must be paid or why there is any insurance expense when the insurance policies of the business have more than two years to run before new insurance must be purchased.

Instructions

a Advise Bob as to how much cash the business will generate each month. Will this amount of cash enable Bob to withdraw $960 per month to meet his living expenses and pay $2,364 per month to the former owner?

b Explain why insurance expense appears on the income statement of the business if no new policies will be purchased within the next two years.

5 Merchandising Transactions and Internal Control

ACCOUNTING FOR A MERCHANDISING BUSINESS

The preceding four chapters have illustrated step by step the complete accounting cycle for Greenhill Real Estate Company, a business rendering personal services. Service-type companies represent an important part of our economy. They include, for example, airlines, railroads, motels, theaters, golf courses, ski resorts, and professional football clubs. In contrast to the service-type business, there are a great many companies whose principal activity is buying and selling merchandise. The term *merchandise* means goods acquired by a business for the purpose of resale to customers. In other words, merchandise consists of the goods in which a business regularly deals. Merchandising companies may be engaged in either the retail or wholesale distribution of goods. The accounting concepts and methods we have studied for a service-type business are also applicable to a merchandising company; however, some additional accounts and techniques are needed in accounting for the purchase and sale of merchandise.

Income statement for a merchandising business

An income statement for a merchandising business consists of three main sections: (1) the revenue section, (2) the cost of goods sold section, and (3) the operating expenses section. This sectional arrangement is illustrated in the income statement for a retail sporting goods store on page 163. We shall assume that the business of the Campus Sports Shop consists of buying sports equipment from manufacturers and selling this merchandise to college students and others. To keep the illustration reasonably short, we shall use a smaller number of expense accounts than would generally be used in a merchandising business.

CAMPUS SPORTS SHOP
Income Statement
For the Year Ended December 31, Year 10

Note distinction between cost of goods sold and operating expenses	Gross sales		$201,000
	Less: Sales returns & allowances		1,000
	Net sales		$200,000
	Cost of goods sold:		
	Inventory, Jan. 1	$ 25,000	
	Purchases	125,000	
	Cost of goods available for sale	$150,000	
	Less: Inventory, Dec. 31	30,000	
	Cost of goods sold		120,000
	Gross profit on sales		$ 80,000
	Operating expenses:		
	Salaries	$ 46,000	
	Advertising	8,000	
	Telephone	1,000	
	Depreciation	4,000	
	Insurance	1,000	
	Total operating expenses		60,000
	Income before income taxes		$ 20,000
	Income taxes expense		4,000
	Net income		$ 16,000

ANALYZING THE INCOME STATEMENT How does this income statement compare in form and content with the income statement of the service-type business presented in the preceding chapters? The most important change is the inclusion of the section entitled Cost of Goods Sold. Note how large the cost of goods sold is in comparison with the other figures on the statement. The cost of the merchandise sold during the year amounts to $120,000, or 60% of the year's sales of $200,000. Another way of looking at this relationship is to say that for each dollar the store receives by selling goods to customers, the sum of 60 cents represents a recovery of the cost of the merchandise. This leaves a *gross profit* of 40 cents from each sales dollar, out of which the store must pay its operating expenses. In our illustration the operating expenses for the year were $60,000, that is, 30% of the net sales figure of $200,000. Therefore, the gross profit of 40 cents contained in each dollar of sales was enough to cover the operating expenses of 30 cents and leave a pretax income of 10 cents from each dollar of sales. After the deduction of income taxes expense, the net income amounted to $16,000, or 8 cents from each dollar of net sales.

Of course the percentage relationship between net sales and cost of goods sold will vary from one type of business to another, but, in all types of merchandising companies the cost of goods sold is one of the largest elements in the income statement. Accountants, investors, bankers, and business managers all have the habit of mentally computing percentage relationships when they look at financial statements. Formation of this habit will be helpful throughout the study of accounting, as well as in many business situations.

Sales of merchandise

If merchandising companies are to succeed or even to survive, they must, of course, sell their goods at prices higher than they pay to the vendors or suppliers from whom they buy. The selling prices charged by a retail store must cover three things: (1) the cost of the merchandise to the store; (2) the operating expenses of the business such as advertising, store rent, and salaries of the sales staff; and (3) a net income to the business.

When a business sells merchandise to its customers, it either receives immediate payment in cash or acquires an account receivable which will soon become cash. As explained in Chapter 3, the inflow of cash and receivables from sales of the current period is equal to the revenue for that period. The entry to record the sale of merchandise consists of a debit to an asset account and a credit to the Sales account, as shown by the following example:

Journal *entry for* *cash sale*	Cash 100	
	Sales	100
	To record the sale of merchandise for cash.	

If the sale was not a cash transaction but called for payment at a later date, the entry would be:

Journal *entry for* *sale on* *credit*	Accounts Receivable 100	
	Sales	100
	To record the sale of merchandise on credit; payment due within *30 days.*	

Revenue from the sale of merchandise is considered as earned in the period in which the merchandise is delivered to the customer, even though payment in cash is not received for a month or more after the sale. Consequently, the revenue earned in a given accounting period may differ considerably from the cash receipts of that period.

The amount and trend of sales are watched very closely by management, investors, and others interested in the progress of a company. A rising volume of sales is evidence of growth and suggests the probability of an increase in earnings. A declining trend in sales, on the other hand, is often the first signal of reduced earnings and of financial difficulties ahead. The amount of sales for each year is compared with the sales of the preceding year; the sales of each month may be compared with the sales of the preceding month and also with the corresponding month of the preceding year. These comparisons bring to light significant trends in the volume of sales. The financial pages of newspapers regularly report on the volume and trend of sales for corporations with publicly owned stock.

NET SALES Note that the key figure used in our analysis of the Campus Sports Shop income statement was *net sales.* Most merchandising companies allow customers to obtain a refund by returning merchandise which is found to be unsatisfactory. When customers find that merchandise purchased has minor defects, they may agree to keep such merchandise if an allowance is made on the sales price. Refunds and allowances have the effect of reversing previously recorded sales and reducing the amount of revenue earned by the business. Thus, net sales is the revenue actually earned after giving consideration to sales returns and allowances. The journal entry to record sales returns and allowances is shown below:

Journal Sales Returns and Allowances *100*
entry for   Cash (or Accounts Receivable) *100*
sales
returns and *Made refund for merchandise returned by customer.*
allowances

The use of a Sales Returns and Allowances account rather than recording refunds by direct debits to the Sales account is advisable because the accounting records then show both the total amount of sales and the amount of sales returns. Management is interested in the percentage relationship between goods sold and goods returned as an indication of customer satisfaction with the merchandise.

The cost of goods sold

In the illustrated income statement of Campus Sports Shop on page 163 the cost of goods sold for the year was computed as follows:

Computing Inventory of merchandise at beginning of year . . . . $ 25,000
cost of
goods Purchases   125,000
sold Cost of goods available for sale $150,000
Less: Inventory at end of year   30,000
Cost of goods sold $120,000

Every merchandising business has *available for sale* during an accounting period the merchandise on hand at the beginning of the period *plus* the merchandise purchased during the period. If all these goods were sold during the period, there would be no ending inventory, and cost of goods sold would be equal to the cost of goods available for sale. Normally, however, some goods remain unsold at the end of the period; *cost of goods sold is then equal to the cost of goods available for sale minus the ending inventory of unsold goods.*

The cost of goods sold is an important concept which requires careful attention. To gain a thorough understanding of this concept, we need to consider the nature of the accounts used in determining the cost of goods sold.

The Purchases account

The cost of *merchandise purchased for resale* to customers is recorded by debiting an account called Purchases, as illustrated below:

Journal	Purchases *10,000*	
entry for *purchase*	Accounts Payable (or Cash).	*10,000*
of mer-	*Purchased merchandise from ABC Supply Co.*	
chandise		

The Purchases account *is used only for merchandise acquired for resale;* assets acquired for *use* in the business (such as a delivery truck, a typewriter, or office supplies) are recorded by debiting the appropriate asset account, not the Purchases account. The Purchases account does not indicate whether the purchased goods have been sold or are still on hand.

At the end of the accounting period, the balance accumulated in the Purchases account represents the total cost of merchandise purchased during the period. This amount is used in preparing the income statement. The Purchases account has then served its purpose and it is closed to the Income Summary account. Since the Purchases account is closed at the end of each period, it has a zero balance at the beginning of each succeeding period.

Inventory of merchandise

An inventory of merchandise consists of the goods on hand and available for sale to customers. In the Campus Sports Shop, the inventory consists of golf clubs, tennis rackets, and skiing equipment; in a pet shop the inventory might include puppies, fish, and parakeets. Inventories are acquired through the purchase of goods from wholesalers, manufacturers, or other suppliers. The goods on hand at the beginning of the period are referred to as the *beginning inventory;* the goods on hand at the end of the period are referred to as the *ending inventory.* Thus in our example of a year's operations of Campus Sports Shop, the beginning inventory on January 1 was $25,000 and the ending inventory on December 31 was $30,000. The ending inventory of one accounting period is, of course, the beginning inventory of the following period. For the following year, Campus Sports Shop would have a beginning inventory of $30,000—the amount determined to be on hand at the close of business on December 31 of the current year.

Inventory of merchandise and cost of goods sold

The cost of the merchandise sold during the year appears in the income statement as a deduction from the sales of the year. The merchandise which is **available for sale but not sold** during the year constitutes the inventory of merchandise on hand at the end of the year. The ending inventory is included in the year-end balance sheet as an asset.

How can a store manager determine, at the end of a year, a month, or other accounting period, the quantity and the cost of the goods remaining on hand? How can management determine the cost of the goods sold during the period? These amounts must be determined before either a balance sheet or an income statement can be prepared. In fact, the determination of inventory value and of the cost of goods sold may be the most important single step in measuring the profitability of a business. There are two alternative approaches to the determination of inventory and of cost of goods sold, namely, the **perpetual inventory method** and the **periodic inventory method**.

THE PERPETUAL INVENTORY SYSTEM A business which sells merchandise of high unit value, such as automobiles or television sets, generally uses a perpetual inventory system. An automobile dealer or a television store may make only a few sales each day. For such a small number of sales transactions, it is possible to look in the records to determine the cost of the individual automobile or television set being sold. This cost figure can easily be recorded as the **cost of goods sold** for each sales transaction. Under this system, records are maintained showing the cost of each article in stock. Units added to inventory and units sold are recorded on a daily basis—hence the name "perpetual inventory system." At the end of the accounting period when financial statements are to be prepared, the total cost of goods sold during the period is easily determined by adding the costs recorded from day to day for the units sold.

Although the perpetual inventory system is definitely worthwhile for a business selling merchandise of high unit value, it is not practicable in a business such as a drugstore which may sell a customer a bottle of aspirin, a candy bar, and a tube of toothpaste. The sales price of this merchandise can quickly be recorded on a cash register, but it would not be practical to look up in the records at the time of each sale the cost of such small items. Instead, stores which deal in merchandise of low unit cost usually wait until the end of the accounting period to determine the cost of goods sold. They rely upon the **periodic inventory system** rather than maintain perpetual inventory records. In this chapter we shall concentrate upon the periodic inventory system. The perpetual inventory system is discussed in Chapter 11.

THE PERIODIC INVENTORY SYSTEM A great many businesses do not maintain perpetual inventory records; they rely instead upon a periodic inventory (a count of merchandise on hand) to determine the inventory at the end of the accounting period and the cost of goods sold during the period. The periodic inventory system may be concisely summarized as follows:

1 A physical count of merchandise on hand is made at the end of each accounting period.

2 The cost value of this inventory is computed by multiplying the quantity of each item by an appropriate unit cost. A total cost figure for the entire inventory is then determined by adding the costs of all the various types of merchandise.

3 The *cost of goods available for sale* during the period is determined by adding the amount of the inventory at the beginning of the period to the amount of the purchases during the period.

4 The *cost of goods sold* is computed by subtracting the inventory at the end of the period from the cost of goods available for sale. In other words, the difference between the cost of goods available for sale and the amount of goods remaining unsold at the end of the period is presumed to have been sold.

A simple illustration of the above procedures for determining the cost of goods sold follows:

Using the periodic inventory method	*Beginning inventory (determined by count)*	*$ 25,000*
	Add: Purchases	*125,000*
	Cost of goods available for sale	*$150,000*
	Less: Ending inventory (determined by count)	*30,000*
	Cost of goods sold	*$120,000*

Because of the importance of the process for determining inventory and cost of goods sold, we shall now consider in more detail the essential steps in using the periodic inventory system.

Taking a physical inventory When the periodic inventory system is in use, there is no day-to-day record of the cost of goods sold. Neither is there any day-to-day record of the amount of goods unsold and still on hand. At the end of the accounting period, however, it is necessary to determine the cost of goods sold during the period and also the amount of unsold goods on hand. The figure for cost of goods sold is used in determining the net income or loss for the period, and the value of the merchandise on hand at the end of the period is included in the balance sheet as an asset.

To determine the cost of the merchandise on hand, a physical inventory is taken. The count of merchandise should be made if possible after the close of business on the last day of the accounting period. It is difficult to make an accurate count during business hours while sales are taking place; consequently, the physical inventory is often taken in the evening or on Sunday. After all goods have been counted, the proper cost price must be assigned to each article. The assignment of a cost price to each item of merchandise in stock is often described as *pricing the inventory.*

The Inventory account After the amount of the ending inventory has been computed by counting and pricing the goods on hand at the end of the period, this amount is entered in the records by *debiting the Inventory account and crediting Income Summary.* (This entry will be illustrated and explained more fully later in this chapter.) Entries are made in the Inventory account only at the end of the accounting period. During the period, the Inventory account shows only the cost of the merchandise which was on hand at the beginning of the current period.

Inflation and the cost of replacing inventories

Inventories have traditionally been valued at their original cost for accounting purposes. However, the rapid inflation of recent years has made original cost figures less relevant in many cases than current value or replacement cost. Consequently, large corporations are now required by the SEC to disclose in their financial statements the *current replacement cost* as well as the original cost for both inventories and cost of goods sold. During a period of rising prices, a company's reported income will be less if the cost of goods sold is expressed in terms of replacement cost rather than original cost. This issue will be discussed more fully along with other aspects of accounting for inventories in Chapter 11.

Other accounts included in cost of goods sold

In the income statement of Campus Sports Shop illustrated earlier, the cost of goods sold was derived from only three items: beginning inventory, purchases, and ending inventory. In most cases, however, some additional accounts will be involved. These include the Transportation-in account and the Purchase Returns and Allowances account.

TRANSPORTATION-IN The cost of merchandise acquired for resale logically includes any transportation charges necessary to place the goods in the purchaser's place of business.

A separate ledger account is used to accumulate transportation charges on merchandise purchased. The journal entry to record transportation charges on inbound shipments of merchandise is as follows:

Journalizing Transportation-in *125*
transporta-
tion charges   Cash (or Accounts Payable) *125*
on pur- *Air freight charges on merchandise purchased from Miller Brothers,*
chases of *Kansas City.*
merchandise

Since transportation charges are part of the *delivered cost* of merchandise purchased, the Transportation-in account is combined with the Purchases account in the income statement to determine the cost of goods available for sale.

Transportation charges on inbound shipments of merchandise must not be confused with transportation charges on outbound shipments of goods to customers. Freight charges and other expenses incurred in making deliveries to customers are regarded as selling expenses; these outlays are debited to a separate account entitled Delivery Expense and are not included in the cost of goods sold.

PURCHASE RETURNS AND ALLOWANCES When merchandise purchased from suppliers is found to be unsatisfactory, the goods may be returned to the seller, or a request may be made for an allowance on the price. A return of goods to the supplier is recorded as follows:

Journal entry for return of goods to supplier

Accounts Payable	1,200	
Purchase Returns and Allowances		1,200
To charge Marvel Supply Co. for the cost of goods returned.		

It is preferable to credit Purchase Returns and Allowances when merchandise is returned to a supplier, rather than crediting the Purchases account directly. The accounts then show both the total amount of purchases and the amount of purchases which required adjustment or return. The percentage relationship between merchandise purchased and merchandise returned is significant, because an excessive number of returns indicates inefficiency in the operation of the purchasing department.

F.O.B. shipping point and F.O.B. destination

The agreement between the buyer and seller of merchandise includes a provision as to which party shall bear the cost of transporting the goods. The term *F.O.B. shipping point* means that the seller will place the merchandise "free on board" the railroad cars or other means of transport, and that the buyer must pay transportation charges from that point. Many people in negotiating for the purchase of a new automobile have encountered the expression "F.O.B. Detroit," meaning that the buyer must pay the freight charges from the manufacturer's location in Detroit, in addition to the basic price of the car. In most merchandise transactions involving wholesalers or manufacturers, the buyer bears the transportation cost. Sometimes, however, as a matter of convenience, the seller prepays the freight and adds this cost to the amount billed to the buyer.

F.O.B. destination means that the seller agrees to bear the freight cost. If the seller prepays the truckline or other carrier, the agreed terms have been met and no action is required of the buyer other than to pay the agreed purchase price of the goods. If the seller does not prepay the freight, the buyer will pay the carrier and deduct this payment from the amount owed the seller when making payment for the merchandise.

Illustration of accounting cycle using periodic inventory method

An annual income statement for the Campus Sports Shop was presented on page 163. Transactions of the Campus Sports Shop for the following year, Year 11, will now be used to illustrate the accounting cycle for a business using the periodic inventory system of accounting for merchandise.

RECORDING SALES OF MERCHANDISE All sales of sports equipment during the year were for cash, and each sales transaction was rung up on a cash register. At the close of each day's business, the total sales for the day were computed by pressing the total key on the cash register. As soon as each day's sales were computed, a journal entry was prepared and posted to the Cash account and to the Sales account in the ledger. The following journal entry is typical:

Cash *600*

Sales *600*

To record today's sales of merchandise.

The daily entering of cash sales in the journal tends to minimize the opportunity for errors or dishonesty by employees in handling the cash receipts. In Chapter 6 a procedure will be described which provides a daily record of sales and cash receipts yet avoids the making of an excessive number of entries in the Cash and Sales accounts.

OTHER OPERATING TRANSACTIONS DURING THE YEAR Other routine transactions carried out by Campus Sports Shop during Year 11 included sales returns and allowances, the purchase of merchandise, the return of goods to suppliers, payment of charges for transportation-in, payment of accounts payable, and payment of operating expenses, such as salaries, telephone, and advertising. To conserve space in this illustration, these transactions are not listed individually but are included in ledger account balances at December 31.

WORK SHEET FOR A MERCHANDISING BUSINESS After the year's transactions of the Campus Sports Shop had been posted to ledger accounts, the work sheet illustrated on page 172 was prepared. The first step in the preparation of the work sheet was, of course, the listing of the balances of the ledger accounts in the Trial Balance columns. In studying this work sheet, note that the Inventory account in the Trial Balance debit column still shows a balance of $30,000, the cost of merchandise on hand at the end of the prior year. No entries were made in the Inventory account during the current year despite the various purchases and sales of merchandise. The significance of the Inventory account in the trial balance is that it shows the amount of merchandise with which the Campus Sports Shop began operations on January 1 of the current year.

Adjustments on the work sheet Salaries to employees and interest on the notes payable were paid to date on December 31; consequently adjustments were not necessary for accrued salaries or accrued interest at

CAMPUS SPORTS SHOP
Work Sheet
For the Year Ended December 31, Year 11

	Trial Balance		Adjustments*		Income Statement		Balance Sheet	
	Dr	Cr	Dr	Cr	Dr	Cr	Dr	Cr
Cash	14,000						14,000	
Inventory, Jan. 1	30,000				30,000			
Land	34,000						34,000	
Building	60,000						60,000	
Accumulated depreciation: building		12,000		(a) 4,000				16,000
Notes payable		42,000						42,000
Accounts payable		15,000						15,000
Capital stock		30,000						30,000
Retained earnings, Dec. 31, Year 10		24,000						24,000
Dividends	10,000						10,000	
Sales		215,000				215,000		
Sales returns and allowances	5,000				5,000			
Purchases	128,000				128,000			
Purchase returns and allowances		2,000				2,000		
Transportation-in	4,000				4,000			
Advertising expense	14,000				14,000			
Salaries expense	38,000				38,000			
Telephone expense	1,100				1,100			
Interest expense	1,900				1,900			
	340,000	340,000						
Depreciation expense: building			(a) 4,000		4,000			
Income taxes expense			(b) 5,000		5,000			
Income taxes payable				(b) 5,000				5,000
			9,000	9,000				
Inventory, Dec. 31						34,000	34,000	
					231,000	251,000	152,000	132,000
Net income					20,000			20,000
					251,000	251,000	152,000	152,000

Note the treatment of the beginning inventory

Note the treatment of the ending inventory

*Adjustments: (a) Depreciation of building during the year.
           (b) To accrue income taxes.

year-end. Only two adjustments were necessary at December 31: one to record depreciation of the building and the other to record the income taxes expense for the year. (The amount of income taxes is given as $5,000. We are not concerned at this point with the procedures for computing income taxes expense.) After these two adjustments were recorded, the Adjustments columns were then totaled to prove the equality of the adjustment debits and credits.

Omission of Adjusted Trial Balance columns In the work sheet previously illustrated in Chapter 4, page 135, the amounts in the Trial Balance columns were combined with the amounts listed in the Adjustments columns and then extended into the Adjusted Trial Balance columns. When there are only a few adjusting entries, many accountants prefer to omit the Adjusted Trial Balance columns and to extend the trial balance figures (as adjusted by the amounts in the Adjustments columns) directly to the Income Statement or Balance Sheet columns. This procedure is used on page 172 in the work sheet for the Campus Sports Shop.

Recording the ending inventory on the work sheet The key points to be observed in this work sheet are (*1*) the method of recording the ending inventory and (*2*) the method of handling the various accounts making up the cost of goods sold.

After the close of business on December 31, a physical inventory was taken of all merchandise in the store. The cost of the entire stock of goods was determined to be $34,000. This ending inventory, dated December 31, does not appear in the trial balance; it is therefore written on the first available line below the trial balance totals. The amount of $34,000 is listed in the Income Statement credit column and also in the Balance Sheet debit column. By entering the ending inventory in the Income Statement *credit* column, we are in effect *deducting* it from the total of the beginning inventory, the purchases, and the transportation-in, all of which are extended from the trial balance to the Income Statement *debit* column.

One of the functions of the Income Statement columns is to bring together all the accounts involved in determining the cost of goods sold. The accounts with debit balances are the beginning inventory, the purchases, and the transportation-in; these accounts total $162,000. Against this total, the two credit items of purchase returns, $2,000, and ending inventory, $34,000, are offset. The three merchandising accounts with debit balances exceed in total the two with credit balances by an amount of $126,000; this amount is the cost of goods sold, as shown in the income statement on page 175.

The ending inventory is also entered in the Balance Sheet debit column, because this inventory of merchandise on December 31 will appear as an asset in the balance sheet bearing this date.

Completing the work sheet When all the accounts on the work sheet have been extended into the Income Statement or Balance Sheet columns (and the ending inventory has been entered), the final four columns should be totaled. The net income of $20,000 is computed by subtracting the Income Statement debit column from the Income Statement credit column. This same amount of $20,000 can also be obtained by subtracting the Balance Sheet credit column from the Balance Sheet debit column. To balance out the four columns, the amount of the net income is entered in the Income Statement debit column and on the same line in the Balance Sheet credit column. (The proof of accuracy afforded by the self-balancing nature of the work sheet was explained in Chapter 4.) Final totals are determined for the Income Statement and Balance Sheet columns, and the work sheet is complete.

Financial statements

The work to be done at the end of the period is much the same for a merchandising business as for a service-type firm. First, the work sheet is completed; then, financial statements are prepared from the data in the work sheet; next, the adjusting and closing entries are entered in the journal and posted to the ledger accounts; and finally, an after-closing trial balance is prepared. This completes the periodic accounting cycle.

INCOME STATEMENT The income statement for Year 11 (page 175) was prepared from the work sheet on page 172. Note particularly the arrangement of items in the cost of goods sold section of the income statement; this portion is more detailed than in the Year 10 income statement previously illustrated and shows many of the essential accounting concepts covered in this chapter. Note also that the amount of $25,000 remaining after deducting operating expenses from gross profit on sales is called "Income before income taxes." A final deduction for the year's income taxes is then made to arrive at the "bottom line" figure of net income.

The related statement of retained earnings and the balance sheet for Campus Sports Shop are not shown because they do not differ significantly from previous illustrations.

Closing entries

The entries used in closing revenue and expense accounts have been explained in preceding chapters. The important new elements in this illustration of closing entries for a trading business are the entries showing the *elimination* of the beginning inventory and the *recording* of the ending inventory. The beginning inventory is cleared out of the Inventory account by a debit to Income Summary and a credit to Inventory. A separate entry could be made for this purpose, but we can save time by making one compound entry which will debit the Income Summary account with the balance of the beginning inventory and with the balances

CAMPUS SPORTS SHOP
Income Statement
For the Year Ended December 31, Year 11

This income statement consists of three major sections	Revenue from sales:		
	Sales		$215,000
	Less: Sales returns and allowances		5,000
	Net sales		$210,000
	Cost of goods sold:		
	Inventory, Jan. 1		$ 30,000
	Purchases	$128,000	
	Transportation-in	4,000	
	Delivered cost of purchases	$132,000	
	Less: Purchase returns and allowances	2,000	
	Net purchases		130,000
	Cost of goods available for sale		$160,000
	Less: Inventory, Dec. 31		34,000
	Cost of goods sold		126,000
	Gross profit on sales		$ 84,000
	Operating expenses:		
	Advertising		$ 14,000
	Salaries		38,000
	Telephone		1,100
	Interest		1,900
	Depreciation		4,000
	Total operating expenses		59,000
	Income before income taxes		$ 25,000
	Income taxes expense		5,000
	Net income		$ 20,000

of all temporary owners' equity accounts having debit balances. The *temporary owners' equity accounts* are those which appear in the income statement. As the name suggests, the temporary owners' equity accounts are used during the period to accumulate temporarily the increases and decreases in the owners' equity resulting from operation of the business.

Closing temporary owners' equity accounts with debit balances	Dec. 31 Income Summary	231,000
	Inventory (Jan. 1)	30,000
	Purchases	128,000
	Sales Returns and Allowances	5,000
	Transportation-in	4,000
	Advertising Expense	14,000
	Salaries Expense	38,000
	Telephone Expense	1,100
	Interest Expense	1,900
	Depreciation Expense	4,000
	Income Taxes Expense	5,000

To close out the beginning inventory and the temporary owners' equity accounts with debit balances.

Note that the above entry closes all the operating expense accounts and Income Taxes Expense as well as the accounts used to accumulate the cost of goods sold, and also the Sales Returns and Allowances account. Although the Sales Returns and Allowances account has a debit balance, it is not an expense account. In terms of account classification, it belongs in the revenue group of accounts because it serves as an offset to the Sales account and appears in the income statement as a deduction from Sales.

To bring the **ending inventory** into the accounting records after taking a physical inventory on December 31, we could make a separate entry debiting Inventory and crediting the Income Summary account. However, it is more convenient to combine this step with the closing of the Sales account and any other temporary proprietorship accounts having credit balances, as illustrated in the following closing entry.

Closing	*Dec. 31* *Inventory (Dec. 31)*	*34,000*
temporary	*Sales*	*215,000*
owners'		
equity	*Purchase Returns and Allowances*	*2,000*
accounts		
with	*Income Summary*	*251,000*
credit	*To record the ending inventory and to close all temporary*	
balances	*owners' equity accounts with credit balances.*	

The remaining closing entries serve to transfer the balance of the Income Summary account to the Retained Earnings account and to close the Dividends account, as follows:

Closing	*Dec. 31* *Income Summary*	*20,000*
Income	*Retained Earnings*	*20,000*
Summary	*To close the Income Summary account.*	
account and		
Dividends		
account	*31* *Retained Earnings*	*10,000*
	Dividends	*10,000*
	To close the Dividends account.	

After the preceding four closing entries have been posted to the ledger, the only accounts left with dollar balances will be balance sheet accounts. An after-closing trial balance should be prepared to prove that the ledger is in balance after the year-end entries to adjust and close the accounts.

Summary of merchandising transactions and related accounting entries

The transactions regularly encountered in merchandising operations and the related accounting entries may be concisely summarized as follows:

	Transactions during the Period	Related Accounting Entries	
		Debit	**Credit**
Typical journal entries relating to merchandise	Purchase merchandise for resale	Purchases	Cash (or Accounts Payable)
	Incur transportation charges on merchandise purchased for resale	Transportation-in	Cash (or Accounts Payable)
	Return unsatisfactory merchandise to supplier, or obtain a reduction from original price	Cash (or Accounts Payable)	Purchase Returns and Allowances
	Sell merchandise to customers	Cash (or Accounts Receivable)	Sales
	Permit customers to return merchandise, or grant them a reduction from original price	Sales Returns and Allowances	Cash (or Accounts Receivable)
	Inventory Procedures at End of Period		
	Transfer the balance of the beginning inventory to the Income Summary account	Income Summary	Inventory
	Take a physical inventory of goods on hand at the end of the period, and price these goods at cost	Inventory	Income Summary

THE SYSTEM OF INTERNAL CONTROL

The meaning of internal control

In this section we shall round out our discussion of a merchandising business by considering the *system of internal control* by which management maintains control over the purchasing, receiving, storing, and selling of merchandise. Strong internal controls are needed not only for purchases and sales transactions, but for all other types of transactions as well. It is particularly important to maintain strong internal controls over transactions involving cash receipts and cash payments. In fact, the concept of internal control is so important that it affects all the assets of a business, all liabilities, the revenue and expenses, and every aspect of operations. *The purpose of internal control is to aid in the efficient operation of a business.*

As defined in Chapter 1, the system of internal control includes all the measures taken by an organization for the purpose of (*1*) protecting its resources against waste, fraud, and inefficiency; (*2*) ensuring accuracy and reliability in accounting and operating data; (*3*) securing compliance with company policies; and (4) evaluating the level of performance in all divisions of the company.

Many people think of internal control as a means of safeguarding cash and preventing fraud. Although internal control is an important factor in protecting assets and preventing fraud, this is only a part of its role. Remember that business decisions are based on accounting data: and the system of internal control provides assurance of the *dependability of the accounting data used in making decisions.*

The decisions made by management are communicated throughout the organization and become company policy. The means of communication include organization charts, manuals of accounting policies and procedures, flow charts, financial forecasts, purchase orders, receiving reports, invoices, and many other documents. The term *documentation* refers to all the charts, forms, reports, and other business papers that guide and describe the working of a company's system of accounting and internal control.

ADMINISTRATIVE CONTROLS AND ACCOUNTING CONTROLS Internal controls fall into two major classes: administrative controls and accounting controls. *Administrative controls* are measures that apply principally to operational efficiency and compliance with established policies in all parts of the organization. For example, an administrative control may be a requirement that traveling salespersons submit reports showing the number of calls made on customers each day. Another example is a directive requiring airline pilots to have an annual medical examination. These internal administrative controls have no direct bearing on the reliability of the financial statements. Consequently, administrative controls are not of direct interest to accountants and independent auditors.

Internal accounting controls are measures that relate to protection of assets and to the reliability of accounting and financial reports. An example is the requirement that a person whose duties involve handling cash shall not also maintain accounting records. More broadly stated, the accounting function must be kept separate from the custody of assets. Another accounting control is the requirement that checks, purchase orders, and other documents be serially numbered.

When certified public accountants perform an audit of a company, they always study and evaluate the system of internal control. However, this work is concentrated on accounting controls rather than administrative controls, because the objective of the CPA is to form an opinion of the company's financial statements and it is the accounting controls which assure reliability in financial statements.

Strong internal control now required by law

In recent years, some American corporations have acknowledged making payments to foreign officials which could be interpreted as bribes. These payments in many cases were legal under the laws of the countries in which they were made, although they were not in conformity with American business ethics. In some cases, the top executives of the corporations involved were not aware that these transactions were taking place.

To put an end to such practices, the United States Congress passed the *Foreign Corrupt Practices Act of 1977.* This Act requires every corporation under the jurisdiction of the SEC to maintain a system of internal control sufficient to provide reasonable assurance that transactions are executed only with the knowledge and authorization of management. The Act also requires the system of internal control to limit the use of corporate assets to those purposes approved by management. Finally, the Act requires that accounting records of assets be compared at reasonable intervals with the assets actually on hand. These requirements are designed to prevent the creation of secret "slush funds" or other misuses of corporate assets. Violations of the Act may result in fines of up to $1 million and imprisonment of the responsible parties. Thus, a strong system of internal control, long recognized as vital to the operation of a large business, is now required by federal law.

GUIDELINES TO STRONG INTERNAL CONTROL

Organization plan to establish responsibility for every function

An organization plan should indicate clearly the departments or persons responsible for such functions as purchasing merchandise, receiving incoming shipments, maintaining accounting records, approving credit to customers, and preparing the payroll. When an individual or department is assigned responsibility for a function, it is imperative that authority to make decisions also be granted. The lines of authority and responsibility can conveniently be shown on an organization chart; a portion of an organization chart of a manufacturing company is illustrated on page 180.

Control of transactions

If management is to direct the activities of a business according to plan, every transaction should go through four basic steps: It should be *authorized, approved, executed,* and *recorded.* These steps may be illustrated by the example of the sale of merchandise on credit. The top management of the company may *authorize* the sale of merchandise on credit to customers who meet certain standards. The manager of the credit and collection department may *approve* a sale of given dollar amount to a particular customer. The sales transaction is *executed* by preparing a sales invoice and delivering the merchandise to the credit customer. The sales transaction is *recorded* in the accounting department by debiting Accounts Receivable and crediting Sales.

Portion of an Organization Chart

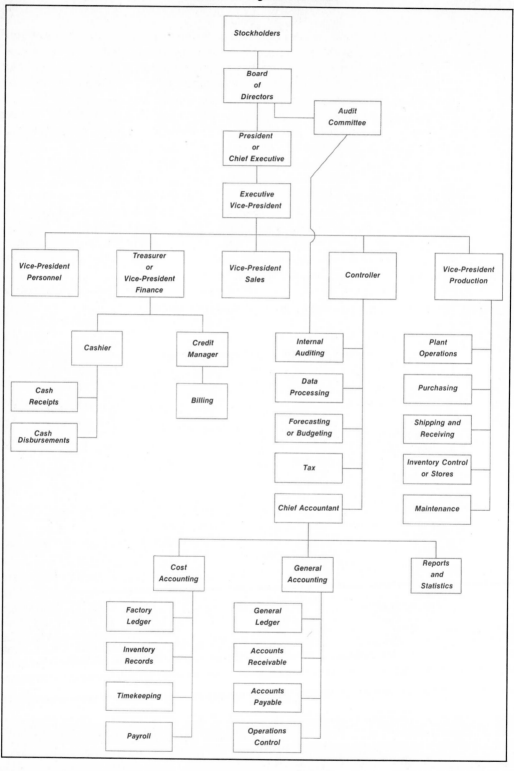

Consider for a moment the losses that would probably be incurred if this internal control of transactions did not exist. Assume, for example, that all employees in a store were free to sell on credit any amount of merchandise to any customer, and responsibility for recording the sales transactions was not fixed on any one person or department. The result no doubt would be many unrecorded sales; of those sales transactions that were recorded, many would represent uncollectible receivables.

Subdivision of duties strengthens internal control

Procedures for controlling the purchase and sale of merchandise emphasize the subdivision of duties within the company so that no one person or department handles a transaction completely from beginning to end. When duties are divided in this manner, the work of one employee serves to verify that of another and any errors which occur tend to be detected promptly.

To illustrate the development of internal control through subdivision of duties, let us review the procedures for a sale of merchandise on account by a wholesaler. The sales department of the company is responsible for securing the order from the customer; the credit department must approve the customer's credit before the order is filled; the stock room assembles the goods ordered; the shipping department packs and ships the goods; and the accounting department records the transaction. Each department receives written evidence of the action of the other departments and reviews the documents describing the transaction to see that the actions taken correspond in all details. The shipping department, for instance, does not release the merchandise until after the credit department has approved the customer as a credit risk. The accounting department does not record the sale until it has received documentary evidence that (1) the goods were ordered, (2) the extension of credit was approved, and (3) the merchandise has been shipped to the customer.

SEPARATION OF ACCOUNTING AND CUSTODY OF ASSETS An employee who has custody of an asset or access to an asset should not maintain the accounting record of that asset. The person having custody of an asset will not be inclined to waste it, steal it, or give it away if he or she is aware that another employee is maintaining a record of the asset. The employee maintaining the accounting record does not have access to the asset and therefore has no incentive to falsify the record. If one person has custody of assets and also maintains the accounting records, there is both opportunity and incentive to falsify the records to conceal a shortage. The following diagram illustrates how separation of duties creates strong internal control.

In this diagram Employee A has custody of assets and Employee B maintains an accounting record of the assets. Employee C periodically counts the assets and compares the count with the record maintained by

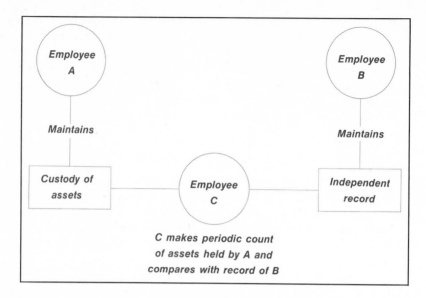

B. This comparison should reveal any errors made by either A or B unless the two have collaborated to conceal an error or irregularity.

Assume for a moment, as an example of unsatisfactory internal control, that one employee was permitted to take the customer's order, approve the credit terms, get the merchandise from the stock room, deliver the goods to the customer, prepare the invoice, enter the transaction in the accounting records, and collect the account receivable. If this employee made errors, such as selling to poor credit risks, forgetting to enter the sale in the accounting records, or perhaps delivering more merchandise to the customer than was charged for, no one would know the difference. By the time such errors came to light, substantial losses would have been incurred.

PREVENTION OF FRAUD If one employee is permitted to handle all aspects of a transaction, the danger of fraud is increased. Studies of fraud cases suggest that many individuals may be tempted into dishonest acts if given complete control of company property. Most of these persons, however, would not engage in fraud if doing so required collaboration with another employee. Losses through employee dishonesty occur in a variety of ways: merchandise may be stolen; payments by customers may be withheld; suppliers may be overpaid with a view to kickbacks to employees; and lower prices may be allowed to favored customers. The opportunities for fraud are almost endless if all aspects of a sale or purchase transaction are concentrated in the hands of one employee.

ROTATION OF EMPLOYEES To the extent practicable, rotation of employees from one job assignment to another may strengthen internal control. When employees know that other persons may soon be taking over their duties, they are more likely to maintain records with care and to follow established procedures. The rotation of employees may also bring to light any errors or irregularities that have occurred. This same line of reasoning indicates that all employees should be required to take annual vacations and all their duties should be performed by others during such vacation periods.

Serially numbered documents—another control device

Another method of achieving internal control, in addition to the subdivision of duties, consists of having the printer include serial numbers on such documents as purchase orders, sales invoices, and checks. The use of serial numbers makes it possible to account for all documents. In other words, if a sales invoice is misplaced or concealed, the break in the sequence of numbers will call attention to the discrepancy.

Competence of personnel

Even the best-designed system of internal control will not work satisfactorily unless the people assigned to operate it are competent. Each person involved must have a level of competence sufficient for the work assigned and a willingness to assume responsibility for performance. Competence and integrity of employees are in part developed through training programs, but they are also related to the policies for selection of personnel, the adequacy of supervision, and the complexity of the system.

Financial forecasts

A financial forecast, as defined in Chapter 1, is a plan of operations for a future period. Specific goals are set for each division of the business as, for example, the expected volume of sales, the amounts of expenses, and the planned cash balance. Actual results achieved month by month can then be compared with the planned results and management's attention is promptly directed to any areas of substandard performance. The system of internal control is strengthened by the use of forecasts because errors or irregularities which cause actual results to differ from planned results will be identified and fully investigated.

Internal auditing

In all large organizations an important element of internal control is the internal auditing staff. *Internal auditors* are professional-level employees with the responsibility of investigating throughout the company the efficiency of operations in every department or other organizational unit. They are continuously studying and testing the system of internal control and reporting to top management on compliance with company standards and on problems which require strengthening of internal controls.

Limitations of internal control

Although internal control is highly effective in increasing the reliability of accounting data and in protecting against fraud, no system of internal control is foolproof. Two or more dishonest employees working in collusion can defeat the system. Carelessness by employees and misunderstanding of instructions can cause a breakdown in controls. The much-publicized Equity Funding management fraud case demonstrated that top management can circumvent the system of internal control if it is determined to do so.

Internal control in the small business

Satisfactory internal control is more difficult to achieve in a small business than a large one because, with only a few employees, it is not possible to arrange extensive subdivision of duties. However, in many small businesses, internal control is unnecessarily weak because management does not understand the basic principles of internal control or neglects to give attention to the problem.

Some internal controls are suitable for even the smallest business, with only one or two employees. An example is the use of serial numbers on checks, sales invoices, and other documents to ensure that no document is misplaced and forgotten. Another example is insistence that documentary evidence be created to verify an invoice before it is paid, and that documents supporting the issuance of a check be marked paid when the check is issued.

An essential element in maintaining a reasonable degree of internal control in the small business is active participation by the owner-manager in strategic control procedures. These procedures will be considered in later chapters dealing with such topics as cash and receivables.

Internal control in perspective

In appraising the merits of various internal control procedures, the question of their cost cannot be ignored. Too elaborate a system of internal control may entail greater operating costs than are justified by the protection gained. For this reason the system of internal control must be tailored to meet the requirements of the individual business. In most organizations, however, proper subdivision of duties and careful design of accounting procedures will provide a basis for adequate internal control and at the same time will contribute to economical operation of the business.

Fidelity bonds

Since no system of internal control can provide absolute protection against losses from dishonest employees, many companies require that employees handling cash or other negotiable assets be bonded. A *fidelity bond* is a type of insurance contract in which a bonding company agrees to reimburse an employer up to agreed dollar limits for losses caused by fraud or embezzlement by bonded employees.

Fidelity bonds are not a substitute for internal control; they do little or nothing to assure reliable accounting data, to prevent wasteful inefficient use of company assets, or to encourage compliance with company policies.

INTERNAL CONTROLS OVER THE PURCHASE AND SALE OF MERCHANDISE

The owner-manager of a small store is sufficiently familiar with the stock of merchandise to know what items need to be replenished. A notebook record of items to be ordered may be maintained by writing down each day any items which the owner observes to be running low. A sales representative of a wholesaler or manufacturer who visits the store will write up the order in an order book. A copy of the order, showing the quantities and prices of all items ordered, is left with the store owner.

Purchase orders

In many businesses and especially in large organizations, the buying company uses its own purchase order forms. A purchase order of the Zenith Company issued to Adams Manufacturing Company is illustrated below.

Serially numbered purchase order

PURCHASE ORDER			Order no. 999
ZENITH COMPANY			
10 Fairway Avenue, San Francisco, California			
To: Adams Manufacturing Company		**Date** Nov. 10, 19___	
19 Union Street		**Ship via** Jones Truck Co.	
Kansas City, Missouri		**Terms:** 2/10, n/30	

Please enter our order for the following:

Quantity	Description	Price	Total
15 sets	Model S irons	$60.00	$900.00
50 dozen	X3Y Shur-Par golf balls	7.00	350.00

Zenith Company

By *B. B. McCarthy*

Note that the illustrated purchase order bears a serial number, 999. When purchase orders are serially numbered, there can be no doubt as to how many orders have been issued. Each department authorized to receive copies of purchase orders should account for every number in the series, thus guarding against the loss or nondelivery of any document.

In large companies in which the functions of placing orders, receiving merchandise, and making payment are lodged in separate departments, several copies of the purchase order are usually prepared, each on a different color paper. The original is sent to the supplier; this purchase order is an authorization to deliver the merchandise and to submit a bill based on the prices listed. Carbon copies of the purchase order are usually routed to the purchasing department, accounting department, receiving department, and finance department.

The issuance of a purchase order does not call for any debit or credit entries in the accounting records of either the prospective buyer or seller. The company which receives an order does not consider (for accounting purposes) that a sale has been made until the merchandise is delivered. At that point ownership of the goods changes, and both buyer and seller should make accounting entries to record the transaction.

Invoices

The supplier (vendor) mails an invoice to the purchaser at the time of shipping the merchandise. An invoice contains a description of the goods being sold, the quantities, prices, credit terms, and method of shipment. The illustration on page 187 shows an invoice issued by Adams Manufacturing Company in response to the purchase order from Zenith Company.

From the viewpoint of the seller, an invoice is a *sales invoice;* from the buyer's viewpoint it is a *purchase invoice.* The invoice is the basis for an entry in the accounting records of both the seller and the buyer because it evidences the transfer of ownership of goods. At the time of issuing the invoice, the selling company makes an entry debiting Accounts Receivable and crediting Sales. The buying company however, does not record the invoice as a liability until after making a careful verification of the transaction, as indicated in the following section.

VERIFICATION OF INVOICE BY PURCHASER Upon receipt of an invoice, the purchasing company should verify the following aspects of the transaction:

1 The invoice agrees with the purchase order as to prices, quantities, and other provisions.
2 The invoice is arithmetically correct in all extensions of price times quantity and in the addition of amounts.
3 The goods covered by the invoice have been received and are in satisfactory condition.

<table>
<tr><td colspan="2" align="center">**INVOICE**</td></tr>
<tr><td colspan="2" align="center">**ADAMS MANUFACTURING COMPANY**</td></tr>
<tr><td colspan="2" align="center">**19 Union Street**</td></tr>
<tr><td colspan="2" align="center">**Kansas City, Missouri**</td></tr>
</table>

Invoice is basis for accounting entry

Sold to Zenith Company

Invoice no. 777

10 Fairway Avenue

Invoice date Nov. 15, 19__

San Francisco, Calif.

Your order no. 999

Shipped to Same

Date shipped Nov. 15, 19__

Terms 2/10, n/30

Shipped via Jones Truck Co.

Quantity	Description	Price	Amount
15 sets	Model S irons	$60.00	$ 900.00
50 dozen	X3Y Shur-Par golf balls	7.00	350.00
			$1,250.00

Evidence that the merchandise has been received in good condition must be obtained from the receiving department. It is the function of the receiving department to receive all incoming goods, to inspect them as to quality and condition, and to determine the quantities received by counting, measuring, or weighing. The receiving department should prepare a separate *receiving report* for each shipment received; this report is sent to the accounting department for use in verifying the invoice.

The verification of the invoice in the accounting department is accomplished by comparing the purchase order, the invoice, and the receiving report. Comparison of these documents establishes that the merchandise described in the invoice was actually ordered, has been received in good condition, and was billed at the prices specified in the purchase order.

Debit and credit memoranda

If merchandise purchased on account is unsatisfactory and is to be returned to the supplier (or if a price reduction is agreed upon), a *debit memorandum* may be prepared by the purchasing company and sent to the supplier. The debit memorandum informs the supplier that his or her account is being debited (reduced) by the buyer and explains the circumstances.

The supplier upon being informed of the return of damaged merchandise (or having agreed to a reduction in price) will issue a *credit memorandum* as evidence that the account receivable from the purchaser is being credited (reduced) by the supplier.

Trade discounts

Many manufacturers and wholesalers publish annual catalogs in which their products are listed at retail prices. Substantial reductions from the *list prices* (listed retail prices) are offered to dealers. These reductions from list prices (often as much as 30 or 40%) are called *trade discounts.* As market conditions change, the schedule of discounts is revised. This is a more convenient way to revise actual selling prices quickly than by publishing a new catalog.

Trade discounts are not recorded in the accounting records of either the seller or the buyer. A sale of merchandise is recorded at the actual selling price and the trade discount is merely a device for computing the actual sales price. From the viewpoint of the company purchasing goods, the significant price is not the list price but the amount which must be paid, and this amount is recorded as the cost of the merchandise.

For example, if a manufacturer sells goods to a retailer at a list price of $1,000 with a trade discount of 40%, the transaction will be recorded by the manufacturer as a $600 sale and by the retailer as a $600 purchase. Because trade discounts are not recorded in the accounts they should be clearly distinguished from the cash discounts discussed below.

Cash discounts

Manufacturers and wholesalers generally offer a cash discount to encourage their customers to pay invoices. For example, the credit terms may be "2% 10 days, net 30 days"; these terms mean that the authorized credit period is 30 days, but that the customer company may deduct 2% of the amount of the invoice if it makes payment within 10 days. On the invoice these terms would appear in the abbreviated form "2/10, n/30"; this expression is read "2, 10, net 30." Some companies issue invoices payable 10 days after the end of the month in which the sale occurs. Such invoices bear the expression "10 e.o.m." The selling company regards a cash discount as a *sales discount;* the buyer calls the discount a *purchase discount.*

To illustrate the application of a cash discount, assume that Adams Manufacturing Company sells goods to the Zenith Company and issues a sales invoice for $1,000 dated November 3 and bearing the terms 2/10, n/30. If Zenith Company mails its check in payment on or before November 13, it is entitled to deduct 2% of $1,000, or $20, and settle the obligation for $980. If Zenith Company decides to forego the discount, it may postpone payment for an additional 20 days until December 3 but must then pay $1,000.

REASONS FOR CASH DISCOUNTS From the viewpoint of the seller, the acceptance of $980 in cash as full settlement of a $1,000 account receivable represents a $20 reduction in the amount of revenue earned. By making this concession to induce prompt payment, the seller collects accounts receivable more quickly and is able to use the money collected to buy additional goods. A greater volume of business can be handled with a given amount of invested capital if this capital is not tied up in accounts receivable for long periods. There is also less danger of accounts receivable becoming uncollectible if they are collected promptly; in other words, the older an account receivable becomes, the greater becomes the risk of nonpayment by the customer.

Is it to the advantage of the Zenith Company to settle the $1,000 invoice within the discount period and thereby save $20? The alternative is for Zenith to conserve cash by postponing payment for an additional 20 days. The question may therefore be stated as follows: Does the amount of $20 represent a reasonable charge for the use of $980 for a period of 20 days? Definitely not; this charge is the equivalent of an annual interest rate of about 36%. (A 20-day period is approximately $\frac{1}{18}$ of a year; 18 times 2% amounts to 36%.)[1] Although interest rates vary widely, most businesses are able to borrow money from banks at an annual interest rate of 10% or less. Well-managed businesses, therefore, generally pay all invoices within the discount period even though this policy necessitates borrowing from banks in order to have the necessary cash available.

RECORDING SALES DISCOUNTS   Sales of merchandise are generally recorded at the full selling price without regard for the cash discount being offered. The discount is not reflected in the seller's accounting records until payment is received. Continuing our illustration of a sale of merchandise by Adams Manufacturing Company for $1,000 with terms of 2/10, n/30, the entry to record the sale on November 3 is as shown by the following:

Sale	*Nov. 3 Accounts Receivable*	*1,000*
entered at full price	*Sales*	*1,000*
	To record sale to Zenith Company, terms 2/10, n/30.	

Assuming that payment is made by Zenith Company on November 13, the last day of the discount period, the entry by Adams to record collection of the receivable is as follows:

Sales	*Nov. 13 Cash*	*980*
discounts recorded	*Sales Discounts*	*20*
at time of collection	*Accounts Receivable*	*1,000*
	To record collection from Zenith Company of invoice	
	of Nov. 3 less 2% cash discount.	

As previously explained, the allowing of a cash discount reduces the amount received from sales. In the income statement, therefore, sales discounts appear as a deduction from sales, as follows:

[1] A more accurate estimate of interest expense on an annual basis can be obtained as follows: ($20 × 18) ÷ $980 = 36.7%.

Partial Income Statement

Sales		$189,788
Less: Sales returns & allowances	$4,462	
Sales discounts	3,024	7,486
Net sales		$182,302

RECORDING PURCHASE DISCOUNTS In the accounts of the Zenith Company, the purchase of merchandise on November 3 was recorded at the gross amount of the invoice, as shown by the following entry:

Purchases	1,000	
Accounts Payable		1,000

To record purchase from Adams Manufacturing Company,
terms 2/10, n/30.

When the invoice was paid on November 13, the last day of the discount period, the payment was recorded as follows:

Accounts Payable	1,000	
Purchase Discounts		20
Cash		980

To record payment to Adams Manufacturing Company of invoice of
Nov. 3, less 2% cash discount.

The effect of the discount was to reduce the cost of the merchandise to the Zenith Company. The credit balance of the Purchase Discounts account should therefore be deducted in the income statement from the debit balance of the Purchase account.

Since the Purchase Discounts account is deducted from Purchases in the income statement, a question naturally arises as to whether the Purchase Discounts account is really necessary. Why not reduce the amount of purchases at the time of taking a discount by crediting Purchases rather than crediting Purchase Discounts? The answer is that management needs to know the amount of discounts taken. The Purchase Discounts account supplies this information. Any decrease in the proportion of purchase discounts to purchases carries the suggestion that the accounts payable department is becoming inefficient. That department has the responsibility of paying all invoices within the discount period, and management should be informed of failure by any department to follow company policies consistently. If management is to direct the business effectively, it needs to receive from the accounting system information indicating the level of performance in every department.

CLASSIFIED FINANCIAL STATEMENTS

The financial statements illustrated up to this point have been rather short and simple because of the limited number of transactions and accounts used in these introductory chapters. Now let us look briefly at a more comprehensive and realistic balance sheet for a merchandising business. A full understanding of all the items on this balance sheet may not be possible until our study of accounting has progressed further, but a bird's-eye view of a fairly complete balance sheet is nevertheless useful at this point.

In the balance sheet of Skymart Company illustrated on page 192, the assets are classified into three groups: (1) current assets, (2) plant and equipment, and (3) other assets. The liabilities are classified into two types: (1) current liabilities and (2) long-term liabilities. This classification of assets and liabilities, subject to minor variations in terminology, is virtually a standard one throughout American business. The inclusion of captions for the balance sheet totals is an optional step.

The purpose of balance sheet classification

The purpose underlying a standard classification of assets and liabilities is to aid management, owners, creditors, and other interested persons in understanding the financial position of the business. Bankers, for example, would have a difficult time in reading the balance sheets of all the companies which apply to them for loans, if each of these companies followed its own individual whims as to the sequence and arrangement of accounts comprising its balance sheet. Standard practices as to the order and arrangement of a balance sheet are an important means of saving the time of the reader and of giving a fuller comprehension of the company's financial position. On the other hand, these standard practices are definitely not iron-clad rules; the form and content of a well-prepared balance sheet today are different in several respects from the balance sheet of 25 years ago. No two businesses are exactly alike and a degree of variation from the conventional type of balance sheet is appropriate for the individual business in devising a clear presentation of its financial position. Standardization of the form and content of financial statements is a desirable goal; but if carried to an extreme, it might prevent the introduction of new improved methods and the constructive changes necessary to reflect changes in business practices.

The analysis and interpretation of financial statements is the subject of Chapter 16. At this point our objective is merely to emphasize that classification of the items on a balance sheet aids the reader greatly in appraising the financial position of the business. Some of the major balance sheet classifications are discussed briefly in the following section.

CURRENT ASSETS Current assets include cash, government bonds and other marketable securities, receivables, inventories, and prepaid expenses. To qualify for inclusion in the current asset category, an asset must be capable of being converted into cash within a relatively short period without interfering with the normal operation of the business. The

SKYMART COMPANY
Balance Sheet
December 31, 19___

Assets

Current assets:

Cash			$ 145,000
U.S. government bonds			100,000
Notes receivable			124,000
Accounts receivable		$269,600	
Less: Allowance for doubtful accounts		8,600	261,000
Inventory			352,000
Short-term prepayments			12,000
Total current assets			$ 994,000

Plant and equipment:

Land		$100,000	
Building	$240,000		
Less: Accumulated depreciation	19,200	220,800	
Store equipment	$ 94,000		
Less: Accumulated depreciation	18,800	75,200	
Delivery equipment	$ 28,000		
Less: Accumulated depreciation	7,000	21,000	
Total plant and equipment			417,000

Other assets:

Land (future building site)			165,000
Total assets			$1,576,000

Liabilities & Stockholders' Equity

Current liabilities:

Notes payable		$ 115,000
Accounts payable		190,400
Income taxes payable		20,000
Deferred revenue		5,100
Total current liabilities		$ 330,500

Long-term liabilities:

Mortgage payable (due in 10 years)		250,000
Total liabilities		$ 580,500

Stockholders' equity:

Capital stock	$600,000	
Retained earnings	395,500	995,500
Total liabilities & stockholders' equity		$1,576,000

Note: A new item introduced in this balance sheet is the Allowance for Doubtful Accounts of $8,600, shown as a deduction from Accounts Receivable. This is an estimate of the uncollectible portion of the accounts receivable and serves to reduce the valuation of this asset to the net amount of $261,000 that is considered collectible.

period is usually one year, but it may be longer for those businesses having an operating cycle in excess of one year. The sequence in which current assets are listed depends upon their liquidity; the closer an asset is to becoming cash the higher is its liquidity. The total amount of a company's current assets and the relative amount of each type give some indication of the company's short-run debt-paying ability.

The term *operating cycle* is often used in establishing the limits of the current asset classification. Operating cycle means the average time period between the purchase of merchandise and the conversion of this merchandise back into cash. The series of transactions comprising a complete cycle often runs as follows: (*1*) purchase of merchandise, (*2*) sale of the merchandise on credit, (*3*) collection of the account receivable from the customer. The word *cycle* suggests the circular flow of capital from cash to inventory to receivables to cash again. This cycle of transactions in a merchandising business is portrayed in the following diagram.

The operating cycle repeats continuously

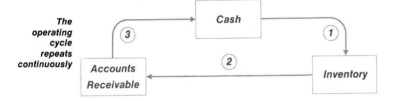

In a business handling fast-moving merchandise (a supermarket, for example) the operating cycle may be completed in a few weeks; for most merchandising businesses the operating cycle requires several months but less than a year. In a business such as a shipyard, however, the operating cycle may require several years.

CURRENT LIABILITIES Liabilities that must be paid within one year or the operating cycle (whichever is longer) are called *current liabilities.* Current liabilities are paid out of current assets, and a comparison of the amount of current assets with the amount of current liabilities is an important step in appraising the ability of a company to pay its debts in the near future.

CURRENT RATIO Many bankers and other users of financial statements believe that for a business to qualify as a good credit risk, the total current assets should be about twice as large as the total current liabilities. In studying a balance sheet, a banker or other creditor will compute the *current ratio* by dividing total current assets by total current liabilities. The current ratio is a convenient measure of the short-run debt-paying ability of a business.

In the illustrated balance sheet of Skymart Company, the current assets of $994,000 are approximately three times as great as the current liabilities of $330,500; the current ratio is therefore 3 to 1, which would generally be regarded as a very strong current position. The current assets could shrink by two-thirds and still be sufficient for payment of the current liabilities. Although a strong current ratio is desirable, an extremely high current ratio (such as 4 to 1 or more) may signify that a company is holding too much of its resources in cash, marketable securities, and other current assets and is not pursuing profit opportunities as aggressively as it might.

WORKING CAPITAL The excess of current assets over current liabilities is called *working capital;* the relative amount of working capital is another indication of short-term financial strength. In the illustrated balance sheet of Skymart Company, working capital is $663,500, computed by subtracting the current liabilities of $330,500 from the current assets of $994,000. The importance of solvency (ability to meet debts as they fall due) was emphasized in Chapter 1. Ample working capital permits a company to buy merchandise in large lots, to carry an adequate stock of goods, and to sell goods to customers on favorable credit terms. Many companies have been forced to suspend business because of inadequate working capital, even though total assets were much larger than total liabilities.

Classification in the income statement

A new feature to be noted in the illustrated income statement of Skymart Company (page 195) is the division of the operating expenses into the two categories of selling expenses and general and administrative expenses. Selling expenses include all expenses of storing merchandise, advertising and sales promotion, sales salaries and commissions, and delivering goods to customers. General and administrative expenses include the expenses of operating the general offices, the accounting department, the personnel office, and the credit and collection department.

This classification aids management in controlling expenses by emphasizing that certain expenses are the responsibility of the executive in charge of sales, and that other types of expenses relate to the business as a whole. Some expenses, such as depreciation of the building, may be divided between the two classifications according to the portion utilized by each functional division of the business. The item of Doubtful Accounts Expense listed under the heading of General and Administrative Expenses is an expense of estimated amount. It will be discussed fully in Chapter 10.

Another feature to note in the income statement of Skymart Company is that interest earned on investments is placed after the figure showing income from operations. Other examples of such *nonoperating revenues* are dividends on shares of stock owned, and rent earned by leasing property not presently needed in the operation of the business. Any items of expense not related to selling or administrative functions may also be placed after *Income from Operations.* Separate group headings of Non-operating Revenue and Nonoperating Expenses are sometimes used.

SKYMART COMPANY
Income Statement
For the Year Ended December 31, 19___

Gross sales			$3,108,900
Sales returns & allowances	$	38,200	
Sales discounts		48,300	86,500
Net sales			$3,022,400
Cost of goods sold:			
Inventory, Jan. 1		$ 300,400	
Purchases	$2,124,000		
Transportation-in	83,000		
Delivered cost of purchases	$2,207,000		
Less: Purchase returns &			
allowances	$24,000		
Purchase discounts	51,000	75,000	
Net purchases		2,132,000	
Cost of goods available for sale		$2,432,400	
Less: Inventory, Dec. 31		352,000	
Cost of goods sold			2,080,400
Gross profit on sales			$ 942,000
Operating expenses:			
Selling expenses:			
Sales salaries	$384,100		
Advertising	101,900		
Depreciation: building	8,400		
Depreciation: store equipment	9,400		
Depreciation: delivery equipment	7,000		
Insurance	11,000		
Miscellaneous	8,200		
Total selling expenses		$ 530,000	
General and administrative expenses:			
Office salaries	$192,000		
Doubtful accounts	7,500		
Depreciation: building	1,200		
Insurance	1,000		
Miscellaneous	9,300		
Total general and administrative expenses		211,000	
Total operating expenses			741,000
Income from operations			$ 201,000
Interest earned on investments			3,000
Income before income taxes			$ 204,000
Income taxes expense			81,600
Net income			$ 122,400

Condensed income statement

In the published annual reports of large corporations, the income statement is usually greatly condensed because the public is presumably not interested in the details of operations. A condensed income statement usually begins with *net* sales. The details involved in computing the cost of goods are also often omitted and only summary figures are given for selling expenses and general and administrative expenses. A condensed income statement for Skymart Company appears below:

SKYMART COMPANY

Income Statement

For the Year Ended December 31, 19___

Net sales		$3,022,400
Cost of goods sold		2,080,400
Gross profit on sales		$ 942,000
Expenses:		
Selling	$530,000	
General and administrative	211,000	741,000
Income from operations		$ 201,000
Interest earned on investments		3,000
Income before income taxes		$ 204,000
Income taxes expense		81,600
Net income		$ 122,400

A condensed income statement

The statement of retained earnings for Skymart Company would not differ significantly from the form shown in previous illustrations.

KEY TERMS INTRODUCED OR EMPHASIZED IN CHAPTER 5

Beginning inventory Goods on hand and available for sale to customers at the beginning of the accounting period.

Cash discount A reduction in price (usually 2% or less) offered by manufacturers and wholesalers to encourage customers to pay invoices within a specified discount period.

Cost of goods sold A computation appearing as a separate section of an income statement showing the cost of goods sold during the period. Computed by adding net delivered cost of merchandise purchases to beginning inventory to obtain cost of goods available for sale, and then deducting from this total the amount of the ending inventory. Usually equal to between 60 and 80% of net sales.

Credit memorandum A document issued to show a reduction in the amount owed by a customer because of goods returned, a defect in the goods or services provided, or an error.

Current assets Cash and other assets that can be converted into cash within one year or the operating cycle (whichever is longer) without interfering with the normal operation of the business.

Current liabilities   Any debts that must be paid within one year or the operating cycle (whichever is longer).

Current ratio   Current assets divided by current liabilities. A measure of short-run debt-paying ability.

Debit memorandum   A document issued by a buyer to show a decrease in the amount previously recorded as owing to a seller. May also be issued by a seller to increase the amount previously recorded as receivable from a customer.

Embezzlement   Theft by a person of assets entrusted to him or her.

Ending inventory   Goods still on hand and available for sale to customers at the end of the accounting period.

Fidelity bond   A form of insurance contract in which a bonding company agrees to reimburse an employer for losses caused by theft by bonded employees.

Financial forecast   A plan of operations for a future period with expected results expressed in dollars.

F.O.B. destination   The seller bears the cost of shipping goods to the buyer's location.

F.O.B. shipping point   The buyer of goods bears the cost of transportation from the seller's location to the buyer's location.

Fraud   Dishonest acts intended to deceive, often involving the theft of assets and falsification of accounting records and financial statements.

General and administrative expenses   Expenses of the general offices, accounting department, personnel office, credit and collection department, and activities other than the selling of goods. A subdivision of operating expenses.

Gross profit on sales   Revenue from sales minus cost of goods sold.

Internal auditing   An activity carried on in large organizations by a professional staff to investigate and evaluate the system of internal control on a year-round basis. Also to evaluate the efficiency of individual departments within the organization.

Internal control   All measures used by a business to guard against errors, waste, or fraud and to assure the reliability of accounting data. Designed to aid in the efficient operation of a business and to encourage compliance with company policies.

Inventory (merchandise)   Goods acquired and held for sale to customers.

Invoice   An itemized statement of goods being bought or sold. Shows quantities, prices, and credit terms. Serves as the basis for an entry in the accounting records of both seller and buyer because it evidences the transfer of ownership of goods.

Operating cycle   The average time period from the purchase of merchandise to its sale and conversion back into cash.

Periodic inventory system   A system of accounting for merchandise in which inventory at the balance sheet date is determined by counting and pricing the goods on hand. Cost of goods sold is computed by subtracting the ending inventory from the cost of goods available for sale.

Perpetual inventory system   A system of accounting for merchandise that provides a continuous record showing the quantity and cost of all goods on hand.

Physical inventory   The process of counting and pricing the merchandise on hand at a given date, usually the end of the accounting period.

Purchase order   A serially numbered document sent by the purchasing department of a business to a supplier or vendor for the purpose of ordering materials or services.

Purchases An account used to record the cost of merchandise purchased for the purpose of sale to customers.

Receiving report An internal form prepared by the receiving department for each incoming shipment showing the quantity and condition of goods received.

Replacement cost The estimated current cost of replacing goods in inventory or goods sold during the period. Large corporations must disclose in financial statements both historical cost and current replacement cost of inventories and cost of goods sold.

Sales The revenue account credited with the sales price of goods sold during the accounting period.

Selling expenses Expenses of marketing the product, such as advertising, sales salaries, and delivery of merchandise to customers. A subdivision of operating expenses.

Working capital Current assets minus liabilities.

DEMONSTRATION PROBLEM FOR YOUR REVIEW

In this demonstration problem for a merchandising company, note that operations for the year result in a loss. Since the revenue for the year is less than the expenses, the Income Summary account has a debit balance. The closing of the Income Summary account into the Retained Earnings account therefore causes a decrease in the amount of stockholders' equity. Because of the loss, no income taxes are owed.

The trial balance of Stone Supply Company at December 31, 19____, appears below. An inventory taken on December 31, 19____, amounted to $32,440. The following adjustments should be made:
(1) Depreciation of buildings, $4,100; of delivery equipment, $1,500.
(2) Accrued salaries: office, $845; sales, $950.
(3) Insurance expired, $250.
(4) Store supplies used, $1,000.

STONE SUPPLY COMPANY
Trial Balance
December 31, 19____

Cash	$ 9,310	
Accounts receivable	10,380	
Inventory, Jan. 1, 19____	28,650	
Store supplies	1,270	
Unexpired insurance	610	
Land	89,700	
Buildings	100,000	
Accumulated depreciation: buildings		$ 17,650
Delivery equipment	45,000	
Accumulated depreciation: delivery equipment		14,800
Accounts payable		22,450
Accrued salaries payable		
Capital stock		100,000
Retained earnings		185,165
Dividends	40,000	

		$171,220
Sales		
Sales returns & allowances	$ 2,430	
Purchases	138,900	
Purchase returns & allowances		1,820
Sales salaries expense	25,050	
Delivery expense	2,800	
Depreciation expense: delivery equipment		
Office salaries expense	19,005	
Depreciation expense: buildings		
Insurance expense		
Store supplies expense		
	$513,105	$513,105

Instructions

a Prepare a 10-column work sheet at December 31, 19____, with pairs of columns for Trial Balance, Adjustments, Adjusted Trial Balance, Income Statement, and Balance Sheet.
b Prepare an income statement for the year.
c Prepare a statement of retained earnings for the year.
d Prepare a classified balance sheet at December 31, 19____.
e Prepare closing journal entries.

SOLUTION TO DEMONSTRATION PROBLEM

a See page 200.

b

STONE SUPPLY COMPANY
Income Statement
For the Year Ended December 31, 19____

Gross sales			$171,220
Less: Sales returns & allowances			2,430
Net sales			$168,790
Cost of goods sold:			
Inventory, Jan. 1, 19____		$ 28,650	
Purchases	$138,900		
Less: Purchase returns & allowances	1,820	137,080	
Cost of goods available for sale		$165,730	
Less: Inventory, Dec. 31, 19____		32,440	
Costs of goods sold			133,290
Gross profit on sales			$ 35,500
Operating expenses:			
Sales salaries		$ 26,000	
Delivery		2,800	
Depreciation: delivery equipment		1,500	
Office salaries		19,850	
Depreciation: buildings		4,100	
Insurance		250	
Store supplies		1,000	
Total operating expenses			55,500
Net loss			$ 20,000

a

STONE SUPPLY COMPANY
Work Sheet
For the Year Ended December 31, 19 ___

	Trial Balance		Adjustments*		Adjusted Trial Balance		Income Statement		Balance Sheet	
	Dr	Cr	Dr	Cr	Dr	Cr	Dr	Cr	Dr	Cr
Cash	9,310				9,310				9,310	
Accounts receivable	10,380				10,380				10,380	
Inventory, Jan. 1, 19	28,650				28,650		28,650			
Store supplies	1,270			(4) 1,000	270				270	
Unexpired insurance	610			(3) 250	360				360	
Land	89,700				89,700				89,700	
Buildings	100,000				100,000				100,000	
Accum. depr.: buildings		17,650		(1) 4,100		21,750				21,750
Delivery equipment	45,000				45,000				45,000	
Accum. depr.: del. eqpt.		14,800		(1) 1,500		16,300				16,300
Accounts payable		22,450				22,450				22,450
Accrued salaries payable				(2) 1,795		1,795				1,795
Capital stock		100,000				100,000				100,000
Retained earnings		185,165				185,165				185,165
Dividends	40,000				40,000				40,000	
Sales		171,220				171,220		171,220		
Sales returns & allowances	2,430				2,430		2,430			
Purchases	138,900				138,900		138,900			
Purchase returns & allowances		1,820				1,820		1,820		
Sales salaries expense	25,050		(2) 950		26,000		26,000			
Delivery expense	2,800				2,800		2,800			
Depr. expense: del. eqpt.			(1) 1,500		1,500		1,500			
Office salaries expense	19,005		(2) 845		19,850		19,850			
Depr. expense: buildings			(1) 4,100		4,100		4,100			
Insurance expense			(3) 250		250		250			
Store supplies expense			(4) 1,000		1,000		1,000			
	513,105	513,105	8,645	8,645	520,500	520,500				
Inventory, Dec. 31, 19 ___								32,440	32,440	
							225,480	205,480	327,460	347,460
Net loss								20,000	20,000	
							225,480	225,480	347,460	347,460

* Adjustments: (1) To record depreciation expense for the year.
(2) To record accrued salaries payable at Dec. 31, 19 ___.
(3) To record insurance expired.
(4) To record store supplies used.

c

STONE SUPPLY COMPANY
Statement of Retained Earnings
For the Year Ended December 31, 19___

Retained earnings, Jan. 1, 19___		$185,165
Less: Net loss	$20,000	
Dividends	40,000	60,000
Retained earnings, Dec. 31, 19___		$125,165

d

STONE SUPPLY COMPANY
Balance Sheet
December 31, 19___

Assets

Current assets:			
Cash			$ 9,310
Accounts receivable			10,380
Inventory			32,440
Store supplies			270
Unexpired insurance			360
Total current assets			$ 52,760
Plant and equipment:			
Land			$ 89,700
Buildings		$100,000	
Less: Accumulated depreciation		21,750	78,250
Delivery equipment		$ 45,000	
Less: Accumulated depreciation		16,300	28,700
Total plant and equipment			196,650
Total assets			$249,410

Liabilities & Stockholders' Equity

Current liabilities:		
Accounts payable		$ 22,450
Accrued salaries payable		1,795
Total current liabilities		$ 24,245
Stockholders' equity:		
Capital stock	$100,000	
Retained earnings	125,165	225,165
Total liabilities & stockholders' equity		$249,410

e			*Closing Entries*		
19___					
Dec.	*31*	Income Summary	225,480	
		Inventory, Jan. 1, 19___		28,650
		Sales Returns & Allowances		2,430
		Purchases		138,900
		Sales Salaries Expense		26,000
		Delivery Expense		2,800
		Depreciation Expense: Delivery Equipment		1,500
		Office Salaries Expense		19,850
		Depreciation Expense: Buildings		4,100
		Insurance Expense		250
		Store Supplies Expense		1,000
		To close the beginning inventory account and all temporary proprietorship accounts having debit balances.		
	31	Sales	171,220	
		Inventory, Dec. 31, 19___	32,440	
		Purchase Returns & Allowances	1,820	
		Income Summary		205,480
		To set up the ending inventory and close all temporary proprietorship accounts having credit balances.		
	31	Retained Earnings	20,000	
		Income Summary		20,000
		To close the Income Summary account.		
	31	Retained Earnings	40,000	
		Dividends		40,000
		To close the Dividends account.		

REVIEW QUESTIONS

1 Hi-Rise Company during its first year of operation had cost of goods sold of $90,000 and a gross profit equal to 40% of sales. What was the dollar amount of sales for the year?

2 Which of the following expenditures by Southside Drugstore should be recorded by a debit to the Purchases account?
   a Purchase of a new delivery truck
   b Purchase of a three-year insurance policy
   c Purchase of drugs from drug manufacturer
   d Purchase of advertising space in local newspaper
   e Payment in advance for three months' guard service by Security Patrol, Inc.

3 Supply the proper terms to complete the following statements:
   a Net sales − cost of goods sold = ?
   b Net purchases + beginning inventory + transportation-in = ?
   c Cost of goods sold + ending inventory = ?
   d Cost of goods sold + gross profit on sales = ?
   e Net income + operating expenses = ?

4 During the current year, Davis Corporation purchased merchandise costing $200,000. State the cost of goods sold under each of the following alternative assumptions:
   a No beginning inventory; ending inventory $40,000
   b Beginning inventory $60,000; no ending inventory
   c Beginning inventory $58,000; ending inventory $78,000
   d Beginning inventory $90,000; ending inventory $67,000

5 Solana Company uses the periodic inventory method and maintains its accounting records on a calendar-year basis. Does the beginning or the ending inventory figure appear in the trial balance prepared from the ledger on December 31?

6 Compute the amount of cost of goods sold, given the following account balances: beginning inventory $25,000, purchases $84,000, purchase returns and allowances $4,500, transportation-in $500, and ending inventory $36,000.

7 Why is it advisable to use a Purchase Returns and Allowances account when the same end result may be achieved by crediting the Purchases account when goods purchased are returned to the supplier?

8 Which party (seller or buyer) bears the transportation costs when the terms of a merchandise sale are (a) F.O.B. shipping point; (b) F.O.B. destination?

9 In which columns of the work sheet for a merchandising company does the ending inventory appear?

10 State briefly the difference between the *perpetual* inventory system and the *periodic* inventory system.

11 When the periodic inventory method is in use, how is the amount of inventory determined at the end of the period?

12 What is the purpose of a closing entry consisting of a debit to the Income Summary account and a credit to the Inventory account?

13 What is the purpose of a system of internal control? List four groups of measures included in a system of internal control.

14 Criticize the following statement: "Internal control may be defined as all those measures which a business uses to prevent fraud."

15 Ross Corporation is a medium-sized business with 20 office employees. State two or three guidelines or principles which should be followed in assigning duties to the various employees so that internal control will be as strong as possible.

16 State a general principle to be observed in assigning duties among employees with respect to the purchase of merchandise so that strong internal control will be achieved.

17 Suggest a control device to protect a business against the loss or nondelivery of invoices, purchase orders, and other documents which are routed from one department to another.

18 Criticize the following statement: "In our company we get things done by requiring that a person who initiates a transaction follow it through in all particulars. For example, an employee who issues a purchase order is held responsible for inspecting the merchandise upon arrival, approving the invoice, and preparing the check in payment of the purchase. If any error is made, we know definitely whom to blame."

19 If a company obtains a fidelity bond protecting it against loss from dishonest actions on the part of any of its officers or employees, would it still be necessary for the company to maintain a system of internal control? Explain.

20 Explain why the operations and custodianship functions should be separate from the accounting function.

21 A system of internal control is often said to include two major types of controls: administrative controls and accounting controls. Explain the nature of each group and give an example of each.

22 Blair Manufacturing Company sells appliances on both a wholesale and a retail basis and publishes an annual catalog listing products at retail prices. At what price should the sale be recorded when an item listed in the catalog at $400 is delivered to a wholesaler entitled to a 30% trade discount?

23 What is meant by the expressions (*a*) 2/10, n/30; (*b*) 10 e.o.m.; (*c*) n/30?

24 Explain the terms *current assets, current liabilities,* and *current ratio.*

25 The Riblet Company has a current ratio of 3 to 1 and working capital of $60,000. What are the amounts of current assets and current liabilities?

26 Define a *condensed income statement* and indicate its advantages and possible shortcomings.

27 What disclosure requirements concerning the cost of inventories have been imposed on large corporations by the Securities and Exchange Commission as a result of continued inflation? Explain.

EXERCISES

Ex. 5-1 Compute the amount of *total* purchases for the period by using the appropriate items from the following list of account balances.

Sales	$222,180
Sales returns and allowances	3,000
Ending inventory	46,200
Beginning inventory	52,368
Purchase returns and allowances	2,580
Transportation-in	2,268
Cost of goods sold	151,680

Ex. 5-2 Use the following data as a basis for computing the amount of the beginning inventory.

Purchase returns and allowances	$ 7,360
Transportation-in	3,840
Cost of goods sold	67,040
Purchases	104,000
Ending inventory	61,520

Ex. 5-3 Key figures taken from the income statement of Blue Spring Company for two successive years are shown below:

	Year 5	Year 4
Sales	$320,000	$240,000
Cost of goods sold	240,000	168,000
Selling expenses	40,000	34,000
General and administrative expenses	16,000	17,000
Income taxes expense	4,800	4,200

Instructions
a The net income increased from $ _____ in Year 4 to $ _____ in Year 5?
b The net income as a percentage of sales was _____ % in Year 4 and decreased to _____ % of sales in Year 5.
c The gross profit as a percentage of sales decreased from _____ % in Year 4 to _____ % in Year 5.

Ex. 5-4 Give the journal entry, if any, to be prepared for each of these events:
a Received a telephone order from a customer for $1,800 worth of merchandise.
b Issued a purchase order to Mack Company for merchandise costing $2,500.
c Received the merchandise ordered from Mack Company and an invoice for $2,500; credit terms 2/10, n/30. (Record at gross amount.)
d Delivered the $1,800 of merchandise ordered in (*a*) above to the customer and mailed an invoice; credit terms 10 e.o.m.
e Mailed check to Mack Company in full settlement of amount owed after taking allowable discount.
f Customer returned $400 of goods delivered in (*d*) above, which were unsatisfactory. A credit memorandum was issued for that amount.

Ex. 5-5 Village Shop prepared a work sheet at December 31, Year 5. Shown on page 206 is the Income Statement pair of columns from that work sheet. To keep this exercise short, expense accounts have been combined. Use this work sheet data to prepare an income statement for the year ended December 31, Year 5.

	Income Statement	
	Debit	Credit
Inventory, Dec. 31, Year 4	10,000	
Sales		120,300
Sales returns & allowances	672	
Purchases	97,200	
Purchase returns & allowances		7,200
Transportation-in	2,400	
Selling expenses	16,000	
General and administrative expenses	8,320	
Income taxes expense	4,000	
Inventory, Dec. 31, Year 5		28,000
	138,592	155,500
Net income	16,908	
	155,500	155,500

Ex. 5-6 A CPA firm performing an audit of a company's financial statements always begins with a study and evaluation of the internal controls in force. List several **documents** which a CPA firm would expect to find at the business which would be helpful in the study and evaluation of internal control.

Ex. 5-7 A strong system of internal control serves to protect a company's assets against waste, fraud, and inefficient use. Fidelity bonds provide a means by which a company may recover losses caused by dishonest acts of employees. Would it be reasonable for a company to maintain a strong system of internal control and also pay for a fidelity bond? Explain.

Ex. 5-8 Jet Auto Supply Store received from a manufacturer a shipment of 200 gasoline cans. Harold Abbott, who handles all purchasing activities, telephoned the manufacturer and explained that he had ordered only 100 cans. The manufacturer replied that two separate purchase orders for 100 cans each had recently been received from Jet Auto Supply Store. Harold Abbott is sure that the manufacturer is in error and is merely trying to justify an excess shipment, but he has no means of proving his point. What is the missing element in internal control over purchases by Jet Auto Supply Store?

Ex. 5-9 Robert Hale, owner of Hale Equipment, a merchandising business, explains to you how he has assigned duties to employees. Hale states: "In order to have clearly defined responsibility for each phase of our operations, I have made one employee responsible for the purchasing, receiving, and storage of merchandise. Another employee has been charged with responsibility for maintaining the accounting records and for making all collections from customers. I have assigned to a third employee responsibility for maintaining personnel records for all our employees and for timekeeping, preparation of payroll records, and distribution of payroll checks. My goal in setting up this organization plan is to have a strong system of internal control."

You are to evaluate Hale's plan of organization and explain fully the reasoning underlying any criticism you may have.

Ex. 5-10 James Company sold merchandise to Bay Company on credit. On the next day, James Company received a telephone call from Bay Company stating that one of the items delivered was defective. James Company immediately issued credit memorandum no. 163 for $100 to Bay Company.

a Give the accounting entry required in James Company's records to record the issuance of the credit memorandum.

b Give the accounting entry required on Bay Company's accounting records when the credit memorandum is received. (Assume that Bay Company had previously recorded the purchase at the full amount of the seller's invoice and had not issued a debit memorandum.)

Ex. 5-11 Hudson Company sold merchandise to River Company for $3,000; terms 2/10, n/30. River Company paid for the merchandise within the discount period. Assume that both companies record invoices at the gross amounts.
  a Give the journal entries by Hudson Company to record the sale and the subsequent collection.
  b Give the journal entries by River Company to record the purchase and the subsequent payment.

Ex. 5-12 The balance sheet of Brush Company contained the following items, among others:

Cash	$137,600
Accounts receivable	48,000
Inventory	198,400
Store equipment (net)	192,000
Other assets	28,800
Mortgage payable (due in 3 years)	48,000
Notes payable (due in 10 days)	115,200
Accounts payable	38,400
Capital stock	220,800

Instructions
  a From the above information compute the amount of current assets and the amount of current liabilities.
  b How much working capital does Brush Company have?
  c Compute the current ratio.
  d Assume that Brush Company pays the notes payable of $115,200, thus reducing cash to $22,400. Compute the amount of working capital and the current ratio after this transaction.

Ex. 5-13 Indicate whether each of the following events would increase, decrease, or have no effect upon (1) the current ratio and (2) the working capital of a business with current assets **greater** than its current liabilities. Example: An account payable is paid in cash.
      (1) Increase current ratio.
      (2) No effect on working capital.
  a Merchandise is purchased on account.
  b An adjusting entry is made to accrue salaries earned by employees but not yet paid.
  c An account receivable is collected.
  d An adjusting entry is prepared to record depreciation for the period.
  e Land is purchased by making a small cash down payment and signing a long-term mortgage payable.

Ex. 5-14 Ryder Company made credit sales during June of $106,000, of which $21,000 was collected in June and the remainder was collected in July. Cash sales in June amounted to $17,000, and an additional $80,000 was received from customers in payment for goods sold to them in May. Sales returns in June amounted to $3,000. Gross profit for the month of June was 40% of net sales, general and administrative expenses were $14,000, and a net loss of $1,000 was incurred.
      Prepare a condensed income statement for Ryder Company for the month ended June 30. (**Hint:** Selling expenses must be computed. Income taxes are to be ignored.)

PROBLEMS

5-1 Carleton Company uses the periodic inventory system. The company completed the following transactions among others during the month of January.

Jan. 3 Purchased merchandise for cash, $1,065.

Jan. 4 Sold merchandise to Tucker Company on open account, $7,800.

Jan. 6 Paid transportation charges on shipment to Tucker Company, $375.

Jan. 8 Purchased office equipment from ABC Corporation for cash, $8,250.

Jan. 14 Permitted Tucker Company to return for credit $630 of the merchandise purchased on Jan. 4 (no reduction in the transportation charges paid on Jan. 6).

Jan. 19 Sold merchandise for cash, $6,450.

Jan. 22 Refunded $390 to a customer who had made a cash purchase on Jan. 19.

Jan. 26 Purchased merchandise from Selzer Company on open account, $3,360.

Jan. 27 Paid by check transportation charges on merchandise purchased from Selzer Company in the amount of $240.

Jan. 29 Returned for credit of $450 merchandise purchased from Selzer Company (no reduction was allowed with respect to the transportation charges paid Jan. 27).

Jan. 30 Purchased stationery and miscellaneous office supplies on open account, $705.

Instructions

Prepare a separate journal entry (including an explanation) for each of the above transactions.

5-2 The income statement of Patrick Corporation contained the following items, among others, for the year ended April 30, 19_____ .

Sales	$1,635,750	Ending inventory	$	?
Purchases	1,041,861	Sales returns &		
Transportation-in	11,580	allowances		43,350
Purchase returns &		Beginning inventory		205,800
allowances	5,250	Purchase discounts		1,815
Sales discounts	13,800	Gross profit on sales		536,724

Instructions

a Compute the amount of net sales.

b Compute the gross profit percentage.

c What percentage of net sales represents the cost of goods sold?

d Prepare a partial income statement utilizing all the accounts listed above, including the determination of the amount of the ending inventory.

5-3 Saddle Shops, Inc., a successful small merchandising corporation, uses the periodic inventory system. The following trial balance was prepared from the ledger at December 31; Year 6.

SADDLE SHOPS, INC.

Trial Balance

December 31, Year 6

Cash	$ 12,800	
Accounts receivable	54,400	
Inventory (Jan. 1, Year 6)	115,200	
Supplies	4,544	
Unexpired insurance	1,728	
Land	64,000	
Buildings	160,000	
Equipment	38,400	
Accounts payable		$ 90,592
Capital stock		100,000
Retained earnings		172,000
Dividends	24,000	
Sales		624,800
Sales returns & allowances	12,800	
Purchases	371,200	
Purchase returns & allowances		9,088
Transportation-in	15,424	
Selling commissions expense	20,016	
Delivery expense	5,600	
Salaries and wages expense	94,768	
Property taxes expense	1,600	
	$996,480	$996,480

A physical inventory was taken at the close of business December 31, Year 6; this count showed merchandise on hand in the amount of $92,800.

Other data
(a) Property taxes accrued but not yet recorded, $2,880.
(b) A physical count showed supplies on hand of $1,344.
(c) The cost of insurance which had expired during the year was $896.
(d) Depreciation rates: 4% on buildings and 10% on equipment.
(e) Income taxes expense for the year was determined to be $22,000.

Instructions Prepare an eight-column work sheet at December 31, Year 6. (Omit columns for an adjusted trial balance).

5-4 The accounting records of Lyon Company are maintained on the basis of a fiscal year ending June 30. After all necessary adjustments had been made at June 30, 19____, the adjusted trial balance appeared as follows:

LYON COMPANY

Adjusted Trial Balance

June 30, 19____

Cash	$ 57,000	
Accounts receivable	102,000	
Inventory (beginning of fiscal year)	86,700	
Unexpired insurance	2,100	
Supplies	3,600	
Furniture and fixtures	60,000	
Accumulated depreciation: furniture and fixtures		$ 3,600
Accounts payable		24,900
Notes payable		21,000
Income taxes payable		40,000
Capital stock		150,000
Retained earnings		106,440
Dividends	90,000	
Sales		879,000
Sales returns and allowances	12,000	
Purchases	574,575	
Purchase returns and allowances		4,635
Transportation-in	30,000	
Salaries and wages expense	136,200	
Rent expense	25,200	
Depreciation expense: furniture and fixtures	3,600	
Supplies expense	4,200	
Insurance expense	2,400	
Income taxes expense	40,000	
	$1,229,575	$1,229,575

The inventory on June 30, 19____, as determined by count, amounted to $107,640.

Instructions

a Prepare an income statement for Lyon Company for the year ended June 30, 19____.

b Prepare the necessary journal entries to close the accounts on June 30, 19____. (*Suggestion:* Use four separate closing entries. The first entry may be used to close the beginning inventory and all nominal accounts having debit balances; the second entry to record the ending inventory and to close nominal accounts having credit balances; the third entry to close the Income Summary account; and the fourth entry to close the Dividends account.)

5-5 On September 30, the close of the fiscal year for Border Corporation, the company's accountant prepared the following trial balance from the ledger.

Cash	$ 37,260	
Accounts receivable	37,827	
Inventory, beginning	67,032	
Unexpired insurance	1,296	
Office supplies	909	
Land	54,792	
Buildings	122,400	
Accumulated depreciation: buildings		$ 34,416
Equipment	35,640	
Accumulated depreciation: equipment		20,880
Accounts payable		19,548
Capital stock		180,000
Retained earnings, beginning of year		47,826
Dividends	18,000	
Sales		386,469
Sales returns & allowances	5,922	
Purchases	260,820	
Purchase returns & allowances		3,861
Transportation-in	5,337	
Salaries & wages expense	44,532	
Property taxes expense	1,233	
	$693,000	$693,000

Other data
(1) The buildings are being depreciated over a 25-year useful life and the equipment over a 12-year useful life.
(2) Accrued salaries payable as of September 30 were $5,040.
(3) Examination of policies showed $810 unexpired insurance on September 30.
(4) Office supplies on hand at September 30 were estimated to amount to $378.
(5) Income taxes expense for the year was determined to be $10,000.
(6) Inventory of merchandise on September 30 was $54,000.

Instructions
a Prepare an eight-column work sheet at September 30. (Omit columns for an adjusted trial balance.)
b Prepare an income statement for the year.
c Prepare a classified balance sheet as of September 30.
d Prepare a statement of retained earnings for the year.
e Prepare closing journal entries.

5-6 The Sunset Corporation maintains its accounting records on the basis of a fiscal year ending April 30. After all necessary adjustments had been made at April 30, 1981, the adjusted trial balance prepared by the company's accountant appeared as follows:

SUNSET CORPORATION
Adjusted Trial Balance
April 30, 1981

Cash	$ 41,877	
Accounts receivable	69,336	
Inventory (Apr. 30, 1980)	61,074	
Unexpired insurance	1,260	
Supplies	2,088	
Furniture & fixtures	89,460	
Accumulated depreciation: furniture & fixtures		$ 7,605
Accounts payable		23,940
Notes payable		12,600
Income taxes payable		25,000
Capital stock, $1 par value		90,000
Retained earnings, April 30, 1980		56,790
Sales		544,698
Sales returns & allowances	7,686	
Purchases	351,945	
Purchase returns & allowances		2,781
Transportation-in	17,730	
Salaries & wages expense	74,610	
Rent expense	15,120	
Depreciation expense: furniture & fixtures	2,259	
Supplies expense	2,547	
Insurance expense	1,422	
Income taxes expense	25,000	
	$763,414	$763,414

The inventory on April 30, 1981, as determined by count, amounted to $69,750.

Instructions
a Prepare an income statement for Sunset Corporation for the year ended April 30, 1981.
b Prepare the necessary entries (in general journal form) to close the accounts at April 30, 1981.
c Assume that the ending inventory of $69,750 was overstated $7,500 as a result of double counting part of the goods on hand at April 30, 1981. Prepare a three-column list of the items in the income statement developed in *a* above which are incorrect as a result of the $7,500 inventory overstatement. List in the second column the reported figures and in the third column the corrected figures. You may assume that the decrease in "Income before income taxes" would cause "Income taxes expense" to decrease by $3,750.

5-7 Casa Grande, a furniture distributor, engaged in the following merchandising transactions during the month of November.

Nov. 1 Purchased merchandise from Rand Co. The list price was $37,500 with a trade discount of 20% and terms of 2/10, n/60.

Nov. 2 Purchased merchandise from National Supply Co. for $16,500, terms 1/10, n/30.

Nov. **5** Sold merchandise to Pachman Company $18,000; terms 2/10, n/30.

Nov. **6** Returned to Rand Co. damaged merchandise having a cost after trade discount of $3,000.

Nov. 11 Paid Rand Co. for invoice of November 1, less discount and returns.

Nov. 15 Received cash in full settlement of Pachman Company account.

Nov. 22 Sold merchandise to Bell Co., $60,000; terms 2/10, n/30.

Nov. 25 Purchased from Stone Co. merchandise with list price of $27,000, subject to trade discount of 25% and credit terms of 1/10, n/30.

Nov. 28 Returned for credit part of merchandise received from Stone Co. Cost of the returned goods (after trade discount) was $600.

Nov. 30 Paid National Supply Co. invoice of November 2.

Instructions

a Journalize the above transactions.

b Prepare a partial income statement, showing gross profit on sales. Assume the following inventories: October 31, $62,700; November 30, $79,650.

c Compute the balance of accounts payable at November 30.

d Compute the effective annual rate of interest Casa Grande would be paying if it failed to take advantage of discount terms on the Rand Co. invoice. (For convenience in calculating an annual rate of interest, assume that a year has 360 days.)

5-8 For several years Jerry Dale had worked as the in-charge accountant for Baxter Company. When he suddenly became ill in late December, his recently employed assistant was called upon to complete the year-end accounting work. The assistant, whose knowledge of accounting was rather limited, prepared the following financial statements. All dollar amounts are correct, although numerous errors exist in the location of accounts in the financial statements.

BAXTER COMPANY

Loss Statement

December 31, 19___

Sales	$918,000	
Purchase returns & allowances	6,840	
Purchase discounts	13,257	
Interest earned on investments	1,710	
Increase in inventory	9,234	$949,041
Purchases	$681,570	
Sales returns & allowances	16,164	
Sales discounts	8,352	
Transportation-in	42,723	
Interest expense	3,006	
Uncollectible accounts expense	3,816	
Depreciation expense: building	3,150	
Depreciation expense: store equipment	4,023	
Depreciation expense: delivery equipment	3,312	
Insurance expense	2,880	
Office salaries expense	27,900	
Executive salaries expense	73,800	
Sales salaries expense	109,575	
Miscellaneous selling expense	1,674	
Miscellaneous general expense	2,826	984,771
Net loss for year		$ 35,730

BAXTER COMPANY
Balance Sheet
December 31, 19____

Current assets:

Notes receivable.	$ 18,000	
Accounts receivable	45,900	
Cash	29,520	
Rent collected in advance	1,440	
Land	36,000	$130,860

Plant and equipment:

Inventory	$ 96,309	
Store equipment	34,380	
Building	86,400	
Delivery equipment	26,100	243,189

Other assets:

Marketable securities held as temporary investments	$ 16,200	
Land held as future building site	22,500	38,700
Total assets		$412,749

Liabilities:

Accounts payable	$ 50,877	
Accrued salaries payable	3,933	
Short-term prepayments	1,440	
Notes payable	27,000	
First mortgage bonds payable	90,000	
Allowance for doubtful accounts	2,952	
Accumulated depreciation: building	28,080	
Accumulated depreciation: store equipment	21,600	
Accumulated depreciation: delivery equipment	20,880	
Total liabilities		$246,762

Stockholders' equity:

Capital stock	$180,000	
Less: Deficit	14,013	165,987
Total liabilities & stockholders' equity		$412,749

Instructions

a Prepare in acceptable form an income statement for the year ended December 31, 19____ . (Allocate to selling expense 60% of building depreciation and $900 of insurance expense.) The remaining portions of these two expense accounts should be classified under the General and Administrative Expenses heading. The Uncollectible Accounts Expense of $3,816 should also be listed under General and Administrative Expenses.

b Prepare a balance sheet as of December 31, 19____ , properly classified. Show the Allowance for Doubtful Accounts as a deduction from Accounts Receivable in the current asset section of the balance sheet.

c What was the balance in the Retained Earnings account at the *beginning* of the current year?

5-9 After spending several years as an executive for a large nationwide finance company, Charles Bell resigned in order to open his own finance business, called Happy Loan Company. The business consists of four very small offices in four cities a few miles apart. The activity of each office consists of making small loans to individual borrowers. The borrowers agree to repay the amount borrowed plus interest in monthly installments over a period of 36 months or less.

Charles Bell has his own office at one of the four loan offices and makes fairly frequent trips to the other offices to provide general supervision and to perform some internal auditing work. Early in the current year Bell called upon a firm of certified public accountants, explained that he was worried about the honesty of his employees, and made the following statement: "In the large nationwide loan company where I worked before starting my own business, we had over 500 offices scattered over 10 states. The system of accounting and internal control in that company made fraud absolutely impossible. I can describe the system to you in detail and I want you to install that system in my own company."

Instructions
a Explain how the CPA firm would probably respond to Bell's request that it install the large finance company's system of internal control in his new business.
b Comment on Bell's statement that the new system would make fraud absolutely impossible.

5-10 At the Uptown Theater, the cashier is located in a box office at the front of the building. The cashier receives cash from customers and operates a ticket machine which ejects serially numbered tickets. The serial number appears on each end of the ticket. The tickets come from the printer in large rolls which fit into the ticket machine and are removed at the end of each cashier's working period.

After purchasing a ticket from the cashier, in order to be admitted to the theater a customer must hand the ticket to a doorman stationed some 50 feet from the box office at the entrance to the theater lobby. The doorman tears the ticket in half, opens the door for the customer, and returns the ticket stub to the customer. The other half of the ticket is dropped by the doorman into a locked box.

Instructions
a Describe the internal controls present in Uptown Theater's method of handling cash receipts.
b What steps should be taken regularly by the theater manager or other supervisor to make these internal controls work most effectively?
c Assume that the cashier and the doorman decided to collaborate in an effort to abstract cash receipts. What action might they take?
d On the assumption made in *(c)* of collaboration between the cashier and the doorman, what features of the control procedures would be most likely to disclose the embezzlement?

5-11 Dave Smith an employee of Jones' Company, is responsible for preparing checks to suppliers in payment for purchases of merchandise. Before submitting the checks to the treasurer for signature, Smith receives a copy of the purchase order, the receiving report, and the supplier's invoice. After determining that all three documents are in agreement and that no arithmetical errors exist, he fills in an invoice approval form and then prepares a check complete except for the treasurer's signature. Smith files the documents (purchase order, purchase invoice, receiving report, and invoice approval form) alphabetically by supplier. As a final step, he forwards the check to the treasurer for signature.

While trying to finish work early on Friday, December 31, Smith accidentally prepared for the treasurer's signature a check payable to Miller Company, a regular supplier, for $96,420, although the invoice and other documents indicated the amount payable was actually $69,420. Smith had previously made another error in recording the invoice, debiting the Purchases account when the debit should have been to Office Equipment because the invoice was for typewriters and other equipment to be used in the business and not to be sold to customers.

The amount of this accounting entry agreed with the invoice but not with the check. The entry was as follows:

Purchases *69,420*

    Accounts Payable *69,420*

To record purchase invoice from Miller Company. Terms,
cash upon delivery.

The check for $96,420 was forwarded to the treasurer, promptly signed, and entered in the accounting records as a debit to Accounts Payable and a credit to Cash in the amount of $96,420. The treasurer mailed the check to the supplier. The supplier did not notice the overpayment and deposited the check.

A physical inventory was taken at the close of business Dec. 31, and financial statements were prepared by Jones Company without discovery of the error. Net income for the year was $100,000 and the retained earnings at December 31 appeared in the balance sheet as $204,000.

On January 20, Smith was processing another invoice from Miller Company and discovered the previous overpayment error. Smith processed the new invoice in a normal manner and then informed Miller Company by telephone of the December overpayment, requesting that a refund check be mailed and the envelope marked for his attention. After receiving the refund check for $27,000, Smith went to a nearby town, opened a new bank account in the name of Jones Company and deposited the check. A short time later he withdrew the amount deposited, closed the bank account, and moved out of town leaving no forwarding address. Jones Company does not carry a fidelity bond on its employees.

Instructions

a Were the figures for net income and retained earnings correct as shown in the financial statements? Explain fully. If you consider these amounts incorrect, compute corrected amounts. Income taxes are to be ignored.

b Assuming that the facts about the overstated check, the refund, and the theft by Smith all came to light late in January, prepare the necessary adjusting entry or entries. Include a full explanation as part of such entries.

c Identify any weaknesses in the system of internal control indicated by the above events and make recommendations for improvements.

5-12 Jim Brown, long-time office manager of North Building Materials, prepares all purchase orders for merchandise in which the company deals. Brown personally owns a large waterfront lot and during the current year was having a marina constructed on this lot. The construction plans included boat slips, a large dock, a restaurant, and a marine supply store.

To obtain building materials for this project, Brown fraudulently issued purchase orders in the name of North Building Materials and instructed the suppliers to deliver the materials at his waterfront site. The suppliers did not question the propriety of these orders since they were accustomed to receiving from North Building Supplies purchase orders signed by Brown. When purchase invoices from the suppliers relating to these materials reached North Building Materials, Brown entered them in the accounting records as debits to Purchases and credits to Accounts Payable. On the appropriate dates, he prepared company checks payable to the suppliers and presented them to the treasurer of North Building Materials for signature. Since the checks were payable to suppliers from whom North Building Materials regularly made purchases, the treasurer signed and mailed the checks without question.

The accounting system used by North Building Materials required that duplicate copies of purchase orders be attached to the related receiving reports and purchase invoices, and then be filed alphabetically by vendor. Since there were no receiving reports for the materials delivered to the marina, Brown removed from the the files the purchase orders and related purchase invoices for these materials and concealed these documents in his desk. During the year, the billed price of the materials which Brown ordered and diverted to his marina totaled $110,000. Of this total, all but $10,000 had been paid for at year-end by North Building Materials and cash discounts of $2,000 had been taken. The remaining $10,000 in unpaid invoices were included in the year-end balance of accounts payable at the gross amount.

North Building Materials uses the periodic inventory system. A complete physical inventory was taken on December 31. In an effort to prevent the theft of materials from having a conspicuous effect on the year's reported earnings, Brown changed figures on the inventory count sheets, thereby causing the ending inventory to be overstated by $100,000.

Condensed financial statements for the company at December 31 of the current year appeared as follows:

NORTH BUILDING MATERIALS
Balance Sheet
December 31, 19___

Assets		Liabilities & Stockholders' Equity	
Cash	$ 32,000	Notes payable	$320,000
Accounts receivable	280,000	Accounts payable	260,000
Inventory	625,000	Accrued salaries	20,000
Office equipment (net)	5,000	Total liabilities	$600,000
Trucks (net)	36,000	Stockholders' equity:	
		Capital stock ... $100,000	
		Retained earnings 278,000	378,000
	$978,000		$978,000

NORTH BUILDING MATERIALS
Income Statement
For the Year Ended December 31, 19___

Net sales			$3,661,000
Cost of goods sold:			
Beginning inventory		$ 520,000	
Purchases	$3,225,000		
Less: Purchase returns & allow.	$72,000		
Purchase discounts	60,000	132,000	3,093,000
Cost of goods available for sale		$3,613,000	
Less: Inventory, Dec. 31, 19___		625,000	
Cost of goods sold			2,988,000
Gross profit on sales			$ 673,000
Operating expenses:			
Selling		$ 409,000	
General and administrative		265,000	674,000
Net loss			$ 1,000

At an office party on New Year's Eve, Jim Brown became somewhat intoxicated and confided to a secretary how he had acquired "free materials" to build a marina. The secretary reported this information to Lee North, president of the company, who immediately demanded an explanation from Brown. Jim Brown confessed to his dishonest actions and returned the purchase orders and purchase invoices he had removed from the files. Also on New Year's Eve, the marina being constructed by Brown was completely destroyed by fire. There was no insurance in force, and Brown had no other assets. Lee North discharged Brown, who left town without any forwarding address. North Building Materials did not have a fidelity bond for its employees. Lee North considers that the entire problem was caused by his failure to establish a satisfactory system of internal control. He does not attach any blame to the suppliers.

Instructions

a Compute the loss to North Building Materials from Jim Brown's dishonest actions. Show how you arrived at this amount. (Income taxes are not to be considered.)

b Prepare a corrected balance sheet and income statement. Omit from the balance of the Purchases account the cost of the materials which were never in the possession of the company. After deducting operating expenses, show Income from Operations followed by the nonoperating item, Loss from Material Shortages.

c Explain the weaknesses in the system of internal control which made possible concealment of the thefts by Brown and recommend any appropriate improvements in the system.

BUSINESS DECISION PROBLEM 5

Bell Company and Harte Corporation are both merchandising companies applying for nine-month bank loans in order to finance the acquisition of new equipment. Both companies are seeking to borrow the amount of $210,000 and have submitted the following balance sheets with their loan applications:

BELL COMPANY

Balance Sheet

January 31, 19___

Assets

Current assets:			
Cash			$ 57,000
Accounts receivable			153,000
Inventories			162,000
Short-term prepayments			6,000
Total current assets			$ 378,000
Plant and equipment:			
Land			$150,000
Building	$600,000		
Less: Accumulated depreciation	90,000	510,000	
Store equipment	$180,000		
Less: Accumulated depreciation	45,000	135,000	
Total plant and equipment			795,000
Total assets			$1,173,000

Liabilities & Stockholders' Equity

Current liabilities:

Accounts payable		$ 135,000
Income taxes payable		45,000
Total current liabilities		$ 180,000

Long-term liabilities:

Mortgage payable (due in 13 months)		330,000
Total liabilities		$ 510,000

Stockholders' equity:

Capital stock	$300,000	
Retained earnings	363,000	663,000
Total liabilities & stockholders' equity		$1,173,000

HARTE CORPORATION
Balance Sheet
January 31, 19____

Assets

Current assets:

Cash		$ 384,000
U.S. government bonds		210,000
Accounts receivable		603,000
Inventories		567,000
Total current assets		$1,764,000

Plant & equipment:

Land		$ 180,000	
Building and equipment	$1,230,000		
Less: Accumulated depreciation	180,000	1,050,000	
Total plant & equipment			1,230,000
Total assets			$2,994,000

Liabilities & Stockholders' Equity

Current liabilities:

Notes payable		$ 600,000
Accounts payable		520,000
Income taxes payable		140,000
Total current liabilities		$1,260,000

Long-term liabilities:

Mortgage payable (due in 10 years)		420,000
Total liabilities		$1,680,000

Stockholders' equity:

Capital stock	$750,000	
Retained earnings	564,000	1,314,000
Total liabilities & stockholders' equity		$2,994,000

Instructions

a Compute the current ratio and amount of working capital for each company as of January 31, 19____.

b Compute the current ratio and amount of working capital that each company would have *after* obtaining the bank loan and investing the borrowed cash in new equipment (assuming no other transactions affecting current accounts).

c From the viewpoint of a bank loan officer, to which company would you prefer to make a $210,000 nine-month loan? Explain. Include in your answer a discussion of the ability of each company to meet its obligations in the near future, and also make a comparison of the relative liquidity of the various current assets held by each company.

6 Accounting Systems: Manual and EDP

In the early chapters of an introductory accounting book, basic accounting principles can most conveniently be discussed in terms of a small business with only a few customers and suppliers. This simplified model of a business has been used in preceding chapters to demonstrate the analysis and recording of the more common types of business transactions.

The recording procedures illustrated thus far call for recording each transaction by an entry in the general journal, and then posting each debit and credit from the general journal to the proper account in the ledger. We must now face the practical problem of streamlining and speeding up this basic accounting system so that the accounting department can keep pace with the rapid flow of transactions in a modern business.

Accounting systems in common use range from manual systems, which use special journals to streamline the journalizing and posting processes, to sophisticated computer systems which maintain accounting records on magnetic tape. The accounting system in use in any given company will be specially tailored to the size and information needs of the business.

MANUAL ACCOUNTING SYSTEMS

In a large business there may be hundreds or even thousands of transactions every day. To handle a large volume of transactions rapidly and efficiently, it is helpful to group the transactions into classes and to use a specialized journal for each class. This will greatly reduce the amount of detailed recording work and will also permit a division of labor, since each special-purpose journal can be handled by a different employee. The great majority of transactions (perhaps as much as 90 or 95%) usually fall into four types. These four types and the four corresponding special journals are as follows:

Type of Transaction	Name of Special Journal
Sales of merchandise on credit	Sales journal
Purchases of merchandise on credit	Purchases journal
Receipts of cash	Cash receipts journal
Payments of cash	Cash payments journal

In addition to these four special journals, a *general journal* will be used for recording transactions which do not fit into any of the above four types. The general journal is the same book of original entry illustrated in preceding chapters; the adjective "general" is added merely to distinguish it from the special journals.

Sales journal

Illustrated below is a sales journal containing entries for all sales on account made during November by the Seaside Company. Whenever merchandise is sold on credit, several copies of a sales invoice are prepared. The information listed on a sales invoice usually includes the date of the sale, the serial number of the invoice, the customer's name, the amount of the sale, and the credit terms. One copy of the sales invoice is used by the seller as the basis for an entry in the sales journal.

Sales Journal

Page 1

	Date		Account Debited	Invoice No.	√	Amount
Entries for sales on credit during November	19___ Nov.	2	John Adams	301	√	450
		4	Harold Black	302	√	1,000
		5	Robert Cross	303	√	975
		11	H. R. Davis	304	√	620
		18	C. D. Early	305	√	900
		23	John Frost	306	√	400
		29	D. H. Gray	307	√	1,850
						6,195
						(5) (41)

Note that the illustrated sales journal contains special columns for recording each of these aspects of the sales transaction, except the credit terms. If it is the practice of the business to offer different credit terms to different customers, a column may be inserted in the sales journal to show the terms of sale. In this illustration it is assumed that all sales are made on terms of 2/10, n/30; consequently, there is no need to write the credit terms as part of each entry. *Only sales on credit are entered in the sales journal.* When merchandise is sold for cash, the transaction is recorded in a *cash receipts journal,* which is illustrated later in this chapter.

ADVANTAGES OF THE SALES JOURNAL Note that each of the above seven sales transactions is recorded on a single line. Each entry consists of a debit to a customer's account; the offsetting credit to the Sales account is understood without being written, because sales on account are the only transactions recorded in this special journal.

An entry in a sales journal need not include an explanation; if more information about the transaction is desired it can be obtained by referring to the file copy of the sales invoice. The invoice number is listed in the sales journal as part of each entry. The one-line entry in the sales journal requires much less writing than would be required to record a sales transaction in the general journal. Since there may be several hundred or several thousand sales transactions each month, the time saved in recording transactions in this streamlined manner becomes quite important.

Every entry in the sales journal represents a debit to a customer's account. Charges to customers' accounts should be posted daily so that each customer's account will always be up-to-date and available for use in making decisions relating to collections and to the further extension of credit. A check mark ($\checkmark$) is placed in the sales journal opposite each amount posted to a customer's account, to indicate that the posting has been made.

Another advantage of the special journal for sales is the great saving of time in posting credits to the Sales account. Remember that every amount entered in the sales journal represents a credit to Sales. In our illustrated sales journal, there are seven transactions (and in practice there might be 700). Instead of posting a separate credit to the Sales account for each sales transaction, we can wait until the end of the month and make one posting to the Sales account for the total of the amounts recorded in the sales journal.

In the illustrated sales journal for November, the sales on account totaled $6,195. On November 30 this amount is posted as a credit to the Sales account, and the ledger account number for Sales (41) is entered under the total figure in the sales journal to show that the posting operation has been performed. The total sales figure is also posted as a debit to ledger account no. 5, Accounts Receivable. To make clear the reason for this posting to Accounts Receivable, an explanation of the nature of controlling accounts and subsidiary ledgers is necessary.

Controlling accounts and subsidiary ledgers

In preceding chapters all transactions involving accounts receivable from customers have been posted to a single account entitled Accounts Receivable. Under this simplified procedure, however, it is not easy to look up the amount receivable from a given customer. In practice, nearly all businesses which sell goods on credit maintain a separate account receivable with each customer. If there are 4,000 customers, this would require a ledger with 4,000 accounts receivable, in addition to the accounts for other assets, and for liabilities, owners' equity, revenue, and expenses. Such a ledger would be cumbersome and unwieldy. Also, the trial balance prepared from such a large ledger would be a very long one. If the trial balance showed the ledger to be out of balance, the task of locating the error or errors would be most difficult. All these factors indicate that it is not desirable to have too many accounts in one ledger. Fortunately, a simple solution is available; this solution is to divide up the ledger into several separate ledgers.

In a business which has a large number of accounts with customers and creditors, it is customary to divide the ledger into three separate ledgers. All the accounts with *customers* are placed in alphabetical order in a separate ledger called the *accounts receivable ledger.* All the accounts with *creditors* are arranged alphabetically in another ledger called the *accounts payable ledger.* Both of these ledgers are known as *subsidiary ledgers,* because they support and are controlled by the general ledger.

After thus segregating the accounts receivable from customers in one subsidiary ledger and placing the accounts payable to creditors in a second subsidiary ledger, we have left in the original ledger all the revenue and expense accounts and also all the balance sheet accounts except those with customers and creditors. This ledger is called the *general ledger,* to distinguish it from the subsidiary ledgers.

When the numerous individual accounts with customers are placed in a subsidiary ledger, an account entitled Accounts Receivable continues to be maintained in the general ledger. This account shows the total amount due from all customers; in other words, this single *controlling* account in the general ledger takes the place of the numerous customers' accounts which have been removed to form a subsidiary ledger. The general ledger is still in balance because the controlling account, Accounts Receivable, has a balance equal to the total of the customers' accounts which were removed from the general ledger. Agreement of the controlling account with the sum of the accounts receivable in the subsidiary ledger also provides assurance of accuracy in the subsidiary ledger.

A controlling account entitled Accounts Payable is also kept in the general ledger in place of the numerous accounts with creditors which have been removed to form the accounts payable subsidiary ledger. Because the two controlling accounts represent the total amounts receivable from customers and payable to creditors, a trial balance can be prepared from the general ledger alone. The following illustration shows the relationship of the subsidiary ledgers to the controlling accounts in the general ledger:

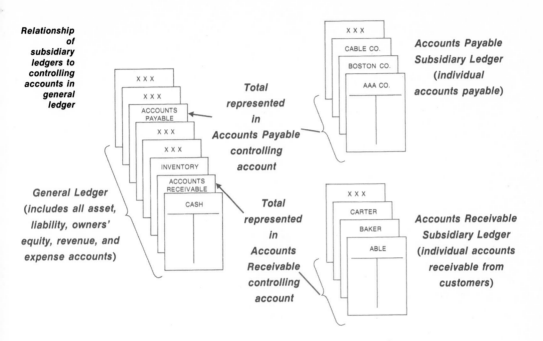

Relationship of subsidiary ledgers to controlling accounts in general ledger

Total represented in Accounts Payable controlling account

Accounts Payable Subsidiary Ledger (individual accounts payable)

CABLE CO.
BOSTON CO.
AAA CO.

General Ledger (includes all asset, liability, owners' equity, revenue, and expense accounts)

ACCOUNTS PAYABLE
INVENTORY
ACCOUNTS RECEIVABLE
CASH

Total represented in Accounts Receivable controlling account

Accounts Receivable Subsidiary Ledger (individual accounts receivable from customers)

CARTER
BAKER
ABLE

POSTING TO SUBSIDIARY LEDGERS AND TO CONTROLLING ACCOUNTS To illustrate the posting of subsidiary ledgers and of controlling accounts, let us refer again to the sales journal illustrated on page 222. Each debit to a customer's account is posted currently during the month from the sales journal to the customer's account in the accounts receivable ledger. The accounts in this subsidiary ledger are usually kept in alphabetical order and are not numbered. When a posting is made to a customer's account, a check mark (✓) is placed in the sales journal as evidence that the posting has been made to the subsidiary ledger.

At month-end the sales journal is totaled. The total amount of sales for the month, $6,195, is posted as a credit to the Sales account and also as a debit to the controlling account, Accounts Receivable, in the general ledger. The controlling account will, therefore, equal the total of all the customers' accounts in the subsidiary ledger.

The following diagram shows the day-to-day posting of individual entries from the sales journal to the subsidiary ledger. The diagram also shows the month-end posting of the total of the sales journal to the two general ledger accounts affected, Accounts Receivable and Sales. Note that the amount of the monthly debit to the controlling account is equal to the sum of the debits posted to the subsidiary ledger.

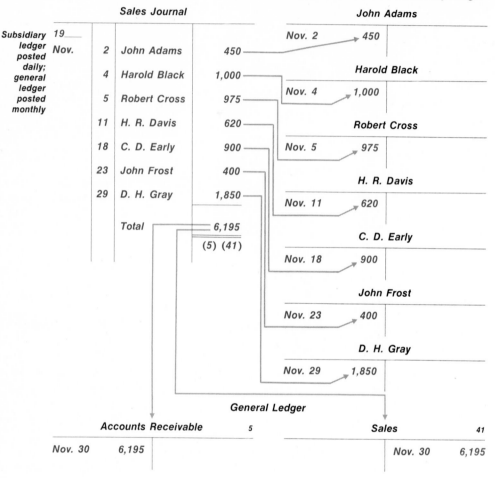

Subsidiary ledger posted daily; general ledger posted monthly

Sales Journal

Accounts Receivable Subsidiary Ledger

19__			
Nov.	2	John Adams	450
	4	Harold Black	1,000
	5	Robert Cross	975
	11	H. R. Davis	620
	18	C. D. Early	900
	23	John Frost	400
	29	D. H. Gray	1,850
		Total	6,195
			(5) (41)

John Adams

Nov. 2 — 450

Harold Black

Nov. 4 — 1,000

Robert Cross

Nov. 5 — 975

H. R. Davis

Nov. 11 — 620

C. D. Early

Nov. 18 — 900

John Frost

Nov. 23 — 400

D. H. Gray

Nov. 29 — 1,850

General Ledger

Accounts Receivable   5

Nov. 30   6,195

Sales   41

Nov. 30   6,195

Purchases journal

The handling of purchase transactions when a purchases journal is used follows a pattern quite similar to the one described for the sales journal.

Assume that the purchases journal illustrated on page 227 contains all purchases of merchandise on credit during the month by the Seaside Company. The invoice date is shown in a separate column because the cash discount period begins on this date.

The five entries are posted as they occur during the month as credits to the creditors' accounts in the subsidiary ledger for accounts payable. As each posting is completed a check mark (✓) is placed in the purchases journal.

At the end of the month the purchases journal is totaled and ruled as

Purchases Journal

	Date		Account Credited	Invoice Date		√	Amount
Entries for purchases on credit during November	19___ Nov.	2 4 10 17 27	Alabama Supply Co. Barker & Bright Canning & Sons Davis Co. Excelsior, Inc.	19___ Nov.	2 4 9 15 25	√ √ √ √ √	3,325 700 500 900 1,825
							7,250
							(50) (21)

shown in the illustration. The total figure, $7,250, is posted to two general ledger accounts as follows:

1 As a debit to the Purchases account
2 As a credit to the Accounts Payable controlling account

The account numbers for Purchases (50) and for Accounts Payable (21) are then placed in parentheses below the column total of the purchases journal to show that the posting has been made.

Under the particular system being described, the only transactions recorded in the purchases journal are purchases of merchandise on credit. The term **merchandise** means goods acquired for resale to customers. If merchandise is purchased for cash rather than on credit, the transaction should be recorded in the **cash payments journal,** as illustrated on pages 232 and 233.

The diagram on page 228 illustrates the day-to-day posting of individual entries from the purchases journal to the accounts with creditors in the subsidiary ledger for accounts payable. The diagram also shows how the column total of the purchases journal is posted at the end of the month to the general ledger accounts, Purchases and Accounts Payable. One objective of this diagram is to emphasize that the amount of the monthly credit to the control account is equal to the sum of the credits posted to the subsidiary ledger.

When assets other than merchandise are being acquired, as, for example, a delivery truck or an office desk for use in the business, the journal to be used depends upon whether a cash payment is made. If assets of this type are purchased for cash, the transaction should be entered in the cash payments journal; if the transaction is on credit, the general journal is used. The purchases journal is not used to record the acquisition of these assets because the total of this journal is posted to the Purchases account and this account (as explained in Chapter 5) is used in determining the cost of goods sold.

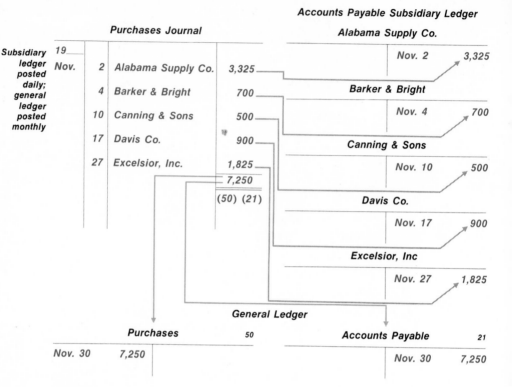

Accounts Payable Subsidiary Ledger

Purchases Journal

Subsidiary ledger posted daily; general ledger posted monthly

19___
Nov.

	2	Alabama Supply Co.	3,325
	4	Barker & Bright	700
	10	Canning & Sons	500
	17	Davis Co.	900
	27	Excelsior, Inc.	1,825
			7,250
			(50) (21)

Alabama Supply Co.

| Nov. 2 | 3,325 |

Barker & Bright

| Nov. 4 | 700 |

Canning & Sons

| Nov. 10 | 500 |

Davis Co.

| Nov. 17 | 900 |

Excelsior, Inc

| Nov. 27 | 1,825 |

General Ledger

Purchases   50

| Nov. 30 | 7,250 |

Accounts Payable   21

| Nov. 30 | 7,250 |

Cash receipts journal

All transactions involving the receipt of cash are recorded in the cash receipts journal. One common example is the sale of merchandise for cash. As each cash sale is made, it is rung up on a cash register. At the end of the day the total of the cash sales is computed by striking the total key on the register. This total is entered in the cash receipts journal, which therefore contains one entry for the total cash sales of the day. For other types of cash receipts, such as the collection of accounts receivable from customers, a separate journal entry may be made for each transaction. The cash receipts journal illustrated on pages 230 and 231 contains entries for selected November transactions, all of which include the receipt of cash.

Nov. 1 R. B. Jones organized the Seaside Company by investing $25,000 cash in exchange for 2,500 shares of $10 par value capital stock.

4 Sold merchandise for cash, $300.

5 Sold merchandise for cash, $400.

8 Collected from John Adams invoice of Nov. 2, $450 less 2% cash discount.

10 Sold portion of land not needed in business for a total price of $7,000, consisting of cash of $1,000 and a note receivable for $6,000. The cost of the land sold was $5,000.

12 Collected from Harold Black invoice of Nov. 4, $1,000 less 2% cash discount.

20 Collected from C. D. Early invoice of Nov. 18, $900 less 2% cash discount.

27 Sold merchandise for cash, $125.

30 Obtained $4,000 loan from bank. Issued a note payable in that amount.

Note that the cash receipts journal illustrated on pages 230 and 231 has three debit columns and three credit columns as follows:

Debits
1 Cash. This column is used for every entry, because only those transactions which include the receipt of cash are entered in this special journal.
2 Sales discounts. This column is used to accumulate the sales discounts allowed during the month. Only one line of the cash receipts book is required to record a collection from a customer who takes advantage of a cash discount.
3 Other accounts. This third debit column is used for debits to any and all accounts other than cash and sales discounts, and space is provided for writing in the name of the account. For example, the entry of November 10 in the illustrated cash receipts journal shows that cash and a note receivable were obtained when land was sold. The amount of cash received, $1,000, is entered in the Cash debit column, the account title Notes Receivable is written in the Other Accounts debit column and the amount of the debit to this account, $6,000. These two debits are offset by credit entries to Land, $5,000, and to Gain on Sale of Land, $2,000, in the Other Accounts credit column.

Credits:
1 Accounts receivable. This column is used to list the credits to customers' accounts as receivables are collected. The name of the customer is written in the space entitled Account Credited to the left of the Accounts Receivable column
2 Sales. The existence of this column will save posting by permitting the accumulation of all sales for cash during the month and the posting of the column total at the end of the month as a credit to the Sales account (41).
3 Other accounts. This column is used for credits to any and all accounts other than Accounts Receivable and Sales. In some instances, a transaction may require credits to two accounts. Such cases are handled by using two lines of the special journal, as illustrated by the transaction of November 10, which required credits to both the Land account and to Gain on Sale of Land.

POSTING THE CASH RECEIPTS JOURNAL It is convenient to think of the posting of a cash receipts journal as being divided into two phases. The first phase consists of the daily posting of individual amounts throughout the month; the second phase consists of the posting of column totals at the end of the month.

Posting during the month Daily posting of the Accounts Receivable credits column is desirable. Each amount is posted to an individual customer's account in the accounts receivable subsidiary ledger. A check mark ($\sqrt{}$) is placed in the cash receipts journal alongside each item posted to a customer's account to show that the posting operation has been performed. When debits and credits to customers' accounts are posted daily,

Cash Receipts Journal

	Date		Explanation	Cash	Sales Discounts	Other Accounts Name	LP	Amount

Includes all transactions involving receipt of cash

Date			Explanation	Cash	Sales Discounts	Name	LP	Amount
Nov.	1		Issued capital stock	25,000				
	4		Cash sales	300				
	5		Cash sales	400				
	8		Invoice Nov. 2, less 2%	441	9			
	10		Sale of land	1,000		Notes Receivable	3	6,000
	12		Invoice Nov. 4, less 2%	980	20			
	20		Invoice Nov. 18, less 2%	882	18			
	27		Cash sales	125				
	30		Obtained bank loan	4,000				
				33,128	47			6,000
				(1)	(43)			(X)

the current status of each customer's account is available for use in making decisions as to further granting of credit and as a guide to collection efforts on past-due accounts.

The debits and credits in the Other Accounts sections of the cash receipts journal may be posted daily or at convenient intervals during the month. If this portion of the posting work is done on a current basis, less detailed work will be left for the busy period at the end of the month. As the postings of individual items are made, the number of the ledger account debited or credited is entered in the LP column of the cash receipts journal opposite the item posted. Evidence is thus provided in the special journal as to which items have been posted.

Posting column totals at month-end At the end of the month, the cash receipts journal is ruled as shown above. Before posting any of the column totals, it is first important to prove that *the sum of the debit column totals is equal to the sum of the credit column totals.*

After the totals of the cash receipts journal have been crossfooted, the following column totals are posted:

1 Cash debit column. Posted as a debit to the Cash account.

2 Sales Discounts debit column. Posted as a debit to the Sales Discounts account.

3 Accounts Receivable credit column. Posted as a credit to the controlling account, Accounts Receivable.

4 Sales credit column. Posted as a credit to the Sales account.

Page 1

	Credits				
	Accounts Receivable			Other Accounts	
Account Credited	√	Amount	Sales	LP	Amount
Capital stock, $10 par				30	25,000
			300		
			400		
John Adams	√	450			
Land				11	5,000 ⎫
Gain on Sale of Land				40	2,000 ⎬
Harold Black	√	1,000			
C. D. Early	√	900			
			125		
Notes Payable				20	4,000
		2,350	825		36,000
		(5)	(41)		(X)

As each column total is posted to the appropriate account in the general ledger, the ledger account number is entered in parentheses just below the column total in the special journal. This notation shows that the column total has been posted and also indicates the account to which the posting was made. The totals of the Other Accounts columns in both the debit and credit sections of the special journal are not posted, because the amounts listed in the column affect various general ledger accounts and have already been posted as individual items. The symbol (X) may be placed below the totals of these two columns to indicate that no posting is made.

Cash payments journal

Another widely used special journal is the cash payments journal, sometimes called the cash disbursements journal, in which all payments of cash are recorded. Among the more common of these transactions are payments of accounts payable to creditors, payment of operating expenses, and cash purchases of merchandise.

The cash payments journal illustrated on pages 232 and 233 contains entries for all November transactions of the Seaside Company which required the payment of cash.

Nov. 1 Paid rent on store building for November, $800.

2 Purchased merchandise for cash, $500.

8 Paid Barker & Bright for invoice of Nov. 4, $700 less 2%.

9 Bought land, $15,000, and building, $35,000, for future use in business. Paid cash of $20,000 and signed a promissory note for the balance of $30,000. (Land and building were acquired in a single transaction.)

17 Paid salesmen's salaries, $600.

26 Paid Davis Co. for invoice of Nov. 16, $900 less 2%.

27 Purchased merchandise for cash, $400.

28 Purchased merchandise for cash, $650.

29 Paid for newspaper advertising, $50.

29 Paid for three-year insurance policy, $720.

Note in the illustrated cash payments journal that the three credit columns are located to the left of the three debit columns; any sequence of columns is satisfactory in a special journal as long as the column headings clearly distinguish debits from credits. The Cash column is often placed first in both the cash receipts journal and the cash payments journal because it is the column used in every transaction.

Good internal control over cash disbursements requires that all payments be made by check. The checks are serially numbered and as each transaction is entered in the cash payments journal, the check number is listed in a special column provided just to the right of the date column. An unbroken sequence of check numbers in this column gives assurance that every check issued has been recorded in the accounting records.

Cash Payments Journal

Includes all transactions involving payment of cash

Date		Check No.	Explanation	Credits				
						Other Accounts		
				Cash	Purchase Discounts	Name	LP	Amount
19__								
Nov.	1	101	Paid November rent	800				
	2	102	Purchased merchandise	500				
	8	103	Invoice of Nov. 4, less 2%	686	14			
	9	104	Bought land and building	20,000		Notes Payable	20	30,000
	17	105	Paid sales salaries	600				
	26	106	Invoice of Nov. 17, less 2%	882	18			
	27	107	Purchased merchandise	400				
	27	108	Purchased merchandise	650				
	29	109	Newspaper advertisement	50				
	29	110	Three-year ins. policy	720				
				25,288	32			30,000
				(1)	(52)			(X)

The use of the six money columns in the illustrated cash payments journal parallels the procedures described for the cash receipts journal.

POSTING THE CASH PAYMENTS JOURNAL   The posting of the cash payments journal falls into the same two phases already described for the cash receipts journal. The first phase consists of the daily posting of entries in the Accounts Payable debit column to the individual accounts of creditors in the accounts payable subsidiary ledger. Check marks (√) are entered opposite these items to show that the posting has been made. If a creditor telephones to inquire about any aspect of his account, information on all purchases and payments made to date is readily available in the accounts payable subsidiary ledger.

The individual debit and credit entries in the Other Accounts columns of the cash payments journal may be posted daily or at convenient intervals during the month. As the postings of these individual items are made, the page number of the ledger account debited or credited is entered in the LP column of the cash payments journal opposite the item posted.

The second phase of posting the cash payments journal is performed at the end of the month. When all the transactions of the month have been journalized, the cash payments journal is ruled as shown below, and the six money columns are totaled. The equality of debits and credits is then proved before posting.

After the totals of the cash payments journal have been proved to be in balance, the totals of the columns for Cash, Purchase Discounts, Ac-

Page 1

		Debits			
	Accounts Payable			Other Accounts	
Account Debited	√	Amount	Purchases	LP	Amount
Store Rent Expense				54	800
			500		
Barker & Bright	√	700			
Land				11	15,000 ⎫
Building				12	35,000 ⎭
Sales Salaries Expense				53	600
Davis Co.	√	900			
			400		
			650		
Advertising Expense				55	50
Unexpired Insurance				6	720
		1,600	1,550		52,170
		(21)	(50)		(X)

counts Payable, and Purchases are posted to the corresponding accounts in the general ledger. The numbers of the accounts to which these postings are made are listed in parentheses just below the respective column totals in the cash payments journal. The totals of the Other Accounts columns in both the debit and credit section of this special journal are not to be posted, and the symbol (X) may be placed below the totals of these two columns to indicate that no posting is required.

The general journal

When all transactions involving cash or the purchase and sale of merchandise are recorded in special journals, only a few types of transactions remain to be entered in the general journal. Examples include the purchase or sale of plant and equipment on credit, the return of merchandise for credit to a supplier, and the return of merchandise by a customer for credit to his account. The general journal is also used for the recording of adjusting and closing entries at the end of the accounting period.

The following transactions of the Seaside Company during November could not conveniently be handled in any of the four special journals and were therefore entered in the general journal.

Nov. 25 A customer, John Frost, was permitted to return for credit $50 worth of merchandise that had been sold to him on Nov. 23.

28 The Seaside Company returned to a supplier, Excelsior, Inc., for credit $300 worth of the merchandise purchased on Nov. 27.

29 Purchased for use in the business office equipment costing $1,225. Agreed to make payment within 30 days to XYZ Equipment Co.

General Journal   *Page 1*

	Date		Account Titles and Explanation	LP	Dr	Cr
Transactions which do not fit any of the four special journals	19___ Nov.	25	Sales Returns and Allowances........................	42	50	
			Accounts Receivable, John Frost.........	5/ √		50
			Allowed credit to customer for return of merchandise from sale of Nov. 23.			
		28	Accounts Payable, Excelsior, Inc...................	21/ √	300	
			Purchase Returns and Allowances......	51		300
			Returned to supplier for credit a portion of merchandise purchased on Nov. 27.			
		29	Office Equipment...	14	1,225	
			Accounts Payable, XYZ Equipment Co.	21/ √		1,225
			Purchased office equipment on 30-day credit.			

Each of the above entries includes a debit or credit to a controlling account (Accounts Receivable or Accounts Payable) and also identifies by name a particular creditor or customer. When a controlling account is debited or credited by a *general journal entry,* the debit or credit must be posted twice: one posting to the controlling account in the general ledger and another posting to a customer's account or a creditor's account in a subsidiary ledger. This double posting is necessary to keep the controlling account in agreement with the subsidiary ledger.

For example, in the illustrated entry of November 25 for the return of merchandise by a customer, the credit part of the entry is posted twice:

1 To the Accounts Receivable controlling account in the general ledger; this posting is evidenced by listing the account number (5) in the LP column of the general journal.

2 To the account of John Frost in the subsidiary ledger for accounts receivable; this posting is indicated by the check mark (√) placed in the LP column of the general journal.

Showing the source of postings in ledger accounts

When a general journal and several special journals are in use, the ledger accounts should indicate the book of original entry from which each debit and credit was posted. An identifying symbol is placed opposite each entry in the reference column of the account. The symbols used in this text are as follows:

S1	meaning page 1 of the sales journal
P1	meaning page 1 of the purchases journal
CR1	meaning page 1 of the cash receipts journal
CP1	meaning page 1 of the cash payments journal
J1	meaning page 1 of the general journal

Subsidiary ledger accounts

The following illustration shows a customer's account in a subsidiary ledger for accounts receivable.

Name of Customer

Date			Ref	Debit	Credit	Balance
19——						
July	1		S1	400		400
	20		S3	200		600
Aug.	4		CR7		400	200
	15		S6	120		320

Subsidiary ledger: account receivable

The advantage of this three-column form of account is that it shows at a glance the present balance receivable from the customer. The current amount of a customer's account is often needed as a guide to collection activities, or as a basis for granting additional credit. In studying the above illustration note also that the Reference column shows the source of each debit and credit.

Accounts appearing in the accounts receivable subsidiary ledger are assumed to have debit balances. If one of these customers' accounts should acquire a credit balance by overpayment or for any other reason, the word *credit* should be written after the amount in the Balance column.

The same three-column form of account is also generally used for creditors' accounts in an accounts payable subsidiary ledger, as indicated by the following illustration:

Name of Creditor

Date			Ref	Debit	Credit	Balance
19___						
July	10		P1		625	625
	25		P2		100	725
Aug.	8		CP4	725		0
	12		P3		250	250

Subsidiary ledger: account payable

Accounts in the accounts payable subsidiary ledger normally have credit balances. If by reason of payment in advance or accidental overpayment, one of these accounts should acquire a debit balance, the word *debit* should be written after the amount in the Balance column.

As previously stated, both the accounts receivable and accounts payable subsidiary ledgers are customarily arranged in alphabetical order and account numbers are not used. This arrangement permits unlimited expansion of the subsidiary ledgers, as accounts with new customers and creditors can be inserted in proper alphabetical sequence.

Ledger accounts

THE GENERAL LEDGER The general ledger accounts of the Seaside Company illustrated on pages 237–238 indicate the source of postings from the various books of original entry. The subsidiary ledger accounts appear on pages 239–240. To gain a clear understanding of the procedures for posting special journals, the student should trace each entry in the illustrated special journals into the general ledger accounts and also to the subsidiary ledger accounts where appropriate. The general ledger accounts are shown in T-account form in order to distinguish them more emphatically from the accounts in the subsidiary ledgers.

Note that the Cash account contains only one debit entry and one credit entry, although there were many cash transactions during the month. The one debit, $33,128, represents the total cash received during the month and was posted from the cash receipts journal on November 30. Similarly, the one credit entry of $25,288 was posted on November 30

Cash 1

General ledger accounts	19__					19__			
	Nov.	30		CR1	33,128	Nov.	30	CP1	25,288

Notes Receivable 3

19__									
Nov.	10		CR1	6,000					

Accounts Receivable 5

19__					19__				
Nov.	30		S1	6,195	Nov.	25		J1	50
						30		CR1	2,350

Unexpired Insurance 6

19__									
Nov.	29		CP1	720					

Land 11

19__					19__				
Nov.	9		CP1	15,000	Nov.	10		CR1	5,000

Building 12

19__									
Nov.	9		CP1	35,000					

Office Equipment 14

19__									
Nov.	29		J1	1,225					

Notes Payable 20

					19__				
					Nov.	9		CP1	30,000
						30		CR1	4,000

Accounts Payable 21

19__					19__				
Nov.	28		J1	300	Nov.	29		J1	1,225
	30		CP1	1,600		30		P1	7,250

Capital Stock, $10 Par   30

				19___				
				Nov.	1		CR1	25,000

Gain on Sale of Land   40

				19___				
				Nov.	10		CR1	2,000

Sales   41

				19___				
				Nov.	30		CR1	825
					30		S1	6,195

Sales Returns and Allowances   42

19___								
Nov.	25		J1	50				

Sales Discounts   43

19___								
Nov.	30		CR1	47				

Purchases   50

19___								
Nov.	30		CP1	1,550				
	30		P1	7,250				

Purchase Returns and Allowances   51

				19___				
				Nov.	28		J1	300

Purchase Discounts   52

				19___				
				Nov.	30		CP1	32

Sales Salaries Expense   53

19___								
Nov.	17		CP1	600				

Store Rent Expense   54

19___								
Nov.	1		CP1	800				

Advertising Expense 55

19__									
Nov.	29		CP1	50					

from the cash payments journal and represents the total of all cash payments made during the month.

ACCOUNTS RECEIVABLE LEDGER   The subsidiary ledger for accounts receivable appears as follows after the posting of the various journals has been completed.

John Adams

Customers' accounts

19__						
Nov.	2		S1	450		450
	8		CR1		450	0

Harold Black

19__						
Nov.	4		S1	1,000		1,000
	12		CR1		1,000	0

Robert Cross

19__						
Nov.	5		S1	975		975

H. R. Davis

19__						
Nov.	11		S1	620		620

C. D. Early

19__						
Nov.	18		S1	900		900
	20		CR1		900	0

John Frost

19__						
Nov.	23		S1	400		400
	25		J1		50	350

D. H. Gray

19__						
Nov.	29		S1	1,850		1,850

ACCOUNTS PAYABLE LEDGER The accounts with creditors in the accounts payable subsidiary ledger are as follows:

Alabama Supply Co.

Creditors' 19____					
accounts Nov.	2		P1	3,325	3,325

Barker & Bright

19____					
Nov.	4		P1	700	700
	8		CP1	700		0

Canning & Sons

19____					
Nov.	10		P1	500	500

Davis Co.

19____					
Nov.	17		P1	900	900
	26		CP1	900		0

Excelsior, Inc.

19____					
Nov.	27		P1	1,825	1,825
	28		J1	300		1,525

XYZ Equipment Co.

19____					
Nov.	29		J1	1,225	1,225

Proving the ledgers

At the end of each accounting period, proof of the equality of debits and credits in the general ledger is established by preparation of a trial balance, as illustrated in preceding chapters. When controlling accounts and subsidiary ledgers are in use, it is also necessary to prove that each subsidiary ledger is in agreement with its controlling account. This proof is accomplished by preparing a schedule of the balances of accounts in each subsidiary ledger and determining that the totals of these schedules agree with the balances of the corresponding controlling accounts.

Variations in special journals

The number of columns to be included in each special journal and the number of special journals to be used will depend upon the nature of the particular business and especially upon the volume of the various kinds of

SEASIDE COMPANY
Trial Balance
November 30, 19___

General Cash	$ 7,840	
ledger Notes receivable	6,000	
trial		
balance Accounts receivable (see schedule below)	3,795	
Unexpired insurance	720	
Land	10,000	
Building	35,000	
Office equipment	1,225	
Notes payable		$34,000
Accounts payable (see schedule below)		6,575
Capital stock, $10 par		25,000
Gain on sale of land		2,000
Sales		7,020
Sales returns and allowances	50	
Sales discounts	47	
Purchases	8,800	
Purchase returns and allowances		300
Purchase discounts		32
Sales salaries expense	600	
Store rent expense	800	
Advertising expense	50	
	$74,927	$74,927

Schedule of Accounts Receivable
November 30, 19___

Subsidiary Robert Cross	$ 975
ledgers in H. R. Davis	620
balance	
with John Frost	350
controlling D. H. Gray	1,850
accounts	
Total (per balance of controlling account)	$3,795

Schedule of Accounts Payable
November 30, 19___

Alabama Supply Co.	$3,325
Canning & Sons	500
Excelsior, Inc.	1,525
XYZ Equipment Co.	1,225
Total (per balance of controlling account)	$6,575

transactions. For example, the desirability of including a Sales Discounts column in the cash receipts journal depends upon whether a business offers discounts to its customers for prompt payment and whether the customers frequently take advantage of such discounts.

A retail store may find that customers frequently return merchandise for credit. To record efficiently this large volume of sales returns, the store may establish a sales returns and allowances journal. A purchase returns and allowances journal also may be desirable if returns of goods to suppliers occur frequently.

Special journals should be regarded as laborsaving devices which may be designed with any number of columns appropriate to the needs of the particular business. A business will usually benefit by establishing a special journal for any type of transaction that occurs quite frequently.

Direct posting from invoices

In many business concerns the efficiency of data processing is increased by posting sales invoices directly to the customers' accounts in the accounts receivable ledger rather than copying sales invoices into a sales journal and then posting to accounts in the subsidiary ledger. If the sales invoices are serially numbered, a file or binder of duplicate sales invoices arranged in numerical order may take the place of a formal sales journal. By accounting for each serial number, it is possible to be certain that all sales invoices are included. At the end of the month, the invoices are totaled on an adding machine, and a general journal entry is made debiting the Accounts Receivable controlling account and crediting Sales for the total of the month's sales invoices.

Direct posting may also be used in recording purchase invoices. As soon as purchase invoices have been verified and approved, credits to the creditors' accounts in the accounts payable ledger may be posted directly from the purchase invoices.

The trend toward direct posting from invoices to subsidiary ledgers is mentioned here as further evidence that accounting records and procedures can be designed in a variety of ways to meet the individual needs of different business concerns.

MECHANICAL ACCOUNTING SYSTEMS

The processing of accounting data may be performed manually, mechanically, or electronically. The term *data processing* includes the preparation of documents (such as invoices and checks) and the flow of the data contained in these documents through the major accounting steps of recording, classifying, and summarizing. A well-designed system produces an uninterrupted flow of all essential data needed by management for planning and controlling business operations.

Unit record for each transaction

Our discussion has thus far been limited to a manual accounting system. One of the points we have emphasized is that an immediate record should be made of every business transaction. The *medium* used to make this record is usually a document or form, such as an invoice or a check. This concept of a unit record for each transaction is an important one as we consider the alternatives of processing these media by accounting machines, by punched cards, or by a computer. Regardless of whether we use mechanical or electronic equipment, the document representing a single transaction is a basic element of the accounting process.

Use of office equipment in a manual data processing system

Manually kept records are a convenient means of demonstrating accounting principles, and they are also used by a great many small businesses. Strictly defined, a manual system of processing accounting data would call for handwritten journals, ledgers, and financial statements. Even in a small business with some handwritten records, however, the use of office machines and laborsaving devices such as cash registers, adding machines, desk calculators, and multicopy forms has become standard practice.

Simultaneous preparation of documents, journals, and ledgers

Traditionally, each business transaction was recorded, copied, and recopied. A transaction was first evidenced by a document such as a sales invoice, then copied into a journal (book of original entry), and later posted to a ledger. This step-by-step sequence of creating accounting records is time-consuming and leaves room for the introduction of errors at each step. Whenever a figure, an account title, or an account number is copied, the danger of introducing errors exists. This is true regardless of whether the copying is done with pen and ink or by punching a machine keyboard. The copying process is subject to human errors. From this premise it follows that if several accounting records can be created by writing a transaction only once, the recording process will be not only faster but also more accurate.

Accounting machines

The development of accounting machines designed to create several accounting records with a single writing of a transaction has progressed at a fantastic rate. Machines with typewriter keyboards and computing mechanisms were early developments useful in preparing journals, invoices, payrolls, and other records requiring the typing of names and the computation of amounts. *Accounting machines* is a term usually applied to mechanical or electronic equipment capable of performing arithmetic functions and used to produce a variety of accounting records and reports.

Punched cards and tabulating equipment

Punched cards are a widely used medium for recording accounting data. Information such as amounts, names, account numbers, and other details is recorded by punching holes in appropriate columns and rows of a standard-sized card, usually by means of a *key-punch machine.* The information punched on the cards can then be read and processed by a variety of machines, including computers.

Every business receives original documents such as invoices and checks in many shapes and sizes. By punching the information on each such document into a card, we create a document of standard size which machines and computers can use in creating records and reports. For example, once the information on sales invoices has been punched into cards, these cards can be run through machines to produce a schedule of accounts receivable, an analysis of sales by product, by territory, and by each salesperson, and a listing of commissions earned by sales personnel.

Processing accounting data by means of punched cards may be viewed as three major steps, with specially designed machines for each step. The first step is that of recording data; a machine often used for this purpose is an electrically operated *key punch* with a keyboard similar to that of a typewriter.

The second major step is classifying or sorting the data into related groups or categories. For this step a machine called a *sorter* is used. The sorter reads the information on each punched card and then arranges the cards in a particular order, or sorts a deck of cards into groups based on the relationship of the data punched into the cards.

The third major step is summarizing the data. This step is performed by a *tabulating machine,* which has an *output* of printed information resulting from the classifying and totaling of the data on the cards.

EDP ACCOUNTING SYSTEMS

The term *electronic data processing* (EDP) refers to the processing of data by electronic computers. A computer-based accounting system processes data in basically the same manner as does a manual or mechanical system. Transactions are initially recorded manually on source documents. The data from these source documents are then keypunched into punched cards which can be read by the computer. The computer processes the information and performs such routine tasks as printing journals (called transaction summaries), posting to ledger accounts, determining account balances, and printing financial statements and other reports.

The primary advantage of the computer is its incredible speed. The number of computations made by an electronic computer is measured in millions per second. In one minute, an electronic printer can produce as much printed material as the average typist in a full day. Because of this speed, ledger accounts may be kept continually up-to-date and current reports may be prepared quickly at any time to assist executives in making decisions.

Elements of an EDP system

An electronic data processing system includes a computer, also called a *central processing unit* (CPU), and a number of related machines, which are often called *peripheral equipment.* The computer is the heart of the system; it performs the processing function which includes the storage of information, arithmetic computations, and control. The other two major elements are (*1*) *input* devices which prepare and insert information into the computer and (*2*) *output* devices which transfer information out of the

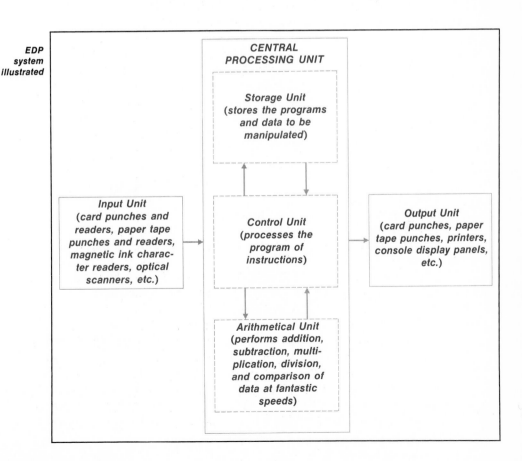

EDP system illustrated

CENTRAL PROCESSING UNIT

Storage Unit
(stores the programs and data to be manipulated)

Input Unit
(card punches and readers, paper tape punches and readers, magnetic ink character readers, optical scanners, etc.)

Control Unit
(processes the program of instructions)

Output Unit
(card punches, paper tape punches, printers, console display panels, etc.)

Arithmetical Unit
(performs addition, subtraction, multiplication, division, and comparison of data at fantastic speeds)

computer to the accountant or other user. Both input and output devices perform the function of *translation.* The machines used to feed information into a computer translate the data into computer language; the output devices translate the processed data back into the language of written words, or of punched cards, paper tape, or magnetic tape.

HARDWARE AND SOFTWARE The machines and related equipment used in an EDP system are called *hardware.* All the other materials utilized in selecting, installing, and operating the system (except the operating personnel) are called *software.* Software includes not only the *computer programs* (the sequence of instructions given to the computer), but also feasibility studies, training materials such as films and manuals, studies of equipment requirements, and everything about the EDP system other than the hardware.

Input devices

Among the input devices used to transfer instructions and accounting data into a computer are card readers, punched-paper-tape readers, magnetic-tape readers, character readers, and terminals. The card-reading device will either transmit information from punched cards into the memory unit of the computer or convert the information to paper or magnetic tape. Punched cards will be read by the card-reading devices at rates of several hundred or even several thousand per minute.

Punched-paper tape can be created as part of the process of recording transactions on cash registers or adding machines. This type of input medium is inexpensive to create and easy to use, but it does not permit the insertion of additional data or the making of corrections after the tape has been punched. Punched-tape readers deliver the data to the computer at high speeds. Both punched-card readers and paper-tape readers are usually connected directly to the computer and are described as part of the *on-line* (direct access) system. They offer the advantage of compatibility with nonelectronic equipment utilizing punched cards or tape.

Magnetic tape is a far faster means of feeding information into a computer and has the advantage of being easily stored. Corrections are also easily made on magnetic tape. Magnetic-tape reels are, however, more expensive than paper tape.

Character-reading machines are perhaps best known in the banking field. They read the account numbers printed in magnetic ink on checks and deposit tickets and convert these data into codes acceptable to the computer. Another type of character-reading device is the optical scanner, with a photoelectric cell which can read a printed document and convert the characters into computer language. This device makes unnecessary the costly step of translating printed matter into punched-card form.

Terminals are keyboard devices which make it possible to enter limited amounts of data into an EDP system without punching the information into cards or tape as a preliminary step. Terminals are extremely slow in comparison with the operating capacity of the computer because they are manually operated. However, terminals have the advantage of allowing the various departments of a business to enter data directly into the accounting system, without having to send their source documents to an EDP department to be keypunched and read into the computer. Some retail stores use terminals in the sales departments to record each sale in the accounting records and to update the accounts receivable from customers. Terminals are also equipped with a printing device which permits output from the computer to be delivered immediately to the user of the terminal.

Output devices

The *printer* is the most important output device. It interprets the computer code and prints several hundred lines per minute, either at the computer center or at remote locations. The printer might be used to produce payroll checks, customers' statements, and many types of accounting reports.

Card-punching machines and paper-tape-punching machines can transfer data from the computer into punch cards and paper tape which later may be used as input data for subsequent analysis or processing.

Processing operations in the computer

The processing operations performed by a computer include storage of information, arithmetic manipulation of data, and control. The computer receives and stores instructions and data; it calls this information from the memory or storage unit as required by the processing routine; it goes through arithmetic operations, makes comparisons of numbers, and takes the action necessary to produce the required output of information.

The term *control* describes the ability of the computer to guide itself through the processing operations utilizing detailed lists of instructions concerning the work to be done.

PROGRAM A *program* is a series of steps planned to carry out a certain process, such as the preparation of a payroll. Each step in the program is a command or instruction to the computer. A program for payroll might be compared with a very detailed written set of instructions given to an inexperienced employee assigned to the payroll function in a manual accounting system. A most important attribute of the computer is its ability to receive and store a set of instructions which controls its behavior.

The preparation of a computer program is a complicated and costly task. A company may employ its own programmers or may rely on outside organizations which specialize in such services.

Differences between mechanical and electronic data processing systems

Mechanical data processing equipment such as electric calculators, mechanical accounting machines, and key-punch machines is extremely slow when compared with electronic equipment. The processing of data in the electronic system is accomplished by electric impulses traveling through electronic circuits. Such equipment functions hundreds of times faster than mechanical devices.

Another point of contrast is that the units of equipment comprising an EDP system are interconnected so that the processing of data is a continuous operation from the point of reading input data to the point of printing the report or other final result. On the other hand, a mechanical data processing system employs separate machines which do not communicate directly with each other. After each machine, such as a key punch, has performed its function, the output media (punched cards or paper tape) must be transported manually to another machine.

Reliability of EDP systems

EDP equipment itself is highly reliable, and the possibility of errors caused by the hardware is very small. However, the use of reliable equipment does not eliminate entirely the possibilities of errors in the accounting records. Errors may still be made in the preparation of source documents. The process of keypunching data into punched cards is comparable to using a typewriter, and making errors is quite possible. Also, the computer program may contain errors which may cause the data to be processed improperly. To reduce the possibility of these types of errors, an EDP system should include both *input controls* and *program controls.*

INPUT CONTROLS Input controls are the precautions taken to ensure that the data being entered into the computer are correct. One important input control is the manual preparation of *control totals,* representing the total dollar amount of all source documents sent to the EDP department for processing. The computer will add up the total dollar amount of all data processed and print this total as part of the computer output. The manually prepared control totals may then be compared to the total printed by the computer to ensure that all source documents sent to the EDP department have been processed.

Another input control is the use of a *verifier key punch.* When data are keypunched into punched cards, there is always the possibility of striking the wrong key, causing a keypunching error. A verifier key punch is used to keypunch the source data into the punched cards a second time; any differences between the first and second keypunching cause the machine to signal that an error has been made.

PROGRAM CONTROLS Program controls are error-detecting measures built into the computer program. An example of a program control is a *limit test,* which compares every item of data processed by the computer to a specified dollar limit. In the event an amount exceeds the dollar limit, the computer does not process that item and prints out an *error report.* A limit test is particularly effective in such computer applications as preparing paychecks, when it is known that none of the paychecks should be for more than a specified amount, such as $1,000.

Another example of a program control is an *item count.* The total number of punched cards to be processed by the computer is determined, and that total is entered as part of the input to the computer. The computer then counts the number of cards it processes, and if this number differs from the predetermined total, an error report is printed. This item count ensures that all the punched cards are actually processed by the computer.

Accounting applications of the computer

The use of electronic data processing equipment is possible for virtually every phase of accounting operations. Even a CPA firm, in conducting an annual audit, may use the computer as an audit tool. For this purpose the auditors may employ specially written computer programs to aid in their work of sampling and analyzing data to determine the fairness of the financial statements.

The most common application of the computer, however, is to process large masses of accounting data relating to routine repetitive operations such as accounts receivable, accounts payable, inventories, payrolls, and posting to ledger accounts.

PAYROLLS In a manual accounting system the preparation of payroll checks is usually separate from the maintenance of records showing pay rates, positions, time worked, payroll deductions, and other personnel data. An EDP system, however, has the capability of maintaining all records relating to payroll as well as turning out the required paychecks. Payroll processing is usually one of the first accounting operations to be placed on the computer.

The payroll procedure consists of determining for each employee the gross earnings, making deductions, computing net pay, preparing the payroll check, and maintaining a record of each individual's earnings. Also, the company needs a payroll summary for each period and usually a distribution of payroll costs by department, by product, or classified by the various productive processes. The payroll function has become increasingly complex and time-consuming in recent years because of the advent of social security taxes, income tax withholding, and other payroll deductions. Each employee must receive not only a payroll check but a statement showing the gross earnings, deductions, and net pay. The company's records must be designed to facilitate filing with the federal and state governments regular payroll reports showing amounts withheld for income taxes, unemployment insurance, and social security. The time and the expense required to prepare payrolls has risen in proportion to the need for more information. The demands by governments, labor unions, credit unions, and other outside agencies have added to the problem.

An EDP payroll system will not only maintain the necessary records, print the checks, and print these reports, but it can also keep management informed of the costs of various functions within the business. For example, data can be produced showing the work-hours and labor costs on each job, labor cost by department for each salesclerk, or the time required by different employees to perform similar work. In other words, much current information can be developed without significant extra expense that will provide management with a detailed breakdown of labor costs. The comparison below illustrates the efficiency of processing payrolls by EDP rather than manually:

	Function	*Payroll Prepared Manually*	*Payroll Prepared by EDP*
Payroll may be prepared either manually or by EDP	1 Timekeeping	Fill in new set of records each period, making extensions manually.	Enter raw data on appropriate forms.
	2 Computation of gross pay	Compute gross pay for each employee, perhaps with desk calculator, and enter manually in records.	Performed electronically.
	3 Calculation of deductions	For each employee, refer to charts and make computations; enter manually in records.	Performed electronically.
	4 Preparation of checks, earnings statements, and payroll register	Write by hand or type checks. Proofread and maintain controls.	Performed electronically.
	5 Bank reconciliation	Reconcile payroll bank account per accounting records with monthly bank statement.	Performed electronically.
	6 Reports to government	Prepare quarterly reports showing for each employee and in total amounts earned, deducted, and paid. Reconcile individual data with controls.	Performed electronically.
	7 Managerial control data	Prepare distribution of hours and labor cost by department or by job. Other analyses may be needed.	Performed electronically.

COMPUTER-BASED JOURNALS AND LEDGERS As mentioned earlier in this chapter, computers also may be used to maintain the journals and ledgers and to prepare financial statements. Transactions and end-of-period adjustments still must be analyzed by persons possessing a knowledge of accounting principles. However, after these transactions have been analyzed and prepared in computer input form, the computer can be used to print the journals, post to the ledger accounts, and print the financial statements and other financial reports. The advantage of maintaining accounting records by computer is that the possibility of mathematical errors is greatly reduced, and the speed of the computer permits the records to be kept continuously up-to-date.

Other accounting applications of computers include forecasting the profit possibilities inherent in alternative courses of action, analyzing gross profit margins by department or by product line, and determining future cash requirements long in advance. Recent developments of accounting applications of the computer provide much more information about business operations than was available to management in the past.

Computer service centers and time-sharing

A computer and related hardware are costly to buy or rent. The employment of personnel qualified to operate the equipment is also a major expense, especially for a small business. One way in which a small business can avoid investing large sums yet gain the operating efficiencies of EDP is to turn over its raw data to a bank, an accounting firm, or a computer center that offers EDP services on a fee basis. The small business may either keypunch its data and send the punched cards to the service center for processing or write the data on special forms and let the service center do the keypunching.

Another method of using EDP services without owning a computer is called *time-sharing.* Time-sharing refers to using a large central computer by means of a portable terminal, which is both an input and output device. Through these terminals, hundreds of businesses may make use of the same central computer. The company which owns the central computer sends each of these users a monthly bill, including a fixed monthly charge plus a per-minute charge for the actual time spent using the computer. Since the portable terminals communicate with the central computer using ordinary telephone lines, the terminals may be thousands of miles away from the central computer.

An advantage of time-sharing is the convenience of direct access to the computer through a portable terminal. A disadvantage, however, is that a terminal enters data into the computer using a manual keyboard. This is a relatively slow way of entering data into a computer. If large quantities of data must be processed, a computer service center may be less expensive than time-sharing.

Do computers make decisions?

Computers can do only what they have specifically been told to do. Computers cannot make decisions in the sense of exercising judgment. They can choose among alternatives only by following the specific instructions contained in the program. When a computer encounters a situation for which it has not been programmed, it is unable to act. Computer programs must therefore be carefully tested to determine that they provide the computer with adequate instructions for all aspects of the data processing.

Information systems

The automation of an accounting system speeds up the production and transmission of information. The term *integrated data processing* (IDP) describes the current trend of providing attachments for typewriters, accounting machines, cash registers, and other conventional equipment which will, as a by-product, produce perforated tape or cards acceptable to a computer. The typewriter, for example, when equipped with such attachments can be used not only to prepare conventional business documents but simultaneously to provide the same information in a form compatible with input requirements of a computer. The *integration* of processes for recording information in conventional form and concurrently providing input media for an EDP system eliminates the intermediate work of transferring information from invoices, checks, and other documents to the tape or cards acceptable for processing by the computer.

The integration of an accounting system requires that forms and procedures be designed not for the needs of a single department but rather as part of a complete *information system* for the entire business. To create such an integrated system, the accounting systems specialist tries to coordinate paper work and procedures in a manner that will provide a rapid and uninterrupted flow of all information needed in the conduct of the business as an entity.

KEY TERMS INTRODUCED OR EMPHASIZED IN CHAPTER 6

Accounts receivable ledger A subsidiary ledger containing an account with each credit customer. The total of the ledger agrees with the general ledger controlling account, Accounts Receivable.

Cash payments journal A special journal used to record all payments of cash.

Cash receipts journal A special journal used to record all receipts of cash.

Central processing unit (CPU) Main section of a computer, including the storage unit, control unit, and arithmetic unit.

Controlling account A general ledger account which is supported by detailed information in a subsidiary ledger.

Data processing The preparation of documents and the flow of data contained in these documents through the major accounting steps of recording, classifying, and summarizing.

Electronic data processing (EDP) A system for processing data by use of electronic computers.

Hardware The machines and related equipment used in an EDP system.

Input controls Internal control measures to ensure accuracy of data entered into a computer (such as control totals, the total dollar amount of documents to be processed).

Input devices An element of a computer used to prepare and insert information into the computer.

Output devices An element of a computer which transfers information out of the computer to the accountant or other user.

Program Instructions to a computer consisting of a series of steps planned to carry out a certain process (such as payroll preparation).

Program controls Error-detecting measures built into a computer program (such as a limit test setting a maximum dollar amount, or item counts specifying the number of cards to be processed).

Punched cards An input device on which accounting data are recorded by using holes in columns and rows to represent numerical and alphabetical data.

Purchases journal A special journal used exclusively to record purchases of merchandise on credit.

Sales journal A special journal used exclusively to record sales of merchandise on credit.

Software All materials (except hardware) utilized in selecting, installing, and operating an EDP system.

Subsidiary ledger A supplementary record used to provide detailed information for a control account in the general ledger. The total of accounts in a subsidiary ledger equals the balance of the related control account in the general ledger.

Terminals Keyboard devices for entering information into a computer without first punching the information into punched cards or tape.

Time-sharing Use of a central computer through a terminal upon payment of a monthly fee by the subscriber.

DEMONSTRATION PROBLEM FOR YOUR REVIEW

The Signal Corporation began operations on November 1, 19___. The chart of accounts used by the company included the following accounts, among others:

Cash	10	*Purchases*	60
Marketable securities	15	*Purchase returns & allowances*	62
Inventory of office supplies	18	*Purchase discounts*	64
Notes payable	30	*Salaries expense*	70
Accounts payable	32	*Utilities expense*	71

November transactions relating to the purchase of merchandise and to accounts payable are listed below, along with selected other transactions.

Nov. 1 Purchased merchandise from Moss Co. for $3,000. Invoice dated today; terms 2/10, n/30.

Nov. 3 Received shipment of merchandise from Wilmer Co. and invoice dated November 2 for $7,600; terms 2/10, n/30.

Nov. 6 Purchased merchandisè from Archer Company at cost of $5,600. Invoice dated November 5; terms 2/10, n/30.

Nov. 9 Purchased marketable securities, $1,200.

Nov. 10 Issued check to Moss Co. in settlement of invoice dated November 1, less discount.

Nov. 12 Received shipment of merchandise from Cory Corporation and an invoice dated November 11 in amount of $7,100; terms net 30 days.

Nov. 14 Issued check to Archer Company in settlement of invoice of November 5.

Nov. 16 Paid cash for office supplies, $110.

Nov. 17 Purchased merchandise for cash, $950.

Nov. 19 Purchased merchandise from Klein Co. for $11,500. Invoice dated November 18; terms 2/10, n/30.

Nov. 21 Purchased merchandise from Belmont Company for $8,400. Invoice dated November 20; terms 1/10, n/30.

Nov. 24 Purchased merchandise for cash, $375.

Nov. 26 Purchased merchandise from Brooker Co. for $6,500. Invoice dated today; terms 1/10, n/30.

Nov. 28 Paid utilities, $150.

Nov. 30 Paid salaries for November, $2,900.

Nov. 30 Paid $2,600 cash to Wilmer Co. and issued 6%, 90-day promissory note for $5,000 in settlement of invoice dated November 2.

Instructions

a Record the transactions in the appropriate journals. Use a single-column purchases journal and a six-column cash payments journal.

b Indicate how postings would be made by placing ledger account numbers and check marks in the appropriate columns of the journals.

c Prepare a schedule of accounts payable at November 30 to prove that the subsidiary ledger is in balance with the controlling account.

SOLUTION TO DEMONSTRATION PROBLEM

a & b   **Purchases Journal**   *Page 1*

Date		Account Credited		Invoice Date		Amount
19___				19___		
Nov.	1	Moss Co.	(terms 2/10, n/30)	Nov.	1	3,000
	3	Wilmer Co.	(terms 2/10, n/30)		2	7,600
	6	Archer Company	(terms 2/10, n/30)		5	5,600
	12	Cory Corporation	(terms net 30)		11	7,100
	19	Klein Co.	(terms 2/10, n/30)		18	11,500
	21	Belmont Company	(terms 1/10, n/30)		20	8,400
	26	Brooker Co.	(terms 1/10, n/30)		26	6,500
						49,700
						(60)(32)

Cash Payments Journal

| Date | Explanation | Credits | | Other Accounts | | | Account Debited | ✓ | Debits | | Other Accounts | |
		Cash	Purchase Discounts	Name	LP	Amount			Accounts Payable	Purchases	LP	Amount
19— Nov. 9	Bought securities	1,200					Marketable Securities				15	1,200
10	Invoice, Nov. 1, less 2%	2,940	60				Moss Co.	√	3,000			
14	Invoice, Nov. 5, less 2%	5,488	112				Archer Company	√	5,600			
16	Purchased office supplies	110					Office Supplies				18	110
17	Cash purchases	950								950		
24	Cash purchases	375								375		
28	Paid utilities	150					Utilities Expense				71	150
30	Paid salaries	2,900					Salaries Expense				70	2,900
30	Invoice, Nov. 2, note issued for unpaid balance	2,600		Notes Payable	30	5,000	Wilmer Co.	√	7,600			
		16,713	172			5,000			16,200	1,325		4,360
		(10)	(64)			(X)			(32)	(60)		(X)

c

SIGNAL CORPORATION
Schedule of Accounts Payable
November 30, 19___

Belmont Company	$ 8,400
Brooker Co.	6,500
Cory Corporation	7,100
Klein Co.	11,500
Total (per general ledger controlling account)	$33,500

REVIEW QUESTIONS

1 What advantages are offered by the use of special journals?

2 Pine Hill General Store makes about 500 sales on account each month, using only a two-column general journal to record these transactions. What would be the extent of the work saved by using a sales journal?

3 When accounts receivable and accounts payable are kept in subsidiary ledgers, will the general ledger continue to be a self-balancing ledger with equal debits and credits? Explain.

4 Explain how, why, and when the cash receipts journal and cash payments journal are crossfooted.

5 During November the sales on credit made by the Hardy Company actually amounted to $41,625, but an error of $1,000 was made in totaling the amount column of the sales journal. When and how will the error be discovered?

6 Considerable copying work may be performed in preparing a sales invoice, a sales journal, and a receivables ledger. Is this step-by-step sequence, with its related opportunity for errors, a characteristic of all types of accounting systems? Explain.

7 What are the principal advantages of electronic data processing in the accounting department of a company?

8 In which phases or areas of accounting can EDP equipment be used to advantage? Which phases can most conveniently and advantageously be converted to electronic data processing?

9 What avenues are open to a small business interested in gaining the efficiencies of electronic data processing, but lacking funds for purchase or rental of a computer and not having employees familiar with computer operations?

10 Evaluate the following quotation: "The computer will ultimately replace both bookkeepers and accountants and will be able to make many of the decisions now made by top management."

11 Distinguish between *hardware* and *software* as these terms are used in data processing systems.

12 Explain the meaning of the term *computer program.*

13 What are the principal elements of an electronic data processing system?

14 Explain the meaning of the term *input control* and give an example.

15 Explain the meaning of the term *program control* and give an example.

EXERCISES

Ex. 6-1 Fall River Company uses a cash receipts journal, a cash payments journal, a sales journal, a purchases journal, and a general journal. Indicate which journal should be used to record each of the following transactions.
a Adjusting entry to record depreciation
b Purchase of delivery truck for cash
c Purchase of merchandise on account
d Return of merchandise by a customer company for credit to its account
e Payment of property taxes
f Purchase of typewriter on account
g Sale of merchandise on account
h Sale of merchandise for cash
i Cash refund to a customer who returned merchandise
j Return of merchandise to a supplier for credit

Ex. 6-2 The accounting system used by Adams Company includes a general journal and also four special journals for cash receipts, cash payments, sales, and purchases of merchandise. On January 31, the Accounts Receivable control account in the general ledger had a debit balance of $160,000, and the Accounts Payable control account had a credit balance of $48,000.

During February the sales journal included transactions which totaled $96,000. The purchases journal included transactions totaling $56,000. In the cash receipts journal the Accounts Receivable column showed a credit total for February of $76,800. In the cash payments journal, the Accounts Payable column showed a debit total of $67,200.
a What posting would be made of the $76,800 total of the Accounts Receivable column in the cash receipts journal at February 28?
b What posting would be made of the $96,000 total of the sales journal at February 28?
c What posting would be made of the $56,000 total of the purchases journal at February 28?
d What posting would be made of the $67,200 total of the Accounts Payable column in the cash payments journal at February 28?
e Based on the above information, state the balances of the Accounts Receivable control account and the Accounts Payable control account in the general ledger after completion of posting at February 28.

Ex. 6-3 The Island Company uses a cash receipts journal, a cash payments journal, a sales journal, a purchases journal, and a general journal.
a In which of the five journals would you expect to find the smallest number of transactions recorded?
b At the end of the accounting period, the total of the sales journal should be posted to what account or accounts? As a debit or credit?
c At the end of the accounting period, the total of the purchases journal should be posted to what account or accounts? As a debit or credit?
d Name two subsidiary ledgers which would probably be used in conjunction with the journals listed above. Identify the journals from which postings would normally be made to each of the two subsidiary ledgers.
e In which of the five journals would adjusting and closing entries be made?

Ex. 6-4 Collins Company uses a sales journal to record all sales of merchandise on credit. At July 31 the transactions in this journal were as follows:

Sales Journal

Date		Account Debited	Invoice No.	Amount
July	6	Robert Baker		$ 3,600
	15	Minden Company		8,610
	17	Pell & Warden		1,029
	26	Stonewall Corporation		17,500
	27	Robert Baker		3,000
				$33,739

Entries in the general journal during July include one for the return of merchandise by a customer, as follows:

July	18	Sales Returns and Allowances		500	
		Accounts Receivable, Minden Com-			
		pany			500
		Allowed credit to customer for return of			
		merchandise from sale of July 15			

a Prepare a subsidiary ledger for accounts receivable by opening a T account for each of the four customers listed above. Post the entries in the sales journal to these individual customers' accounts. From the general journal, post the credit to the account of Minden Company.

b Prepare general ledger accounts in T form as follows: a controlling account for Accounts Receivable, a Sales account, and a Sales Returns and Allowances account. Post to these accounts the appropriate entries from the sales journal and general journal.

c Prepare a schedule of accounts receivable at July 31 to prove that this subsidiary ledger is in agreement with its controlling account.

Ex. 6-5 A check for $13,230 was received from a customer within 10 days from the date of sending a sales invoice for $13,500, with terms of 2/10, n/30. In recording the receipt of the check, Robert Hall, the employee maintaining the cash receipts journal, entered $13,230 in the Cash column and $13,500 in the Accounts Receivable column. He made no entry in the Sales Discounts column. What procedure should bring this error to light?

Ex. 6-6 Jason Company maintains its sales journal and accounts receivable subsidiary ledger by EDP. Each day the accounting department prepares a control total of total credit sales and sends the sales invoices to the EDP department. The sales data are keypunched in the EDP department, and the punched cards and a control figure representing the total number of sales transactions (per the invoices) are entered into the computer.

The computer prepares the sales journal, posts to the accounts receivable ledger (maintained on magnetic tape), and performs an item count. Any discrepancy in the item count is printed out on an error report. A copy of the sales journal for each day is sent back to the accounting department for comparison with the daily control totals.

What control procedure will first detect the following independent errors?

a A sales invoice of $760 is accidentally keypunched as $7,600.

b A sales invoice is lost on the way from the accounting department to the EDP department.

c Several punched cards are lost before being processed by the computer.

PROBLEMS

6-1 The accounting system used by Lake Company, a small business, includes a two-column general journal and four special journals. The four special journals are:
1 A one-column sales journal
2 A one-column purchases journal
3 A six-column cash receipts journal
4 A six-column cash payments journal
  Lake Company maintains a general ledger, an accounts receivable subsidiary ledger, and an accounts payable subsidiary ledger. All the ledgers are in the three-column, running balance form.
  At November 30, the subsidiary ledger for accounts receivable consisted of the accounts with customers shown below.

L. Lawrence

Date		Explanation	Ref	Debit	Credit	Balance
19—						
Nov.	3		S4	2240		2240
	9		S4	4160		6400
	27		CR2		3840	2560

M. Mooney

Date		Explanation	Ref	Debit	Credit	Balance
19—						
Oct.	31	Balance				2073 6
Nov.	8		CR1		12800	7936
	8		J1		2560	5376
	28		CR2		5376	-0-

N. Nathan

Date		Explanation	Ref	Debit	Credit	Balance
19—						
Oct.	31	Balance				14080
Nov.	10		J1		3200	10880
	11		S4	8000		18880
	30		CR2		10240	8640

O. Osmond

Date		Explanation	Ref	Debit	Credit	Balance
19—						
Nov.	4		S4	28160		28160
	29		S4	7680		35840
	29		CR2		28160	7680

Instructions You are to make all appropriate entries in the general ledger controlling account, Accounts Receivable, for the month of September. Use a three-column, running balance form of ledger account. (Remember that a controlling account is posted on a daily basis for transactions recorded in the general journal, but is posted only at the end of the month for the *monthly totals* of special journals such as the sales journal and the cash receipts journal.) Include in the controlling account the balance at October 31, the transactions from the general journal during November in chronological order, and the running balance of the account after each entry. For each amount entered in the Accounts Receivable controlling account, the date and source (name of journal and journal page) should be listed. Use the symbols shown on page 235 to identify the various journals.

6-2 Ozark Corporation has a chart of accounts which includes the following accounts, among others.

Cash	10	Accounts payable	30
Office supplies	18	Purchases	50
Land	20	Purchase returns & allowances	52
Building	22	Purchase discounts	53
Notes payable	28	Salaries expense	60

The December transactions relating to the purchase of merchandise for resale and to accounts payable are listed below along with selected other transactions.

Dec. **1** Purchased merchandise from Sawyer Company at a cost of $9,360. Invoice dated today; terms 2/10, n/30.

Dec. **4** Purchased merchandise from Bright Company for $30,240. Invoice dated December 3; terms 2/10, n/30.

Dec. **5** Returned for credit to Sawyer Company defective merchandise having a list price of $2,880.

Dec. **6** Received shipment of merchandise from Trojan Co. and their invoice dated December 5 in amount of $20,520. Terms net 30 days.

Dec. **8** Purchased merchandise from Wayne Associates, $24,480. Invoice dated today with terms 1/10, n/60.

Dec. 10 Purchased merchandise from King Corporation, $29,880. Invoice dated December 9; terms 2/10, n/30.

Dec. 10 Issued check to Sawyer Company in settlement of balance resulting from purchase of December 1 and purchase return of December 5.

Dec. 11 Issued check to Bright Company in payment of December 3 invoice.

Dec. 18 Issued check to King Corporation in settlement of invoice dated December 9.

Dec. 20 Purchased merchandise for cash, $1,080.

Dec. 21 Bought land, $64,800, and building, $144,000, for expansion of business. Paid cash of $36,000 and signed a promissory note for the balance of $172,800. (Land and building were acquired in a single transaction from R. M. Wilson.)

Dec. 23 Purchased merchandise for cash, $900.

Dec. 26 Purchased merchandise from Taper Company for $32,400. Invoice dated December 25, terms 2/10, n/30.

Dec. 28 Paid cash for office supplies, $270.

Dec. 29 Purchased merchandise for cash, $1,890.

Dec. 31 Paid salaries for December, $7,920.

Instructions

a Record the transactions in the appropriate journals. Use a single-column purchases journal, a six-column cash payments journal, and a two-column general journal. Foot and rule the special journals. Make all postings to the proper general ledger accounts and to the accounts payable subsidiary ledger. Round all amounts to the nearest dollar.

b Prepare a schedule of accounts payable at December 31 to prove that the subsidiary ledger is in balance with the controlling account for accounts payable.

6-3 The chart of accounts used by the Hunt Corporation included the following accounts, among others:

Cash	10	Sales	50
Notes receivable	15	Sales returns & allowances	52
Accounts receivable	17	Sales discounts	54
Land	20	Purchases	60
Office equipment	25	Purchase returns & allowances	62
Notes payable	30	Interest revenue	82
Accounts payable	32	Gain on sale of land	85

The sales activity, cash receipts, and certain other transactions for the month of June are presented below:

June 1 Sold merchandise to Miley Company for cash, $7,725.

June 4 Sold merchandise to Presto Company, $26,500. Invoice no. 618; terms 2/10, n/30.

June 5 Returned $3,400 of merchandise to a supplier for a cash refund.

June 8 Sold merchandise to Topper Company for $13,500. Invoice no. 619; terms 2/10, n/30.

June 9 Received a check from Hartman Company in payment of a $7,500 invoice, less 2% discount.

June 11 Received $3,500 from Gray Company in payment of a past-due invoice.

June 13 Received check from Presto Company in settlement of invoice dated June 4, less discount.

June 16 Sold merchandise to Mexical Company, $13,000. Invoice no. 620; terms 2/10, n/30.

June 16 Returned $3,000 of merchandise to supplier, ICM Corporation, for reduction of account payable.

June 18 Purchased office equipment at a cost of $9,500, signing a 8%, 90-day note payable for the full amount.

June 20 Sold merchandise to Johnston Company for $24,000. Invoice no. 621; terms 2/10, n/30.

June 21 Mexical Company returned for credit $2,000 of merchandise purchased on June 16.

June 23 Borrowed $75,000 cash from a local bank, signing an 8%, six-month note payable.

June 25 Received payment in full from Mexical Company in settlement of invoice dated June 16, less return and discount.

June 29 Sold land costing $95,000 for $35,000 cash and a 9%, two-year note receivable for $105,000. (Credit Gain on Sale of Land for $45,000.)

June 30 Collected from Johnston Company amount of invoice dated June 20, less 2% discount.

June 30 Collected $40,600 in full settlement of a $40,000, 9%, 60-day note receivable held since May 1. (No interest revenue has yet been recorded.)

June 30 Received a 60-day, non-interest-bearing note from Topper Company in settlement of invoice dated June 8.

Instructions

Record the above transactions in the appropriate journals. Use a single-column sales journal, a six-column cash receipts journal, and a two-column general journal. Foot and rule the special journals and indicate how postings would be made by placing ledger account numbers and check marks in the appropriate columns of the journals.

6-4 Frost Company uses multicolumn cash receipts and cash payments journals similar to those illustrated in this chapter. The cash activities for the month of May are presented below:

May 1 Sold additional capital stock in the company for $45,000 cash.

May 1 Purchased U.S. government bonds, $9,000.

May 2 Paid May rent, $3,600.

May 2 Cash sales of merchandise, $12,300.

May 4 Purchased fixtures, $10,500, making a down payment of $1,500 and issuing a note payable for the balance.

May 9 Received $2,100 as partial payment of Bee Co. invoice of $6,300 and 60-day, 10% note for the balance.

May 12 Paid Dallas Co. invoice, $9,000 less 2%.

May 13 Sold land costing $7,500 for $8,850 cash.

May 15 Received $3,822 in full settlement of Bing Company invoice after allowing 2% discount.

May 19 Cash purchase of merchandise, $7,200.

May 20 Paid note due today, $5,100, and accrued interest amounting to $102.

May 21 Sold U.S. government bonds costing $3,000 for $2,925.

May 23 Paid installment on note payable due today, $1,440, of which $702 represented interest expense.

May 25 Cash sales of merchandise, $9,045.

May 25 Paid Post Company invoice, $9,900 less 2%.

May 26 Purchased three-year fire insurance policy, $1,170.

May 28 Cash purchase of merchandise, $6,450.

May 30 Received payment in full settlement of Baker Company invoice, $7,800, less 2%.

May 31 Paid monthly salaries, $8,034.

Instructions

Enter the above transactions in a six-column journal for cash receipts and a six-column journal for cash payments. Compute column totals and rule the journals. Determine the equality of debits and credits in column totals.

6-5 Skyline, Inc., began operations on May 1, and established an accounting system using the following accounts:

Cash	10	Sales	50
Marketable securities	13	Sales returns & allowances	52
Notes receivable	14	Sales discounts	54
Accounts receivable	15	Purchases	60
Merchandise inventory	17	Purchase returns & allowances	62
Unexpired insurance	19	Purchase discounts	64
Land	20	Transportation-in	66
Building	21	Rent expense	70
Furniture and fixtures	24	Salaries expense	72
Notes payable	30	Taxes expense	74
Accounts payable	32	Supplies expense	76
Mortgage payable	36	Insurance expense	78
Capital stock	40	Interest earned	80
Retained earnings	42	Interest expense	83
Income summary	45	Loss on sale of securities	84

The transactions for the month of May are listed below.

May 1 Sold capital stock for $180,000, and deposited this amount in the bank under the name Skyline, Inc.

May 3 Purchased land and building on contract, paying $90,000 cash and signing a mortgage for the remaining balance of $285,000. Estimated value of the land was $165,000.

May 6 Purchased merchandise from Fast Company, $18,300. Invoice dated today; terms 2/10, n/30.

May 7 Sold merchandise to W. B. Allen, $9,000. Invoice no. 1; terms 2/10, n/60.

May 7 Sold merchandise for cash, $2,220.

May 7 Paid $810 for a two-year fire insurance policy.

May 10 Paid freight charges of $615 on Fast Company purchase of May 6.

May 12 Sold merchandise to Connors Company, $14,700. Invoice no. 2; terms 2/10, n/60.

May 13 Purchased merchandise for cash, $4,260.

May 15 Received payment in full from W. B. Allen; Invoice no. 1, less 2% discount.

May 15 Purchased securities for cash, $4,800.

May 16 Issued credit memorandum no. 1 to Connors Company, $1,200 for goods returned today.

May 16 Paid Fast Company invoice of May 6, less discount.

May 18 Purchased merchandise from Hope Corporation, $11,100. Invoice dated today; terms 2/10, n/30.

May 20 A portion of merchandise purchased from Hope Corporation was found to be substandard. After discussion with the vendor, a price reduction of $300 was agreed upon and debit memorandum no. 1 was issued in that amount.

May 22 Received payment in full from Connors Company; Invoice no. 2, less returns and discount.

May 23 Purchased merchandise from Fast Company, $12,600. Invoice dated today; terms 2/10, n/60.

May 25 Sold for $4,260 the securities purchased on May 15.

May 27 Sold merchandise for cash, $1,545.

May 28 Borrowed $9,000 from the bank, issuing a 60-day, 10% note payable as evidence of indebtedness.

May 28 Paid Hope Corporation invoice dated May 18, less discount and return of $300.

May 30 Paid first installment on mortgage, $3,300. This payment included interest of $2,070.

May 30 Purchased merchandise for cash, $2,760.

May 31 Paid monthly salaries of $6,345.

May 31 Sold merchandise to J. Jones, $8,250. Invoice no. 3; terms 2/10, n/60.

Instructions

Enter the May transactions in the following journals:

    Two-column general journal

    One-column sales journal

    One-column purchases journal

    Six-column cash receipts journal

    Six-column cash payments journal

Foot and rule all special journals and show how postings would be made by placing ledger account numbers and check marks in the appropriate columns of the journals.

6-6 Sand Castle Company uses the following accounts in recording transactions:

Cash	10	Dividends	53
Notes receivable	14	Sales	60
Accounts receivable	16	Sales returns and allowances	62
Supplies	17	Sales discounts	64
Unexpired insurance	18	Purchases	70

Equipment	26	Purchase returns and allowances	72
Accumulated depreciation: equip-		Purchase discounts	74
ment	28	Transportation-in	76
Notes payable	30	Salaries expense	80
Accounts payable	32	Supplies expense	84
Dividends payable	34	Insurance expense	86
Mortgage payable	40	Depreciation expense: equipment	88
Capital stock	50	Gain on sale of equipment	90
Retained earnings	52	Interest expense	92

The schedules of accounts receivable and accounts payable for the company at October 31, 19____, are shown below:

Schedule of Accounts Receivable October 31, 19____		Schedule of Accounts Payable October 31, 19____	
Ace Contractors	$20,800	Durapave, Inc.	$30,000
Reliable Builders, Inc.	8,750		
Total	$29,550		

The November transactions of Sand Castle Company were as follows:

Nov. 2 Purchased merchandise on account from Durapave, Inc., $28,000. Invoice was dated today with terms of 2/10, n/30.

Nov. 3 Sold merchandise to Ace Contractors $16,000. Invoice no. 428; terms 2/10, n/30.

Nov. 4 Purchased supplies for cash, $875. (Debit the asset account, Supplies.)

Nov. 5 Sold merchandise for cash, $5,600.

Nov. 7 Paid the Durapave, Inc., invoice for $30,000, representing October purchases. No discount is allowed by Durapave, Inc.

Nov. 10 Purchased merchandise from Tool Company, $32,500. Invoice dated November 9 with terms of 1/10, n/30.

Nov. 10 Collected from Ace Contractors for invoice no. 428 for $16,000, and for October sales of $20,800 on which the discount had lapsed.

Nov. 12 Sold merchandise to Rex Company, $21,750. Invoice no. 429; terms 2/10, n/30.

Nov. 14 Paid freight charges of $2,050 on goods purchased November 10 from Tool Company.

Nov. 14 Sold equipment for $9,000, receiving cash of $1,500 and a 30-day, 10% note receivable for the balance. Equipment cost $20,000 and accumulated depreciation was $13,000. (Debit Accumulated Depreciation: Equipment for $13,000 and credit Gain on Sale of Equipment for $2,000.)

Nov. 15 Issued credit memorandum no. 38 in favor of Rex Company upon return of $1,000 of merchandise.

Nov. 18 Paid for one-year fire insurance policy, $1,425.

Nov. 18 Purchased merchandise for cash, $7,625.

Nov. 19 Paid the Tool Company invoice dated November 9, less the 1% discount.

Nov. 20 Sold merchandise on account to Vincent Co., $13,650; invoice no. 430. Required customer to sign a 30-day, non-interest-bearing note. (Record this sale by a debit to Accounts Receivable, then transfer from Accounts Receivable to Notes Receivable by means of an entry in the general journal.)

Nov. 22 Purchased merchandise for cash, $4,050.

Nov. 22 Sold merchandise for cash, $4,675.

Nov. 22 Received payment from Rex Company for invoice no. 429. Customer made deduction for credit memorandum no. 38 issued November 15, and a 2% discount.

Nov. 23 Sold merchandise on account to Waite, Inc., $9,950. Invoice no. 431; terms 2/10, n/30.

Nov. 24 Declared a cash dividend of $37,500 on capital stock, payable December 20, 19____.

Nov. 25 Purchased merchandise from Smith Company, $26,500. Invoice dated November 24 with terms of 2/10, n/60.

Nov. 26 Issued debit memorandum no. 42 to Smith Company in connection with merchandise returned today amounting to $2,125.

Nov. 27 Purchased equipment having a list price of $60,000. Paid $10,000 down and signed a promissory note for the balance of $50,000.

Nov. 30 Paid monthly salaries of $14,800 for services rendered by employees during November.

Nov. 30 Paid monthly installment on mortgage, $3,500, of which $1,020 was interest.

Instructions

a Record the November transactions in the following journals:

General journal—2 columns
Sales journal—1 column
Purchases journal—1 column
Cash receipts journal—6 columns
Cash payments journal—6 columns

Foot and rule all special journals and show how postings would be made by placing ledger account numbers and check marks in the appropriate columns of the journals.

b Prepare a schedule of accounts receivable and accounts payable as of November 30, 19____.

6-7 Smoke Tree, Inc., maintains special journals for sales, purchases, cash receipts, and cash payments. All sales and purchases are made on account. During the month of July, all transactions were recorded in the special journals; no entries were made in the general journal. The after-closing trial balance on June 30 and the unadjusted trial balance on July 31 are shown below:

	After-closing Trial Balance, June 30		Trial Balance, July 31	
Cash	$ 178,000		$ 134,000	
Accounts receivable	240,000		261,000	
Inventory	252,000		252,000	
Equipment	350,000		368,000	
Accumulated depreciation:				
equipment		$ 75,000		$ 75,000
Accounts payable		195,000		130,000
Capital stock		500,000		600,000
Retained earnings		250,000		250,000
Sales				170,000
Purchases			125,000	
Salaries expense			40,000	
Advertising expense			10,000	
Supplies expense			7,500	
Property tax expense			12,500	
Miscellaneous expense			15,000	
	$1,020,000	$1,020,000	$1,225,000	$1,225,000

Instructions

a Prepare a schedule of cash receipts for July listing separately the amount of cash collected from customers and the amount of cash receipts from any other source.

b Prepare a schedule of cash payments for July including cash payments to suppliers and the amounts of cash paid for all other purposes.

c Prepare one compound journal entry (general journal form) summarizing all July transactions involving the receipt of cash. The entry should include a debit to Cash and credits to other accounts for the amounts indicated in **a.**

d Prepare one compound journal entry (general journal form) summarizing all July transactions involving the payment of cash. The entry should include a credit to Cash and debits to other accounts for amounts indicated in **b.**

BUSINESS DECISION PROBLEM 6

Leisure Clothing is a mail-order company which sells clothes to the public at discount prices. Recently Leisure Clothing initiated a new policy allowing a 10-day free trial on all clothes bought from the company. At the end of the 10-day period, the customer may either pay cash for the purchase or return the goods to Leisure Clothing. The new policy caused such a large boost in sales that, even after considering the many sales returns, the policy appeared quite profitable.

The accounting system of Leisure Clothing includes a sales journal, purchases journal, cash receipts journal, cash payments journal, and a general journal. As an internal control procedure, an officer of the company reviews and initials every entry in the general journal before the amounts are posted to the ledger accounts. Since the 10-day free trial policy has been in effect, hundreds of entries recording sales returns have been entered in the general journal each week. Each of these entries has been reviewed and initialed by an officer of the firm, and the amounts have been posted to Sales Returns & Allowances and to the Accounts Receivable control account in the general ledger, and also to the customer's account in the accounts receivable subsidiary ledger.

Since these sales return entries are so numerous, it has been suggested that a special journal be designed to handle them. This could not only save time in journalizing and posting the entries, but also eliminate the time-consuming individual review of each of these repetitive entries by an officer of the company.

Instructions

a How many amounts are entered in the general journal to describe a single sales return transaction? Are these amounts the same?

b Explain why these transactions are suited to the use of a special journal. Explain in detail how many money columns the special journal should have, and what postings would have to be done either at the time of the transaction or at the end of the period.

c Assume that there were 3,000 sales returns during the month. How many postings would have to be made during the month if these transactions were entered in the general journal? How many postings would have to be made if the special journal you designed in **b** were used? (Assume a one-month accounting period.)

d Assume that a general journal entry requires 40 seconds to write and a special journal entry can be written in 15 seconds. Also assume that each posting requires an average of 20 seconds and that the officer of the company averages 20 seconds to review and initial a general journal entry for a sales return. The officer estimates the entire sales return special journal could be reviewed in 10 minutes. How much time (expressed in hours, minutes, and seconds) would be required to journalize, review, and post 3,000 entries in (*1*) general journal form and (2) special journal form? What is the time saving resulting from using the special journal?

e If the estimated cost of designing a sales returns journal and training employees in its use were $300, would you recommend adopting such a journal? Present a case to support your decision, assuming that the labor cost of operating either system averages $8 per hour.

7 Forms of Business Organization

Three forms of business organization are common to American industry: the single proprietorship, the partnership, and the corporation. When these forms of organization were introduced in Chapter 1, it was emphasized that most accounting principles apply to all three forms and that the main area of difference lies in the accounting for owners' equity. In this chapter we shall describe briefly some accounting processes peculiar to single proprietorships and partnerships, and then move to a discussion of corporations. Our consideration of accounting and reporting problems relating to corporations will be continued in Chapter 8.

SINGLE PROPRIETORSHIPS

Accounting for the owner's equity in a single proprietorship

A balance sheet for a single proprietorship shows the entire ownership equity as a single dollar amount without any effort to distinguish between the amount originally invested by the owner and the later increase or decrease in owner's equity as a result of profitable or unprofitable operations. A corporation must maintain separate accounts for capital stock and retained earnings, because distributions to owners in the form of dividends cannot legally exceed the earnings of the corporation. In an unincorporated business, however, the owner is free to withdraw assets from the business at any time and in any amount.

The accounting records for a single proprietorship do not include accounts for capital stock, retained earnings, or dividends. Instead of these accounts, a *capital* account and a *drawing* account are maintained for the owner.

THE OWNER'S CAPITAL ACCOUNT In a single proprietorship, a single owner's capital account is used in place of the two corporate accounts for capital stock and retained earnings. The total owner's equity in the business, therefore, appears as a single amount in the balance sheet. The title of the capital account includes the name of the owner, as, for example, *John Jones, Capital.*

The capital account is credited with the amount of the proprietor's original investment in the business and also with any subsequent investments. When the accounts are closed at the end of each accounting period, the Income Summary account is closed into the owner's capital account. Thus the capital account is credited with the net income earned (or debited with the net loss incurred). Withdrawals by the proprietor during the period are debited to a drawing account and later closed to the capital account.

THE OWNER'S DRAWING ACCOUNT A withdrawal of cash or other assets by the owner reduces the owner's equity in the business and could be recorded by debiting the owner's capital account. However, a clearer record is created if a separate Drawing account is maintained. This drawing account (entitled, for example, *John Jones, Drawing*) replaces the Dividends account used by a corporation.

The drawing account is debited for any of the following transactions:

1 Withdrawals of cash or other assets. If the proprietor of a clothing store, for example, withdraws merchandise for personal use, the Drawing account is debited for the cost of the goods withdrawn. The offsetting credit is to the Purchases account (or to Inventory if a perpetual inventory system is maintained).

2 Payment of the proprietor's personal bills out of the business bank account.

3 Collection of an account receivable of the business, with the cash collected being retained personally by the proprietor.

Withdrawals by the proprietor (like dividends to stockholders) are not an expense of the business. Expenses are incurred for the purpose of generating revenue, and a withdrawal of cash or other assets by the proprietor does not have this purpose.

Closing the accounts

The revenue and expense accounts of a single proprietorship are closed into the Income Summary account in the same way as for a corporation. However, the net income or net loss is closed to the proprietor's Capital account rather than to a Retained Earnings account. To complete the closing of the accounts, the balance of the Drawing account is transferred into the proprietor's Capital account.

Financial statements for a single proprietorship

The balance sheet of a single proprietorship differs from the balance sheet of a corporation only in the owner's equity section. An illustration of the ownership equity portion of the balance sheet for a proprietorship, a partnership, and a corporation was presented in Chapter 1 on pages 20 and 21.

A statement of owner's equity may be prepared in a form similar to the statement of retained earnings used by a corporation. The statement of owner's equity, however, shows additional investments made by the owner as well as the earnings retained in the business. An illustration follows:

JONES INSURANCE AGENCY
Statement of Owner's Equity
For the Year Ended December 31, 19____

John Jones, capital, Jan. 1, 19____	$ 80,400
Add: Additional investments	10,000
Net income for year	30,500
Subtotal	$120,900
Less: Withdrawals	34,000
John Jones, capital, Dec. 31, 19____	$ 86,900

Note that withdrawals may exceed net income

The income statement for a single proprietorship does not include any salary expense representing managerial services rendered by the owner. One reason for not including among the expenses a salary to the owner-manager is the fact that individuals in such a position are able to set their own salaries at any amount they choose. The use of an unrealistic salary to the proprietor would tend to destroy the significance of the income statement as a device for measuring the earning power of the business. It is more logical to regard the single proprietor as working to earn the entire net income of the business than as working for a salary.

Another distinctive feature of the income statement for a single proprietorship is that income tax is not included. The proprietor reports on his or her individual tax return the taxable income from the business and from other sources such as personal investments. The rate of tax is determined by the proprietor's total taxable income; consequently, the tax applicable to the income from the business is influenced by factors unrelated to the business enterprise. As explained later in this chapter, the financial statements for a corporation will include income tax expense in the income statement and income taxes payable among the current liabilities in the balance sheet.

PARTNERSHIPS

A *partnership* may be defined as "an association of two or more persons to carry on, as co-owners, a business for profit." In the professions and in businesses which stress the factor of personal service, the partnership form of organization is widely used. The laws of some states may even deny the incorporation privilege to persons engaged in such professions as law and public accounting, because the personal responsibility of the professional practitioner to clients might be lost behind the impersonal corporate entity. However, an increasing number of states are now affording professionals the privilege of incorporating. In the fields of manufacturing, wholesaling, and retail trade, the partnership form is popular, because it affords a convenient means of combining the capital and abilities of two or more persons.

Significant features of a partnership

Before taking up the accounting problems peculiar to partnerships, it will be helpful to consider briefly some of the distinctive characteristics of the partnership form of organization. These characteristics (such as limited life and unlimited liability) all stem from the basic point that a partnership is not a separate legal entity in itself but merely a voluntary association of individuals.

EASE OF FORMATION A partnership can be created without any legal formalities. When two persons agree to become partners, a partnership is automatically created. The voluntary aspect of a partnership agreement means that no one can be forced into a partnership or forced to continue as a partner.

LIMITED LIFE A partnership may be ended at any time by the death or withdrawal of any member of the firm. Other factors which may bring an end to a partnership include the bankruptcy or incapacity of a partner or the completion of the project for which the partnership was formed. The admission of a new partner or the retirement of an existing partner means an end to the old partnership, although the business may be continued by the formation of a new partnership.

MUTUAL AGENCY Each partner acts as an agent of the partnership, with authority to bind the partnership to contracts. The partnership is bound by the acts of any partner as long as these acts are within the scope of normal operations. The factor of mutual agency suggests the need for exercising great caution in the selection of a partner. To be in partnership with an irresponsible person or one lacking in integrity is an intolerable situation.

UNLIMITED LIABILITY Each partner in a *general partnership* is personally responsible for the debts of the partnership. The lack of any ceiling on the liability of a general partner may deter a wealthy person from entering a general partnership. In a *limited partnership* one (or more) of the partners has no personal liability for the debts of the partnership.

A new member joining an existing partnership may or may not assume liability for debts incurred by the firm prior to his or her admission. A partner withdrawing from membership must give adequate public notice of withdrawal; otherwise the former partner may be held liable for partnership debts incurred subsequent to withdrawal. The retiring partner remains liable for partnership debts existing at the time of withdrawal unless the creditors agree to a release of this obligation.

CO-OWNERSHIP OF PARTNERSHIP PROPERTY AND PROFITS When a partner invests a building, inventory, or other property in a partnership, he or she does not retain any personal right to the assets contributed. The property becomes jointly owned by all partners. Each member of a partnership also has an ownership right in the profits.

Advantages and disadvantages of a partnership

Perhaps the most important advantage and the principal reason for the formation of most partnerships is the opportunity to bring together sufficient capital to carry on a business. The opportunity to combine special skills, as, for example, the specialized talents of engineers, accountants, or lawyers may also induce individuals to join forces in a partnership. Members of a partnership enjoy more freedom and flexibility of action than do the owners of a corporation; the partners may withdraw funds and make business decisions of all types without the necessity of formal meetings or legalistic procedures. Finally, operating as a partnership may, in certain instances, result in significant income tax advantages.

Offsetting these advantages of a partnership are such serious disadvantages as limited life, unlimited liability, and mutual agency. Furthermore, if a business is to require a very large amount of capital, the partnership is a less effective device for raising the capital than is a corporation.

Partnership accounting

An adequate accounting system and an accurate measurement of income are needed by every business, but they are especially important in a partnership because the net income is divided among two or more owners. All partners need current, accurate information on profits so that they can make intelligent decisions on such questions as additional investments, expansion of the business, or sale of their respective interests in the partnership.

Partnership accounting requires the maintenance of a separate capital account for each partner; a separate drawing account for each partner is also needed. The other distinctive feature of partnership accounting is the division of each year's net profit or loss among the partners in the proportions specified by the partnership agreement. In the study of partnership accounting, the new concepts lie almost entirely in the owners' equity section; accounting for partnership assets and liabilities follows the same principles as for other forms of business organization.

RECORDING INITIAL INVESTMENTS When a partner invests assets other than cash, a question always arises as to the value of such assets; the valuations assigned to noncash assets should be their *fair market values* at the date of transfer to the partnership. The valuations assigned must be agreed to by all the partners.

To illustrate the opening entries for a newly formed partnership, assume that on January 1 Janet Blair and Richard Cross, who operate competing retail stores, decide to form a partnership by consolidating their two businesses. A capital account will be opened for each partner and credited with the agreed valuation of the *net assets* (total assets less total liabilities) that the partner contributes. The journal entries to open the accounts of the partnership of Blair and Cross are as follows:

Entries for formation of partnership

Cash	40,000	
Accounts Receivable	60,000	
Inventory	90,000	
Accounts Payable		30,000
Janet Blair, Capital		160,000

To record the investment by Janet Blair in the partnership of Blair and Cross.

Cash	10,000	
Land	60,000	
Building	100,000	
Inventory	60,000	
Accounts Payable		70,000
Richard Cross, Capital		160,000

To record the investment by Richard Cross in the partnership of Blair and Cross.

The values assigned to assets in the accounts of the new partnership may be quite different from the amounts at which these assets were carried in the accounts of their previous owners. For example, the land contributed by Cross and valued at $60,000 might have appeared in his accounting records at a cost of $20,000. The building which he contributed was valued at $100,000 by the partnership, but it might have cost

Cross only $80,000 some years ago and might have been depreciated on his records to a net value of $60,000. Assuming that market values of land and buildings had risen sharply while Cross owned this property, it is no more than fair to recognize the *present market value* of these assets at the time of transfer to the partnership and to credit his capital account accordingly. Depreciation of the building for financial accounting purposes will begin anew in the partnership accounts and will be based on the assigned value of $100,000 at the date of acquisition by the partnership.

ADDITIONAL INVESTMENTS Assume that after six months of operation the firm is in need of more cash, and the partners make an additional investment of $10,000 each on July 1. These additional investments are credited to the capital accounts as shown below:

Entry for additional investment

Cash	20,000	
Janet Blair, Capital		10,000
Richard Cross, Capital		10,000

To record additional investments by partners.

WITHDRAWALS BY PARTNERS The drawing account maintained for each partner serves the same purpose as the drawing account of the owner of a single proprietorship. The transactions calling for debits to the drawing accounts of partners may be summarized as follows:

1 Cash or other assets withdrawn by a partner
2 Payments from partnership funds of the personal debits of a partner
3 Partnership cash collected on behalf of the firm by a partner but retained by the partner personally

Credits to the drawing accounts are seldom encountered; one rather unusual transaction requiring such an entry consists of the payment of a partnership liability by a partner out of personal funds.

In our example of the Blair and Cross partnership, we might assume that the partners made numerous withdrawals during the year. Partners may make withdrawals at any time; there is no need for a formal "declaration" as in the case of dividends paid by a corporation. The amounts withdrawn need not be the same for all partners. The withdrawals by Blair and Cross are represented by the following summary entry:

Recording withdrawals by partners

Janet Blair, Drawing	12,000	
Richard Cross, Drawing	8,000	
Cash		20,000

To record withdrawals by partners.

CLOSING ENTRIES The revenue and expense accounts of a partnership are closed into the Income Summary account in the same way as for a corporation. However, the net income or net loss shown by the Income Summary account is closed into the partners' Capital accounts rather than to a Retained Earnings account. If the partnership agreement does not mention how profits are to be divided, the law assumes that the intention of the partners was for an equal division of profits and losses. If the partnership agreement specifies a method of dividing profits but does not mention the possibility of losses, any losses are divided in the proportions provided for sharing profits.

In the previous illustration of the firm of Blair and Cross, an equal sharing of profits was agreed upon. Assuming that a profit of $60,000 was realized during the first year of operations, the entry to close the Income Summary account would be as follows:

Closing In-	*Income Summary*	*60,000*	
come Summary;	*Janet Blair, Capital*		*30,000*
profits	*Richard Cross, Capital*		*30,000*
shared			
equally	*To divide net income for 19___ in accordance with partnership*		
	agreement to share profits equally.		

The final step in closing the accounts is to transfer the debit balances of the Drawing accounts into the partners' Capital accounts, as follows:

Closing the	*Janet Blair, Capital*	*12,000*	
drawing ac-	*Richard Cross, Capital*	*8,000*	
counts to	*Janet Blair, Drawing*		*12,000*
capital	*Richard Cross, Drawing*		*8,000*
accounts	*To transfer debit balances in partners' drawing accounts to their*		
	respective capital accounts.		

INCOME STATEMENT FOR A PARTNERSHIP The income statement for a partnership may include a final section to show the division of the net income between the partners, as illustrated at the top of page 276 for the firm of Blair and Cross.

BLAIR AND CROSS
Income Statement
For the Year Ended December 31, 19___

<table>
<tr><td rowspan="2" style="text-align:right;">*Note distri-
bution of
net income*</td><td>*Sales* . . . .</td><td></td><td>*$600,000*</td></tr>
<tr><td>*Cost of goods sold:*</td><td></td><td></td></tr>
<tr><td></td><td>Inventory, Jan. 1 . . . .</td><td>*$150,000*</td><td></td></tr>
<tr><td></td><td>Purchases . . . .</td><td>310,000</td><td></td></tr>
<tr><td></td><td>Cost of goods available for sale . . . .</td><td>*$460,000*</td><td></td></tr>
<tr><td></td><td>Less: Inventory, Dec. 31 . . . .</td><td>200,000</td><td></td></tr>
<tr><td></td><td>Cost of goods sold . . . .</td><td></td><td>260,000</td></tr>
<tr><td></td><td>*Gross profit on sales* . . . .</td><td></td><td>*$340,000*</td></tr>
<tr><td></td><td>*Operating expenses:*</td><td></td><td></td></tr>
<tr><td></td><td>Selling expenses . . . .</td><td>*$200,000*</td><td></td></tr>
<tr><td></td><td>General & administrative expenses . . . .</td><td>80,000</td><td>280,000</td></tr>
<tr><td></td><td>*Net income* . . . .</td><td></td><td>*$ 60,000*</td></tr>
<tr><td></td><td>*Distribution of net income:*</td><td></td><td></td></tr>
<tr><td></td><td>To Janet Blair (50%) . . . .</td><td>*$ 30,000*</td><td></td></tr>
<tr><td></td><td>To Richard Cross (50%) . . . .</td><td>30,000</td><td>*$ 60,000*</td></tr>
</table>

STATEMENT OF PARTNERS' CAPITALS The partners will usually want an explanation of the change in their capital accounts from one year-end to the next. A financial statement called a *statement of partners' capitals* is prepared to show this information and is illustrated below for the partnership of Blair and Cross:

BLAIR AND CROSS
Statement of Partners' Capitals
For the Year Ended December 31, 19___

<table>
<tr><td></td><td></td><td style="text-align:center;">*Blair*</td><td style="text-align:center;">*Cross*</td><td style="text-align:center;">*Total*</td></tr>
<tr><td rowspan="3" style="text-align:right;">*Changes in
capital ac-
counts dur-
ing the year*</td><td>*Investment, Jan. 1, 19___* . . . .</td><td>*$160,000*</td><td>*$160,000*</td><td>*$320,000*</td></tr>
<tr><td>*Add: Additional investment* . . . .</td><td>10,000</td><td>10,000</td><td>20,000</td></tr>
<tr><td>Net income for the year . . . .</td><td>30,000</td><td>30,000</td><td>60,000</td></tr>
<tr><td></td><td>*Subtotals* . . . .</td><td>*$200,000*</td><td>*$200,000*</td><td>*$400,000*</td></tr>
<tr><td></td><td>*Less: Drawings* . . . .</td><td>12,000</td><td>8,000</td><td>20,000</td></tr>
<tr><td></td><td>*Balances, Dec. 31, 19___* . . . .</td><td>*$188,000*</td><td>*$192,000*</td><td>*$380,000*</td></tr>
</table>

The balance sheet for Blair and Cross would show the capital balance for each partner, as well as the total ownership equity of $380,000.

Partnership profits and income taxes

Partnerships are not required to pay income taxes. However, a partnership is required to file an information tax return showing the amount of the partnership net income ($60,000 in our example), and the share of each partner in the net income. The partners must include their share of the partnership profit on their individual income tax returns. Partnership net income is thus taxable to the partners individually in the year in which it is earned. In the partnership of Blair and Cross illustrated above, each would report and pay tax on $30,000 of partnership net income.

Note that partners report and pay tax on their respective shares of the profits earned by the partnership during the year and not on the amounts which they have drawn out of the business during the year. *The entire net income of the partnership is taxable to the partners each year,* even though there may have been no withdrawals. This treatment is consistent with that accorded a single proprietorship.

Alternative methods of dividing partnership income

In the preceding illustration, the partners divided net income equally. Partners can, however, share net income in any way they wish. Factors that partners might consider in arriving at an equitable plan to divide net income include (*1*) the amount of time each partner devotes to the business, (*2*) the amount of capital invested by each partner, and (*3*) any other contribution by each partner to the success of the partnership. Net income, for example, may be shared in any agreed ratio such as 4 to 1, in the ratio of average capital invested, or in a fixed ratio after an allowance is made to each partner for salary and interest on capital invested.

Assume that the partnership of Adams and Barnes earned $48,000 (before interest and salary allowances to partners) in Year 1 and that they had agreed to share net income as follows:

1 Salary allowances of $12,000 per year to Adams and $24,000 per year to Barnes. (Partners' salaries are merely a device for sharing net income and are not necessarily withdrawn from the business.)

2 Interest at 6% on average capitals to be allowed to each partner. Average capital balances for Adams and Barnes amounted to $80,000 and $20,000, respectively.

3 Any amount in excess of the foregoing salary and interest allowances to be divided equally.

Pursuant to this agreement, the net income of $48,000 would be divided between Adams and Barnes as follows:

Distribution of Net Income

Income sharing; salaries, interest, and fixed ratio as basis

Net income to be divided.			$48,000
Salaries to partners:			
Adams	$12,000		
Barnes	24,000	$36,000	
Interest on average invested capital:			
Adams ($80,000 x 0.06)	$ 4,800		
Barnes ($20,000 x 0.06)	1,200	6,000	42,000
Remaining net income to be divided equally.			$ 6,000
Adams	$ 3,000		
Barnes	3,000	6,000	

This three-step division of the year's profit of $48,000 has resulted in giving Adams a total of $19,800 and Barnes a total of $28,200. The amounts credited to each partner may be summarized as follows:

	Adams	Barnes	Together
Salaries	$12,000	$24,000	$36,000
Interest on average capitals	4,800	1,200	6,000
Remaining profit divided equally	3,000	3,000	6,000
Totals	$19,800	$28,200	$48,000

Income allocated to each partner . . .

The journal entry to close the Income Summary account will be

. . .may be recorded in a single journal entry

Income Summary	48,000	
Adams, Capital		19,800
Barnes, Capital		28,200

To close the Income Summary account by crediting partners' capital accounts with authorized salaries and interest on average capitals at 6%, and by dividing the remaining net income equally.

AUTHORIZED SALARIES AND INTEREST IN EXCESS OF NET INCOME In the preceding example the total of the authorized salaries and interest was $42,000 and the net income to be divided was $48,000. Suppose that the net income had been only $30,000; how should the division have been made?

If the partnership agreement provides for salaries and interest on invested capital, these provisions are to be followed even though the net income for the year is less than the total of the authorized salaries and interest. If the net income of the firm of Adams and Barnes amounted to only $30,000, this amount would be distributed as shown on page 279:

Distribution of Net Income

Authorized	Net income to be divided			*$30,000*
salaries and	Salaries to partners:			
interest may				
exceed net	Adams	$12,000		
income	Barnes	24,000	$36,000	
	Interest on average invested capitals:			
	Adams ($80,000 × 0.06)	$ 4,800		
	Barnes ($20,000 × 0.06)	1,200	6,000	42,000
	Residual loss to be divided equally			$12,000
	Adams		$ 6,000	
	Barnes		6,000	12,000

The residual loss of $12,000 must be divided equally because the partnership agreement states that profits and losses are to be divided equally after providing for salaries and interest.

The result of this distribution of the net income of $30,000 has been to give Adams a total of $10,800 and Barnes a total of $19,200.

Other aspects of partnership accounting

The foregoing discussion of partnership accounting is by no means exhaustive. The admission of a new partner to the partnership, the withdrawal of a partner, and the liquidation of a partnership, for example, may raise some very complex accounting issues. These issues are primarily of interest to advanced accounting students and for that reason are not included in this introductory text.

CORPORATIONS

The corporation has become the dominant form of business organization on the American economic scene, probably because it gathers together large amounts of capital more readily than single proprietorships or partnerships. Because of its efficiency as a device for pooling the savings of many individuals, the corporation is an ideal means of obtaining the capital necessary for large-scale production and its inherent economies. Virtually all large businesses are corporations.

Definition of corporation

A corporation has been defined as "an artificial being, invisible, intangible, and existing only in contemplation of the law." A corporation is regarded as a legal entity having a continuous existence apart from that of its owners. By way of contrast, a partnership is a relatively unstable type of organization which is dissolved by the death or retirement of any one of its members, whereas the continuous existence of a corporation is not interrupted by the death of a stockholder.

Ownership in a corporation is evidenced by transferable shares of stock, and the owners are called *stockholders* or *shareholders.* To administer the affairs of the corporation, the stockholders elect a *board of directions.* The directors in turn select a president and other corporate officers to carry on active management of the business.

Advantages of the corporate form of organization

The corporation offers a number of advantages not available in other forms of organization. Among these advantages are the following:

1 **Greater amounts of capital can be gathered together** Some corporations have a million or more stockholders. The sale of stock is a means of obtaining funds from the general public; both small and large investors find stock ownership a convenient means of participating in ownership of business enterprise.

2 **Limited liability** Creditors of a corporation have a claim against the assets of the corporation only, not against the personal property of the owners of the corporation. Since stockholders have no personal liability for the debts of the corporation, they can never lose more than the amount of their investment.

3 **Shares of stock in a corporation are readily transferable** The ease of disposing of all or part of one's stockholdings in a publicly owned corporation makes this form of investment particularly attractive.

4 **Continuous existence** A corporation is a separate legal entity with a perpetual existence. The continuous life of the corporation despite changes in ownership is made possible by the issuance of transferable shares of stock.

5 **Centralized authority** The power to make all kinds of operating decisions is lodged in the president of a corporation. The president may delegate to others limited authority for various phases of operations but retains final authority over the entire business.

6 **Professional management** The person who owns a few shares of stock in a large corporation usually has neither the time nor the knowledge of the business necessary for intelligent participation in operating problems. Because of this the functions of management and of ownership are sharply separated in the corporate form of organization, and the corporation is free to employ as executives the best managerial talent available.

Disadvantages of the corporate form of organization

Among the disadvantages of the corporation are:

1 **Heavy taxation** A corporation must pay a high rate of taxation on its income. If part of its net income is distributed to the owners in the form of dividends, the dividends are considered to be personal income to the stockholders and are subject to personal income tax. This practice of first taxing corporate income to the corporation and then taxing dividends to the stockholder is sometimes referred to as *double taxation.*

2 **Greater regulation** Corporations come into existence under the terms of state laws and these same laws may provide for considerable regulation of the corporation's activities. Also, large corporations have gradually come to accept the necessity for extensive public disclosure of their affairs.

3 **Separation of ownership and control** The separation of the functions of ownership and management may be an advantage in some cases but a disadvantage in others. On the whole, the excellent record of growth and earnings in most large corporations indicates that the separation of ownership and control has benefited rather than injured stockholders. In a few instances, however, a management group has chosen to operate a corporation for the benefit of insiders. The stockholders may find it difficult in such cases to take the concerted action necessary to oust the officers.

Formation of a corporation

To form a corporation, an application signed by at least three incorporators is submitted to the corporation commissioner (or other designated official) of the state in which the company is to be incorporated. The approved application contains the *articles of incorporation* and becomes the company *charter.* The incorporators (who have subscribed for capital stock and therefore are now stockholders) hold a meeting to elect *directors* and to pass *bylaws* as a guide to the company's affairs. The directors in turn hold a meeting at which officers of the corporation are appointed. Capital stock certificates are then issued and the formation of the corporation is complete.

ORGANIZATION COSTS The formation of a corporation is a much more costly step than the organization of a partnership. The necessary costs include the payment of an incorporation fee to the state, the payment of fees to attorneys for their services in drawing up the articles of incorporation, payments to promoters, and a variety of other outlays necessary to bring the corporation into existence. These costs are charged to an asset account called Organization Costs.

The incurring of these organization costs leads to the existence of the corporate entity; consequently, the benefits derived from these costs may be regarded as extending over the entire life of the corporation. Since the life of a corporation may continue indefinitely, one might argue that organization costs should be carried at the full amount until the corporation is liquidated. Because present income tax law permits organization costs to be written off over a period of five years or more, most companies elect to write off organization costs over a five-year period. Accountants have been willing to accept this practice, despite the lack of theoretical support, on the grounds that such costs usually are not material in relation to other assets.

RIGHTS OF STOCKHOLDERS The ownership of stock in a corporation usually carries the following basic rights:

1 To vote for directors, and thereby to be represented in the management of the business. The approval of a majority of stockholders may also be required for such important corporate actions as mergers and acquisitions, the selection of independent auditors, the incurring of long-term debts, the establishment of stock option plans, or the splitting of capital stock into a larger number of shares.

2 To share in profits by receiving dividends declared by the board of directors.

3 To share in the distribution of assets if the corporation is liquidated. When a corporation ends its existence, the creditors of the corporation must first be paid in full; any remaining assets are divided among stockholders in proportion to the number of shares owned.

4 To subscribe for additional shares in the event that the corporation decides to increase the amount of stock outstanding. This *preemptive right* entitles stockholders to maintain their percentages of ownership in the company by subscribing, in proportion to their present stockholdings, to any additional shares issued. Corporations organized in certain states do not grant preemptive rights to their stockholders. In other cases stockholders sometimes agree to waive their preemptive rights in order to grant more flexibility to management in negotiating mergers.

The ownership of stock does not give a stockholder the right to intervene in the management of a corporation or to transact business in its behalf. Although the stockholders as a group own the corporation, they do not personally own the assets of the corporation; neither do they personally owe the debts of the corporation. The stockholders have no direct claim on income earned; income earned by a corporation does not become income to the stockholders unless the board of directors orders the distribution of the income to stockholders in the form of a cash dividend.

Stockholders' meetings are usually held once a year. Each share of stock is entitled to one vote. In large corporations, these annual meetings are usually attended by relatively few persons, often by less than 1% of the stockholders. Prior to the meeting, the management group will request stockholders who do not plan to attend in person to send in *proxy statements* assigning their votes to the existing management. Through this use of the proxy system, management may secure the right to vote as much as, perhaps, 90% or more of the total outstanding shares.

FUNCTIONS OF THE BOARD OF DIRECTORS The primary functions of the board of directors are to manage the corporation and to protect the interests of the stockholders. At this level, management may consist principally of formulating policies and reviewing acts of the officers. Specific duties of the directors include declaring dividends, setting the salaries of officers, authorizing officers to arrange loans from banks, and authorizing important contracts of various kinds.

The extent of active participation in management by the board of directors varies widely from one company to another. In some corporations the officers also serve as directors and a meeting of directors may differ only in form from a conference of operating executives. In other corporations the board may consist of outsiders who devote little time to the corporation's affairs and merely meet occasionally to review and approve policies which have been formed and administered by the officers. In recent years increased importance has been attached to the need for electing as directors some individuals who were not officers of the company and who could thus have a view independent of that of active managers.

The official actions of the board are recorded in minutes of their meetings. The *minutes book* is the source of many of the accounting entries affecting the owners' equity accounts.

FUNCTIONS OF CORPORATE OFFICERS Corporate officers usually include a president, one or more vice-presidents, a controller, a treasurer, and a secretary. A vice-president is often made responsible for the sales function; other vice-presidents may be given responsibility for such important functions as personnel, finance, production, and research and development.

The responsibilities of the controller, treasurer, and secretary are most directly related to the accounting phase of business operation. The *controller,* or chief accounting officer, is responsible for the maintenance of adequate internal control and for the preparation of accounting records and financial statements. Such specialized activities as budgeting, tax planning, and preparation of tax returns are usually placed under the controller's jurisdiction. The *treasurer* has custody of the company's funds and is generally responsible for planning and controlling the company's cash position. The *secretary* represents the corporation in many contractual and legal matters and maintains minutes of the meetings of directors and stockholders. Another responsibility of the secretary is to coordinate the preparation of the annual report, which includes the financial statements and other information relating to corporate activities. In small corporations, one officer frequently acts as both secretary and treasurer. The following organization chart indicates lines of authority extending from stockholders to the directors to the president and other officers.

Typical corporate organization

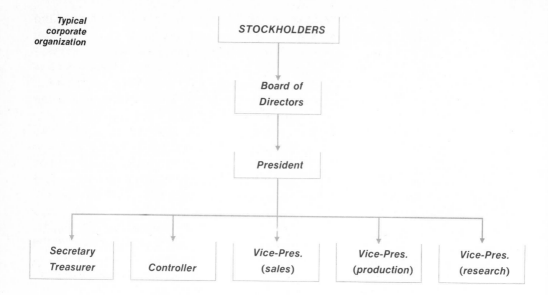

AUTHORIZATION AND ISSUANCE OF CAPITAL STOCK

The articles of incorporation specify the number of shares of capital stock which a corporation is authorized to issue and the *par value,* if any, per share. The corporation may secure authorization for a larger number of shares than presently needed. In future years, if more capital is needed, the previously authorized shares will be readily available for issue; otherwise, the corporation would be forced to apply to the state for permission to increase the number of authorized shares.

In previous chapters we have seen that corporations use separate owners' equity accounts (Capital Stock and Retained Earnings) to represent (*1*) the capital invested by the stockholders (called *paid-in capital*) and (2) the capital acquired and retained through profitable operations (earned capital).

Up to this point we have assumed that each of these two categories of stockholders' equity may be represented by a single ledger account. In this chapter we shall see that different classes of capital stock may be issued by a corporation and that capital stock may be issued at a price which differs from its par value. In these situations, additional ledger accounts will be necessary to show the various elements of stockholders' equity received from investors.

Par value

The chief significance of par value is that it represents the *legal capital* per share, that is, the amount below which stockholders' equity cannot be reduced except by (*1*) losses from business operations or (2) legal action taken by a majority vote of stockholders. A dividend cannot be declared by a corporation if such action would cause the stockholders' equity to fall below the par value of the outstanding shares. Par value, therefore, may be regarded as a minimum cushion of capital existing for the protection of creditors.

Par value may be $1 per share, $5, $100, or any other amount decided upon by the corporation. The par value of the stock is no indication of its market value; the par value merely indicates the amount per share to be entered in the Capital Stock account. The par value of most common stocks is relatively low. Polaroid Corporation common stock, for example, has a par value of $1; General Motors Corporation common stock has a par value of $1⅔; Avon Products stock has a par value of 50 cents per share. The market value of all these securities is far above their par value.

In an earlier period of the history of American corporations, all capital stock had par value, but in more recent years state laws have permitted corporations to choose between par value stock and no-par value stock. The corporate charter always states the par value, if any, of the shares to be issued.

Issuance of capital stock

Mere authorization of a stock issue does not bring an asset into existence, nor does it give the corporation any capital. The obtaining of authorization from the state for a stock issue merely affords a legal opportunity to obtain assets through the sale of stock.

When par value stock is *issued,* the Capital Stock account is credited with the par value of the shares issued, regardless of whether the issuance price is more or less than par. Assuming that 10,000 shares of $10 par value stock have been authorized and that 6,000 of these authorized shares are issued at a price of $10 each, Cash would be debited and Capital Stock would be credited for $60,000. When stock is sold for more than par value, the Capital Stock account is credited with the par value of the shares issued, and a separate account, Paid-in Capital in Excess of Par Value, is credited for the excess of selling price over par. If, for example, the issuance price is $15, the entry is as follows:

Stock-holders' investment in excess of par value	Cash	*90,000*
	Capital Stock	*60,000*
	Paid-in Capital in Excess of Par Value	*30,000*
	Issued 6,000 shares of $10 par value stock at a price of $15 a share.	

The amount received in excess of par value does not represent a profit to the corporation. It is part of the invested capital and it will be added to the capital stock in the balance sheet to show the total paid-in capital. The stockholders' equity section of the balance sheet would be as follows (the existence of $10,000 in retained earnings is assumed in order to present a complete illustration):

Stockholders' equity:

Capital stock, $10 par value, authorized 10,000 shares, issued and outstanding 6,000 shares	$ 60,000
Paid-in capital in excess of par value	30,000
Total paid-in capital	$ 90,000
Retained earnings	10,000
Total stockholders' equity	$100,000

If stock is issued by a corporation for less than par, the account Discount on Capital Stock should be debited for the difference between the issuance price and the par value. The issuance of stock at a discount is seldom encountered; it is illegal in many states.

No-par value stock

An understanding of no-par stock can best be gained by reviewing the reasons why par value was originally required in an earlier period of American corporate history. The use of the par value concept in state laws was intended for the protection of creditors and of public stockholders. In some states stock could not be issued at less than par value; in most states if stock was issued at less than par value the purchaser was contingently liable for the discount below par. Because of these statutes concerning par value, a creditor of a corporation could tell by inspection of the balance sheet the amount which owners had invested permanently in the corporation. This permanent investment of capital (par value times the number of outstanding shares) represented a buffer which protected the creditors of the corporation from the impact of any losses sustained by the corporation. Such protection for creditors was considered necessary because stockholders have no personal liability for the debts of the corporation.

The par value device proved rather ineffective in achieving its avowed objective of protecting creditors and stockholders, and most states later enacted legislation permitting corporations to issue stock without par value. With the advent of no-par stock, state legislatures attempted to continue the protection of corporate creditors by designating all or part of the amount received by the corporation for its no-par shares as **stated capital** not subject to withdrawal.

Assume that a corporation is organized in a state which permits the board of directors to establish a **stated value** on no-par stock, and that the board passed a resolution setting the stated value per share at $5. If a total of 80,000 shares were issued at $12 per share, the journal entry to record the issuance would be:

Note the
stated
value per
share

Cash		960,000
Capital Stock, $5 stated value		400,000
Paid-in Capital in Excess of Stated Value		560,000

Issued 80,000 shares of no-par value capital stock at $12 each.
Stated value set by directors at $5 per share.

In the absence of a stated value, the entire proceeds on the issuance of no-par stock would be credited to the Capital Stock account and would be viewed as legal capital. However, most companies which issue no-par capital stock do establish a stated value per share.

Preferred and common stock

In order to appeal to as many investors as possible, a corporation may issue more than one kind of capital stock, just as an automobile manu-facturer may make sedans, convertibles, and station wagons in order to appeal to various groups of car buyers. The basic type of capital stock issued by every corporation is called *common stock.* Common stock has the four basic rights previously mentioned. Whenever these rights are modified, the term *preferred stock* (or sometimes Class B Common) is used to describe this second type of stock. A few corporations issue two or three classes of preferred stock, each class having certain distinctive features designed to interest a particular type of investor. In summary, we may say that every business corporation has common stock; a good many corporations also issue preferred stock; and some companies have two or more types of preferred stock.

Common stock may be regarded as the basic, residual element of ownership. It carries voting rights and, therefore, is the means of exer-cising control over the business. Common stock has unlimited possibili-ties of increase in value; during periods of business expansion the market prices of common stocks of some leading corporations may rise to two or three times their former values. On the other hand, common stocks lose value more rapidly than other types of securities when corporations encounter periods of unprofitable business.

The following stockholders' equity section illustrates the balance sheet presentation for a corporation having both preferred and common stock; note that the item of retained earnings is not apportioned between the two groups of stockholders.

Balance
sheet
presentation

Stockholders' equity:

8% cumulative preferred stock, $100 par value, authorized and issued 100,000 shares	$10,000,000
Common stock, $5 par value, authorized and issued 1 million shares	5,000,000
Retained earnings	3,500,000
Total stockholders' equity	$18,500,000

CHARACTERISTICS OF PREFERRED STOCK Most preferred stocks have the following distinctive features:

1 Preferred as to dividends

2 Preferred as to assets in event of the liquidation of the company

3 Callable at the option of the corporation

4 No voting power

Another very important but less common feature is a clause permitting the *conversion* of preferred stock into common at the option of the holder. Preferred stocks vary widely with respect to the special rights and privileges granted. Careful study of the terms of the individual preferred stock contract is a necessary step in the evaluation of any preferred stock.

Stock preferred as to dividends Stock preferred as to dividends is entitled to receive each year a dividend of specified amount before any dividend is paid on the common stock. The dividend is usually stated as a dollar amount per share. For example, the balance sheet of General Motors Corporation shows two types of preferred stock outstanding, one paying $5.00 a year and the other $3.75 a year, as shown below:

Dividend stated as dollar amount

Capital stock:

Preferred, without par value (authorized 6 million shares):

$5.00 series; stated value $100 per share, redeemable at $120 per share, outstanding 1,835,644 shares	*$183,564,400*
$3.75 series; stated value $100 per share, redeemable at $101 per share, outstanding 1,000,000 shares	*100,000,000*

Some preferred stocks state the dividend preference as a percentage of par value. For example, a 9% preferred stock with a par value of $100 per share would mean that $9 must be paid yearly on each share of preferred stock before any dividends are paid on the common. An example of the percentage method of stating the dividend on a preferred stock is found in the balance sheet of Georgia-Pacific Corporation:

Dividend stated as percentage

Capital stock:

Preferred, $5\frac{1}{2}$% cumulative, par value $100 per share	*$10,000,000*

The holders of preferred stock have no assurance that they will always receive the indicated dividend. A corporation is obligated to pay dividends to stockholders only when the board of directors declares a dividend. Dividends must be paid on preferred stock before anything is paid to the common stockholders, but if the corporation is not prospering, it may decide not to pay dividends on either preferred or common stock. For a corporation to pay dividends, profits must be earned and cash must be available. However, preferred stocks in general offer more assurance of regular dividend payments than do common stocks.

Cumulative preferred stock   The dividend preference carried by most preferred stocks is a *cumulative* one. If all or any part of the regular dividend on the preferred stock is omitted in a given year, the amount *in arrears* must be paid in a subsequent year before any dividend can be paid on the common stock. Assume that a corporation was organized January 1, Year 1, with 1,000 shares of $4 cumulative preferred stock and 1,000 shares of common stock. Dividends paid in Year 1 were at the rate of $4 per share of preferred stock and $3 per share of common. In Year 2, earnings declined sharply and the only dividend paid was $1 per share on the preferred stock. No dividends were paid in Year 3. What is the status of the preferred stock at December 31, Year 3? Dividends are in arrears in the amount of $7 a share ($3 omitted during Year 2 and $4 omitted in Year 3). On the entire issue of 1,000 shares of preferred stock, the dividends in arrears amount to $7,000.

In Year 4, we shall assume that the company earned large profits and wished to pay dividends on both the preferred and common stocks. Before paying a dividend on the common, the corporation must pay the $7,000 in arrears on the cumulative preferred stock plus the regular $4 a share applicable to the current year. The preferred stockholders would, therefore, receive a total of $11,000 in dividends in Year 4; the board of directors would then be free to declare dividends on the common stock.

Dividends in arrears *are not listed among the liabilities of a corporation,* because no liability exists until a dividend is declared by the board of directors. Nevertheless, the amount of any dividends in arrears on preferred stock is an important factor to investors and should always be disclosed. This disclosure is usually made by a note accompanying the balance sheet such as the following:

"As of December 31, Year 3, dividends on the $4 cumulative preferred stock were in arrears to the extent of $7 per share and amounted in total to $7,000."

For a *noncumulative preferred stock,* any unpaid or omitted dividend is lost forever. Because of this factor, investors view the noncumulative feature as an unfavorable element, and very few noncumulative preferred stocks exist.

Participating clauses in preferred stock   Because participating preferred stocks are seldom issued, discussion of them will be brief. A fully participating preferred stock is one which, in addition to the regular specified dividend, is entitled to participate with the common stock in any additional dividends paid. For example, a $5 fully participating preferred stock would be entitled to receive $5 a share before the common stock received anything. After $5 a share had been paid to the preferred stockholders, a $5 dividend could be paid on the common stock. If the company desired to pay an additional dividend to the common, say, an extra $3 per share, the preferred stock would also be entitled to receive an extra $3 dividend. In brief, a fully participating preferred stock participates dollar for dollar with the common stock in any dividends paid in excess of the stated rate on the preferred stock.

Stock preferred as to assets   Most preferred stocks carry a preference as to assets in the event of liquidation of the corporation. If the business is terminated, the preferred stock is entitled to payment in full of its par value or a higher stated liquidation value before any payment is made on the common stock. This priority also includes any dividends in arrears.

Callable preferred stock   Most preferred stocks are callable at the option of the corporation at a stipulated price, usually slightly above the issuance price. The *call price* or *redemption price* for a $100 par value preferred stock is often $103 or $104 per share.

In the financing of a new or expanding corporation, the organizers usually hold common stock, which assures them control of the company because only the common stock has voting rights. However, it is often necessary to obtain outside capital. One way of doing this, without the loss of control or any serious reduction in possible future earnings on the common stock, is to issue a callable preferred stock.

It may be argued that the position of the holders of a callable preferred stock is more like that of creditors than that of owners. They supply capital to the company for an agreed rate of return, have no voice in management, and may find their relationship with the company terminated at any time through the calling in of their certificates. If a company is so fortunate as to enter upon a period of unusually high earnings, it will probably increase the dividend payments on its common stock, but it will not consider increasing the dividends paid to the preferred stockholders. On the contrary, the corporation may decide that this era of prosperity is a good time to eliminate the preferred stock through exercise of the call provision.

Regardless of the fact that preferred stock lacks many of the traditional aspects of ownership, it is universal practice to include all types of preferred stock in the stockholders' equity section of the balance sheet.

Convertible preferred stock   In order to add to the attractiveness of preferred stock as an investment, corporations sometimes offer a conversion privilege which entitles the preferred stockholders to exchange their shares for common stock in a stipulated ratio. If the corporation prospers, its common stock will probably rise in market value, and dividends on the common stock will probably be increased. The investor who buys a convertible preferred stock rather than common stock has greater assurance of regular dividends. In addition, through the conversion privilege, the investor is assured of sharing in any substantial increase in value of the company's common stock.

As an example, assume that the Remington Corporation issued a 5%, $100 par, convertible preferred stock on January 1, at a price of $100 a share. Each share was convertible into four shares of the company's $10 par value common stock at any time. The common stock had a market price of $20 a share on January 1, and an annual dividend of 60 cents a share was being paid. The yield on the preferred stock was 5% ($5 ÷ $100); the yield on the common stock was only 3% ($0.60 ÷ $20).

During the next few years, the Remington Corporation's earnings increased, the dividend on the common stock was raised to an annual rate of $1.50, and the market price of the common stock rose to $40 a share. At this point the preferred stock would have a market value of at least $160, since it could be converted at any time into four shares of common stock with a market value of $40 each. In other words, the market value of a convertible preferred stock will tend to move in accordance with the price of the common. When the dividend rate is increased on the common stock, some holders of the preferred stock may convert their holdings into common stock in order to obtain a higher cash return on their investments.

If the holder of 100 shares of the preferred stock presented these shares for conversion, the Remington Corporation would make the following journal entry:

Conversion of preferred stock into common	*5% Convertible Preferred Stock*	*10,000*	
	Common Stock		*4,000*
	Paid-in Capital in Excess of Par Value		*6,000*

To record the conversion of 100 shares of preferred stock, par $100, into 400 shares of $10 par value common stock.

Note that the issue price recorded for the 400 shares of common stock is based upon the carrying value of the preferred stock in the accounting records, not upon market prices at the date of conversion.

The preceding illustration was based on the assumption that the Remington Corporation enjoyed larger earnings after the issuance of its convertible preferred. Let us now make a contrary assumption and say that shortly after issuance of the convertible preferred stock, the company's profits declined and the directors deemed it necessary to cut the annual dividend on the common stock from 60 cents a share to 20 cents a share. Stockholders who acquired common stock at a cost of $20 a share now find that their dividend income has dropped to a rate of 1% ($0.20 ÷ $20 cost). The dividend on the preferred stock remains at $5 a share.

These two illustrations indicate that the convertible preferred stock has two important advantages from the viewpoint of the investor: It increases in value along with the common stock when the company prospers, and it offers greater assurance of steady dividend income during a period of poor earnings.

The underwriting of stock issues

When a large amount of stock is to be issued, the corporation will probably utilize the services of an investment banking firm, frequently referred to as an *underwriter.* The underwriter guarantees the issuing corporation a specific price for the stock and makes a profit by selling the stock to the investing public at a higher price. For example, an issue of 1,270,000 shares of $1 par value common stock might be sold to the public at a price of $47 a share, of which $2.35 a share is retained by the underwriter and $44.65 represents the net proceeds to the issuing corporation.[1] The corporation would enter in its accounts only the net amount received from the underwriter ($44.65) for each share issued. The use of an underwriter assures the corporation that the entire stock issue will be sold without delay, and the entire amount of funds to be raised will be available on a specific date.

Market price of common stock

The preceding sections concerning the issuance of stock at prices above and below par value raise a question as to how the market price of stock is determined. The price which the corporation sets on a new issue of stock is based on several factors including (1) an appraisal of the company's expected future earnings, (2) the probable dividend rate per share, (3) the present financial position of the company, and (4) the current state of the investment market.

After the stock has been issued, the price at which it will be traded among investors will rise and fall in response to all the forces of the marketplace. The market price per share will tend to reflect the progress of the company, with primary emphasis being placed on earnings and dividends per share. *Earnings per share* of common stock, for example, is computed by dividing the annual net income available to the common stock by the number of shares outstanding. At this point in our discussion, the significant fact to emphasize is that market price is not related to par value, and that it tends to reflect current and future earnings and dividends. (Earnings per share is discussed in some detail in Chapter 8.)

---

[1] These figures are taken from a prospectus issued by Levi Strauss & Co. covering the issuance of 1,070,000 shares by the corporation and 200,000 shares by stockholders in an initial public offering by the corporation. Figures taken from the face of the prospectus follow:

	Price to Public	Underwriting Discounts and Commissions*	Proceeds to the Company†	Proceeds to Selling Stockholders
Per share	$47.00	$2.35	$44.65	$44.65
Total	$59,690,000	$2,984,500	$47,775,500	$8,930,000

*The Company has agreed to indemnify the Underwriters against certain liabilities under the Securities Act of 1933.
†Before deducting expenses payable by the Company estimated at $200,000.

Stock issued for assets other than cash

Corporations generally sell their capital stock for cash and use the cash obtained in this way to buy the various types of assets needed in the business. Sometimes, however, a corporation may issue shares of its capital stock in a direct exchange for land, buildings, or other assets. Stock may also be issued in payment for services rendered by attorneys and promoters in the formation of the corporation.

When a corporation issues capital stock in exchange for services or for assets other than cash, a question arises as to the proper valuation of the property or services received. For example, assume that a corporation issues 1,000 shares of its $1 par value common stock in exchange for a tract of land. A problem may exist in determining the fair market value of the land, and consequently in determining the amount received for the stock. If there is no direct evidence of the value of the land, we may value it by using indirect evidence as to the alternative amount of cash for which the shares might have been sold. Assume that the company's stock is listed on a stock exchange and is presently selling at $90 a share. The 1,000 shares which the corporation exchanged for the land could have been sold for $90,000 cash, and the cash could have been used to pay for the land. The direct exchange of stock for land may be considered as the equivalent of selling the stock for cash and using the cash to buy the land. It is therefore logical to say that the cost of the land to the company was $90,000, the market value of the stock given in exchange for the land. *Note that the par value of the stock is not any indication of the fair value of the stock or of the land.*

Once the valuation question has been decided, the entry to record the issuance of stock in exchange for noncash assets can be made as follows:

How were	*Land*	*90,000*	
dollar	*Common Stock*		*1,000*
amounts			
determined?	*Paid-in Capital in Excess of Par Value*		*89,000*

To record the issuance of 1,000 shares of $1 par value common stock in exchange for land. Current market value of stock ($90 a share) used as basis for valuing the land.

Subscriptions to capital stock

Small corporations sometimes sell stock on a subscription plan, in which the investor agrees to pay the subscription price at a future date or in a series of installments. For example, Subscriptions Receivable: Common would be debited and Common Stock Subscribed would be credited when the subscription contract was signed. Collections would be credited to Subscriptions Receivable: Common; when the entire subscription price had been collected and the stock issued, Common Stock Subscribed would be debited and Common Stock would be credited. The following illustration demonstrates the accounting procedures for stock subscriptions.

In this example, 10,000 shares of $10 par value stock are subscribed at a price of $15. Subscriptions for 6,000 of these shares are then collected in full. A partial payment is received on the other 4,000 shares.

Subscription price above par

Subscriptions Receivable: Common	150,000	
Common Stock Subscribed		100,000
Paid-in Capital in Excess of Par Value		50,000
Received subscriptions for 10,000 shares of $10 par value stock		
at price of $15 a share.		

When the subscriptions for 6,000 shares are collected in full, certificates for 6,000 shares will be issued. The following entries are made:

Certificates issued for fully paid shares

Cash	90,000	
Subscriptions Receivable: Common		90,000
Collected subscriptions in full for 6,000 shares at $15 each.		

Common Stock Subscribed	60,000	
Common Stock		60,000
Issued certificates for 6,000 fully paid $10 par value shares.		

The subscriber to the remaining 4,000 shares paid only half of the amount of the subscription but promised to pay the remainder within a month. Stock certificates will not be issued until the subscription is collected in full, but the partial collection is recorded by the following entry:

Partial collection of subscription

Cash	30,000	
Subscriptions Receivable: Common		30,000
Collected partial payment on subscription for 4,000 shares.		

From the corporation's point of view, Subscriptions Receivable is a current asset, which ordinarily will be collected within a short time. If financial statements are prepared between the date of obtaining subscriptions and the date of issuing the stock, the Common Stock Subscribed account will appear in the stockholders' equity section of the balance sheet.

Retained earnings or deficit

Capital provided to a corporation by stockholders in exchange for shares of either preferred or common stock is called paid-in capital, or contributed capital. The second major type of stockholders' equity is retained earnings. The amount of the Retained Earnings account at any balance sheet date represents the accumulated earnings of the company since the date of incorporation, minus any losses and minus all dividends distributed to stockholders.

For a corporation with $1,000,000 of paid-in capital and $600,000 of retained earnings, the stockholders' equity section of the balance sheet may appear as follows:

Paid-in capital and earned capital

Stockholders' equity:	
Capital stock, $10 par value, 100,000 shares authorized,	
20,000 shares issued	$ 200,000
Paid-in capital in excess of par value	800,000
Total paid-in capital	$1,000,000
Retained earnings	600,000
Total stockholders' equity	$1,600,000

If this same company had been unprofitable and incurred losses of $300,000 since its organization, the stockholders' equity section of the balance sheet would be as follows:

Paid-in capital reduced by losses incurred

Stockholders' equity:	
Capital stock, $10 par value, 100,000 shares authorized,	
20,000 shares issued	$ 200,000
Paid-in capital in excess of par value	800,000
Total paid-in capital	$1,000,000
Less: Deficit	300,000
Total stockholders' equity	$ 700,000

This second illustration tells us that $300,000 of the original $1,000,000 invested by stockholders has been lost. Note that the presentation of total paid-in capital in both illustrations remains at the fixed amount of $1,000,000, the stockholders' original investment. The accumulated profits or losses since the organization of the corporation are shown as *retained earnings* or as a *deficit* and are not intermingled with the paid-in capital. The term *deficit* indicates a negative amount of retained earnings.

Special records of corporations

The financial page of today's newspaper reports that the most actively traded stocks on the New York Stock Exchange today were the following:

Today's stock market

	Number of Shares Sold	Closing Price
Texaco	340,200	$25\frac{3}{8}$
General Electric	282,500	$52\frac{1}{2}$
General Motors	179,300	65

The three corporations listed did not necessarily buy or sell any shares of their stock today. The quantities of shares listed above were probably sold by existing stockholders to other investors. When a corporation first issues its stock, the transaction is between the corporation and the investor; once the stock is outstanding, most further stock transactions are between individuals and do not affect the corporation which issued the stock.[2] However, the corporation must be informed of each such stock transaction so that it can correct its records of stock ownership by eliminating the name of the former owner and adding the name of the new owner.

STOCK CERTIFICATES Ownership of a corporation is evidenced by stock certificates. A large corporation with stock listed on an organized stock exchange usually has many millions of shares outstanding and may have several hundred thousand stockholders. The number of shares changing hands on a typical business day may be as many as 200,000 to 300,000 shares. Exxon Corporation, for example, has over 200 million shares of stock outstanding. These shares are owned by approximately 700,000 investors. (The term *investor* as used in this discussion is meant to include investment groups or entities such as pension funds, investment clubs, and similar organizations, as well as individual investors.)

A stock certificate and the related stub are shown on page 297. This certificate is ready to be detached from the stub and delivered to the shareholder, Richard Warren. Note that the certificate has been signed by the officers of the company and that the following information is listed on both the certificate and the stub:

Certificate number	*901*
Name of shareholder	*Richard Warren*
Number of shares	*100*
Date issued	*Jan. 10, 1978*
Type of stock	*Common*

The certificate is now detached from the stub and delivered to Richard Warren. The open stubs in the certificate book (stubs without any certificates attached) represent outstanding certificates. If a stockholder sells his or her shares, the certificate is returned to the company, canceled, and attached to the corresponding stub in the stock certificate book. The total number of shares of stock outstanding at any time can be determined by adding up the number of shares listed on all the open stubs.

STOCKHOLDERS' LEDGER For a company with a large number of stockholders, it is not practicable to include in the general ledger an account with each stockholder. Instead a single controlling account entitled Common Stock is carried in the general ledger and a subsidiary stockholders' ledger with individual stockholders is maintained. In this stock-

---

[2] A corporation may reacquire some of its own shares by purchase in the open market. Shares reacquired by a corporation are called *treasury stock* (see Chap. 8).

Certificate No. 901	Certificate No. 901	−100− Shares

Certificate No.   901

For ....−100−.......... Shares
Of the Common Stock of
The Gold Cup Corporation

ISSUED TO:
    Richard Warren

Date.. January 10, 1978

FROM WHOM TRANSFERRED:

    −−Original issue−−

No. of Original Certificate	No. of Original Shares	No. of Shares Transferred

Certificate No.   901   −100− Shares

THE GOLD CUP CORPORATION

Par Value $5 per Share Common Stock
Incorporated under the Laws of the State of California

THIS IS TO CERTIFY that   Richard Warren
is the owner of ....−one hundred−.... fully paid and non-
assessable shares of the common capital stock of The Gold
Cup Corporation, transferable only on the books of this corporation by the said owner hereof in person or by attorney,
upon surrender of this certificate properly endorsed.
    Witness the seal of the corporation and the signatures
of its duly authorized officers on this ....−10th−.... day of
  −January−...., 1978

THE GOLD CUP CORPORATION
INCORPORATED
1967

Murray Whitehall
President

Byron Bannock
Secretary

holders' ledger, each stockholder's account shows the number of shares which he or she owns, the certificate numbers, and the dates of acquisition and sale. Entries are not made in dollars but in number of shares.

The stockholders' ledger contains essentially the same information as the stock certificate book, but the arrangement of the information is in an alphabetical listing of stockholders rather than in the sequence of stock certificate numbers. One stockholder may own a number of certificates, acquired at various dates. The entire holdings of any one stockholder would be summarized in one account in the stockholders' ledger.

STOCK TRANSFER AGENT AND STOCK REGISTRAR The large corporation with thousands of stockholders and a steady flow of stock transfers usually turns over the function of maintaining capital stock records to an independent stock transfer agent and a stock registrar. A bank or trust company serves as stock transfer agent and another bank acts as the stock registrar. When certificates are to be transferred from one owner to another, the certificates are sent to the transfer agent, who cancels them, makes the necessary entries in the stockholders' ledger, and signs new certificates which are forwarded to the stock registrar. The function of the registrar is to prevent any improper issuance of stock certificates.

Income taxes in corporate financial statements

A corporation is a legal entity subject to corporation income tax; consequently, the ledger of a corporation should include accounts for recording income taxes. No such accounts are needed for a business organized as a single proprietorship or partnership.

Income taxes are based on a corporation's earnings. At year-end, before preparing financial statements, income taxes are recorded by an adjusting entry such as the following:

Recording corporate income taxes

Income Taxes Expense	*45,650*	
Income Taxes Payable		*45,650*
To record the income taxes payable for the year ended		
Dec. 31, 19____.		

The account debited in this entry, Income Taxes Expense, is an expense account and usually appears as the very last deduction in the income statement as follows:

Final step in income statement

Income before income taxes	*$100,000*
Income taxes	*45,650*
Net income	*$ 54,350*

The liability account, Income Taxes Payable, will ordinarily be paid within a few months and should, therefore, appear in the current liability section of the balance sheet. More detailed discussion of corporation taxes is presented in Chapter 17.

Balance sheet for a corporation illustrated

A fairly complete corporation balance sheet is presented on page 299. In studying this balance sheet, the student should bear in mind that current practice includes many alternatives in the choice of terminology and the arrangement of items in financial statements. Some of these alternatives are illustrated in the Appendix at the end of this book.

DEL RIO CORPORATION
Balance Sheet
December 31, Year 10

Assets

Current assets:

Cash		$ 305,600
U.S. government securities, at cost (market value $812,800)		810,000
Accounts receivable (net of allowance for doubtful accounts)		1,165,200
Subscriptions receivable: preferred stock		50,000
Inventories (lower of fifo cost or market)		1,300,800
Short-term prepayments		125,900
Total current assets		$3,757,500
Investments: Common stock of Price Corporation		444,900

Plant and equipment:

Land		$ 500,000	
Buildings	$2,482,100		
Less: Accumulated depreciation	400,000	2,082,100	
Equipment	$1,800,000		
Less: Accumulated depreciation	800,000	1,000,000	3,582,100
Intangibles: Patents and trademarks			110,000
Total assets			$7,894,500

Liabilities & Stockholders' Equity

Current liabilities:

Accounts payable		$1,037,800
Income taxes payable		324,300
Dividends payable		70,000
Interest payable		20,000
Total current liabilities		$1,452,100
Long-term liabilities: Bonds payable, 8%, due Oct. 1, Year 20		1,000,000
Total liabilities		$2,452,100

Stockholders' equity:

Cumulative 5% preferred stock, $100 par, authorized 10,000 shares:

8,000 shares issued	$ 800,000	
2,000 shares subscribed	200,000	$1,000,000

Common stock, $1 par, authorized

1,000,000 shares: 600,000 shares issued	600,000	
Paid-in capital in excess of par: common	2,200,000	
Total paid-in capital	$3,800,000	
Retained earnings	1,642,400	
Total stockholders' equity		5,442,400
Total liabilities & stockholders' equity		$7,894,500

KEY TERMS INTRODUCED OR EMPHASIZED IN CHAPTER 7

Board of directors Persons elected by common stockholders to direct the affairs of a corporation.

Call price The price to be paid by a corporation for each share of callable preferred stock if the corporation decides to call (redeem) the preferred stock.

Capital stock Transferable units of ownership in a corporation. A broad term which may refer to common stock, preferred stock, or both.

Common stock A type of capital stock which possesses the basic rights of ownership including the right to vote. Represents the residual element of ownership in a corporation.

Convertible preferred stock Preferred stock which entitles the owner to exchange his or her shares for common stock in a specified ratio.

Corporation A business organized as a legal entity separate from its owners. Chartered by the state with ownership divided into shares of transferable stock. Stockholders are not liable for debts of the corporation.

Cumulative preferred stock A class of stock with a provision that if dividends are reduced or omitted in any year, this amount accumulates and must be paid prior to payment of dividends on the common stock.

Deficit Accumulated losses incurred by a corporation. A negative amount of retained earnings.

Dividend A distribution of cash by a corporation to its stockholders.

Drawing account The account used to record the withdrawals of cash or other assets by the owner (or owners) of an unincorporated business. Closed at the end of the period by transferring its balance to the owner's capital account.

Limited liability An important characteristic of the corporate form of organization. The corporation as a separate legal entity is responsible for its own debts; the stockholders are not personally liable for the corporation's debts.

Minutes book Formal record of official actions taken in meetings of stockholders and of the board of directors.

Mutual agency Authority of each partner to act as agent for the partnership within its normal scope of operations and to enter into contracts which bind the partnership.

No-par stock Stock without par value. Usually has a stated value which is similar to par value.

Organization costs Costs incurred to form a corporation.

Paid-in capital The amounts invested in a corporation by its stockholders.

Partnership An association of two or more persons to carry on as co-owners a business for profits.

Par value The legal capital of a corporation. Also the face amount of a share of capital stock. Represents the minimum amount per share to be invested in the corporation when shares are originally issued.

Preferred stock A class of capital stock usually having preferences as to dividends and in the distribution of assets in event of liquidation.

Retained earnings That portion of stockholders' equity resulting from profits earned and retained in the business.

Single proprietorship An unincorporated business owned by one person.

Stated capital That portion of capital invested by stockholders which cannot be withdrawn. Provides protection for creditors. Also called *legal capital.*

Statement of partners' capitals An annual financial statement which shows for each partner and for the firm the amounts of beginning capitals, additional investments, net income, drawings, and ending capitals.

Stock certificate A document issued by a corporation as evidence of the ownership of the number of shares stated on the certificate.

Stock registrar An independent fiscal agent, usually a large bank, retained by a corporation to control the issuance of stock certificates and provide assurance against overissuance.

Stock transfer agent A bank or trust company retained by a corporation to maintain its records of capital stock ownership and make transfers from one investor to another.

Stockholders' ledger A subsidiary record showing the number of shares owned by each stockholder.

Subscriptions to capital stock Formal promises to buy shares of stock from a corporation with payment at a later date. Stock certificates delivered when full payment received.

Underwriter An investment banking firm which handles the sale of a corporation's stock to the public.

DEMONSTRATION PROBLEM FOR YOUR REVIEW

At the close of the current year, the stockholders' equity section of the Rockhurst Corporation's balance sheet appeared as follows:

Stockholders' equity:

$1.50 preferred stock, $25 par value, authorized 1,500,000 shares:		
Issued	*$10,800,000*	
Subscribed	*5,400,000*	*$16,200,000*
Common stock, no par, $5 stated value, authorized		
6,000,000 shares		*12,300,000*
Paid-in capital in excess of par or stated value:		
On preferred stock	*$ 810,000*	
On common stock	*7,626,000*	*8,436,000*
Retained earnings (deficit)		*(600,000)*
Total stockholders' equity		*$36,336,000*

Among the assets of the corporation appears the following item: Subscriptions Receivable: Preferred, $1,123,200.

Instructions On the basis of this information, write a brief answer to the following questions, showing any necessary supporting computations.
a How many shares of preferred and common stock have been issued?
b How many shares of preferred stock have been subscribed?
c What was the average price per share received (including stock subscribed) by the corporation on its preferred stock?
d What was the average price per share received by the corporation on its common stock?
e What is the average amount per share that subscribers of preferred stock have yet to pay on their subscriptions?
f What is the total paid-in capital including stock subscribed?
g What is the total legal or stated value of the capital stock including stock subscribed?

SOLUTION TO DEMONSTRATION PROBLEM

a *Preferred stock issued* <u>432,000 shares</u> *($10,800,000 ÷ $25)*

Common stock issued <u>2,460,000 shares</u> *($12,300,000 ÷ $5)*

b *Preferred stock subscribed* <u>216,000 shares</u> *($5,400,000 ÷ $25)*

c *Preferred stock par value ($10,800,000 + $5,400,000)* $16,200,000
   Paid-in capital in excess of par   810,000
     Total paid-in and subscribed $17,010,000
   Total shares (432,000 + 216,000)   648,000
   Average price per share ($17,010,000 ÷ 648,000 as
   computed in a and b). **$26.25**

d *Common stock stated value* $12,300,000
   Paid-in capital in excess of par   7,626,000
     Total paid in. $19,926,000
   Total shares (see a)   2,460,000
   Average price per share ($19,926,000 ÷ 2,460,000) **$8.10**

e *Subscriptions receivable, preferred* . . . . $ 1,123,200
   Shares subscribed   216,000
   Average price per share ($1,123,200 ÷ 216,000). **$5.20**

f <u>$36,936,000</u> *(preferred $16,200,000 + common $12,300,000 +*

paid-in capital in excess of par or stated value $8,436,000)

g <u>$28,500,000</u> *(preferred $16,200,000 + common $12,300,000)*

REVIEW QUESTIONS

1 Is it possible that a partnership agreement containing interest and salary allowances as a step toward distributing income could cause a partnership net loss to be distributed so that one partner's capital account would be decreased by more than the amount of the entire partnership net loss?

2 Jane Miller is the proprietor of a small manufacturing business. She is considering the possibility of joining in partnership with Sarah Bracken, whom she considers to be thoroughly competent and congenial. Prepare a brief statement outlining the advantages and disadvantages of the potential partnership to Miller.

3 Scott has land having a book value of $5,000 and a fair market value of $8,000, and a building having a book value of $50,000 and a fair market value of $40,000. The land and building become Scott's sole capital contribution to a partnership. What is Scott's capital balance in the new partnership? Why?

4 Partner Tom Jones withdraws $25,000 from a partnership during the year. When the financial statements are prepared at the end of the year, Jones's share of the partnership income is $15,000. Which amount must Jones report on his income tax return?

5 Partner John Young has a choice to make. He has been offered by the partners a choice between no salary allowance and a one-third share in the partnership income or a salary of $6,000 per year and a one-quarter share of residual profits. Write a brief memorandum explaining the factors to be considered in reaching a decision.

6 What factors should be considered in drawing up an agreement as to the way in which income shall be shared by two or more partners?

7 What factors should be considered when comparing the net income figure of a partnership to that of a corporation of similar size?

8 State the effect of each of the transactions given below on a partner's capital or drawing accounts:

a Partner borrows cash from the business and signs a promissory note.

b Partner collects a partnership account receivable while on vacation and uses the cash for personal purposes.

c Partner receives in cash the salary allowance provided in the partnership agreement.

d Partner takes home merchandise (cost $100; selling price $125) for personal use.

e Partner has loaned money to the partnership. The loan, together with interest at 8%, is now repaid to the partner in cash.

9 Distinguish between corporations and partnerships in terms of the following characteristics:

a Owners' liability

b Transferability of ownership interest

c Continuity of existence

d Federal taxation on income

10 What are the basic rights of the owner of a share of corporate stock? In what way are these basic rights commonly modified with respect to the owner of a share of preferred stock?

11 Describe three kinds of costs that may be incurred in the process of *organizing* a corporation. How are such expenditures treated for accounting purposes? Why?

12 Distinguish between *paid-in capital* and *retained earnings* of a corporation. Why is such a distinction useful?

13 Smith owns 200 of the 8,000 shares of common stock issued and outstanding in X Company. The company issued 2,000 additional shares of stock. What is Smith's position with respect to the new issue if he is entitled to preemptive rights?

14 In theory, a corporation may sell its stock for an amount greater or less than par value; in practice, stock is seldom if ever issued for less than par. Explain the significance of par value and why shares are seldom issued for less than par.

15 When stock is issued by a corporation in exchange for assets other than cash, accountants face the problem of determining the dollar amount at which to record the transaction. Discuss the factors they should consider and explain their significance.

16 Rosemead Company sold 300,000 shares of no-par common stock through underwriters at $21 per share. The company paid $408,000 in underwriting discounts and commissions, thus receiving only $5,892,000. In addition, the company paid other costs of $82,000 in connection with the underwriting.

a What benefits did the company receive from the $490,000 of costs and how should these costs be reported in the balance sheet?

b Is this a steep price to pay for new financing by an established company?

17 State the classification (asset, liability, stockholders' equity, revenue, or expense) of each of the following accounts:

a Subscriptions receivable: common stock

b Capital stock

     c Retained earnings
     d Common stock subscribed
     e Paid-in capital in excess of par
     f Income taxes

18 Explain the following terms:
     a Stock transfer agent   **d** Minutes book
     b Stockholders' ledger   **e** Stock registrar
     c Underwriter

19 Describe the usual nature of the following features as they apply to a share of preferred stock:
     a Cumulative
     b Participating
     c Convertible
     d Callable

EXERCISES

Ex. 7-1 A business owned by John Rogers was short of cash and Rogers therefore decided to form a partnership with Steve Wilson, who was able to contribute cash to the new partnership. The assets contributed by Rogers appeared as follows in the balance sheet of his business: cash, $900; accounts receivable, $18,900, with an allowance for doubtful accounts of $600; inventory, $42,000; and store equipment, $15,000. Rogers had recorded depreciation of $1,500 during his use of the store equipment in his single proprietorship.

    Rogers and Wilson agreed that the allowance for doubtful accounts was inadequate and should be $1,000. They also agreed that a fair value for the inventory was its replacement cost of $46,000 and that the fair value of the store equipment was $12,000. You are to open the partnership accounts by making a general journal entry to record the investment by Rogers.

Ex. 7-2 On July 31, 19____, A and B agreed to combine their single proprietorships into a partnership. The partnership will take over all assets and assume all liabilities of A and B. The balance sheets for A and B are shown below:

	A's Business		B's Business	
	Book Value	**Fair Value**	**Book Value**	**Fair Value**
Assets				
Cash	$ 2,500	$ 2,500	$ 9,000	$ 9,000
Accounts receivable . . .	12,000	11,600	30,000	29,000
Inventory	18,000	20,400	40,000	35,000
Equipment (net)	23,000	23,500	62,000	76,200
Total	$55,500	$58,000	$141,000	$149,200
Liabilities & Owners' Capital				
Accounts payable	$20,500	$20,500	$ 39,500	$ 41,000
Accrued wages payable .	600	600	1,000	1,000
A, capital	34,400	36,900		
B, capital			100,500	107,200
Total	$55,500	$58,000	$141,000	$149,200

Accounts receivable of $1,400 are written off as uncollectible. This write-off explains the difference in amounts and accounts receivable shown in the Book Value and Fair Value column. The book value of B's accounts payable was less than fair value because liabilities of $1,500 had not been recorded.

Prepare a *classified* balance sheet in good form for the new entity of A-B Company immediately following formation of the partnership.

Ex. 7-3 Marsh and Nelson form a partnership by investing $40,000 and $60,000, respectively. Determine how the first year's net income of $45,000 would be divided under each of the following assumptions:

a The partnership agreement does not mention profit sharing.

b Net income to be divided in the ratio of the original investments.

c Interest at 8% to be allowed on original capital investments and balance to be divided equally.

d Salaries of $18,000 to Marsh and $15,000 to Nelson, balance to be divided equally.

e Interest at 9% to be allowed on original capital investments, salaries of $18,000 to Marsh and $15,000 to Nelson, balance to be divided equally.

Ex. 7-4 Redmond and Ancil form a partnership, with Redmond investing $45,000 and Ancil $30,000. They agree to share net income as follows:

(1) Interest at 8% on beginning capital balances.

(2) Salary allowances of $24,000 to Redmond and $18,000 to Ancil.

(3) Any partnership earnings in excess of the amount required to cover the interest and salary allowances to be divided 45% to Redmond and 55% to Ancil.

The partnership net income for the first year of operations amounted to $60,000 before interest and salary allowances. Show how this $60,000 should be divided between the two partners. Use a three-column schedule with a separate column for each partner and a total column. List on separate lines the amounts of interest, salaries, and the residual amount divided.

Ex. 7-5 Clawson Corporation was organized on July 1, 19____. The corporation was authorized to issue 10,000 shares of $100 par value, 8% cumulative preferred stock, and 200,000 shares of no-par common stock with a stated value of $5 per share.

All the preferred stock was issued at par and 160,000 shares of the common stock were sold for $22 per share. Prepare the stockholders' equity section immediately after the issuance of the securities but prior to any operation of the company.

Ex. 7-6 Wolfe Company has outstanding two classes of $100 par value stock: 5,000 shares of 6% cumulative preferred and 25,000 shares of common. The company had a $50,000 deficit at the beginning of the current year, and preferred dividends had not been paid for two years. During the current year, the company earned $250,000. What will be the balance in retained earnings at the end of the current year, if the company pays a dividend of $1.50 per share on the common stock?

Ex. 7-7 A portion of the stockholders' equity section from the balance sheet of Barnes Corporation appears below:

Stockholders' equity:

Preferred stock, 6% cumulative, $50 par, 40,000 shares authorized and issued	*$2,000,000*
Preferred stock, 9% noncumulative, $100 par, 8,000 shares authorized and issued	*800,000*
Common stock, $5 par, 400,000 shares authorized and issued	*2,000,000*
Total paid-in capital	*$4,800,000*

Instructions Assume that all the stock was issued on January 1, 19____, and that no dividends were paid during the first two years of operations. During the third year, Barnes Corporation paid total cash dividends of $532,000.

a Compute the amount of cash dividends paid during the third year to each of the three classes of stock.

b Compute the dividends paid *per share* during the third year for each of the three classes of stock.

Ex. 7-8 Jim Anderson owns 500 shares of convertible preferred stock of Gravity Research, Inc. Each share is convertible into 1.5 shares of common stock. The preferred stock is selling at $80 per share and pays a dividend of $2.50 per year. The common stock is selling for $50 and pays an annual dividend of $2 per share. Anderson wants to convert the preferred stock in order to increase his total dividend income, but an accounting student suggests that he sell his preferred stock and then buy 750 shares of common stock on the open market. Anderson objects to the student's suggestion on the grounds that he would have to pay income taxes at the rate of 25% on the gain from sale of preferred stock, which he had acquired at $68 per share a year ago. Prepare a schedule showing the results under the two alternatives. (Brokers' commissions on the proposed transactions are to be ignored.)

Ex. 7-9 The stockholders' equity section of the balance sheet appeared as follows in a recent annual report of Samoa Corporation:

Stockholders' equity:

  Capital stock:

    $5.50 dividend cumulative preferred stock; no-par value, 300,000

shares authorized, 180,000 shares outstanding, stated at	*$ 18,000,000*
Common stock; no-par value, 5,000,000 shares authorized,	
4,300,000 shares issued, stated at	*32,250,000*
Retained earnings	*75,800,000*
Total stockholders' equity	*$126,050,000*

Instructions From this information compute answers to the following questions:

a What is the stated value per share of the preferred stock?

b What was the average issuance price of a share of common stock?

c What is the amount of the total legal capital and the amount of the total paid in capital?

d What is the total amount of the annual dividend requirement on the preferred stock issue?

e Total dividends of $5,200,000 were declared on the preferred and common stock during the year, and the balance in retained earnings at the beginning of the year amounted to $67,800,000. What was the amount of net income for the year?

Ex. 7-10 Orange Corporation has only one issue of capital stock, consisting of 50,000 outstanding shares of $5 par value. The net income in the first year of operations was $88,000. No dividends were paid in the first year. On January 15 of the second year, a dividend of 80 cents per share was declared by the board of directors payable February 15.

a Prepare the journal entry at December 31 of Year 1 to close the Income Summary account.

b Prepare the journal entries for declaration of the dividend on January 15 and payment of the dividend on February 15.

c Assuming that operations for Year 2 resulted in a net loss of $25,000, prepare the journal entry to close the Income Summary account at December 31, Year 2.

d Compute the balance of the Retained Earnings account as it would appear in the balance sheet at December 31, Year 2.

PROBLEMS

7-1 The partnership of Hale and Boston was formed on July 1, Year 1, when Richard Hale and John Boston agreed to invest equal amounts and to share profits and losses equally. The investment by Hale consists of $46,080 cash and an inventory of merchandise valued at $69,120. Boston also is to contribute a total of $115,200. However, it is agreed that his contribution will consist of the following assets of his business along with the transfer to the partnership of his business liabilities. The agreed values of the various items as well as their carrying values on Boston's records are listed below. Boston also contributes enough cash to bring his capital account to $115,200.

	Investment by Boston	
	Balances on Boston's Records	Agreed Value
Accounts receivable	$107,520	$107,520
Allowance for doubtful accounts	4,608	9,600
Inventory	11,520	15,360
Office equipment (net)	15,360	9,600
Accounts payable	34,560	34,560

Instructions

a Draft entries (in general journal form) to record the investments of Hale and Boston in the new partnership.

b Prepare the beginning balance sheet of the partnership (in report form) at the close of business July 1, reflecting the above transfers to the firm.

c On the following June 30 after one year of operation, the Income Summary account showed a credit balance of $153,600 and the Drawing account for each partner showed a debit balance of $38,400. Prepare journal entries to close the Income Summary account and the drawing accounts at June 30.

7-2 The account balances of Adams Company, arranged in alphabetical order, at the end of the current year are as follows:

Accounts payable	$ 38,520
Accounts receivable	81,000
Accrued liabilities	2,880
Accumulated depreciation	18,000
Adams, capital (beginning of year)	74,400
Adams, drawing	10,080
Administrative expenses	91,620
Cash	37,020
Equipment	90,000
Finley, capital (beginning of year)	60,000
Finley, drawing	7,200
Inventory (beginning of year)	27,360
Notes payable	9,600
Purchases (including transportation-in)	391,800
Sales	648,960
Selling expenses	112,380
Short-term prepayments	3,900

There were no changes in partners' capital accounts during the year. The inventory at the end of the year was $28,200. The partnership agreement provided that partners are to be allowed 10% interest on invested capital as of the beginning of the year and that the "residual" net income is to be divided equally.

Instructions

a Prepare an income statement for the current year, showing the distribution of net income as illustrated on page 276.

b Prepare a statement of partners' capitals for the current year.

c Prepare a balance sheet at the end of the current year.

7-3 The two cases described below are independent of each other.

(1) Early in Year 3 Marine Corporation was formed with authorization to issue 320,000 shares of $5 par value common. The stock was issued at par, and the corporation reported a net loss of $96,000 for Year 3 and a net loss of $224,000 in Year 4. In Year 5 net income was $4.20 per share.

(2) Pacific Corporation was organized early in Year 1 and authorized to issue 200,000 shares of $10 par value common and 32,000 shares of cumulative preferred stock. All the preferred and 192,000 shares of common were issued at par. The preferred stock was callable at 105% of its $100 par value and was entitled to dividends of 6% before any dividends were paid to common. During the first five years of its existence, the corporation earned a total of $2,304,000 and paid dividends of 50 cents per share each year on the common stock.

Instructions For each of the independent situations described, prepare in good form the stockholders' equity section of the balance sheet as of December 31, Year 5. Include a supporting schedule for each case showing your determination of the balance of retained earnings that should appear in the balance sheet.

7-4 Shown below is the stockholders' equity section of the balance sheet of Reno Corporation at the end of the current year.

RENO CORPORATION

Stockholders' Equity

December 31, Current Year

$2.75 preferred stock, $50 par value, authorized 40,000 shares:		
Issued	$720,000	
Subscribed	360,000	$1,080,000
Common stock, no par, $5 stated value, authorized 320,000 shares:		
Issued	$680,000	
Subscribed	140,000	820,000
Paid-in capital in excess of par or stated value:		
On preferred	$108,000	
On common	164,000	272,000
Retained earnings (deficit)		(300,000)
Total stockholders' equity		$1,872,000

Among the assets of the corporation appear the following items: Subscriptions Receivable: Preferred, $180,000; Subscriptions Receivable: Common, $91,000.

Instructions On the basis of this information, write a brief answer to the following questions, showing any necessary supporting computations.

a How many shares of preferred and common have been issued?
b How many shares of preferred and common have been subscribed?
c What was the average price per share received by the corporation on its preferred stock including preferred stock subscribed?
d What was the average price per share received by the corporation on its common stock including common stock subscribed?
e What is the average amount per share that subscribers of preferred stock have yet to pay on their subscriptions?
f What is the total contributed capital of the Reno Corporation?
g What is the total legal or stated value of its capital stock?
h What is the average amount per share that common stock subscribers have already paid on their subscriptions? (Assume common subscribed at $6.)

7-5 In January, Year 10, London Corporation was organized with authorization to issue both preferred stock and common stock. The preferred stock consisted of 50,000 authorized shares of $100 par value and a cumulative annual dividend of 8%. The common stock had a par value of $1 and 400,000 shares were authorized. Since London Corporation planned to sell its stock for cash to a small number of investors and to issue the shares without delay, subscription contracts were not used. The following transactions (among others) occurred during Year 10.

Jan. **6** Issued for cash 50,000 shares of common stock at $8 a share.
Jan. **7** Issued 5,000 shares of preferred stock for cash of $500,000.
June **1** Acquired land as a building site in exchange for 1,000 shares of London Corporation preferred stock and 10,000 shares of the common stock. In view of the appraised value of the land and the progress of London Corporation, the parties agreed that the preferred stock was to be valued for purposes of this transaction at $100 a share and the common stock at $10 a share. The shares were issued.
Dec. 20 The first annual dividend of $8 per share was declared on the preferred stock to be paid January 20 of Year 11.
Dec. 31 After the revenue and expenses (except income taxes) were closed into the Income Summary account, that account showed a before-tax profit of $90,000. Income taxes were determined to be $32,000.

Instructions
a Prepare journal entries for Year 10 in general journal form to record the above transactions. Include entries at December 31 to (*1*) record the income tax liability; (*2*) close the income tax expense into the Income Summary account; and (*3*) close the Income Summary account.
b Prepare the stockholders' equity section of the balance sheet at December 31, Year 10.

7-6 Ventura Corporation was organized early in Year 1 and was authorized to issue 160,000 shares of $5 par value common stock. The stock was issued at $30 per share. The corporation reported a net loss of $120,000 in Year 1 and a net loss of $90,000 in Year 2. In Year 3, net income was $2.20 per share of common stock. No dividends were declared in Years 1 and 2; a dividend of 40 cents per share was declared in Year 3.

Rowland Corporation was organized early in Year 1 and was authorized to issue 200,000 shares of $10 par value common stock and 20,000 shares of $100 par value cumulative preferred stock. All the preferred stock was issued at $102 per share, and 120,000 shares of common stock were issued at $19.50 per share. The preferred stock is callable at $105 per share and is entitled to dividends of $8 per year before any dividends are paid on the common stock. During the first five years of its existence, the Rowland Corporation earned a total of $1,320,000. The dividends paid each year included 30 cents per share on the common stock.

Instructions Prepare in good form the stockholders' equity section of the balance sheet at December 31, Year 3, for the Ventura Corporation and at

December 31, Year 5, for the Rowland Corporation. Include a supporting schedule for each company showing your determination of the balance of retained earnings reported in the balance sheet.

7-7 Notch Corporation was authorized to issue 500,000 shares of $5 par value common stock and 20,000 shares of $6 convertible and cumulative, no-par value, preferred stock. Each share of preferred stock is convertible, at the option of the shareholder, into four shares of common stock. All of the preferred stock was issued at $103 per share, and 300,000 shares of common stock were issued at $15 per share. The balance in Retained Earnings at January 1, Year 10, is $670,000, and there are no dividends in arrears.

Instructions

a Prepare the stockholders' equity section of the balance sheet at January 1, Year 10.

b Assume that on January 1, Year 10, all of the preferred stock is converted into shares of common stock. Prepare a journal entry to record the conversion.

c Prepare a revised stockholders' equity section of the balance sheet at January 1, Year 10, after the conversion of the preferred stock.

7-8 Dale Corporation was organized on July 1 of Year 1 with the following two types of capital stock:

9% Preferred stock, cumulative, $100 par value, 10,000 shares authorized

Common stock, $2.50 par value, 200,000 share authorized

On July 1, 50 shares of preferred stock and 500 shares of common stock were issued to Jill Dale in payment for her services in organizing the corporation. Market value of these securities on July 1 were $100 per share for the preferred stock and $5 per share for the common stock. Attorneys' fees of $2,400 incurred in connection with the formation of the corporation had been billed to Dale Corporation but not yet paid.

On July 10, Jill Dale transferred to Dale Corporation certain assets (formerly used in another business) and received in exchange 6,000 shares of the 9%, cumulative preferred stock. The current fair value of the assets transferred to Dale Corporation was as follows: notes receivable, $360,000; inventory, $60,000; and equipment, $180,000.

On July 31, common stock consisting of 160,000 shares was sold for cash at $5.50 per share. Also on July 31, Dale Corporation purchased land and a building for $1,520,000. The total purchase price was allocated $120,000 to the land and $1,400,000 to the building. Payment for this property consisted of $720,000 in cash and the issuance of an 8% mortgage note payable for $800,000 due in 10 years.

Dale Corporation did not begin regular operations until after July 31, so no revenue from sales was earned during July. On July 31, miscellaneous expenses of $2,500 were paid but were not considered as organization costs. The attorneys' fee of $2,400 mentioned previously remained unpaid. Interest revenue of $1,500 was recognized as having accrued during July on the notes receivable. The terms of the mortgage note payable provided that interest did not begin to accrue until August 1. (Income taxes are to be ignored.)

Instructions

a Prepare journal entries to record the above transactions in the accounts of Dale Corporation. Include a closing entry to transfer the net income or loss to the Retained Earnings account.

b Prepare a classified balance sheet for Dale Corporation at July 31, Year 1.

7-9 Each of the cases described below is independent of the others.

Case A Adams Corporation was organized in 1982 and was authorized to issue 200,000 shares of $5 par value common stock. All shares were issued at a price of

$16 per share. The corporation reported a net loss of $120,000 for 1982 and a net loss of $280,000 in 1983. In 1984, the net income was $3.60 per share. No dividends were declared during the three-year period.

Case B Barker Corporation was organized in 1980. The company was authorized to issue 250,000 shares of $10 par value common stock and 20,000 shares of cumulative preferred stock. All the preferred stock was issued at par and 240,000 shares of the common stock were issued at $24. The preferred stock was callable at 105% of its $100 par value and was entitled to dividends of 8% before any dividends were paid on the common stock. During the first five years of its existence, the corporation earned a total of $2,880,000 and paid dividends of 70 cents per share each year on the common stock, in addition to regular dividends on the preferred stock.

Case C Cross Corporation was organized in 1981, issuing at $44 per share one-half of the 200,000 shares of $20 par common stock authorized. On January 1, 1982, the company sold at par the entire 10,000 authorized shares of $100 par value, 7% cumulative preferred. On January 1, 1983, the company issued 10,000 shares of an authorized 20,000 shares of $6 no-par, cumulative preferred stock for $1,050,000. The company suffered losses and paid no dividends in 1981 and 1982, reporting a deficit of $600,000 at the end of 1982. During the years 1983 and 1984 combined, the company earned a total of $3,000,000. Dividends of $2 per share were paid on the common stock in 1983 and $8.50 in 1984.

Instructions For each of the independent cases described, prepare in good form the stockholders' equity section of the balance sheet at December 31, 1984. Include a supporting schedule for each case showing your determination of the balance of retained earnings at December 31, 1984.

BUSINESS DECISION PROBLEM 7

Southern Electric and Eastern Power are two utility companies with very stable earnings. Southern Electric consistently has a net income of approximately $96 million per year, and Eastern Power's net income consistently approximates $84 million per year. Southern Electric has 5,400,000 shares of 6% preferred stock, $50 par value, and 26,600,000 shares of $50 par value common stock outstanding. Eastern Power has 2,400,000 shares of 6% preferred stock, $100 par value, and 17,400,000 shares of $10 par value common stock outstanding. Assume that both companies distribute all net income as dividends every year, and will continue to do so. Neither company plans to issue additional shares of capital stock.

Instructions
a Compute the annual dividend which would be paid on the common stock of each company, assuming that Southern Electric has a net income of $96 million and Eastern Power has a net income of $84 million.
b What company's common stock would you expect to have the higher *market price per share?* Support your answer with information provided in the problem.

8

Corporations: Earnings Per Share, Retained Earnings, and Dividends

The most important aspect of corporate financial reporting, in the view of most stockholders, is the determination of periodic net income. Both the market price of common stock and the amount of cash dividends per share depend to a considerable extent on the current level of earnings. The amount of *earnings per share* of common stock for a year, or for an *interim* period such as three months, is of particular interest to stockholders and financial analysts. Even more important than the absolute amount of earnings per share is the *trend* of such earnings. Are earnings per share in an upward or downward trend? The common stocks of those companies which regularly achieve higher earnings per share year after year become the favorite securities of the investment community. Such stature helps greatly in raising new capital, in attracting and retaining highly competent management, and in many other ways.

Developing predictive information

An income statement tells us a great deal about the performance of a company over the past year. For example, study of the income statement makes clear the rate of gross profit on sales, the net income for the year, the percentage of profit per dollar of sales, and the net income earned on each share of common stock. Can we expect the income statement for *next year* to indicate about the same level of performance? If the transactions summarized in the income statement for the year just completed were of a normal recurring nature, such as selling merchandise, paying employees, and incurring other normal expenses, we can reasonably assume that the operating results were typical and that somewhat similar results can be expected in the following year. However, in any business, unusual and nonrecurring events may occur which cause the current year's net income to be quite different from the income we should expect the company to earn in the future. For example, the company may have sustained large losses in the current year from an earthquake, a strike, or some other event which is not likely to recur in the near future.

Ideally, the results of unusual and nonrecurring transactions should be shown in a separate section of the income statement *after* the income or loss from normal business activities has been determined. Income from *normal and recurring* activities presumably should be a more useful figure for predicting future earnings than is a net income figure which includes the results of nonrecurring events. The problem in creating such an income statement, however, is in determining which events are so unlikely to recur that they should be excluded from the results of "normal" operations.

The question of how unusual an event should be to require separate presentation has long been debated by accountants and other interested parties. Current accounting practice recognizes three categories of unusual transactions and accords each category a different treatment in the income statement. These categories are (*1*) the results of discontinued operations, (*2*) extraordinary items, and (*3*) other nonoperating items. The criteria which define these categories and the related income statement presentation are still being debated and may well change in future years.

Discontinued operations of a segment of a business

Assume that a corporation sells a major segment of its operations to another company late in the current year. A problem would arise in making the income statements comparable for this year and next year since the operations would be of different scope and magnitude after disposal of a segment of the business.

Current accounting standards include rather precise guidelines for measuring and reporting the operating results of discontinued segments of a business. This topic is covered in **APB Opinion No. 30** entitled "Reporting the Results of Operations." A *segment of a business* is "a component of a company whose activities represent a major line of business or class of customer."[1] The assets and operating results of a segment of a business should be clearly identifiable from the other assets and results of operations of the company. Several examples of segments of a business are:

---

[1] *APB Opinion No. 30,* "Reporting the Results of Operations—Reporting the Effects of Disposal of a Segment of a Business, and Extraordinary, Unusual and Infrequently Occurring Events and Transactions," AICPA (New York: 1973).

1 An electronics division of a highly diversified manufacturing company
2 A professional sports team owned by a newspaper publishing company
3 A wholesale milk distributorship owned by a retail food chain

The income statement is probably more useful if the results of the **continuing operations** of a business entity are reported separately from the results of operations which have been discontinued. Thus, the operating results of a discontinued segment of a business (including any gain or loss on the disposal of the segment) for the current period are reported separately in the income statement **after** determining the **income from continuing operations.** The purpose of such separate disclosure is to enable users of financial statements to make better predictive judgments as to the future earnings performance of the company.

For example, assume that the Childs Company reported a net income of $10 million for Year 10, including $4 million net income earned on sales of $100 million by an exporting division which was sold near the end of the year. Would the Childs Company be able to earn $10 million in Year 11 without the exporting business? Before answering this question, let us make an alternative assumption, that is, that the exporting division lost $8 million (after income taxes) in Year 10 instead of earning $4 million. What income might the Childs Company be expected to earn in Year 11 without the drain on earnings from the exporting business? The following partial income statement would be helpful to investors contemplating answers to these two questions:

CHILDS COMPANY
Partial Income Statement
For Year 10

	Assuming Exporting Division Earned $4 Million	Assuming Exporting Division Lost $8 Million
Income from continuing operations	$ 6,000,000	$18,000,000
Income (or loss) from discontinued operations*	4,000,000	(8,000,000)
Net income	$10,000,000	$10,000,000

Income or loss from discontinued operations in the income statement

*The revenue in Year 10 from the discontinued segment was $100 million.

The income from continuing operations is a logical starting point in forecasting the probable earnings of the Childs Company for Year 11. However, other variables (such as price changes, increase in sales volume, and the acquisition of new lines of business) may cause the income from continuing operations in Year 11 to change materially under either assumption above.

The **revenue** and **expenses** shown in an income statement for the year in which a segment of a business is eliminated should consist only of the *revenue and expenses from continuing operations.* The net income or loss from discontinued operations is reported separately in the income statement, and the revenue from the discontinued segment is disclosed in the notes to the financial statements. Any gain or loss on the disposal of a segment should be reported with the results of the discontinued operations.

ALLOCATION OF INCOME TAXES BETWEEN CONTINUING AND DISCONTINUED OPERATIONS When an income statement includes sections for both continuing and discontinued operations, the company's income tax expense should be *allocated* between these sections. Only the income tax expense applicable to continuing operations should be deducted as an expense in arriving at income from continuing operations. Income taxes attributable to the discontinued operations should be considered, along with other expenses of the discontinued segment, in computing income (or loss) from discontinued operations.

To illustrate, assume that Alpha Corporation earns income *before* income taxes of $300,000 from continuing operations and $100,000 from operations discontinued during the year. If all income is taxable at a rate of 40%, the company's total income tax expense is 40% of $400,000, or $160,000. However, only $120,000 of this amount is attributable to continuing operations (computed as $300,000 × 40%); the remaining $40,000 of income tax expense stems from the discontinued operations. The following partial income statement illustrates the allocation of Alpha's total income tax expense.

ALPHA CORPORATION
Partial Income Statement
For Year 6

Income before taxes from continuing operations	$300,000
Income tax expense (total taxes are $160,000, of which $40,000 are	
attributable to discontinued operations)	120,000
Income from continuing operations	$180,000
Income from discontinued operations, net of taxes ($100,000 − $40,000) . . .	60,000
Net income	$240,000

As a separate case, assume that Alpha's discontinued operations had incurred a before-tax *loss* of $50,000. Total before-tax income would be $250,000 ($300,000 − $50,000) and total income tax expense would be $100,000. The amount of income taxes applicable to the $300,000 before-tax income from continuing operations is still $120,000; however, the before-tax loss from discontinued operations creates a $20,000 *tax savings.* This tax savings should be subtracted from the before-tax loss to show the loss from discontinued operations on an after-tax basis. The income statement presentation follows:

ALPHA CORPORATION
Partial Income Statement
For Year 6

Income before taxes from continuing operations	$300,000
Income tax expense (total taxes are $100,000 as a result of a $20,000 tax savings attributable to discontinued operations)	120,000
Income from continuing operations	$180,000
Loss from discontinued operations, net of taxes ($50,000 – $20,000)	(30,000)
Net income	$150,000

Note that in both income statements for Alpha Corporation income from continuing operations is $180,000. *The amount of income reported from continuing operations is not affected by the operating results of the discontinued operations.* Thus, the subtotal Income from Continuing Operations should be a useful figure for evaluating the earning power of those segments of the company which are remaining in operation.

Extraordinary items

Some gains and losses are so unusual in nature that it may be useful to include in the income statement a subtotal showing what net income *would have been* if these extraordinary events had not occurred. Such events are called *extraordinary items,* and the subtotal developed in the income statement is termed *Income before Extraordinary Items.* If an extraordinary item is segregated in the income statement, that is, shown separately from the results of normal recurring operations of the business, it will be easier for us to use the income statement as a measure of "normal" performance.

An event or transaction must be *material in dollar amount* to warrant separate disclosure as an extraordinary item. For many years there was much argument over what kinds of events should be considered extraordinary. The definition was narrowed considerably by *APB Opinion No. 30.* Extraordinary items are now defined as material transactions and events that are both *unusual in nature and occur infrequently* in the operating environment of the business.

In order to be considered unusual in nature, the underlying event or transaction should be abnormal and clearly unrelated to the ordinary and typical activities of the entity. The scope of operations, lines of business, operating policies, and the environment in which an entity operates should be considered in applying this criterion. The environment of a business includes such factors as the characteristics of the industry, the geographic location of activities, and the degree of government regulation.

"Occurring infrequently," according to *APB Opinion 30,* means that the event or transaction is not reasonably expected to take place again in the foreseeable future. Past experience of the entity is generally a helpful guide in determining the frequency of an event or transaction.

To illustrate these criteria, consider the case of a farming enterprise located along river bottomland subject to severe flood damage every few years. A large loss from a flood would not qualify as an extraordinary item in the income statement of this agricultural business, because it is not unusual and infrequent in the environment in which this particular business operates. Thus only those events which are both *unusual and infrequent* lead to extraordinary gains and losses. These qualitative standards are difficult to apply in practice, and differences of opinion still exist as to what is and what is not an extraordinary item. Listed below are some examples of gains or losses which are viewed as extraordinary and some which are not.

Extraordinary Items	*Not Extraordinary Items*
1 *Effects of major casualties such as earthquake (if rare in the area)*	1 *Write-down or write-off of receivables, inventories, or intangible assets*
2 *Expropriation of assets by foreign governments*	2 *Gains or losses on disposal of a segment of a business or from sale or abandonment of plant assets*
3 *Effects of a prohibition under a newly enacted law or regulation*	3 *Effects of labor strikes or shortages of raw materials*
	4 *Changes in estimates of accumulated depreciation, accrued expenses, and profits or losses on long-term construction contracts*

Few extraordinary items currently appear in corporate income statements as a result of the rigorous criteria established in *APB Opinion No. 30.* The presentation of extraordinary items in the income statement is illustrated on page 318.

ATLANTA CORPORATION
Income Statement
For the Year Ended December 31, 19___

Net sales		$10,000,000
Cost of goods sold		6,000,000
Gross profit on sales		$ 4,000,000
Operating expenses:		
Selling	$1,200,000	
General and administrative	600,000	
Loss from suspension of operations during strike	200,000	2,000,000
Income before income taxes		$ 2,000,000
Deduct: Income taxes (actual taxes are $575,000 as a result of a		
$225,000 tax savings attributable to extraordinary loss)		800,000
Income before extraordinary item		$ 1,200,000
Extraordinary item: Loss from earthquake, net of reduction in income		
taxes ($925,000 − $225,000)		700,000
Net income		$ 500,000
Earnings per share of common stock:		
Earnings before extraordinary item		$1.20
Extraordinary item		0.70
Net earnings		$0.50

The income or loss from a discontinued segment of the business (including any gain or loss on disposal of the segment) is **not** an extraordinary item. When discontinued operations and an extraordinary item appear in the same income statement, the income or loss from the discontinued operations is presented **before** the extraordinary item. Thus, the subtotal Income before Extraordinary Items includes the operating results of any segments of the business which have been discontinued during the year.

ALLOCATION OF INCOME TAXES BETWEEN REGULAR OPERATIONS AND EXTRAORDINARY ITEMS If income before extraordinary items is to represent what net income would have been without the extraordinary loss, we must separate the tax effect of the earthquake loss from the income tax expense attributable to regular operations. Thus, the amount of the earthquake loss is shown **net of the related tax effects.** In the preceding illustration, we have assumed the before-tax earthquake loss to be $925,000 and the related tax savings $225,000. This tax savings is deducted from the before-tax loss to show the extraordinary item in the income statement on an after-tax basis.

If these tax allocation procedures had not been used, the income tax expense shown in arriving at income before extraordinary items would have been understated in relation to the before-tax income from normal operations.

Other nonoperating gains and losses

Some transactions are not typical of normal operations but also do not meet the criteria for separate presentation as extraordinary items. Among such events are uninsured fire losses and the gains or losses resulting from the sale of securities held for investment. Such items, if material, should be individually listed as items of revenue or expense, rather than being combined with other items in broad categories such as sales revenue or general and administrative expenses.

In the income statement illustrated on page 318, the nonoperating loss of $200,000 resulting from a strike was disclosed separately in the income statement but was not listed as an extraordinary item. This strike loss was important enough to bring to the attention of readers of the financial statements, but strikes are not sufficiently unusual or infrequent to be considered extraordinary items. Since this strike loss is included in the "normal operations" section of the income statement, the $200,000 figure is a before-tax loss and the related tax effects are included in the $800,000 income tax expense relating to normal operations.

Earnings per share (EPS)

Perhaps the most widely used of all accounting statistics is *earnings per share* of common stock. Since a purchase or sale of common stock is executed on the basis of the market price per share, it is helpful to know the amount of earnings applicable to a single share. The concept of earnings per share applies only to common stock; preferred stock has no claim to earnings beyond the stipulated preferred stock dividends.

The amounts of quarterly and annual earnings per share are useful in investment decisions. By computing the *price-earnings ratio* (market price of a share of common stock divided by the annual earnings per share), investors can determine whether the market price of the stock appears reasonable in relation to the underlying amount of earnings. Because of the wide publicity given to earnings per share data in newspapers and business journals, it is important that these data be computed in a consistent and logical manner.

WEIGHTED-AVERAGE NUMBER OF SHARES OUTSTANDING The simplest example of computing earnings per share is found when a company has issued only common stock and the number of shares outstanding has not changed during the year. In this situation, the net income for the year divided by the number of shares outstanding at year-end equals earnings per share.

In many companies, however, the number of shares of stock outstanding is changed one or more times during the year. When additional shares are issued in exchange for assets during the year, the computation of earnings per share is based upon the **weighted-average** number of shares outstanding.[2]

The weighted-average number of shares for the year is determined by multiplying the number of shares outstanding by the fraction of the year that said number of shares outstanding remained unchanged. For example, assume that 100,000 shares of common stock were outstanding during the first nine months of Year 1 and 140,000 shares during the last three months. Assume also that the increase in shares outstanding resulted from the sale of 40,000 shares for cash. The weighted-average number of shares outstanding during Year 1 would be 110,000, determined as follows:

100,000 shares × $\frac{3}{4}$ of a year	*75,000*
140,000 shares × $\frac{1}{4}$ of a year	*35,000*
Weighted-average number of common shares outstanding	*110,000*

This procedure gives more meaningful earnings per share data than if the total number of shares outstanding at the end of the year were used in the calculations. By using the weighted-average number of shares, we recognize that the proceeds from the sale of the 40,000 shares were available to generate earnings only during the last three months of the year. The contribution to earnings made by 40,000 shares outstanding during one-fourth of the year is equivalent to that of 10,000 shares outstanding for a full year. In other words, the weighted-average number of shares outstanding consists of 100,000 shares outstanding during the entire year plus the 10,000 share full-year equivalent of the shares issued during the year.

Primary and fully diluted earnings per share

The computation of earnings per share is easily done for companies with common stock only, that is, companies not having convertible preferred stock or other obligations capable of being converted into additional common shares. In companies with such simple capital structures there is no risk of conversion which would increase the number of common shares and **dilute** (reduce) earnings per share of common stock.

When preferred stock is outstanding, the preferred stockholders participate in net income to the extent of the preferred stock dividends. To determine the portion of earnings **applicable to common stock,** we must deduct from net income the amount of any preferred stock dividends. To illustrate, let us assume that a company with a net income of $100,000 for Year 1 has 5,000 shares of $2 preferred stock and 40,000 shares of

[2] When the number of shares outstanding changes as a result of a stock split or a stock dividend (discussed later in this chapter), the computation of the weighted-average number of shares outstanding should be adjusted **retroactively** rather than weighted for the period the new shares were outstanding. Earnings per share data for prior years thus will be consistently stated in terms of the current capital structure.

common stock outstanding throughout the year. Earnings per share of common stock would be computed as follows:

Earnings	*Net income*	*$100,000*
per share when	*Less: Dividend on preferred stock for current period, 5,000 × $2*	*10,000*
preferred	*Income available for common stock*	*$ 90,000*
stock is outstanding	*Weighted-average number of common shares outstanding*	*40,000*
	Earnings per share of common stock, $90,000 ÷ 40,000 shares	*$2.25*

Let us now assume that each of the 5,000 shares of preferred stock is **convertible** into two shares of common stock. Conversion of the preferred stock would increase the number of common shares outstanding and might dilute earnings per share. Any common stockholder interested in the trend of earnings per share will want to know what effect conversion of the preferred stock would have upon this statistic.

To inform investors of the potential dilution which might occur, two earnings per share figures are presented. In computing the first figure, called **primary** earnings per share, we ignore the potential dilution represented by the convertible preferred stock.[3] In computing the second figure, called **fully diluted** earnings per share, we show the effect that conversion of the preferred shares would have had on primary earnings per share in the current year.

Primary earnings per share are computed in the same manner illustrated in our preceding calculation. In computing fully diluted earnings per share, **we assume that the preferred stock was converted into common stock at the beginning of the current year.**[4] Under this assumption, there would have been no preferred stock dividends; however, there would have been an additional 10,000 shares of common stock outstanding throughout the year. The computation of primary earnings per share and fully diluted earnings per share is shown below:

		Primary	*Fully Diluted*
Primary and	*Net income*	*$100,000*	*$100,000*
fully diluted earnings	*Less: Dividends on preferred stock, 5,000 × $2*	*10,000*	*–0–*
per share	*Earnings available for common stock*	*$ 90,000*	*$100,000*
	Number of shares of common stock outstanding:		
	In computing primary earnings per share	*40,000*	
	In computing fully diluted earnings per share, 40,000 +		
	(5,000 × 2)		*50,000*
	Earnings per share of common stock	*$2.25*	*$2.00*

[3]If certain criteria are met, convertible securities qualify as **common stock equivalents** and enter into the computation of primary earnings per share. Common stock equivalents and other complex issues relating to earnings per share are discussed in *APB Opinion No. 15*, "Earnings per Share," AICPA (New York, 1969), and in *Intermediate Accounting* of this series.

[4] If the preferred stock had been issued during the current year, we would assume that it was converted into common stock on the date it was issued.

It is important to remember that fully diluted earnings per share represent a *hypothetical case.* The preferred stock actually was not converted during the year. The presentation of fully diluted earnings per share merely warns common stockholders what *could* have happened. When the difference between primary and fully diluted earnings per share is significant, investors should recognize the risk that future earnings per share may be diluted by conversions of other securities into common stock.

Presentation of earnings per share in the income statement

All publicly owned corporations are required to present earnings per share data in their income statements.[5] If an income statement includes subtotals for income from continuing operations or income before extraordinary items, per-share figures are shown for these amounts as well as for net income. The presentation of earnings per share for a company reporting discontinued operations and having a complex capital structure is illustrated below:

Income from continuing operations	*$4,800,000*
Loss from discontinued operations, net of related tax savings	*(1,200,000)*
Net income	*$3,600,000*

Earnings per share of common stock:	
Primary:	
Earnings from continuing operations	*$2.20*
Loss from discontinued operations	*(0.60)*
Net earnings for the year	*$1.60*
Fully diluted:	
Earnings from continuing operations	*$2.00*
Loss from discontinued operations	*(0.50)*
Net earnings for the year	*$1.50*

Note that both income from continuing operations and net income are expressed on a per-share basis. In addition, each of these amounts is shown on both a primary and a fully diluted basis. (We have also shown the amount of the loss from discontinued operations on a per-share basis, but this is merely a reconciling amount and may be omitted in a formal income statement.)

To informed users of financial statements, each of these figures has a different significance. Earnings per share from continuing operations represents the results of continuing and ordinary business activity. Presumably, this figure is the most useful one for predicting future operating results. Net earnings per share, on the other hand, shows the overall

---

[5] In 1978 the FASB exempted closely held corporations (those not publicly owned) from the requirement of computing and reporting earnings per share.

operating results of the current year, including any discontinued operations or extraordinary items. The fully diluted per-share figures indicate the extent to which primary earnings per share could be diluted by the conversion of other securities into common stock.

Unfortunately the term *earnings per share* often is used without qualification in referring to various types of per-share data. When using per-share information, it is important to know exactly which per-share statistic is being presented. The *Wall Street Journal,* for example, uses *net earnings* per share in computing the *price-earnings ratio* for common stocks listed on the major stock exchanges. When a company reports both primary and fully diluted earnings per share, the *Wall Street Journal* uses the fully diluted figure.

Income statement for a corporation illustrated

In order to highlight important changes and trends in operating results, most corporations present *comparative* income statements in their quarterly and annual reports to stockholders. In a comparative income statement, the operating results of the current year are shown together with those of the preceding year.

A comparative income statement which includes losses from discontinued operations and extraordinary losses is illustrated on page 324. Fully diluted earnings per share are not presented because the company has a simple capital structure which does not create a potential for dilution of earnings per common share.

CALIFORNIA INDUSTRIES, INC.

Comparative Income Statement

For Years Ended September 30

	Year 2	Year 1
Net sales	$81,853,000	$57,167,000
Cost of goods sold	68,649,000	46,114,000
Gross profit on sales	$13,204,000	$11,053,000
Expenses:		
Selling, administrative, and general	$10,072,000	$ 8,493,000
Interest	1,504,000	1,325,000
Other expense, net of miscellaneous income	66,000	101,000
Total expenses	$11,642,000	$ 9,919,000
Income (before income taxes) from continuing		
operations	$ 1,562,000	$ 1,134,000
Federal and state income taxes	658,000	505,000
Income from continuing operations	$ 904,000	$ 629,000
Loss from discontinued operations, net of income		
tax benefit of $80,000 in Year 2 and $362,000 in		
Year 1	(94,000)	(342,000)
Income before extraordinary items	$ 810,000	$ 287,000
Extraordinary items: expropriation loss, net of taxes .	–0–	(203,000)
Net income	$ 810,000	$ 84,000
Earnings per share of common stock:		
Earnings from continuing operations	$3.85	$2.68
Loss from discontinued operations	(0.40)	(1.46)
Earnings before extraordinary items	$3.45	$1.22
Extraordinary items	–0–	(0.86)
Net earnings	$3.45	$0.36

Income statement with loss from discontinued operations and extraordinary items

Cash dividends

The prospect of receiving cash dividends is a principal reason for investing in the stocks of corporations. An increase or decrease in the established rate of dividends will usually cause an immediate rise or fall in the
market price of the company's stock. Stockholders are keenly interested
in prospects for future dividends and as a group are generally strongly in
favor of more generous dividend payments. The board of directors, on the
other hand, is primarily concerned with the long-run growth and financial
strength of the corporation; it may prefer to restrict dividends to a minimum in order to conserve cash for purchase of plant and equipment or for
other needs of the company. Many of the so-called "growth companies"
plow back into the business most of their earnings and pay only very small
cash dividends.

The preceding discussion suggests three requirements for the payment
of a cash dividend. These are:

1 *Retained earnings.* Since dividends represent a distribution of earnings to stockholders, the theoretical maximum for dividends is the total net income of the company. As a practical matter, many corporations limit dividends to somewhere near 40% of earnings, in the belief that a major portion of the net income must be retained in the business if the company is to grow and to keep pace with its competitors.

2 *An adequate cash position.* The fact that the company reports large earnings does not mean that it has a large amount of cash on hand. Earnings may have been invested in new plant and equipment, or in paying off debts, or in acquiring a larger inventory. There is no necessary relationship between the balance in the Retained Earnings account and the balance in the Cash account. The traditional expression of "paying dividends out of retained earnings" is misleading. Cash dividends can be paid only "out of" cash.

3 *Dividend action by the board of directors.* Even though the company's net income is substantial and its cash position seemingly satisfactory, dividends are not paid automatically. A positive action by the directors is necessary to declare a dividend.

Dividend dates

Four significant dates are involved in the distribution of a dividend. These dates are:

1 *Date of declaration.* On the day on which the dividend is declared by the board of directors, a liability to make the payment comes into existence.

2 *Date of record.* The date of record always follows the date of declaration, usually by a period of two or three weeks, and is always stated in the dividend declaration. In order to be eligible to receive the dividend, a person must be listed as the owner of the stock on the date of record.

3 *Ex-dividend date.* The ex-dividend date is significant for investors in companies with stocks traded on the stock exchanges. To permit the compilation of the list of stockholders as of the record date, it is customary for the stock to go "ex-dividend" three business days before the date of record. A stock is said to be selling ex-dividend on the day that it loses the right to receive the latest declared dividend. A person who buys the stock before the ex-dividend date is entitled to receive the dividend; conversely, a stockholder who sells shares in the period between the date of declaration and the ex-dividend date does not receive the dividend.

4 *Date of payment.* The declaration of a dividend always includes announcement of the date of payment as well as the date of record. Usually the date of payment comes from two to four weeks after the date of record.

The journal entries to record the declaration and payment of a cash dividend were illustrated in Chapter 3 but are repeated here with emphasis on the date of declaration and date of payment.

Entries *made on* *declaration* *date* *and . . .*	*June 1*	*Dividends*	*100,000*	
		Dividends Payable		*100,000*
		To record declaration of a cash dividend of $1 per *share on the 100,000 shares of common stock out-* *standing. Payable July 10 to stockholders of record* *on June 20.*		

<table>
<tr><td>*. . . on</td><td>*July 10*</td><td>*Dividends Payable* . . . .</td><td>*100,000*</td><td></td></tr>
<tr><td>*payment*</td><td></td><td>*Cash* . . . .</td><td></td><td>*100,000*</td></tr>
<tr><td>*date*</td><td></td><td>*To record payment of $1 per share dividend declared*</td><td></td><td></td></tr>
<tr><td></td><td></td><td>*June 1 to stockholders of record on June 20.*</td><td></td><td></td></tr>
</table>

If a company has one or more issues of preferred stock as well as common stock, it will use separate dividend accounts for each issue. The account debited when a dividend is declared may have a title such as Dividends on Preferred Stock; such an account would be closed to Retained Earnings at the end of the year.

Property and liquidating dividends

Most dividends are paid in cash, but occasionally a dividend declaration calls for payment in assets other than cash. A large distillery once paid a dividend consisting of a bottle of whiskey for each share of stock. When a corporation goes out of existence (particularly a small corporation with only a few stockholders), it may choose to distribute noncash assets to its owners rather than to convert all its assets into cash.

A *liquidating* dividend occurs when a corporation returns to stockholders all or part of their paid-in capital investment. Liquidating dividends are usually paid only when a corporation is going out of existence or is making a permanent reduction in the size of its operations. Normally dividends are paid as a result of profitable operations, and the recipients of a dividend are entitled to assume that the dividend represents a distribution of income unless they are specifically notified that the dividend is a return of invested capital.

Stock dividends

Stock dividend is an important but confusing term which requires close attention. It is confusing because all dividends are distributions to stockholders and "stock dividend" may suggest to some people merely a dividend on capital stock. *A stock dividend is a distribution of additional shares of stock to a company's stockholders in proportion to their present holdings.* In brief, the dividend consists of shares of stock rather than cash. Perhaps a better term for a stock dividend would be a "dividend payable in capital stock," but the expression "stock dividend" is too firmly entrenched to be easily replaced. Most stock dividends consist of additional shares of common stock distributed to holders of common stock, and our discussion will be limited to this type of stock dividend.

What is the effect of a stock dividend on the company's financial position? Why does a corporation choose to pay a dividend in shares of stock rather than in cash? Would you as an investor prefer to receive a stock dividend or a cash dividend? These questions are closely related, and a careful analysis of the nature of a stock dividend should provide a basis for answering them.

A cash dividend reduces the assets of a corporation and reduces the stockholders' equity by the same amount. A stock dividend, on the other hand, causes no change in assets and no change in the *total* amount of the stockholders' equity. The only effect of a stock dividend on the accounts is to transfer a portion of the retained earnings into the Common Stock and Paid-in Capital from Stock Dividends accounts. In other words, a stock dividend merely "reshuffles" the stockholders' equity accounts, increasing the permanent capital accounts and decreasing the Retained Earnings account. A stockholder who receives a stock dividend will own an increased number of shares, but his or her total ownership equity in the company will be *no larger than before.*

To illustrate this point, assume that a corporation with 2,000 shares of stock is owned equally by James Davis and Susan Miller, each owning 1,000 shares of stock. The corporation declares a stock dividend of 10% and distributes 200 additional shares (10% of 2,000 shares), with 100 shares going to each of the two stockholders. Davis and Miller now hold 1,100 shares apiece, but each still owns one-half of the business. The corporation has not changed; its assets and liabilities and its total stockholders' equity are exactly the same as before the dividend. From the stockholder's viewpoint, the ownership of 1,100 shares out of a total of 2,200 outstanding shares represents no more than did the ownership of 1,000 shares out of a total of 2,000 shares previously outstanding.

Assume that the fair market value of this stock was $11 per share prior to the stock dividend. Total market value of all the outstanding shares was, therefore, 2,000 times $11, or $22,000. What would be the market value per share and in total after the additional 200 dividend shares were issued? The 2,200 shares now outstanding should have the same total market value as the previously outstanding 2,000 shares, because the "pie" has merely been divided into more but smaller pieces. The value per share should have dropped from $11 to $10, and the aggregate market value of outstanding shares would consequently be computed as 2,200 shares times $10, or $22,000. Whether the market price per share will, in all cases, decrease in proportion to the change in number of outstanding shares is another matter. The market prices of stocks listed on a stock exchange are subject to many conflicting influences, some as unpredictable as the state of mind of investors.

REASONS FOR DISTRIBUTION OF STOCK DIVIDENDS Many reasons have been given for the popularity of stock dividends; for example:

1 To conserve cash. When the trend of profits is favorable but cash is needed for expansion, a stock dividend may be an appropriate device for "passing along the earnings" to stockholders without weakening the corporation's cash position.[6]

---

[6] For example, the Standard Oil Company of California, in a letter to its stockholders, gave the following reason for the "payment" of a 5% stock dividend: "Payment of this stock dividend recognizes the continuing increase in your stockholder's equity in the Company's assets, resulting from reinvestment of part of the Company's earnings. Reinvestment of earnings has helped to sustain the Company's long-range program of capital and exploratory expenditures and investments aimed to increase future income and enhance further the value of your shareholding."

2 To reduce the market price of a corporation's stock to a more convenient trading range by increasing the number of shares outstanding. This objective is usually present in large stock dividends (25 to 100% or more).

3 To avoid income tax on stockholders. For income tax purposes, stock dividends are not considered as income to the recipients; therefore, no income tax is levied.

Some critics of stock dividends argue that a stock dividend is not really a dividend at all. These critics say that a company which cannot afford to pay a cash dividend should declare no dividends, rather than trying to deceive stockholders by increasing the number of outstanding shares. The popularity of stock dividends, according to such critics, is based on a lack of understanding on the part of stockholders.

Regardless of the merit of the arguments for and against stock dividends, most stockholders welcome these distributions. In many cases a small stock dividend has not caused the market price per share to decline appreciably; consequently, the increase in the number of shares in the hands of each stockholder has, regardless of logic, resulted in an increase in the total market value of his or her holdings.

ENTRIES TO RECORD STOCK DIVIDENDS Assume that a corporation had the following stockholders' equity accounts on December 15, Year 1, just prior to declaring a 10% stock dividend:

Stock-holders' equity before stock dividend

Stockholders' equity:

Common stock, $10 par value, 300,000 shares authorized, 100,000	
shares issued and outstanding	*$1,000,000*
Paid-in capital in excess of par	*500,000*
Retained earnings	*2,000,000*
Total stockholders' equity	*$3,500,000*

Assume also that the closing market price of the stock on December 15, Year 1, was $30 a share. The company declares and distributes a 10% stock dividend, consisting of 10,000 common shares (10% × 100,000 = 10,000). The entry to record the **declaration** of the dividend is as follows:

Stock dividend declared; note use of market price of stock

Year 1

Dec. 15	*Retained Earnings*	*300,000*	
	Stock Dividend to Be Distributed		*100,000*
	Paid-in Capital from Stock Dividends		*200,000*

To record declaration of a 10% stock dividend consisting of 10,000 shares of $10 par value common stock. To be distributed on Feb. 9, Year 2, to stockholders of record on Jan. 15, Year 2. Amount of retained earnings transferred to permanent capital is based on market price of $30 a share on Dec. 15, Year 1.

The Stock Dividend to Be Distributed account is *not a liability,* because there is no obligation to distribute cash or any other asset. If a balance sheet is prepared between the date of declaration of a stock dividend and the date of distribution of the shares, this account, as well as Paid-in Capital from Stock Dividends, should be presented in the stockholders' equity section of the balance sheet.

The entry to record *distribution* of the dividend shares is as follows:

Year 2

Stock Feb. 9 Stock Dividend to Be Distributed 100,000
dividend   Common Stock 100,000
distributed   *To record distribution of stock dividend of 10,000 shares.*

Note that the amount of retained earnings transferred to permanent capital accounts by the above entries is not the par value of the new shares, but the *market value,* as indicated by the market price prevailing at the date of declaration. The reasoning behind this practice is simple: Since stockholders tend to measure the "worth" of a small stock dividend (say, 20 to 25% or less) in terms of the market value of the additional shares issued, then Retained Earnings should be reduced by this amount.

Large stock dividends (for example, those in excess of 20 to 25%) should be recorded by transferring only the par or stated value of the dividend shares from the Retained Earnings account to the Common Stock account. Large stock dividends generally have the effect of proportionately reducing the market price of the stock. For example, a 100% stock dividend would reduce the market price by about 50%, because twice as many shares would be outstanding. A 100% stock dividend is very similar to the 2 for 1 stock split discussed in the following section of this chapter.

Stock splits

Most large corporations are interested in as wide as possible a distribution of their securities among the investing public. If the market price reaches very high levels as, for example, $150 per share, the corporation may feel that, by splitting the stock 5 for 1 and thereby reducing the price to $30 per share, the number of shareholders may be increased. The bulk of trading in securities occurs in 100-share lots and an extra commission is charged on smaller transactions. Many investors with limited funds prefer to make their investments in 100-share lots of lower-priced stocks. The majority of leading American corporations have split their stock; some have done so several times. Generally the number of shareholders has increased noticeably after the stock has been split.

A stock split consists of increasing the number of outstanding shares and reducing the par or stated value per share in proportion. For example, assume that a corporation has outstanding 1 million shares of $10 par value stock. The market price is $90 per share. The corporation now reduces the par value from $10 to $5 per share and increases the number of shares from 1 million to 2 million. This action would be called a 2 for 1 stock split. A stockholder who formerly owned 100 shares of the $10 par old stock would now own 200 shares of the $5 par new stock. Since the number of outstanding shares has been doubled without any change in the affairs of the corporation, the market price will probably drop from $90 to approximately $45 a share.

A stock split does not change the balance of any ledger account; consequently, the transaction may be recorded merely by a memorandum notation in the general journal and in the Common Stock account.

DISTINCTION BETWEEN STOCK SPLITS AND LARGE STOCK DIVIDENDS What is the difference between a 2 for 1 stock split and a 100% stock dividend? There is very little difference; both will double the number of outstanding shares without changing total stockholders' equity, and both will serve to cut the market price of the stock in half. The stock dividend, however, will cause a transfer from the Retained Earnings account to the Common Stock account equal to the par or stated value of the dividend shares, whereas the stock split does not change the dollar balance of any account.

After an increase in the number of shares as a result of a stock split or stock dividend, earnings per share are computed in terms of the increased number of shares. In presenting five- or ten-year summaries, the earnings per share for earlier years are *retroactively revised* to reflect the increased number of shares currently outstanding and thus make the trend of earnings per share from year to year a valid comparison.

Retained earnings

Throughout this book the term *retained earnings* is used to describe that portion of stockholders' equity derived from profitable operations. Retained earnings is a historical concept, representing the accumulated earnings (including prior period adjustments) minus dividends declared from the date of incorporation to the present. If we assume that there are no *prior period adjustments,* the major sources of entries in the Retained Earnings account will be (1) the periodic transfer of net income (or loss) from the Income Summary account and (2) the debit entries for dividend declarations.

Prior period adjustments to the Retained Earnings account

On occasion, a company may discover that a material error was made in the measurement of net income in a prior year. Since net income is the source of retained earnings, an error in reported net income will cause an error in the amount of retained earnings shown in all subsequent balance sheets. When such an error comes to light, it should be corrected. However, if the error in measuring the net income of a prior year is corrected in the current period's income statement, net income for the current period will be distorted. Therefore, material errors in the amount of net income reported in prior periods are corrected by adjusting the balance of the Retained Earnings account. Such adjustments are called *prior period adjustments.*

Material errors in the financial statements of prior years may arise as a result of mathematical errors, failure to properly interpret the accounting effects of transactions, or the use of inappropriate accounting principles and concepts. Assume, for example, that in Year 10 Vista Corporation is audited for the first time by a firm of certified public accountants. During the audit, the CPAs discover that in Year 6 land costing $120,000 had been written up in Vista Corporation's accounting records to an appraised value of $180,000 and a $60,000 gain had been included in net income. Since land should be valued in accounting records at cost rather than appraised value, the recognition of this $60,000 gain constitutes a material error in Vista Corporation's Year 6 financial statements.

What effect does this error have upon the Vista Corporation's financial statements in Year 10? Since the net income of Year 6 has been closed into the Retained Earnings account, both land and retained earnings are overstated in Year 10 by $60,000. The entry to correct this error is shown below:

Retained Earnings	*60,000*
Land	*60,000*

Prior period adjustment to correct error made in the valuation of land and recognition of income in Year 6.

PRESENTATION OF PRIOR PERIOD ADJUSTMENTS IN FINANCIAL STATEMENTS Corrections of the operating results of prior years are *not* included in the income statement of the current year. Prior period adjustments are shown in the *statement of retained earnings* as an adjustment to the balance of retained earnings at the beginning of the current year. The amount of the prior period adjustment should be shown net of any related tax effects. The presentation of the prior period adjustment in the statement of retained earnings of Vista Corporation is illustrated on page 333.

Most companies present comparative financial statements; that is, financial statements of the preceding year are presented along with those of the current year. If the financial statements for the year in which the error occurred are being presented for comparative purposes, these statements should be revised to eliminate the error. A footnote to the comparative statements should explain that the financial statements for the earlier year have been revised to reflect correction of the error.

NEW CRITERIA MAKE PRIOR PERIOD ADJUSTMENTS RARE Until recently the items treated as prior period adjustments were not limited to the correction of errors. For example, when contract disputes, income tax disputes, or lawsuits were finally resolved, many companies reported the settlements as prior period adjustments. Other companies, however, viewed these events as affecting income for the current year. To resolve these differences, the FASB issued *Statement of Financial Accounting Standards No. 16,* which limits prior period adjustments to the correction of errors in prior years' financial statements and certain income tax adjustments.[7]

Under the criteria set forth in *Statement No. 16,* prior period adjustments should be extremely rare. Large corporations which are audited annually by certified public accountants are not likely to have material errors in their financial statements which subsequently will require correction by prior period adjustments.

Appropriations and restrictions of retained earnings

A few corporations transfer a portion of their retained earnings into separate accounts called *appropriations.* The purpose of such appropriations is to indicate to users of financial statements that a portion of retained earnings is not available for the declaration of cash dividends. The limitation on cash dividends may be established voluntarily by the board of directors (perhaps to provide for some contingency) or it may be required by law or contract. An appropriation of retained earnings is recorded by a debit to Retained Earnings and a credit to the appropriation account such as Retained Earnings Appropriated for Contingencies. Appropriation accounts are still a part of total retained earnings, as indicated by the following partial stockholders' equity section which appeared in a recent balance sheet of Wm. Wrigley Jr. Company:

Appropriations in the balance sheet

Stockholders' equity:

Capital stock, no-par value—authorized and issued—2,000,000 shares	*$ 19,200,000*
Accumulated earnings retained for use in the business	*109,130,000*
Accumulated earnings appropriated for guarantees under employment assurance contracts	*2,000,000*

When the restriction on retained earnings is no longer needed, the appropriation account is eliminated by transferring its balance back to the Retained Earnings account.

Instead of establishing appropriations of retained earnings, most corporations disclose restrictions on the declaration of cash dividends in

---

[7] *Statement of Financial Accounting Standards No. 16,* "Prior Period Adjustments," FASB (Stamford, Conn.: 1977).

notes accompanying the financial statements.[8] An example of such disclosure is shown below.

Alternative disclosure of restrictions placed on retained earnings

Rockwell International Corporation:
Among other covenants, certain of the long-term debt agreements contain limitations on creation of additional long-term debt and restrictions on payment of dividends and acquisition of treasury stock. Retained earnings . . . not so restricted amounted to approximately $117,000,000.

Since the only purpose of appropriating retained earnings is to inform readers of the financial statements that a portion of the retained earnings is "reserved" for a specific purpose and is not available for declaration of cash dividends, this information can be conveyed more directly, with less danger of misunderstanding, by a note accompanying the financial statements.

Statement of retained earnings

In addition to the balance sheet and the income statement, most corporations include a statement of retained earnings and a statement of changes in financial position in their annual reports to stockholders. (The latter statement will be illustrated in Chapter 15.) The statement of retained earnings is usually presented in comparative form covering two years. This format and the treatment of a *prior period adjustment* are illustrated below for Vista Corporation.

VISTA CORPORATION
Statement of Retained Earnings
For Years Ended June 30

	Year 10	Year 9
Retained earnings at beginning of year:		
As originally reported	$ 810,000	$ 780,000
Prior period adjustment—to correct error in		
valuation of land recorded in Year 6	(60,000)	(60,000)
As restated	$ 750,000	$ 720,000
Net income	360,000	210,000
Subtotal	$1,110,000	$ 930,000
Less: Cash dividends on common stock:		
$2.40 per share in Year 10	(240,000)	
$1.80 per share in Year 9		(180,000)
Retained earnings at end of year	$ 870,000	$ 750,000

Statement of retained earnings shows prior period adjustments, net income, and dividends

[8] According to a recent issue of *Accounting Trends & Techniques* published by the AICPA, very few of the 600 annual reports surveyed showed appropriated retained earnings while a large majority of the annual reports referred to restrictions on retained earnings.

The error in the Year 6 financial statements was discovered in Year 10 and is shown as a correction to the beginning balance in retained earnings for both Year 10 and Year 9, since both beginning amounts were overstated. The statement of retained earnings thus provides a useful vehicle for the disclosure of prior period adjustments and for the explanation of all changes in retained earnings during the accounting period.

An alternative presentation of net income and retained earnings is used by some companies. The reconciliation of retained earnings may be shown in the body of a *combined statement of income and retained earnings,* as illustrated below for Lacey Corporation.

LACEY CORPORATION
Combined Statement of Income and Retained Earnings
For Years Ended December 31

	Year 10	Year 9
Net sales	$2,900,000	$2,700,000
Cost of goods sold	1,730,000	1,650,000
Gross profit on sales	$1,170,000	$1,050,000
Operating expenses	620,000	590,000
Income before income taxes	$ 550,000	$ 460,000
Income taxes	260,000	215,000
Net income	$ 290,000	$ 245,000
Retained earnings at beginning of year	730,000	665,000
	$1,020,000	$ 910,000
Dividends: $1 per share in Year 10 and		
$0.90 per share in Year 9	210,000	180,000
Retained earnings at end of year	$ 810,000	$ 730,000
Earnings per share of common stock	$1.38	$1.22

The statement for the Lacey Corporation emphasizes the close relationship of operating results and retained earnings. Some readers of financial statements, however, object to the fact that net income (or loss) is "buried" in the body of a combined statement of income and retained earnings rather than being prominently displayed as the final figure before reporting earnings per share.

Treasury stock

Corporations frequently reacquire shares of their own capital stock by purchase in the open market. The effect of reacquiring shares is to reduce the assets of the corporation and to reduce the stockholders' equity by the same amount. One reason for such purchases is to have stock available to reissue to officers and employees under bonus plans. Other reasons may include a desire to increase the reported earnings per share, to support the market price of the stock, and to have shares available for the acquisition of other companies.

Treasury stock may be defined as a corporation's own capital stock which has been issued, fully paid, and reacquired but not canceled. Treasury shares may be held indefinitely or may be issued again at any time. Shares of capital stock held in the treasury are not entitled to receive dividends, vote, or receive cash or other assets upon dissolution of the company. In the computation of earnings per share, shares held in the treasury are not regarded as outstanding shares.

Recording purchases and reissuance of treasury stock

Purchases of treasury stock should be recorded by debiting the Treasury Stock account with the cost of the stock. For example, if a corporation reacquires 100 shares of its own $10 par stock at a price of $150 per share, the entry is as follows:

Treasury stock recorded at cost	Treasury Stock	15,000	
	Cash		15,000
	Purchased 100 shares of $10 par treasury stock at $150 per share.		

Treasury stock is customarily recorded *at cost* regardless of whether it is par value stock or no-par stock. When the treasury shares are reissued, the Treasury Stock account is credited for *the cost* of the shares reissued, and Paid-in Capital from Treasury Stock Transactions is debited or credited for the difference between cost and reissuance price.

To illustrate the reissuance of treasury stock at a price above cost, assume that the 100 shares acquired at a cost of $15,000 are reissued for a higher price, $18,000. The journal entry is:

Reissued at a price above cost	Cash	18,000	
	Treasury Stock		15,000
	Paid-in Capital from Treasury Stock Transactions		3,000
	Sold 100 shares of treasury stock, which cost $15,000, at a price of $180 each.		

If treasury stock is reissued at a price below cost and a paid-in capital account exists as a result of previous treasury stock transactions, this account may be debited. If there is no paid-in capital as a result of previous treasury stock transactions, the excess of the cost of the treasury shares over reissuance price could be recorded as a debit in any other paid-in capital account. If the company had no paid-in capital in excess of par from any source, the debit would be entered in the Retained Earnings account.

Treasury stock is not an asset

Corporations sometimes list treasury stock among the assets, on the grounds that the shares could be sold for cash just as readily as shares owned in another corporation. The same argument could be made for treating unissued shares as assets. Treasury shares are basically the same as unissued shares, and an unissued share of stock is definitely not an asset.

When treasury stock is purchased, the corporation is eliminating a part of the stockholders' equity by paying off one or more stockholders. It is, therefore, reasonable to think of the purchase of treasury stock not as the acquisition of an asset, but as the returning of capital to stockholders. For this reason treasury stock should appear in the balance sheet *as a deduction in the stockholders' equity section.*

Conversely, if the treasury shares are later reissued, this is a separate transaction in which the corporation is securing additional invested capital. Assume, for example, that a corporation pays $10 to acquire a share of treasury stock and later reissues this share for $15. Has the corporation made a $5 profit on this transaction with its owners? Definitely not; *there is no profit or loss on treasury stock transactions.* When the treasury share was reissued for $15, the corporation was merely receiving a larger amount of invested capital than was previously withdrawn when a stockholder surrendered the share to the company. A corporation earns profits by selling goods and services to outsiders at a price above cost, not by issuing or reissuing shares of its own stock.

Restriction of retained earnings when treasury stock is acquired

If a corporation is to maintain its paid-in capital intact, it must not pay out to its stockholders any more than it earns. As previously stated in the section dealing with dividends, the amount of dividends to be paid must not exceed the corporation's accumulated earnings, or the corporation will be returning a portion of the stockholders' original investment to them.

The payment of cash dividends and the acquisition of treasury stock have a good deal in common. In both transactions, the corporation is disbursing cash to its stockholders. Of course, the dividend payment is spread out among all the stockholders, whereas the payment to purchase treasury stock may go to only a few stockholders, but this does not alter the fact that the corporation is turning over some of its assets to its owners. The total amount which a corporation may pay to its stockholders without reducing paid-in capital is shown by the balance in the Retained Earnings account. Consequently, it is important that a corporation keep track of the total amount disbursed in payment for treasury stock and make sure that this amount plus any dividends paid does not exceed the company's accumulated earnings. This objective is conveniently accomplished by restricting the availability of retained earnings for dividends to the extent of the cost of treasury stock purchased. The restriction should be disclosed in a note accompanying the financial statements.

Book value per share of common stock

Earlier in this chapter, we emphasized that most stockholders are much interested in earnings per share and dividends per share. Another accounting measurement of interest to stockholders is **book value per share of common stock.** In a corporation which has issued common stock only, the book value per share is computed by dividing total stockholders' equity by the number of shares of stock outstanding. Thus book value per share is equal to the **net assets** represented by one share of stock. The term **net assets** means total assets minus total liabilities; in other words, the total net assets are equal to the total stockholders' equity.

Book value is usually computed only for common stock. If a company has both preferred and common stock outstanding, the computation of book value per share of common stock requires two steps. First the redemption value or call price of the entire preferred stock issue and any dividends in arrears are deducted from total stockholders' equity. Secondly, the remaining amount of stockholders' equity is divided by the number of common shares outstanding to determine book value per common share. This procedure reflects the fact that the common stockholders are the residual owners of the corporate entity.

To illustrate, assume that the stockholders' equity is as follows:

Two classes of stock *8% preferred stock, $100 par, callable at $110*	*$1,000,000*
Common stock, no-par; $5 stated value; authorized 100,000 shares,	
issued and outstanding 80,000 shares	*400,000*
Paid-in capital in excess of par value	*800,000*
Retained earnings	*900,000*
Total stockholders' equity	*$3,100,000*

All the capital belongs to the common stockholders, except the $1.1 million call price ($110 × 10,000 shares) applicable to the preferred stock (and any dividends in arrears on preferred stock). The calculation of book value per share of common stock can therefore be made as follows:

Compute *Total stockholders' equity*	*$3,100,000*
book value *Less: Preferred stock (at call price of $110 per share)*	*1,100,000*
per share of	
common *Equity of common stockholders*	*$2,000,000*
stock *Number of shares of common stock outstanding*	*80,000*
Book value per share of common stock $\dfrac{\$2,000,000}{80,000}$	*$25*

The concept of book value is of vital importance in many contracts. For example, a majority stockholder might obtain an option to purchase the shares of the minority stockholders at book value at a specified future date. Many court cases have hinged on definitions of book value.

Book value is also used in judging the reasonableness of the market price of a stock. However, it must be used with great caution; the fact that a stock is selling at less than its book value does not necessarily indicate a bargain. The disparity between book value and market price per share is indicated by the following data currently available for three well-known corporations: General Motors, book value $54, market price $63; American Airlines, book value $24, market price $13; Johnson & Johnson, book value $25, market price $77. Earnings per share, dividends per share, and prospects for future earnings are usually more important factors affecting market price than is book value.

Book value does *not* indicate the amount which the holder of a share of stock would receive if the corporation were to be dissolved. In liquidation, the assets would probably be sold at prices quite different from their carrying values in the accounts, and the stockholders' equity would go up or down accordingly.

Illustration of stockholders' equity section

The following illustration of a stockholders' equity section of a balance sheet shows a fairly detailed classification by source of the various elements of corporate capital:

Stockholders' Equity

Compare with published financial statements

Capital stock:			
9% preferred stock, $100 par value, authorized and issued 1,000 shares		$100,000	
Common stock, no-par, stated value $5 a share, authorized 100,000 shares, issued 60,000 shares, of which 1,000 are held in treasury		300,000	
Common stock subscribed, 6,000 shares		30,000	$430,000
Additional paid-in capital:			
Paid-in capital from stock dividends		$ 50,000	
Paid-in capital in excess of stated value: common stock		290,000	
Paid-in capital from treasury stock transactions		5,000	345,000
Total paid-in capital			$775,000
Retained earnings (of which $12,000, an amount equal to the cost of treasury stock purchased, is unavailable for dividends)			162,000
			$937,000
Less: Treasury stock, common, 1,000 shares at cost			12,000
Total stockholders' equity			$925,000

The published financial statements of leading corporations indicate that there is no one standard arrangement for the several items making up the stockholders' equity section. Variations occur in the selection of titles, in the sequence of items, and in the extent of detailed classification. Many companies, in an effort to avoid excessive detail in the balance sheet, will combine several related ledger accounts into a single balance sheet item. An example of published financial statements appears in the Appendix.

KEY TERMS INTRODUCED OR EMPHASIZED IN CHAPTER 8

Book value per share The net assets per share of common stock, computed by dividing common stockholders' equity by the number of common shares outstanding.

Comparative financial statements Financial statements of current year and the preceding year which are presented together to facilitate comparison.

Date of record The date on which a person must be listed as a shareholder in order to be eligible to receive a dividend. Follows the date of declaration of a dividend by two or three weeks.

Discontinued operations The operations (revenue and expenses) of a segment of a company which has been or is being sold.

Earnings per share (EPS) Net income available to the common stock divided by the weighted-average number of common shares outstanding during the year.

Ex-dividend date A date three days prior to the date of record specified in a dividend declaration. A person buying a stock prior to the ex-dividend date also acquires the right to receive the dividend. The three-day interval permits the compilation of a list of stockholders as of the date of record.

Extraordinary items Transactions and events that are both unusual in nature and occur infrequently; for example, a large earthquake loss.

Fully diluted earnings per share Net income available to the common stock divided by the weighted-average number of common shares outstanding during the year plus any other securities convertible into common shares (if conversion would decrease EPS).

Liquidating dividend A return to shareholders of all or part of their paid-in capital investment. To be distinguished from a distribution of earnings.

Price-earnings ratio Market price of a share of common stock divided by annual earnings per share.

Primary earnings per share Net income available to the common stock divided by weighted-average number of common shares outstanding.

Prior period adjustment A correction of a material error in the earnings reported in the financial statements of a prior year. Prior period adjustments are recorded directly in the Retained Earnings account and are not included in the income statement of the current period.

Restrictions of retained earnings Action by the board of directors to classify a portion of retained earnings as unavailable for dividends.

Segment of a business A component of a business. The activities of the component represent a major line of business or class of customer.

Statement of retained earnings A basic financial statement showing the change in retained earnings during the year.

Stock dividend A distribution of additional shares to common stockholders in proportion to their holdings.

Stock split An increase in the number of shares outstanding with a corresponding decrease in par value per share. Distributed proportionately to all common shareholders. Purpose is to reduce market price per share and encourage wider public ownership of the company's stock. A 2 for 1 stock split will give each stockholder twice as many shares as previously owned.

Treasury stock Shares of a corporation's own stock which have been issued, fully paid, and reacquired but not canceled.

DEMONSTRATION PROBLEM FOR YOUR REVIEW

A comparative summary of the stockholders' equity of Sutton Corporation, together with certain additional information, is shown below:

	Dec. 31, Year 10		Dec. 31, Year 9
Stockholders' equity:			
Common stock, 100,000 shares author-			
ized; issued:			
At Dec. 31, Year 10, 70,000 shares, $8			
par value (1,000 held in treasury)	*$560,000*		
At Dec. 31, Year 9, 40,000 shares,			
$10 par value			*$ 400,000*
Stock dividend to be distributed			
(6,900 shares)	*55,200*	*$ 615,200*	
Additional paid-in capital:			
From issuance of common stock in			
excess of par value	*$940,000*		*200,000*
From stock dividends distributed	*276,000*		
From treasury stock transactions	*8,000*	*1,224,000*	
Total paid-in capital		*$1,839,200*	*$ 600,000*
Retained earnings		*1,276,800*	*1,500,000*
Total paid-in capital and retained earnings		*$3,116,000*	
Less: Treasury stock, 1,000 shares at cost		*37,000*	
Total stockholders' equity		*$3,079,000*	*$2,100,000*

Transactions affecting stockholders' equity during Year 10:
Mar. 1 A 5 for 4 stock split proposed by the board of directors was approved by vote of the stockholders.
Mar. 31 Additional shares were distributed to stockholders pursuant to the 5 for 4 split.
Apr. 1 The company purchased 2,000 shares of its common stock on the open market at $37 per share.
July 1 The company reissued 1,000 shares of treasury stock at $45 per share.
July 1 Issued for cash 20,000 shares of previously unissued $8 par value common stock at a price of $45 per share.
Dec. 1 A cash dividend of $1 per share was declared, payable on December 30, to stockholders of record at December 14.
Dec. 22 A 10% stock dividend was declared; the dividend shares to be distributed on January 24, Year 11. The market price of the stock on December 22 was $48 per share.

The net income for the year ended December 31, Year 10, amounted to $177,000, after an extraordinary loss of $35,400 (net of income tax reduction of $30,000).

Instructions
a Prepare journal entries to record the transactions relating to stockholders' equity that took place during Year 10.
b Prepare the lower section of the income statement for the year ended December 31, Year 10, beginning with the income before extraordinary items and showing the extraordinary loss and the net income. Also illustrate the presentation of earnings per share in the income statement, assuming that earnings per share is determined on the basis of the weighted-average number of shares outstanding during the year.
c Prepare a statement of retained earnings for the year ended December 31, Year 10.

SOLUTION TO DEMONSTRATION PROBLEM

a   *General Journal*

Mar.	1	Memorandum: Stockholders approved a 5 for 4 stock split. This action increased the number of shares of common stock outstanding from 40,000 to 50,000 and reduced the par value from $10 to $8 per share.		
	31	Common Stock, $10 par	400,000	
		Common Stock, $8 par		400,000
		Distributed 10,000 additional shares of stock pursuant to 5 for 4 stock split, and reduced par value.		
Apr.	1	Treasury Stock	74,000	
		Cash		74,000
		Acquired 2,000 shares of treasury stock at $37 per share.		
July	1	Cash	45,000	
		Treasury Stock		37,000
		Paid-in Capital from Treasury Stock Transactions		8,000
		Sold 1,000 shares of treasury stock at $45 per share.		
	1	Cash	900,000	
		Common Stock, $8 par		160,000
		Paid-in Capital in Excess of Par		740,000
		Issued 20,000 shares of previously unissued $8 par value stock for cash.		

Dec. 1	Dividends	69,000	
	Dividends Payable		69,000

To record declaration of cash dividend of $1 per share on
69,000 shares of common stock outstanding (1,000 shares
in treasury are not entitled to receive dividends).

Note: Entry to record the payment of the cash dividend is not shown here since
the action does not affect the stockholders' equity.

Dec. 22	Retained Earnings	331,200	
	Stock Dividends to be Distributed		55,200
	Paid-in Capital from Stock Dividends		276,000

To record declaration of 10% stock dividend consisting of
6,900 shares of $8 par value common stock to be distributed
on Jan. 24, Year 11. Excess of fair market value of stock
over par value, $40 ($48 − $8), is credited to Paid-in Capital
from Stock Dividends.

31	Income Summary	177,000	
	Retained Earnings		177,000

To close Income Summary account.

Dec. 31	Retained Earnings	69,000	
	Dividends		69,000

To close Dividends account.

b

SUTTON CORPORATION
Partial Income Statement
For Year Ended December 31, Year 10

Income before extraordinary items	$212,400
Extraordinary loss, net of income tax reduction of $30,000	(35,400)
Net income	$177,000

Earnings per share:*

Income before extraordinary items	$3.60
Extraordinary loss, net of tax	(0.60)
Net income	$3.00

*On 59,000 weighted-average number of shares of common stock outstanding during Year 10: determined as follows:

Jan. 1–Mar. 31: (40,000 + 10,000 shares issued pursuant to a 5 for 4 split) × $\frac{1}{4}$ of year	12,500
Apr. 1–June 30: (50,000 − 2,000 shares of treasury stock) × $\frac{1}{4}$ of year	12,000
July 1–Dec. 31: (50,000 + 20,000 shares of new stock − 1,000 shares of treasury stock) × $\frac{1}{2}$ of year	34,500
Weighted-average number of shares outstanding	59,000

c

SUTTON CORPORATION
Statement of Retained Earnings
For the Year Ended December 31, Year 10

Retained earnings, Jan. 1, Year 10		$1,500,000
Net income		177,000
Subtotal		$1,677,000
Dividends:		
Cash, $1 per share	$ 69,000	
Stock, 10% (to be distributed Jan. 24, Year 11)	331,200	400,200
Retained earnings, Dec. 31, Year 10		$1,276,800

REVIEW QUESTIONS

1 Why is the reporting of the results of operations so important to users of financial statements?

2 Define a *segment of a business* and *extraordinary items* for purposes of reporting the results of operations.

3 Give some examples of *segments of a business* and *extraordinary losses.*

4 Briefly describe how each of the following should be reported in the income statement for the current year:
a Write-off of a large account receivable from a bankrupt customer
b Large loss from sale of a major segment of a business
c Large gain from sale of one of many investments in common stock
d Large write-off of obsolete inventory
e Large uninsured loss from earthquake
f Correction of a material error in the reported net income of an earlier year

5 How should the effect of a material event or transaction which is either unusual in nature or occurs infrequently, but not both, be disclosed?

6 Briefly define each of the following:
a Price-earnings ratio
b Primary earnings per share
c Fully diluted earnings per share

7 Explain the significance of the following dates relating to dividends: date of declaration, date of record, date of payment, ex-dividend date.

8 Distinguish between a *stock split* and a *stock dividend.* Is there any reason for the difference in accounting treatment of these two events?

9 If the Retained Earnings account has a debit balance, how is it presented in the balance sheet and what is it called?

10 What are prior period adjustments? How are they presented in financial statements?

11 What is the purpose of an appropriation of retained earnings? What are the arguments for and against the use of such appropriations?

12 What type of transaction most frequently appears as a deduction in a statement of retained earnings?

13 What is *treasury stock?* Why do corporations purchase their own shares? Is treasury stock an asset? How should it be reported in the balance sheet?

14 In many states, the corporation law requires that retained earnings be restricted for dividend purposes to the extent of the cost of treasury shares. What is the reason for this legal rule?

15 What would be the effect, if any, on book value per share of common stock as a result of each of the following independent events: a corporation (*a*) obtains a bank loan, (*b*) is assessed additional income taxes applicable to prior years, and (*c*) distributes a 5% stock dividend?

16 How is book value per share of common stock computed when a company has both preferred and common stock outstanding?

17 If a statement of retained earnings consisted of only four items, what would these four items most probably be?

18 What is the most effective method of disclosing in financial statements the fact that a portion of the retained earnings is restricted by the terms of a long-term debt agreement and therefore not available for payment of dividends or acquisition of treasury stock?

19 "In a long-established, successful corporation the Cash account would normally have a dollar balance equal to or larger than the Retained Earnings account." Do you agree with this quotation? Explain.

EXERCISES

Ex. 8-1 In Year 5, Salarno Company had net sales of $1,200,000, costs and other expenses (including income taxes) of $720,000, and an extraordinary loss (net of income tax) of $200,000. Prepare a condensed income statement (including earnings per share) for Year 5, assuming that an average of 100,000 shares of common stock were outstanding during Year 5.

Ex. 8-2 Fred Johnson purchased 100 shares of stock in Mills Corporation at the time it was organized. At the end of the first year's operations, the corporation reported earnings (after taxes) of $6 per share, and declared a dividend of $3 per share. Johnson complains that he is entitled to the full distribution of the amount earned on his investment. Is there any reason why a corporation that earns $6 per share may not be able to pay a dividend of this amount? Are there any advantages to Johnson in the retention by the company of one-half of its earnings?

Ex. 8-3 San Lorenzo Corporation has been in existence for three years and at the end of Year 3 intends to report earnings per share for each of the three years on a *comparable basis.* During Years 1 and 2 the common stock outstanding remained unchanged at 2,000,000 shares. In Year 3, the stock was split 3 for 1 on March 1, and 1,200,000 new shares were sold for cash on July 1. (Note that the company had the use of additional funds paid in by stockholders for the last half of Year 3.) The corporation had 7,200,000 shares outstanding at the end of Year 3.

  a Compute the *weighted-average number* of shares outstanding for each year that should be used in reporting *comparative earnings per share data* in the financial statements at the end of Year 3.

  b Assuming that net earnings were $4,500,000 in Year 1, $600,000 in Year 2, and $9,900,000 in Year 3, compute the earnings per share for each year to be reported on a comparable basis at the end of Year 3.

Ex. 8-4 Lee Company has 180,000 shares of $10 par common stock and 10,000 shares of $6.60 cumulative preferred stock outstanding at the end of the current year. Each share of preferred stock is convertible into four shares of common stock. Net income for the current year is $660,000. Show how the primary and fully diluted earnings per share should appear in the income statement for the current year.

Ex. 8-5 Martin Corporation has a total of 20,000 shares of common stock outstanding and no preferred stock. The net assets of the Martin Corporation at the end of the current year are $750,000 and the market value of the stock is $48 per share. At year-end, the company declares a stock dividend of one share for each five shares held. If all parties concerned clearly recognized the nature of the stock dividend, what would you expect the market price per share of Martin's common stock to be on the ex-dividend date?

Ex. 8-6 Glass Corporation has 1 million shares of $5 par value capital stock outstanding. You are to prepare the journal entries to record the following transactions:

June 1 Declared a cash dividend of 20 cents per share.
July 1 Paid the 20-cent cash dividend to stockholders.
Aug. 1 Declared a 5% stock dividend. Market price of stock was $18 per share.
Sept. 10 Issued 50,000 shares pursuant to the 5% stock dividend.
Dec. 1 Declared a 50% stock dividend. Market price of stock was $30 per share.

Ex. 8-7 Sharon Reed owns 1,000 out of a total of 20,000 outstanding common shares of McNerney Corporation. The McNerney Corporation reports total assets of $1,360,000 and total liabilities of $480,000 at the end of the current year, and at that time the board declares a stock dividend of one share for each 10 shares held. Compute the book value *per share* of Reed's stock and the total book value of Reed's investment in the corporation: (*a*) before the stock dividend; (*b*) after the stock dividend.

Ex. 8-8 The following data are taken from the records of the Brunner Corporation:

9% cumulative preferred stock, $100 par (callable at $110)	*$200,000*
Common stock, no par, 51,500 shares issued, 1,500 held in treasury	*760,000*
Paid-in capital from treasury stock transactions	*2,100*
Dividends in arrears on preferred stock, 2 full years	*18,000*
Deficit	*126,800*
Organization costs	*10,000*
Treasury stock, common, 1,500 shares, at cost	*17,300*
Total liabilities	*423,000*

Instructions
a Compute the amount of net assets (stockholders' equity).
b Compute the book value per share of common stock.

PROBLEMS

8-1 The operations for Replacement Parts, Inc., are summarized below for Year 10:

	From Continuing Operations	*From Discontinued Operations*
Net sales	*$14,000,000*	*$3,000,000*
Costs and expenses (including applicable income tax effects)	*11,200,000*	*3,850,000*
Loss on disposal of discontinued segment, net of income taxes		*450,000*

Instructions Assuming that the company had an average of 500,000 shares of a single class of capital stock outstanding during Year 10, prepare a condensed income statement (including earnings per share).

8-2 The accountant for Santa Rosa Corporation *improperly* prepared the following income statement for Year 3:

SANTA ROSA CORPORATION
Income Statement
For Year 3

Net sales.		$ 8,800,000
Sales of treasury stock in Year 3 (cost, $650,000; proceeds,		
$800,000)		150,000
Excess of proceeds over par value of capital stock issued in		
Year 3		960,000
Reduction in appropriation of retained earnings (for treasury stock		
owned)		650,000
Total revenue.		$10,560,000
Less:		
Cost of goods sold	$4,970,000	
Operating expenses.	2,040,000	
Loss from earthquake (before tax reduction of		
$200,000)	460,000	
Dividends declared on capital stock	300,000	
Estimated income tax expense, after reduction of		
$200,000 as a result of the loss from		
earthquake	650,000	8,420,000
Net income		$ 2,140,000

At the beginning of Year 3, the audited financial statements of the company show unappropriated retained earnings of $3,250,000 and a balance in the Appropriated Retained Earnings (for Treasury Stock Owned) account of $1,000,000. The treasury stock transaction is not taxable, and the earthquake loss is fully deductible in computing taxable income. Income tax expense has been properly estimated by a tax advisor. The earthquake loss should be reported in the income statement as an extraordinary item **net of income taxes.**

Instructions

a Prepare a corrected income statement for Year 3. Show data for earnings per share of capital stock in the income statement. Santa Rosa Corporation had a weighted average of 200,000 shares of a single class of capital stock outstanding during the year.

b Prepare a statement of retained earnings for Year 3. [Use three columns as follows: Appropriated Retained Earnings (for Treasury Stock Owned), Unappropriated Retained Earnings, and Total Retained Earnings.]

8-3 John Thorpe, a part-time employee of Whaleboat Corporation, prepared a balance sheet at December 31, Year 7, which included the following stockholders' equity accounts:

6% cumulative preferred stock (40,000 shares issued and outstanding) . . .	$2,000,000
Common stock (60,000 shares outstanding)	546,000
Surplus	1,614,000

The company was authorized to issue 50,000 shares of $50 par value preferred and 100,000 shares of $10 par value common stock. Of the 40,000 shares of preferred issued, 36,000 were issued at par and 4,000 were issued at $53 per share. A total of 66,000 shares of common stock were issued at an average price of $22 per share. Of this total, 6,000 shares have been reacquired by the company at a cost of $114,000, which amount the accountant deducted from the Common Stock account. The preferred stock is callable at any time at $55 per share.

The Surplus account contains the excess of issuance price over par on preferred and common stock and $810,000 of retained earnings.

Instructions Prepare a corrected stockholders' equity section of the balance sheet at December 31, Year 7. Include a full description of each stock issue with respect to par value, call provision, and number of shares authorized, issued, outstanding, and held in the treasury.

8-4 Coastal Airlines, Inc., operated both an airline service and several motels located near airports. During Year 4, all motel operations were discontinued and the following operating results were reported:

Income before taxes from continuing operations	*$4,500,000*
Loss before taxes from discontinued operations	*1,000,000*
Extraordinary loss, before tax	*400,000*

All income is taxable at a rate of 40% (the loss from discontinued operations and the extraordinary loss are deductible in determining the amount of taxable income).

Coastal Airlines, Inc., had 400,000 shares of common stock and 50,000 shares of 6%, $100 par value, convertible preferred stock outstanding throughout Year 4. Each share of the preferred stock is convertible into two shares of common stock.

Instructions Prepare a partial income statement for Year 4, beginning with Income before taxes from continuing operations . . . $4,500,000. The loss from discontinued operations and the extraordinary loss are to be shown net of income taxes. Include all appropriate earnings per share figures.

8-5 Transactions affecting the stockholders' equity section of Skyline, Inc., from the date of its incorporation have been as follows:
   (1) Received from investors $756,000 in payment for 12,000 shares of $50 par value 8% preferred stock. The total preferred stock authorized was 36,000 shares.
   (2) The company has received from stockholders $1,650,000 in exchange for 60,000 outstanding shares of no-par value common stock having a stated value of $10 per share (authorized: 300,000 shares).
   (3) Total net income since the date of incorporation has been $1,146,000.
   (4) Cash dividends paid since the date of incorporation, $468,000.
   (5) Stock dividends declared (but not yet distributed to stockholders) amount to 6,000 shares of common. The market value of the common at the date of record was $40 per share.
   (6) Certain land having an assessed valuation of $60,000 was donated to the corporation by the city as a site for a manufacturing plant. The fair market value of the land at the time of the gift was $192,000. The company properly credited Donated Capital for $192,000.
   (7) The amount of $120,000 was recently transferred by order of the board of directors from the Retained Earnings account to Retained Earnings Appropriated for Contingencies.

Instructions On the basis of this information, prepare in good form the stockholders' equity section of the Skyline, Inc., balance sheet at the end of the current year.

8-6 Ramada Corporation was organized early in Year 1 and was authorized to issue 160,000 shares of $10 par value common stock and 80,000 shares of $50 par value 7% preferred stock. During Year 1 the company sold 112,000 shares of common stock, at an average price of $30 per share, and issued an additional 16,000 shares of common stock in exchange for patents valued at $512,000. The company earned a net income of $168,000 in Year 1 and paid dividends of 40 cents per share of common stock at the end of Year 1.

On January 1 of Year 2, the company issued 32,000 shares of preferred stock in exchange for land valued at $1,616,000. Quarterly dividends were declared and paid on preferred shares in March, June, and September of Year 2. On December 28, Year 2, the company declared the fourth quarterly dividend on preferred stock and a 10% stock dividend to be distributed in Year 3 to common stockholders. Net income for Year 2 was $572,800. The market price of common stock at the end of Year 2 was $40 per share.

Instructions Prepare the stockholders' equity section of the balance sheet at
a December 31, Year 1
b December 31, Year 2

8-7 On January 1 of the current year Offshore Industries had retained earnings of $5,920,000. On July 31, the company declared and paid a cash dividend of 50 cents per share.

At November 30 of the current year, the stockholders' equity was as follows:

Capital stock, $10 par value, authorized 1,200,000 shares, issued and outstanding 700,000 shares	*$ 7,000,000*
Paid-in capital in excess of par value	*4,200,000*
Retained earnings	*6,790,000*
Total stockholders' equity	*$17,990,000*

During December the company earned net income of $138,400, and on December 30 the board of directors declared a cash dividend of 60 cents per share. The equity accounts were also affected during December by the company's action in reacquiring 10,000 shares of its own capital stock for $300,000. Later in the month (and prior to the December 30 dividend declaration), the company sold 6,000 shares of the treasury stock at $33 per share.

Instructions
a Prepare a statement of retained earnings for the year.
b Prepare the stockholders' equity section of the balance sheet at December 31.
c Compute book value per share at November 30 and at December 31.

8-8 On January 1 of the current year, Great Plains Corporation showed the following amounts in the stockholders' equity section of the balance sheet.

Stockholders' equity:	
8% cumulative preferred stock, $100 par, 80,000 shares authorized, 8,000 shares issued	*$ 800,000*
Common stock, $5 par, 800,000 shares authorized, 300,000 shares issued	*1,500,000*
Paid-in capital in excess of par:	
Preferred stock	*16,000*
Common stock	*1,200,000*
Total paid-in capital	*$3,516,000*
Retained earnings	*2,080,000*
Total stockholders' equity	*$5,596,000*

The transactions relating to the stockholders' equity accounts during the current year are shown below:

Jan. 18 Paid regular semiannual dividend on preferred stock and $1 per share cash dividend on common stock. Both dividends were declared in December of the prior year and properly recorded at that time.

June 5 Declared semiannual dividend on preferred stock to stockholders of record on July 12, payable on July 26. (Debit Dividends on Preferred Stock.)

July 26 Paid preferred dividend declared on June 5.

Oct. 14 Declared 5% stock dividend on common stock to stockholders of record on October 31, to be distributed November 15; market price, $14 a share.

Nov. 15 Distributed 5% stock dividend declared on October 14.

Nov. 30 Sold 32,000 shares of common stock for $16 per share.

Dec. 23 Declared regular semiannual dividend on preferred stock and a dividend of $1 per share on common stock of record at January 10, payable on January 21.

Dec. 31 Net income for the current year amounted to $672,000. (Close the Income Summary account into the Retained Earnings account.)

Dec. 31 Closed dividend accounts to Retained Earnings account.

Instructions

a Prepare in general journal form the entries necessary to record these transactions.

b Comment on whether Great Plains Corporation increased or decreased the total amount of cash dividends *declared* on the common stock during the current year in comparison with the dividends declared in the past year.

c Prepare a balance sheet for Great Plains Corporation at the end of the current year, assuming that total assets amount to $9.6 million. (*Hint:* Prepare the stockholders' equity section of the balance sheet and "plug" the amount of other liabilities after computing the amount of dividends payable.)

BUSINESS DECISION PROBLEM 8

Near the end of the current year, the board of directors of the Shadetree Corporation is presented with the following statement of stockholders' equity:

Capital stock (120,000 shares issued)	$2,400,000
Paid-in capital in excess of par	1,440,000
Retained earnings	1,920,000
Total stockholders' equity	$5,760,000

Shadetree Corporation has paid dividends of $3.60 per share in each of the last five years. After careful consideration of the company's cash needs, the board of directors declared a stock dividend of 24,000 shares. Shortly after the stock dividend had been distributed and before the end of the year, the company declared a cash dividend of $3 per share.

John Joseph owned 10,000 shares of Shadetree Corporation's stock which he acquired several years ago. The market price of this stock before any dividend action in the current year was $60 per share.

Instructions Based on the information given above, answer each of the following questions, showing all relevant computations.

a What is Joseph's share (in dollars) of the net assets as reported in the balance sheet of the Shadetree Corporation before the stock dividend action? What is his share after the stock dividend action? Explain why there is or is not any change as a result of the 20% stock dividend.

b What are the probable reasons why the market value of Joseph's stock differs from the amount of net assets per share shown in the accounting records?

c How does the amount of cash dividends that Joseph received in the current year compare with dividends received in prior years?

  d On the day the stock went ex-dividend (with respect to the 20% stock dividend), its quoted market price fell from $60 to $50 per share. Did this represent a loss to Joseph? Explain.

  e If the Shadetree Corporation had announced that it would continue its regular cash dividend of $3.60 per share on the increased number of shares outstanding after the 20% stock dividend, would you expect the market price of the stock to react in any way different from the change described in ***d?*** Why?

9

Cash and Marketable Securities

CASH

Accountants use the word *cash* to include coins, paper money, checks, money orders, and money on deposit with banks. However, cash does not include postage stamps, IOU's, or postdated checks.

In deciding whether a particular item comes within the classification of cash, the following rule is a useful one: *Any medium of exchange which a bank will accept for deposit is included in cash.* As an example, checks and money orders are accepted by banks for deposit and are considered as cash. Postage stamps and postdated checks are not acceptable for deposit at a bank and are not included in the accountant's definition of cash.

Balance sheet presentation

Cash is a current asset. In fact, cash is the most current and most liquid of all assets. In judging whether other types of assets qualify for inclusion in the current assets section of the balance sheet, we consider the length of time required for the asset to be converted into cash.

The banker, credit manager, or investor who studies a balance sheet critically will always be interested in the total amount of cash as compared with other balance sheet items, such as accounts payable. These outside users of a company's financial statements are not interested, however, in such details as the number of separate bank accounts, or in the distinction between cash on hand and cash in banks. A business that carries checking accounts with several banks will maintain a separate ledger account for each bank account. On the balance sheet, however, the entire amount of cash on hand and cash on deposit with the several banks will be shown as a single amount. One objective in preparing financial statements is to keep them short, concise, and easy to read.

Some bank accounts are restricted as to their use, so that they are not available for making payments to meet normal operating needs of the business. An example (discussed in Chapter 13) is a bond sinking fund, consisting of cash being accumulated by a corporation for the specific purpose of paying off bonded indebtedness at a future date and not available for any other use. A bank account located in a foreign country may also be restricted if monetary regulations prevent the transfer of funds between the two countries. Restricted bank accounts are not regarded as current assets because they are not available for use in paying current liabilities.

Management responsibilities relating to cash

Efficient management of cash includes measures that will:

1 Prevent losses from fraud or theft
2 Provide accurate accounting for cash receipts, cash payments, and cash balances
3 Maintain a sufficient amount of cash at all times to make necessary payments, plus a reasonable balance for emergencies
4 Prevent unnecessarily large amounts of cash from being held idle in bank accounts which produce no revenue

Internal control over cash is sometimes regarded merely as a means of preventing fraud or theft. A good system of internal control, however, will also aid in achieving management's other objectives of accurate accounting for cash transactions and the maintenance of adequate but not excessive cash balances.

Basic requirements for internal control over cash

Cash is more susceptible to theft than any other asset. Furthermore, a large portion of the total transactions of a business involve the receipt or disbursement of cash. For both these reasons, internal control over cash is of great importance to management and also to the employees of a business. If a cash shortage arises in a business in which internal controls are weak or nonexistent, every employee is under suspicion. Perhaps no one employee can be proved guilty of the theft, but neither can any employee prove his or her innocence.

On the other hand, if internal controls over cash are adequate, theft without detection is virtually impossible except through the collusion of two or more employees. To achieve internal control over cash or any other group of assets requires first of all that *the custody of assets be clearly separated from the recording of transactions.* Secondly, the recording function should be subdivided among employees, so that the work of one person is verified by that of another. This subdivision of duties discourages fraud, because collusion among employees would be necessary to conceal an irregularity. Internal control is more easily achieved in large companies than in small companies, because extensive subdivision of duties is more feasible in the larger business.

The major steps in establishing internal controls over cash include the following:

1 Separate the function of handling cash from the maintenance of accounting records. Employees who handle cash should not have access to the accounting records, and accounting personnel should not have access to cash.
2 Establish separate and specific routines to be followed in the handling of cash receipts, the making of cash payments, and the recording of cash transactions.
3 Require that all cash receipts be deposited daily in the bank and that all significant cash payments be made by check. Cash payments should *not* be made directly from cash receipts on hand.
4 Require that the validity and amount of every expenditure be verified before payment is made.
5 Separate the function of approving expenditures from the function of signing checks.

The application of these principles in building an adequate system of internal control over cash can best be illustrated by considering separately the topics of cash receipts and cash disbursements.

Cash receipts

Cash receipts consist of two major types: cash received over the counter at the time of a sale and cash received through the mail as collections on accounts receivable.

USE OF CASH REGISTERS Cash received over the counter at the time of a sale should be rung up on a cash register, so located that the customer will see the amount recorded. If store operations can be so arranged that two employees must participate in each sales transaction, stronger internal control will be achieved than when one employee is permitted to handle a transaction in its entirety. In some stores this objective is accomplished by employing a central cashier who rings on a cash register the sales made by all salespeople.

At the end of the day, the store manager or other supervisor should compare the cash register tape, showing the total sales for the day, with the total cash collected.

USE OF PRENUMBERED SALES TICKETS Internal control may be further strengthened by writing out a prenumbered sales ticket in duplicate at the time of each sale. The original is given to the customer and the carbon copy retained. At the end of the day an employee computes a total sales figure from these duplicate tickets, and also makes sure that no tickets are missing from the series. The total amount of sales as computed from the duplicate sales tickets is then compared with the total sales recorded on the cash register.

CASH RECEIVED THROUGH THE MAIL The procedures for handling checks and currency received through the mail are also based on the internal control principle that two or more employees should participate in every transaction.

The employee who opens the mail should prepare a list of the checks received. In order that this list shall represent the total receipts of the day, the totals recorded on the cash registers may be added to the list. One copy of the list is forwarded with the cash (currency and checks) to the cashier, who will deposit in the bank all the cash received for the day. Another copy of the list is sent to the accounting department, which will record the amount of cash received.

The total cash receipts recorded each day in the accounting records should agree with the amount of the cashier's deposit, and also with the list of total cash receipts for the day.

CASH OVER AND SHORT In handling over-the-counter cash receipts, a few errors in making change will inevitably occur. These errors will cause a cash shortage or overage at the end of the day, when the cash is counted and compared with the reading on the cash register.

For example, assume that the total cash sales for the day as recorded by the cash register amount to $500, but that the cash in the drawer when counted amounts to only $490. The following entry would be made to record the day's sales and the cash shortage of $10.

Recording cash shortage

Cash	490	
Cash Over and Short	10	
Sales		500

The account entitled Cash Over and Short is debited with shortages and credited with overages. If the cash shortages during an entire accounting period are in excess of the cash overages, the Cash Over and Short account will have a debit balance and will be shown as a miscellaneous expense in the income statement. On the other hand, if the overages exceed the shortages, the Cash Over and Short account will show a credit balance at the end of the period and should be treated as an item of miscellaneous revenue.

Cash disbursements

An adequate system of internal control requires that each day's cash receipts be deposited intact in the bank and that all disbursements be made by check. Checks should be prenumbered. Any spoiled checks should be marked "Void" and filed in sequence so that all numbers in the series can be accounted for.

Every transaction requiring a cash disbursement should be verified and approved before payment is made. Assume, for example, that a company merely paid without question every bill that arrived in the mail. Dishonest employees or outsiders could send the company invoices at excessive prices or invoices for goods and services which had never even been delivered.

The voucher system

One widely used method of establishing control over cash disbursements is the voucher system. This system provides that every transaction requiring a cash payment be verified and approved before a check is issued. A written authorization called a *voucher* is prepared for every expenditure, regardless of whether the expenditure is for payment of an expense, purchase of an asset, or payment of a liability.

A voucher is attached to each incoming invoice and given an identification number. The voucher has spaces for listing the data from the invoice and specifying the ledger accounts to be debited and credited in recording the transaction. Space is also provided for approval signatures for each step in the verification and approval process. A completed voucher provides a description of the transaction and also of the work performed in verifying the liability and approving the cash disbursement.

PREPARING A VOUCHER To illustrate the functioning of a voucher system, let us begin with the receipt of an invoice from a supplier. A voucher is prepared by filling in the appropriate blanks with information taken from the invoice, such as the invoice date, invoice number, and amount, and the creditor's name and address. The voucher with invoice attached is then sent to the employees responsible for verifying the extensions and footings on the invoice and for comparing prices, quantities, and terms with those specified in the purchase order and receiving report. When completion of the verification process has been evidenced by approval signatures of the persons performing these steps, the voucher and supporting documents are sent to an employee of the accounting department, who indicates on the voucher the accounts to be debited and credited.

The voucher is now reviewed by an accounting official to provide assurance that the verification procedures have been satisfactorily completed and that the liability is a proper one. After receiving this executive approval, the voucher is entered in a journal called a *voucher register.*

Entries in the voucher register indicate the nature of the expenditure by debiting the appropriate asset, expense, or liability accounts. The credit portion of each entry is always to a short-term liability account entitled

Vouchers Payable. Note that the entry in the voucher register is not made until the liability has been verified and approved.

In the voucher system, the ledger account, Vouchers Payable, replaces Accounts Payable. For purposes of balance sheet presentation, however, most companies continue to use the more widely understood term Accounts Payable.

PAYING THE VOUCHER WITHIN THE DISCOUNT PERIOD After the voucher has been entered in the voucher register, it is placed (with the supporting documents attached) in an unpaid voucher file according to the date of required payment. The voucher system emphasizes the required *time for payment* of liabilities rather than the identity of the creditors; for this reason, vouchers are filed by required date of payment. In computing future cash requirements of a business, the amount of a liability and the required date of payment are of basic significance; the identity of the creditor has no bearing on the problem of maintaining a proper cash position.

Cash discount periods generally run from the date of the invoice. Since a voucher is prepared for each invoice, the required date of payment is the last day on which a check can be prepared and mailed to the creditor in time to qualify for the discount.

When the payment date arrives, the approved voucher with supporting documents (such as purchase order and receiving report) attached is removed from the unpaid file and sent to the office of the cashier in the finance department. The cashier, after inspecting the voucher and attached documents for completeness, prepares a check (except for signature) and enters the check number and date on the voucher. The unsigned check, voucher, and all supporting documents are then sent to the treasurer or other financial executive authorized to sign checks.

The treasurer reviews the voucher to determine that the cash disbursement has been authorized, signs the check, and mails the check directly to the creditor. (Note that the check does not come back into the possession of the employee who prepared it.) When the check is signed, the supporting documents and voucher are perforated or stamped "Paid" to eliminate any possibility of their being presented later in support of another check. The paid voucher and documents then are returned to the accounting department where the cash disbursement is recorded in the *check register* and the date and serial number of the check are noted in the Payment column of the voucher register.

A check register is merely a simplified version of the cash payments journal illustrated in Chapter 6. When a voucher system is in use, checks are issued only in payment of approved and recorded vouchers. Consequently, every check issued is recorded by a debit to Vouchers Payable and a credit to Cash. The check register, therefore, may be a single column special journal.

Internal control is strong in a voucher system because every expenditure must be verified and approved before a check is issued. Also, the check is prepared by one person and signed by another. Thus, no one employee is in a position to make cash disbursements without other employees reviewing and approving the transaction.

Petty cash

As previously emphasized, adequate internal control over cash requires that all receipts be deposited in the bank and all significant disbursements be made by check. However, every business finds it convenient to have a small amount of cash on hand with which to make some minor expenditures. Examples include payments for small purchases of office supplies, postage stamps, and taxi fares. Internal control over these small cash payments can best be achieved through a petty cash fund.

ESTABLISHING THE PETTY CASH FUND   To create a petty cash fund, a check is written for a round amount such as $50 or $100, which will cover the small expenditures to be paid in cash for a period of two or three weeks. This check is cashed and the money kept on hand in a petty cash box under the control of an employee designated as *custodian* of the fund.

The entry for the issuance of the check is:

Creating the petty cash fund

Petty cash	100	
Cash		100
To establish a petty cash fund.		

MAKING DISBURSEMENTS FROM THE PETTY CASH FUND   As cash payments are made out of the petty cash box, the custodian of the fund is required to fill out a *petty cash voucher* for each expenditure. A petty cash voucher shows the amount paid, the purpose of the expenditure, the date, and the signature of the person receiving the money. A petty cash voucher should be prepared for every payment made from the fund. The petty cash box should, therefore, always contain cash and/or vouchers totaling the exact amount of the fund.

The petty cash custodian should be informed that occasional surprise counts of the fund will be made and that he or she is personally responsible for the fund being intact at all times.

REPLENISHING THE PETTY CASH FUND   Assume that a petty cash fund of $100 was established on June 1 and that payments totaling $89.75 were made from the fund during the next two weeks. Since the $100 originally placed in the fund is nearly exhausted, the fund should be replenished. A check is drawn payable to Petty Cash for the exact amount of the expenditures, $89.75. This check is cashed and the money placed in the petty cash box. The vouchers totaling that amount are perforated to prevent their reuse and filed in support of the replenishment check. The journal entry to record the issuance of the check will debit the expense accounts indicated by inspection of the vouchers, as follows:

Office Supplies Expense		*40.60*
Telephone & Telegraph Expense		*4.80*
Freight-in		*6.00*
Postage Expense		*25.25*
Miscellaneous Expense		*13.10*
Cash		*89.75*

Replenishment of petty cash fund

To replenish the petty cash fund.

Notice that *expense accounts* are debited each time the fund is replenished. The Petty Cash account is debited only when the fund is first established. There will ordinarily be no further entries in the Petty Cash account after the fund is established, unless the fund is discontinued or a decision is made to change its size from the original $100 amount.

The petty cash fund is usually replenished at the end of an accounting period, even though the fund is not running low, so that all vouchers in the fund are charged to expense accounts before these accounts are closed and financial statements prepared.

BANK CHECKING ACCOUNTS

Since adequate internal control over cash requires that all significant payments be made by check rather than in currency, every business, large or small, will maintain one or more bank checking accounts. The use of checks not only eliminates the need for keeping large amounts of cash on hand, but also provides documentary evidence of payments because all paid checks bear the endorsements of the payees and are returned by the bank to the makers of the checks at the end of each month.

Opening a bank account

When a depositor first opens a bank account, he must sign his name on a signature card, exactly as he will sign checks. The signature card is kept on file by the bank, so that any check bearing a signature not familiar to bank employees may be compared with the depositor's signature card. When a corporation opens a bank account, the board of directors will pass a resolution designating the officers or employees authorized to sign checks. A copy of this resolution is given to the bank.

Making deposits

The depositor fills out a *deposit ticket* (usually in duplicate) for each deposit. The deposit ticket includes a listing of each check deposited and the code number of the bank on which it is drawn. Space is also provided for listing the amounts of coin and currency deposited.

The bank statement

Each month the bank will provide the depositor with a statement of his or her account, accompanied by the checks paid and charged to the account during the month. The bank statement illustrated below shows the balance on deposit at the beginning of the month, the deposits, the checks paid, any other debits and credits during the month, and the new balance at the end of the month. Certain items in the bank statement of The Parkview Company warrant explanation and are discussed in the following paragraphs.

STATEMENT OF ACCOUNT WITH

WESTERN NATIONAL BANK

PERIOD ENDING

July 31, 1980

ACCOUNT NO.

7 00532

The Parkview Company
19101 Parkview Road
Los Angeles, Calif. 90018

FOLD HERE

CHECKS—LISTED IN ORDER OF PAYMENT—READ ACROSS				DEPOSITS	DATE	NEW BALANCE
				300 00	7–1–80	5329 30
100 00				250 00	7–2–80	5479 30
415 20	10 00				7–3–80	5054 10
25 00	90 00	36 50		185 10	7–5–80	5087 70
				60 00	7–7–80	5147 70
96 00	400 00				7–10–80	4651 70
500 00				147 20	7–12–80	4298 90
425 00					7–15–80	3873 90
95 75				200 00	7–18–80	3978 15
85 00				101 19	7–21–80	3994 34
150 27				83 25	7–24–80	3927 32
50 25M				500 00M	7–30–80	4377 07
2 00S				625 10	7–31–80	5000 17

SUMMARY OF ACTIVITY

BALANCE FORWARD	DEBITS		CREDITS		SERVICE CHARGE		NEW BALANCE
	NUMBER	AMOUNT	NUMBER	AMOUNT	ITEMS	AMOUNT	
5 029 30	14	2 478 97	10	2 451 84	1	2 00	5 000 17

Please examine this statement at once. If no error is reported in ten days the account will be considered correct. All items are credited subject to final payment.

EXPLANATION OF SYMBOLS

S SERVICE CHARGE   M MISCELLANEOUS ENTRY

NSF CHECKS Deposits made by a business include checks received from customers. Occasionally a customer's check may not clear because the customer's bank balance is less than the amount of the check. For example, on July 24 The Parkview Company received a check for $50.25 from J. B. Ball, and the check was included in the bank deposit made on that day. The Ball check was returned to Western National Bank by the bank on which it was drawn marked NSF (Not Sufficient Funds), indicating that Ball did not have a sufficient balance on deposit to cover the check. Western National Bank therefore charged the NSF check against The Parkview Company's account as shown by the July 30 item of $50.25. (The letter M alongside this entry stands for Miscellaneous Entry.)

Upon receipt of the NSF check returned by the bank, The Parkview Company should remove this item from the cash classification by a journal entry debiting an account receivable from J. B. Ball and crediting Cash. The NSF check is thus regarded as a receivable until it is collected directly from the drawer, or redeposited, or is determined to be worthless.

BANK SERVICE CHARGES Under the date of July 31 on the illustrated bank statement is a debit for $2 accompanied by the symbol S. This symbol means Service Charge, a charge made by the bank to cover the expense of handling the account. The amount of the service charge is based upon such considerations as the average balance of the account and the number of checks and deposits. Most banks would probably not make a service charge on The Parkview Company's account because the balance is substantial and the activity is low. However, a service charge is shown here for the purpose of illustrating its use. When the bank sends the monthly statement and paid checks to the depositor, it will include debit memoranda for service charges and any other charges not represented by checks.

MISCELLANEOUS CHARGES Other charges which may appear on the bank statement include rental fees for safe deposit boxes, charges for printing checks, collection charges on notes left with the bank for collection, and interest charges on funds borrowed from the bank.

Reconciling the bank account

The balance shown on the monthly statement received from the bank will usually not agree with the balance of cash shown by the depositor's accounting records. Certain transactions recorded by the depositor will not yet have been recorded by the bank. The most common examples are:

1 Outstanding checks. These are checks written by the depositor and deducted on the depositor's records but not yet presented to the bank for payment and deduction.

2 Deposits in transit. Deposits mailed to the bank are usually not received by the bank and not entered on the bank's records until a day or two later than the entry on the depositor's accounting records.

Transactions which may appear on the bank statement but which have not yet been recorded by the depositor include:

1 Service charges

2 Charges for NSF checks

3 Miscellaneous bank charges and credits

In some cases the bank reconciliation will be complete after such items as outstanding checks, deposits in transit, and miscellaneous bank charges have been taken into account. Other cases may require the correction of errors by the bank or by the depositor to complete the reconciliation. When a company maintains accounts in several banks, one possible type of error is to record a check drawn on one bank as a payment from another bank account. Similar errors may occur in recording deposits.

Procedures for preparing a bank reconciliation

Preparing a bank reconciliation means determining those items which make up the difference between the balance appearing on the bank statement and the balance of cash according to the depositor's records. By listing and studying these discrepancies, it is possible to determine the correct figure for cash to appear on the balance sheet. Specific steps to be taken in preparing a bank reconciliation are:

1 Compare the deposits listed on the bank statement with the deposits shown in the company's records. Place check marks in the company's cash records and on the bank statement beside the items which agree. Any unchecked item in the company's records of deposits will be deposits not yet recorded by the bank, and should be added to the balance reported by the bank. Determine that any deposits in transit listed in last month's bank reconciliation are included in the current month's bank statement.

2 Arrange the paid checks in numerical order and compare each check with the corresponding entry in the cash payments journal. (In the case of personal bank accounts for which the only record maintained is the checkbook, compare each paid check with the check stub.) Place a check mark in the depositor's cash payments journal opposite each entry for which a paid check has been returned by the bank. The unchecked entries should be listed in the bank reconciliation as outstanding checks to be deducted from the balance reported by the bank. Determine whether the checks listed as outstanding in the bank reconciliation for the preceding month have been returned by the bank this month. If not, such checks should be listed as outstanding in the current reconciliation.

3 Deduct from the balance per the depositor's records any debit memoranda issued by the bank which have not been recorded by the depositor. In the illustrated bank reconciliation on page 363, examples are the NSF check for $50.25 and the $2 service charge.

4 Add to the balance per the depositor's records any credit memoranda issued by the bank which have not been recorded by the depositor. An example in the illustrated bank reconciliation on page 363 is the credit of $500 for a note receivable collected by the bank in behalf of The Parkview Company.

5 Prepare a bank reconciliation, reflecting the preceding steps, similar to the illustration on page 363.

6 Make journal entries for any items on the bank statement which have not yet been recorded in the depositor's accounts.

ILLUSTRATION The July bank statement prepared by the bank for The Parkview Company was illustrated on page 359. This statement shows a balance of cash on deposit at July 31 of $5,000.17. We shall assume that The Parkview Company's records at July 31 show a bank balance of $4,172.57. Our purpose in preparing the bank reconciliation is to identify the items that make up this difference and to determine the correct cash balance.

Assume that the specific steps to be taken in preparing a bank reconciliation have been carried out and that the following reconciling items have been discovered:

1 A deposit of $310.90 mailed to the bank on July 31 does not appear on the bank statement.

2 A credit memorandum issued by the bank on July 30 in the amount of $500 was returned with the July bank statement and appears in the Deposits column of that statement. This credit represents the proceeds of a note receivable left with the bank by The Parkview Company for the purpose of collection. The collection of the note has not yet been recorded by The Parkview Company.

3 Four checks issued in July or prior months have not yet been paid by the bank. These checks are:

Check No.	Date	Amount
801	June 15	$100.00
888	July 24	10.25
890	July 27	402.50
891	July 30	205.00

4 A debit memorandum issued by the bank on July 31 for a $2 service charge was enclosed with the July bank statement.

5 Check no. 875 was issued July 20 in the amount of $85 but was erroneously listed on the check stub and in the cash payments journal as $58. The check, in payment of telephone service, was paid by the bank, returned with the July bank statement, and correctly listed on the Bank statement as an $85 charge to the account. The Cash account in the depositor's ledger is overstated because of this $27 error ($85 − $58).

6 No entry has as yet been made in The Parkview Company's accounts to reflect the bank's action on July 30 of charging against the account the NSF check for $50.25 drawn by J. B. Ball.

The July 31 bank reconciliation for The Parkview Company follows:

THE PARKVIEW COMPANY
Bank Reconciliation
July 31, 19___

Balance per depositor's records, July 31, 19___			$4,172.57
Add: Note receivable collected for us by bank			500.00
			$4,672.57
Less: Service charge		$ 2.00	
NSF check of J. B. Ball		50.25	
Error on check stub no. 875		27.00	79.25
Adjusted balance			$4,593.32
Balance per bank statement, July 31, 19___			$5,000.17
Add: Deposit of July 31 not recorded by bank			310.90
			$5,311.07
Less: Outstanding checks			
No. 801	$100.00		
No. 888	10.25		
No. 890	402.50		
No. 891	205.00		717.75
Adjusted balance (as above)			$4,593.32

The adjusted balance of $4,593.32 is the amount of cash owned by The Parkview Company and is, therefore, the amount which should appear as cash on the July 31 balance sheet.

Note that the adjusted balance of cash differs from both the bank statement and the depositor's records. This difference is explained by the fact that neither set of records is up-to-date as of July 31, and also by the existence of an error in The Parkview Company's records.

ADJUSTING THE RECORDS AFTER THE RECONCILIATION To make The Parkview Company's records up-to-date and accurate, four journal entries affecting the Cash account are necessary for the four items that make up the difference between the $4,172.57 balance per the depositor's records and the adjusted balance of $4,593.32. These four reconciling items call for the following entries:

Cash	500.00	
Notes Receivable		500.00
To record the note receivable collected for us by the bank.		
Miscellaneous Expense	2.00	
Cash		2.00
To record the service charge by the bank.		

Accounts Receivable, J. B. Ball	*50.25*	
Cash		*50.25*

To record as a receivable from J. B. Ball the amount of the NSF check returned to us by the bank.

Telephone Expense	*27.00*	
Cash		*27.00*

To correct the error by which check no. 875 for an $85 payment for telephone service was recorded as $58 ($85 − $58 = $27).

Instead of making four separate journal entries affecting the Cash account, one compound journal entry can be made to record all four of the above items.

Electronic funds transfer systems (EFTS)

Our discussion of cash transactions and bank accounts would be incomplete without mention of the many new systems for transferring funds electronically rather than by delivery of physical documents. In the banking field, for example, automated clearing houses may eliminate the need for banks to exchange bundles of customers' checks each day. If you pay your telephone bill by a check written on Bank A, the telephone company traditionally has deposited your check in its bank (Bank B). Bank B would then deliver your check and others like it to Bank A in order to collect. At the same time Bank A would be presenting a bundle of checks deposited with it but drawn on Bank B. In reality many banks, not just Bank A and Bank B, would be involved in this "clearing house" activity. Since the number of checks written each day is roughly 50 million, this exchange of paper represents a great opportunity for saving through electronic transfer of funds. Electronic equipment now exists which enables banks to transfer funds from the account of one depositor to the account of another without all this cumbersome exchange of paper.

Many other applications of electronic funds transfer are now in use. For example, a company may pay all its employees (if they agree) by delivering payroll information to its bank on magnetic tape. The bank's computer debits the employer's account and credits the bank account of each employee without any paper changing hands.

POINT-OF-SALE (POS) TERMINALS   Supermarkets and other stores cash more checks than banks do. To cut down on paper work, a bank can issue plastic identification cards to its depositors. The depositor when shopping can have the store's employees use this card at a computer terminal to obtain cash or to pay for purchases. The terminal is connected to the bank's computer which will approve the transaction and transfer funds immediately from the customer's account to the store's account.

The further development of electronic funds transfer systems seems to be impeded more by government regulations, legislative barriers, and public attitudes than by lack of technology. A considerable portion of the public appears to be reluctant to move into a "checkless society."

INVESTMENTS IN MARKETABLE SECURITIES

In Chapters 7 and 8, the issuance of securities and such related transactions as the payment of dividends and interest have been considered primarily from the viewpoint of the issuing corporation. Now we shall consider these transactions from the viewpoint of the investor.

Reasons for investing in marketable securities

The term *marketable securities* refers primarily to U.S. government bonds and the bonds and stocks of large corporations. Investments in these types of securities are almost as liquid as cash itself. In fact, investments in marketable securities are often called "secondary cash resources." If cash is needed for any operating purpose, these securities may quickly be converted into cash; in the meantime, investments in marketable securities are preferable to cash because of the interest or dividend revenue which they produce. Most companies watch their cash balances very carefully and invest any cash not needed for current operations in high-grade marketable securities.

When an investor owns several different marketable securities, the group of securities is termed an investment *portfolio.* In deciding upon the securities to include in the portfolio, the investor seeks to maximize return while minimizing risk. Risk often can be reduced by *diversification,* that is, by including in the portfolio a variety of securities, especially securities of companies in different industries.

Some corporations buy stocks of other corporations in sufficient quantity that a *degree of control* may be exercised over the issuing corporation. Sometimes a substantial investment in stock of a customer company may be helpful in maintaining good business relations. Investments of this type cannot be sold without disturbing established policies; therefore, such investments should not be considered marketable securities. Investments for purposes of control will be discussed later in this chapter.

Securities exchanges

The stocks and bonds of most large corporations are listed on organized securities exchanges, such as the *New York Stock Exchange.* Among the investors in these securities are mutual funds, pension funds, banks, insurance companies, industrial corporations, and a great number of individuals. An investor may either buy or sell these listed securities through any brokerage house which is a member of the exchange. The brokerage company represents the investor and negotiates with other exchange members either to buy or sell the securities on behalf of its customer. The price at which the broker negotiates the transaction represents the current market value of the security and is publicly quoted for reference by other investors. The stocks and bonds of many smaller companies are not listed on an organized securities exchange, but brokerage firms also arrange for the purchase and sale of these unlisted or over-the-counter securities.

At the time of issuance of stocks or bonds, the transaction is between the investor and the issuing corporation (or its underwriting agent). The great daily volume of transactions in securities, however, consists of the sale of stocks and bonds by investors to other investors. Virtually all these security transactions are made through a stockbroker acting as intermediary.

QUOTED MARKET PRICES The market price of stocks is quoted in terms of dollars per share. Bond prices, however, are quoted as a *percentage* of their face value or *maturity* value, which is usually $1,000. The maturity value is the amount the issuing company must pay to redeem the bond at the date it matures (becomes due). A bond quoted at *96* would therefore have a market price of $960 (96% of $1,000). The following line from the financial page of a daily newspaper summarizes the previous day's trading in bonds of Sears, Roebuck and Co.

	Bonds	*Sales*	*High*	*Low*	*Close*	*Net Change*
What is the market value of this bond?	Sears R $8\frac{5}{8}$ 95	45	103	102	$102\frac{1}{2}$	−1

This line of condensed information indicates that 45 of Sears, Roebuck and Co.'s $8\frac{5}{8}$, $1,000 bonds maturing in 1995 were traded. The highest price is reported as 103, or $1,030 for a bond of $1,000 face value. The lowest price was 102 or $1,020 for a $1,000 bond. The closing price (last sale of the day) was $102\frac{1}{2}$, or $1,025. This was one point below the closing price of the previous day, a decrease of $10 in the price of a $1,000 bond.

The primary factors which determine the market value of a bond are (*1*) the relationship of the bond's interest rate to other investment opportunities and (*2*) investors' confidence that the issuing company will be able to meet its obligations for future interest and principal payments. A bond selling at a market price greater than its maturity value is said to be selling at a *premium;* a bond selling at a price below its maturity value is selling at a *discount.* As a bond nears its maturity date, the market price of the bond approaches its maturity value. At the maturity date the market price of the bond should be exactly equal to its maturity value, and the issuing corporation will redeem the bond for that amount.

LISTED CORPORATIONS REPORT TO A MILLION OWNERS When a corporation invites the public to purchase its stocks and bonds, it accepts an obligation to keep the public informed on its financial condition and the profitability of operations. This obligation of disclosure includes public distribution of financial statements. The Securities and Exchange Commission is the government agency responsible for seeing that corporations make adequate disclosure of their affairs so that investors have a basis for intelligent investment decisions. The flow of corporate accounting data distributed through newspapers and financial advisory services to millions of investors is a vital force in the functioning of our economy; in fact, the successful working of a profit-motivated economy rests upon the quality and dependability of the accounting information being reported.

LISTED CORPORATIONS ARE AUDITED BY CERTIFIED PUBLIC ACCOUNT-ANTS Corporations with securities listed on organized stock exchanges are required to have regular audits by independent public accountants. The financial statements distributed each year to stockholders are accompanied by a report by a firm of certified public accountants indicating that an audit has been made and expressing an opinion as to the fairness of the company's financial statements. It is the *independent status* of the auditing firm that enables investors to place confidence in audited financial statements.

Marketable securities as current assets

A recent balance sheet of International Business Machines Corporation shows the following items listed first in the current asset section.

Current assets:

Cash	*$ 208,607,210*
Marketable securities, at lower of cost or market	*5,947,653,848*

The large investment by IBM in marketable securities is in no way unusual; many corporations have large holdings of marketable securities. In the balance sheet, marketable securities are usually listed immediately after the asset Cash, because these securities are almost as liquid as cash itself. In the event that cash is needed for any operating purpose, the marketable securities can be sold quickly and thus transformed into cash. A recent balance sheet of Gulf Oil Corporation shows as the very first current asset: "Cash and marketable securities. . . .$1,989,000,000." This practice of lumping together cash and marketable securities reflects the general attitude that these two assets are essentially similar. From the viewpoint of creditors, it is often said in appraising a company's financial strength that "cash and marketable securities" amount to so many dollars. To a loan officer in a bank reviewing an application for a loan, there is no more impressive or reassuring asset on the balance sheet of a prospective borrower than a large amount of high-quality marketable securities.

In *Statement of Financial Accounting Standards No. 12,* the FASB considered the possibility that a company may choose to separate its investments in marketable securities into two groups: one group considered as temporary investments and classified as current assets, and the other group considered to be permanent investments and classified as noncurrent assets.[1] In practice, however, this distinction is seldom made. Most published balance sheets show marketable securities as one group in the current asset section.

If a company has a definite intention to hold certain marketable securities on a long-term basis, it can justifiably show them in the balance sheet below the current asset section under a caption such as Long-Term Investments. More realistically, however, management usually stands ready to sell marketable securities whenever company needs require it, or whenever favorable stock market movements make such action appropriate. Consequently, marketable securities are generally viewed as current assets.

Determining the cost of investments in stocks and bonds

When securities are purchased, an account entitled Marketable Securities is debited for the entire purchase price, including any commissions to stockbrokers and any transfer taxes. A subsidiary ledger must also be maintained which shows for each type of security owned the acquisition date, total cost, number of shares (or bonds) owned, and cost per share (or bond). This subsidiary ledger provides the information necessary to determine the amount of gain or loss when all or part of the investment is sold.

The principal distinction between the recording of an investment in bonds and an investment in stocks is that interest on bonds accrues from day to day. The interest accrued since the last semiannual interest payment date is paid for by the purchaser and should be recorded separately from the cost of the bond itself. Dividends on stock, however, *do not accrue* and the entire purchase price paid by the investor in stocks is recorded in the Marketable Securities account.

BOND INTEREST PAYMENTS The amount of interest paid to bondholders is equal to a stated percentage of the bond's maturity value. Thus, the owner of an 8% bond would receive $80 interest (8% of $1,000) every year. Since bond interest usually is paid semiannually, the bondholder would receive two semiannual interest payments of $40 each.

PURCHASE OF BONDS BETWEEN INTEREST DATES When bonds are purchased between interest dates, the purchaser pays the quoted market price for the bond *plus* the interest accrued since the last interest payment date. By this arrangement the new owner becomes entitled to receive in

[1] *Statement of Financial Accounting Standards No. 12,* "Accounting for Certain Marketable Securities," Financial Accounting Standards Board (Stamford, Conn.: 1975).

full the next semiannual interest payment. An account called Accrued Bond Interest Receivable should be debited for the amount of interest purchased. For example, assume that an investor purchases ten 9%, $1,000 bonds at a price of 98 plus a brokerage commission of $50 and two months' accrued interest of $150 (9% $\times$ $10,000 $\times$ $\frac{2}{12}$ = $150). The entry is as follows:

Separate	Marketable Securities	*9,850*	
account for	Accrued Bond Interest Receivable	*150*	
accrued			
bond	Cash		*10,000*
interest	Purchased ten 9% bonds of Rider Co. at 98 plus a brokerage		
purchased	commission of $50 and two months' accrued interest.		

Four months later at the semiannual interest payment date, the investor will receive an interest check for $450, which will be recorded as follows:

Note portion	Cash	*450*	
of interest	Accrued Bond Interest Receivable		*150*
check			
earned	Bond Interest Revenue		*300*
	Received semiannual interest on Rider Co. bonds.		

This $300 credit to Bond Interest Revenue represents the amount actually earned during the four months the bond was owned (9% $\times$ $10,000 $\times$ $\frac{4}{12}$ = $300).

ENTRIES TO RECORD BOND INTEREST EARNED EACH PERIOD If the investor in bonds is to determine bond interest earned each year on an accrual basis, an adjusting entry will be necessary at the balance sheet date for any interest earned but not yet received. The following series of entries illustrates the accounting for bond interest earned by a company on a calendar-year basis of accounting. The investment consists of $100,000 face value of 9% bonds with interest dates of February 28 and August 31.

	Year 1		
Allocating	Dec. 31 Accrued Bond Interest Receivable	*3,000*	
bond	Bond Interest Revenue		*3,000*
interest	To accrue four months' interest earned (Sept. 1–Dec. 31)		
earned by	on $100,000 face value of 9% bonds.		
years			

Year 2		
Feb. 28 Cash	*4,500*	
Accrued Bond Interest Receivable		*3,000*
Bond Interest Revenue		*1,500*
Received semiannual bond interest.		

Aug. 31 Cash	*4,500*	
Bond Interest Revenue		*4,500*
Received semiannual bond interest.		

> Dec. 31 Accrued Bond Interest Receivable 3,000
>
>   Bond Interest Revenue 3,000
>
>   To accrue four months' interest earned (Sept. 1–Dec. 31)
>
>   on $100,000 face value of 9% bonds.

INCOME ON INVESTMENTS IN STOCKS Cash dividends are seldom recorded as income until received. The entry upon receipt of a dividend check consists of a debit to Cash and a credit to Dividend Revenue.

Additional shares of stock received in stock splits or stock dividends *are not income* to the stockholder, and only a *memorandum entry* needs to be made to record the increase in the number of shares owned. The *cost basis per share* is decreased, however, because of the larger number of shares comprising the investment after distribution of a stock split or a stock dividend. As an example, assume that an investor paid $72 a share for 100 shares of stock, a total cost of $7,200. Later the investor received 20 additional shares as a stock dividend. The cost per share is thereby reduced to $60 a share, computed by dividing the total cost of $7,200 by the 120 shares owned after the 20% stock dividend. The memorandum entry to be made in the general journal follows:

> July 10 Memorandum: Received 20 additional shares of Delta Co. common stock as a
>
>   result of 20% stock dividend. Now own 120 shares with a cost basis of $7,200, or
>
> $60 per share.

Gains and losses from sale of investments in securities

The sale of an investment in stocks is recorded by debiting Cash for the amount received and crediting the Marketable Securities account for the carrying value of the securities sold. Any difference between the proceeds of the sale and the carrying value of the investment is recorded by a debit to Loss on Sale of Marketable Securities or by a credit to Gain on Sale of Marketable Securities.

At the date of sale of an investment in bonds, any interest accrued since the last interest payment date should be recognized as interest revenue. For example, assume that 10 bonds of the Elk Corporation carried in the accounts of an investor at $9,600 are sold at a price of 94 and accrued interest of $90. The commission on the sale is $50. The following entry should be made:

Investment in bonds sold at a loss

Cash	9,440	
Loss on Sale of Marketable Securities	250	
Marketable Securities		9,600
Bond Interest Revenue		90

Sold 10 bonds of Elk Corporation at 94 and accrued interest of $90
less broker's commission of $50.

Balance sheet valuation of marketable securities

Although the market price of a bond may fluctuate from day to day, we can be reasonably certain that when the maturity date arrives the market price will be equal to the bond's maturity value. Stocks, on the other hand, do not have maturity values. When the market price of a stock declines, there is no way that we can be certain whether the decline will be temporary or permanent. For this reason, different valuation standards are applied in accounting for investments in marketable *debt* securities (bonds) and investments in marketable *equity* securities (stocks).

VALUATION OF MARKETABLE DEBT SECURITIES A short-term investment in bonds is generally carried in the accounting records at cost and a gain or loss is recognized when the investment is sold. If bonds are held as a long-term investment and the difference between the cost of the investment and its maturity value is substantial, the valuation of the investment becomes more complex. The valuation of long-term investments in bonds is discussed in Chapter 13.

VALUATION OF MARKETABLE EQUITY SECURITIES The market values of stocks may rise or fall dramatically during an accounting period. An investor who sells an investment at a price above or below cost will recognize a gain or loss on the sale. But what if the investor continues to hold the securities after a significant change in their market value? In this case, should any gain or loss be recognized in the financial statements?

In *Statement No. 12,* the FASB ruled that a portfolio of marketable equity securities should be shown in the balance sheet at the *lower* of aggregate cost or current market value. The effect of the *lower-of-cost-or-market* rule is to recognize losses from drops in market value without recognizing gains from rising market prices.

Note that this rule does not accord the same treatment to market gains and losses. Accountants traditionally have applied different criteria in recognizing gains and losses. One of the basic principles in accounting is that gains shall not be recognized until they are *realized,* and the usual test of realization is the sale of the asset in question. Losses, on the other hand, are recognized as soon as objective evidence indicates that a loss has been incurred.

Lower of cost or market

In applying the lower-of-cost-or-market rule, the total cost of the portfolio of marketable equity securities is compared with its current market value, and the lower of these two amounts is used as the balance sheet valuation. If the market value of the portfolio is below cost, an entry is made to reduce the carrying value of the portfolio to current market value and to recognize an *unrealized loss* for the amount of the market decline. The write-down of an investment in marketable securities to a market value below cost is an end-of-period adjusting entry and should be based upon market prices at the balance sheet date.

To illustrate the lower-of-cost-or-market adjustment, assume the following facts for the investment portfolio of Eagle Corporation at December 31, Year 1:

	Cost	Market Value
Common stock of Adams Corporation	$100,000	$106,000
Common stock of Barnes Company	60,000	52,000
Preferred stock of Parker Industries	200,000	192,000
Other marketable equity securities	25,000	25,000
Totals	$385,000	$375,000

Since the total market value of the securities in our example is less than their cost to Eagle Corporation, the proper balance sheet valuation would be the lower amount of $375,000. This downward adjustment of $10,000 means that an unrealized loss of $10,000 will be included in the determination of the year's net income. The accounting entry would be as follows:

Year 1

Dec. 31	Unrealized Loss on Marketable Securities	10,000	
	Valuation Allowance for Marketable Securities		10,000
	To reduce the carrying value of the investment in marketable securities to the lower of cost or market.		

The loss from the decline in the market value of securities owned is termed an unrealized loss to distinguish it from a loss which is realized by an actual sale of securities.

THE VALUATION ACCOUNT The Valuation Allowance for Marketable Securities is a *contra-asset* account or *valuation* account. In the balance sheet, this valuation account is offset against the asset Marketable Securities in the same manner as the Accumulated Depreciation account is offset against the asset Building. The following partial balance sheet illustrates the use of the Valuation Allowance for Marketable Securities:

Cash		$ 80,000
Marketable securities	$385,000	
Less: Valuation allowance for marketable securities	10,000	375,000

The end result of crediting the Valuation Allowance for Marketable Securities is much the same as if we had credited the Marketable Securities account; that is, the net amount shown in the balance sheet for marketable equity securities is the current market value of the portfolio. The use of the valuation account, however, highlights in the financial statements the fact that marketable securities have been written down to a market value below cost.

THE VALUATION ACCOUNT IS ADJUSTED EVERY PERIOD At the end of every period, the balance of the valuation account is adjusted to cause marketable equity securities to be shown in the balance sheet at the lower of cost or current market value. If the valuation allowance must be increased because of further declines in market value, the adjusting entry will recognize an additional unrealized loss. On the other hand, if market prices have increased since the last balance sheet date, the adjusting entry will reduce or eliminate the valuation allowance and recognize an *unrealized gain.*

To illustrate the adjustment of the valuation account, let us assume that by the end of Year 2 the market value of Eagle Corporation's portfolio has increased to an amount greater than cost. Since market value is no longer below cost, the valuation allowance, which has a credit balance of $10,000, is no longer needed. Thus, the following entry would be made to eliminate the balance of the valuation allowance:

Year 2

Unrealized gain cannot exceed the former balance of the valuation account

Dec. 31	Valuation Allowance for Marketable Securities	10,000	
	Unrealized Gain on Marketable Securities		10,000
	To increase the carrying value of marketable securities		
	to original cost following recovery of market value.		

Note that the amount of unrealized gain recognized is limited to the amount in the valuation account. Increases in market value above cost are not recognized in the accounting records. In brief, when marketable securities have been written down to the lower of cost or market, they can be written back up to original cost if the market prices recover. However, current rules of the FASB do not permit recognition of a market rise above the original cost of the portfolio.

Because the valuation allowance is based upon a comparison of aggregate portfolio cost and market value, the allowance cannot be directly associated with individual investments. The valuation allowance reduces the carrying value of the total portfolio but does not affect the individual carrying values of the investments which comprise the portfolio. Lower-of-cost-or-market adjustments, therefore, have *no effect* upon the gain or loss recognized when an investment is sold. When specific securities are sold, the gain or loss realized from the sale is determined by comparing the *cost* of the securities (without regard to lower-of-cost-or-market adjustments) to their selling price.[2]

[2] The reader may notice that a decline in the market value of securities owned could be reported in the income statement on two separate occasions: first, as an unrealized loss in the period in which the price decline occurs; and second, as a realized loss in the period in which the securities are sold. However, after securities with market values below cost have been sold, the valuation allowance may be reduced or eliminated. The entry to reduce the valuation allowance involves the recognition of an unrealized gain which offsets the unrealized losses reported in earlier periods.

INCOME TAX RULES FOR MARKETABLE SECURITIES The FASB rules described above are not acceptable in determining income subject to income tax. The only gains or losses recognized for income tax purposes are realized gains and losses resulting from sale of an investment.

The argument for valuation at market value

A weakness in the position taken by the FASB is that some increases in the market value of securities owned are recognized in the financial statements while others are ignored. For this reason, many accountants believe that investments in marketable securities should be valued in the balance sheet at current market price regardless of whether this price is above or below cost. Increases and decreases in market value would then be recognized as gains or losses as these changes occur.

Several strong arguments exist for valuing marketable securities at market value:

1 Market value is a better indicator of the current debt-paying ability represented by the securities than is their original cost.
2 Market values may be objectively determined from market price quotations.
3 The market price may be realized at any time without interfering with the normal operations of the business.
4 Changes in market price may constitute a major portion of the economic benefit resulting from investments in marketable securities.

At this point it is important to stress that valuation of marketable securities at current market values which exceed cost is not in accordance with the present accounting practices of most companies.[3] However, the valuation of marketable securities is a controversial issue in the accounting profession and may be an area of forthcoming change in generally accepted accounting principles.

Presentation of marketable securities in financial statements

Gains and losses on the sale of investments, as well as interest and dividend revenue, are nonoperating types of income. These items should be specifically identified in the income statement and shown after the determination of operating income.

Although marketable securities are usually classified as current assets in the balance sheet, they may alternatively be classified as long-term investments if management has a definite intention to hold the securities for more than one year. Regardless of how marketable equity securities are classified in the balance sheet, they are shown at the lower-of-cost-or-market value.

The unrealized gains and losses resulting from application of the

[3] Companies whose principal business activity includes investing in marketable securities (such as mutual funds and brokerage houses) currently use market values in accounting for their investment portfolios.

lower-of-cost-or-market rule, however, are presented differently in the financial statements depending upon whether the securities portfolio is classified as a current asset or a long-term investment. When the portfolio is viewed as a current asset, the related gains and losses are closed into the Income Summary account and shown in the income statement along with other types of investment income.

In *Statement No. 12,* the FASB ruled that holding gains and losses on long-term investments should *not* be included in the measurement of the current year's income because management does not intend to sell these securities in the near future. Therefore, any unrealized loss recognized on long-term investments is shown in the balance sheet as a *reduction in stockholders' equity* instead of being closed into the Income Summary account. The account Unrealized Loss on Long-Term Investments appears as a reduction in stockholders' equity only when the long-term portfolio is shown in the balance sheet at a price below cost. The debit balance of this contra-equity account is equal in amount to the credit balance of the contra-asset account Valuation Allowance for Long-Term Investments. When the market value of long-term investments exceeds cost, both the unrealized loss account and the valuation account have zero balances and do not appear in the financial statements.

The presentation of unrealized losses as a reduction in stockholders' equity is not often seen in published financial statements, because most investors classify marketable securities as current assets. A weakness in the FASB's position is that some investors are required to include unrealized losses in the income statement while other investors show them only in the balance sheet.

Investments for purposes of control

When an investor owns enough common stock to exercise a degree of control over the issuing company (called the investee), the investment is not included in the portfolio of marketable securities. Such investments are shown in the balance sheet under the caption Long-Term Investments, which follows the current asset section.

If an investor is able to exercise significant control over the investee's management, dividends paid by the investee may no longer be a good measure of the investor's income from the investment. This is because the investor may control the investee's dividend policy. In such cases, dividends paid by the investee are likely to reflect the *investor's* cash needs and tax considerations, rather than the profitability of the investment.

For example, assume that Sigma Company owns all the common stock of Davis Company. For three years Davis Company is very profitable but pays no dividends, because Sigma Company has no need for additional cash. In the fourth year, Davis Company pays a large cash dividend to Sigma Company despite operating at a loss for that year. Clearly, it would be misleading for Sigma Company to report no investment income while the company it owns is operating profitably, and then to show large investment income in a year when Davis Company incurred a net loss.

The investor does not have to own 100% of the common stock of the investee to exercise a significant degree of control. An investor with much less than 50% of the voting stock may have effective control, since the remaining shares are not likely to vote as an organized block. In the absence of other evidence (such as another large stockholder), owner-ship of 20% or more of the investee's common stock is considered an investment for purposes of control. In such cases, the investor should account for the investment by using the *equity method.*[4]

The equity method

When the equity method is used, an investment in common stock is initially recorded at cost but is then adjusted for changes in the underlying stockholders' equity of the investee subsequent to acquisition. As the investee earns net income, the stockholders' equity in the company increases. An investor using the equity method recognizes his *proportionate share of the investee's net income* as an increase in the carrying value of his investment. A proportionate share of a net loss reported by the investee is recognized as a decrease in the investment.

When the investee pays dividends, the stockholders' equity in the company is reduced. The investor, therefore, treats dividends received from the investee as a conversion of the investment into cash, thereby reducing the carrying value of the investment. Investments accounted for by the equity method are *not* adjusted to the lower of cost or market value. In effect, the equity method causes the carrying value of the investment to rise and fall with changes in the book value of the underlying shares.

ILLUSTRATION OF THE EQUITY METHOD Assume that Post Corporation purchases 25% of the common stock of Sun Company for $200,000, which corresponds to the underlying book value. During the following year, Sun Company earns net income of $60,000 and pays dividends of $40,000. Post Corporation would account for its investment as follows:

Investment in Sun Company	200,000	
Cash		200,000

To record acquisition of 25% of the common stock of
Sun Company.

Investment in Sun Company	15,000	
Investment Income		15,000

To increase the investment for 25% share of net income earned
by Sun Company (25% × $60,000).

[4] Accounting Principles Board, *Opinion No. 18*, "The Equity Method of Accounting for Investments in Common Stock," AICPA (New York: 1971).

Cash *10,000*

     Investment in Sun Company *10,000*

To reduce investment for dividends received from Sun Company
(25% × $40,000).

Note that the net effect of Post Corporation's accounting for Sun Company's reported income and dividends was to increase the carrying value of the Investment in Sun Company account by $5,000. This corresponds to 25% of the increase reported in Sun Company's retained earnings during the period [25% × ($60,000 − $40,000) = $5,000].

In this illustration of the equity method, we have made several simplifying assumptions: (1) Post Corporation purchased the stock of Sun Company at a price equal to the underlying book value; (2) Sun Company had issued common stock only and the number of shares outstanding did not change during the year; and (3) there were no intercompany transactions between Post Corporation and Sun Company. If we were to change any of these assumptions, the computations in applying the equity method would become more complicated. Application of the equity method in more complex situations will be discussed in *Intermediate Accounting* of this series.

KEY TERMS INTRODUCED OR EMPHASIZED IN CHAPTER 9

Bank reconciliation A statement listing the items which make up the difference between the balance shown on the bank statement and the balance of cash according to the depositor's records.

Bond A formal certificate (or debt instrument) issued by a corporation to borrow money on a long-term basis.

Carrying value The value at which an asset is shown in the balance sheet.

Cash receipts The inflow of cash to a business.

Check register A simplified version of the cash payments journal (see Chapter 6) used for recording cash payments when a voucher system is in use.

Contra-asset account An account with a credit balance which is offset against or deducted from an asset account to produce the proper balance sheet valuation for the asset. Also called a *valuation* account.

Deposits in transit Cash receipts which have been entered in the depositor's accounting records and mailed to the bank or left in the bank's night depository, but which reached the bank too late to be credited to the depositor's current monthly bank statement.

Electronic funds transfer system The electronic transfer of funds from the bank account of one depositor to the account of another without the delivery of checks. Many related applications are in use to reduce paper work in cash transactions.

Equity method The method of accounting used when the investment by one corporation in another is large enough to influence the policies of the investee. The investor recognizes as investment income its proportionate share of the investee's net income, rather than considering dividends received as income.

Investee When an investor owns a sufficient amount of the voting stock in a company to exercise a significant degree of control over the company's policies, the controlled company is termed the investee.

Lower of cost or market The technique of valuing a portfolio of marketable equity securities in the balance sheet at the lower of cost or current market value. A write-down to a market value below cost involves recognition of an **unrealized loss.**

Marketable securities A highly liquid type of investment which can be sold at any time without interfering with normal operation of the business. Usually classified as a current asset second only to cash in liquidity.

Maturity value The amount (usually $1,000 per bond) which the issuing company must pay to redeem its bonds at the date they mature (become due). Bond prices and interest rates are stated as percentages of maturity value.

NSF check A customer's check which was deposited but returned because of a lack of funds (Not Sufficient Funds) in the account on which the check was drawn.

Outstanding checks Checks issued by a business to suppliers, employees, or other payees but not yet presented to the bank for payment.

Petty cash fund A small amount of cash set aside for making minor cash payments for which writing of checks is not practicable.

Portfolio An investment in various marketable securities which is managed and accounted for as a single unit rather than as a number of separate investments. An investor may have both short-term and long-term investment portfolios.

Realization principle The principle of recognizing revenue and gains in the accounting records only when the earning process is virtually complete. The usual criterion for realization is a sales transaction.

Unrealized losses and gains An unrealized loss results from writing down marketable equity securities to a market value below cost. An unrealized gain results from restoring a former write-down because of a recovery in market price. Securities cannot be written up above aggregate cost. Unrealized losses and gains on marketable securities classified as current assets are included in the determination of the year's net income. The net unrealized loss on marketable securities classified as long-term investments is excluded from the determination of net income and is shown in the balance sheet as a reduction in stockholders' equity.

Valuation allowance for marketable securities The contra-asset account used to reduce the carrying value of marketable equity securities from cost to a market value below cost. Adjusted at each balance sheet date.

Voucher A document prepared to authorize and describe an expenditure.

Voucher register A special journal used to record all liabilities which have been approved for payment.

Voucher system A method of controlling expenditures and the payment of liabilities. Requires that every liability be recorded as soon as it is incurred, and that checks be issued only in payment of approved liabilities.

DEMONSTRATION PROBLEM FOR YOUR REVIEW

The information listed below is available in reconciling the bank statement for the White River Company on November 30, 19____.

(1) The ledger account for Cash showed a balance at November 30 of $7,766.64, including a $100 petty cash fund. Petty cash should be transferred to a separate account. The bank statement at November 30 indicated a balance of $9,734.70.

(2) The November 30 cash receipts of $5,846.20 had been mailed to the bank on that date and did not appear among the deposits on the November bank statement. The receipts include a check for $4,000 from a brokerage house for the sale of 150 shares of stock of the Axe Co. which cost $6,270. Neither

the proceeds on the sale of stock nor the collections on accounts receivable ($1,846.20) has been recorded in the accounts of the White River Company.

(3) Included with the November bank statement was an NSF check for $220 signed by a customer, J. Wilson. This amount had been charged against the bank account on November 30.

(4) Of the checks issued in November, the following were not included among the paid checks returned by the bank:

Check No.	Amount	Check No.	Amount
924	$136.25	944	$ 95.00
940	105.00	945	716.15
941	11.46	946	60.00
943	826.70		

(5) A service charge for $340 by the bank had been made in error against the White River Company account.

(6) A non-interest-bearing note receivable for $690 owned by the White River Company had been left with the bank for collection. On November 30 the company received a memorandum from the bank indicating that the note had been collected and credited to the company's account after deduction of a $5 collection charge. No entry has been made by the company to record collection of the note.

(7) A debit memorandum for $7.50 was enclosed with the paid checks at November 30. This charge covered the printing of checkbooks bearing the White River Company name and address.

Instructions

a Prepare a bank reconciliation at November 30, 19____.

b Prepare journal entries required as of November 30, 19____, to bring the company's records up to date. Use one journal entry to record all increases in the cash account and another journal entry to record all decreases.

SOLUTION TO DEMONSTRATION PROBLEM

a

WHITE RIVER COMPANY

Bank Reconciliation

November 30, 19____

Balance per depositor's records, Nov. 30		$ 7,766.64
Add: Proceeds on sale of stock	$4,000.00	
Collection on accounts receivable	1,846.20	
Note receivable collected by bank, $690, less collection charge, $5	685.00	6,531.20
		$14,297.84
Less: Petty cash fund reported separately	$ 100.00	
NSF check, J. Wilson	220.00	
Charge by bank for printing checks	7.50	327.50
Adjusted balance		$13,970.34
Balance per bank statement, Nov. 30		$ 9,734.70
Add: Deposit of Nov. 30 not recorded by bank	$5,846.20	
Service charge made by bank in error	340.00	6,186.20
		$15,920.90

Less: Outstanding checks on Nov. 30:

No. 924	$ 136.25	
No. 940	105.00	
No. 941	11.46	
No. 943	826.70	
No. 944	95.00	
No. 945	716.15	
No. 946	60.00	1,950.56
Adjusted balance (*as above*)		$13,970.34

b

General Journal

19___

Nov. 30	Cash	6,531.20	
	Loss on Sale of Marketable Securities	2,270.00	
	Miscellaneous Expense	5.00	
	Investment in Marketable Securities		6,270.00
	Notes Receivable		690.00
	Accounts Receivable		1,846.20
	To record increase in Cash account as indicated by bank reconciliation.		
Nov. 30	Petty Cash	100.00	
	Miscellaneous Expense	7.50	
	Accounts Receivable, J. Wilson	220.00	
	Cash		327.50
	To record cash disbursements as indicated by bank reconciliation and to record petty cash in a separate account.		

REVIEW QUESTIONS

1 In bidding for some surplus property offered at auction by a government agency, the Argus Company on December 28 drew a check for $3,000 and mailed it with the bid. The government agency on January 3 rejected the bid and returned the check. Should the $3,000 be included as cash in the December 31 balance sheet, which was prepared by the Argus Company on January 5 after the check had been returned? Explain.

2 Does the expression "efficient management of cash" mean anything more than procedures to prevent losses from fraud or theft? Explain.

3 Mention some principles to be observed by a business in establishing strong internal control over cash receipts.

4 Explain how internal control over cash transactions is strengthened by compliance with the following rule: "Deposit each day's cash receipts intact in the bank, and make all disbursements by check."

5 Name three internal control practices relating to cash which would be practicable even in a small business having little opportunity for division of duties.

6 With respect to a *voucher system,* what is meant by the terms *voucher, voucher register,* and *check register?*

7 What is the greatest single advantage of the voucher system?

8 Randall Company uses a voucher system to control its cash disbursements. With respect to a purchase of merchandise, what three documents would need to be examined to verify that the voucher should be approved?

9 Suggest an internal control procedure to prevent the documents supporting a paid voucher from being resubmitted later in support of another cash disbursement.

10 Pico Stationery Shop has for years maintained a petty cash fund of $75, which is replenished twice a month.
   a How many debit entries would you expect to find in the Petty Cash account each year?
   b When would expenditures from the petty cash fund be entered in the ledger accounts?

11 Classify each of the numbered reconciling items listed below under one of the following headings: (*a*) an addition to the balance per depositor's records; (*b*) a deduction from the balance per depositor's records; (*c*) an addition to the balance per bank statement; (*d*) a deduction from the balance per bank statement.
   (*1*) Deposits in transit
   (*2*) Outstanding checks
   (*3*) Customer's check deposited but returned by bank marked NSF
   (*4*) Bank service charges
   (*5*) Collection by bank of note receivable left with bank for collection in behalf of depositor

12 A check for $455 issued in payment of an account payable was erroneously listed in the cash payments journal as $545. The error was discovered early in the following month when the paid check was returned by the bank. What corrective action is needed?

13 In the reconciliation of a bank account, what reconciling items necessitate a journal entry in the depositor's accounting records?

14 It is standard accounting practice to treat as cash all checks received from customers. When a customer's check is received, recorded, and deposited, but later returned by the bank marked NSF, what accounting entry or entries would be appropriate?

15 Why must an investor who owns numerous marketable securities maintain a marketable securities subsidiary ledger?

16 If an investor buys a bond between interest dates he or she pays, as a part of the purchase price, the accrued interest since the last interest date. On the other hand, if the investor buys a share of common or preferred stock, no "accrued dividend" is added to the quoted price. Explain why this difference exists.

17 Writing down securities to market value when market is below cost, but refusing to write up securities to market prices above cost, is inconsistent procedure. What arguments may be given *in favor* of this treatment?

18 Should stock dividends received be considered revenue to an investor? Explain.

19 "To substitute current market value for cost as a basis for valuing marketable securities would represent a departure from traditional accounting practice." Discuss the case for and against using market value consistently as the basis of valuation in accounting for marketable securities.

20 *Statement on Financial Accounting Standards No. 12,* issued by the FASB, requires that marketable securities classified as current assets be valued at the lower of cost or market. What effect, if any, does this practice have upon the determination of net income?

21 Because of a decline in market prices, National Corporation had to write down the carrying value of its investment in marketable securities by $70,000 in the current year. In the determination of net income for the current year, does it make any difference if National Corporation's investment portfolio is classified as a current asset or a long-term investment? Explain fully.

22 How does the financial reporting requirement of valuing marketable securities at the lower-of-cost-or-market value compare with income tax rules concerning marketable securities?

23 In the current asset section of its balance sheet, Delta Industries shows marketable securities at a market value $12,000 below cost. If the market value of these securities rises by $19,000 during the next accounting period, how large an unrealized gain (if any) should Delta Industries include in its next income statement? Explain fully.

24 When should investors use the equity method to account for an investment in common stock?

25 Dividends on stock owned are usually recognized as income when they are received. Does an investor using the *equity method* to account for an investment in common stock follow this policy? Explain fully.

EXERCISES

Ex. 9-1 Solana Corporation maintains a petty cash fund of $400. At December 31, the end of the company's fiscal year, the fund contained the following:

Currency and coins	*$278.82*
Expense vouchers:	
Flowers for funeral of deceased customer	*20.80*
Box of cigars for purchasing agent of the Powell Co.	*14.18*
Office supplies expense	*46.20*
Salary advance to employee	*40.00*
Total	*$400.00*

a Since there is a substantial amount of cash in the petty cash fund, is there any reason to replenish it at December 31? Explain.

b Prepare the entry (in general journal form) to replenish the petty cash fund.

Ex. 9-2 At July 31 the Cash account in the ledger of Art Mart, Inc., showed a balance of $36,500. The bank statement, however, showed a balance of $43,700 at the same date. If the only reconciling items consisted of a $2,400 deposit in transit, a bank service charge of $4, and 30 outstanding checks, what was the total amount of the outstanding checks?

Ex. 9-3 At the end of the month Matson Company received a bank statement showing a balance of $28,000 on deposit. Among the reconciling items were outstanding checks totaling $5,800, bank service charges of $6, a deposit in transit of $4,400, and a memorandum showing that a $2,400 note receivable owned by Matson Company and left with the bank for collection had been collected and credited to the company's account.

a What is the adjusted amount of cash which should appear on the Matson Company's balance sheet?

b What was the balance per the depositor's records before making adjusting entries for any of the reconciling items?

Ex. 9-4 The following information relates to the Truesdale Company's September 30 cash balance:
(1) As of September 30, cash per books was $5,810; per bank statement, $4,697.
(2) Cash receipts of $1,451 on September 30 were not deposited until October 1.
(3) Among the paid checks returned by the bank was a stolen check for $630 paid in error by the bank after Truesdale Company had issued a "stop payment" order to the bank.
(4) The following memoranda accompanied the bank statement:
  (a) A debit memo for service charges for the month of September, $3.
  (b) A debit memo attached to a $200 check for Susan Scott, marked NSF.
(5) The following checks had been issued but were not included among the paid checks returned by the bank: No. 921 for $326, No. 924 for $684, and No. 925 for $161.

Instructions
a Prepare a bank reconciliation as of September 30.
b Prepare the necessary adjusting journal entries.

Ex. 9-5 Yamato Company purchased as a short-term investment $10,000 face value of the 9% bonds of Lorenzo, Inc., on March 31 of the current year, at a total cost of $10,125, including interest accrued since January 1. Interest is paid by Lorenzo, Inc., on June 30 and December 31. On July 31, four months after the purchase, Yamato Company sold the bonds and interest accrued since July 1 for a total price of $10,105.

Prepare all entries required in the accounting records of Yamato Company relating to the investment in Lorenzo, Inc., bonds. (Commissions are to be ignored.)

Ex. 9-6 Portofino Corporation acquired a portfolio of marketable equity securities in Year 1. The portfolio is regarded as a current asset, and securities are purchased and sold from the portfolio as part of the company's cash management program. The cost and market value of the portfolio at year-end is shown below for Years 1, 2, and 3:

	Cost	Market Value
Year 1	$118,000	$115,200
Year 2	109,600	108,700
Year 3	115,300	116,800

Instructions
a For each of the three years, prepare the year-end adjusting entry to value the portfolio at the lower of cost or market.
b Show how the portfolio would appear in the balance sheet at the end of Year 2. (Use a valuation account in your presentation.)

Ex. 9-7 Target Corporation owns marketable equity securities which cost $100,000 and are classified in the balance sheet as a long-term investment. In the current year, the market value of the securities declined from an amount greater than cost to $90,000, and Target Corporation correctly made the following year-end adjusting entry:

Unrealized Loss on Long-Term Investments	*10,000*	
Valuation Allowance for Long-Term Investments		*10,000*
To adjust carrying value of long-term investment in equity securities to lower of cost or market.		

Instructions
For each of the financial statement items or relationships listed below, explain

what change (if any) would result if the marketable securities were classified as a current asset instead of a long-term investment.

(1) Current assets
(2) Total assets
(3) Current ratio (With the portfolio classified as a long-term investment, current assets total $180,000 and current liabilities total $100,000.)
(4) Net income
(5) Retained earnings
(6) Total stockholders' equity

The type of explanation desired is illustrated below, using item (1) as an example:

(1) Current assets would be increased by $90,000 if the securities were classified as a current asset.

Ex. 9-8 On January 1, Year 4, Travis Corporation purchases 40% of the common stock of Comoy, Inc. for $300,000, which corresponds to the underlying book value. Comoy, Inc., has issued common stock only. During Year 4, Comoy, Inc., earns net income of $70,000 and pays dividends of $30,000. Travis Corporation uses the equity method to account for this investment.

Instructions
a Prepare all journal entries in the accounting records of Travis Corporation relating to the investment during Year 4.
b During Year 5, Comoy, Inc., reports a net loss of $90,000 and pays no dividends. Compute the carrying value of Travis Corporation's investment in Comoy, Inc., at the end of Year 5.

PROBLEMS

9-1 In order to handle small cash disbursements in an efficient manner, Capital Ventures, Inc., established a petty cash fund on July 1, 19 ____ . The company does not use a voucher system. The following transactions occurred relating to petty cash.

July 1 A check for $300 was issued and cashed to establish a petty cash fund.
July 15 The fund was replenished after a count which revealed the following cash and petty cash vouchers for disbursements:

Office supplies expense	$89.25
Postage expense	65.00
Travel expense	78.12
Miscellaneous expense	21.00
Telephone expense	31.75
Currency and coin	14.88

July 31 A count of the fund at month-end disclosed the following:

Office supplies expense	$59.40
Postage expense	60.00
Travel expense	59.38
Miscellaneous expense	40.62
Currency and coin	80.60

A check was issued on July 31 to replenish the petty cash fund and to increase the amount of the fund to $375.

Instructions

a Prepare entries in general journal form to record the above transactions.

b Explain why the petty cash fund should be replenished at the end of the accounting period even though the fund contains considerable cash.

9-2 Robert Smith, a trusted employee of Novelty Sales Co., found himself in personal financial difficulties and carried out the following plan to steal $1,000 from the company and to conceal the fraud.

Smith removed $1,000 in currency from the cash register. This amount represented the bulk of the cash received in over-the-counter sales during the three business days since the last bank deposit. Smith then removed a $1,000 check from the day's incoming mail; this check had been mailed in by a customer, Larry Jansen, in full payment of his account. Smith made no entry in the cash receipts journal for the $1,000 collection from Jansen but deposited the check in Novelty Sales Co.'s bank account in place of the $1,000 of over-the-counter cash receipts he had stolen. In order to keep Jansen from protesting when his month-end statement reached him, Smith made a general journal entry debiting Sales Returns and Allowances and crediting Accounts Receivable—Larry Jansen. Smith posted this entry to the two general ledger accounts affected and also to Jansen's account in the subsidiary ledger for accounts receivable.

Instructions

a Did these actions by Smith cause the general ledger to be out of balance or the subsidiary ledger to disagree with the control account? Explain.

b Several weaknesses in internal control apparently exist in the Novelty Sales Co. Indicate the corrective actions needed.

9-3 The cash transactions and cash balances of Roland Company for April, 19____, are summarized below.

(1) As of April 30, cash per accounting records was $7,059.12; per bank statement, $6,678.67.

(2) Cash receipts of $2,187.03 on April 30 were not deposited until May 1.

(3) The following memoranda accompanied the bank statement:

(a) A debit memo for service charges for the month of April, $7.56.

(b) A debit memo attached to a check for G. Herron, marked NSF, for $149.88.

(c) A credit memo for $1,452, representing the proceeds of a non-interest-bearing note collected by the bank for Roland Company. The note was for $1,464; the bank deducted a collection fee of $12.

(4) The following checks had been issued but were not included in the canceled checks returned by the bank: no. 348 for $302.40, no. 351 for $124.32, and no. 356 for $85.30.

Instructions

a Prepare a bank reconciliation as of April 30.

b Draft in general journal form the journal entries necessary to adjust the accounts.

c State the amount of cash which should appear in the balance sheet at April 30.

9-4 Information necessary for the preparation of a bank reconciliation and related journal entries for the Stonehenge Corporation at November 30 is listed below:

(1) The balance per records of the Stonehenge Corporation is $10,423.09.

(2) The bank statement shows a balance of $9,168.57 as of November 30.

(3) Two debit memoranda accompanied the bank statement: one for $13 was for service charges for the month; the other for $864.60 was attached to an NSF check from R. B. Thomas.

(4) The paid checks returned with the November bank statement disclosed two errors in the cash records. Check no. 832 for $456.30 had been erroneously recorded as $465.30 in the cash payments journal, and check no. 851 for $77.44 had been recorded as $44.77. Check no. 832 was issued in payment for a store display counter; check no. 851 was for telephone expense.

(5) A collection charge for $126.00 (not applicable to Stonehenge Corporation) was erroneously deducted from the account by the bank.

(6) Cash receipts of November 30 amounting to $585.25 were mailed to the bank too late to be included in the November bank statement.

(7) Checks outstanding as of November 30 were as follows: no. 860 for $151.93, no. 867 for $82.46, and no. 869 for $123.61.

Instructions

a Prepare a bank reconciliation at November 30.

b Prepare the necessary adjusting entries in general journal form.

9-5 Rancho Lumber Co. had never given much attention to internal control concepts and the internal controls over cash transactions were not adequate. Donna Jones, the cashier-bookkeeper, handled cash receipts, made small disbursements from the cash receipts, maintained accounting records, and prepared the monthly reconciliations of the bank account.

At April 30, the statement received from the bank showed a balance on deposit of $30,510. The outstanding checks were as follows: no. 7062 for $371.16, no. 7183 for $306, no. 7284 for $470.61, no. 8621 for $315.34, no. 8623 for $613.80, and no. 8632 for $311.04. The balance of cash shown by the company's ledger account for Cash was $35,474.96, which included the cash on hand. The bank statement for April showed a credit of $360 arising from the collection of a note left with the bank; the company's accounts did not include an entry to record this collection.

Recognizing the weakness existing in internal control over cash transactions, Jones removed all the cash on hand in excess of $6,025.14, and then prepared the following reconciliation in an attempt to conceal this theft.

Balance per accounting records, Apr. 30		*$35,474.96*
Add: Outstanding checks:		
No. 8621	*$315.34*	
No. 8623	*613.80*	
No. 8632	*311.04*	*1,060.18*
		$36,535.14
Less: Cash on hand		*6,025.14*
Balance per bank statement, Apr. 30		*$30,510.00*
Less: Unrecorded credit		*360.00*
True cash, Apr. 30		*$30,150.00*

Instructions

a Determine how much cash Jones took and explain how she attempted to conceal her theft. Prepare a bank reconciliation in a form which first shows the balance per the accounting records after adding the cash from collection of the note and, second, shows an adjusted bank balance after deducting the proper amount for all outstanding checks. The two adjusted balances will not agree; the difference is the amount of undeposited cash which should be on hand. Comparison of the undeposited cash which should be on hand with the actual amount on hand of $6,025.14 will indicate the amount of the cash shortage.

b Suggest some specific internal control devices for the Rancho Lumber Co.

9-6 During the current year, Apache Company engaged in the following transactions relating to marketable securities:

Feb. 28 Purchased 1,000 shares of National Products common stock for $63 per share plus a broker's commission of $600.

Mar. 15 National Products paid a cash dividend of 50 cents per share which had been declared on February 20 payable on March 15 to stockholders of record on March 6.

May 31 National Products distributed a 20% stock dividend.

Nov.15 National Products distributed additional shares as the result of a 2 for 1 stock split.

Dec.10 Apache Company sold 600 shares of its National Products stock at $28 per share, less a broker's commission of $150.

Dec.10 National Products paid a cash dividend of 25 cents per share. Dividend was declared November 20 payable December 10 to stockholders of record on November 30.

As of December 31, National Products common stock had a market value of $25 per share. Apache Company classifies its National Products stock as a current asset and owns no other marketable securities.

Instructions Prepare journal entries to account for this investment in Apache Company's accounting records. Include memorandum entries when appropriate to show changes in the cost basis per share. Also include the year-end adjusting entry, if one is necessary, to reduce the investment to the lower of cost or market value. For journal entries involving computations, the explanation portion of the entry should include the computation.

9-7 In the current asset section of its most recent balance sheet, Mirage Corporation showed marketable securities as follows:

Marketable securities $72,400

Less: Valuation allowance for marketable securities . . . . <u>1,250</u> $71,150

Shortly after the above balance sheet date, Mirage Corporation sold for $44,000 marketable securities which had cost $42,600.

Instructions

a Prepare a journal entry to record the above sale for $44,000 of marketable securities which had cost $42,600.

b The following numbered items are *independent* assumptions as to the current market value of the equity securities which remain in Mirage Corporation's portfolio at the next balance sheet date after the sale recorded in part *a*. For each assumption, prepare the journal entry required to adjust the carrying value of the portfolio to the lower of cost or market as of the balance sheet date. Show computations supporting each entry.

(1) Assume current market value is $27,100.

(2) Assume current market value is $29,270.

(3) Assume current market value is $31,800.

9-8 The portfolio of marketable securities owned by Blue Marlin Corporation at January 1 of the current year consisted of the four securities listed below. All marketable securities are classified as current assets.

$100,000 maturity value Bay Resort Corp. $7\frac{1}{2}$% bonds due Dec. 31, 1986.

Interest is payable on June 30 and Dec. 31 of each year. Cost basis

$976 per bond $97,600

$50,000 maturity value Copper Products Co. 9% bonds due Apr. 30, 1990.

Interest is payable on Apr. 30 and Oct. 31 of each year. Cost basis

$990 per bond 49,500

1,200 shares of Aztec Corporation common stock. Cost basis $38.50

per share 46,200

800 shares of Donner-Pass, Inc., $4.80 cumulative preferred stock. Cost

basis $65 per share 52,000

Transactions relating to investments that were completed during the first six months of the current year follow:

Jan. 10 Acquired 500 shares of Rhodes Co. common stock at $76 per share. Brokerage commissions paid amounted to $250.

Jan. 21 Received quarterly dividend of $1.20 per share on 800 shares of Donner-Pass, Inc., preferred stock.

Mar. 5 Sold 200 shares of Donner-Pass, Inc., preferred stock at $62 per share less commissions and transfer taxes amounting to $105.

Apr. 1 Received additional 500 shares of Rhodes Co. common stock as a result of a 2 for 1 split.

Apr. 20 Received quarterly dividend of $1.20 per share on 600 shares of Donner-Pass, Inc., preferred stock.

Apr. 30 Received semiannual interest on Copper Products Co. 9% bonds. Accrued interest of $750 had been recorded on December 31 of last year in the Accrued Bond Interest Receivable account.

May 1 Sold $25,000 face value of Copper Products Co. 9% bonds at 103, less a commission of $125.

May 10 Received additional 120 shares of Aztec Corporation common stock as a result of 10% stock dividend.

June 4 Received a cash dividend of 90 cents per share on Rhodes Co. common stock.

June 24 Sold 800 shares of Aztec Corporation common stock at $38 per share, less a brokerage commission and transfer taxes amounting to $280.

June 30 Received semiannual interest on Bay Resorts Corp. $7\frac{1}{2}$% bonds.

On June 30 of the current year, the quoted market prices of the marketable equity securities owned by Blue Marlin Corporation were as follows: Aztec Corporation common stock, $37; Donner-Pass, Inc., preferred stock, $62\frac{1}{2}$; and Rhodes Co. common stock. $43.

Instructions

a Prepare journal entries to record the transactions listed above. Include an adjusting entry to record accrued interest on the remaining Copper Products Co. bonds through June 30. (Do not consider a lower-of-cost-or-market adjustment in part *a*.)

b Prepare a schedule showing the cost and market value of the marketable equity securities owned by Blue Marlin Corporation at June 30. Prepare the adjusting entry, if one is required, to reduce the portfolio to the lower of cost or market. (At January 1, the market value of the portfolio was above cost and the Valuation Allowance for Marketable Securities account had a zero balance.)

9-9 Carolina Mills was organized on January 1, Year 1, to manufacture carpeting. On this date, the corporation issued 200,000 shares of common stock at a price of $25 per share; 40,000 of these shares were issued to Discount Carpet Sales, Inc.

Discount Carpet Sales, Inc., regards its investment in Carolina Mills as long term. Shown below are the net income (or loss) earned and dividends paid by Carolina Mills during Years 1 and 2. Also shown is the market price per share of common stock at the end of each year.

	Net Income (Loss)	Dividends Paid	Market Price per Share (Year-End)
Year 1	$420,000	$120,000*	$37
Year 2	(270,000)	None	21

*60 cents per share.

Instructions

a Prepare all journal entries relating to this investment in Years 1 and 2 in the accounting records of Discount Carpet Sales, Inc. Assume that dividends are recognized as income when received and that the investment is valued at the lower of cost or market.

b Prepare all journal entries relating to this investment in Years 1 and 2 assuming that Discount Carpet Sales, Inc., uses the *equity method* to account for its investment in Carolina Mills.

c For each ledger account used in parts *a* and *b,* explain briefly the nature of the account and where it will appear in the financial statements. Prepare a separate explanation for each account, but explain each account only once. You may omit an explanation of the Cash account.

An example of the type of explanation desired follows: "Marketable Securities—Long-Term: This is an asset account which appears in the balance sheet under the caption Long-Term Investments."

9-10 The cash receipts journal and the cash payments journal maintained by Rainbow Company showed transactions during September as listed on page 390. On October 1, Rainbow Company received from its bank a bank statement covering the month of September. Enclosed with the bank statement were 23 checks paid by the bank during September and a $4.25 debit memorandum for service charges. The September bank statement appears below.

Instructions

a Prepare a bank reconciliation at September 30. (The balance of the general ledger account for Cash at August 31 was in agreement with the ending balance shown on the bank statement for August.)

b Prepare a general journal entry to adjust the Cash account at September 30.

RAINBOW COMPANY

4200 Badger Road

Rainbow, California

THE FIRST NATIONAL BANK

OF RAINBOW

Vouchers Returned   *24*

Checks			Deposits	Date	Balance
				Sept. 1	7,658.75
31.15	35.48	130.00	72.80	Sept. 2	7,534.92
60.00			361.00	Sept. 5	7,835.92
70.00	515.00		280.00	Sept. 7	7,530.92
90.00				Sept. 8	7,440.92
13.30	62.50		510.00	Sept. 9	7,875.12
28.00			205.60	Sept. 12	8,052.72
650.00			180.14	Sept. 14	7,582.86
			345.00	Sept. 16	7,927.86
85.00			427.50	Sept. 19	8,270.36
24.10	125.06			Sept. 20	8,121.20
40.00	65.00		90.00	Sept. 21	8,106.20
162.40			360.00	Sept. 23	8,303.80
15.00			625.00	Sept. 26	8,913.80
355.00	270.00	225.00	130.25	Sept. 28	8,194.05
155.00	25.00	4.25S	280.50	Sept. 30	8,290.30

Cash Receipts		
Date		Cash Dr
Sept.	1	72.80
	3	361.00
	6	280.00
	8	510.00
	10	205.60
	13	180.14
	15	345.00
	17	427.50
	20	90.00
	22	360.00
	24	625.00
	27	130.25
	29	280.50
	30	315.25
		4,183.04

Cash Payments			
Date		Ck. No.	Cash Cr
Sept.	1	65	130.00
	1	66	90.00
	1	67	35.48
	2	68	31.15
	4	69	60.00
	4	70	70.00
	5	71	515.00
	9	72	62.50
	10	73	13.30
	10	74	28.00
	13	75	650.00
	19	76	125.06
	19	77	40.00
	19	78	85.00
	20	79	24.10
	21	80	38.60
	22	81	65.00
	22	82	162.40
	23	83	150.00
	26	84	15.00
	28	85	270.00
	28	86	105.20
	28	87	225.00
	28	88	355.00
	30	89	25.00
	30	90	45.00
	30	91	155.00
			3,570.79

BUSINESS DECISION PROBLEM 9

June Davis inherited a highly successful business, Glacier Corporation, shortly after her twenty-second birthday and took over the active management of the business. A portion of the company's business consisted of over-the-counter sales for cash, but most sales were on credit and were shipped by truck. Davis had no knowledge of internal control practices and relied implicitly upon the bookkeeper-cashier, J. K. Wiley, in all matters relating to cash and accounting records. Wiley, who had been with the company for many years, maintained the accounting records and prepared all financial statements with the help of two assistants, made bank deposits, signed checks, and prepared bank reconciliations.

The monthly income statements submitted to Davis by Wiley showed a very satisfactory rate of net income; however, the amount of cash in the bank declined steadily during the first 18 months after Davis took over the business. To meet the company's weakening cash position, a bank loan was obtained and a few months later when the cash position again grew critical, the loan was increased.

On April 1, two years after Davis assumed the management of the company, Wiley suddenly left town, leaving no forwarding address. Davis was immediately deluged with claims of creditors who stated their accounts were several months past due and that Wiley had promised all debts would be paid by April 1. The bank telephoned to notify Davis that the company's account was overdrawn and that a number of checks had just been presented for payment.

In an effort to get together some cash to meet this emergency, Davis called on two of the largest customers of the company, to whom substantial sales on account had recently been made, and asked if they could pay their accounts at once. Both customers informed her that their accounts were paid in full. They produced paid checks to substantiate their payments and explained that Wiley had offered them reduced prices on merchandise if they would pay within 24 hours after delivery.

To keep the business from insolvency, Davis agreed to sell at a bargain price a half interest in the company. The sale was made to Helen Smith, who had had considerable experience in the industry. One condition for the sale was that Smith should become the general manager of the business. The cash investment by Smith for her half interest was sufficient for the company to meet the demands on it and continue operations.

Immediately after Smith entered the business, she launched an investigation of Wiley's activities. During the course of this investigation the following irregularities were disclosed:

(1) During the last few months of Wiley's employment with the company, bank deposits were much smaller than the cash receipts. Wiley had abstracted most of the receipts and substituted for them a number of worthless checks bearing fictitious signatures. These checks had been accumulated in an envelope marked "Cash Receipts—For Deposit Only."

(2) Numerous legitimate sales of merchandise on account had been charged to fictitious customers. When the actual customer later made payment for the goods, Wiley abstracted the check or cash and made no entry. The account receivable with the fictitious customer remained in the records.

(3) When checks were received from customers in payment of their accounts, Wiley had frequently recorded the transaction by debiting an expense account and crediting Accounts Receivable. In such cases Wiley had removed from the cash receipts an equivalent amount of currency, thus substituting the check for the currency and causing the bank deposit to agree with the recorded cash receipts.

(4) More than $3,000 a month had been stolen from petty cash. Fraudulent petty cash vouchers, mostly charged to the Purchases account, had been created to conceal these thefts and to support the checks cashed to replenish the petty cash fund.

(5) For many sales made over the counter, Wiley had recorded lesser amounts on the cash register or had not rung up any amount. He had abstracted the funds received but not recorded.

(6) To produce income statements that showed profitable operations, Wiley had recorded many fictitious sales. The recorded accounts receivable included many from nonexistent customers.

(7) In preparing bank reconciliations, Wiley had omitted many outstanding checks, thus concealing the fact that the cash in the bank was less than the amount shown by the ledger.

(8) Inventory had been recorded at inflated amounts in order to increase reported profits from the business.

Instructions

a For each of the numbered paragraphs, describe one or more internal control procedures you would recommend to prevent the occurrence of such fraud.

b Apart from specific internal controls over cash and other accounts, what general precaution could June Davis have taken to assure herself that the accounting records were properly maintained and the company's financial statements complete and dependable? Explain fully.

10

Receivables
and Payables

One of the key factors underlying the tremendous expansion of the American economy has been the trend toward selling all types of goods and services on credit. The automobile industry has long been the classic example of the use of retail credit to achieve the efficiencies of large-scale output. Today, however, in nearly every field of retail trade it appears that sales and profits can be increased by granting customers the privilege of making payment a month or more after the date of sale. The sales of manufacturers and wholesalers are made on credit to an even greater extent than in retail trade.

ACCOUNTS RECEIVABLE

The credit department

No business concern wants to sell on credit to a customer who will prove unable or unwilling to pay his or her account. Consequently, most business organizations include a credit department which must reach a decision on the credit worthiness of each prospective customer. The credit department investigates the debt-paying ability and credit record of each new customer and determines the maximum amount of credit to be extended.

If the prospective customer is a business concern as, for example, a retail store, the financial statements of the store will be obtained and analyzed to determine its financial strength and the trend of operating results. The credit department naturally prefers to rely upon financial statements which have been audited by certified public accountants.

Regardless of whether the prospective customer is a business concern or an individual consumer, the investigation by the credit department will probably include the obtaining of a credit report from a local credit agency or from a national credit-rating institution such as Dun & Bradstreet, Inc. A credit agency compiles credit data on individuals and business concerns, and distributes this information to its clients. Most companies that make numerous sales on credit find it worthwhile to subscribe to the services of one or more credit agencies.

Uncollectible accounts

A business that sells its goods or services on credit will inevitably find that some of its accounts receivable are uncollectible. Regardless of how thoroughly the credit department investigates prospective customers, some uncollectible accounts will arise as a result of errors in judgment or because of unexpected developments. As a matter of fact, a limited amount of uncollectible accounts is evidence of a sound credit policy. If the credit department should become too cautious and conservative in rating customers, it might avoid all credit losses but, in so doing, lose profitable business by rejecting many acceptable customers.

Reflecting uncollectible accounts in the financial statements

In measuring business income, one of the most fundamental principles of accounting is that *revenue must be matched with the expenses incurred in generating that revenue.*

Uncollectible accounts expense is caused by selling goods on credit to customers who fail to pay their bills; such expenses, therefore, are incurred in the year in which the sales are made, even though the accounts are not determined to be uncollectible until the following year. An account receivable which originates from a sale on credit in the year 1981 and is determined to be uncollectible sometime during 1982 represents an expense of the year 1981. Unless each year's uncollectible accounts expense is *estimated* and reflected in the year-end balance sheet and income statement, both of these financial statements will be seriously deficient.

To illustrate, let us assume that Arlington Corporation began business on January 1, Year 1, and made most of its sales on credit throughout the year. At December 31, Year 1, accounts receivable amounted to $200,000. On this date the management reviewed the status of the accounts receivable, giving particular study to accounts which were past due. This review indicated that the collectible portion of the $200,000 of accounts receivable amounted to approximately $190,000. In other words, management estimated that uncollectible accounts expense for the first year of operations amounted to $10,000. The following adjusting entry should be made at December 31, Year 1:

<table>
<tr><td rowspan="4">*Provision for uncollectible accounts*</td><td>*Uncollectible Accounts Expense* . . . .</td><td>*10,000*</td><td></td></tr>
<tr><td>*Allowance for Doubtful Accounts* . . . .</td><td></td><td>*10,000*</td></tr>
<tr><td>*To record the estimated uncollectible accounts expense for*</td><td></td><td></td></tr>
<tr><td>*Year 1.*</td><td></td><td></td></tr>
</table>

The Uncollectible Accounts Expense account created by the debit part of this entry is closed into the Income Summary account in the same manner as any other expense account. The Allowance for Doubtful Accounts which was credited in the above journal entry will appear in the balance sheet as a deduction from the face amount of the accounts receivable. It serves to reduce the accounts receivable to their *realizable value* in the balance sheet, as shown by the following illustration:

ARLINGTON CORPORATION
Partial Balance Sheet
December 31, Year 1

<table>
<tr><td rowspan="8">*How much is the estimated realizable value of the accounts receivable?*</td><td colspan="3">*Current assets:*</td></tr>
<tr><td>*Cash* . . . .</td><td></td><td>*$ 75,000*</td></tr>
<tr><td>*Accounts receivable* . . . .</td><td>*$200,000*</td><td></td></tr>
<tr><td>*Less: Allowance for doubtful accounts* . . . .</td><td>*10,000*</td><td>*190,000*</td></tr>
<tr><td>*Inventory* . . . .</td><td></td><td>*100,000*</td></tr>
<tr><td>*Total current assets* . . . .</td><td></td><td>*$365,000*</td></tr>
</table>

The allowance for doubtful accounts

There is no way of telling in advance which accounts receivable will be collected and which ones will prove to be worthless. It is therefore not possible to credit the account of any particular customer to reflect our overall estimate of the year's credit losses. Neither is it possible to credit the Accounts Receivable control account in the general ledger. If the Accounts Receivable control account were to be credited with the estimated amount of doubtful accounts, this control account would no longer be in balance with the total of the numerous customers' accounts in the subsidiary ledger. The only practicable alternative, therefore, is to credit a separate account called Allowance for Doubtful Accounts with the amount estimated to be uncollectible.

The Allowance for Doubtful Accounts is sometimes described as a *contra-asset* account, an *offset* account, an *asset reduction* account, a *negative asset* account, and most frequently of all, a *valuation* account. All these terms are derived from the fact that the Allowance for Doubtful Accounts is an account with a credit balance, which is offset against an asset account to produce the proper balance sheet value of an asset.

Estimating uncollectible accounts expense

Before the accounts are closed and financial statements are prepared at the end of the accounting period, an estimate of uncollectible accounts expense must be made. This estimate will usually be based upon past experience, perhaps modified in accordance with current business conditions.

Since the allowance for doubtful accounts is necessarily an estimate and not a precise calculation, the factor of personal judgment may play a considerable part in determining the size of this valuation account. There is a fairly wide range of reasonableness within which the amount may be set. Most companies intend that the allowance shall be adequate to cover probable losses. The term *adequate,* when used in this context, suggests an amount somewhat larger than the minimum probable amount.

CONSERVATISM AS A FACTOR IN VALUING ACCOUNTS RECEIVABLE The larger the allowance established for doubtful accounts, the lower the net valuation of accounts receivable will be. Some accountants and some business executives tend to favor the most conservative valuation of assets that logically can be supported. Accountants necessarily make decisions under conditions of uncertainty. Conservatism in the preparation of a balance sheet implies a tendency to resolve uncertainties in the valuation of assets by reporting assets at the lower end of the range of reasonable values rather than by establishing values in a purely objective manner.

The valuation of assets at conservative amounts is a long-standing tradition in accounting, stemming from the days when creditors were the major users of financial statements. From a theoretical point of view, the doctrine of balance sheet conservatism is difficult to support, but from the viewpoint of bankers and others who use financial statements as a basis for granting loans, conservatism in valuing assets has long been regarded as a desirable policy.

Assume that the balance sheet of Company A presents optimistic, exaggerated values for the assets owned. Assume also that this "unconservative" balance sheet is submitted to a banker in support of an application for a loan. The banker studies the balance sheet and makes a loan to Company A in reliance upon the values listed. Later the banker finds it impossible to collect the loan and also finds that the assets upon which the loan was based had been greatly overstated in the balance sheet. The banker will undoubtedly consider the overly optimistic character of the balance sheet as partially responsible for the loss. Experiences of this type have led creditors as a group to stress the desirability of conservatism in the valuation of assets.

In considering the argument for balance sheet conservatism, it is important to recognize that the income statement is also affected by the estimates made of uncollectible accounts expense. The act of providing a relatively large allowance for doubtful accounts involves a correspond-ingly heavy charge to expense. Setting asset values at a minimum in the balance sheet has the related effect of stating the current year's net income at a minimum amount.

Two methods of estimating uncollectible accounts expense

The provision for uncollectible accounts is an estimate of expense to be sustained. Two alternative approaches are widely used in making the annual estimate for uncollectible accounts. One method consists of adjusting the valuation account to a new balance equal to the estimated uncollectible portion of the existing accounts receivable. This method is referred to as the *balance sheet* approach and rests on an *aging of the accounts receivable.* The adjusting entry takes into consideration the existing balance in the Allowance for Doubtful Accounts.

The alternative method requires an adjusting entry computed as a percentage of the year's net sales. This method may be regarded as the *income statement* approach to estimating uncollectible accounts expense. This *percentage of sales* method emphasizes the expense side of the adjustment and leaves out of consideration any existing balance in the valuation-allowance account. If any substantial balance should accumu-late in the allowance account, however, a change in the percentage figure being applied to sales might be appropriate. These two methods are explained below.

AGING THE ACCOUNTS RECEIVABLE A past-due account receivable is always viewed with some suspicion. The fact that a receivable is past due suggests that the customer is either unable or unwilling to pay. The analysis of accounts receivable by age is known as aging the accounts, as illustrated by the schedule below.

Analysis of Accounts Receivable by Age
December 31, 19____

Customer	Total	Not Yet Due	1–30 Days Past Due	31–60 Days Past Due	61–90 Days Past Due	Over 90 Days Past Due
A. B. Adams	$ 500	$ 500				
B. L. Baker	150			$ 150		
R. D. Carl	800	800				
H. V. Davis	900				$ 800	$ 100
R. M. Evans	400	400				
Others	32,250	16,300	$10,000	4,200	200	1,550
Totals	$35,000	$18,000	$10,000	$4,350	$1,000	$1,650
Percentage . . .	100	51	29	12	3	5

If you were credit man-ager . . . ?

This analysis of accounts receivable gives management a useful picture of the status of collections and the probabilities of credit losses. Almost half of the total accounts receivable are past due. The question "How long past due?" is pertinent, and is answered by the bottom line of the aging analysis. About 29% of the total receivables are past due from 1 to 30 days; another 12% are past due from 31 to 60 days; about 3% are past due from 61 to 90 days; and 5% of the total receivables consist of accounts past due more than three months. If an analysis of this type is prepared at the end of each month, management will be informed continuously on the trend of collections and can take appropriate action to ease or to tighten credit policy. Moreover, a yardstick is available to measure the effectiveness of the persons responsible for collection activities.

The longer past due an account receivable becomes, the greater the likelihood that it will not be collected in full. In recognition of this fact, the analysis of receivables by age groups can be used as a stepping-stone in determining a reasonable amount to add to the Allowance for Doubtful Accounts. To determine this amount, it is desirable to estimate the percentage of probable expense for each age group of accounts receivable. This percentage, when applied to the dollar amount in each age group, gives a probable expense for each group. By adding together the probable expense for all the age groups, the required balance in the Allowance for Doubtful Accounts is determined. The following schedule lists the group totals from the preceding illustration and shows how the total probable expense from uncollectible accounts is computed.

Accounts Receivable by Age Groups

		Amount	*Percentage Considered Uncollectible*	*Allowance for Doubtful Accounts*
Estimate of probable uncollectible accounts expense	*Not yet due*	$18,000	1	$ 180
	1–30 days past due	10,000	3	300
	31–60 days past due	4,350	10	435
	61–90 days past due	1,000	20	200
	Over 90 days past due	1,650	50	825
	Totals	$35,000		$1,940

This summary indicates that an allowance for doubtful accounts of $1,940 is required. Before making the adjusting entry, it is necessary to consider the existing balance in the allowance account. If the Allowance for Doubtful Accounts presently has a credit balance of, say, $500, the adjusting entry should be for $1,440 in order to bring the account up to the required balance of $1,940. This entry is as follows:

Increasing	Uncollectible Accounts Expense	1,440
allowance for	Allowance for Doubtful Accounts	1,440
doubtful accounts	To increase the valuation account to the estimated	

required total of $1,940, computed as follows:

Present credit balance of valuation account	$ 500
Current provision for doubtful accounts	1,440
New credit balance in valuation account	$1,940

On the other hand, if the Allowance for Doubtful Accounts contained a *debit* balance of $500 before adjustment, the adjusting entry would be made in the amount of $2,440 ($1,940 + $500) in order to create the desired credit balance of $1,940. (The circumstances which could lead to a temporary debit balance in the Allowance for Doubtful Accounts will be explained later in this chapter.)

ESTIMATING UNCOLLECTIBLE ACCOUNTS AS A PERCENTAGE OF NET SALES An alternative approach preferred by some companies in providing for uncollectible accounts consists of computing the charge to uncollectible accounts expense as a percentage of the net sales for the year. The question to be answered is not "How large a valuation allowance is needed to reduce our receivables to realizable value?" Instead, the question is stated as "How much uncollectible accounts expense is associated with this year's volume of sales?" This method may be regarded as the *income statement* approach to estimating uncollectible accounts.

As an example, assume that for several years the expense of uncollectible accounts has averaged 1% of net sales (sales minus returns and allowances and sales discounts). At the end of the current year, before adjusting entries, the following account balances appear in the ledger:

	Dr	Cr
Sales		$1,260,000
Sales returns and allowances	$40,000	
Sales discounts	20,000	
Allowance for doubtful accounts		1,500

The *net sales* of the current year amount to $1,200,000; 1% of this amount is $12,000. The existing balance in the Allowance for Doubtful Accounts *should be ignored in computing the amount of the adjusting entry,* because the percentage of net sales method stresses the relationship between uncollectible accounts expense and net sales rather than the valuation of receivables at the balance sheet date. The entry is:

Provision for un-collectible accounts based on percentage of net sales	Uncollectible Accounts Expense	12,000
	Allowance for Doubtful Accounts	12,000
	To record uncollectible accounts expense of 1% of the year's net sales (.01 × $1,200,000).	

If a company makes both cash sales and credit sales, it may be desirable to exclude the cash sales from consideration and to compute the percentage relationship of uncollectible accounts expense to credit sales only.

This approach of estimating uncollectible accounts receivable as a percentage of credit sales is easier to apply than the method of aging accounts receivable. The aging of receivables, however, tends to give a more reliable estimate of uncollectible accounts because of the consideration given to the age and collectibility of the specific accounts receivable at the balance sheet date. Some companies use the income statement approach for preparing interim financial statements and internal reports but use the balance sheet method for preparing annual financial statements.

Writing off an uncollectible account receivable

Whenever an account receivable from a specific customer is determined to be uncollectible, it no longer qualifies as an asset and should immediately be written off. To write off an account receivable is to reduce the balance of the customer's account to zero. The journal entry to accomplish this consists of a credit to the Accounts Receivable control account in the general ledger (and to the customer's account in the subsidiary ledger), and an offsetting debit to the Allowance for Doubtful Accounts.

Referring again to the example of the Arlington Corporation as shown on page 394, the ledger accounts were as follows after the adjusting entry for estimated uncollectible accounts had been made on December 31, Year 1:

Accounts receivable	*$200,000*
Less: Allowance for doubtful accounts	*10,000*

Next let us assume that on January 27, Year 2, a customer by the name of William Benton became bankrupt and the account receivable from him in the amount of $1,000 was determined to be worthless. The following entry should be made by the Arlington Corporation:

Writing off an uncol- lectible account

Allowance for Doubtful Accounts	*1,000*	
* Accounts Receivable, William Benton*		*1,000*
To write off the receivable from William Benton as uncollectible.		

The important thing to note in this entry is that the debit is made to the Allowance for Doubtful Accounts and **not** to the Uncollectible Accounts Expense account. The estimated expense of customer credit losses is charged to the Uncollectible Accounts Expense account at the end of each accounting period. When a particular account receivable is later ascertained to be worthless and is written off, this action does not represent an additional expense but merely confirms our previous estimate of the expense. If the Uncollectible Accounts Expense account were first charged with *estimated* credit losses and then later charged with *proven* credit losses, we would be double counting the actual uncollectible accounts expense.

After the entry writing off William Benton's account has been posted, the Accounts Receivable control account and the Allowance for Doubtful Accounts appear as follows:

Accounts Receivable

Year 1		Year 2	
Dec. 31	200,000	Jan. 27 (Benton write-off)	1,000

Both accounts reduced by write-off of worthless receivable

Allowance for Doubtful Accounts

Year 2		Year 1	
Jan. 27 (Benton write-off)	1,000	Dec. 31	10,000

Note that the *net* amount of the accounts receivable was unchanged by writing off William Benton's account against the Allowance for Doubtful Accounts.

Net value of receivables unchanged by write-off

Before the Write-off		After the Write-off	
Accounts receivable	$200,000	Accounts receivable	$199,000
Less: Allowance for		Less: Allowance for	
doubtful accounts	10,000	doubtful accounts	9,000
Net value of receivables . . .	$190,000	Net value of receivables . . .	$190,000

The fact that writing off a worthless receivable against the Allowance for Doubtful Accounts does not change the net carrying value of accounts receivable shows that no expense is entered in the accounting records when an account receivable is written off. This example bears out the point stressed earlier in the chapter: *Credit losses belong in the period in which the sale is made, not in a later period in which the account receivable is discovered to be uncollectible.*

WRITE-OFFS SELDOM AGREE WITH PREVIOUS ESTIMATES   The total amount of accounts receivable written off in a given year will seldom, if ever, be exactly equal to the estimated amount previously credited to the Allowance for Doubtful Accounts.

If the amounts written off as uncollectible turn out to be less than the estimated amount, the Allowance for Doubtful Accounts will continue to show a credit balance. If the amounts written off as uncollectible are greater than the estimated amount, the Allowance for Doubtful Accounts will acquire a *temporary debit balance,* which will be eliminated by the adjustment at the end of the period.

Recovery of an account previously written off

Occasionally an account which has been written off as worthless will later be collected in full or in part. Such collections are often referred to as **recoveries** of bad debts. Collection of an account receivable previously written off is evidence that the write-off was an error; the write-off entry should therefore be reversed.

Let us assume, for example, that a past-due account receivable in the amount of $400 from J. B. Barker was written off by the following entry:

Barker Allowance for Doubtful Accounts *400*
account   Accounts Receivable, J. B. Barker *400*
considered
uncol- To write off the receivable from J. B. Barker as uncollectible.
lectible

At some later date the customer, J. B. Barker, pays the account in full. The entry to restore Barker's account will be:

Barker Accounts Receivable, J. B. Barker *400*
account   Allowance for Doubtful Accounts *400*
reinstated
To reverse the entry writing off J. B. Barker's account.

A separate entry will be made in the cash receipts journal to record the collection from Barker. This entry will debit Cash and credit Accounts Receivable, J. B. Barker.

Direct charge-off method of recognizing uncollectible accounts expense

Instead of making adjusting entries to record uncollectible accounts expense on the basis of estimates, some concerns merely charge uncollectible accounts to expense at the time such receivables are determined to be worthless. This method makes no attempt to match revenue and related expenses. Uncollectible accounts expense is recorded in the period in which individual accounts receivable are determined to be worthless rather than in the period in which the sales were made.

When the direct charge-off method is in use, the accounts receivable will be listed in the balance sheet at their gross amount, and *no valuation allowance* will be used. The receivables, therefore, are not stated at their probable realizable value.

In the determination of taxable income under present federal income tax regulations, both the direct charge-off method and the allowance method of estimating uncollectible accounts expense are acceptable. From the standpoint of accounting theory, the allowance method is much the better, for it enables expenses to be matched with related revenue and thus aids in making a logical measurement of net income.

Credit card sales

Many retailing businesses avoid the risk of uncollectible accounts by making credit sales to customers who use well-known credit cards, such as

American Express, Visa, and Master Charge. A customer who makes a purchase using one of these cards must sign a multipart form, which includes a *credit card draft.* A credit card draft is similar to a check which is drawn upon the funds of the credit card company rather than upon the personal bank account of the customer. The credit card company promptly pays cash to the merchant to redeem these drafts. At the end of each month, the credit card company bills the credit card holder for all the drafts it has redeemed during the month. If the credit card holder fails to pay the amount owed, it is the credit card company which sustains the loss.

By making sales through credit card companies, merchants receive cash more quickly from credit sales and avoid uncollectible accounts expense. Also, the merchant avoids the expenses of investigating customers' credit, maintaining an accounts receivable subsidiary ledger, and making collections from customers.

BANK CREDIT CARDS Some widely used credit cards (such as Visa and Master Charge) are issued by banks. When the credit card company is a bank, the retailing business may deposit the signed credit card drafts directly in its bank account, along with the currency and personal checks received from customers. Banks accept these credit card drafts for immediate deposit; consequently, a business making sales to customers using bank credit cards can enter these transactions in the accounting records as cash sales.

In exchange for handling the credit card drafts, the bank makes a monthly service charge which usually runs between $1\frac{1}{4}$ and $3\frac{1}{2}\%$ of the amount of the drafts deposited by the merchant during the month. This monthly service charge is automatically deducted from the merchant's bank account and appears with other bank service charges in the merchant's monthly bank statement.

OTHER CREDIT CARDS When customers use nonbank credit cards (such as American Express, Diners' Club, and Carte Blanche), the retailing business cannot deposit the credit card drafts directly in its bank account. Instead of debiting Cash, the merchant records an account receivable from the credit card company. Periodically, the credit card drafts are mailed to the credit card company, which then sends a check to the merchant. Credit card companies, however, do not redeem the drafts at the full sales price. The agreement between the credit card company and the merchant usually allows the credit card company to take a discount of between $3\frac{1}{2}$ and 5% when redeeming the drafts.

To illustrate the procedures in accounting for these credit card sales, assume that Bradshaw Camera Shop sells a camera for $200 to a customer who uses a Quick Charge credit card. The entry would be:

Receivable	*Accounts Receivable, Quick Charge Co.*	*200*	
is from the	*Sales*		*200*
credit card			
company	*To record sale to customer using Quick Charge Credit card.*		

At the end of the week, Bradshaw Camera Shop mails credit card drafts totaling $1,200 to Quick Charge Co., which redeems the drafts less a 5% discount. When payment is received, the entry is:

Cash	*1,140*	
Credit Card Discount Expense	*60*	
Accounts Receivable, Quick Charge Co.		*1,200*
To record collection of account receivable from Quick Charge Co.,		
less 5% discount.		

The expense account, Credit Card Discount Expense, should be included among the selling expenses in the income statement of Bradshaw Camera Shop.

From a theoretical viewpoint, one might argue that the credit card discount expense should be recorded at the date of sale rather than at the date of collection. In this case, the sale of the camera for $200 would have been recorded by debiting Credit Card Discount Expense for $10 and Accounts Receivable, Quick Charge Co. for $190. Although this procedure would be theoretically preferable in terms of matching revenue with related expenses, it requires computing the discount expense separately for each sales transaction. For this reason, it is common practice to record the discount expense at the date of collection. Since the discount expense is small and collection usually occurs shortly after the date of sale, the difference between the two methods does not have a material effect upon the financial statements.

Analysis of accounts receivable

What dollar amount of accounts receivable would be reasonable for a business making annual credit sales of $1,200,000? Comparison of the average amount of accounts receivable with the sales made on credit during the period indicates how long it takes to convert receivables into cash. For example, if annual credit sales of $1,200,000 are made at a uniform rate throughout the year and the accounts receivable at year-end amount to $200,000, we can see at a glance that the receivables represent one-sixth of the year's sales, or about 60 days of uncollected sales. Management naturally wants to make efficient use of the available capital in the business, and therefore is interested in a rapid "turnover" of accounts receivable. If the credit terms offered by the business in the above example were, say, 30 days net, the existence of receivables equal to 60 days' sales would warrant investigation. The analysis of receivables is considered more fully in Chapter 16.

NOTES RECEIVABLE

Definition of a promissory note

A promissory note is an unconditional promise in writing to pay on demand or at a future date a definite sum of money.

The person who signs the note and thereby promises to pay is called the *maker* of the note. The person to whom payment is to be made is called the *payee* of the note. In the illustration below, G. L. Smith is the maker of the note and A. B. Davis is the payee.

Simplified form of promissory note

$1,000	Los Angeles, California	July 10, 19—

One month .... *after date* .... I .... *promise to pay*

to the order of .... A. B. Davis ....

------One thousand and no/100------- *dollars*

payable at .... First National Bank of Los Angeles ....

for value received, with interest at 10%

G. L. Smith

From the viewpoint of the maker, G. L. Smith, the illustrated note is a liability and is recorded by crediting the Notes Payable account. However, from the viewpoint of the payee, A. B. Davis, this same note is an asset and is recorded by debiting the Notes Receivable account. The maker of a note expects to pay cash at the maturity date; the payee expects to receive cash at that date.

Nature of interest

Interest is a charge made for the use of money. To the borrower (maker of a note) interest is an expense; to the lender (payee of a note) interest is revenue.

COMPUTING INTEREST A formula used in computing interest is as follows:

Principal × Rate of Interest × Time = Interest

(Often expressed as **P × R × T = I**)

Interest rates are usually stated on an annual basis. For example, the interest on a $1,000, one-year, 12% note is computed as follows:

$1,000 × 0.12 × 1 = $120

If the term of the note were only four months instead of a year, the interest charge would be $40, computed as follows:

$1,000 × 0.12 × $\frac{4}{12}$ = $40

If the term of the note is expressed in days, the exact number of days must be used in computing the interest. The day on which a note is dated is not included; the day on which a note falls due is included. Thus, a note dated today and maturing tomorrow involves only one day's interest. It is customary to assume that a year contains 360 days. Suppose, for example, that a 60-day, 12% note for $1,000 is drawn on June 10. The interest charge could be computed as follows:

$1,000 × 0.12 × $\frac{60}{360}$ = $20

The principal of the note ($1,000) plus the interest ($20) equals $1,020, and this amount (the *maturity value*) will be payable on August 9. The computation of days to maturity is as follows:

Days remaining in June (30 − 10; date of origin is not included)	20
Days in July	31
Days in August to maturity date (date of payment is included)	9
Total days called for by note	60

PREVAILING INTEREST RATES Interest rates, like the prices of goods and services, are always in a process of change. The Federal Reserve Board has a policy of deliberately causing interest rates to rise or fall in an effort to keep our economy running at a reasonable level of activity. At present, you can earn 5 to 6% a year interest on money deposited in a bank savings account. If you obtain a long-term mortgage loan on a residence, you will probably pay about 9 or 10% as an annual interest rate. For a six-month personal loan from a bank, you may pay an annual interest rate of perhaps 10 to 12%, depending upon whether you provide collateral to secure payment of the loan and depending upon your personal credit rating. On an unsecured bank loan payable in monthly installments, the annual interest rate is now about 16%. Many retail stores charge interest on installment accounts at $1\frac{1}{2}$% a month, which is equivalent to 18% a year. On the other hand, the largest and strongest corporations borrow millions of dollars in bank loans at interest rates of perhaps 7 to 9%. In brief, interest rates vary widely depending upon the nature of the loan and the financial strength of the borrower.

SIXTY-DAY, 6% METHOD FOR COMPUTING INTEREST Considerable saving of time is often possible by using the 60-day, 6% method of computing interest. If the interest rate is 6% a year, the interest for 60 days on any amount of money may be determined merely by *moving the decimal point two places to the left.* For example,

The interest at 6% for 60 days on $1,111.00 is $11.11

The interest at 6% for 60 days on $9,876.43 is $98.76

The reasoning underlying the 60-day, 6% shortcut may be summarized as follows:

Since interest on $1.00 for one year is $0.06
And 60 days is $\frac{1}{6}$ of a year
Interest on $1.00 for 60 days is $0.01 ($\frac{1}{6}$ of $0.06)

If the interest on $1.00 at 6% for 60 days can be computed by moving the decimal point two places to the left, then the interest on any amount at 6% for 60 days can be computed in the same manner.

The 60-day, 6% method can be used for time periods other than 60 days. The time of the note can be stated as a fraction or a multiple of 60 days and the interest quickly computed. For example, assuming an annual interest rate of 6%, what is the interest on $8,844 for 15 days?

Interest for 60 days on $8,844 is $88.44
Interest for 15 days on $8,844 is $\frac{1}{4}$ of $88.44, or $22.11

The 60-day, 6% method can also be applied when the interest rate is higher or lower than 6%. If the interest rate is something other than 6%, the interest is first computed at 6%, and an adjustment is then made for the difference between 6% and the actual rate. For example, what is the interest at 8% on $963 for 60 days?

Interest at 6% on $963 for 60 days is $ 9.63
Interest at 2% on $963 for 60 days is   3.21   ($\frac{1}{3}$ × $9.63)
Interest at 8% on $963 for 60 days is $12.84

Although this shortcut method of computing interest can be used for almost any rate and any time period, not much time is saved by using it in cases in which elaborate computations are required.

Accounting for notes receivable

In some lines of business, notes receivable are seldom encountered; in other fields they occur frequently and may constitute an important part of total assets. Business concerns that sell high-priced durable goods such as automobiles and farm machinery often accept notes receivable from their customers. Many companies obtain notes receivable in settlement of past-due accounts receivable.

All notes receivable are usually posted to a single account in the general ledger. A subsidiary ledger is not essential because the notes themselves, when filed by due dates, are the equivalent of a subsidiary ledger and provide any necessary information as to maturity, interest rates, collateral pledged, and other details. The amount debited to Notes Receivable is always the **face amount** of the note, regardless of whether or not the note bears interest. When an interest-bearing note is collected, the amount of cash received will be larger than the face amount of the note. The interest collected is credited to an Interest Revenue account, and only the face amount of the note is credited to the Notes Receivable account.

ILLUSTRATIVE ENTRIES Assume that a 6%, 90-day note receivable is acquired from a customer, Marvin White, in settlement of an existing account receivable of $2,000. The entry for acquisition of the note is as follows:

Note received to replace account receivable

Notes Receivable	2,000	
Accounts Receivable, Marvin White		2,000
Accepted 6%, 90-day note in settlement of account receivable.		

The entry 90 days later to record collection of the note will be:

Collection of principal and interest

Cash	2,030	
Notes Receivable		2,000
Interest Revenue		30
Collected 6%, 90-day note from Marvin White.		

When a note is received from a customer at the time of making a sale of merchandise on account, two entries may be made, as follows:

Sale may be run through accounts receivable when note is received from customer

Accounts Receivable, Russ Company	7,500	
Sales		7,500
To record sale of merchandise on account.		
Notes Receivable	7,500	
Accounts Receivable, Russ Company		7,500
To record receipt of note from customer.		

When this procedure is employed, the account with a particular customer in the subsidiary ledger for accounts receivable provides a complete record of all transactions with that customer, regardless of the fact that some sales may have been made on open account and others may have involved a note receivable. Having a complete history of all transactions with a customer on a single ledger card may be helpful in reaching decisions as to collection efforts or further extensions of credit.

IF THE MAKER OF A NOTE DEFAULTS A note receivable which cannot be collected at maturity is said to have been *defaulted* by the maker. Immediately after the default of a note, an entry should be made by the holder to transfer the amount due from the Notes Receivable account to an account receivable from the debtor.

Assuming that a 60-day, 6% note receivable from Robert Jones is not collected at maturity, the following entry would be made:

Default of note receivable

Accounts Receivable, Robert Jones	1,010	
Notes Receivable		1,000
Interest Revenue		10
To record default by Robert Jones of a 6%, 60-day note.		

The interest earned on the note is recorded as a credit to Interest Revenue and is also included in the account receivable from the maker. The interest receivable on a defaulted note is just as valid a claim against the maker as is the principal of the note; if the principal is collectible, then presumably the interest too can be collected.

By transferring past-due notes receivable into Accounts Receivable, two things are accomplished. First, the Notes Receivable account is limited to current notes not yet matured and is, therefore, regarded as a highly liquid type of asset. Secondly, the account receivable ledger card will show that a note has been defaulted and will present a complete picture of all transactions with the customer.

RENEWAL OF A NOTE RECEIVABLE Sometimes the two parties to a note agree that the note shall be renewed rather than paid at the maturity date. If the old note does not bear interest, the entry could be made as follows:

Renewal	*Notes Receivable* *10,000*	
of note	*Notes Receivable*	*10,000*
should be		
recorded	*A 60-day, non-interest-bearing note from Bell Company renewed*	
	today with new 60-day, 6% note.	

Since the above entry causes no change in the balance of the Notes Receivable account, a question may arise as to whether the entry is necessary. The renewal of a note is an important transaction requiring managerial attention; a general journal entry is needed to record the action taken by management and to provide a permanent record of the transaction. If journal entries were not made to record the renewal of notes, confusion might arise as to whether some of the notes included in the balance of the Notes Receivable account were current or defaulted.

ADJUSTMENTS FOR INTEREST AT END OF PERIOD Notes receivable acquired in one accounting period often do not mature until a following period. Interest is being earned throughout the life of the note, and this revenue should be apportioned between the two accounting periods on a time basis. At the end of the accounting period, interest earned to date on notes receivable should be accrued by an adjusting entry debiting the asset account, Accrued Interest Receivable, and crediting Interest Revenue. When the note matures and the interest is received in the following period, the entry to be made consists of a debit to Cash, a credit to Accrued Interest Receivable for the amount of the accrual, and a credit to Interest Revenue for the remainder of the interest collected.

Discounting notes receivable

Many business concerns which obtain notes receivable from their customers prefer to sell the notes to a bank for cash rather than to hold them until maturity. Selling a note receivable to a bank or finance company is often called *discounting* a note receivable. The holder of the note endorses the back of the note (as in endorsing a check) and delivers the note to the bank. The bank expects to collect the *maturity value* (principal plus interest) from the maker of the note at the maturity date, but if the maker fails to pay, the bank can demand payment from the endorser.

When a business endorses a note and turns it over to a bank for cash, it is promising to pay the note if the maker fails to do so. The endorser is therefore contingently liable to the bank. A *contingent liability* may be regarded as a potential liability which either will develop into a full-fledged liability or will be eliminated entirely by a future event. The future event in the case of a discounted note receivable is the payment (or default) of the note by the maker. If the maker pays, the contingent liability of the endorser is thereby ended. If the maker fails to pay, the contingent liability of the endorser becomes a real liability. In either case the period of contingent liability ends at the maturity date of the note.

The discounting of notes receivable with a bank may be regarded by a company as an alternative to borrowing by issuing its own note payable. To issue its own note payable to the bank would, of course, mean the creation of a liability; to obtain cash by discounting a note receivable creates only a contingent liability.

COMPUTING THE PROCEEDS The amount of cash obtained from the bank by discounting a note receivable is termed the *proceeds* of the note. The proceeds are computed by applying an interest rate (termed the *discount rate*) to the maturity value of the note for the time remaining before the note matures.

To illustrate, assume that on July 1 Retail Sales Company receives a 75-day, 6% note for $8,000 from Raymond Kelly. The note will mature on September 14 (30 days in July, 31 days in August, and 14 days in September). On July 16, Retail Sales Company discounts this note receivable with its bank, which charges a discount rate of 8% a year. How much cash will Retail Sales Company receive? The computation is as follows:

Face of the note	*$8,000*
Add: Interest from date of note to maturity ($8,000 × .06 × $\frac{75}{360}$)	*100*
Maturity value	*$8,100*
Less: Bank discount at 8% for the discount period of 60 days	
(July 16 to Sept. 14) ($8,100 × .08 × $\frac{60}{360}$)	*108*
Proceeds (cash received from bank)	*$7,992*

The entry made by Retail Sales Company to record the discounting of the Kelly note would be as follows:

Cash	*7,992*	
Interest Expense	*8*	
Note Receivable		*8,000*
Discounted Raymond Kelly note at bank at 8%.		

In this illustration, the cash of $7,992 received from the bank was less than the $8,000 face amount of the note. The proceeds received from discounting a note may be *either more or less* than the face amount of the note, depending upon the interest rates and time periods involved. The difference between the face amount of the note being discounted and the cash proceeds is usually recorded as either Interest Expense or Interest Revenue. If the proceeds are less than the face value, the difference is debited to Interest Expense. However, if the proceeds exceed the face value of the note, the difference is credited to Interest Revenue.

Classification of receivables in the balance sheet

Accounts receivable from customers will ordinarily be collected within the operating cycle; they are therefore listed among the current assets on the balance sheet. Receivables may also arise from miscellaneous transactions other than the sale of goods and services. These miscellaneous receivables, such as advances to officers and employees, and claims against insurance companies for losses sustained, should be listed separately on the balance sheet and should not be merged with trade accounts receivable. If an account receivable from an officer or employee originates as a favor to the officer or employee, efforts at collection may await the convenience of the debtor. Consequently, it is customary to include such receivables in the balance sheet as noncurrent assets under a caption such as Other Assets.

Notes receivable usually appear among the current assets; however, if the maturity date of a note is more than a year distant and beyond the operating cycle of the business, the note should be listed as noncurrent under a heading such as Long-Term Investments. Any accrued interest receivable at the balance sheet date is a current asset but may be combined on the balance sheet with other accrued items such as accrued rents receivable or royalties receivable.

DISCLOSURE OF CONTINGENT LIABILITIES Since contingent liabilities are potential liabilities rather than full-fledged liabilities, they are not included in the liability section of the balance sheet. However, these potential liabilities may affect the financial position of the business if future events cause them to become real liabilities. Therefore, contingent liabilities should be disclosed in footnotes to the financial statements. The contingent liability arising from the discounting of notes receivable could be disclosed by the following footnote:

Note 6: Contingencies and commitments

At December 31, 19____, the Company was contingently liable for notes receivable discounted with maturity values in the amount of $250,000.

CURRENT LIABILITIES

Current liabilities are obligations that must be paid within the operating cycle or one year (whichever is longer). Comparison of the amount of current liabilities with the amount of current assets is one means of appraising the financial position of a business. In other words, a comparison of the amount of current liabilities with the amount of current assets available for paying these debts helps us in judging a company's short-run debt-paying ability.

In accounting for current liabilities, we are especially interested in making certain that all such obligations are included in the balance sheet. Fraud may be concealed by deliberate understatement of a liability. The omission or understatement of a liability will usually be accompanied by an overstatement of owners' equity or else by an understatement of assets. Depending on the nature of the error, the net income of the business may also be overstated.

Among the more common current liabilities are notes payable, accounts payable, and accrued or estimated liabilities such as wages, interest, and taxes. An *estimated* liability is an obligation known to exist but for which the dollar amount is uncertain. In this chapter we shall consider the accounting problems relating to notes payable; the liabilities arising from payrolls will be considered in Chapter 13.

NOTES PAYABLE

Notes payable are issued whenever bank loans are obtained. Other transactions which may give rise to notes payable include the purchase of real estate or costly equipment, the purchase of merchandise, and the substitution of a note for a past-due account payable.

Notes payable issued to banks

Assume that on November 1 Porter Company borrows $10,000 from its bank for a period of six months at an interest rate of 9%. Six months later on May 1, Porter Company will have to pay the bank the *principal* amount of $10,000 plus $450 interest ($10,000 × .09 × $\frac{6}{12}$). The directors of Porter Company have authorized John Caldwell, the company's treasurer, to sign notes payable issued by the company. The note issued by Porter Company could read as shown on page 412 (omitting a few minor details).

The journal entry in Porter Company's accounting records for this borrowing is:

Face amount of note   *Cash* *10,000*
        Notes Payable *10,000*
    Borrowed $10,000 for six months at 9% interest per year.

> | Miami, Florida | November 1, Year 1 |
> | --- | --- |
>
> Six months .... **after this date** .... Porter Company ....
>
> **promises to pay to Security National Bank the sum of $** .... 10,000 ....
>
> **with interest at the rate of** ...... 9% ...... **per annum.**
>
> **Signed** ... John Caldwell
>
> **Title** ...... Treasurer

This note is for the principal amount with interest stated separately

Notice that no liability is recorded for the interest charges when the note is issued. At the date that money is borrowed, the borrower has a liability only for the principal amount of the loan; the liability for interest charges comes into existence gradually over the life of the loan. At December 31, two months' interest expense has been incurred, and the following entry is made:

A liability arises for accrued interest

Interest Expense	150	
Accrued Interest Payable		150

To record interest expense incurred through year-end on 9%, six-month note dated Nov. 1 ($10,000 × .09 × $\frac{2}{12}$ = $150).

When the note is paid on May 1, the entry to be made is:

Payment of principal and interest

Notes Payable	10,000	
Accrued Interest Payable	150	
Interest Expense	300	
Cash		10,450

To record payment of 9%, six-month note on maturity date and to recognize interest expense incurred since year-end ($10,000 × 9% × $\frac{4}{12}$ = $300).

Notes payable with interest charges included in the face amount

Instead of stating the interest rate separately as in the preceding illustration, the note payable issued by Porter Company could have been drawn so as to include the interest charge in the face amount of the note, as shown on page 413.

Notice that the face amount of this note ($10,450) is greater than the amount borrowed ($10,000). Porter Company's liability at November 1 is only $10,000; the other $450 included in the face amount of the note represents *future interest charges.* As interest expense is incurred over the life of the note, Porter Company's liability will grow to $10,450, just as in the preceding illustration.

The entry to record Porter Company's $10,000 borrowing from the bank at November 1 is shown below the illustrated note.

This note shows interest included in face amount of note

Miami, Florida	November 1, Year 1

Six months **after this date** .... Porter Company

promises to pay to Security National Bank the sum of $10,450

Signed *John Caldwell*

Title .... Treasurer

Interest included in face of note

Cash	10,000	
Discount on Notes Payable	450	
Notes Payable		10,450

Issued to bank a 9%, six-month note payable with interest charge included in face amount of note.

The liability account, Notes Payable, was credited with the full face amount of the note ($10,450). It is therefore necessary to debit a ***contra-liability*** account, ***Discount on Notes Payable,*** for the amount of the future interest charges included in the face amount. Discount on Notes Payable is shown in the balance sheet as a deduction from the Notes Payable account. In our illustration, the amounts in the balance sheet would be Notes Payable, $10,450, minus Discount on Notes Payable, $450, or a net liability of $10,000 at November 1.

DISCOUNT ON NOTES PAYABLE The balance of the account Discount on Notes Payable represents ***interest charges applicable to future periods.*** As this interest expense is incurred, the balance of the discount account gradually is transferred into the Interest Expense account. Thus, at the maturity date of the note, Discount on Notes Payable will have a zero balance, and the net liability will have increased to $10,450. The process of transferring the amount in the Discount on Notes Payable account into the Interest Expense account is called ***amortization*** of the discount.

AMORTIZATION OF THE DISCOUNT The discount on short-term notes payable usually is amortized by the straight-line method, which allocates a proportionate amount of the discount to interest expense in each accounting period.[1] If the $450 discount on the Porter Company note payable is amortized by the straight-line method, the discount will be transferred from the Discount on Notes Payable account into Interest Expense at the rate of $75 per month ($450 discount ÷ 6 months). Alternatively, we can compute the monthly interest expense by applying the rate of interest included in the face amount of the note (9% in our example) to the principal amount of the note, as follows: $10,000 \times 9\% \times \frac{1}{12} = \$75$.

[1] When an interest charge is included in the face amount of a long-term note, the effective interest method of amortizing the discount is often used instead of the straight-line method. The effective interest method of amortization is discussed in Chapter 13.

Entries should be made to amortize an appropriate portion of the discount at the end of each accounting period and at the date the note matures. At December 31, Year 1, Porter Company will make the following adjusting entry to recognize the two months' interest expense incurred since November 1.

Amortiza-	*Interest Expense*	*150*	
tion of *discount*	*Discount on Notes Payable*		*150*

To record interest expense incurred to end of year on 9%, six-month note dated Nov. 1 ($450 discount × $\frac{2}{6}$).

Note that the liability for accrued interest is recorded by crediting Discount on Notes Payable rather than Accrued Interest Payable. The credit to Discount on Notes Payable reduces the debit balance in this contra-liability account from $450 to $300, thereby increasing the *net liability* for notes payable by $150.

At December 31, Porter Company's net liability for the bank loan will appear in the balance sheet as shown below:

Liability	*Current liabilities:*		
shown net *of discount*	*Notes payable*	*$10,450*	
	Less: Discount on notes payable	*300*	*$10,150*

The net liability of $10,150 consists of the $10,000 principal amount of the debt plus the $150 interest which has accrued since November 1.

When the note matures on May 1, Year 2, Porter Company will recognize the four months' interest expense incurred since year-end and will pay the bank $10,450. The entry is

Two-thirds	*Notes Payable*	*10,450*	
of interest *applicable*	*Interest Expense*	*300*	
to second	*Discount on Notes Payable*		*300*
year	*Cash*		*10,450*

To record payment of six-month note due today and recognize interest expense incurred since year-end ($10,000 × 9% × $\frac{4}{12}$ = $300).

Comparison of the two forms of notes payable

We have illustrated two alternative methods which Porter Company could use in accounting for its $10,000 bank loan, depending upon the form of the note payable. The journal entries for both methods, along with the resulting balance sheet presentations of the liability at November 1 and December 31, are summarized on page 415. Note that both methods result in Porter Company recognizing the same amount of interest expense and the same total liability in its balance sheet. The form of the note does not change the economic substance of the transaction.

Note written for $10,000 plus 9% interest

Entry to record borrowing on Nov. 1

Cash	10,000	
Notes Payable		10,000

Partial balance sheet at Nov. 1

Current liabilities:

Notes payable	$10,000

Adjusting entry at Dec. 31

Interest Expense	150	
Accrued Interest Payable		150

Partial balance sheet at Dec. 31

Current liabilities:

Notes payable	$10,000	
Accrued interest payable	150	$10,150

Entry to record payment of note on May 1

Notes Payable	10,000	
Accrued Interest Payable	150	
Interest Expense	300	
Cash		10,450

Note written with interest included in face amount

Entry to record borrowing on Nov. 1

Cash	10,000	
Discount on Notes Payable	450	
Notes Payable		10,450

Partial balance sheet at Nov. 1

Current liabilities:

Notes payable	$10,450	
Less: Discount on notes payable	450	$10,000

Adjusting entry at Dec. 31

Interest Expense	150	
Discount on Notes Payable		150

Partial balance sheet at Dec. 31

Current liabilities:

Notes payable	$10,450	
Less: Discount on notes payable	300	$10,150

Entry to record payment of note on May 1

Notes Payable	10,450	
Interest Expense	300	
Discount on Notes Payable		300
Cash		10,450

The concept of present value applied to long-term notes

When a note payable is issued in exchange for cash, it is easy to determine whether an interest charge is included in the face amount of the note. Any difference between the face amount of the note and the amount of cash borrowed should be viewed as an interest charge. However, when a note is issued in exchange for other kinds of assets, such as land or equipment, the amount of interest (if any) included in the face amount of the note may be less apparent.

If a realistic rate of interest is stated in a long-term note, we may assume that no interest charge is included in the face amount. If no interest charge is specified, however, or if the specified interest rate is unrealistically low (such as 2% a year), a portion of the face amount of the note must be assumed to represent an interest charge. When such a note is issued or received, the transaction should be recorded at the *present value* of the note rather than at the face amount.

The concept of present value is based upon the "time value" of money—the idea that an amount of money which will not be received until some future date is equivalent to a smaller amount of money received today. The present value of a future cash receipt is the amount of money which, if received today, would be considered equivalent to the future receipt. The present value is always less than the future amount, because money available today can be invested to earn interest and thereby become equivalent to a larger amount in the future.[2]

When a note does not call for the payment of interest, the present value of the note is less than its face amount, because the face amount of the note will not be received until the maturity date. The difference between the present value of a note and its face amount should be viewed as an interest charge included in the face amount. Often we can determine the present value of a note by the fair market value of the asset acquired when the note is issued. Alternatively, the present value can be computed using mathematical techniques which will be discussed in later accounting courses.

The *effective rate of interest* associated with a note is that interest rate which will cause the note's present value to increase to the full maturity value of the note by the time the note matures.

An illustration of notes recorded at present value

To illustrate the use of present value in transactions involving long-term notes, let us assume that on September 1 Everts Company buys equipment from Tru-Tool, Inc., by issuing a one-year note payable in the face amount of $330,000 with no mention of an interest rate. It is not logical to assume that Tru-Tool, Inc., would finance Everts Company's purchase of the equipment for one year without charging any interest. Therefore,

---

[2] The concept of present value will be discussed further in Chapter 13.

some portion of the $330,000 face amount of the note should be regarded as a charge for interest. In the accounting records of Everts Company, the amount of this interest charge should be debited to the contra-liability account Discount on Notes Payable, instead of being treated as part of the cost of the equipment.

If Everts Company were to debit Equipment and credit Notes Payable for the full $330,000 face amount of the note, the following errors would result: (1) the cost of the equipment and the amount of the related liability would be overstated by the amount of the interest charge included in the face amount of the note; (2) interest expense would be understated over the life of the note; and (3) depreciation expense would be overstated throughout the estimated service life of the equipment.

Let us assume that the regular sales price of this equipment is $300,000. In this case, the present value of the note is apparently $300,000, and the remaining $30,000 of the face amount represents a charge for interest. The rate of interest which will cause the $300,000 present value of the note to increase to the $330,000 maturity value in one year is 10%. Thus, the face amount of the note actually includes an interest charge computed at the effective interest rate of 10%.

Everts Company should use the present value of the note in determining the cost of the equipment and the amount of the related net liability, as shown by the following journal entry:

Equipment	300,000	
Discount on Notes Payable	30,000	
Notes Payable		330,000

Purchased equipment for $300,000 by issuing a one-year note payable with a 10% interest charge included in the face amount.

Over the next 12 months, the $30,000 recorded as a discount on the note payable will be amortized into interest expense.

It is equally important for the selling company, Tru-Tool, Inc., to use the present value of the note in determining the amount of revenue to be recognized from the sale. The $30,000 interest charge included in the face amount of the note receivable from Everts Company represents **unearned interest** to Tru-Tool, Inc., and is **not part of the sales price of the equipment.** If Tru-Tool, Inc., were to treat the entire face amount of the note receivable as the sales price of the equipment, the result would be to overstate sales revenue and notes receivable by $30,000, and also to understate interest revenue by this amount over the life of the note. Tru-Tool, Inc., should record the sale at the present value of the note received, as shown below and on page 418:

Accounts Receivable, Everts Company	300,000	
Sales		300,000

To record sale of equipment to Everts Company.

Notes Receivable	*330,000*	
Discount on Notes Receivable		*30,000*
Accounts Receivable, Everts Company		*300,000*

Obtained from Everts Company a one-year note with a 10%
interest charge included in the face amount.

Note that the interest charge included in the face amount of the note receivable is credited to **Discount on Notes Receivable.** Discount on Notes Receivable represents unearned interest and is a contra-asset account which appears in the balance sheet as a deduction from notes receivable. As the interest is earned, the balance of the discount account will gradually be transferred into Interest Revenue. As of December 31, Tru-Tool, Inc., will have earned four months' interest revenue and will make the following entry:

Discount on Notes Receivable	*10,000*	
Interest Revenue		*10,000*

To record interest earned through Dec. 31 on Everts Company note
($300,000 × 10% × $\frac{4}{12}$).

On August 31 of the following year, when the note receivable is collected from Everts Company, the required entry will be:

Cash	*330,000*	
Discount on Notes Receivable	*20,000*	
Interest Revenue		*20,000*
Notes Receivable		*330,000*

To record collection of Everts Company note and to recognize
interest earned since year-end.

In past years, failure to use the concept of present value in recording transactions involving long-term notes occasionally resulted in large overstatements of assets and sales revenue, especially by real estate development companies. In recognition of this problem, the Financial Accounting Standards Board now requires the use of present value in recording transactions involving **long-term** notes receivable or payable which do not bear reasonable stated rates of interest.[3]

When a note is issued for a short period of time, any interest charge included in its face amount is likely to be relatively small. Therefore, the use of present value is not required in recording normal transactions with customers or suppliers involving notes due within one year. Notes given or received in such transactions which do not specify an interest rate may be considered non-interest bearing.

Installment receivables

Another application of present value is found in the recording of **installment sales.** Many retailing businesses sell merchandise on installment

[3] *APB Opinion No. 21,* "Interest on Receivables and Payables," AICPA (New York: 1971).

sales plans, which permit customers to pay for their credit purchases through a series of periodic payments. The importance of installment sales is emphasized by a recent balance sheet of Sears, Roebuck, and Co., which shows about $6 billion of customer accounts receivable, nearly all of which call for collection in periodic monthly installments.

When merchandise is sold on an installment plan, substantial interest charges are usually added to the "cash selling price" of the product in determining the total dollar amount to be collected in the series of installment payments. The amount of sales revenue recognized at the time of sale, however, is limited to the *present value* of these installment payments. In most cases, the present value of these future payments is equal to the regular sales price of the merchandise. The portion of the installment account receivable which represents unearned finance charges is credited to the contra-asset account, Discount on Installment Receivables. The balance of this contra-asset account is then amortized into Interest Revenue over the length of the collection period.

Although the collection period for an installment receivable often runs as long as 24 to 36 months, such receivables are regarded as current assets if they correspond to customary credit terms of the industry. In published balance sheets, the Discount on Installment Receivables is often called Deferred Interest Income or Unearned Finance Charges. A typical balance sheet presentation of installment accounts receivable is illustrated below:

Trade accounts receivable:	
Accounts receivable	$ 75,040,500
Installment contracts receivable, including $31,000,000 due after	
one year	52,640,788
	$127,681,288
Less: Deferred interest income ($8,070,000) and allowance for	
doubtful accounts	9,942,600
Total trade accounts and notes receivable	$117,738,688

INCOME TAX ASPECTS OF INSTALLMENT SALES Current provisions of the federal income tax law permit sellers to spread the recognition of the gross profit from installment sales over the years in which collections are received. The result of this treatment is to postpone the recognition of taxable income and the payment of income tax. For financial statement purposes, however, the entire gross profit from installment sales is recognized *in the period in which the sale occurs.* The method of recognizing gross profit from installment sales for income tax purposes will be illustrated in Chapter 14. There are a number of other more complex issues relating to installment sales; these are covered in *Modern Advanced Accounting* of this series.

KEY TERMS INTRODUCED OR EMPHASIZED IN CHAPTER 10

Aging the accounts receivable The process of classifying accounts receivable by age groups such as current, past due 1–30 days, past due 31–60 days, etc. A step in estimating the uncollectible portion of the accounts receivable.

Allowance for Doubtful Accounts A valuation account or contra account relating to accounts receivable and showing the portion of the receivables estimated to be uncollectible.

Amortization of discount on notes payable The process of gradually transferring the balance of the Discount on Notes Payable account (which represents future interest expense) into the Interest Expense account as the interest expense is incurred.

Amortization of discount on notes receivable The process of transferring the balance of the Discount on Notes Receivable account (which represents future interest revenue) into the Interest Revenue account as the interest revenue is earned.

Contingent liability A potential liability which either will develop into a full-fledged liability or will be eliminated entirely by a future event.

Contra account A ledger account which is deducted from or offset against a related account in the financial statements, for example, Allowance for Doubtful Accounts, Discount on Notes Payable, and Discount on Notes Receivable.

Default Failure to pay interest or principal of a promissory note at the due date.

Direct charge-off method A method of accounting for uncollectible receivables in which no expense is recognized until individual accounts are determined to be worthless. At that point the account receivable is written off with an offsetting debit to uncollectible accounts expense. Fails to match revenue and related expenses.

Discount on Notes Payable A contra-liability account representing any interest charges applicable to future periods included in the face amount of a note payable. Over the life of the note, the balance of the Discount on Notes Payable account is amortized into Interest Expense.

Discount on Notes Receivable A contra-asset account representing any un-earned interest included in the face amount of a note receivable. Over the life of the note, the balance of the Discount on Notes Receivable account is amortized into Interest Revenue.

Discounting notes receivable Selling a note receivable prior to its maturity date.

Effective interest rate The rate of interest which will cause the present value of a note to increase to the maturity value by the maturity date.

Installment sales Sales on credit in which the customer agrees to make a series of installment payments, including substantial interest charges.

Interest A charge made for the use of money. The formula for computing interest is Principal $\times$ Rate of Interest $\times$ Time $=$ Interest ($P \times R \times T = I$).

Maker (of a note) A person or entity who issues a promissory note.

Maturity date The date on which a note becomes due and payable.

Maturity value The value of a note at its maturity date, consisting of principal plus interest.

Notes payable A liability evidenced by issuance of a formal written promise to pay a certain amount of money, usually with interest, at a future date.

Notes receivable A receivable (asset) evidenced by a formal written promise to pay a certain amount of money, usually with interest, at a future date.

Payee The person named in a promissory note to whom payment is to be made (the lender).

Present value concept Based upon the time value of money. The basic premise is that an amount of money which will not be received until a future date is equivalent to a smaller amount of money available today.

Present value of a future cash receipt The amount of money which an informed investor would pay today for the right to receive that future cash receipt. The present value is always less than the future amount, because money available today can be invested to earn interest and thereby become equivalent to a larger amount in the future.

Principal amount That portion of the maturity value of a note which is attributable to the amount borrowed or to the cost of the asset acquired when the note was issued, rather than being attributable to interest charges.

Proceeds The amount received from selling a note receivable prior to its maturity. Maturity value minus discount equals proceeds.

DEMONSTRATION PROBLEM FOR YOUR REVIEW

The Monastery, Inc., sells custom wood furniture to decorators and the general public. Selected transactions relating to the company's receivables and payables for the month of August are shown below. The company uses the allowance method in accounting for uncollectible accounts.

Aug. 1 Borrowed $48,000 from Central Bank by issuing a 90-day note payable with a stated interest rate of $7\frac{1}{2}$%.

Aug. 5 Sold merchandise for $960 to R. Lucas on the installment plan. Lucas signed an installment contract requiring 12 monthly payments of $90 each, beginning September 5. (Record transaction by debiting Installment Contracts Receivable rather than Accounts Receivable.)

Aug. 8 A $420 account receivable from S. Wilson was determined to be worthless and was written off.

Aug. 10 Sold merchandise to Century Interiors on account, $15,200. It was agreed that Century Interiors would issue a 60-day, 8% note upon receipt of the merchandise and could deduct any freight it paid on the goods.

Aug. 11 Received a 60-day note from StyleCraft Co. in settlement of $3,600 open account. Interest computed at the effective rate of 8% was included in the face amount of the note.

Aug. 13 Received a letter from Century Interiors stating that it had paid $200 freight on the shipment of August 10. Enclosed was a 60-day, 8% note dated August 13 for $15,000.

Aug. 16 Purchased land for $92,000, making a cash down payment of $20,000 and issuing a one-year note payable for the balance. The face amount of the note was $78,480, which included interest computed at an effective rate of 9%.

Aug. 20 Received full payment from J. Porter of a $4,500, 60-day, 6% note dated June 21. Accrued interest receivable of $30 had been recorded in prior months.

Aug. 23 Discounted the Century Interiors note dated August 13 at the bank. The bank discount rate of 9% was applied to the maturity value of the note for the 50 days remaining to maturity.

Aug. 25 An account receivable of $325 from G. Davis had been written off in June; full payment was unexpectedly received from Davis.

Aug. 29 Sales to ExtraCash credit card customers during August amounted to $14,800. (Summarize all credit card sales in one entry. ExtraCash Co. is not a bank.)

Aug. 30 Collected cash from ExtraCash Co. for the August credit card sales, less a 5% discount charged by ExtraCash.

Aug. 31 The Discount on Installment Receivables account is amortized to reflect $3,960 of finance charges earned during August.

Aug. 31 As a result of substantial write-offs, the Allowance for Doubtful Accounts has a debit balance of $320. Aging of the accounts receivable indicates that the allowance account should have a $1,200 credit balance at the end of August.

Instructions Prepare journal entries to record the transactions listed above and to make any adjusting entries necessary at August 31.

SOLUTION TO DEMONSTRATION PROBLEM

General Journal

19___

Aug. 1	Cash		48,000	
	Notes Payable			48,000
	Borrowed $48,000 from Central Bank; issued a 90-day, 7½% note payable.			
5	Installment Contracts Receivable, R. Lucas		1,080	
	Discount on Installment Receivables			120
	Sales			960
	Installment sale, due in 12 monthly installments of $90 each.			
8	Allowance for Doubtful Accounts		420	
	Accounts Receivable, S. Wilson			420
	Wrote off uncollectible account from S. Wilson.			
10	Accounts Receivable, Century Interiors		15,200	
	Sales			15,200
	Sale of merchandise on account.			
11	Notes Receivable		3,648	
	Discount on Notes Receivable			48
	Accounts Receivable, StyleCraft Co.			3,600
	Received 60-day note with interest at effective rate of 8% included in face amount in settlement of open account.			
13	Notes Receivable		15,000	
	Delivery Expense		200	
	Accounts Receivable, Century Interiors			15,200
	To record credit to Century Interiors for freight paid by them and receipt of 60-day, 8% note for balance of amount owed.			

16	Land	92,000	
	Discount on Notes Payable	6,480	
	Notes Payable		78,480
	Cash		20,000

Purchased land for $92,000, paying $20,000 cash and
issuing a one-year note payable with a 9% interest charge
included in the face amount.

20	Cash	4,545	
	Notes Receivable		4,500
	Accrued Interest Receivable		30
	Interest Revenue		15

Collected note from J. Porter, including $45 interest.

23	Cash	15,010	
	Notes Receivable		15,000
	Interest Revenue		10

Discounted Century Interiors' note at bank, proceeds
computed as follows: Maturity value $15,200 − bank charge
of $190 ($15,200 × .09 × $\frac{50}{360}$) = $15,010.

| 25 | Account Receivable, G. Davis | 325 | |
| | Allowance for Doubtful Accounts | | 325 |

To reverse entry writing off Davis' account.

| 25 | Cash | 325 | |
| | Accounts Receivable, G. Davis | | 325 |

To record collection of Davis account.

| 29 | Accounts Receivable, ExtraCash Co. | 14,800 | |
| | Sales | | 14,800 |

To record credit card sales for August.

30	Cash	14,060	
	Credit Card Discount Expense	740	
	Accounts Receivable, ExtraCash Co.		14,800

Collected August credit card sales invoices, less 5%.

| 31 | Discount on Installment Receivables | 3,960 | |
| | Interest Revenue | | 3,960 |

To record finance charges earned on installment contracts
receivable during August.

31	Uncollectible Accounts Expense	1,520	
	Allowance for Doubtful Accounts		1,520
	To provide for estimated uncollectibles as follows:		
	Balance required $1,200		
	Present balance (debit) 320		
	Required increase in allowance $1,520		

31	Interest Expense	300	
	Accrued Interest Payable		300
	To record interest expense on note payable to Central		
	Bank ($48,000 × $7\frac{1}{2}$% × $\frac{30}{360}$).		

31	Discount on Notes Receivable	16	
	Interest Revenue		16
	To record interest earned through Aug. 31 on StyleCraft		
	note receivable ($48 discount × $\frac{20}{60}$ = $16).		

31	Interest Expense	270	
	Discount on Notes Payable		270
	To amortize discount through Aug. 31 on one-year note		
	payable dated Aug. 16 ($6,480 × $\frac{1}{12}$ × $\frac{1}{2}$).		

REVIEW QUESTIONS

1 Adams Company determines at year-end that its Allowance for Doubtful Accounts should be increased by $6,500. Give the adjusting entry to carry out this decision.

2 In making the annual adjusting entry for uncollectible accounts, a company may utilize a *balance sheet approach* to make the estimate or it may use an *income statement approach.* Explain these two alternative approaches.

3 At the end of its first year in business, Baxter Laboratories had accounts receivable totaling $148,500. After careful analysis of the individual accounts, the credit manager estimated that $146,100 would ultimately be collected. Give the journal entry required to reflect this estimate in the accounts.

4 In February of its second year of operations, Baxter Laboratories (question *3* above) learned of the failure of a customer, Sterling Corporation, which owed Baxter $800. Nothing could be collected. Give the journal entry to recognize the uncollectibility of the receivable from Sterling Corporation.

5 What is the *direct charge-off method* of handling credit losses as opposed to the *allowance method?* What is its principal shortcoming?

6 Morgan Corporation has decided to write off its account receivable from Brill Company because the latter has entered bankruptcy. What general ledger accounts should be debited and credited, assuming that the allowance method is in use? What general ledger accounts should be debited and credited if the direct charge-off method is in use?

7 Mill Company, which has accounts receivable of $309,600 and an allowance for doubtful accounts of $3,600, decides to write off as worthless a past-due account receivable for $1,500 from J. D. North. What effect will the write-off have upon total current assets? Upon net income for the period? Explain.

8 Describe a procedure by which management could be informed each month of the status of collections and the overall quality of the accounts receivable on hand.

9 What are the advantages to a retailer of making credit sales only to customers who use nationally recognized credit cards?

10 Alta Mine Co. is a restaurant that had always made cash sales only until a new policy was adopted to honor several nationally known credit cards. Sales did not increase, but many of Alta Mine Co.'s regular customers began charging dinner bills on the credit cards. Has the new policy been beneficial to Alta Mine Co.? Explain.

11 Determine the maturity date of the following notes:
   a A three-month note dated March 10
   b A 30-day note dated August 15
   c A 90-day note dated July 2

12 X Company acquires a 9%, 60-day note receivable from a customer, Robert Waters, in settlement of an existing account receivable of $4,000. Give the journal entry to record acquisition of the note and the journal entry to record its collection at maturity.

13 Distinguish between
   a Current and long-term liabilities
   b Estimated and contingent liabilities

14 Does a contingent liability appear on a balance sheet? If so, in what part of the balance sheet?

15 Jonas Company issues a 90-day, 12% note payable to replace an account payable to Smith Supply Company in the amount of $8,000. Draft the journal entries (in general journal form) to record the issuance of the note payable and the payment of the note at the maturity date.

16 Howard Benson applied to the City Bank for a loan of $20,000 for a period of three months. The loan was granted at an annual interest rate of 12%. Write a sentence illustrating the wording of the note signed by Benson if
   a Interest is stated separately in the note.
   b Interest is included in the face amount of the note.

17 With reference to question *16* above, give the journal entry required on the books of Howard Benson for issuance of each of the two types of notes.

18 Rager Products sold merchandise to Baron Company in exchange for a one-year note receivable. The note was made out in the face amount of $13,189, *including* a 9% interest charge. Compute the amount of sales revenue to be recognized by Rager Products. (*Hint:* $13,189 equals 109% of sales amount.)

19 Sylmar Industries buys a substantial amount of equipment having an estimated service life of five years by issuing a two-year note payable. The note includes no mention of an interest charge. Explain the errors which will result in the future financial statements of Sylmar Industries if the equipment and related liability are recorded at the face value, rather than the present value, of the note.

20 Maxline Stores sells merchandise with a sales price of $1,260 on an install-ment plan requiring 12 monthly payments of $120 each. How much revenue will this sale ultimately generate for Maxline Stores? Explain the nature of this revenue and when it should be recognized in the accounting records.

21 With reference to question *20* above, make the journal entries required in the accounting records of Maxline Stores to record
   a Sale of the merchandise on the installment plan.
   b Collection of the first monthly installment payment. (Assume that an equal portion of the discount is amortized at the time that each installment payment is received.)

EXERCISES

Ex. 10-1 The general ledger control account for accounts receivable shows a balance of $98,000 at the end of the year. An aging analysis of the individual customers' accounts indicates doubtful accounts totaling $2,440. Draft the year-end adjusting entry for uncollectible accounts under each of the following independent assumptions:

a The Allowance for Doubtful Accounts had a credit balance of $1,760.
b The Allowance for Doubtful Accounts had a debit balance of $592.

Ex. 10-2 The unadjusted trial balance for Nashville Corporation at the end of the current year includes the following accounts:

	Debit	Credit
Accounts receivable	$144,000	
Allowance for doubtful accounts		$ 1,092
Sales (25% represent cash sales)		576,000

Compute the uncollectible accounts expense for the current year, assuming that uncollectible accounts expense is determined as follows:
a 1% of total sales.
b $1\frac{1}{2}$% of credit sales.
c Allowance for doubtful accounts is increased to equal 3% of gross accounts receivable.

Ex. 10-3 Lyons Mane, Inc., reported the following amounts on its balance sheet at the end of last year:

Notes receivable from customers	$12,000
Accrued interest on notes receivable	240
Accounts receivable	50,400
Less: Allowance for doubtful accounts	1,200

You are to record the following events of the current year in general journal entries:
a Accounts receivable of $1,152 are written off as uncollectible.
b A customer's note for $330 on which interest of $18 has been accrued in the accounts is deemed uncollectible, and both balances are written off against the Allowance for Doubtful Accounts.
c An account receivable for $156 previously written off is collected.
d Aging of accounts receivable at the end of the current year indicates a need for an $1,800 allowance to cover possible failure to collect accounts currently outstanding.

Ex. 10-4 Alpine Outfitters, Inc., has been in business for three years and has charged off accounts receivable as they proved to be uncollectible. At the end of Year 3, management decides to adopt the allowance method of accounting for uncollectible accounts and asks you to help them determine the proper balance in the Allowance for Uncollectible Accounts. The following information is available for your consideration:

Year	Sales	Accounts Written Off	Year 1	Year 2	Year 3	Net Income
			Year of Origin of Accounts Written Off			
1	$300,000	$2,400	$2,400			$20,000
2	500,000	5,200	1,200	$4,000		40,000
3	880,000	9,000		3,600	$5,400	50,000

Accounts receivable at the end of Year 3 amount to $160,000, all from sales.

 a Based on the average experience for Years 1 and 2, compute the amount of the **total** uncollectible accounts that can reasonably be anticipated on the sales for Year 3.

 b Since $5,400 of accounts receivable originating in Year 3 have already been written off, compute the amount of the allowance that should be established at the end of Year 3 to cover estimated uncollectible accounts.

 c In comparison with the actual write-off of receivables originating in Year 1 and Year 2 and in comparison with the estimated uncollectibles for Year 3, the use of the direct charge-off method caused the income before taxes to be overstated in each of the three years. Compute the amount of the overstatement for each year and in total. Show computations.

Ex. 10-5 Use the 60-day, 6% method to compute interest on the following notes:

 a $6,501 at 6% for 60 days
 b $12,838 at 6% for 90 days
 c $21,472 at 6% for 30 days
 d $24,045 at 8% for 60 days
 e $4,612 at 12% for 120 days
 f $10,220 at 18% for 90 days

Ex. 10-6 Three notes receivable, each in the amount of $20,000, were discounted by a company at its bank on May 10. The bank charged a discount rate of 6%, applied to the maturity value. From the following data, compute the proceeds of each note. (Answers should be rounded to the nearest cent wherever necessary.)

Date of Note	Interest Rate, %	Life of Note
a Apr. 10	6	3 months
b Mar. 31	10	60 days
c Mar. 11	8	90 days

Ex. 10-7 On November 1, Ward Corporation borrowed $100,000 from a local bank, agreeing to repay that amount plus 9% interest (per annum) in six months. Show the presentation of the bank loan on Ward Corporation's December 31 balance sheet, assuming that the company signed a note as follows:

 a For $100,000, interest payable at maturity.
 b With the interest charge included in the face amount of the note.

Ex. 10-8 Dale Motors, an automobile dealer, sold three trucks to Zorro Truck Lines on April 1, Year 1, for a total price of $68,000. Under the terms of the sale, Dale Motors received $20,000 cash and a promissory note due in full 18 months later. The face amount of the note was $53,760, which included interest on the note for the 18 months.

 Prepare all entries (in general journal form) for Dale Motors relating to the sales transaction and to the note for the fiscal year ended September 30, Year 1. Include the adjusting entry needed to record interest earned to September 30.

Ex. 10-9 Based upon the information in Exercise **10-8,** above, prepare all entries (in general journal form) for Zorro Truck Lines relating to the purchase of the trucks and the note for the fiscal year ended December 31, Year 1. Include the adjusting entries to record interest expense and depreciation expense to December 31. (The trucks are to be depreciated over an 8-year service life by the straight-line method. There is no estimated salvage value.)

PROBLEMS

10-1 Books, Etc., owned by Linda Snow, has for the past three years been engaged in selling paper novelty goods to retail stores. Sales are made on credit and the company has regularly estimated its uncollectible accounts expense as a percentage of net sales. The percentage used has been $\frac{1}{2}$ of 1% of net sales. However, it appears that this provision has been inadequate because the Allowance for Doubtful Accounts has a debit balance of $2,693.90 at May 31 prior to making the annual provision. Snow has therefore decided to change the method of estimating uncollectible accounts expense and to rely upon an analysis of the age and character of the accounts receivable at the end of each accounting period.

At May 31, the end of the company's fiscal year, the accounts receivable totaled $178,816. This total amount included past-due accounts in the amount of $36,982. None of these past-due accounts was considered hopeless; all accounts regarded as worthless had been written off as rapidly as they were determined to be uncollectible. These write-offs had totaled $5,113.90 during the year. After careful investigation of the past-due accounts at May 31, Linda Snow decided that the probable loss contained therein was 10%, and that in addition she should anticipate a loss of 1% of the current accounts receivable.

Instructions

a Compute the probable uncollectible accounts expense applicable to the accounts receivable at May 31, based on the analysis by the owner.

b Prepare the journal entry necessary to carry out the change in company policy with respect to providing for uncollectible accounts expense.

10-2 The balance sheet prepared by Milagros Santos at December 31 last year included $504,000 in accounts receivable and an allowance for doubtful accounts of $26,400. During January of the current year selected transactions are summarized as follows:

(1) Sales on account	*$368,000*
(2) Sales returns & allowances	*7,360*
(3) Cash payments by customers (no cash discounts)	*364,800*
(4) Account receivable from Acme Company written off as worthless	*9,280*

After a careful aging and analysis of all customers' accounts at January 31, it was decided that the allowance for doubtful accounts should be adjusted to a balance of $29,280 in order to reflect accounts receivable at net realizable value in the January 31 balance sheet.

Instructions

a Prepare a journal entry (in general journal form) to *summarize* each of the four numbered items above and the adjusting entry at January 31 to provide for uncollectible accounts.

b Show the amounts of accounts receivable and the allowance for doubtful accounts as they would appear in a partial balance sheet at January 31.

c Assume that three months after the receivable from Acme Company had been written off as worthless, Acme Company won a large award in the settlement of patent litigation and immediately paid the $9,280 debt to Milagros Santos. Give the journal entry or entries (in general journal form) to reflect this recovery of a receivable previously written off.

10-3 The balance sheet prepared by Muirland Associates at December 31, Year 6, included accounts receivable of $380,640, and an allowance for doubtful accounts of $9,720. The company's sales volume in Year 7 reached a new high of $2,562,000 all on credit, and cash collections from customers amounted to $2,478,768. Among these collections was the recovery in full of a $4,680 receivable from Anthony Walker, a customer whose account had been written off as worthless late in Year 6. During Year 7, it was necessary to write off as uncollectible customers' accounts totaling $10,098.

On December 1, Year 7, Muirland Associates sold for $216,000 a tract of land acquired as a building site several years earlier at a cost of $144,000. The land was now considered unsuitable as a building site. Terms of sale were $60,000 cash and a 6%, six-month note for $156,000. The buyer was a large corporation and the note was regarded as fully collectible.

At December 31, Year 7, the accounts receivable included $60,174 of past-due accounts. After careful study of all past-due accounts, the management estimated that the probable loss contained therein was 20% and that, in addition, 2% of the current accounts receivable might prove uncollectible.

Instructions

a Prepare journal entries in general journal form, for all transactions in Year 7 relating to accounts and notes receivable.

b Prepare the necessary adjusting entries at December 31, Year 7. Round amounts to the nearest dollar for uncollectible accounts expense.

c What amount should appear in the income statement for Year 7 as uncollectible accounts expense?

d Prepare a partial balance sheet at December 31, Year 7, showing the accounts indicated above.

10-4 Leather Products sells to retail stores on 30-day open account, but requires customers who fail to pay invoices within 30 days to substitute promissory notes for their past-due accounts. No sales discount is offered. Among recent transactions were the following:

Oct. 17 Sold merchandise to Harris Shops, Inc., on account, $72,000, terms n/30.

Nov. 16 Received a 60-day, 9% note from Harris Shops, Inc., dated today in settlement of open account of $72,000.

Dec. 26 Discounted the Harris Shops note at the bank. The bank discount rate was 6% applied to the maturity value of the note for the 20 days remaining to maturity.

Jan. 15 Received notice from the bank that the Harris Shops note due today was in default. Paid the bank the maturity value of the note. Since Harris Shops, Inc., is a rapidly growing chain of retail stores, the management of Leather Products is confident that no loss will be incurred on the defaulted note.

Jan. 25 Made a $48,000 loan to Superior Saddlery on a 30-day, 9% note.

Instructions

a Prepare in general journal form the entries necessary to record the above transactions.

b Prepare the adjusting journal entry needed at January 31, the end of the company's fiscal year, to record interest accrued on the two notes receivable. (Accrue interest at 9% per annum for the 16 days from date of default on the maturity value of the Harris Shops note.)

10-5 Several transactions involving notes payable were carried out by Dunleer Corporation during the fiscal year ended October 31.

June 6 Borrowed $11,200 from T. Hutchins, issuing to him a 45-day, 6% note payable.

July 13 Purchased office equipment from Harper Company. The invoice amount was $16,800 and the Harper Company agreed to accept as full payment a 7%, three-month note for the invoiced amount.

July 21 Paid the Hutchins note plus accrued interest.

Sept. 1 Borrowed $235,200 from Sun National Bank at an interest rate of 6% per annum; signed a 90-day note with interest included in the face amount of the note.

Oct. 1 Purchased merchandise in the amount of $2,700 from Kramer Co. Gave in settlement a 90-day note bearing interest at 8%.

Oct. 13 The $16,800 note payable to Harper Company matured today. Paid the interest accrued and issued a new 30-day, $7\frac{1}{2}$% note to replace the maturing note.

Instructions

a Prepare journal entries (in general journal form) to record the above transactions.

b Prepare the adjusting entries needed at October 31, prior to closing the accounts. (*Reminder:* In accruing interest, do not include the day the note is issued.)

10-6 The following information concerning the receivables of the Foxdale Corporation appeared in the accounts on December 1, Year 7:

Accounts receivable:

C. L. Laurence	$ 2,425
E. D. Nemson	3,870
C. A. Shively	6,200
Total	$12,495

Notes receivable:

A. P. Marra, 8%, 45-day note, dated Nov. 4, Year 7	$ 6,000
C. M. Hines, 9%, 90-day note, dated Nov. 30, Year 7	4,000
Total	$10,000

Installment contracts receivable:

M. Moyers (*monthly payment $150*)	$ 2,850

Unearned interest on installment contracts:

Applicable to M. Moyers contract	$ 386

During the month of December, the following additional transactions took place:

Dec.   7 E. D. Nemson paid $870 on account and gave a 30-day, 8% note to cover the balance.

Dec. 12 Received a 60-day, 8% note from C. L. Laurence in full settlement of his account.

Dec. 19 A. P. Marra wrote that he would be unable to pay the note due today and included a check to cover the interest due and a new 30-day, 7% note renewing the old note. No accrued interest has been recorded in prior months.

Dec. 28 Discounted the C. L. Laurence note at the bank. The proceeds on the note amounted to $2,432.

Dec. 31 Received the monthly payment on the M. Moyers contract. The payment of $150 includes $20 of interest revenue earned during December. The interest charges included in the face amount of the installment contract had originally been credited to the contra-asset account, Unearned Interest on Installment Contracts.

Instructions

a Prepare journal entries (in general journal form) for December, including an adjusting entry relating to accrued interest at December 31. (*Hint:* Three notes require adjustment. Number of days' interest does not include the day a note is dated.)

b Show how the accounts relating to notes receivable, accounts receivable, installment contracts receivable, and accrued interest receivable would appear in the balance sheet as of December 31. Show the actual balances.

10-7 On April 1, Year 8, Merrimack Corporation sold merchandise to West Supply Co. in exchange for a note receivable due in one year. The note was drawn in the face amount of $47,300, which included the principal amount and an interest charge. In its December 31, Year 8, balance sheet, Merrimack Corporation correctly presented the note receivable as follows:

Note receivable, due Mar. 31, Year 9	*$47,300*	
Less: Discount on note receivable	*825*	*$46,475*

Instructions

a Determine the monthly interest revenue earned by Merrimack Corporation from this note receivable. (*Hint:* The balance in the discount account represents unearned interest as of December 31, Year 8.)

b Compute the amount of interest revenue recognized by Merrimack Corporation from the note during Year 8.

c Compute the amount of sales revenue recognized by Merrimack Corporation on April 1, Year 8, when this note was received.

d Compute the effective annual rate of interest (stated as a percentage) represented by the interest charge originally included in the face amount of the note.

e Prepare all journal entries relating to this note in the accounting records of Merrimack Corporation for Years 8 and 9. Assume that adjusting entries are made only at December 31.

10-8 J. Roberts, controller of Wood Products, became concerned over the company's weak cash position. To improve this situation, Roberts decided to minimize the amount tied up in receivables by discounting at the bank the notes receivable from customers. The bank applies a discount rate to the maturity value of the notes, which varies with the quality of the note and the general level of interest rates.

Wood Products makes some sales on 30-day open account, but any customer who does not pay in full within 30 days is asked to substitute an interest-bearing note for the past-due account. Some customers are required to sign promissory notes at the time of sale. The company uses the allowance method of accounting for uncollectible accounts.

A partial list of transactions for the six months ended December 31 is given below.

July 1 Sale of merchandise to G. Adler on account, $3,863. It was agreed that Adler would submit a 60-day, 8% note upon receipt of the merchandise and would deduct any freight paid on the goods.

July 3 Received from Adler a letter stating that he had paid $113 freight on the shipment of July 1 and enclosing a 60-day, 8% note dated July 3 for $3,750.

July 18 Sold merchandise on account, $5,500, to Ward Company; terms 2/10, n/30.

July 27 Discounted Adler note at bank and received $3,770 in cash.

July 28 Ward Company paid account in full.

Aug. 8 Sold merchandise to W. Patrick on account, $3,000; terms 2/10, n/30.

Sept. 1 Received notice from the bank that Adler had defaulted on the note due today. The bank charged the company's account for $3,800, the maturity value of the note.

Sept. 7 Received a 60-day, 7% note from W. Patrick in settlement of open account.

Sept. 10 It was ascertained that an account receivable from H. B. Gilkes amounting to $300 could not be collected and it was written off.

Oct. 15 An account receivable of $750 from Elaine Anderson had been written off in June; full payment was unexpectedly received from Anderson.

Oct. 25 Received cash from G. Adler in full settlement of his account due today, including interest of 8% on $3,800 from September 1, maturity date of note.

Nov. 6 W. Patrick paid the note due today.

Dec. 31 As a result of substantial write-offs, the Allowance for Doubtful Accounts has a *debit* balance of $500. Aging of the accounts receivable (which amount to $200,000) indicates that a credit balance of $3,000 in the Allowance for Doubtful Accounts is required.

Instructions Prepare journal entries (in general journal form) to record the transactions and adjustments listed above.

10-9 During the three months ended June 30, Solar Corporation had the following transactions relating to notes payable.

Apr. **1** Purchased equipment from Copper-Weld, Inc., for $13,000, making an $1,800 cash down payment and issuing a one-year note payable for the balance. The face amount of the note was $12,040, which included a $7\frac{1}{2}$% interest charge.

Apr. **16** Gave $5,000 cash and a 90-day, 8% note to Lees Company in settlement of open account due today in the amount of $14,000.

Apr. **25** Purchased factory machinery from ADM Company for $17,400, giving a 60-day, 9% note in settlement thereof.

May **11** Borrowed $72,000 from Manufacturers Bank, giving a 90-day note as evidence of indebtedness. An interest charge computed at the effective rate of $8\frac{1}{2}$% per annum was included in the face amount of the note.

June 15 Purchased merchandise on account from Phoenix Co., $18,000.

June 18 Issued a 60-day note bearing interest at 9% in settlement of the Phoenix Co. account.

June 24 Paid the 60-day, 9% note due to ADM Company.

Instructions

a Prepare journal entries (in general journal form) to record the listed transactions for the three months ended June 30.

b Prepare an adjusting entry to record the interest expense on notes payable through June 30. (*Hint:* Four notes must be considered. The computation of interest on each can be shown as part of the explanation of the adjusting entry.)

c Prepare a partial balance sheet as of June 30 reflecting the above transactions. Show Notes Payable to Bank (minus the discount) as one item and Notes Payable: Other (minus the discount) as a separate liability.

10-10 During the month of August, Delux Office Supply Co. engaged in the following transactions involving receivables and payables:

Aug. **1** Sold merchandise to C. Reed for $4,500. Reed issued a 90-day, 8% note for the amount of the purchase.

Aug. **4** Received a 60-day, 9% note from Reno Corporation for $6,200 in settlement of open account.

Aug. **11** Issued a 60-day, $7\frac{1}{2}$% note payable to Magnum Company for $5,040 in settlement of open account.

Aug. **16** Borrowed $12,000 from First Charter Bank and signed a six-month, 9% note payable which included the interest in the face amount.

Aug. **17** Discounted the Reno Corporation note. The proceeds from the bank amounted to $6,221.

Aug. **21** Sold merchandise to Howard Wright. As payment, Wright issued a 60-day note for a face amount of $6,318, which included an interest charge of $468.

Aug. **24** Received payment from W. Harned of a $4,000, 60-day, 9% note dated June 25. Accrued interest receivable of $36 had been recorded in prior months.

Aug. **26** A long overdue account receivable from J. Bartlett in the amount of $720 was written off as uncollectible against the allowance for doubtful accounts.

Aug. **28** Full payment of a $290 account receivable was unexpectedly received from J. Kievits. This account had been written off as uncollectible several months ago.

Aug. **30** Sales to HandyCharge credit card customers in August amounted to $9,500. (Summarize all credit card sales in one entry. HandyCharge Co. is not a bank.)

Aug. **31** Collected cash from HandyCharge for August credit card sales, less 3% discount charged by HandyCharge.

Aug. 31 An aging of accounts receivable on August 31 indicates the allowance for doubtful accounts should be increased to $1,950. On September 30, the balance in the allowance account had been $1,830. No entries other than those described above have been made in the allowance account during August.

Instructions

a Prepare in general journal form the entries necessary to record the above transactions.

b Prepare any adjusting entries needed at August 31. (*Hint:* Four notes require adjusting entries.)

c Draft the appropriate footnote to the financial statements to disclose the contingent liability relating to the discounted note receivable.

BUSINESS DECISION PROBLEM 10

Record House and Concert Sound are two companies engaged in selling stereo equipment to the public. Both companies sell equipment at a price 50% greater than cost. Customers may pay cash, purchase on 30-day accounts, or make installment payments over a 36-month period. The installment receivables include a three-year interest charge (which amounts to 30% of the sales price) in the face amount of the contract. Condensed income statements prepared by the companies for their first year of operations are shown below:

	Record House	Concert Sound
Sales	$387,000	$288,000
Cost of goods sold	210,000	192,000
Gross profit on sales	$177,000	$ 96,000
Operating expenses	63,000	60,000
Operating income	$114,000	$ 36,000
Interest earned	–0–	10,800
Net income	$114,000	$ 46,800

When Record House makes a sale of stereo equipment on the installment plan it immediately credits the Sales account with the face amount of the installment receivable. In other words, the interest charges are included in sales revenue at the time of the sale. The interest charges included in Record House's installment receivables originating in the first year amount to $72,000, of which $59,100 is unearned at the end of the first year. Record House uses the direct charge-off method to recognize uncollectible accounts expense. During the year, accounts receivable of $2,100 were written off as uncollectible, but no entry was made for $37,200 of accounts estimated to be uncollectible at year-end.

Concert Sound records sales revenue equal to the present value of its installment receivables and recognizes the interest *earned during the year* as interest revenue. Concert Sound provides for uncollectible accounts by the allowance method. The company recognized uncollectible accounts expense of $11,100 during the year and this amount appeared to be adequate.

Instructions

a Prepare a condensed income statement for Record House for the year, using the same methods of accounting for installment sales and uncollectible accounts as were used by Concert Sound. The income statement you prepare should contain the same seven items shown in the illustrated income statements. Provide footnotes showing the computations you made in revising the amount of sales and any other figures you decide to change.

b Compare the income statement you have prepared in part *a* to the one originally. prepared by Record House. Which income statement do you believe better reflects the results of the company's operations during the year? Explain.

c What do you believe to be the key factor responsible for making one of these companies more profitable than the other? What corrective action would you recommend be taken by the less profitable company to improve future performance?

11 Inventories

Some basic questions relating to inventory

In earlier sections of this book the procedures for recording inventory at the end of the accounting period have been illustrated. The use of the inventory figure in both the balance sheet and the income statement has been demonstrated, and particular emphasis has been placed on the procedure for computing the cost of goods sold by deducting the ending inventory from the cost of goods available for sale during the period.

In all the previous illustrations, the dollar amount of the ending inventory has been given with only a brief explanation as to how this amount was determined. The valuation of inventory, as for most other types of assets, has been stated to be at cost, but the concept of *cost* as applied to inventories of merchandise has not been explored or defined.

In this chapter we shall consider some of the fundamental questions involved in accounting for inventories. Among the questions to be considered are these:

1 What goods are to be included in inventory?
2 How is the amount of the ending inventory determined?
3 What are the arguments for and against each of several alternative methods of inventory valuation?
4 What are the advantages of a perpetual inventory system?

Inventory defined

One of the largest assets in a retail store or in a wholesale business is the inventory of merchandise, and the sale of this merchandise at prices in excess of cost is the major source of revenue. For a merchandising company, *the inventory consists of all goods owned and held for sale in the regular course of business.* Merchandise held for sale will normally be converted into cash within less than a year's time and is therefore regarded as a current asset. In the balance sheet, inventory is listed immediately after accounts receivable, because it is just one step further removed from conversion into cash than are the accounts receivable.

In manufacturing businesses there are three major types of inventories: *raw materials, goods in process of manufacture,* and *finished goods.* All three classes of inventories are included in the current asset section of the balance sheet.

To expand our definition of inventory to fit manufacturing companies as well as merchandising companies, we can say that inventory means "the aggregate of those items of tangible personal property which (*1*) are held for sale in the ordinary course of business, (*2*) are in process of production for such sale, or (*3*) are to be currently consumed in the production of goods or services to be available for sale."[1]

Inventory valuation and the measurement of income

In measuring the gross profit on sales earned during an accounting period, we subtract the *cost of goods sold* from the total *sales* of the period. The figure for sales is easily accumulated from the daily record of sales transactions, but in many businesses no day-to-day record is maintained showing the cost of goods sold.[2] The figure representing the cost of goods sold during an entire accounting period is computed at the end of the period by separating the *cost of goods available for sale* into two elements:

1 The cost of the goods sold
2 The cost of the goods not sold, which therefore comprise the ending inventory

This idea, with which you are already quite familiar, may be concisely stated in the form of an equation as follows:

Finding cost of goods sold

$$\text{Cost of Goods Available for Sale} - \text{Ending Inventory} = \text{Cost of Goods Sold}$$

Determining the amount of the ending inventory is the key step in establishing the cost of goods sold. In separating the *cost of goods available for sale* into its components of *goods sold* and *goods not sold,* we are just as much interested in establishing the proper amount for cost of goods sold as in determining a proper figure for inventory. Throughout this chapter you should bear in mind that the procedures for determining the

[1] American Institute of Certified Public Accounts, *Accounting Research and Terminology Bulletins,* Final Edition (New York: 1961), p. 28.
[2] As explained in Chap. 5, a company that maintains perpetual inventory records will have a day-to-day record of the cost of goods sold and of goods in inventory. Our present discussion, however, is based on the assumption that the periodic system of inventory is being used.

amount of the ending inventory are also the means for determining the cost of goods sold. The valuation of inventory and the determination of the cost of goods sold are in effect the two sides of a single coin.

The American Institute of Certified Public Accountants has summarized this relationship between inventory valuation and the measurement of income in the following words: "A major objective of accounting for inventories is the proper determination of income through the process of matching appropriate costs against revenues." [3] The expression "matching costs against revenues" means determining what portion of the cost of goods available for sale should be deducted from the revenue of the current period and what portion should be carried forward (as inventory) to be matched against the revenue of the following period.

Importance of an accurate valuation of inventory

The most important current assets in the balance sheets of most companies are cash, accounts receivable, and inventory. Of these three, the inventory of merchandise is usually much the largest. Because of the relatively large size of this asset, an error in the valuation of inventory may cause a material misstatement of financial position and of net income. An error of 20% in valuing the inventory may have as much effect on the financial statements as would the complete omission of the asset cash.

An error in inventory will of course lead to other erroneous figures in the balance sheet, such as the total current assets, total assets, owners' equity, and the total of liabilities and owners' equity. The error will also affect key figures in the income statement, such as the cost of goods sold, the gross profit on sales, and the net income for the period. Finally, it is important to recognize that *the ending inventory of one year is also the beginning inventory of the following year.* Consequently, the income statement of the second year will also be in error by the full amount of the original error in inventory valuation.

ILLUSTRATION OF THE EFFECTS OF AN ERROR IN VALUING INVENTORY
Assume that on December 31, Year 5, the inventory of the Hillside Company is actually $100,000 but, through an accidental error, it is recorded as $90,000. The effects of this $10,000 error on the income statement for Year 5 are indicated in the first illustration on page 438 showing two income statements side by side. The left-hand set of figures shows the inventory of December 31, Year 5, at the proper value of $100,000 and represents a correct income statement for Year 5. The right-hand set of figures represents an incorrect income statement, because the ending inventory is erroneously listed as $90,000. Note the differences between the two income statements with respect to net income, gross profit on sales, and cost of goods sold. Income taxes have purposely been omitted in this illustration.

[3] AICPA, op. cit.

HILLSIDE COMPANY
Income Statement
For the Year Ended December 31, Year 5

		With Correct Ending Inventory		With Incorrect Ending Inventory
Sales			$240,000	$240,000
Cost of goods sold:				
Inventory, December 31,				
Year 4	$ 75,000		$ 75,000	
Purchases (net)	210,000		210,000	
Cost of goods available for sale	$285,000		$285,000	
Less: Inventory, December 31,				
Year 5	100,000		90,000	
Cost of goods sold		185,000		195,000
Gross profit on sales		$ 55,000		$ 45,000
Operating expenses		30,000		30,000
Net income		$ 25,000		$ 15,000

Effect of error in inventory

This illustration shows that an understatement of $10,000 in the ending inventory for Year 5 caused an understatement of $10,000 in the net income for Year 5. Next, consider the effect of this error on the income statement of the following year. The ending inventory of Year 5 is, of course, the beginning inventory of Year 6. The preceding illustration is now continued to show side by side a correct statement and an incorrect statement for Year 6. The ending inventory of $120,000 for Year 6 is the same in both statements and is to be considered correct. Note that the $10,000 error in the beginning inventory of the right-hand statement causes an error in the cost of goods sold, in gross profit, and in net income for Year 6.

HILLSIDE COMPANY
Income Statement
For the Year Ended December 31, Year 6

		With Correct Beginning Inventory		With Incorrect Beginning Inventory
Sales			$265,000	$265,000
Cost of goods sold:				
Inventory, December 31,				
Year 5	$100,000		$ 90,000	
Purchases (net)	230,000		230,000	
Cost of goods available for sale	$330,000		$320,000	
Less: Inventory, December 31,				
Year 6	120,000		120,000	
Cost of goods sold		210,000		200,000
Gross profit on sales		$ 55,000		$ 65,000
Operating expenses		33,000		33,000
Net income		$ 22,000		$ 32,000

Effect on succeeding year

COUNTERBALANCING ERRORS The illustrated income statements for Years 5 and 6 show that an understatement of the ending inventory in Year 5 caused an understatement of net income in that year and an offsetting overstatement of net income for Year 6. Over a period of two years the effects of an inventory error on net income will *counterbalance,* and the total net income for the two years together is the same as if the error had not occurred. Since the error in reported net income for the first year is exactly offset by the error in reported net income for the second year, it might be argued that an inventory error has no serious consequences. Such an argument is not sound, for it disregards the fact that accurate yearly figures for net income are a primary objective of the accounting process. Moreover, many actions by management and many decisions by creditors and owners are based upon *trends* indicated in the financial statements for two or more years. Note that the inventory error has made the Year 6 net income appear to be more than twice as large as the Year 5 net income, when in fact *less* net income was earned in Year 6 than in Year 5. Anyone relying on the erroneous financial statements would be greatly misled as to the trend of Hillside Company's earnings.

To produce dependable financial statements, inventory must be accurately determined at the end of each accounting period. The counterbalancing effect of the inventory error by the Hillside Company is illustrated below:

		With Inventory Correctly Stated	With Inventory at Dec. 31, Year 5. Understated	
			Reported Net Income Will Be	Reported Net Income Will Be Overstated (Understated)
Counter-balancing effect on net income	Net income for Year 5	$25,000	$15,000	($10,000)
	Net income for Year 6	22,000	32,000	10,000
	Total net income for two years	$47,000	$47,000	$ –0–

RELATION OF INVENTORY ERRORS TO NET INCOME The effects of errors in inventory upon net income may be summarized as follows:

1 When the *ending* inventory is understated, the net income for the period will be understated.

2 When the *ending* inventory is overstated, the net income for the period will be overstated.

3 When the *beginning* inventory is understated, the net income for the period will be overstated.

4 When the *beginning* inventory is overstated, the net income for the period will be understated.

Taking a physical inventory

At the end of each accounting period the ledger accounts will show up-to-date balances for most of the assets. For inventory, however, the balance in the ledger account represents the *beginning* inventory, because no entry has been made in the Inventory account since the end of the preceding period. All purchases of merchandise during the present period have been recorded in the Purchases account. The ending inventory does not appear anywhere in the ledger accounts; it must be determined by a physical count of merchandise on hand at the end of the accounting period.

Establishing a balance sheet valuation for the ending inventory requires two steps: (*1*) determining the quantity of each kind of merchandise on hand, and (*2*) multiplying the quantity by the cost per unit. The first step is called *taking the inventory;* the second is called *pricing the inventory.* Taking inventory, or more precisely, taking a physical inventory, means making a systematic count of all merchandise on hand.

In most merchandising businesses the taking of a physical inventory is a year-end event. In some lines of business an inventory may be taken at the close of each month. It is common practice to take inventory after regular business hours or on Sunday. By taking the inventory while business operations are suspended, a more accurate count is possible than if goods were being sold or received while the count was in process.

PLANNING THE PHYSICAL INVENTORY Unless the taking of a physical inventory is carefully planned and supervised, serious errors are apt to occur which will invalidate the results of the count. To prevent such errors as the double counting of items, the omission of goods from the count, and other quantitative errors, it is desirable to plan the inventory so that the work of one person serves as a check on the accuracy of another.

There are various methods of counting merchandise. One of the simplest procedures is carried out by the use of two-member teams. One member of the team counts and calls the description and quantity of each item. The other person lists the descriptions and quantities on an inventory sheet. (In some situations, a tape recorder is useful in recording quantities counted.) When all goods have been counted and listed, the items on the inventory sheet are priced at cost, and the unit prices are multiplied by the quantities to determine the valuation of the inventory.

To assure the accuracy of the recorded counts, a representative number of items should be recounted by supervisors. Some businesses make a practice of counting all merchandise a second time and comparing the quantities established by the different teams. The initials of the persons making both the first and the second counts should be placed on an inventory tag attached to each lot of merchandise counted. Once it is known that all merchandise has been tagged and that the counts are accurate, the tags are gathered and sent to the accounting office so that all the information can be summarized and the dollar valuation of inventory can be computed.

INCLUDING ALL GOODS OWNED All goods to which the company has title should be included in the inventory, regardless of their location. Title to merchandise ordinarily passes from seller to buyer at the time the goods are delivered. No question usually arises as to the ownership of merchandise on the shelves, in stock rooms, or in warehouses. A question of ownership often does arise, however, for merchandise en route from suppliers but not yet received on the last day of the year. A similar question of ownership concerns goods in the process of shipment to customers at year-end.

Goods in transit Do goods in transit belong in the inventory of the seller or of the buyer? If the selling company makes delivery of the merchandise in its own trucks, the merchandise remains its property while in transit. If the goods are shipped by rail, air, or other public carrier, the question of ownership of the goods while in transit depends upon whether the public carrier is acting as the agent of the seller or of the buyer. If the terms of the shipment are *F.O.B.* (free on board) *shipping point,* title passes at the point of shipment and the goods are the property of the buyer while in transit. If the terms of the shipment are *F.O.B. destination,* title does not pass until the shipment reaches the destination, and the goods belong to the seller while in transit. In deciding whether goods in transit at year-end should be included in inventory, it is therefore necessary to refer to the terms of the agreements with vendors (suppliers) and customers.

At the end of the year a company may have received numerous orders from customers, for which goods have been segregated and packed but not yet shipped. These goods should generally be included in inventory. An exception to this rule is found occasionally when the goods have been prepared for shipment but are being held for later delivery at the request of the customer.

Passage of title to merchandise The debit to the customer's account and the offsetting credit to the Sales account should be made *when title to the goods passes to the customer.* It would obviously be improper to set up an account receivable and at the same time to include the goods in question in inventory. Great care is necessary at year-end to ensure that all last-minute shipments to customers are recorded as sales of the current year and, on the other hand, that no customer's order is recorded as a sale until the date when the goods are shipped. Sometimes, in an effort to meet sales quotas, companies have recorded sales on the last day of the accounting period, when in fact the merchandise was not shipped until early in the next period. Such practices lead to an overstatement of the year's earnings and are not in accordance with generally accepted principles of accounting.

Merchandise in inventory is valued at *cost,* whereas accounts receivable are stated at the *sales price* of the merchandise sold. Consequently, the recording of a sale prior to delivery of the goods results in an unjustified increase in the total assets of the company. The increase will equal the difference between the cost and the selling price of the goods in question. The amount of the increase will also be reflected in the income statement, where it will show up as additional earnings. An unscrupulous company, which wanted to make its financial statements present a more favorable picture than actually existed, might do so by treating year-end orders from customers as sales even though the goods were not yet shipped.

Pricing the inventory

One of the most interesting and widely discussed problems in accounting is the pricing of inventory. Even those business executives who have little knowledge of accounting are usually interested in the various methods of pricing inventory, because inventory valuation has a direct effect upon reported net income. Federal income taxes are based on income, and the choice of inventory method may have a considerable effect upon the amount of income taxes payable. Federal income tax authorities are therefore very interested in the problem of inventory valuation and have taken a definite position on the acceptability of various alternative methods of pricing inventory.

In approaching our study of inventory valuation, however, it is important that we do not overemphasize the income tax aspects of the problem. It is true that in selected cases one method of inventory valuation may lead to a substantially lower income tax liability than would another method, but there are other important considerations in pricing inventory apart from the objective of minimizing the current income tax burden.

Proper valuation of inventory is one part of a larger undertaking, that is, to measure net income accurately and to provide all those persons interested in the financial position and operating results of a business with accounting data which are dependable and of maximum usefulness as a basis for business decisions.

Accounting for inventories involves determination of cost and of current fair value or replacement cost. An understanding of the meaning of the term *cost* as applied to inventories is a first essential in appreciating the complexity of the overall problem of inventory valuation.

Cost basis of inventory valuation

''The primary basis of accounting for inventory is cost, which has been defined generally as the price paid or consideration given to acquire an asset. As applied to inventories, cost means in principle the sum of the applicable expenditures and charges directly or indirectly incurred in bringing an article to its existing condition and location''[4]

INCLUSION OF INDIRECT EXPENDITURES IN INVENTORY COST—A QUESTION OF MATERIALITY The starting point in determining the cost of inventory is the *net invoice price* of the goods in inventory. From a conceptual point of view, all indirect expenditures incurred in the acquisition of these goods should be added to the invoice prices in determining the cost of inventory. For example, part of the expenditure during the period for transportation-in is applicable to ending inventory and should be included in the inventory cost. In determining the cost of the ending inventory, many businesses add to the net invoice price of the goods a reasonable portion of the transportation charges incurred during the period.

In some lines of business, however, it is customary to price the year-end inventory without giving any consideration to transportation charges, because these charges are *not material in amount.* Although this practice results in a slight understatement of inventory cost, the understatement is so small that it does not affect the usefulness or reliability of the financial statements. Thus, the omission of transportation charges from the cost of inventory often may be justified by the factors of convenience and economy. Accounting textbooks stress theoretical concepts of cost and income determination. The student of accounting should be aware, however, that in many business situations a close *approximation* of cost will serve the purpose at hand. The extra work involved in developing more precise accounting data must be weighed against the benefits that will result.

If transportation-in is part of the cost of merchandise purchased, what about the other incidental charges relating to the acquisition of merchandise, such as the salary of the purchasing agent, insurance of goods in transit, cost of receiving and inspecting the merchandise, etc.? Although in theory these incidental charges should be identified and apportioned among the various items of merchandise purchased, the expense of computing cost on such a precise basis would usually outweigh the benefits to be derived. The costs of operating the purchasing department and the receiving department are customarily treated as expense of the period in which incurred, rather than being carried forward to another period by inclusion in the balance sheet amount for inventory.

Inventory valuation methods

The prices of many kinds of merchandise are subject to frequent change. When identical lots of merchandise are purchased at various dates during the year, each lot may be acquired at a different cost price.

---

[4] Ibid.

To illustrate the several alternative methods in common use for determining which purchase prices apply to the units remaining in inventory at the end of the period, assume the data shown below.

	Number of Units	Cost per Unit	Total Cost
Beginning inventory	100	$ 80	$ 8,000
First purchase (Mar. 1)	50	90	4,500
Second purchase (July 1)	50	100	5,000
Third purchase (Oct. 1)	50	120	6,000
Fourth purchase (Dec. 1)	50	130	6,500
Available for sale	300		$30,000
Units sold	180		
Units in ending inventory	120		

This schedule shows that 180 units were sold during the year and that 120 units are on hand at year-end to make up the ending inventory. In order to establish a dollar amount for cost of goods sold and for the ending inventory, we must make an assumption as to which units were sold and which units remain on hand at the end of the year. There are several acceptable assumptions on this point; four of the most common will be considered. Each assumption made as to the cost of the units in the ending inventory leads to a different method of pricing inventory and to different amounts in the financial statements. The four assumptions (and inventory valuation methods) to be considered are known as (1) specific identification, (2) average cost, (3) first-in, first-out, and (4) last-in, first-out.

Although each of these four methods will produce a different answer as to the cost of goods sold and the cost of the ending inventory, the valuation of inventory in each case is said to be at "cost." In other words, *these methods represent alternative definitions of inventory cost.*

SPECIFIC IDENTIFICATION METHOD If the units in the ending inventory can be identified as coming from specific purchases, they *may* be priced at the amounts listed on the purchase invoices. Continuing the example already presented, if the ending inventory of 120 units can be identified as, say, 50 units from the purchase of March 1, 40 units from the purchase of July 1, and 30 units from the purchase of December 1, the cost of the ending inventory may be computed as follows:

Specific	50 units from the purchase of Mar. 1 @ $90	$ 4,500
identifica-	40 units from the purchase of July 1 @ $100	4,000
tion	30 units from the purchase of Dec. 1 @ $130	3,900
method and . . .	Ending inventory (specific identification)	$12,400

The cost of goods sold during the period is determined by subtracting the ending inventory from the cost of goods available for sale.

... cost of goods sold computation

Cost of goods available for sale	*$30,000*
Less: Ending inventory	*12,400*
Cost of goods sold (specific identification method)	*$17,600*

A business may prefer not to use the specific identification method even though the cost of each unit sold could be identified with a specific purchase. The flow of cost factors may be more significant than the flow of specific physical units in measuring the net income of the period.

As a simple example, assume that a coal dealer purchased 100 tons of coal at $60 a ton and a short time later made a second purchase of 100 tons of the same grade of coal at $80 a ton. The two purchases are in separate piles and it is a matter of indifference as to which pile is used in making sales to customers. Assume that the dealer makes a retail sale of one ton of coal at a price of $100. In measuring the gross profit on the sale, which cost figure should be used, $60 or $80? To insist that the cost depended on which of the two identical piles of coal was used in filling the delivery truck is an argument of questionable logic.

A situation in which the specific identification method is more likely to give meaningful results is in the purchase and sale of such high-priced articles as boats, automobiles, and jewelry.

AVERAGE-COST METHOD Average cost is computed by dividing the total cost of goods available for sale by the number of units available for sale. This computation gives a *weighted-average unit cost,* which is then applied to the units in the ending inventory.

Average-cost method and ...

Cost of goods available for sale	*$30,000*
Number of units available for sale	*300*
Average unit cost	*$ 100*
Ending inventory (at average cost, 120 units @ $100)	*$12,000*

Note that this method, when compared with the specific identification method, leads to a different amount for cost of goods sold as well as a different amount for the ending inventory.

... cost of goods sold computation

Cost of goods available for sale	*$30,000*
Less: Ending inventory	*12,000*
Cost of goods sold (average-cost method)	*$18,000*

When the average-cost method is used, the cost figure of $12,000 determined for the ending inventory is influenced by all the various prices paid during the year. The price paid early in the year may carry as much weight in pricing the ending inventory as a price paid at the end of the year. A common criticism of the average-cost method of pricing inventory is that it attaches no more significance to current prices than to prices which prevailed several months earlier.

FIRST-IN, FIRST-OUT METHOD The first-in, first-out method, which is often referred to as *fifo,* is based on the assumption that the first merchandise acquired is the first merchandise sold. In other words, each sale is made out of the *oldest* goods in stock; *the ending inventory therefore consists of the most recently acquired goods.* The fifo method of determining inventory cost may be adopted by any business, regardless of whether or not the physical flow of merchandise actually corresponds to this assumption of selling the oldest units in stock. Using the same data as in the preceding illustrations, the 120 units in the ending inventory would be regarded as consisting of the most recently acquired goods, as follows:

First-in, first-out method and . . .	*50 units from the Dec. 1 purchase @ $130*	*$ 6,500*
	50 units from the Oct. 1 purchase @ $120	*6,000*
	20 units from the July 1 purchase @ $100	*2,000*
	Ending inventory, 120 units (at fifo cost)	*$14,500*

During a period of *rising prices* the first-in, first-out method will result in a larger amount ($14,500) being assigned as the cost of the ending inventory than would be assigned under the average-cost method. When a relatively large amount is allocated as cost of the ending inventory, a relatively small amount will remain as cost of goods sold, as indicated by the following calculation:

. . . cost of goods sold computation	*Cost of goods available for sale*	*$30,000*
	Less: Ending inventory	*14,500*
	Cost of goods sold (first-in, first-out method)	*$15,500*

It may be argued in support of the first-in, first-out method that the inventory valuation reflects recent costs and is therefore a realistic value in the light of conditions prevailing at the balance sheet date.

LAST-IN, FIRST-OUT METHOD The title of this method of pricing suggests that the most recently acquired goods are sold first, and that the ending inventory consists of "old" merchandise acquired in the earliest purchases. Such an assumption is, of course, not in accord with the actual physical movement of goods in most businesses, but there is nevertheless a strong logical argument to support this method. As merchandise is sold, more goods must be purchased to replenish the stock on hand. Since the making of a sale necessitates a replacement purchase of goods, the cost of replacement should be offset against the sales price to determine the gross profit realized.

The supporters of last-in, first-out, or *lifo,* as it is commonly known, contend that the accurate determination of income requires that primary emphasis be placed on the **matching of current costs of merchandise against current sales prices,** regardless of which physical units of merchandise are being delivered to customers. Keeping in mind the point that the **flow of costs** may be more significant than the **physical movement** of merchandise, we can say that, under the lifo method, the cost of goods sold consists of the cost of the most recently acquired goods, and the ending inventory consists of the cost of the oldest goods which were available for sale during the period.

Using the same data as in the preceding illustrations, the 120 units in the ending inventory would be priced as if they were the oldest goods available for sale during the period, as follows:

Last-in,	*100 units from the beginning inventory @ $80*	*$8,000*
first-out	*20 units from the purchase of Mar.1 @ $90*	*1,800*
method		
and . . .	*Ending inventory, 120 units (at lifo cost)*	*$9,800*

Note that the lifo cost of the ending inventory ($9,800) is very much lower than the fifo cost ($14,500) of ending inventory in the preceding example. Since a relatively small part of the cost of goods available for sale is assigned to ending inventory, it follows that a relatively large portion must have been assigned to cost of goods sold, as shown by the following computation:

. . . cost	*Cost of goods available for sale*	*$30,000*
of goods	*Less: Ending inventory*	*9,800*
sold com-		
putation	*Cost of goods sold (last-in, first-out method)*	*$20,200*

COMPARISON OF THE ALTERNATIVE METHODS OF PRICING INVENTORY
We have now illustrated four common methods of pricing inventory at cost; the specific identification method, the average-cost method, the first-in, first-out method, and the last-in, first-out method. By way of contrasting the results obtained from the four methods illustrated, especially during a period of rapid price increases, let us summarize the amounts computed for ending inventory, cost of goods sold, and gross profit on sales under each of the four methods. Assume that sales for the period amounted to $27,500.

	Specific Identifi-cation Method	Average-Cost Method	First-in, First-out Method	Last-in, First-out Method
Sales	$27,500	$27,500	$27,500	$27,500
Cost of goods sold:				
Beginning inventory	$ 8,000	$ 8,000	$ 8,000	$ 8,000
Purchases	22,000	22,000	22,000	22,000
Cost of goods available for sale	$30,000	$30,000	$30,000	$30,000
Less: Ending inventory	12,400	12,000	14,500	9,800
Cost of goods sold	$17,600	$18,000	$15,500	$20,200
Gross profit on sales	$ 9,900	$ 9,500	$12,000	$ 7,300

Four methods of determining inventory cost compared

This comparison of the four methods makes it apparent that during periods of *rising prices,* the use of lifo will result in lower reported profits and lower income taxes than would be the case under the other methods of inventory valuation. Perhaps for this reason many businesses have adopted lifo. Current income tax regulations permit virtually any business to use the last-in, first-out method in determining taxable income.[5]

During a period of *declining prices,* the use of lifo will cause the reporting of relatively large profits as compared with fifo, which will hold reported profits to a minimum. Obviously, the choice of inventory method becomes of greatest significance during prolonged periods of drastic changes in price levels.

WHICH METHOD OF INVENTORY VALUATION IS BEST? All four of the inventory methods described are regarded as acceptable accounting practices and all four are acceptable in the determination of taxable income. No one method of inventory valuation can be considered as the "correct" or the "best" method. In the selection of a method, consideration should be given to the probable effect upon the balance sheet, upon the income statement, upon the amount of taxable income, and upon such business decisions as the establishment of selling prices for goods.

The specific identification method has the advantage of portraying the actual physical flow of merchandise. However, this method permits manipulation of income by selecting which items to deliver in filling a sales order. Also, the specific identification method may lead to faulty pricing decisions by implying that identical items of merchandise have different economic values.

Identical items will have the same accounting values only under the average-cost method. Assume for example that a hardware store sells a given size nail for 65 cents per pound. The hardware store buys the nails in 100-pound quantities at different times at prices ranging from 40 to 50 cents per pound. Several hundred pounds of nails are always on hand,

---

[5] Income tax laws require the use of lifo for financial reporting if it is used for tax purposes.

stored in a large bin. The average-cost method properly recognizes that when a customer buys a pound of nails it is not necessary to know exactly which nails the customer happened to select from the bin in order to measure the gross profit on the sale.

A shortcoming in the average-cost method is that changes in current replacement costs of inventory are concealed because these costs are averaged with older costs. As a result of this averaging, the reported gross profit may not reflect current market conditions. This problem is illustrated in the discussion of *inventory profits* later in this chapter.

The inflation of recent years is a strong argument for the use of the lifo method. When prices are rising drastically, the most significant cost data to use as a guide to sales policies are probably the *current replacement costs* of the goods being sold. The lifo method of inventory valuation comes closer than any of the other methods described to measuring net income in the light of current selling prices and replacement costs.

On the other hand, the use of lifo during a period of rising prices is apt to produce a balance sheet figure for inventory which is far below the current replacement cost of the goods on hand. The fifo method of inventory valuation will lead to a balance sheet valuation of inventory more in line with current replacement costs.

Some business concerns which adopted lifo more than 30 years ago now show a balance sheet figure for inventory which is less than half the present replacement cost of the goods in stock. An inventory valuation method which gives significant figures for the income statement may thus produce misleading amounts for the balance sheet, whereas a method which produces a realistic figure for inventory on the balance sheet may provide less realistic data for the income statement.

The search for the "best" method of inventory valuation is rendered difficult because the inventory figure is used in both the balance sheet and the income statement, and these two financial statements are intended for different purposes. In the income statement the function of the inventory figure is to permit a matching of costs and revenue. In the balance sheet the inventory and the other current assets are regarded as a measure of the company's ability to meet its current debts. For this purpose a valuation of inventory in line with current replacement cost would appear to be more significant.

Consistency in the valuation of inventory

A business has considerable latitude in selecting a method of inventory valuation best suited to its needs; once a method has been selected, however, that method should be followed consistently from year to year. A change from one inventory method to another will ordinarily cause reported income to vary considerably in the year in which the change occurs. Frequent switching of methods would therefore make the income statements undependable as a means of portraying operating results.

The need for consistency in the valuation of inventory does not mean that a business should *never* make a change in inventory method. However, when a change is made, the approval of tax authorities must be obtained, and full disclosure of the nature of the change and of its effect upon the year's net income should be included in the financial statements or in a footnote to the statements. Even when the same method of inventory pricing is being followed consistently, the financial statements should include a disclosure of the pricing method in use.

The environment of inflation

The inflationary policies and high income tax rates of recent years have stimulated the interest of business management in the choice of inventory methods. Most business executives and government officials expect the trend of rising prices to continue; in other words, an environment of inflation has come to be considered as normal. The lifo method of inventory valuation causes reported net income to reflect the increasing cost of replacing the merchandise sold during the year and also tends to avoid basing income tax payments on an exaggerated measurement of taxable income. Therefore, the existence of inflation is an argument for the lifo method of inventory.

Inventory profits

Many accountants believe that the use of fifo or of average cost during a period of inflation results in the reporting of fictitious profits and consequently in the payment of excessive income taxes. A portion of the reported profits are considered to be fictitious because under both the fifo and average-cost methods, the gross profit is computed by subtracting old inventory costs rather than current replacement costs from sales revenue. These old costs are relatively low, resulting in a high reported gross profit. However, the company must pay the higher current cost in order to replenish its inventory.

To illustrate this concept, assume that TV Sales Shop has an inventory of 20 television sets which were acquired at an average cost of $270. During the current month, 10 television sets are sold for cash at a sales price of $350 each. Using the average-cost method to value inventory, the company will report the following gross profit for the month:

Sales (10 × $350)	*$3,500*
Cost of goods sold (10 × $270)	*2,700*
Gross profit on sales	*$ 800*

However, TV Sales Shop must replace its inventory of television sets to continue in business. Because of inflation, TV Sales Shop can no longer buy 10 television sets for $2,700. Let us assume that the current replacement cost of television sets is $325 each; TV Sales Shop must pay $3,250 to replenish its inventory. Thus, TV Sales Shop is able to keep only $250 ($3,500 − $3,250) of the reported $800 gross profit; the remaining $550 has to be reinvested in inventory because of the increasing cost of television sets. This $550 would be considered a fictitious profit, or an *inventory profit,* by many accountants and business executives.

The inventory profit included in the reported net income of a business may be computed by deducting the cost of goods sold shown in the income statement from the *replacement cost* (computed at the date of sale) of these goods.

In periods of rapid inflation, a significant portion of the reported net income of companies using fifo or average cost may actually be inventory profits. The net income of companies using lifo will include much less inventory profit because lifo causes more current costs to be included in the cost of goods sold.

The SEC rules on replacement cost

The Securities and Exchange Commission recently adopted disclosure requirements to spotlight the effect of inflation on the nation's largest corporations. The Commission required the 1,000 largest nonfinancial corporations to disclose what it would cost to replace their inventories at current prices and what their cost of goods sold would be if computed by using current replacement cost at the date of sale. The disclosure of replacement costs can be in a special section of the financial statements or in a footnote. This information thus supplements rather than replaces the use of historical cost as a basis of accounting for inventories and cost of goods sold.

The disclosure of cost of goods sold computed on the basis of replacement cost has revealed that a substantial portion of the net income reported in the financial statements of many large corporations is actually inventory profit. In other words, net income tends to be overstated and fictitious profits reported when companies rely solely on historical cost values during a period of inflation. The SEC action to adopt replacement cost accounting may prove to be one of the most significant changes in accounting practice in many years. Some accountants view it as a major step away from cost-based accounting toward current-value accounting.

The lower-of-cost-or-market rule

Although cost is the primary basis for valuation of inventories, circumstances may arise under which inventory may properly be valued at less than its cost. If the *utility* of the inventory has fallen below cost by reason of physical deterioration, obsolescence, or decline in the price level, a loss has occurred. This loss may appropriately be recognized as a loss of the current period by reducing the accounting value of the inventory from cost to a lower level designated as market. The word *market* as used in this context means *current replacement cost.* For a merchandising company, *market* is the amount which the concern would have to pay at the present time for the goods in question, purchased in the customary quantities through the usual sources of supply and including transportation-in. To avoid misunderstanding, the rule might better read "lower of actual cost or replacement cost."

In the early days of accounting when the principal users of financial statements were creditors and attention was concentrated upon the balance sheet, conservatism was a dominant consideration in asset valuation. The lower-of-cost-or-market rule was then considered justifiable because it tended to produce a "safe" or minimum value for inventory. The rule was widely applied for a time without regard for the possibility that although replacement costs had declined, there might be no corresponding and immediate decline in selling prices.

As the significance of the income statement has increased, considerable dissatisfaction with the lower-of-cost-or-market rule has developed. If ending inventory is written down from cost to a lower market figure but the merchandise is sold during the next period at the usual selling prices, the effect of the write-down will have been to reflect a fictitious loss in the first period and an exaggerated profit in the second period. Arbitrary application of the lower-of-cost-or-market rule ignores the historical fact that selling prices do not always drop when replacement prices decline. Even if selling prices do follow replacement prices downward, they may not decline by a proportionate amount.

Because of these objections, the lower-of-cost-or-market rule has undergone some modification and is now qualified in the following respects. If the inventory can probably be sold at prices which will yield a *normal profit,* the inventory should be carried at cost even though current replacement cost is lower. Assume, for example, that merchandise is purchased for $1,000 with the intention of reselling it to customers for $1,500. The replacement cost then declines from $1,000 to $800, but it is believed that the merchandise can still be sold to customers for $1,450. In other words, the normal anticipated profit has shrunk by $50. The carrying value of the inventory could then be written down from $1,000 to $950. There is no justification for reducing the inventory to the replacement cost of $800 under these circumstances.

Another qualification of the lower-of-cost-or-market rule is that inventory should never be carried at an amount greater than *net realizable value,* which may be defined as prospective selling price minus anticipated selling expenses. Assume, for example, that because of unstable market conditions, it is believed that goods acquired at a cost of $500 and having a current replacement cost of $450 will probably have to be sold for no more than $520 and that the selling expenses involved will amount to $120. The inventory should then be reduced to a carrying value (net realizable value) of $400, which is less than current replacement cost.

APPLICATION OF THE LOWER-OF-COST-OR-MARKET RULE The lower of cost or market for inventory is often computed by determining the cost and the market figures for each item in inventory and using the lower of the two amounts in every case. If, for example, item A cost $100 and replacement cost is $90, the item should be priced at $90. If item B cost $200 and replacement cost is $225, this item should be priced at $200. The total cost of the two items is $300 and total replacement cost is $315, but the total inventory value determined by applying the lower-of-cost-or-market rule to each item in inventory is only $290. This application of the lower-of-cost-or-market rule is illustrated by the tabulation shown below.

Application of Lower-of-Cost-or-Market Rule, Item-by-Item Method

	Item	Quantity	Unit Cost		Total Cost		Lower of Cost or Market
			Cost	Market	Cost	Market	
Pricing	A	10	$100	$ 90	$ 1,000	$ 900	$ 900
inventory at lower	B	8	200	225	1,600	1,800	1,600
of cost or	C	50	50	60	2,500	3,000	2,500
market	D	80	90	70	7,200	5,600	5,600
	Totals				$12,300	$11,300	$10,600

If the lower-of-cost-or-market rule is applied item by item, the carrying value of the above inventory would be $10,600. However, an alternative and less rigorous version of the lower-of-cost-or-market rule calls for applying it to the total of the entire inventory rather than to the individual items. If the above inventory is to be valued by applying the lower-of-cost-or-market rule to the total of the inventory, the balance sheet amount for inventory is determined merely by comparing the total cost of $12,300 with the total replacement cost of $11,300 and using the lower of the two figures. Still another alternative method of using the lower-of-cost-or-market concept is to apply it to categories of the inventory rather than item by item. These alternative methods of applying the lower-of-cost-or-market rule are appropriate when no loss of income is anticipated, because the decline in replacement costs of certain goods is fully offset by higher replacement costs for other items.

Gross profit method of estimating inventories

The taking of a physical inventory is a time-consuming and costly job in many lines of business; consequently, a physical inventory may be taken only once a year. Monthly financial statements are needed, however, for intelligent administration of the business, and the preparation of monthly statements requires a determination of the amount of inventory at the end of each month. In many cases this dilemma may be solved satisfactorily by estimating the inventory each month by using the **gross profit method.**

The gross profit method of estimating the inventory is based on the assumption that the rate of gross profit remains approximately the same from year to year. This assumption is a realistic one in many fields of business. The first step in using the gross profit method is to obtain from the ledger the figures for beginning inventory, net purchases, and net sales. **Cost of goods sold is then computed by reducing the sales figure by the usual gross profit rate.** The difference between the cost of goods available for sale and the cost of goods sold represents the estimated ending inventory.

To illustrate, let us assume that the beginning inventory is $25,000, the net purchases of the period $70,000, and the net sales $100,000. The gross profit rate is assumed to have approximated 40% of net sales for the past several years. This information is now assembled in the customary form of an income statement as follows:

Gross profit method ...	*Net sales*	*$100,000* *(100%)*
	Beginning inventory $25,000	
	Net purchases 70,000	
	Cost of goods available for sale $95,000	
	Less: Ending inventory . . . . ?	
	Cost of goods sold	*60,000* *(60%)*
	Gross profit on sales (40% × $100,000)	*$ 40,000* *(40%)*

Customarily, in preparing an income statement, the ending inventory is deducted from the cost of goods available for sale to determine the cost of goods sold. In this case our calculation to determine the ending inventory consists of deducting the estimated cost of goods sold from the cost of goods available for sale.

. . . to estimate ending inventory	*Cost of goods available for sale*	*$95,000*
	Less: Cost of goods sold (60% of $100,000 of sales)	*60,000*
	Ending inventory (estimate)	*$35,000*

The gross profit method of estimating inventory has several uses apart from the preparation of monthly financial statements. This calculation may be used after the taking of a physical inventory to confirm the overall reasonableness of the amount determined by the counting and pricing process. In the event of a fire which destroys the inventory, the approximate amount of goods on hand at the date of the fire may also be computed by the gross profit method.

The retail method of inventory valuation

The retail method of estimating ending inventory is somewhat similar to the gross profit method. It is widely used by chain stores, department stores, and other types of retail business. Goods on sale in retail stores are marked at the retail prices; it is therefore more convenient to take inventory at current retail prices than to look up invoices to find the unit cost of each item in stock. After first determining the value of the inventory at retail price, the next step is to convert the inventory to cost price by applying the ratio prevailing between cost and selling price during the current period. This method of approximating an inventory may also be carried out by using data from the accounts without taking any physical count of the goods on hand. The underlying basis for the *retail method* of inventory valuation is the ratio of cost to selling price for the *current period,* whereas the *gross profit method* of estimating inventory rests on the rate of gross profit experienced in *preceding periods.*

When the retail method of inventory is to be used, it is necessary to maintain records of the beginning inventory and of all purchases during the period in terms of selling price as well as at cost. Goods available for sale during the period can then be stated both at cost and at selling price. By deducting the sales for the period from the sales value of the goods available for sale, the ending inventory at selling price may be determined without the need for a physical count. The ending inventory at selling price is then converted to a cost basis by using the percentage of cost to selling price for the current period.

In practice, the application of this method may be complicated because the originally established sales prices are modified by frequent price markups and markdowns. These frequent changes in retail price present some difficulties in determining the correct rate to use in reducing the inventory from selling price to cost. The following illustration shows the calculation of inventory by the retail method, without going into the complications which would arise from markups and markdowns in the original retail selling price.

	Cost Price	Selling Price
Used by many department stores		
Beginning inventory	$20,000	$30,000
Net purchases during the month	11,950	15,000
Goods available for sale	$31,950	$45,000
Less: Net sales for the month		20,000
Ending inventory at selling price		$25,000
Cost ratio ($31,950 ÷ $45,000)		71%
Ending inventory at cost (71% × $25,000)	$17,750	

Perpetual inventory system

Throughout our discussion thus far we have emphasized the periodic inventory system. Under that system, we have demonstrated that acquisitions of merchandise are recorded by debits to a Purchases account and that no entry is made to record the cost of goods sold at the date of a sales transaction. Under the periodic system, the Inventory account is brought up to date only at the end of the accounting period when all the goods on hand are counted and priced.

However, as explained earlier in Chapter 5, companies which deal in merchandise of high unit cost, such as television sets or outboard motors, find a perpetual inventory system worthwhile and efficient. Since inventory may be one of the largest assets in a business and has a rapid rate of turnover, strong internal control is especially important. A perpetual inventory system can provide the strongest possible internal control over the inventory of merchandise.

The information required for a perpetual inventory system can be processed electronically or manually. In a manual system a subsidiary record card, as shown below, is used for each type of merchandise on hand. If the company has 100 different kinds of products in stock, then 100 inventory record cards will make up the subsidiary inventory record. Shown below is an inventory record card for item XL-2000.

Perpetual inventory record card

Item: XL–2000							Maximum: 20		
Location: Storeroom 2							Minimum: 8		
	PURCHASED			**SOLD**			**BALANCE**		
Date	Units	Unit Cost	Total	Units	Unit Cost	Total	Units	Unit Cost	Balance
Jan. 1							12	$50.00	$600.00
7				2	$50.00	$100.00	10	50.00	500.00
9	10	$55.00	$550.00				10	50.00	
							10	55.00	1,050.00
12				8	50.00	400.00	2	50.00	
							10	55.00	650.00
13				2	50.00	100.00			
				1	55.00	55.00	9	55.00	495.00

On this card, the quantity and cost of units received will be listed at the date of receipt; the quantity and cost of units sold will be recorded at the date of sale; and after each purchase or sales transaction, the balance remaining on hand will be shown. This running balance will be shown in number of units, cost per unit, and total dollar amount.

The information on the illustrated inventory record shows that the first-in, first-out basis of pricing the inventory is being used. After the sale of two units on January 7, the remaining inventory consisted of 10 units at a cost of $50 each. The purchase on January 9 of 10 units carried a unit cost of $55, rather than $50, hence must be accounted for separately. The balance on hand after the January 9 purchase appears on two lines: 10 units at $50 and 10 units at $55. When eight units were sold on January 12, they were treated as coming from the oldest stock on hand and therefore had a cost of $50 each. The balance remaining on hand then consisted of two units at $50 and 10 units at $55. When three units were sold on January 13, the cost consisted of two units at $50 and one unit at $55. The remaining inventory of nine units consists of the most recently acquired units with a cost of $55 each.

Perpetual inventory records may also be maintained on a last-in, first-out basis or on an average-cost basis, but these systems involve some complexities which are considered in advanced accounting courses.

Control over the amount invested in inventory can be strengthened by listing on each inventory card the maximum and minimum quantities that should be kept in stock. By maintaining quantities within these limits, overstocking and out-of-stock situations can be avoided.

GENERAL LEDGER ENTRIES FOR A PERPETUAL INVENTORY SYSTEM The general ledger control account entitled *Inventory* is continuously (perpetually) updated when a perpetual inventory system is in use. This Inventory account controls the many subsidiary record cards discussed above. A continuously updated Cost of Goods Sold account is also maintained in the general ledger.

The purchase of merchandise by a company using a perpetual inventory system requires a journal entry affecting general ledger control accounts as follows:

Inventory *550*
    Accounts Payable, Lake Company *550*
To record purchase of merchandise on credit.

This purchase transaction would also be recorded in the subsidiary ledger (the perpetual inventory cards) showing the quantity of each kind of merchandise purchased. The $550 purchase from Lake Company might affect only one or perhaps a dozen of the subsidiary records, depending on how many types of merchandise were included in this purchase transaction.

For every sales transaction, we can determine the cost of the goods sold by referring to the appropriate perpetual inventory card record.

Therefore, at the time of a sale, we can record both the amount of the selling price and the *cost* of the goods sold, as illustrated in the following pair of related entries.

Accounts Receivable, J. Williams 140
    Sales 140
To record the sale of merchandise on credit.

Cost of Goods Sold 100
    Inventory 100
To record the cost of goods sold and the related
decrease in inventory.

To avoid making a large number of entries in the general journal, a special column can be entered in the Sales Journal to show the cost of the goods involved in each sales transaction. At the end of the month the total of this "Cost" column can be posted as a debit to Cost of Goods Sold and a credit to Inventory.

A company maintaining perpetual inventory records will also conduct a physical count of all merchandise once a year and compare the amount of the physical inventory with the perpetual inventory records. An adjusting entry can be made to bring the inventory records into agreement with the physical inventory. For example, if shoplifting or other factors have caused an inventory shortage, the adjusting entry will consist of a debit to the loss account, Inventory Shortage, and a credit to Inventory.

When a perpetual inventory system is in use, the Inventory account is increased by purchases of merchandise. It is decreased by the cost of goods sold, by purchase returns and allowances, and by purchase discounts. At the end of the year the dollar balances of all the subsidiary inventory record cards should be added to see that the total is in agreement with the general ledger control account. The only adjustment necessary at year-end will be to correct the Inventory control account and the subsidiary records for any discrepancies indicated by the taking of a physical inventory.

The advantages of a perpetual inventory system as indicated in the preceding discussion include:

1 Stronger internal control. By comparing the physical inventory with the perpetual records, management will be made aware of any shortages or errors and can take corrective action.

2 A physical inventory can be taken at dates other than year-end, or it can be taken for different products or different departments at various dates during the year, since the perpetual records always show the amounts which *should* be on hand.

3 Quarterly or monthly financial statements can be prepared more readily because of the availability of dollar amounts for inventory and cost of goods sold in the accounting records.

Inventories for a manufacturing business

A typical manufacturing firm buys raw materials and converts them into a finished product. The raw materials purchased by an aircraft manufacturer, for example, include sheet aluminum, steel, paint, and a variety of electronic gear and control instruments. The completed airplanes assembled from these components are the *finished goods* of the aircraft manufacturer. The terms *raw materials* and *finished goods,* as used in accounting, are defined from the viewpoint of each manufacturing firm. Sheet aluminum, for example, is a raw material from the viewpoint of an aircraft company, but it is a finished product of an aluminum company.

In converting raw materials into finished goods, the manufacturer employs factory labor, uses machinery, and incurs many other manufacturing costs, such as heat, light, and power, machinery repairs, and supervisory salaries. These production costs are added to the cost of raw materials to determine the cost of the finished goods manufactured during any given period. The accounting records of a manufacturing firm must be expanded to include ledger accounts for these various types of factory costs. Financial statements must also be changed to reflect the costs of manufacturing and several new classes of inventories. At any given moment, a manufacturer will have on hand a stock of raw materials, finished goods awaiting shipment and sale, and partially completed products in various stages of manufacture. Inventories of each of these three classes of items must be taken at the end of each accounting period in order to measure the cost of goods that have been completed and the cost of goods sold during the period.

In place of the single inventory account found on the balance sheet of a retail or wholesale business, a manufacturing concern has three separate inventory accounts, all of which are current assets.

1 *Raw materials inventory.* This account represents the unused portion of the raw materials purchased. As a matter of convenience, factory supplies on hand (oil, grease, sweeping compounds) acquired for use in maintaining and servicing the factory building and machinery are often merged with raw materials.

2 *Goods in process inventory.* This inventory consists of the partially completed goods on hand in the factory at year-end. The cost of these partially manufactured goods is determined by estimating the costs of the raw materials, direct labor, and factory overhead associated with these units.

3 *Finished goods inventory.* This account shows the cost of finished goods on hand and awaiting sale to customers as of the end of the year. The cost of these finished units is composed of the factory costs of raw material, direct labor, and factory overhead.

COMPARISON OF INCOME STATEMENTS FOR MANUFACTURING AND MERCHANDISING COMPANIES The treatment of sales, selling expenses, general administrative expenses, and income taxes is the same on the income statement of a manufacturing company as for a merchandising company. The only difference in the two partial income statements shown on page 460 lies in the cost of goods sold section. In the income statement of the manufacturing company, Cost of Finished Goods Manufactured replaces the item labeled Purchases in the income statement of the merchandising company.

MERCHANDISING COMPANY
Partial Income Statement
For the Current Year

Sales		$1,000,000
Cost of goods sold:		
Beginning inventory of merchandise	$300,000	
Purchases	600,000	
Cost of goods available for sale	$900,000	
Less: Ending inventory of merchandise	250,000	
Cost of goods sold		650,000
Gross profit on sales		$ 350,000

MANUFACTURING COMPANY
Partial Income Statement
For the Current Year

Sales		$1,000,000
Cost of goods sold:		
Beginning inventory of finished goods	$300,000	
Cost of finished goods manufactured (Exhibit A)	600,000	
Cost of goods available for sale	$900,000	
Less: Ending inventory of finished goods	250,000	
Cost of goods sold		650,000
Gross profit on sales		$ 350,000

STATEMENT OF COST OF FINISHED GOODS MANUFACTURED The principal new item in the illustrated income statement for a manufacturing company is the item: "Cost of finished goods manufactured . . . $600,000." This amount was determined from the Statement of Cost of Finished Goods Manufactured, a statement prepared to accompany and support the income statement. This statement is illustrated in condensed form on page 461.

Observe that the final amount of $600,000 on the statement of cost of finished goods manufactured (page 461) is carried forward to the income statement and is used in determining the cost of goods sold, as illustrated in the income statement for the manufacturing company.

MANUFACTURING COMPANY		**Exhibit A**
Statement of Cost of Finished Goods Manufactured		
For the Current Year		

Goods in process inventory, beginning of year		$ 70,000
Raw materials used:		
Beginning raw materials inventory	$ 50,000	
Purchases of raw materials	$100,000	
Less: Purchase returns and allowances	3,000 97,000	
Transportation-in	5,000	
Cost of raw materials available for use	$152,000	
Less: Ending raw materials inventory	42,000	
Cost of raw materials used	$110,000	
Direct labor	230,000	
Factory overhead (detail omitted)	250,000	
Total manufacturing costs		590,000
Total cost of goods in process during the year		$660,000
Less: Goods in process inventory, end of year		60,000
Cost of finished goods manufactured		$600,000

PREPARING A STATEMENT OF COST OF FINISHED GOODS MANUFACTURED

The following steps briefly describe the preparation of a statement of cost of finished goods manufactured:

1 The starting point of the statement is the cost of goods in process at the beginning of the period. These items represent *partially* completed goods.

2 To complete the goods in process and to manufacture more goods a company incurs **manufacturing costs,** consisting of **raw materials used, direct labor,** and **factory overhead.**

3 The sum of the cost of goods in process at the beginning of the period plus the total manufacturing costs represents the **total cost of goods in process during the period.** However, not all the goods in process during the period are finished and available for sale at year-end.

4 To determine the **cost of finished goods manufactured** during the period, it is necessary to subtract the cost of goods still in process at the end of the period from the total cost of goods in process during the period.

The accounting procedures for a manufacturing business are discussed thoroughly in courses on cost accounting.

KEY TERMS INTRODUCED OR EMPHASIZED IN CHAPTER 11

Average-cost method A method of inventory valuation. Weighted-average unit cost is computed by dividing the total cost of goods available for sale by the number of units available for sale.

Consistency in inventory valuation An accounting standard that calls for the use of the same method of inventory pricing from year to year, with full disclosure of the effects of any change in method. Intended to make financial statements comparable.

Cost of inventory The price paid for the inventory plus the costs of bringing the goods to the point where they are offered for sale.

Direct labor Labor costs which can be directly associated with manufacturing items for inclusion in inventory. These costs become part of the cost of the completed inventory items.

Factory overhead All manufacturing costs other than the costs of raw materials used and direct labor. Examples include the cost of factory utilities and repairs to factory equipment.

First-in, first-out (fifo) A method of computing the cost of inventory and the cost of goods sold based on the assumption that the first merchandise acquired is the first merchandise sold, and that the ending inventory consists of the most recently acquired goods.

F.O.B. destination A term meaning the seller bears the cost of shipping goods to the buyer's location. Title to the goods remains with the seller while the goods are in transit.

F.O.B. shipping point The buyer of goods bears the cost of transportation from the seller's location to the buyer's location. Title to the goods passes at the point of shipment and the goods are the property of the buyer while in transit.

Gross profit method A method of estimating the cost of the ending inventory based on the assumption that the rate of gross profit remains approximately the same from year to year.

Inventory Goods acquired or produced for sale in the regular operation of a business. Goods in which a business deals.

Inventory profits The amount by which the cost of replacing goods sold (computed at the date of sale) *exceeds* the reported cost of goods sold. Many accountants consider inventory profits to be a "fictitious" profit, because this amount usually must be reinvested in inventories and therefore is not available for distribution to stockholders.

Last-in, first-out (lifo) method A method of computing the cost of goods sold by use of the prices paid for the most recently acquired units. Ending inventory is valued on the basis of prices paid for the units first acquired.

Lower-of-cost-or-market method A method of inventory pricing in which goods are valued at original cost or replacement cost (market), whichever is lower.

Manufacturing costs The costs incurred by a manufacturing business in manufacturing its products. Manufacturing costs consist of the costs of raw materials used, direct labor, and factory overhead.

Net realizable value The prospective selling price minus anticipated selling expenses. Inventory should not be carried at more than net realizable value.

Perpetual inventory system Provides a continuous (perpetual) running record of the goods on hand. As goods are sold their cost is transferred to a Cost of Goods Sold account.

Physical inventory A systematic count of all goods on hand, followed by the application of unit prices to the quantities counted and development of a dollar value for ending inventory.

Retail method A method of estimating inventory in a retail store based on the assumption that the cost of goods on hand bears the same percentage relationship to retail prices as does the cost of all goods available for sale to the original retail prices. Inventory is first priced at retail and then converted to cost by application of a cost-to-retail percentage.

Specific identification method A method of pricing inventory by identifying the units in the ending inventory as coming from specific purchases.

Statement of cost of finished goods manufactured A financial statement prepared by a manufacturing business to support the computation of the cost of goods sold in the income statement. Shows the manufacturing costs incurred in the production of finished goods during the period.

DEMONSTRATION PROBLEM FOR YOUR REVIEW

The operating results (ignoring income taxes) achieved by Bond Company for the years ended December 31, Year 6 and Year 7, are summarized as follows:

Net sales	$760,000	$710,000
Cost of goods sold:		
Beginning inventory	$253,040	$240,000
Net purchases	426,960	409,326
Cost of goods available for sale	$680,000	$649,326
Ending inventory	260,000	253,040
Cost of goods sold	$420,000	$396,286
Gross profit on sales	$340,000	$313,714
Expenses	180,000	143,714
Net income	$160,000	$170,000

The balance sheets of the company showed retained earnings as follows: December 31, Year 5, $300,000; December 31, Year 6, $370,000; and December 31, Year 7, $410,000.

Other data In December, Year 7, Jim Klein, accountant for the Bond Company, decided to make a careful review of the documents and procedures which had been used in taking the physical inventory at December 31, Year 6. Klein felt that this review might disclose errors which still required correction or, at least, should be given consideration to assure maximum accuracy in the taking of the next annual physical inventory. Klein's investigation disclosed three questionable items which are described below. No adjustment or correction of any kind was made for these possible errors prior to preparing the Year 7 income statement.

(1) Merchandise costing $9,840, which had been received on December 31, Year 6, had been included in the inventory taken on that date, although the purchase was not recorded until January 4, when the vendor's invoice arrived. The invoice was then recorded in the purchases journal as a January transaction.

(2) Merchandise shipped to a customer on December 31, Year 6, F.O.B. shipping point, was included in the physical inventory taken that day. The cost of the merchandise was $2,600 and the sales price was $3,600. Because of the press of year-end work, the sales invoice was not prepared until January 6, Year 7. On that date the sale was recorded as a January transaction by entry in the sales journal, and the sales invoice was mailed to the customer.

(3) An error of $2,000 had been made in footing one of the inventory sheets at December 31, Year 6. This clerical error had caused the inventory total to be overstated.

Instructions
a Prepare corrected income statements for the years ended December 31, Year 6 and Year 7. It may be helpful to set up T accounts for Sales, Year 6; Sales, Year

7; Purchases, Year 6; Purchases, Year 7; and Inventory, December 31, Year 6. Corrections may then be entered in these accounts. Ignore income taxes.

b Compute corrected amounts for retained earnings at December 31, Year 6 and Year 7.

c Prepare any correcting journal entries that you consider should have been made at December 12, Year 7, the date these items came to Klein's attention. Any items relating to the net income for Year 6 should be entered in the Retained Earnings account.

d Assume that the $9,840 worth of merchandise described in item (1) had not been included in inventory on December 31, Year 6. Would this handling of the transaction have caused an error in the cost of goods sold for Year 6?

SOLUTION TO DEMONSTRATION PROBLEM

a

BOND COMPANY

Income Statement

For the Years Ended December 31, Year 6 and Year 7

	Year 7	Year 6
Net sales ($3,600 represents sales of Year 6, not Year 7)	$756,400	$713,600
Cost of goods sold:		
Beginning inventory	$248,440 (2)	$240,000
Net purchases	417,120 (3)	419,166 (1)
Cost of goods available for sale	$665,560	$659,166
Ending inventory	260,000	248,440 (2)
Cost of goods sold	$405,560	$410,726
Gross profit on sales	$350,840	$302,874
Expenses	180,000	143,714
Net income	$170,840	$159,160

(1) $409,326 + $9,840 = $419,166
(2) $253,040 − $2,600 − $2,000 = $248,440
(3) $426,960 − $9,840 = $417,120

b

Retained earnings, Dec. 31, Year 5	$300,000
Add: Corrected net income for Year 6	159,160
Less: Dividends for Year 6 (see note below)	(100,000)
Retained earnings as corrected, Dec. 31, Year 6	$359,160
Add: Corrected net income for Year 7	170,840
Less: Dividends for Year 7 ($370,000 + $160,000 − $410,000)	(120,000)
Retained earnings as corrected, Dec. 31, Year 7	$410,000

Note: The amount of dividends declared in Year 6 is determined as follows: Retained earnings on December 31, Year 5, $300,000 plus net income for Year 6 as reported, $170,000, less retained earnings at the end of Year 6, $370,000. The difference, $100,000, represents dividends declared. Similar calculations for Year 7 indicate dividends declared of $120,000.

The errors counterbalanced between Years 6 and 7; therefore, the amount of retained earnings reported at Dec. 31, Year 7, $410,000, was correct.

c   *Correcting Journal Entry*

Year 7

Dec. 12 Sales *3,600*

  Retained Earnings *10,840*

   Purchases *9,840*

   Inventory, Dec. 31, Year 6 ($2,600 + $2,000) *4,600*

  To correct errors in cutoff of sales and purchases at

  Dec. 31, Year 6, and to correct clerical error in

  compiling physical inventory on that date.

d No. If the $9,840 worth of merchandise described in item (*1*) had not been included in inventory on December 31, Year 6, the error of not including the goods in inventory would have offset the error of failing to record the purchase, with no net effect on cost of goods sold for Year 6. However, the current ratio and other balance sheet relationships would have been slightly distorted through understatement of $9,840, both in inventory and in accounts payable.

REVIEW QUESTIONS

1 Which of the seven items listed below are used in computing the *cost of goods available for sale?*

  a Ending inventory   **e** Transportation-in
  b Sales   **f** Purchase returns and allowances
  c Beginning inventory   **g** Delivery expense
  d Purchases

2 Through an error in counting of merchandise at December 31, Year 4, the Trophy Company overstated the amount of goods on hand by $8,000. Assuming that the error was not discovered, what was the effect upon net income for Year 4? Upon the owners' equity at December 31, Year 4? Upon the net income for Year 5? Upon the owners' equity at December 31, Year 5?

3 Is the establishment of an appropriate valuation for the merchandise inventory at the end of the year more important in producing a dependable income statement, or in producing a dependable balance sheet?

4 Explain the meaning of the term *physical inventory.*

5 Near the end of December, Hadley Company received a large order from a major customer. The work of packing the goods for shipment was begun at once but could not be completed before the close of business on December 31. Since a written order from the customer was on hand and the goods were nearly all packed and ready for shipment, Hadley felt that this merchandise should not be included in the physical inventory taken on December 31. Do you agree? What is probably the reason behind Hadley's opinion?

6 During a prolonged period of rising prices, will the fifo or lifo method of inventory valuation result in higher reported profits?

7 Throughout several years of strongly rising prices, Company A used the lifo method of inventory valuation and Company B used the fifo method. In which company would the balance sheet figure for inventory be closer to current replacement cost of the merchandise on hand? Why?

8 You are making a detailed analysis of the financial statements and accounting records of two companies in the same industry, Adams Corporation and Bar Corporation. Price levels have been rising steadily for several years. In the course of your investigation, you observe that the inventory value shown on the Adams Corporation balance sheet is quite close to the current replacement cost of the merchandise on hand. However, for Bar Corporation, the carrying value of the inventory is far below current replacement cost. What method of inventory valuation is probably used by Adams Corporation? By Bar Corporation? If we assume that the two companies are identical except for the inventory valuation method used, which company has probably been reporting higher net income in recent years?

9 Why do some accountants consider a portion of the income reported by businesses during a period of rising prices to be "fictitious profits"?

10 Assume that a business uses the first-in, first-out method of accounting for inventories during a prolonged period of inflation and that the business pays dividends equal to the amount of reported net income. Suggest a problem that may arise in continued successful operation of the business. What does this situation have to do with "inventory profits"?

11 The Securities and Exchange Commission requires large corporations to disclose the cost of replacing their inventories and to disclose what their cost of goods sold would be if computed by using replacement costs. Do you think this policy indicates that corporate profits have tended to be overstated or understated in recent years? Explain.

12 One of the items in the inventory of Grayline Stores is marked for sale at $125. The purchase invoice shows the item cost $95, but a newly issued price list from the manufacturer shows the present replacement cost to be $90. What inventory valuation should be assigned to this item if Grayline Stores follows the lower-of-cost-or-market rule?

13 Explain the meaning of the term *market* as used in the expression "lower of cost or market."

14 Explain the usefulness of the *gross profit method* of estimating inventories.

15 A store using the *retail inventory method* takes its physical inventory by applying current retail prices as marked on the merchandise to the quantities counted. Does this procedure indicate that the inventory will appear in the financial statements at retail selling price? Explain.

16 Estimate the ending inventory by the gross profit method, given the following data: beginning inventory $40,000, net purchases $100,000, net sales $106,667, average gross profit rate 25% of net sales.

17 Summarize the difference between the *periodic system* and the *perpetual system* of accounting for inventory. Which system would usually cost more to maintain? Which system would be most practicable for a restaurant, a retail drugstore, a new car dealer?

18 Identify each of the four statements shown below as true or false. In the accounting records of a company using a perpetual inventory system:

a The Inventory account will ordinarily remain unchanged until the end of an accounting period.

b The Cost of Goods Sold account is debited with the sales price of merchandise sold.

c The Inventory account and the Cost of Goods Sold account will both normally have debit balances.

d The Inventory account and the Cost of Goods Sold account will normally have equal but offsetting balances.

19 What are the three basic types of *manufacturing costs?*

20 Distinguish between *total manufacturing costs* and the *cost of finished goods manufactured.*

EXERCISES

Ex. 11-1 The condensed income statements prepared by Blaze Company for two years are shown below:

Sales	$183,400	$168,000
Cost of goods sold	106,400	134,400
Gross profit on sales	$ 77,000	$ 33,600
Operating expenses	28,000	28,000
Net income	$ 49,000	$ 5,600

The inventory at the end of Year 1 was understated by $16,800, but the error was not discovered until after the accounts had been closed and financial statements prepared at the end of Year 2. The balance sheets for the two years showed owners' equity of $71,400 at the end of Year 1 and $86,800 at the end of Year 2.

Compute the correct net income figures for Year 1 and Year 2 and the gross profit percentage for each year based on corrected data. What correction, if any, should be made in owners' equity at the end of Year 1 and at the end of Year 2?

Ex. 11-2 The beginning inventory balance of item X on January 1 and the purchases of this item during the current year were as follows:

Jan. 1	Beginning inventory	500 units @ $10.00	$ 5,000
Feb. 23	Purchase	1,600 units @ $11.00	17,600
Apr. 20	Purchase	1,000 units @ $11.20	11,200
May 4	Purchase	1,000 units @ $11.60	11,600
Nov. 30	Purchase	400 units @ $12.50	5,000
Totals	. . . .	4,500 units	$50,400

At December 31 the ending inventory consisted of 675 units.

Determine the cost of the ending inventory, based on each of the following methods of inventory valuation:

a Average cost
b First-in, first-out
c Last-in, first-out

Ex. 11-3 Marantz Corporation sells only one product; sales and purchases occur at a uniform rate throughout the year. The following items appear in the company's financial statements for Year 4:

Purchases	$2,000,000
Cost of goods sold	1,900,000
Inventory, Jan. 1, Year 4 (fifo basis)	520,000
Inventory, Dec. 31, Year 4 (fifo basis)	620,000

A footnote to the financial statements disclosed that the replacement cost of inventory at December 31, Year 4, was $650,000 and that the cost of goods sold computed using replacement costs at the date of sale amounted to $2,150,000.

a Compute the amount of inventory profit included in Marantz Corporation's reported operating results for Year 4.

b Did the number of units in Marantz Corporation's inventory increase or decrease during Year 4? Explain your reasoning.

Ex. 11-4 Ruger Company has compiled the following information concerning items in its inventory at December 31:

		Unit Cost	
Item	Quantity	Cost (fifo)	Market
A	120	$ 46	$ 50
B	70	160	136
C	62	100	110
D	81	280	290

Determine the total inventory value to appear on Ruger Company's balance sheet under the lower-of-cost-or-market rule, assuming (**a**) that the rule is applied to inventory as a whole and (**b**) that the rule is applied on an item-by-item basis.

Ex. 11-5 When Ellen Sharp arrived at her store on the morning of May 29, she found empty shelves and display racks; thieves had broken in during the night and stolen the entire inventory. Sharp's accounting record showed that she had $48,000 inventory on May 1 (cost value). From May 1 to May 29, she had made sales of $192,000 and purchases of $151,200. The gross profit during the past several years had consistently averaged 30% of sales. Sharp wishes to file an insurance claim for the theft loss. What is the estimated cost of her inventory at the time of the theft? Show computations.

Ex. 11-6 Vagabond Shop wishes to determine the approximate month-end inventory using data from the accounting records without taking a physical count of merchandise on hand. From the following information, estimate the cost of the September 30 inventory by the retail method of inventory valuation.

	Cost Price	Selling Price
Inventory of merchandise, Aug. 31	$264,800	$400,000
Purchases (net) during September	170,400	240,000
Sales (net) during September		275,200

Ex. 11-7 Santa Cruz Wholesale Company uses a **perpetual inventory system.** On January 1, the Inventory account had a balance of $87,500. During the first few days of January the following transactions occurred.
Jan. 2 Purchased merchandise on credit from Bell Company for $12,500.
Jan. 3 Sold merchandise for cash, $9,000. The cost of this merchandise was $6,300.
a Prepare entries in general journal form to record the above transactions.
b What was the balance of the Inventory account at the close of business January 3?

Ex. 11-8 The records of the Scott Mfg. Co. include the following information:

	July 1	July 31
Raw materials inventory	$19,000	$24,000
Goods in process inventory	8,000	7,500
Finished goods inventory, July 1 (2,000 units)	38,000	
Purchases of raw materials in July		57,000
Direct labor cost for July		79,000
Factory overhead costs for July		48,500

During July 9,000 units were produced and 8,000 units were sold.

Instructions
a Prepare a statement of cost of finished goods manufactured for July.
b Compute the cost of producing a single unit during July.
c Compute the cost of goods sold during July, assuming that the first-in, first-out method of inventory costing is used.
d Compute the finished goods inventory at July 31, assuming that the first-in, first-out method of inventory costing is used.

PROBLEMS

11-1 Fantasy Ventures is being offered for sale as a going concern. Its income statements for the last three years include the following key figures.

	Year 3	Year 2	Year 1
Net sales.	$390,000	$375,000	$360,000
Cost of goods sold	253,500	255,000	252,000
Gross profit on sales	$136,500	$120,000	$108,000
Gross profit percentage	35%	32%	30%

In discussions with prospective buyers, the owners are emphasizing the rising trends of gross profit and gross profit percentage as very favorable factors.
Assume that you are retained by a prospective purchaser of the business to make an investigation of the fairness and reliability of Fantasy Ventures' accounting records and financial statements. You find everything in order except for the following: (1) The inventory was understated by $7,500 at the end of Year 1 and (2) it was overstated by $27,300 at the end of Year 3. The company uses the periodic inventory system and these errors had not been brought to light prior to your investigation.

Instructions
a Prepare a revised three-year schedule along the lines of the one illustrated above.
b Comment on the trend of gross profit and gross profit percentage before and after the revision.

11-2 Information relating to the inventory quantities, purchases, and sales of item KG200 by Palisades Corporation during Year 4 is shown below:

	Number of Units	Cost per Unit	Total Cost
Inventory, Jan. 1, Year 4	8,000	$5.89	$ 47,120
First purchase (Mar. 15)	10,300	6.20	63,860
Second purchase (June 6)	12,400	6.60	81,840
Third purchase (Sept. 20)	9,600	6.80	65,280
Fourth purchase (Dec. 31)	7,700	7.00	53,900
Goods available for sale . . . :	48,000		$312,000
Units sold during Year 4	37,200		
Inventory, Dec. 31, Year 4	10,800		

Instructions
a Compute the cost of the December 31, Year 4, inventory and the cost of goods sold for item KG200 in Year 4 using:
(1) The first-in, first-out method
(2) The last-in, first-out method
(3) The weighted-average method

b Which of the three inventory pricing methods provides the most realistic balance sheet valuation of inventory in light of the current replacement cost of item KG200? Does this same method also produce the most realistic measure of income in light of the costs being incurred by Palisades Corporation to replace units of KG200 when they are sold? Explain.

11-3 Rotor Corporation specializes in the sale of a single product. During Year 9, 106,000 units were sold for a total price of $800,000. The inventory at January 1, Year 9, consisted of 9,100 units valued at cost of $36,400. Purchases during the year were as follows: 20,000 units @ $4.10; 30,000 units @ $4.25; 50,000 units @ $4.60; and 10,900 units @ $5.00.

Instructions
a Compute the December 31, Year 9, inventory using:
  (1) The first-in, first-out method
  (2) The last-in, first-out method
  (3) The weighted-average method
b Prepare partial income statements for each of the above three methods of pricing inventory. The income statements are to be carried only to the determination of gross profit on sales.
c Which of the three methods of pricing inventory would be most advantageous from an income tax standpoint during a period of rising prices? Comment on the significance of the inventory figure under the method you recommend with respect to current replacement cost.

11-4 On May 15, Year 4, an early morning fire destroyed the entire inventory of Suburban Associates. The inventory was stored in a rented warehouse; the offices occupied by the company were not damaged and the accounting records were intact. Suburban Associates did not maintain perpetual inventory records, and the last physical inventory taken had been on December 31 of the prior year.

An estimate of the inventory value at May 15, the date of the fire, must be prepared in order to file an insurance claim. The following income statement for the prior year is available to aid you in estimating the amount of the inventory at the date of the fire.

SUBURBAN ASSOCIATES

Income Statement

For the Year Ended December 31, Year 3

Net sales		$740,000
Cost of goods sold:		
Inventory, Jan. 1	$144,000	
Purchases	520,000	
Cost of goods available for sale	$664,000	
Less: Inventory, Dec. 31	163,000	501,000
Gross profit on sales		$239,000
Expenses		149,000
Net income		$ 90,000

Other data Included in the purchases figure shown in the income statement was $12,600 of office equipment which Suburban Associates had acquired late in December for its own use from a competing concern which was quitting business. The bookkeeper of Suburban Associates had not understood the nature of this transaction and had recorded it by debiting the Purchases account. The office equipment, however, was not included in the inventory at December 31, Year 3.

The accounting records revealed the merchandise transactions from December 31, Year 3, to the date of the fire to be: sales, $306,000; sales returns and allowances, $2,700; transportation-in, $1,800; purchases, $196,200; purchase returns and allowances, $3,600.

Instructions

a Prepare a report directed to the insurance adjuster summarizing your findings. Include an estimate of the inventory value as of the date of the fire and a computation of the applicable gross profit rate.

b Explain how the gross profit method of estimating inventories may be used other than in case of a fire loss.

c Is the rate of gross profit customarily computed as a percentage of the cost of goods sold or as a percentage of sales? Show how the gross profit rate in this problem would vary if based on cost of goods sold rather than on sales.

11-5 Income statements prepared by Sunflower Paints for Year 4 and Year 5 are shown below.

	Year 5	Year 4
Net sales	$630,000	$594,000
Cost of goods sold:		
Beginning inventory	$227,736	$216,000
Net purchases	384,264	368,393
Cost of goods available for sale	$612,000	$584,393
Ending inventory	234,000	227,736
Cost of goods sold	$378,000	$356,657
Gross profit on sales	$252,000	$237,343
Expenses	90,000	81,000
Net income	$162,000	$156,343

The owners' equity as shown in the company's balance sheet was as follows: December 31, Year 3, $180,000; December 31, Year 4, $336,343; and December 31, Year 5, $498,343.

Early in Year 6, Alan Frank, accountant for Sunflower Paints, made a review of the documents and procedures used in taking the physical inventory at December 31 for both Year 4 and Year 5. This investigation disclosed the two questionable items listed below:

(1) Merchandise shipped to a customer on December 31, Year 4, F.O.B. shipping point, was included in the physical inventory taken that date. The cost of the merchandise was $2,610 and the sales price was $3,240. Because of the press of year-end work, the sales invoice was not prepared until January 6, Year 5. On that date the sale was recorded as a January transaction by entry in the sales journal, and the sales invoice mailed to the customer.

(2) Merchandise costing $6,156, which had been received on December 31, Year 4, had been included in the inventory taken on that date, although the purchase was not recorded until January 8 when the vendor's invoice arrived. The invoice was then recorded in the purchases journal as a January transaction.

Instructions

a Prepare corrected income statements for the years ended December 31, Year 4 and Year 5. (Show computations for corrected figures for Sales, Year 4, and Sales, Year 5; Purchases, Year 4, and Purchases, Year 5; and Inventory, December 31, Year 4.)

b Compute corrected amounts for owners' equity at December 31, Year 4 and Year 5.

11-6 Toy Castle, a retail business, had net sales during January of $32,600. Purchases of merchandise from suppliers during January amounted to $20,620. Of these January purchases, invoices totaling $13,620 were paid during the month; the remaining January invoices totaling $7,000 were still unpaid at January 31. The merchandise purchased during January had a retail sales value of $29,500.

On January 1 the merchandise on hand represented a cost of $21,200 as determined by the year-end physical inventory. The retail sales value of this inventory was $32,000. The retail selling price was plainly marked on every item of merchandise in the store.

At January 31 the manager of Toy Castle wished to estimate the cost of inventory on hand without taking time to count the merchandise and look up the cost prices as shown on purchase invoices.

Instructions

a Use the retail inventory method to estimate the cost of the inventory at January 31.

b What effect, if any, does the fact that January purchase invoices in the amount of $7,000 were unpaid at January 31 have upon the determination of the amount of inventory at January 31?

11-7 Porterfield's, a retail store, carries a wide range of merchandise consisting mostly of articles of low unit price. The selling price of each item is plainly marked on the merchandise. At each year-end, the company has taken a physical count of goods on hand and has priced these goods at cost by looking up individual purchase invoices to determine the unit cost of each item in stock. Stevens, the store manager, is anxious to find a more economical method of assigning dollar values to the year-end inventory, explaining that it takes much more time to price the inventory than to count the merchandise on hand.

By analyzing the accounting records you are able to determine that the sales of Year 4 amounted to $1,625,000. During the year, net purchases of merchandise totaled $1,330,000; the retail selling price of this merchandise was $1,750,000. At the end of Year 4, a physical inventory showed goods on hand priced to sell at $375,000. This represented a considerable increase over the inventory of a year earlier. At December 31, Year 3, the inventory on hand had appeared in the balance sheet at cost of $170,000, although it had a retail value of $250,000.

Instructions

a Outline a plan whereby the inventory can be computed without the necessity of looking up individual purchase invoices. List step by step the procedures to be followed. Ignore the possibility of markups and markdowns in the original retail price of merchandise.

b Compute the cost of the inventory at December 31, Year 4, using the method described in *a.*

c Explain how the adoption of the inventory method you have described would facilitate the preparation of monthly financial statements.

11-8 Oaktree Wholesale Company uses a perpetual inventory system, including a perpetual inventory record card for each of the 60 types of products it keeps in stock. The following transactions show the purchases and sales of one of these products (XK3) during September.

Sept.			
1	*Balance on hand, 50 units, cost $60 each*		*$3,000*
4	*Purchase, 20 units, cost $65 each*		*1,300*
8	*Sale, 35 units, sales price $100 each*		*3,500*
9	*Purchase, 40 units, cost $65 each*		*2,600*
20	*Sale, 60 units, sales price $100 each*		*6,000*
25	*Purchase, 40 units, cost, $70 each*		*2,800*
30	*Sale, 5 units, sales price $110 each*		*550*

Instructions

a Record the beginning inventory, the purchases, the cost of goods sold, and the running balance on an inventory record card like the one illustrated on page 456. Use the first-in, first-out method.

b Assume that all sales were made on credit. Compute the total sales and total cost of goods sold of product XK3 for September. Prepare an entry in general journal form to record these sales and a second entry to record the cost of goods sold for September.

c Compute the gross profit on sales of product XK3 for the month of September.

11-9 The following information was taken from the accounting records of Solar Manufacturing Company for the month of February, Year 7.

	Feb. 28	Feb. 1
Inventories:		
Raw materials	$159,700	$174,300
Goods in process	32,400	41,400
Finished goods	554,200	643,400

	Month of February
Purchases of raw materials	$251,400
Transportation-in on raw materials	5,600
Factory overhead	163,200
Direct labor	217,600
Selling expenses	177,200
Raw material purchase discounts	4,600
Raw material purchase returns	4,800
General expenses	203,600
Income taxes	90,000

Instructions

a Prepare a statement of cost of finished goods manufactured for the month of February.

b Prepare a schedule showing the cost of goods sold for the month of February.

BUSINESS DECISION PROBLEM 11

You are the sales manager of Import Motors, an automobile dealership specializing in European imports. Among the automobiles in Import Motors' showroom are two Italian sports cars, which are identical in every respect except for color; one is red and the other white. The red car had been ordered last February, at a cost of $6,300 American dollars. The white car had been ordered early last March, but because of a revaluation of the Italian lira relative to the dollar, the white car had cost only $5,850 American dollars. Both cars arrived in the United States on the same boat and had just been delivered to your showroom. Since the cars were identical except for color and both colors were equally popular, you had listed both cars at the same suggested retail price, $9,000.

Paul Davis, one of your best salesmen, comes into your office with a proposal. He has a customer in the showroom who wants to buy the red car for $9,000. However, when Davis pulled the inventory card on the red car to see what options were included, he happened to notice the inventory card of the white car. Import Motors, like most automobile dealerships, uses the specific identification method to value inventory. Consequently, Davis noticed that the red car had cost $6,300, while the white one had cost Import Motors only $5,850. This gave Davis the idea for the following proposal.

"If I sell the red car for $9,000, Import Motors makes a gross profit of $2,700. But if you'll let me discount that white car $150, I think I can get my customer to buy that one instead. If I sell the white car for $8,850, the gross profit will be $3,000, so Import Motors is $300 better off than if I sell the red car for $9,000. Since I came up with this plan, I feel I should get part of the benefit, so Import Motors should split the extra $300 with me. That way, I'll get an extra $150 commission, and the company still makes $150 more than if I sell the red car."

Instructions

a Prepare a schedule which shows the total revenue, cost of goods sold, and gross profit to Import Motors if *both* cars are sold for $9,000 each.

b Prepare a schedule showing the revenue, cost of goods sold, and gross profit to Import Motors if both cars are sold but Davis's plan is adopted and the white car is sold for $8,850. Assume the red car is still sold for $9,000. To simplify comparison of this schedule to the one prepared in part *a,* include the extra $150 commission to Davis in the cost of goods sold of the part *b* schedule.

c Write out your decision whether or not to accept Davis's proposal, and explain to Davis why the proposal either would or would not be to the advantage of Import Motors. (*Hint:* Refer to your schedules prepared in parts *a* and *b* in your explanation.)

12

Plant and Equipment, Depreciation, Natural Resources, and Intangible Assets

PLANT AND EQUIPMENT

The term **plant and equipment** is used to describe long-lived assets acquired for use in the operation of the business and not intended for resale to customers. Among the more common examples are land, buildings, machinery, furniture and fixtures, office equipment, and automobiles. A delivery truck in the showroom of an automobile dealer is inventory; when this same truck is sold to a drugstore for use in making deliveries to customers, it becomes a unit of plant and equipment.

The term **fixed assets** has long been used in accounting literature to describe all types of plant and equipment. This term, however, has virtually disappeared from the published financial statements of large corporations. **Plant and equipment** appears to be a more descriptive term. Another alternative title used on many corporation balance sheets is **property, plant, and equipment.**

Plant and equipment represent bundles of services to be received

It is convenient to think of a plant asset as a bundle of services to be received by the owner over a period of years. Ownership of a delivery truck, for example, may provide about 100,000 miles of transportation. The cost of the delivery truck is customarily entered in a plant and equipment account entitled Delivery Truck, which in essence represents payment in advance for several years of transportation service. Similarly, a building may be regarded as payment in advance for several years' supply of housing services. As the years go by, these services are utilized by the business and the cost of the plant asset is gradually transferred into depreciation expense.

An awareness of the similarity between plant assets and prepaid expenses is essential to an understanding of the accounting process by which the cost of plant assets is allocated to the years in which the benefits of ownership are received.

Major categories of plant and equipment

Plant and equipment items are often classified into one of the following groups:

1 Tangible plant assets. The term *tangible* denotes physical substance, as exemplified by land, a building, or a machine. This category may be subdivided into two distinct classifications:
  a Plant property subject to depreciation; included are plant assets of limited useful life such as buildings and office equipment.
  b Land. The only plant asset not subject to depreciation is land, which has an unlimited term of existence.
2 Intangible assets. Examples are patents, copyrights, trademarks, franchises, organization costs, leaseholds, and goodwill. Current assets such as accounts receivable or prepaid rent are not included in the intangible classification, even though they are lacking in physical substance. The term *intangible assets* is used to describe assets which are used in the operation of the business but have no physical substance, and are noncurrent.

Accounting problems relating to plant and equipment

Some major accounting problems relating to plant and equipment are indicated by the following questions:

1 How is the cost of plant and equipment determined?
2 How should the costs of plant and equipment be allocated against revenue?
3 How should expenditures for repairs and maintenance be treated?
4 How does inflation affect the measurement of depreciation expense?
5 Should financial statements include disclosure of depreciation computed on the basis of replacement cost?
6 How should disposal of plant assets be recorded?

We are presently concerned with answering the first of these questions; an understanding of how the cost of plant and equipment is determined will be helpful in subsequent study of depreciation.

Determining the cost of plant and equipment

The cost of plant and equipment includes all expenditures reasonable and necessary in acquiring the asset and placing it in a position and condition for use in the operations of the business. Only *reasonable* and *necessary* expenditures should be included. For example, if the company's truck driver receives a traffic ticket while hauling a new machine to the plant, the traffic fine is *not* part of the cost of the new machine. If the machine is dropped and damaged while being unloaded, the cost of repairing the damage should be recognized as expense in the current period and should *not* be added to the cost of the machine.

Cost is most easily determined when an asset is purchased for cash. The cost of the asset is then equal to the cash outlay necessary in acquiring the asset plus any expenditures for freight, insurance while in transit, installation, trial runs, and any other costs necessary to make *the asset ready for use.* If plant assets are purchased on the installment plan or by issuance of notes payable, the interest element or carrying charge should be recorded as interest expense and not as part of the cost of the plant assets.

This principle of including in the cost of a plant asset all the incidental charges necessary to put the asset in use is illustrated by the following example. A factory in Minneapolis orders a machine from a San Francisco tool manufacturer at a list price of $10,000, with terms of 2/10, n/30. A sales tax of 6% must be paid, also freight charges of $1,250. Transportation from the railroad station to the factory costs $150, and installation labor amounts to $400. The cost of the machine to be entered in the Machinery account is computed as follows:

Items	*List price of machine*	*$10,000*
included in	*Less: Cash discount (2% × $10,000)*	*200*
cost of		
machine	*Net cash price*	*$ 9,800*
	Sales tax (6% × $9,800)	*588*
	Freight	*1,250*
	Transportation from railroad station to factory.	*150*
	Installation labor	*400*
	Cost of machine	*$12,188*

Why should all the incidental charges relating to the acquisition of a machine be included in its cost? Why not treat these incidental charges as expenses of the period in which the machine is acquired?

The answer is to be found in the basic accounting principle of *matching costs and revenue.* The benefits of owning the machine will be received over a span of years, 10 years, for example. During those 10 years the operation of the machine will contribute to revenue. Consequently, the total costs of the machine should be recorded in the accounts as an asset and allocated against the revenue of the 10 years. All costs incurred in acquiring the machine are costs of the services to be received from using the machine.

LAND When land is purchased, various incidental costs are generally incurred, in addition to the purchase price. These additional costs may include commissions to real estate brokers, escrow fees, legal fees for examining and insuring the title, delinquent taxes paid by the purchaser, and fees for surveying, draining, clearing, grading, and landscaping the property. All these expenditures are part of the cost of the land. Special assessments for local improvements, such as the paving of a street or the installation of sewers, should also be charged to the Land account, for the reason that a more or less permanent value is being added to the land.

Apportionment of a lump-sum purchase Separate ledger accounts are necessary for land and buildings, because buildings are subject to depreciation and land is not. The treatment of land as a nondepreciable asset is based on the premise that land used as a building site has an unlimited life. When land and building are purchased for a lump sum, the purchase price must be apportioned between the land and the building. An appraisal may be necessary for this purpose. Assume, for example, that land and a building are purchased for a bargain price of $100,000. The apportionment of this cost on the basis of an appraisal may be made as follows:

	Value per Appraisal	Percentage of Total	Apportionment of Cost
Land	$ 48,000	40%	$ 40,000
Building	72,000	60%	60,000
Total	$120,000	100%	$100,000

Apportioning cost between land and building

Sometimes a tract of land purchased as a building site has on it an old building which is not suitable for the buyer's use. The Land account should be charged with the entire purchase price *plus any costs incurred in tearing down or removing the building.* Proceeds received from sale of the materials salvaged from the old building are recorded as a credit in the Land account.

Land acquired as a future building site should be reported under Investments or Other Assets, rather than as part of Plant and Equipment, because it is not currently used in operations.

LAND IMPROVEMENTS Improvements to real estate such as driveways, fences, parking lots, and sprinkler systems have a limited life and are therefore subject to depreciation. For this reason they should be recorded not in the Land account but in a separate account entitled Land Improvements. On the other hand, any improvements such as grading or leveling, which will last indefinitely and are not to be depreciated, are entered in the Land account.

BUILDINGS Old buildings are sometimes purchased with the intention of repairing them prior to placing them in use. Repairs made under these circumstances are charged to the Buildings account. After the building has been placed in use, *ordinary repairs* are considered as maintenance expense when incurred.

When a building is constructed by the business itself, rather than being purchased, cost includes the materials and labor used plus an equitable portion of overhead or other indirect costs, such as executive salaries. Any other outlays specifically relating to the construction such as architectural fees, insurance during the construction period, and building permits should also be included in the cost of the building. A building or machine constructed by a company for its own use should be recorded in the accounts at cost, not at the price which might have been paid to outsiders if the asset had been acquired through purchase.

LEASED PROPERTY Many companies lease buildings and equipment rather than buying these assets. There are two methods of accounting for leased property, depending upon the terms of the lease. Under one method, the *lessee* views the periodic lease payments as rent expense and does not record the leased property as an asset in the accounting records. Under the other method, lease agreements are viewed as creating both an asset and a liability which are recorded in the accounts of the lessee at the *present value* of the future lease payments. The asset, which might be called *leased equipment,* will appear in the balance sheet with other types of plant and equipment and will be depreciated over the life of the lease. Accounting for leases will be discussed further in Chapter 13.

LEASEHOLD IMPROVEMENTS When buildings or other improvements are constructed on leased property by the lessee, the costs should be recorded in a Leasehold Improvements account and written off as expense during the remaining life of the lease or of the estimated useful life of the building, whichever is shorter. This procedure is usually followed even though the lessee has an option to renew the lease, because there is no assurance in advance that conditions will warrant the exercise of the renewal clause.

Capital expenditures and revenue expenditures

The term *expenditure* means making a payment or incurring an obligation to make a future payment for an asset or service received. The acquisition of an asset (such as an automobile) or of a service (such as repairs to the automobile) may be for cash or on credit. In either situation the transaction is properly referred to as an expenditure.

Expenditures for the purchase or expansion of plant assets are called *capital expenditures* and are recorded in asset accounts. Expenditures for ordinary repairs, maintenance, fuel, and other items necessary to the ownership and use of plant and equipment are called *revenue expenditures* and are recorded by debits to expense accounts. The charge to an expense account is based on the assumption that the benefits from the expenditure will be used up in the current period, and the cost should therefore be deducted from the revenue of the current period in determining the net income.

A business may purchase many items which will benefit several accounting periods, but which have a relatively low cost. Examples of such items include auto batteries, wastebaskets, and pencil sharpeners. Such items are theoretically capital expenditures, but if they are recorded as assets in the accounting records it will be necessary to compute and record the related depreciation expense in future periods. We have previously mentioned the idea that the extra work involved in developing more precise accounting information should be weighed against the benefits that result. Thus, for reasons of convenience and economy, expenditures which are *not material* in dollar amount are treated in the accounting records as expenses of the current period. In brief, *any material expenditure that will benefit several accounting periods is considered a capital expenditure. Any expenditure that will benefit only the current period or which is not material in amount is referred to as a revenue expenditure.*

EXTRAORDINARY REPAIRS The term *extraordinary repairs* has a specific meaning in accounting terminology; it means a reconditioning or major overhaul that will *extend the useful life* of a plant asset beyond the original estimate. For example, a new automobile may be depreciated on the basis of an estimated useful life of four years. Assume that after three years of use, a decision is made to install a new engine in the automobile and thereby to extend its overall useful life from the original estimate of four years to a total of six years.

An extraordinary repair of this type may be recorded by *debiting the Accumulated Depreciation account.* This entry is sometimes explained by the argument that the extraordinary repair cancels out some of the depreciation previously recorded. The effect of this reduction (debit entry) in the Accumulated Depreciation account is to *increase* the carrying value of the asset by the cost of the extraordinary repair. Since an extraordinary repair causes an increase in the carrying value of the asset and has no immediate direct effect upon net income, it may be regarded as a form of capital expenditure.

DEPRECIATION

Allocating the cost of plant and equipment over the years of use

Plant assets, with the exception of land, are of use to a company for only a limited number of years, and the cost of each plant asset is allocated as an expense of the years in which it is used. Accountants use the term *depreciation* to describe this gradual conversion of the cost of a plant asset into expense.

Depreciation, as the term is used in accounting, does not mean the physical deterioration of an asset. Neither does depreciation mean the decrease in market value of a plant asset over a period of time. *Depreciation means the allocation of the cost of a plant asset to the periods in which services are received from the asset.*

When a delivery truck is purchased, its cost is first recorded as an asset. This cost becomes expense over a period of years through the accounting process of depreciation. When gasoline is purchased for the truck, the price paid for each tankful is immediately recorded as expense. In theory, both outlays (for the truck and for a tank of gas) represent the acquisition of assets, but since it is reasonable to assume that a tankful of gasoline will be consumed in the accounting period in which it is purchased, we record the outlay for gasoline as an expense immediately. It is important to recognize, however, that *both the outlay for the truck and the payment for the gasoline become expense in the period or periods in which each renders services.*

A separate Depreciation Expense account and a separate Accumulated Depreciation account are generally maintained for each group of depreciable assets such as factory buildings, delivery equipment, and office equipment so that a proper allocation of depreciation expense can be made between functional areas of activity such as sales and manufacturing. Depreciation on manufacturing facilities is not necessarily an expense of the period in which it is recorded; the depreciation charge is first embodied in the inventory of finished goods manufactured, and the cost of this inventory is later deducted from revenue as an expense of the period when the goods are sold.

Depreciation differs from most expenses in that it does not require a cash payment at or near the time it is recorded. The entry to record depreciation (a debit to Depreciation Expense and a credit to Accumulated Depreciation) has no effect on current assets or current liabilities. However, when depreciable assets wear out, a large cash payment must be made in order to replace them.

Because of the noncash nature of depreciation expense and because the dollar amount is materially affected by the depreciation method selected, it is generally desirable that the total amount of depreciation expense for the year be disclosed in the income statement.

Depreciation not a process of valuation

Accounting records do not purport to show the constantly fluctuating market values of plant and equipment. Occasionally the market value of a building may rise substantially over a period of years because of a change in the price level, or for other reasons. Depreciation is continued, however, regardless of the increase in market value. The accountant recognizes that the building will render useful services for only a limited number of years, and that its full cost must be allocated as expense of those years regardless of fluctuations in market value.

The **book value** or **carrying value** of a plant asset is its cost minus the related accumulated depreciation. Plant assets are shown in the balance sheet at their book values, representing the portion of their cost which will be allocated to expense in future periods. Accumulated depreciation represents the portion of the assets' cost which has already been recognized as expense.

Accumulated depreciation does not consist of cash

Many readers of financial statements who have not studied accounting mistakenly believe that accumulated depreciation accounts (depreciation reserves) represent money accumulated for the purpose of buying new equipment when the present equipment wears out. Perhaps the best way to combat such mistaken notions is to emphasize that a credit balance in an accumulated depreciation account represents the **expired cost** of assets acquired in the past. The amounts credited to the accumulated depreciation account could, as an alternative, have been credited directly to the plant and equipment account. An accumulated depreciation account has a **credit** balance; it does not represent an asset; and it cannot be used in any way to pay for new equipment. To buy a new plant asset requires cash; the total amount of cash owned by a company is shown by the asset account for cash.

Causes of depreciation

There are two major causes of depreciation, physical deterioration and obsolescence.

PHYSICAL DETERIORATION Physical deterioration of a plant asset results from use, and also from exposure to sun, wind, and other climatic factors. When a plant asset has been carefully maintained, it is not uncommon for the owner to claim that the asset is as "good as new." Such statements are not literally true. Although a good repair policy may greatly lengthen the useful life of a machine, every machine eventually reaches the point at which it must be discarded. In brief, the making of repairs does not lessen the need for recognition of depreciation.

OBSOLESCENCE The term **obsolescence** means the process of becoming out of date or obsolete. An airplane, for example, may become obsolete even though it is in excellent physical condition; it becomes obsolete because better planes of superior design and performance have become available. Obsolescence relates to the capacity of a plant asset to render services to a particular company for a particular purpose.

The usefulness of plant assets may also be reduced because the rapid growth of a company renders such assets inadequate. Inadequacy of a plant asset may necessitate replacement with a larger unit even though the asset is in good physical condition and is not obsolete. Obsolescence and inadequacy are often closely associated; both relate to the opportunity for economical and efficient use of an asset rather than to its physical condition. Obsolescence is probably a more significant factor than physical deterioration in putting an end to the usefulness of most depreciable assets. Current accounting practice, however, does not usually attempt to separate the effects of physical deterioration and obsolescence.

Methods of computing depreciation

A business need not use the same method of depreciation for all its various assets. For example, a company may use straight-line depreciation on some assets and a declining-balance method for other assets. Management also has the option of using different methods of depreciation in the accounting records and financial statements than are employed in the determination of taxable income. The most widely used methods (straight-line, units-of-output, declining-balance, and sum-of-the-years'-digits) are explained and illustrated in the following sections.

STRAIGHT-LINE METHOD The simplest and most widely used method of computing depreciation is the straight-line method. This method was described in Chapter 3 and has been used repeatedly in problems throughout this book. Under the straight-line method, an equal portion of the cost of the asset is allocated to each period of use; consequently, this method is most appropriate when usage of an asset is fairly uniform from year to year.

The computation of the periodic charge for depreciation is made by deducting the estimated *residual* or *salvage value* from the cost of the asset and dividing the remaining *depreciable cost* by the years of estimated useful life. For example, if a depreciable asset has a cost of $5,200, a residual value of $400, and an estimated useful life for four years, the annual computation of depreciation expense will be as follows:

$$\frac{\text{Cost} - \text{Residual Value}}{\text{Years of Useful Life}} = \frac{\$5,200 - \$400}{4} = \$1,200$$

This same depreciation computation is shown on page 484 in tabular form.

Computing depreciation by straight-line method

Cost of the depreciable asset $5,200
Less: Estimated residual value (amount to be realized by sale of asset
   when it is retired from use) 400
Total amount to be depreciated (depreciable cost) $4,800
Estimated useful life . . . . 4 years
Depreciation expense each year ($4,800 ÷ 4) $1,200

The following schedule summarizes the accumulation of depreciation over the useful life of the asset. The amount to be depreciated is $4,800 (cost of $5,200 minus estimated residual value of $400).

Depreciation Schedule: Straight-Line Method

Year	Computation	Depreciation Expense	Accumulated Depreciation	Book Value
				$5,200
First	($\frac{1}{4}$ × $4,800)	$1,200	$1,200	4,000
Second	($\frac{1}{4}$ × $4,800)	1,200	2,400	2,800
Third	($\frac{1}{4}$ × $4,800)	1,200	3,600	1,600
Fourth	($\frac{1}{4}$ × $4,800)	1,200	4,800	400
		$4,800		

Constant annual depreciation expense

Depreciation rates for various types of assets can conveniently be stated as percentages. In the above example the asset had an estimated life of four years, so the depreciation expense each year was $\frac{1}{4}$ of the depreciable amount. The fraction "$\frac{1}{4}$" is of course equivalent to an annual rate of 25%. Similarly, an asset with a 20-year life would call for annual depreciation expense of $\frac{1}{20}$, or 5%. A 10-year life would require a depreciation rate of $\frac{1}{10}$, or 10%, and an eight-year life a depreciation rate of $\frac{1}{8}$, or $12\frac{1}{2}$%.

In the preceding illustration we assumed that the company maintained its accounts on a calendar-year basis and that the asset was acquired on January 1, the beginning of the accounting period. If the asset had been acquired sometime during the year, on October 1 for example, it would have been in use for only three months, or $\frac{3}{12}$ of a year. Consequently, the depreciation to be recorded at December 31 would be only $\frac{3}{12}$ of $1,200, or $300. Stated more precisely, the depreciation expense in this situation is computed as follows: $\frac{3}{12}$ × 25% × $4,800 = $300.

In practice, the possibility of residual value is sometimes ignored and the annual depreciation charge computed by dividing the total cost of the asset by the number of years of estimated useful life. This practice may be justified in those cases in which residual value is not material and is difficult to estimate accurately. Under this approach the yearly depreciation expense in the above example would be $5,200 ÷ 4, or $1,300. The percentage rate would still be 25%, since one-fourth of the depreciable amount becomes expense each year.

UNITS-OF-OUTPUT METHOD For certain kinds of assets, more equitable allocation of the cost can be obtained by dividing the cost (minus salvage value, if significant) by the estimated units of output rather than by the estimated years of useful life. A truck line or bus company, for example, might compute depreciation on its vehicles by a mileage basis. If a truck costs $11,000 and has a residual value of $1,000 and a useful life of 100,000 miles, the depreciation rate per mile of operation is 10 cents ($10,000 ÷ 100,000). This calculation of the depreciation rate may be stated as follows:

$$\frac{\text{Cost} - \text{Residual Value}}{\text{Estimated Units of Output (Miles)}} = \frac{\text{Depreciation per}}{\text{Unit of Output (Mile)}}$$

or

$$\frac{\$11,000 - \$1,000}{100,000 \text{ miles}} = \$0.10 \text{ depreciation per mile}$$

At the end of each year, the amount of depreciation to be recorded would be determined by multiplying the 10-cent rate by the number of miles the truck had operated during the year. This method is suitable only when the total units of output of the asset over its entire useful life can be estimated with reasonable accuracy.

ACCELERATED DEPRECIATION METHODS The term *accelerated depreciation* means recognition of relatively large amounts of depreciation in the early years of use and reduced amounts in the later years. Many types of plant and equipment are most efficient when new and therefore provide more and better services in the early years of useful life. If we assume that the benefits derived from owning an asset are greatest in the early years when the asset is relatively new, then the amount of the asset's cost which we allocate as depreciation expense should be greatest in these same years. This is consistent with the basic accounting concept of matching costs with related revenue. Another reason for using accelerated depreciation is the pleasing prospect of reducing the current year's income tax burden by recognizing a relatively large amount of depreciation expense.

Declining-balance method For income tax purposes one of the acceptable methods of "rapid write-off" of depreciable assets consists of doubling the normal rate of depreciation and applying this doubled rate each year to the undepreciated cost (book value) of the asset. The term *double-declining-balance* is often applied to this form of accelerated depreciation.

Assume, for example, that an automobile is acquired for business use at a cost of $8,000. Estimated useful life is four years; therefore, the depreciation rate under the straight-line method would be 25%. To depreciate the automobile by the declining-balance method, we double the straight-line rate of 25% and apply the doubled rate of 50% to the book value. Depreciation expense in the first year would then amount to $4,000. In the second year the depreciation expense would drop to $2,000, computed at 50% of the remaining book value of $4,000. In the third year depreciation would be $1,000, and in the fourth year only $500. The following table shows the allocation of cost under this method of depreciation.

Depreciation Schedule: Declining-Balance Method

	Year	Computation	Depreciation Expense	Accumulated Depreciation	Book Value
					$8,000
Accelerated depreciation: declining-balance	First	*(50% × $8,000)*	*$4,000*	*$4,000*	*4,000*
	Second	*(50% × $4,000)*	*2,000*	*6,000*	*2,000*
	Third	*(50% × $2,000)*	*1,000*	*7,000*	*1,000*
	Fourth	*(50% × $1,000)*	*500*	*7,500*	*500*

If the automobile is continued in use beyond the estimated life of four years, depreciation may be continued at the 50% rate on the book value. In the fifth year, for example, the depreciation expense would be $250 (50% × $500), and in the sixth year $125 (50% × $250). When the declining-balance method is used, the cost of a depreciable asset will never be entirely written off as long as the asset continues in use. Perhaps because of the existence of this undepreciated balance of original cost, the tax regulations do not require any deduction from original cost for residual value when this method of depreciation is used. However, if the asset has a residual value, depreciation must stop at this point. For example, if the $8,000 automobile illustrated above has a residual value of $800, the depreciation for the fourth year would be restricted to $200, which is the amount of depreciation required to reduce the carrying value of the automobile to its residual value.

If the asset in the above illustration had been acquired on April 1 rather than on January 1, depreciation for only nine months (April–December) would be recorded in the first year. The computation would be $\frac{9}{12}$ × (50% × $8,000) or $3,000. For the next calendar year the calculation would be 50% × ($8,000 − $3,000), or $2,500.

Sum-of-the-years'-digits method This is another method of allocating a large portion of the cost of an asset to the early years of its use. The depreciation rate to be used is a fraction, of which the numerator is the remaining years of useful life (as of the beginning of the year) and the denominator is the sum of the years of useful life. Consider again the example of an automobile costing $8,000, having an estimated life of four years and an estimated residual value of $800. (Present income tax regulations require that residual value be taken into account when either the straight-line method or the sum-of-the-years'-digits method of depreciation is used.) Since the asset has an estimated life of four years, the denominator of the fraction will be 10, computed as follows: $1 + 2 + 3 + 4 = 10$. For the first year, the depreciation will be $\frac{4}{10} \times \$7,200$, or \$2,880. For the second year, the depreciation will be $\frac{3}{10} \times \$7,200$, or \$2,160; in the third year $\frac{2}{10} \times \$7,200$, or \$1,440; and in the fourth year, $\frac{1}{10} \times \$7,200$, or \$720. In tabular form this depreciation program will appear as follows:

Depreciation Schedule: Sum-of-the-Years'-Digits Method

	Year	Computation	Depreciation Expense	Accumulated Depreciation	Book Value
					$8,000
Accelerated depreciation: sum-of-the-years'-digits	First	($\frac{4}{10} \times \$7,200$)	$2,880	$2,880	5,120
	Second	($\frac{3}{10} \times \$7,200$)	2,160	5,040	2,960
	Third	($\frac{2}{10} \times \$7,200$)	1,440	6,480	1,520
	Fourth	($\frac{1}{10} \times \$7,200$)	720	7,200	800

Assume that the asset being depreciated by the sum-of-the-years'-digits method was acquired on April 1 and the company maintains its accounts on a calendar-year basis. Since the asset was in use for only nine months during the first accounting period, the depreciation to be recorded in this first period will be for only $\frac{9}{12}$ of a full year, that is, $\frac{9}{12} \times \$2,880$, or \$2,160. For the second accounting period the depreciation computation will be:

$\frac{3}{12} \times (\frac{4}{10} \times \$7,200)$ . . . . \$ 720

$\frac{9}{12} \times (\frac{3}{10} \times \ 7,200)$ 1,620

Depreciation expense, second period \$2,340

A similar pattern of allocation will be followed for each accounting period of the asset's life.

DEPRECIATION FOR FRACTIONAL PERIODS In the case of depreciable assets acquired sometime during the year, it is customary to figure depreciation to the nearest month. For example, if an asset is acquired on July 12, depreciation would be computed from July 1; if the asset had been acquired on July 18 (or any other date in the latter half of July), depreciation would be recorded for only five months (August through December) for the current calendar year.

Some businesses prefer to begin depreciation on the first of the month following the acquisition of a depreciable asset. This method, or any one of many similar variations, is acceptable so long as it is followed consistently.

Revision of depreciation rates

Depreciation rates are based on estimates of the useful life of assets. These estimates of useful life are seldom precisely correct and sometimes are grossly in error. Consequently, the annual depreciation expense based on the estimated useful life may be either excessive or inadequate. What action should be taken when, after a few years of using a plant asset, it is decided that the asset actually is going to last for a considerably longer or shorter period than was originally estimated? When either of these situations arises, a revised estimate of useful life should be made and the periodic depreciation expense decreased or increased accordingly.

The procedure for correcting the depreciation program may be stated in a very few words: *Spread the remaining undepreciated cost of the asset over the years of remaining useful life.* The annual depreciation expense is increased or decreased sufficiently so that the depreciation program will be completed in accordance with the revised estimate of remaining useful life. The following data illustrate a revision which increases the estimate of useful life and thereby decreases the annual depreciation expense.

Data prior to revision of depreciation rate	Cost of asset	$10,000
	Estimated useful life (no residual value)	10 years
	Annual depreciation expense (prior to revision)	$ 1,000
	Accumulated depreciation at end of six years ($1,000 × 6)	$ 6,000

At the beginning of the seventh year, it is decided that the asset will last for eight more years. The revised estimate of useful life is, therefore, a total of 14 years. The depreciation expense to be recognized for the seventh year and for each of the remaining years is $500, computed as follows:

Revision of depreciation program	Undepreciated cost at end of sixth year ($10,000 − $6,000)	$4,000
	Revised estimate of remaining years of useful life	8 years
	Revised amount of annual depreciation expense ($4,000 ÷ 8)	$ 500

The method described above for the revision of a depreciation program is generally used and is acceptable in the determination of taxable income. The Financial Accounting Standards Board also supports this approach for financial reporting purposes.

Depreciation and income taxes

Different methods of depreciation may be used for the purpose of preparing financial statements and the purpose of preparing income tax returns. The vast majority of businesses use straight-line depreciation in their financial statements, possibly motivated in part by a desire to report higher earnings per share of stock. For income tax purposes, however, many businesses use an accelerated depreciation method.

Accelerated methods of depreciation became quite popular some years ago when the federal government approved their use for income tax purposes. By offering businesses the opportunity of writing off as depreciation expense a large portion of the cost of a new asset during its early years of use, the government has provided a powerful incentive for investment in new productive facilities. Since an increased charge for depreciation expense will reduce taxable income, business executives may feel that by purchasing new assets and writing off a large part of the cost in the early years of use, they are in effect paying for the new assets with dollars that otherwise would have been used to pay income taxes.

In theory, the ideal depreciation policy is one that allocates the cost of a depreciable asset to the several periods of its use in proportion to the services received each period. Accelerated methods of depreciation sometimes fail to allocate the cost of an asset in proportion to the flow of services from the property and therefore prevent the determination of annual net income on a realistic basis. If annual net income figures are misleading, stockholders, creditors, management, and others who use financial statements as a basis for business decisions may be seriously injured. For income tax purposes, however, accelerated methods of depreciation may be effective in encouraging business organizations to invest in new productive facilities and thereby to raise the level of economic activity.

Inflation and depreciation

The valuation of plant and equipment on a cost basis and the computation of depreciation in terms of cost work very well during periods of stable price levels. However, the substantial rise in the price level in recent years has led many government officials and business executives to suggest that a more realistic measurement of net income could be achieved by basing depreciation on the *estimated replacement cost* of plant assets rather than on the original cost of the assets presently in use.

As a specific illustration, assume that a manufacturing company purchased machinery in 1965 at a cost of $1,000,000. Estimated useful life was 15 years and straight-line depreciation was used. Throughout this 15-year period the price level rose sharply. By 1980 the machinery purchased in 1965 was fully depreciated; it was scrapped and replaced by new machinery in 1980. Although the new machines were not significantly different from the old, they cost $3,000,000, or three times as much as the old machinery. Many accountants would argue that the depreciation expense for the 15 years was in reality $3,000,000, because this was the outlay required for new machinery if the company was merely to "stay even" in its productive facilities. It is also argued that reported profits will be **overstated** during a period of rising prices if depreciation is based on the lower plant costs of some years ago. An overstatement of profit causes higher income taxes and perhaps larger demands for wage increases than are justified by the company's financial position and earnings. A more general criticism is that financial statements which show overstated earnings are misleading and do not serve as a useful basis for decisions by management, investors, or others.

Historical cost versus replacement cost

The above criticism of depreciation accounting based on the historical cost of assets is a convincing one. (*Historical cost* means the cost actually incurred by a company in acquiring an asset, as evidenced by paid checks and other documents.) However, this criticism does not mean that business enterprise in general is on the verge of abandoning the cost principle in accounting for assets and computing depreciation. To substitute estimated current replacement cost for the historical cost of plant and equipment would create many new difficulties and a great deal of confusion. Current replacement cost cannot be determined easily or with precision for many assets. For example, the current cost of replacing a steel mill with its great variety of complex, made-to-order machinery would involve making many assumptions and unprovable estimates. Or, as another example, consider the difficulty of estimating the replacement cost of a large tract of timber or of a gold mine. The price level is constantly changing; consequently, estimates of replacement cost which took a long time to develop for certain complex plant assets might be out-of-date by the time they were completed.

Another difficulty in substituting replacement cost for historical cost of plant assets would be that the whole process of establishing estimated cost data would presumably need to be repeated each year. In contrast, historical cost (which we presently use as the basis of accounting for plant and equipment) is determined at the time of acquiring an asset and remains unchanged throughout the useful life of the asset.

These difficulties connected with the possible adoption of replacement cost as a basis of accounting for assets do not mean that such a change cannot or should not be attempted. However, these difficulties do explain why American business has continued to use historical cost as a primary basis of accounting for assets even during continued inflation. The authors believe that accountants and business leaders should continue to search for means of making accounting data more *relevant* and should be willing to experiment with new methods. It appears probable that business organizations in the United States will increasingly make use of replacement cost in accounting for plant and equipment.

The SEC requirement for disclosure of replacement cost

The Securities and Exchange Commission recently adopted a rule requiring large corporations to *disclose* the estimated current replacement cost of plant and equipment. Also required to be disclosed is depreciation expense based on the replacement cost of the assets. *This rule does not mean that replacement cost is to be used instead of historical cost, but rather that additional supplementary information is to be disclosed.* The disclosure can be made in a footnote to the financial statements or as a supplementary section accompanying the financial statements. The methods used in determining the estimated amounts must be explained.

This action by the SEC is viewed by many accountants as an important first step which eventually may lead to *current-value accounting* on a widespread basis rather than the traditional reliance upon historical cost. The degree of inflation we experience in future years will be an important factor in determining whether such changes in accounting standards actually take place.

Disposal of plant and equipment

When depreciable assets are disposed of at any date other than the end of the year, an entry should be made to record depreciation for the *fraction of the year* ending with the date of disposal. In the following illustrations of the disposal of items of plant and equipment, it is assumed that any necessary entries for fractional-period depreciation have been recorded.

As units of plant and equipment wear out or become obsolete, they must be scrapped, sold, or traded in on new equipment. Upon the disposal or retirement of a depreciable asset, the cost of the property is removed from the asset account, and the accumulated depreciation is removed from the related valuation account. Assume, for example, that office equipment purchased 10 years ago at a cost of $5,000 has been fully depreciated and is no longer useful. The entry to record the scrapping of the worthless equipment is as follows:

Scrapping fully depreciated asset

Accumulated Depreciation: Office Equipment 5,000
  Office Equipment 5,000
To remove from the accounts the cost and the accumulated depreciation on fully depreciated office equipment now being scrapped. No salvage value.

Once an asset has been fully depreciated, no more depreciation should be recorded on it, even though the property is in good condition and is continued in use. The objective of depreciation is to spread the *cost* of an asset over the periods of its usefulness; in no case can depreciation expense be greater than the amount paid for the asset. When a fully depreciated asset is continued in use beyond the original estimate of useful life, the asset account and the Accumulated Depreciation account should remain in the accounting records without further entries until the asset is retired.

GAINS AND LOSSES ON DISPOSAL OF PLANT AND EQUIPMENT Since the residual value and useful life of plant assets are only estimates, it is not uncommon for plant assets to be sold at a price which differs from their book value at the date of disposal. When plant assets are sold, any gain or loss on the disposal is computed by comparing the book value with the amount received from the sale. A sales price in excess of the book value produces a gain; a sales price below the book value produces a loss. These gains or losses, if material in amount, should be shown separately in the income statement in computing the income from operations.

Disposal at a price above book value Assume that a machine which cost $10,000 and has a book value of $2,000 is sold for $3,000. The journal entry to record this disposal is as follows:

Gain on disposal of plant asset

Cash	*3,000*	
Accumulated Depreciation: Machinery	*8,000*	
Machinery		*10,000*
Gain on Disposal of Plant Assets		*1,000*

To record sale of machinery at a price above book value.

Disposal at a price below book value Now assume that the same machine is sold for $500. The journal entry in this case would be as follows:

Loss on disposal of plant asset

Cash	*500*	
Accumulated Depreciation: Machinery	*8,000*	
Loss on Disposal of Plant Assets	*1,500*	
Machinery		*10,000*

To record sale of machinery at a price below book value.

The disposal of a depreciable asset at a price equal to book value would result in neither a gain nor a loss. The entry for such a transaction would consist of a debit to Cash for the amount received, a debit to Accumulated Depreciation for the balance accumulated, and a credit to the asset account for the original cost.

Trading in used assets on new

Certain types of depreciable assets, such as automobiles and office equipment, are customarily traded in on new assets of the same kind. The trade-in allowance granted by the dealer may differ materially from the book value of the old asset. If the dealer grants a trade-in allowance in excess of the book value of the asset being traded in, there is the suggestion of a gain being realized on the exchange. The evidence of a gain is not conclusive, however, because the list price of the new asset may purposely have been set higher than a realistic cash price to permit the offering of inflated trade-in allowances.

For the purpose of determining taxable income, no gain or loss is recognized when a depreciable asset is traded in on another similar asset. The tax regulations provide that *the cost of the new asset shall be the sum of the book value of the old asset traded in plus the additional amount paid or to be paid in acquiring the new asset.*

To illustrate the handling of an exchange transaction in this manner, assume that a delivery truck is acquired at a cost of $8,000. The truck is depreciated on the straight-line basis with the assumption of a five-year life and no salvage value. Annual depreciation expense is ($8,000 ÷ 5), or $1,600. After four years of use, the truck is traded in on a new model having a list price of $10,000. The truck dealer grants a trade-in allowance of $2,400 for the old truck; the additional amount to be paid to acquire the new truck is, therefore, $7,600 ($10,000 list price minus $2,400 trade-in allowance). The *cost basis* of the new truck is computed as follows:

Trade-in:	*Cost of old truck*	*$8,000*
cost of new equipment	*Less: Accumulated depreciation ($1,600 × 4)*	*6,400*
	Book value of old truck	*$1,600*
	Add: Cash payment for new truck (list price, $10,000 – $2,400 trade-in	
	allowance)	*7,600*
	Cost basis of new truck	*$9,200*

The trade-in allowance and the list price of the new truck are not recorded in the accounts; their only function lies in determining the amount which the purchaser must pay in addition to turning in the old truck. The journal entry for this exchange transaction is as follows:

Entry for	*Delivery Truck (new)*	*9,200*	
trade-in	*Accumulated Depreciation: Delivery Truck (old)*	*6,400*	
	Delivery Truck (old)		*8,000*
	Cash		*7,600*

To remove from the accounts the cost of old truck and accumulated depreciation thereon, and to record new truck at cost equal to book value of old truck traded in plus cash paid.

Note that the method used above to record the trade-in of an old productive asset for a new one is different from the usual assumption that the cost of a newly acquired asset is equal to its implied cash price. The reason (as approved by the Financial Accounting Standards Board) for not recognizing a gain on a trade-in is that revenue is not realized merely by the act of substituting a new productive asset for an old one. Revenue flows from the production and sale of the goods or services which the productive asset makes possible.[1] The nonrecognition of a suggested gain on a trade-in causes the recorded cost of the new asset to be less than if the gain were recognized. Consequently, depreciation expense will be less because of the reduced amount recorded as cost of the new asset, and the net income in future years will be correspondingly greater.

Although income tax regulations and financial accounting rules are alike in not recognizing a *gain* on a trade-in, they differ in the case of a trade-in which involves a material *loss.* Tax regulations do not permit recognition of the loss, but for financial statements *the loss should be recognized.* For example, assume that a company received a trade-in allowance of only $10,000 for old machinery which has a book value of $100,000. A journal entry illustrating this situation follows:

Machinery (new)	*600,000*	
Accumulated Depreciation: Machinery (old)	*300,000*	
Loss on Trade-in of Plant Assets	*90,000*	
Machinery (old)		*400,000*
Cash		*590,000*

To recognize for financial reporting purposes a material loss on trade-in of machinery. Loss not recognized in determining taxable income.

If a trade-in transaction involved only a very small loss, most companies would probably follow the income tax rules and not recognize the loss. This treatment would avoid the need for a double record of depreciable assets and depreciation expense, and the departure from financial accounting rules would be permissible if the amount of the loss was not material.

NATURAL RESOURCES

Accounting for natural resources

Mining properties, oil and gas wells, and tracts of standing timber are leading examples of natural resources or "wasting assets." The distinguishing characteristics of these assets are that they are physically consumed and converted into inventory. In a theoretical sense, a coal mine might even be regarded as an "underground inventory of coal"; however, such an inventory is certainly not a current asset. In the balance sheet, mining property and other natural resources are usually listed as a separate group of tangible assets.

Natural resources should be recorded in the accounts at cost. As the resource is removed through the process of mining, cutting, or drilling,

[1] *APB Opinion No. 29,* "Accounting for Nonmonetary Transactions," AICPA (New York: 1973).

the asset account must be proportionately reduced. The carrying value (book value) of a coal mine, for example, is reduced by a small amount for each ton of coal mined. The original cost of the mine is thus gradually transferred out of the asset account and becomes part of the cost of the coal mined and sold.

The cost of a mine or other natural resource may include not only the purchase price but also payments for surveying and various exploratory and developmental activities. Many companies in such industries as oil, gas, and mining carry on a continuous program of exploration and development as, for example, the much-discussed development of off-shore oil fields. Since expenditures for exploration and development thus become normal and continuous, these payments are generally charged to expense in the year in which the exploration or development is performed. If the payments for exploration and development were reasonably certain to produce future revenue, the theoretically preferrable accounting policy would be to capitalize these costs so that they could be matched against the related revenue which they would produce in later years.

DEPLETION The term *depletion* is used to describe the pro rata allocation of cost of a natural resource to the units removed. Depletion is computed by dividing the cost of the natural resource by the estimated available number of units, such as barrels of oil or tons of coal. The depletion charge per unit is them multiplied by the number of units actually removed during the year to determine the total depletion charge for that period.

To illustrate the computation of depletion expense, assume that the sum of $2,000,000 is paid for a coal mine believed to contain 1 million tons of coal. The depletion charge per unit is $2,000,000 ÷ 1,000,000 tons, or $2 a ton. If we assume that 200,000 tons of coal were mined and sold during the first year of operation, the depletion charge for the year would be $2 × 200,000 tons, or $400,000. The journal entry necessary at the end of the year to record depletion of the mine would be as follows:

Recording *Depletion Expense* *400,000*
depletion   *Accumulated Depletion: Coal Mine* *400,000*
    To record depletion expense for the year; 200,000 tons mined
    @ $2 per ton.

In reporting natural resources in the balance sheet, accumulated depletion should be deducted from the cost of the property. A recent balance sheet of Anaconda Company, for example, reports its natural resources as follows:

Natural *Mines and mining claims, water rights and lands, less accumulated*
resources   *depletion of $149,874,000* *$138,410,000*
in the
balance *Timberlands and phosphate and gravel deposits, less accumulated*
sheet   *depletion of $5,602,000* *2,111,000*

Depletion expense in a mining business might be compared with the Purchases account in the ledger of a retail store. The Purchases account represents part of the cost to the store of the goods available for sale; the Depletion Expense account in a mining company represents a part of the cost of the coal or other product available for sale. To the extent that coal produced during the year is not sold but is carried forward as inventory for sale in the following year, *the depletion charge will also be carried forward as part of the inventory value.* In other words, depletion is recorded in the year in which extraction of the product occurs but becomes a deduction from revenue in the period in which the product is sold. Of course, the cost of the inventory of coal or other extracted product on hand at the end of the year includes not only the depletion charge but also the labor cost and other expenditures incurred in bringing the coal to the surface.

PERCENTAGE DEPLETION VERSUS COST DEPLETION For the determination of taxable income, the Internal Revenue Code permits a deduction for depletion expense equal to a specified *percentage of the revenue* from production from mineral deposits such as gold, silver, lead, and zinc ore. Depletion as a percentage of revenue was formerly allowed for the oil and gas industry, but this provision of the tax laws was repealed by Congress except for certain small producers.

Depletion computed as a percentage of revenue *is used only for income tax purposes, not for financial statements.* In terms of generally accepted accounting principles, depletion is always based on the *cost* of the mine or other natural resource.

DEPRECIATION OF BUILDINGS AND EQUIPMENT CLOSELY RELATED TO NATURAL RESOURCES Buildings and equipment installed at a mine or drilling site may be useful only at that particular location. Consequently, such assets should be depreciated over their normal useful lives, or over the life of the natural resource, *whichever is shorter.* Often depreciation on such assets is computed using the units-of-output method, thus relating the depreciation expense to the rate at which units of the natural resource are removed.

INTANGIBLE ASSETS

Characteristics

As the word *intangible* suggests, assets in this classification have no physical substance. Leading examples are goodwill, leaseholds, copyrights, franchises, licenses, and trademarks. Intangible assets are classified on the balance sheet as a subgroup of plant assets. However, not all assets which lack physical substance are regarded as intangible assets; an account receivable, for example, or a short-term prepayment is of nonphysical nature but is classified as a current asset and is not regarded as an intangible. In brief, intangible assets are assets which are used in the operation of the business but which have no physical substance and are noncurrent.

The basis of valuation for intangible assets is cost. In some companies, certain intangible assets such as trademarks may be of great importance but may have been acquired without the incurring of any cost. An intangible asset should appear on the balance sheet *only* if a cost of acquisition or development has been incurred.

However, accounting for an intangible asset is rendered somewhat difficult because the lack of physical substance makes evidence of its existence more elusive, may make its value more debatable, and may make the length of its useful life more questionable. These characteristics of intangible assets suggest that realizable value may be undeterminable or even nonexistent. Perhaps because of the lack of clear support for precise valuation of intangibles, many companies choose to carry their intangible assets on the balance sheet at a nominal valuation of $1; Jantzen, Inc., and the Polaroid Corporation are prominent examples.

There is little doubt, however, that in some companies the intangible assets, such as goodwill or trademarks, may be vitally important to profitable operations. The carrying of intangible assets on the balance sheet is justified only when there is good evidence that future earnings will be derived from these assets.

Operating expenses versus intangible assets

Many types of expenditures offer at least a half promise of yielding benefits in subsequent years, but the evidence is so doubtful and the period of usefulness so hard to define that most companies treat these expenditures as expense when incurred. Another reason for charging these outlays to expense is the practical difficulty of separating them from the recurring expenses of current operations.

Examples are the expenditures for intensive advertising campaigns to introduce new products, and the expense of training employees to work with new types of machinery or office equipment. There is little doubt that some benefits from these outlays continue beyond the current period, but because of the indeterminable duration of the benefits, it is almost universal practice to treat expenditures of this nature as expense of the current period.

Amortization

The term *amortization* is used to describe the systematic write-off to expense of the cost of an intangible asset over the periods of its economic usefulness. The usual accounting entry for amortization consists of a debit to Amortization Expense and a credit to the intangible asset account. There is no theoretical objection to crediting an accumulated amortization account rather than the intangible asset account, but this method is seldom encountered in practice.

For many years some accountants argued that certain intangibles, such as trademarks, had *unlimited* useful lives and therefore should not be amortized. However, the FASB supports the view that the value of intangible assets at any one date eventually disappears, and that *all* intangible assets must be amortized over their useful lives.[2]

Although it is difficult to estimate the useful life of an intangible such as goodwill, it is highly probable that such an asset will not contribute to future earnings on a permanent basis. The cost of the intangible asset should, therefore, be deducted from revenue during the years in which it may be expected to aid in producing revenue.[3] The maximum period of amortization cannot exceed 40 years under the rules presently enforced by the Financial Accounting Standards Board.[4] The straight-line method of amortization is generally used for intangible assets.

ARBITRARY WRITE-OFF OF INTANGIBLES Arbitrary, lump-sum write-off of intangibles (leaving a nominal balance of $1 in the accounts) is a practice sometimes found in companies which have not adopted a systematic amortization program. Arguments for this practice emphasize the element of conservatism, the practical difficulty of estimating an appropriate period for amortization, and the absence of any realizable value for intangibles. Accountants generally agree that whenever any event occurs which indicates that an intangible has lost all value, immediate write-off of the entire cost is warranted regardless of whether an amortization program has previously been followed.

On the other hand, arbitrary write-offs of valuable, revenue-producing intangible assets are no more in accordance with accounting theory than would be the arbitrary write-off of land or buildings.

Goodwill

Business executives used the term *goodwill* in a variety of meanings before it became part of accounting terminology. One of the most common meanings of goodwill in a nonaccounting sense concerns the benefits derived from a favorable reputation among customers. To accountants, however, goodwill has a very specific meaning not necessarily limited to customer relations. It means the *present value of future earnings in excess of the normal return on net identifiable assets.* Above-average earnings may arise not only from favorable customer relations but also from such factors as location, monopoly, manufacturing efficiency, and superior management.

---

[2] *APB Opinion No. 17,* "Intangible Assets," AICPA (New York: 1970), par. 27.
[3] Present tax regulations do not permit the amortization of goodwill in computing taxable income.
[4] *APB Opinion No. 17,* op. cit., par. 29.

The phrase **normal return on net identifiable assets** requires explanation. Net assets means the owners' equity in a business, or assets minus liabilities. Goodwill, however, is not an **identifiable** asset. The existence of goodwill is implied by the ability of a business to earn an above-average return; however, the cause and precise dollar value of goodwill are largely matters of personal opinion. Therefore, **net identifiable assets** means all assets except goodwill minus liabilities. A **normal return** on net identifiable assets is the rate of return which investors demand in a particular industry to justify their buying a business at the **fair market value** of its net identifiable assets. A business has goodwill when investors will pay a higher price because the business earns more than the normal rate of return.

Assume that two businesses in the same line of trade are offered for sale and that the normal return on the fair market value of net identifiable assets in this industry is 12% a year. The relative earning power of the two companies during the past five years is shown below:

	Company X	Company Y
Fair market value of net identifiable assets	$1,000,000	$1,000,000
Normal rate of return on net assets	12%	12%
Average net income for past five years	$ 120,000	$ 160,000
Normal earnings, computed as 12% of net identifiable assets	$ 120,000	$ 120,000
Earnings in excess of normal	$ –0–	$ 40,000

A prospective investor would be willing to pay $1,000,000 to buy Company X, because Company X earns the normal 12% return which justifies the fair market value of its net identifiable assets. Although Company Y has the same amount of net identifiable assets, a prospective investor would be willing to pay **more** for Company Y than for Company X because Company Y has a record of superior earnings which will presumably continue for some time in the future. The extra amount that a prospective buyer would pay to purchase Company Y represents the value of Company Y's goodwill.

ESTIMATING GOODWILL How much will an investor pay for goodwill? Above-average earnings in past years are of significance to prospective purchasers only if they believe that these earnings will continue after they acquire the business. Investors' appraisals of goodwill, therefore, will vary with their estimates of the future earning power of the business. Very few businesses, however, are able to maintain above-average earnings for more than a few years. Consequently, the purchaser of a business will usually limit any amount paid for goodwill to not more than four or five times the amount by which annual earnings exceed normal earnings.

Arriving at a fair value for the goodwill of a going business is a difficult and subjective process. Any estimate of goodwill is in large part a matter of personal opinion. The following are several methods which a prospective purchaser might use in estimating a value for goodwill:

1 Negotiated agreement between buyer and seller of the business may be reached on the amount of goodwill. For example, it might be agreed that the fair market value of net identifiable assets is $1,000,000 and that the total purchase price for the business will be $1,180,000, thus providing a $180,000 payment for goodwill.

2 Goodwill may be determined as a multiple of the amount by which average annual earnings exceed normal earnings. Referring to our example involving Company Y, a prospective buyer may be willing to pay four times the amount by which average earnings exceed normal earnings, indicating a value of $160,000 (4 × $40,000) for goodwill. The purchase price of the business, therefore, would be $1,160,000.

The multiple applied to the excess annual earnings will vary widely from perhaps 1 to 10. An investor who pays four times the excess earnings for goodwill must, of course, expect these earnings to continue for at least four years.

3 Goodwill may be estimated by *capitalizing* the amount by which average earnings exceed normal earnings. Capitalizing an earnings stream means dividing those earnings by the investor's required rate of return. The result is the maximum amount which the investor could pay for the earnings and have them represent the required rate of return on the investment. To illustrate, assume that the prospective buyer decides to capitalize the $40,000 annual excess earnings of Company Y at a rate of 20%. This approach results in a $200,000 estimate ($40,000 ÷ .20 = $200,000) for the value of goodwill. (Note that $40,000 per year represents a 20% return on a $200,000 investment.)

A weakness in the capitalization method is that *no provision is made for the recovery* of the investment. If the prospective buyer is to earn a 20% return on the $200,000 investment in goodwill, either the excess earnings must continue *forever* (an unlikely assumption) or the buyer must be able to recover the $200,000 investment at a later date by selling the business at a price above the fair market value of net identifiable assets.

RECORDING GOODWILL IN THE ACCOUNTING RECORDS Goodwill is recorded in the accounting records *only when it is purchased;* this situation usually occurs only when a going business is purchased in its entirety. After the fair market values of all identifiable assets have been recorded in the accounting records of the new owners, any additional amount paid for the business may properly be debited to an asset account entitled Goodwill. This intangible asset must then be amortized over a period not to exceed 40 years, although a much shorter amortization period usually is appropriate.

Many businesses have never purchased goodwill but have generated it internally through developing good customer relations, superior management, or other factors which result in above-average earnings. Because there is no objective means of determining the dollar value of goodwill unless the business is sold, internally developed goodwill is *not recorded* in the accounting records. Thus, goodwill may be a very important asset of a successful business but may not even appear on the company's balance sheet.

Patents

A patent is an exclusive right granted by the federal government for manufacture, use, and sale of a particular product. The purpose of this exclusive grant is to encourage the invention of new machines and processes. When a company acquires a patent by purchase from the inventor or other holder, the purchase price should be recorded by debiting the intangible asset account Patents. The cost of a successful lawsuit to defend the validity of a patent is also capitalized by charge to the Patents account.

Patents are granted for a period of 17 years, and the period of amortization must not exceed that period. However, if the patent is likely to lose its usefulness in less than 17 years, amortization should be based on the shorter period of estimated useful life. Assume that a patent is purchased from the inventor at a cost of $100,000, after five years of the legal life have expired. The remaining *legal* life is, therefore, 12 years, but if the estimated *useful* life is only five years, amortization should be based on this shorter period. The entry to be made to record the annual amortization expense would be:

Entry for amortization of patent

Amortization Expense: Patents	*20,000*	
Patents		*20,000*

To amortize cost of patent on a straight-line basis and estimated life of five years.

Franchises

A franchise is a right granted by a company or a governmental unit to conduct a certain type of business in a specific geographical area. An example of a franchise is the right to operate a McDonald's restaurant in a specific neighborhood. The cost of franchises varies greatly and often may be quite substantial. When the cost of a franchise is small, it may be charged immediately to expense or amortized over a short period such as five years. When the cost is substantial, amortization should be based upon the life of the franchise (if limited); the amortization period, however, may not exceed 40 years.

Trademarks

A permanent exclusive right to the use of a trademark, brand name, or commercial symbol may be obtained by registering it. If the use of the trademark is abandoned or if its contribution to earnings becomes doubtful, immediate write-off of the cost is called for. The outlay for securing a trademark is often not consequential, and it is common practice to treat such outlays as expense when incurred.

Other intangibles and deferred charges

Many other types of intangible assets are found in the published balance sheets of large corporations. Some examples are formulas, processes, designs, copyrights, name lists, and film rights.

Intangibles, particularly those with limited lives, are sometimes classified as "deferred charges" in the balance sheet. A *deferred charge* is an expenditure that is expected to yield benefits for several accounting periods, and should be amortized over its estimated useful life. Included in this category are such items as bond issuance costs, plant rearrangement and moving costs, start-up costs, and organization costs. The distinction between intangibles and deferred charges is not an important one; both represent "bundles of services" in the form of long-term prepayments awaiting allocation to those accounting periods in which the services will be consumed.

KEY TERMS INTRODUCED OR EMPHASIZED IN CHAPTER 12

Accelerated depreciation   Methods of depreciation that call for recognition of relatively large amounts of depreciation in the early years of an asset's useful life and relatively small amounts in the later years.

Amortization   The systematic write-off to expense of the cost of an intangible asset over the periods of its economic usefulness.

Book value   The cost of a plant asset minus the total recorded depreciation, as shown by the Accumulated Depreciation account. The remaining undepreciated cost is also known as *carrying value.*

Capital expenditure   A cost incurred to acquire a long-lived asset. An expenditure that will benefit several accounting periods.

Declining-balance depreciation   An accelerated method of depreciation in which the rate is a multiple of the straight-line rate, which is applied each year to the *undepreciated cost* of the asset. Most commonly used is double the straight-line rate.

Deferred charge   An expenditure expected to yield benefits for several accounting periods and therefore capitalized and written off during the periods benefited.

Depletion   Allocating the cost of a natural resource to the units removed as the resource is mined, pumped, cut, or otherwise consumed.

Depreciable cost   The cost of an asset minus the estimated residual or salvage value.

Depreciation   The systematic allocation of the cost of an asset to expense over the years of its estimated useful life.

Extraordinary repairs   A reconditioning or major overhaul that will extend the useful life of a plant asset beyond the original estimate. Recorded by debiting the Accumulated Depreciation account.

Goodwill   The present value of expected future earnings of a business in excess of the earnings normally realized in the industry. Recorded when a business entity is purchased at a price in excess of the fair value of its net identifiable assets (excluding goodwill) less liabilities.

Intangible assets   Those assets which are used in the operation of a business but which have no physical substance and are noncurrent.

Lessee   The tenant of leased property.

Lessor   The owner of leased property.

Natural resources   Mines, oil fields, standing timber, and similar assets which are physically consumed and converted into inventory.

Net identifiable assets   Total of all assets *except goodwill* minus liabilities.

Percentage depletion   For income tax purposes only, a deduction for depletion expense equal to a specified percentage of the revenue from a natural resource. Eliminated or reduced by recent legislation.

Present value of future receipts or payments   The amount of money which informed investors would pay *today* for the right to receive the future amounts. The present value is always less than the future amount, because money available today can be invested to become equivalent to a larger amount in the future. The present value concept has many applications in accounting. As shown in Chapter 10, it is used in the valuation of long-term receivables and payables which do not include realistic stated rates of interest. Another application is the valuation of the asset and the liability which arise from certain lease arrangements. Also, *goodwill* is defined as the *present value* of future earnings in excess of a normal rate of return.

Replacement cost   The estimated cost of replacing an asset at the current balance sheet date. Disclosure of such data is required of large companies.

Residual (salvage) value   The portion of an asset's cost expected to be recovered through sale or trade-in of the asset at the end of its useful life.

Revenue expenditure   Any expenditure that will benefit only the current accounting period.

Straight-line depreciation   A method of depreciation which allocates the cost of an asset (minus any residual value) equally to each year of its useful life.

Sum-of-the-years'-digits depreciation   An accelerated method of depreciation. The depreciable cost is multiplied each year by a fraction of which the numerator is the remaining years of useful life (as of the beginning of the current year) and the denominator is the sum of the years of useful life.

Units-of-output depreciation   A depreciation method in which cost (minus residual value) is divided by the estimated units of lifetime output. The units' depreciation cost is multiplied by the actual units of output each year to compute the annual depreciation expense.

DEMONSTRATION PROBLEM FOR YOUR REVIEW

The ledger of Cypress Company contained an account entitled Property, which had been used to record a variety of expenditures. At the end of Year 5, the Property account contained the following entries:

Debit entries:

4/3 Amount paid to acquire building site	$ 62,500
4/15 Cost of removing old unusable building from site	5,000
9/30 Contract price for new building completed Sept. 30	200,000
9/30 Insurance, inspection fees, and other costs directly related to con-	
struction of new building	10,000
Total debits	$277,500

Credit entries:

4/15 Proceeds from sale of old lumber and other material from	
demolition of old building	$ 7,500
12/31 Depreciation for Year 5, computed at 5% of balance in	
Property account ($270,000). Debit was to Deprecia-	
tion Expense 13,500	
Total credits	21,000
12/31 Balance in Property account at year-end	$256,500

Instructions

a List the errors made in the application of accounting principles or practices by Cypress Company.

b Prepare a compound correcting journal entry at December 31, Year 5, assuming that the estimated life of the new building is 20 years and that depreciation is to be recognized for three months of Year 5 using the straight-line method. The accounts have not been closed for Year 5.

SOLUTION TO DEMONSTRATION PROBLEM

a Errors in accounting principles or practices were:
(*1*) Including land (a nondepreciable asset) in the same account with building (a depreciable asset).
(*2*) Using the total of land and building as a base for applying the depreciation rate on building.
(*3*) Recording a full year's depreciation on a new building that was in use only the last three months of the year.
(*4*) Crediting the depreciation for the period directly to the asset account (Property) rather than to a valuation account (Accumulated Depreciation: Building).

b   *Correcting Journal Entry*

Year 5

Dec. 31	Land	60,000	
	Building	210,000	
	Property		256,500
	Accumulated Depreciation: Building		2,625
	Depreciation Expense		10,875
	To correct the accounts reflecting land, building,		
	and depreciation in accordance with the computations		
	shown in the following schedule:		

	Land	Building
Amount paid to acquire building site	$62,500	
Cost of removing old building from site	5,000	
Less: Proceeds from salvaged materials	(7,500)	
Contract price for new building		$200,000
Insurance, inspection fees, and other costs		
directly related to construction of new		
building		10,000
Totals	$60,000	$210,000

Depreciation: $210,000 × 5% × $\frac{3}{12}$ = $2,625$

Correction of depreciation expense: $13,500 − $2,625 = $10,875$

REVIEW QUESTIONS

1 Which of the following characteristics would prevent an item from being included in the classification of plant and equipment? (*a*) Intangible, (*b*) limited life, (*c*) unlimited life, (*d*) held for sale in the regular course of business, (*e*) not capable of rendering benefits to the business in the future.

2 The following expenditures were incurred in connection with a large new machine acquired by a metals manufacturing company. Identify those which should be included in the cost of the asset. (*a*) Freight charges, (*b*) sales tax on the machine, (*c*) payment to a passing motorist whose car was damaged by the equipment used in unloading the machine, (*d*) wages of employees for time spent in installing and testing the machine before it was placed in service, (*e*) wages of employees assigned to lubrication and minor adjustments of machine one year after it was placed in service.

3 What is the distinction between a *capital expenditure* and a *revenue expenditure*?

4 Identify the following expenditures as capital expenditures or revenue expenditures:

a Purchased new spark plugs at a cost of $9.20 for two-year-old delivery truck.

b Installed an escalator at a cost of $14,800 in a three-story building which had previously been used for some years without elevators or escalators.

c Purchased an electric pencil sharpener at a cost of $19.95.

d Immediately after acquiring new delivery truck at a cost of $5,800, paid $75 to have the name of the store and other advertising material painted on the truck.

e Painted delivery truck at a cost of $140 after two years of use.

5 Which of the following statements best describes the nature of depreciation?

a Regular reduction of asset value to correspond to changes in market value as the asset ages.

b A process of correlating the carrying value of an asset with its gradual decline in physical efficiency

c Allocation of cost in a manner that will ensure that plant and equipment items are not carried on the balance sheet at amounts in excess of net realizable value

d Allocation of the cost of a plant asset to the periods in which services are received from the asset

6 Should depreciation continue to be recorded on a building when ample evidence exists that the current market value is greater than original cost and that the rising trend of market values is continuing? Explain.

7 What connection exists between the choice of a depreciation method for expensive new machinery and the amount of income taxes payable in the near future?

8 What is an *extraordinary repair* and how is it recorded in the accounts?

9 Company A's balance sheet shows accumulated depreciation on machinery and equipment of $100,000 and Company B shows accumulated depreciation of $50,000. Both companies are considering the acquisition of new equipment costing $60,000. From the information given, can you determine which company is in a better position to purchase the new equipment for cash? Explain.

10 Criticize the following quotation:
"We shall have no difficulty in paying for new plant assets needed during the coming year because our estimated outlays for new equipment amount to only $20,000, and we have more than twice that amount in our depreciation reserves at present."

11 A factory machine acquired at a cost of $94,200 was to be depreciated by the sum-of-the-years'-digits method over an estimated life of eight years. Residual salvage value was estimated to be $15,000. State the amount of depreciation during the first year and during the eighth year.

12 After four years of using a machine acquired at a cost of $15,000, Ohio Construction Company determined that the original estimated life of 10 years had been too short and that a total useful life of 12 years was a more reasonable estimate. Explain briefly the method that should be used to revise the depreciation program, assuming that straight-line depreciation has been used.

13 *a* Give some reasons why a company may change its depreciation policy for financial reporting purposes from an accelerated depreciation method to the straight-line method.

b Is it possible for a corporation to use accelerated depreciation for income tax purposes and straight-line depreciation for financial reporting purposes?

14 Explain what is meant by the following quotation: "In periods of rising prices companies do not recognize adequate depreciation expense, and reported corporate profits are substantially overstated."

15 LoveMatch Company traded in its old computer on a new model. If the trade-in allowance for the old computer is greater than its book value, would LoveMatch Company recognize a gain on the exchange? Explain.

16 Fargo Corporation traded in an old machine on a similar new one, but received a trade-in allowance less than the book value of the old machine. The Internal Revenue Service did not permit the company to recognize any loss on the transaction in computing its taxable income. How will Fargo benefit in future years for income tax purposes as a result of the indicated loss on the trade-in not being allowed by the IRS?

17 Dell Company traded in an old machine on a similar new one. The original cost of the old machine was $30,000 and the accumulated depreciation was $24,000. The list price of the new machine was $40,000 and the trade-in allowance was $8,000. How much cash must Dell pay to acquire the new machine? Compute the indicated gain or loss (regardless of whether it should be recorded in the accounts). Compute the cost basis of the new machine to be used in figuring depreciation for determination of income subject to federal income tax.

18 Lead Hill Corporation recognizes $1 of depletion for each ton of ore mined. During the current year the company mined 600,000 tons but sold only

500,000 tons, as it was attempting to build up inventories in anticipation of a possible strike by employees. How much depletion should be deducted from revenue of the current year?

19 Define *intangible assets.* Would an account receivable arising from a sale of merchandise under terms of 2/10, n/30 qualify as an intangible asset under your definition?

20 Under what circumstances should *goodwill* be recorded in the accounts?

21 Over what period of time should the cost of various types of intangible assets be amortized by regular charges against revenue? (Your answer should be in the form of a principle or guideline rather than a specific number of years.) What method of amortization is generally used?

22 In reviewing the financial statements of Digital Products Co. with a view to investing in the company's stock, you notice that net identifiable assets total $1 million, that goodwill is listed at $100,000, and that average earnings for the past five years have been $20,000 a year. How would these relationships influence your thinking about the company?

EXERCISES

Ex. 12-1 New office equipment was purchased by the Barker Company at a list price of $36,000 with credit terms of 2/10, n/30. Payment of the invoice was made within the discount period; it included 5% sales tax on the net price. Transportation charges of $430 on the new equipment were paid by Barker Company as well as labor cost of $760 for installing the equipment in the appropriate locations. During the unloading and installation work, some of the equipment fell from a loading platform and was damaged. Repair of the damaged parts cost $2,180. After the equipment had been in use for three months, it was thoroughly cleaned and lubricated at a cost of $260. Prepare a list of the items which should be capitalized by debit to the Office Equipment account and state the total cost of the new equipment.

Ex. 12-2 Henry Morgan, general manager of Catalog Printers, attended an auction of used machinery and was the successful bidder on a lot consisting of three machines for a total price of $17,100. Freight charges of $900 were incurred to have the three machines delivered to Catalog Printers plant. In anticipation of this auction the company had borrowed $15,000 in order to be able to make cash bids for the equipment being auctioned. The interest charge on the borrowing amounted to $500.

The estimated fair market values of the machines and the costs of installations and trial runs necessary to prepare them for regular operations were as follows:

	Machine No. 1	Machine No. 2	Machine No. 3
Fair market value	$10,000	$6,000	$4,000
Installation cost	400	800	300
Cost of trial runs	100	150	None

Determine the cost of each machine for accounting purposes, assuming that the auction and delivery cost is apportioned to the three machines on the basis of relative market value.

Ex. 12-3 Machinery with a useful life of five years was acquired by Gulf Converters at a cost of $50,000. The estimated residual salvage value was $5,000. You are to compute the annual depreciation charges applicable to the machinery under each of the following methods of depreciation:
a Straight-line

    b Sum-of-the-years'-digits
    c Double-declining-balance

Ex. 12-4 An airplane with a book value of $30,000 was traded in on a new airplane with a list price of $300,000. The trade-in allowance (not necessarily the fair market value) for the old airplane was $45,000.
    a How much cash must be paid for the new airplane?
    b What is the cost basis of the new airplane for income tax purposes?
    c How much depreciation should be recorded on the new airplane for the first year of use, assuming a four-year life, a residual value of $33,000, and the use of straight-line depreciation?

Ex. 12-5 A tractor which cost $24,800 had an estimated useful life of five years and an estimated salvage value of $4,800. Straight-line depreciation was used. Give the entry required by each of the following alternative assumptions:
    a The tractor was sold for cash of $15,000 after two years' use.
    b The tractor was traded in after three years on another tractor with a list price of $36,000. Trade-in allowance was $14,600. The trade-in was recorded in a manner acceptable for income tax purposes.
    c The tractor was scrapped after four years' use. Since scrap dealers were unwilling to pay anything for the tractor, it was given to a scrap dealer for his services in removing it.

Ex. 12-6 Automat Corporation on July 1 purchased machinery priced at $290,000 but received a trade-in allowance of $44,000 for used machinery. Cash of $60,000 was paid and a 12%, one-year note payable given for the balance. The machinery traded in had an original cost of $180,000 and had been depreciated at the rate of $18,000 a year. Residual value had been ignored on the grounds of not being material. Accumulated depreciation amounted to $139,500 at December 31 prior to the year of the exchange. No depreciation had been recorded between the closing of the accounts on December 31 and the exchange for the new machinery on July 1.
    In general journal form, give the entries to record:
    a Depreciation for the fraction of a year prior to the July 1 transaction
    b The acquisition of the new machinery on July 1 under the rules acceptable for income tax purposes

Ex. 12-7 Yellow Knife Mines started mining activities early in Year 1. At the end of the year its accountant prepared the following summary of its mining costs:

Labor	$2,380,000
Materials	245,000
Miscellaneous	539,280

These costs do not include any charges for depletion or depreciation. Data relating to assets used in mining the ore follow:

Cost of mine (*estimated deposit, 10 million tons; residual value of the mine estimated at $420,000*)	$2,100,000
Buildings (*estimated life, 15 years; no residual value*)	184,800
Equipment (*useful life, six years regardless of number of tons mined; residual value $42,000*)	336,000

    During the year 800,000 tons (8%) of ore were mined, of which 600,000 tons were sold. It is estimated that it will take at least 15 years to extract the ore.
    Determine the cost that should be assigned to the inventory of unsold ore at the end of Year 1.

Ex. 12-8 During the past several years the net sales of Goldtone Appliance Co. have averaged $4,500,000 annually and net income has averaged 6% of net sales. At the present time the company is being offered for sale. Its accounting records show net assets (total assets minus all liabilities) to be $1,500,000.

An investor negotiating to buy the company offers to pay an amount equal to the book value for the net assets and to assume all liabilities. In addition, the investor is willing to pay for goodwill an amount equal to net earnings in excess of 15% on net assets, capitalized at a rate of 25%.

On the basis of this agreement, what price should the inventor offer for the Goldtone Appliance Co.?

Ex. 12-9 Edison Company acquired its plant and equipment 20 years ago at a cost of $200,000 paid in cash. After paying for the plant and equipment, the company had about $15,000 cash for use in operations. The company has consistently used straight-line depreciation based on historical cost and an estimated useful life of 20 years. Residual or salvage value was estimated to be virtually zero. The company has reported a net income each year. However, each year Edison Company paid cash dividends equal to the reported net income.

The plant and equipment are now worn out and must be replaced. Replacement cost is approximately four times the cost of the original plant and equipment.

a Based solely on the above information, about how much cash would you expect Edison Company to have today? Explain the basis for your answer. (Bear in mind that the company had $15,000 cash after paying for the plant and equipment 20 years ago and that depreciation is a noncash expense.)

b What is the prospect for Edison Company being able to pay for the new plant and equipment it needs?

c On what grounds might the accounting measurement of net income by Edison Company be criticized in the light of 20 years of operation in an inflationary environment?

PROBLEMS

12-1 Fontana Corporation, a newly organized business, purchased equipment at a cost of $146,560. The estimated life of these assets is five years and the residual value $2,560. The company is considering whether to use straight-line depreciation, the sum-of-the-years'-digits method, or the double-declining-balance method. Consideration is also being given to the possibility of using one method for the preparation of income tax returns and another method for financial reporting to stockholders.

The president of Fontana Corporation informs you that the company wants to keep income taxes at a minimum during the coming year (Year 1), but to report the largest possible earnings per share in the company's first annual report to its stockholders. (Earnings per share is computed by dividing net income by the number of shares of stock outstanding; therefore, the higher the net income, the higher the earnings per share.)

Instructions
a Compute the annual depreciation expense throughout the five-year life of the equipment under each of the three methods under consideration. (Use a work sheet with three money columns headed, respectively, Straight-line, Sum-of-the-years'-digits, and Double-declining-balance. Also show the total depreciation under each method and show in footnotes how the calculations were made.) Round off depreciation calculations to the nearest dollar.

b Advise the president of Fontana Corporation which method of depreciation should be used for income tax purposes and which method for the company's financial statements in order to achieve the stated objectives of holding income taxes to a minimum in Year 1 while showing the maximum earnings per share in the company's financial statements.

12-2 North Star Manufacturing showed the following information in its ledger account for Machinery for the current year.

Jan.	2 Acquired four identical machines @ $10,800 each	$43,200
Jan.	4 Installation costs	1,440
	Total debits	$44,640
Dec. 31	Less: Credit for proceeds from sale of one machine	(8,280)
31	Balance in Machinery account	$36,360

The corporation's policy for depreciating the machines is to use the straight-line method with an estimated useful life of five years and an estimated residual value of $1,260 per machine. The December 31 transaction for the sale of one machine was recorded by a debit to Cash for the full sales price of $8,280 and a credit to machinery for $8,280.

Instructions
a Prepare one journal entry at December 31 to record depreciation expense for the year on all four machines.
b What was the amount of the gain or loss on the sale of the machine on December 31? Show computations.
c Prepare one journal entry to **correct the accounts** at December 31. In drafting your correcting entry, give consideration to the debit and credit already entered in the accounts on December 31 to record the sale of one of the machines. Your entry should reduce the Machinery account and the Accumulated Depreciation account and should record the gain or loss on the disposal of the machine which was not recognized in the entry made at the time of the sale.

12-3 Old Dominion Company adjusts and closes its accounts at the end of each calendar year and uses the straight-line method of depreciation on all its plant and equipment. On January 1, Year 1, machinery was purchased for cash at a cost of $427,350. Useful life was estimated to be 10 years and residual value $7,350.

Three years later in December, Year 3, after steady use of the machinery, the company decided that because of rapid technological change, the estimated total useful life should be revised from 10 years to six years. No change was made in the estimate of residual value. The revised estimate of useful life was decided upon prior to recording depreciation for the period ended December 31, Year 3.

On June 30, Year 4, Old Dominion Company decided to lease new, more efficient machinery; consequently, the machinery described above was sold on this date for $105,000 cash.

Instructions Prepare journal entries to record the purchase of the machinery, the recording of depreciation for each of the four years, and the disposal of the Machinery on June 30, Year 4. Do not prepare closing entries.

12-4 Mt. Hood Supply Co. early in the current year purchased some hilly land with old abandoned buildings. The old buildings were removed, the land was leveled, and a new building was constructed. The company moved from its former rented quarters into the new building on October 1. Transactions relating to these events were recorded in an account entitled Property, which contained the following entries at the end of the current year:

Debit entries:

3/9	Purchase for cash of building site	$ 68,750
4/28	Payment for demolition of old building	7,500
5/15	Payment for leveling of land	25,000
9/28	Payment for insurance of building during	
	construction	15,000
9/28	Payment for new building completed today	300,000
10/7	Payment to caterer for office party for	
	employees, customers, and friends to	
	celebrate the move to new building	3,750
	Total debits	$420,000

Credit entries:

4/28	Cash received from sale of materials from		
	demolished building	$11,250	
12/31	Depreciation for the current year, computed at		
	4% of balance in Property account ($408,750).		
	Debit was to Depreciation Expense	16,350	
	Total credits		27,600
12/31	Balance in Property account at year-end		$392,400

Instructions

a List the errors made in the application of accounting principles or practices by Mt. Hood Supply Co.

b Prepare a compound journal entry to **correct the accounts** at December 31 of the current year, assuming that the estimated life of the new building is 25 years and that depreciation is to be recognized for the three months the building was in use during the current year, using the straight-line method. The accounts have not been closed for the current year.

12-5 During the last few years, Sunhill Corporation has acquired four costly machines but has given little consideration to depreciation policies. At the time of acquisition of each machine, a different accountant was employed; consequently, various methods of depreciation have been adopted for the several machines. Information concerning the four machines appears below:

Machine	Date Acquired	Cost	Estimated Useful Life, Years	Estimated Residual Value	Method of Depreciation
A	Jan. 1, Year 4	$145,800	6	None	Declining-balance
B	June 30, Year 4	302,400	8	10%	Straight-line
C	Jan. 1, Year 5	201,600	10	$3,600	Sum-of-the-years'-digits
D	Jan. 1, Year 6	237,600	12	None	Declining-balance

Instructions

a Compute the amount of accumulated depreciation, if any, on each machine at December 31, Year 5. For machines A and D, assume that the depreciation rate was double the rate which would be applicable under the straight-line method.

b Prepare a depreciation schedule for use in the computation of the depreciation expense. Use the following column headings:

Machine	Method of Depreciation	Date of Acquisition	Cost	Estimated Residual Value	Amount to Be Depreciated	Useful Life, Years	Accumulated Depreciation, Dec. 31, Year 5	Depreciation Expense, Year 6

c Prepare a journal entry to record the depreciation expense for Year 6.

12-6 Machinery with an estimated useful life of 10 years had been acquired by Chain Fence Company at a cost of $108,000. Straight-line depreciation had been used with no provision for residual salvage value because the expense of dismantling and removing the machinery at the end of its useful life was expected to be as much as any salvage received.

After several years of using the machinery, Chain Fence Company traded it in on new machinery priced at $162,000. A trade-in allowance of $14,400 was received. The accumulated depreciation on the old machinery amounted to $86,400 at December 31 prior to the year of the trade-in. No depreciation had been recorded between the closing of the accounts at December 31 and the exchange for the new machinery on April 1. The remainder of the trade-in transaction consisted of a $36,000 cash payment and the signing of a 10% one-year note payable for the balance of the purchase price of the new machine.

Instructions Prepare entries in general journal form to record the following:
a Depreciation for the fraction of a year prior to the April 1 transaction
b The acquisition of the new machinery on April 1 under the rules acceptable for income tax purposes
c The acquisition of the new machinery on April 1 under the assumption that the trade-in allowance represents the fair market value of the old machinery being traded in and the loss is to be recognized for financial reporting purposes

12-7 Rialto Corporation purchased new machinery on July 1, Year 7, at the advertised price of $32,500. The terms of payment were 2/10, n/30 and payment was made immediately, including a 4% state sales tax on $31,850. On July 3, the machinery was delivered; Rialto Corporation paid freight charges of $608 and assigned its own employees to the task of installation. The labor costs for installing the machinery amounted to $2,268. During the process of installation, carelessness by a workman caused damage to an adjacent machine, with resulting repairs of $288.

On October 15, after more than three months of satisfactory operation, the machinery was thoroughly inspected, cleaned, and oiled at a cost of $378.

The useful life of the machinery was estimated to be 10 years and the residual scrap value to be zero. The policy of the Rialto Corporation is to use straight-line depreciation and to begin depreciation as of the first of the month in which a plant asset is acquired. During Year 7 and Year 8, however, numerous changes in the company's accounting personnel were responsible for a number of errors and deviations from policy.

Depreciation expense recorded on the machinery for Year 7 was $1,593 and for Year 8, $3,185. At December 31, Year 8, the unaudited financial statements of the Rialto Corporation showed the machinery to be carried at a cost of $31,850 and the accumulated depreciation as $4,778. Net income reported for Year 7 was $89,280 and for Year 8, $99,540.

Instructions
a Prepare entries in general journal form for all the above transactions from July 1 to December 31, Year 7. Include the year-end entry for depreciation and the related closing entry.
b Compute the correct balances for the Machinery account and for accumulated depreciation at December 31, Year 8.
c Compute revised figures for new income for Year 7 and Year 8. (The only errors in the reported net income figures are those indicated by information given in

the problem.) Use a separate column for each year and begin with the reported net income for each year, followed by the necessary additions and deductions to arrive at corrected net income for each year. Disregard income taxes.

12-8 On January 1, Year 10, Midwest Petroleum, an established concern, borrowed $9 million from the First National Bank, issuing a note payable in five years with interest at 9%, payable annually on December 31. Also on January 1, the company purchased for $4,800,000 an undeveloped oil field estimated to contain at least 2 million barrels of oil. Movable equipment having an estimated useful life of five years and no scrap value was also acquired at a cost of $156,000.

During January the company spent $750,000 in developing the field, and several shallow wells were brought into production. The established accounting policy of the company was to treat drilling and development charges of this type as expense of the period in which the work was done.

Construction of a pipeline was completed on May 1, Year 10, at a cost of $1,440,000. Although this pipeline was physically capable of being used for 10 years or more, its economic usefulness was limited to the productive life of the wells; therefore, the depreciation method employed was based on the estimated number of barrels of oil to be produced.

Operating costs incurred during Year 10 (other than depreciation, depletion, and interest on the bank loan) amounted to $960,000, and 230,000 barrels of oil were produced and sold.

In January, Year 11, further drilling expense was incurred in the amount of $600,000, and the estimated total capacity of the field was raised from the original 2,000,000 barrels to 2,590,000 barrels, including oil produced to date.

Cash operating costs for Year 11 (excluding interest expense) amounted to $1,500,000, in addition to the $600,000 of drilling expense mentioned above. Oil production totaled 800,000 barrels, of which all but 80,000 barrels were sold during the year.

Instructions Prepare journal entries to record the transactions of Year 10 and Year 11, including the setting up of the inventory at December 31, Year 11. Do not prepare entries for sales. The inventory valuation should include an appropriate portion of the operating costs of the year, including depreciation and depletion. (Debit Inventory of Oil and credit respective expense accounts for costs allocable to ending inventory.)

12-9 Classic Furniture is considering purchasing the net assets, exclusive of cash, of Antique Reproductions on January 2, Year 7. Antique Reproductions, a single proprietorship owned by Francis Taylor, has been in business for six years and has reported an average annual net income of $41,000 during this period.

After any necessary adjustments have been made to the accounting records of Antique Reproductions, Classic Furniture will pay a price equal to the book value of net assets, excluding the cash of $35,000, plus an amount for goodwill. Classic Furniture will assume all liabilities of Antique Reproductions. The goodwill is to be determined as four times the amount by which average earnings exceed a normal rate of return of 12% on the present net identifiable assets (owner's equity less goodwill) of Antique Reproductions. The purchase plan calls for Classic Furniture to make a cash down payment of $100,000 and issue a promissory note for the balance of the purchase price.

The balance sheet for Antique Reproductions on December 31, Year 6, follows:

Assets

Cash			$ 35,000
Other current assets			71,000
Plant and equipment:			
Land		$113,600	
Buildings	$146,400		
Less: Accumulated depreciation	38,400	108,000	
Equipment	$186,000		
Less: Accumulated depreciation	117,000	69,000	290,600
Patent			54,000
Goodwill			15,000
Total assets			$465,600

Liabilities & Owner's Equity

Accounts payable	$ 74,000
Long-term liabilities:	
Mortgage note payable	110,000
Francis Taylor, capital	281,600
Total liabilities & owner's equity	$465,600

Other data
(1) The $15,000 of goodwill was recorded in the accounts three years ago when Taylor decided that the increasing profitability of the business should be recognized. Since profitability continued to increase, the goodwill was not amortized.
(2) The patent appears at original cost. It was acquired by purchase six years ago from a competitor who had owned the patent for two years of its legal life. The patent is considered very valuable to the business and should have a useful life equal to its legal life (15 years from the date Antique Reproductions acquired it).

Instructions
a Prepare any adjusting entries needed in the accounts of Antique Reproductions to bring the amounts shown in the balance sheet into accord with generally accepted accounting principles. (Two corrections are required.)
b Compute the amount of goodwill to be paid by Classic Furniture after considering the effects of the adjustments in a above. (The reported average net income should be adjusted to reflect amortization of the patent.) Also compute the total purchase price Classic Furniture will pay for the net assets of Antique Reproductions.
c Prepare a compound journal entry in the accounting records of antique Reproductions to record the sale to Classic Furniture. The entry should record:
(1) The closing of the asset and liability accounts (except Cash) to reflect the transfer of these items to Classic Furniture. (The "other current assets" of $71,000 may be treated as the title of a ledger account.)
(2) The receipt of the cash and the note receivable from Classic Furniture.
(3) The gain on the sale of the business.
d Prepare a compound journal entry in the accounting records of Classic Furniture to record the purchase of the assets (including goodwill as determined in b) and the assumption of the liabilities of Antique Reproductions. Classic Furniture records the assets acquired net of accumulated depreciation.

BUSINESS DECISION PROBLEM 12

Samuel Slater is interested in buying a manufacturing business and has located two similar companies being offered for sale. Both companies are single proprietorships which began operations three years ago, each with invested capital of $400,000. A considerable part of the assets in each company is represented by a building with an original cost of $100,000 and an estimated life of 40 years, and by machinery with an original cost of $200,000 and an estimated life of 20 years. Residual value is negligible.

Bay Company uses straight-line depreciation and Cove Company uses fixed-percentage-on-declining-balance depreciation (double the straight-line rate). In all other respects the accounting policies of the two companies are quite similar. Neither company has borrowed from banks or incurred any indebtedness other than normal trade payables. The nature of products and other characteristics of operations are much the same for the two companies.

Audited financial statements for the three years show net income as follows:

Year	Bay Company	Cove Company
1	$ 62,000	$ 59,000
2	65,200	63,200
3	68,400	66,900
Totals	$195,600	$189,100

Slater asks your advice as to which company to buy. They are offered for sale at approximately the same price, and Slater is inclined to choose Bay Company because of its consistently higher earnings. On the other hand, the fact that Cove Company has more cash and a stronger working capital position is impressive. The audited financial statements show that withdrawals by the two owners have been approximately equal during the three-year life of the two companies.

Instructions
a Compute the depreciation recorded by each company in the first three years. Round off depreciation expense for each year to the nearest dollar.
b Write a memorandum to Slater advising which company in your judgment represents the more promising purchase. Give specific reasons to support your recommendation.

13 Bonds Payable, Leases, and Other Liabilities

One of the most important functions of management is providing the funds required to operate the business. Several alternatives are generally available in meeting the temporary and the more permanent cash and working capital needs of a business. Management evaluates the cost and availability of each form of financing and selects the type most advantageous to the company and to its stockholders.

Inventories needed to meet seasonal peaks of activity may be obtained on account from trade creditors. Accounts payable, however, seldom constitute a sufficient source of financing. Cash needed for seasonal peaks of activity may be obtained through borrowing from banks. For example, a six-month bank loan might be arranged in order to buy merchandise for the peak selling season. The sale of the merchandise would provide cash with which to repay the bank loan.

If funds are needed for long-term purposes such as the construction of a new factory building, the borrowing may take the form of long-term mortgage notes or bonds. This will allow time for the increased earnings from the new plant facilities to be used in retiring the debt. A small business in need of permanent financing will often issue a long-term note secured by a mortgage on its plant assets; a large corporation in need of permanent financing will probably consider the issuance of bonds or additional shares of capital stock.

BONDS PAYABLE

A corporation may obtain money for a long-term purpose, such as construction of a new plant, by issuing long-term mortgage notes or bonds payable. Usually the amount of money needed is greater than any single lender can supply. In this case the corporation may sell bonds to the investing public, thus splitting the loan into a great many units, usually of $1,000 each. An example of corporation bonds is the 8% sinking fund debentures of The Singer Company due January 15, 1999, by which The Singer Company borrowed $100 million.

Characteristics of a bond

A bondholder is a creditor of the corporation; a stockholder is an owner. From the viewpoint of the issuing corporation, bonds payable constitute a long-term liability. Throughout the life of this liability the corporation makes semiannual payments of interest to the bondholders for the use of their money.

Formal approval of the board of directors and of the stockholders is usually required before bonds can be issued. The contract between the corporation and the *trustee* (usually a bank) representing the bondholders may place some limitation on the payment of dividends to stockholders during the life of the bonds. For example, dividends may be permitted only when working capital is above specified amounts. In the event that the corporation encounters financial difficulties and is unable to make the required payments of interest or principal, the bondholders may force the corporation into bankruptcy.

Mortgage bonds are secured by the pledge of specific assets. An unsecured bond is called a *debenture bond;* its value rests upon the general credit of the corporation. A debenture bond issued by a very large and strong corporation may have a higher investment rating than a secured bond issued by a corporation in less satisfactory financial condition.

Some bonds have a single fixed maturity date for the entire issue. Other bond issues, called *serial bonds,* provide for varying maturity dates to lessen the problem of accumulating cash for payment. For example, serial bonds in the amount of $10 million issued in 1975 might call for $1 million of bonds to mature in 1985, and an additional $1 million to become due in each of the succeeding nine years. Almost all bonds are *callable,* which means that the corporation has the right to pay off the bonds in advance of the scheduled maturity date. The call price is usually somewhat higher than the face value of the bonds.

As an additional attraction to investors, corporations sometimes include a conversion privilege in the bond indenture. A *convertible bond* is one which may be exchanged for common stock at the option of the bondholder. The advantages to the investor of the conversion feature in the event of increased earnings for the company were described in Chapter 7 with regard to convertible preferred stock.

REGISTERED BONDS AND COUPON BONDS Most corporation bonds issued in recent years have been *registered* bonds; that is, the name of the owner is registered with the issuing corporation. Payment of interest is made by semiannual checks mailed to the registered owner. *Coupon* bonds were more popular some years ago and many are still outstanding. Coupon bonds have interest coupons attached; each six months during the life of the bond one of these coupons becomes due. The bondholder detaches the coupon and deposits it with a bank for collection. The names of the bondholders are not registered with the corporation.

TRANSFERABILITY OF BONDS Corporation bonds, like capital stocks, are traded daily on organized securities exchanges. The holders of a 25-year bond issue need not wait 25 years to convert their investment into cash. By placing a telephone call to a broker, an investor may sell bonds within a matter of minutes at the going market price. This quality of liquidity is one of the most attractive features of an investment in corporation bonds.

QUOTED MARKET PRICES As illustrated in Chapter 9, corporate bond prices are quoted as a *percentage* of the bond's maturity value (or par value), which generally is $1,000. Thus, a bond quoted at 102 has a market value of $1,020 ($1,000 × 102%). Bond prices are quoted at the nearest one-eighth of a percentage point.

Effect of bond financing on holders of capital stock

Interest payments on bonds payable are deductible as an expense by the issuing company in determining the income subject to corporation income tax, but dividends paid on capital stock are not. High tax rates on corporate earnings thus encourage the use of bonds to obtain long-term capital.

Assume that a growing and profitable corporation with 100,000 shares of capital stock outstanding is in need of $10 million cash to finance a new plant. The management is considering whether to issue an additional 100,000 shares of stock or to issue 8% bonds. Assume also that after acquisition of the new plant, the annual earnings of the corporation, before deducting interest expense or income taxes will amount to $2 million. From the viewpoint of the stockholders, which financing plan is preferable? The following schedule shows the earnings per share of capital stock under the two alternative methods of financing:

	If Capital Stock Is Issued	If 8% Bonds Are Issued
Annual earnings before bond interest and income taxes	$2,000,000	$2,000,000
Less: Interest on bonds (8% of $10,000,000)		800,000
Earnings before income taxes	$2,000,000	$1,200,000
Less: Income taxes (assume 50% rate)	1,000,000	600,000
Net income	$1,000,000	$ 600,000
Number of shares of capital stock outstanding	200,000	100,000
Earnings per share of capital stock	$5.00	$6.00

Which financing plan is better?

Financing through issuance of additional capital stock rather than issuance of bonds saves $400,000 (after taxes) but results in *lower earnings per share* because of the *dilution* caused by doubling the number of shares outstanding.

The use of borrowed capital by business firms is referred to as *leverage* or *trading on the equity;* this concept is discussed further in Chapter 16.

Accounting entries for a bond issue

Assume that Wells Corporation on January 1, 1979, after proper authorization by the board of directors and approval by the stockholders, issues $1,000,000 of 20-year, 9% bonds payable. All the bonds bear the January 1, 1979, date, and interest is computed from this date. Interest on the bonds is payable semiannually, each July 1 and January 1. If all the bonds are sold at par value (face value), the sale will be recorded by the following entry:

Jan. 1	Cash	1,000,000
	Bonds Payable	1,000,000
	To record issuance of 9%, 20-year bonds at 100 on	
	the interest date.	

The first semiannual interest payment of $45,000 would be due on July 1. The computation is ($1,000,000 × .09) ÷ 2 = $45,000. The interest payment would be recorded by the following entry:

July 1	Bond Interest Expense	45,000
	Cash	45,000
	Paid semiannual interest on 9%, 20-year bonds with face	
	amount of $1,000,000.	

When the bonds mature 20 years later on January 1, 1999, the entry to record payment of the principal amount will be:

Jan. 1	Bonds Payable	1,000,000
	Cash	1,000,000
	Paid face amount of bonds at maturity.	

RECORDING THE ISSUANCE OF BONDS BETWEEN INTEREST DATES The semiannual interest dates (such as January 1 and July 1, or April 1 and October 1) are printed on the bond certificates. However, bonds are often issued between the specified interest dates. The investor is then required to pay the interest accrued to date of issuance in addition to the stated price of the bond. This practice enables the corporation to pay a full six months' interest on all bonds outstanding at the semiannual interest payment date. The accrued interest collected from investors purchasing bonds between interest payment dates is thus returned to them on the next interest payment date. To illustrate, let us modify our previous example for Wells Corporation and assume that the $1,000,000 face value of 9% bonds were issued at par and accrued interest, *two months after the interest date printed on the bonds.* The entry will be:

Bonds issued between interest dates

Cash	1,015,000	
Bonds Payable		1,000,000
Bond Interest Payable		15,000

Issued $1,000,000 face value of 9%, 20-year bonds at 100 plus accrued interest for two months.

Four months later on the regular semiannual interest payment date, a full six months' interest ($45 per each $1,000 bond) will be paid to all bondholders, regardless of when they purchased their bonds. The entry for the semiannual interest payment is illustrated below:

What is the net interest expense?

Bond Interest Payable	15,000	
Bond Interest expense	30,000	
Cash		45,000

Paid semiannual interest on $1,000,000 face value of 9% bonds.

Now consider these interest transactions from the standpoint of the investors. They paid for two months' accrued interest at the time of purchasing the bonds, and they received checks for six months' interest after holding the bonds for only four months. They have, therefore, been reimbursed properly for the use of their money for four months.

When bonds are subsequently sold by one investor to another, they sell at the quoted market price *plus accrued interest* since the last interest payment date. This practice enables the issuing corporation to pay all the interest for an interest period to the investor owning the bond at the interest date. Otherwise, the corporation would have to make partial payments to every investor who bought or sold the bond during the interest period.

The amount which investors will pay for bonds is the *present value* of the principal and interest payments they will receive. Before going further in our discussion of bonds payable, it will be helpful to review the concepts of present value and effective yield.

The concept of present value

The concept of present value is based upon the "time value" of money—the idea that receiving money today is preferable to receiving money at some later date. Assume, for example, that a bond has a maturity value of $1,000 in five years but pays no interest in the meantime. Investors would not pay $1,000 for this bond today, because they would receive no return on their investment over the next five years. There are prices less than $1,000, however, at which investors would buy the bond. For example, if the bond could be purchased for $600, the investor could expect a return (interest) of $400 from the investment over the five-year period.

The present value of a future cash receipt is the amount that a knowledgeable investor would pay *today* for the right to receive that future payment. The exact amount of the present value depends upon (*1*) the amount of the future payment, (*2*) the length of time until the payment will be received, and (*3*) the rate of return required by the investor. However, the present value will always be less than the future amount. This is because money received today can be invested to earn interest and thereby become equivalent to a larger amount in the future.

The rate of interest which will cause a given present value to grow to a given future amount is called the discount rate or *effective interest rate.* The effective interest rate required by investors at any given time determines the going *market rate* of interest.

The present value concept and bond prices

The price at which bonds will sell is the present value to investors of the future principal and interest payments. If the bonds sell at par, the effective interest rate is equal to the *nominal interest rate* (or contract rate) printed on the bonds. The higher the effective interest rate investors require, the less they will pay for bonds with a given nominal rate of interest. For example, if investors insist upon a 9% return, they will pay less than $1,000 for an 8%, $1,000 bond. Thus, if investors require an effective interest rate *greater* than the nominal rate of interest for the bonds, the bonds will sell at a *discount* (price less than face value). On the other hand, if investors require an effective interest rate of *less* than the nominal rate, the bonds will sell at a *premium* (price above face value).

A corporation wishing to borrow money by issuing bonds must pay the going market rate of interest. On any given date, the going market rate of interest is in reality a whole schedule of rates corresponding to the financial strength of different borrowers. Since market rates of interest are constantly fluctuating, it must be expected that the contract rate of interest printed on the bonds will seldom agree with the market rate of interest at the date the bonds are issued.

Bonds sold at a discount

To illustrate the sale of bonds at a discount, assume that a corporation plans to issue $1 million face value of 7%, 10-year bonds. At the issuance date, however, the going market rate of interest is slightly above 7% and the bonds sell at a price of only 98 ($980 for each $1,000 bond). The issuance of the bonds will be recorded by the following entry:

Issuing bonds at discount

Cash	980,000	
Discount on Bonds Payable	20,000	
Bonds Payable		1,000,000

Issued $1,000,000 face value of 7%, 10-year bonds at 98.

If a balance sheet is prepared immediately after the issuance of the bonds, the liability for bonds payable will be shown as follows:

Liability shown net of discount

Long-term liabilities:

7% bonds payable, due Dec. 31, Year 10	$1,000,000	
Less: Discount on bonds payable	20,000	$980,000

The amount of the discount is deducted from the face value of the bonds payable to show the present value or **carrying value** of the liability. At the date of issuance, the carrying value of bonds payable is equal to the amount for which the bonds were sold. In other words, the amount of the company's liability at the date of issuing the bonds is equal to the amount of money borrowed. Over the life of the bonds, however, we shall see that this carrying value gradually increases until it reaches the face value of the bonds at the maturity date.

BOND DISCOUNT AS PART OF THE COST OF BORROWING In Chapter 10, we illustrated two ways in which interest charges can be specified in a note payable: the interest may be stated as an annual percentage rate of the face amount of the note, or it may be included in the face amount. Bonds issued at a discount include **both** types of interest charge. The $1 million bond issue in our example calls for cash interest payments of $70,000 per year ($1,000,000 × 7% nominal interest rate), payable semi-annually. In addition to making the semiannual interest payments, the corporation must redeem the bond issue for $1 million on December 31, Year 10. This maturity value is $20,000 greater than the $980,000 received when the bonds were issued. Thus, the $20,000 discount in the issue price may be regarded as an **interest charge included in the maturity value of the bonds.**

Although the interest charge represented by the discount will not be paid to bondholders until the bonds mature, the corporation benefits from this cost during the entire period that it has the use of the bondholders' money. Therefore, the cost represented by the discount should be allocated over the life of the bond issue. The process of allocating bond discount to interest expense is termed **amortization** of the discount.

In short, whenever bonds are issued at a discount, the total interest cost over the life of the bonds is equal to the total regular cash interest payments **plus the amount of the discount.** For the $1 million bond issue in our example, the total interest cost over the 10-year life of the bonds is $720,000, of which $700,000 represents the 20 semiannual cash interest payments and $20,000 represents the discount. The average annual interest expense, therefore, is $72,000 ($720,000 ÷ 10 years), consisting of $70,000 paid in cash and $2,000 amortization of the bond discount. This analysis is illustrated below:

Total cash interest payments to bondholders ($1,000,000 × 7% × 10 years)		$700,000
Add: Interest charge included in face amount of bonds:		
Maturity value of bonds	$1,000,000	
Amount borrowed	980,000	20,000
Total cost of borrowing over life of bond issue		$720,000
Average annual interest expense ($720,000 ÷ 10 years)		$ 72,000

Amortization of bond discount

The simplest method of amortizing bond discount is the **straight-line method,** which allocates an equal portion of the discount to Bond Interest Expense in each period.[1] In our example, the Discount on Bonds Payable account has an initial debit balance of $20,000; each year one-tenth of this amount, or $2,000, will be amortized into Bond Interest Expense. Assuming that the interest payment dates are June 30 and December 31, the entries to be made each six months to record bond interest expense are as follows:

Payment of bond interest and straight-line amortization of bond discount

Bond Interest Expense	35,000	
Cash		35,000
Paid semiannual interest on $1,000,000 of 7%, 10-year bonds.		
Bond Interest Expense	1,000	
Discount on Bonds Payable		1,000

Amortized discount for six months on 10-year bond issue ($20,000 discount × $\frac{1}{20}$).

The two entries shown above to record the cash payment of bond interest and to record the amortization of bond discount can conveniently be combined into one compound entry, as follows:

Bond Interest Expense	36,000	
Cash		35,000
Discount on Bonds Payable		1,000

To record payment of semiannual interest on $1,000,000 of 7%, 10-year bonds ($1,000,000 × 7% × $\frac{1}{2}$) and to amortize $\frac{1}{20}$ of the discount on the 10-year bond issue.

---

[1] An alternative method of amortization, called the *effective interest method,* is illustrated later in this chapter. Although the effective interest method is theoretically preferable to the straight-line method, the resulting differences generally are not material in dollar amount.

Regardless of whether the cash payment of interest and the amortization of bond discount are recorded in separate entries or combined in one entry, the amount recognized as Bond Interest Expense is the same— $36,000 each six months, or a total of $72,000 a year. An accounting procedure that provides the same results is to amortize the bond discount only at year-end rather than at each interest-payment date.

Note that the additional interest expense resulting from amortization of the discount does not involve any additional cash payment. The credit portion of the entry is to the contra-liability account, Discount on Bonds Payable, rather than to the cash account. Crediting this contra-liability account *increases the carrying value of bonds payable.* The original $20,000 discount will be completely written off by the end of the tenth year, and the net liability (carrying value) will be the full face value of the bonds.

Bonds sold at a premium

Bonds will sell above par if the contract rate of interest specified on the bonds is higher than the current market rate for bonds of this grade. Let us now change our basic illustration by assuming that the $1 million issue of 7%, 10-year bonds is sold at a price of 102 ($1,020 for each $1,000 bond). The entry is shown below:

Issuing	Cash	1,020,000	
bonds at	Bonds Payable		1,000,000
premium	Premium on Bonds Payable		20,000
	Issued $1,000,000 face value of 7%, 10-year bonds at price		
	of 102.		

If a balance sheet is prepared immediately following the sale of the bonds, the liability will be shown as follows:

Carrying	Long-term liabilities:		
value			
increased	7% bonds payable, due Dec. 31, Year 10	$1,000,000	
by premium	Add: Premium on bonds payable	20,000	$1,020,000

The amount of any unamortized premium is *added* to the maturity value of the bonds payable to show the current carrying value of the liability. Over the life of the bond issue, this carrying value will be reduced toward the maturity value of $1,000,000.

BOND PREMIUM AS REDUCTION IN THE COST OF BORROWING We have illustrated how issuing bonds at a discount increases the cost of borrowing above the amount of the regular cash interest payments. Issuing bonds at a premium, on the other hand, *reduces the cost of borrowing below the amount of the regular cash interest payments.*

The amount received from issuance of the bonds is $20,000 greater than the amount which must be repaid at maturity. This $20,000 premium is not a gain but is to be offset against the periodic interest payments in determining the net cost of borrowing. Whenever bonds are issued at a premium, the total interest cost over the life of the bonds is equal to the regular cash interest payments *minus the amount of the premium.* In our example, the total interest cost over the life of the bonds is computed as $700,000 of cash interest payments minus $20,000 of premium amortized, or a net borrowing cost of $680,000. The annual interest expense will be $68,000, consisting of $70,000 paid in cash less an offsetting $2,000 transferred from the Premium on Bonds Payable account to the credit side of the Bond Interest Expense account.

The semiannual entries on June 30 and December 31 to record the payment of bond interest and amortization of bond premium are as follows:

Payment of	*Bond Interest Expense*	*35,000*	
bond	*Cash*		*35,000*
interest and			
straight-line	*Paid semiannual interest on $1,000,000 of 7%, 10-year bonds.*		
amortization			
of bond			
premium	*Premium on Bonds Payable*	*1,000*	
	Bond Interest Expense		*1,000*
	Amortized premium for six months on 10-year bond issue		
	($20,000 × $\frac{1}{20}$).		

Year-end adjustments for bond interest expense

In the preceding illustration, it was assumed that one of the semiannual dates for payment of bond interest coincided with the end of the company's accounting year. In most cases, however, the semiannual interest payment dates will fall during an accounting period rather than on the last day of the year.

For purposes of illustration, assume that $1 million of 8%, 10-year bonds are issued at a price of 97 on October 1, Year 1. Interest payment dates are April 1 and October 1. The total discount to be amortized amounts to $30,000, or $1,500 in each six-month interest period. The company keeps its accounts on a calendar-year basis; consequently, the adjusting entries shown below will be necessary at December 31 for the accrued interest and the amortization of discount applicable to the three-month period since the bonds were issued.

Bond Interest Expense	*20,750*	
Bond Interest Payable		*20,000*
Discount on Bonds Payable		*750*
To adjust for accrued interest on bonds and to amortize discount		
for period from Oct. 1 to Dec. 31. Accrued interest: $1,000,000 ×		
.08 × $\frac{3}{12}$ = $20,000. Amortization: $30,000 × $\frac{3}{120}$ = $750.		

If the above bonds had been issued at a premium, similar entries would be made at the end of the period for any accrued interest and for amortization of premium for the fractional period from October 1 to December 31.

In the December 31, Year 1, balance sheet, the $20,000 of Accrued Bond Interest Payable will appear as a current liability; the long-term liability for bonds payable will appear as follows:

Long-term liabilities:
8% Bonds payable, due Oct. 1, Year 11 . . . . $1,000,000
Less: Discount on bonds payable 29,250 $970,750

When the bonds were issued on October 1, the net liability for bonds payable was $970,000. Note that the carrying value of the bonds has *increased* over the three months by the amount of discount amortized. When the entire discount has been amortized, the carrying value of the bonds will be $1,000,000, which is equal to their maturity value.

At April 1, Year 2, it is necessary to record interest expense and discount amortization only for the three-month period since year-end. Of the semiannual $40,000 cash payment to bondholders, one-half, or $20,000, represents payment of the liability for Bond Interest Payable recorded on December 31, Year 1. The entry on April 1 is:

Bond Interest Expense *20,750*
Bond Interest Payable *20,000*
  Discount on Bonds Payable *750*
  Cash *40,000*
To record bond interest expense and amortization of discount for
three-month period since year-end and to record semiannual
payment to bondholders.

Straight-line amortization: a theoretical shortcoming

Although the straight-line method of amortizing bond discount or premium recognizes the full cost of borrowing over the life of a bond issue, the method has one conceptual weakness: the same dollar amount of interest expense is recognized each year. Amortizing a discount, however, causes a gradual increase in the liability for bonds payable; amortizing a premium causes a gradual decrease in the liability. If the uniform annual interest expense is expressed as a percentage of either an increasing or a decreasing liability, it appears that the borrower's cost of capital is changing over the life of the bonds.

This problem can be avoided by using the *effective interest method* of amortizing bond discount or premium. The effective interest method recognizes annual interest expense equal to a **constant percentage of the carrying value of the related liability**. This percentage is the effective rate of interest incurred by the borrower. For this reason, the effective interest method of amortization is considered theoretically preferable to the straight-line method. Whenever the two methods would produce *materially different* annual results, the Financial Accounting Standards Board requires the use of the effective interest method.

Over the life of the bonds, both amortization methods recognize the same total amount of interest expense. Even on an annual basis, the results produced by the two methods usually are very similar. Consequently, either method generally would meet the requirements of the FASB. Because of its simplicity, the straight-line method is widely used despite the theoretical arguments favoring the effective interest method.

Effective interest method of amortization

When bonds are sold at a discount, the effective interest rate incurred by the issuing corporation is *higher* than the contract rate printed on the bonds. Conversely, when bonds are sold at a premium, the effective rate of interest is *lower* than the contract rate.

When the effective interest method is used, bond interest expense is determined by multiplying the *carrying value of the bonds* at the beginning of the period by the *effective rate of interest* for the bond issue. The amount of discount or premium to be amortized is the *difference* between the interest expense computed in this manner and the amount of interest paid (or payable) to bondholders for the period. The computation of effective interest expense and the amount of discount or premium amortization for the life of the bond issue is made in advance on a schedule called an *amortization table.*

SALE OF BONDS AT A DISCOUNT To illustrate the effective interest method, assume that on May 1, Year 1, a corporation issues $100,000 face value, 7%, 10-year bonds with interest dates of November 1 and May 1. The bonds sell for $93,205, a price resulting in an effective interest rate of 8%.[2] An amortization table for this bond issue is shown on page 528. (Amounts of interest expense have been rounded to the nearest dollar.)

[2] Computation of the exact effective interest rate involves mathematical techniques beyond the scope of this course. A very close estimate of the effective interest rate can be obtained by dividing the *average* annual interest expense by the *average* carrying value of the bonds. Computation of average annual interest expense was illustrated on page 523. The average carrying value of the bonds is found by adding the issue price and the maturity value of the bond issue and dividing this sum by 2. Applying these procedures to the bond issue in our example provides an estimated effective interest rate of 7.95%, computed [($70,000 interest + $6,795 discount) ÷ 10 years] divided by [($93,205 + $100,000) ÷ 2].

Amortization Table for Bonds Sold at a Discount

($100,000, 10-year bonds, 7% interest payable semiannually, sold at $93,205, to yield 8% compounded semiannually)

Six-Month Interest Period	(A) Interest Paid Semiannually ($3½% of Face Value)	(B) Effective Semiannual Interest Expense (4% of Bond Carrying Value)	(C) Discount Amortization (B − A)	(D) Bond Discount Balance	(E) Carrying Value of Bonds, End of Period ($100,000 − D)
				$6,795	$ 93,205
1	$3,500	$3,728	$228	6,567	93,433
2	3,500	3,737	237	6,330	93,670
3	3,500	3,747	247	6,083	93,917
4	3,500	3,757	257	5,826	94,174
5	3,500	3,767	267	5,559	94,441
6	3,500	3,778	278	5,281	94,719
7	3,500	3,789	289	4,992	95,008
8	3,500	3,800	300	4,692	95,308
9	3,500	3,812	312	4,380	95,620
10	3,500	3,825	325	4,055	95,945
11	3,500	3,838	338	3,717	96,283
12	3,500	3,851	351	3,366	96,634
13	3,500	3,865	365	3,001	96,999
14	3,500	3,880	380	2,621	97,379
15	3,500	3,895	395	2,226	97,774
16	3,500	3,911	411	1,815	98,185
17	3,500	3,927	427	1,388	98,612
18	3,500	3,944	444	944	99,056
19	3,500	3,962	462	482	99,518
20	3,500	3,982*	482	−0−	100,000

*In the last period, interest expense is equal to interest paid to bondholders plus the remaining balance on the bond discount. This compensates for the accumulated effects of rounding amounts.

This amortization table can be used to illustrate the concepts underlying the effective interest method of determining interest expense and discount amortization. Note that the "interest periods" in the table are the semiannual (six-month) interest periods. Thus, the interest payments (column A), interest expense (column B), and discount amortization (column C) are for six-month periods. Similarly, the balance of the Discount on Bonds Payable account (column D) and the carrying value of the liability (column E) are shown as of each semiannual interest payment date.

The original issuance price of the bonds ($93,205) is entered at the top of Column E. This represents the carrying value of the liability throughout the first six-month interest period. The semiannual interest payment, shown in Column A, is $3\frac{1}{2}$% (one-half of the annual contract rate) of the $100,000 face value of the bond issue. The semiannual cash interest payment does not change over the life of the bonds. The interest expense shown in Column B, however, *changes every period.* This expense is always a constant percentage of the carrying value of the liability as of the end of the preceding period. The "constant percentage" is the effective interest rate of the bond issue. The bonds have an effective annual interest rate of 8%, indicating a semiannual rate of 4%. Thus, the effective interest expense for the first six-month period is $3,728 (4% of $93,205). The discount amortization for period 1 is the difference between this effective interest expense and the contract rate of interest paid to bondholders.

Note that after the discount is reduced by $228 at the end of period 1, the carrying value of the bonds in Column E *increases* by $228 (from $93,205 to $93,433). In period 2, the effective interest expense is determined by multiplying the effective semiannual interest rate of 4% by this new carrying value of $93,433 (4% $\times$ $93,433 = $3,737).

Semiannual interest expense may be recorded every period directly from the date in the amortization table. For example, the entry to record bond interest expense at the end of the first six-month period is:

Bond Interest Expense	*3,728*	
Discount on Bonds Payable		*228*
Cash		*3,500*
To record semiannual interest payment and amortize discount		
for six months.		

Similarly, interest expense at the end of the fifteenth six-month period would be recorded by:

Bond Interest Expense	*3,895*	
Discount on Bonds Payable		*395*
Cash		*3,500*
To record semiannual interest payment and amortize discount		
for six months.		

When a bond discount is amortized, the carrying value of the liability for bonds payable *increases* every period toward the maturity value. Since the effective interest expense in each period is a constant percentage of this increasing carrying value, the interest expense also increases from one period to the next. This is the basic difference between the effective interest method and straight-line amortization.

SALE OF BONDS AT A PREMIUM Let us now change our basic illustration by assuming that the $100,000 issue of 7%, 10-year bonds is sold on May 1, Year 1, at a price of $107,443, resulting in an effective interest rate of 6% annually (3% per six-month interest period). An amortization table for this bond issue is shown on page 530.

Amortization Table for Bonds Sold at a Premium

**($100,000, 10-year bonds, 7% interest payable semiannually,
sold at $107,443, to yield 6% compounded semiannually)**

	(A)	(B) Effective Semiannual Interest	(C)	(D)	(E)
Six-Month Interest Period	Interest Paid Semiannually ($3\frac{1}{2}$% of Face Value)	Expense (3% of Bond Carrying Value)	Premium Amortization (A − B)	Bond Premium Balance	Carrying Value of Bonds, End of Period ($100,000 + D)
				$7,443	$107,443
1	$3,500	$3,223	$277	7,166	107,166
2	3,500	3,215	285	6,881	106,881
3	3,500	3,206	294	6,587	106,587
4	3,500	3,198	302	6,285	106,285
5	3,500	3,189	311	5,974	105,974
6	3,500	3,179	321	5,653	105,653
7	3,500	3,170	330	5,323	105,323
8	3,500	3,160	340	4,983	104,983
9	3,500	3,149	351	4,632	104,632
10	3,500	3,139	361	4,271	104,271
11	3,500	3,128	372	3,899	103,899
12	3,500	3,117	383	3,516	103,516
13	3,500	3,105	395	3,121	103,121
14	3,500	3,094	406	2,715	102,715
15	3,500	3,081	419	2,296	102,296
16	3,500	3,069	431	1,865	101,865
17	3,500	3,056	444	1,421	101,421
18	3,500	3,043	457	964	100,964
19	3,500	3,029	471	493	100,493
20	3,500	3,007*	493	−0−	100,000

*In the last period, interest expense is equal to interest paid to bondholders minus the remaining balance of the bond premium. This compensates for the accumulated effects of rounding amounts.

In this amortization table, the interest expense for each six-month period is equal to 3% of the carrying value at the beginning of that period. This amount of interest expense is less than the amount of cash being paid to bondholders, illustrating that the effective interest rate is less than the nominal rate.

Based upon this amortization table, the entry to record the interest payment and amortization of the premium for the first six months of the bond issue is:

Amortization of premium decreases interest expense	Bond Interest Expense	3,223	
	Premium on Bonds Payable	277	
	Cash		3,500
	To record semiannual interest payment and amortization of premium.		

Note that as the carrying value of the liability declines, so does the amount recognized as bond interest expense.

YEAR-END ADJUSTING ENTRIES Since the amounts recognized as interest expense change from one period to the next, we must refer to the appropriate interest period in the amortization table to obtain the dollar amounts for use in year-end adjusting entries. To illustrate, consider our example of the bonds sold at a premium on May 1, Year 1. The entry to record interest and amortization of the premium through November 1, Year 1, was shown on page 530. If the company keeps its accounts on a calendar-year basis, two months' interest has accrued as of December 31, Year 1, and the following adjusting entry is made (amounts rounded to nearest dollar):

Bond Interest Expense	*1,072*	
Premium on Bonds Payable	*95*	
Bond Interest Payable		*1,167*

To record two months' accrued interest and amortize one-third of the premium for the interest period.

This adjusting entry covers one-third (two months) of the second interest period. Consequently, the amounts shown as bond interest expense and amortization of premium are one-third of the amounts shown in the amortization table for the second interest period. Similar adjusting entries must be made at the end of every accounting period while the bonds are outstanding. The dollar amounts of these adjusting entries will vary, however, since the amounts of interest expense and premium amortization change in every interest period. The amounts applicable to any given adjusting entry will be the appropriate fraction of the amounts for the interest period then in progress.

Amortization of bond discount or premium from the investor's viewpoint

We have discussed the need for the corporation issuing bonds payable to amortize any bond discount or premium to measure correctly the bond interest expense. But what about the **purchaser** of the bonds? Should an investor in bonds amortize any difference between the cost of the investment and its future maturity value in order to measure investment income correctly? The answer to this question depends upon whether the investor considers the bonds to be a **short-term** or a **long-term** investment.

A short-term investment in bonds generally is carried in the investor's accounting records at **cost,** and a gain or a loss is recognized when the investment is sold. Short-term investments in bonds usually will be sold before the bonds mature and the sales price will be determined by the current state of the bond market. Under these conditions, there is no assurance that amortization of premium or discount would give any more accurate measurement of investment income than would be obtained by carrying the bonds at cost.

When bonds are owned for the long-term, however, it becomes more probable that the market price of the investment will move toward the maturity value of the bonds. At the maturity date, of course, the market value will be the maturity value of the bonds. Thus, companies making long-term investments in bonds *should* amortize any difference between the cost of the investment and its maturity value over the life of the bonds. If the effective interest method of amortization would produce results materially different from those obtained by the straight-line method, the effective interest method should be used.[3]

Investments in bonds are usually recorded in a single account; that is, the investing company does not use separate accounts to record the face value of the investment and any related premium or discount. Amortization of the difference between cost and maturity value is recorded by direct adjustment to the Investment account. When a long-term investment in bonds is purchased at a discount, the amortization entries consist of a debit to Investment in Bonds and a credit to Interest Revenue. When the bonds are purchased at a premium, amortization is recorded by debiting Interest Revenue and crediting Investment in Bonds.

Retirement of bonds payable

Bonds are sometimes retired before the scheduled maturity date. The principal reason for retiring bonds prior to their maturity date is to relieve the issuing corporation of the obligation to make future interest payments. If interest rates decline to the point where a corporation can borrow at an interest rate below that being paid on a particular bond issue, the corporation may benefit from retiring those bonds and borrowing from an alternative source.

Most bond issues contain a call provision, permitting the corporation to redeem the bonds by paying a specified price, usually a few points above par. Even without a call provision, the corporation may retire its bonds before maturity by purchasing them in the open market. If the bonds can be purchased by the issuing corporation at less than their carrying value, a gain is realized on the retirement of the debt. If the bonds are reacquired by the issuing corporation at a price in excess of their carrying value, a loss must be recognized. In *Statement No. 4,* the FASB ruled that these gains and losses, if *material* in amount, should be shown separately in the income statement as extraordinary items.[4]

For example, assume that the Briggs Corporation has outstanding a $1 million bond issue with unamortized premium in the amount of $20,000. The bonds are callable at 105 and the company exercises the call provi-

---

[3]*APB Opinion No. 21,* "Interest on Receivables and Payables," AICPA (New York: 1971), p. 423.

[4]Financial Accounting Standards Board, *Statement No. 4,* "Reporting Gains and Losses from Extinguishment of Debt," FASB (Stamford, Conn.: 1975).

sion on 100 of the bonds, or 10% of the issue. The entry would be as follows:

<table>
<tr><td rowspan="5">*Bonds called at price above carrying value*</td><td>*Bonds Payable* . . . .</td><td>*100,000*</td><td></td></tr>
<tr><td>*Premium on Bonds Payable* . . . .</td><td>*2,000*</td><td></td></tr>
<tr><td>*Loss on Retirement of Bonds* . . . .</td><td>*3,000*</td><td></td></tr>
<tr><td>*Cash* . . . .</td><td></td><td>*105,000*</td></tr>
</table>

To record retirement of $100,000 face value of bonds called at 105.

The carrying value of each of the 100 called bonds was $1,020, whereas the call price was $1,050. For each bond called the company incurred a loss of $30, or a total loss of $3,000. Note that when 10% of the total issue was called, 10% of the unamortized premium was written off.

If bonds remain outstanding until the maturity date, the discount or premium will have been completely amortized and the accounting entry to retire the bonds (assuming that interest is paid separately) will consist of a debit to Bonds Payable and a credit to Cash.

One year before the maturity date, the bonds payable may be reclassified from long-term debt to a current liability in the balance sheet if payment is to be made from current assets rather than from a bond sinking fund.

Conversion of bonds payable into common stock

Convertible bonds represent a popular form of financing, particularly during periods when common stock prices are rising. The conversion feature gives bondholders an opportunity to profit from a rise in the market price of the issuing company's common stock while still maintaining their status of creditors rather than stockholders. Because of this potential gain, convertible bonds generally carry lower interest rates than nonconvertible bonds.

The conversion ratio is typically set at a price above the current market price of the common stock at the date the bonds are authorized. For example, if common stock with a par value of $10 a share has a current market price of $42 a share, the **conversion price** might be set at $50 per share, thus enabling a holder of a $1,000 par value convertible bond to exchange the bond for 20 shares of common stock.[5] Let us assume that $5 million of such bonds are issued at par, and that some time later when the common stock has risen in price to $60 per share, the holders of 100 bonds decide to convert their bonds into common stock. The conversion transaction would be recorded as follows:

---

[5] $1,000 ÷ $50 conversion price = 20 shares of common stock.

Conversion of bonds into common stock

Convertible Bonds Payable	100,000	
Common Stock, $10 par		20,000
Paid-in Capital in Excess of Par		80,000

To record the conversion of 100 bonds into 2,000 shares of common stock.

No gain or loss is recognized by the issuing corporation upon conversion of bonds; the carrying value of the bonds is simply assigned to the common stock issued in exchange. If the bonds had been issued at a price above or below par, the unamortized premium or discount relating to the bonds would be written off at the time of conversion in order to assign the carrying value of the bonds to the common stock.

Bond sinking fund

To make a bond issue attractive to investors, corporations may agree to create a sinking fund, exclusively for use in paying the bonds at maturity. A bond sinking fund is created by setting aside a specified amount of cash at regular intervals. The cash is usually deposited with a trustee, who invests it and adds the earnings to the amount of the sinking fund. The periodic deposits of cash plus the earnings on the sinking fund investments should cause the fund to equal approximately the amount of the bond issue by the maturity date. When the bond issue approaches maturity, the trustee sells all the securities in the fund and uses the cash proceeds to pay the holders of the bonds. Any excess cash remaining in the fund will be returned to the corporation by the trustee.

A bond sinking fund is not included in current assets because it is not available for payment of current liabilities. The cash and securities comprising the fund are usually shown as a single amount under Investments, placed just below the current asset section. Interest earned on sinking fund securities constitutes revenue to the corporation.

LEASES

A company may purchase the assets needed for use in its business or it may choose to lease them. Examples of assets often acquired by lease include buildings, office equipment, automobiles, and factory machinery. A *lease* is a contract in which the *lessor* gives the *lessee* the right to use an asset in return for periodic rental payments. Accounting for the many forms of lease transactions and the disclosure of lease obligations by lessees are among the more important issues facing accountants today.

Operating lease

When the lessor gives the lessee the right to use the leased property for a limited period of time but retains the usual risks and rewards of ownership, the contract is known as an *operating lease.* In accounting for an operating lease, the lessor accounts for the monthly lease payments received as rental revenue. The lessee accounts for the lease payments as rental expense; no asset or liability (other than a short-term liability for accrued rent payable) relating to the lease is recorded in the lessee's accounts.

Capital lease

When the objectives of the lease contract are to provide financing to the lessee for the eventual purchase of the property, or for use of the property over most of its useful life, the contract is referred to as a *capital lease* (or a *financing lease*). Even though title to the leased property has not been transferred, capital leases are regarded as *essentially equivalent to a sale* of the property by the lessor to the lessee. Thus, a capital lease should be recorded as a *sale* of property by the lessor and as a *purchase* by the lessee. In such lease agreements, an appropriate interest charge usually is added to the regular sales price of the property in determining the total amount of the lease payments.

Some manufacturing companies frequently use capital lease agreements as a means of financing the sale of their products to customers. In accounting for merchandise "sold" through a capital lease, the lessor would debit Lease Payments Receivable and credit Sales for an amount equal to the present value of the future lease payments. In most cases, the present value of these future payments is equal to the regular sales price of the merchandise. In addition, the lessor would transfer the cost of the leased merchandise into the Cost of Goods Sold account. When lease payments are received, the lessor should recognize an appropriate portion of the payment as representing interest revenue and the remainder as a reduction in Lease Payments Receivable.

When equipment is acquired through a capital lease, the lessee should debit an asset account, Leased Equipment, and credit a liability account, Lease Payment Obligation, for the present value of the future lease payments. Lease payments made by the lessee are allocated between Interest Expense and a reduction in the liability Lease Payment Obligation. The asset account, Leased Equipment, is depreciated over the life of the equipment rather than the life of the lease.

DISTINGUISHING BETWEEN CAPITAL LEASES AND OPERATING LEASES In *Statement No. 13,* the FASB required that a lease which meets at least one of the following criteria be accounted for as a capital lease:[6]

1 The lease transfers ownership of the property to the lessee at the end of the lease term.

2 The lease contains a "bargain purchase option."

---

[6]*FASB Statement No. 13,* "Accounting for Leases," FASB (Stamford, Conn: 1976), pp. 9–10.

3 The lease term is equal to 75% or more of the estimated economic life of the property.

4 The present value of the minimum lease payments is at least 90% of the fair value of the leased property.

Only those leases which meet none of the above criteria may be accounted for as operating leases.

NEW STANDARDS REDUCE OFF-BALANCE-SHEET FINANCING Prior to the issuance of *FASB Statement No. 13,* the criteria defining capital leases were much narrower. As a result, a great number of long-term leases were accounted for as operating leases by the lessees. Operating leases often are called *off-balance-sheet financing,* because the obligation for future lease payments does not appear as a liability in the balance sheet of the lessee. As a result of the criteria set forth in *Statement No. 13,* the number of lease contracts qualifying as operating leases has been greatly reduced. In the opinion of the authors, accounting for long-term lease contracts as capital leases significantly improves the usefulness of the balance sheet in evaluating the resources and obligations of those companies which lease substantial portions of their productive assets.

A number of more complex issues and special situations are involved in accounting for leases; these are covered in *Intermediate Accounting* of this series.

OTHER LIABILITIES

Mortgages payable

Mortgages are usually payable in equal monthly installments. A portion of each payment represents interest on the unpaid balance of the loan and the remainder of the monthly payment reduces the amount of the unpaid balance (principal). Since the principal is being reduced each month, the portion of each successive payment representing interest will decrease and the portion of the payment going toward retirement of the principal will increase. This process is illustrated by the following schedule of payments for a three-month period on a 6.6% mortgage note with an unpaid balance of $100,000 at September 11 of the current year.

	Monthly Payment	Interest for One Month at 6.6% on Unpaid Balance	Reduction in Principal	Unpaid Principal Balance
Monthly Sept. 11				$100,000.00
payments Oct. 11	$1,000.00	$550.00	$450.00	99,550.00
on a Nov. 11	1,000.00	547.53	452.47	99,097.53
mortgage Dec. 11	1,000.00	545.04	454.96	98,642.57
note				

On December 31 of the current year, the portion of the unpaid principal balance of $98,642.57 that is due within one year should be classified as a current liability and the remainder as a long-term liability. In addition, the accrued interest for 20 days, amounting to $361.69 ($98,642.57 × 6.6% × $\frac{20}{360}$), would be included under current liabilities.

Pension plans

A *pension plan* is a contract between a company and its employees under which the company agrees to pay retirement benefits to eligible employees. An employer company generally provides for the payment of retirement benefits by making payments at regular intervals to an insurance company or some other outside agency. Pension obligations currently accruing are recorded by the employer company as a debit to Pension Expense and as a credit to Cash. When employees retire, the retirement benefits are paid by the insurance company. This type of arrangement is known as a *funded pension plan* and does not create a long-term pension liability in the balance sheet of the employer company.

When a company does not engage an outside agent to administer the pension plan, the entry to record the pension obligation currently accruing calls for a debit to Pension Expense and a credit to Liability under Pension Plan. Payments to retired employees would be recorded by debits to Liability under Pension Plan and credits to Cash. In the balance sheet, the portion of the *unfunded* pension liability expected to be paid currently would be shown as a current liability; the balance of the pension liability would be shown as long-term debt. Occasionally, a company-administered pension fund may be established to accumulate resources for payment of retirement benefits.

Among the more important accounting and reporting problems relating to pension plans are (*1*) determining the proper accounting period which should be charged for the pension benefits accruing to employees, (*2*) measuring the amount of pension expense in the determination of periodic net income, and (*3*) presenting the significant pension plan information in the financial statements and the accompanying notes. A discussion of these issues is appropriate in advanced accounting courses.[7]

Payroll accounting

Labor costs and related payroll taxes constitute a large and constantly increasing portion of the total costs of operating most business organizations. In the commercial airlines, for example, labor costs represent over 50% of total operating expenses.

The task of accounting for payroll costs would be an important one

---

[7] Accounting principles for pension plans are discussed in detail in *Intermediate Accounting* of this series and in *APB Opinion No. 8,* "Accounting for the Cost of Pension Plans," AICPA (New York: 1966).

simply because of the large amounts involved; however, it is further complicated by the many federal and state laws which require employers to maintain certain specific information in their payroll records not only for the business as a whole but also for each individual employee. Regular reports of total wages and amounts withheld must be filed with government agencies, accompanied by payments of the amounts withheld from employees and payroll taxes levied on the employer.

A distinction must be drawn between *employees* and *independent contractors.* Public accountants, architects, attorneys, and other persons who render services to a business for a fee but are not controlled or directed by the client are not employees but independent contractors, and the amounts paid to them are not subject to payroll taxes.

Deductions from earnings of employees

The take-home pay of most employees is considerably less than their gross earnings. Major factors explaining this difference between the amount earned and the amount received are social security tax, federal income tax withheld, and other deductions discussed below.

SOCIAL SECURITY TAX (FICA) Under the terms of the Social Security Act, qualified workers in covered industries who retire after reaching a specified age receive monthly retirement payments and Medicare benefits. Benefits are also provided for the family of a worker who dies before or after reaching this retirement age. Funds for the operation of this program are obtained through a tax levied under the Federal Insurance Contributions Act, often referred to as FICA taxes, or simply as *social security taxes.*

Employers are required by the Federal Insurance Contributions Act to withhold a portion of each employee's earnings as a contribution to the social security program. A tax at the same rate is levied against the employer. For example, assume that an employee earns $10,000 subject to FICA taxes of 6%. The employer will withhold $600 ($10,000 × .06) from the employee's earnings. The employer will then pay to the government the amount of $1,200, consisting of the $600 withheld from the employee plus an additional $600 of tax on the employer.

Two factors are involved in computing the FICA tax: the *base* or amount of earnings subject to tax, and the *rate* which is applied to the base. Both the base and the rate have been increased many times in recent years and future increases have already been legislated by Congress.[8] The following table indicates that individuals are required to pay approximately 36 times as much in 1981 as they were 30 years earlier.

---

[8] In 1977 Congress scheduled increases in the base earnings subject to social security taxes through 1981 and specified that thereafter the base would rise at the rate of inflation.

Year	Base (Earnings Subject to FICA Tax)	Tax Rate	Amount of Tax
1937	$ 3,000	1.0%	$ 30
1951	3,600	1.5%	54
1966	6,600	4.2%	277
1972	9,000	5.2%	468
1977	16,500	5.85%	965
1979	22,900	6.13%	1,404
1981	29,700	6.65%	1,975
1983	?	?	?

These changes in rates and in the base do not affect the accounting principles or procedures involved. For illustrative purposes in this book, we shall assume the rate of tax to be 6% on both the employee and the employer, applicable to a base of $24,000 (the first $24,000 of wages received by each employee in each calendar year). This assumption of round amounts for both the tax and the base is a convenient one for the purpose of illustrations and for the solution of problems by the student, regardless of frequent changes in the rate and base.

INCOME TAX WITHHOLDING The pay-as-you-go system of federal income tax requires employers to withhold a portion of the earnings of their employees. The amount withheld depends upon the amount of the earnings and upon the number of *exemptions* allowed the employee. The employee is entitled to one exemption for himself, and an additional exemption for each person qualifying as a dependent. (More extensive consideration of exemptions and other aspects of federal income taxes is found in Chapter 17.) The government provides withholding tax tables which indicate the amount to withhold for any amount of earnings and any number of exemptions.

The graduated system of withholding is designed to make the amount of tax withheld closely approximate the rates used in computing the individual's tax liability at the end of the year. Since persons in higher income brackets are subject to higher rates of taxation, the withholding rates are correspondingly higher for them.

States and cities which levy income taxes may also require the employer to withhold the tax from employees' earnings; the accounting for such withholdings would be similar to the procedures used for federal income taxes withheld.

OTHER DEDUCTIONS FROM EMPLOYEES' EARNINGS In addition to the compulsory deductions for taxes, many other deductions are voluntarily authorized by employees. Union dues and insurance premiums are among the most common of these payroll deductions. Others include charitable contributions, supplementary retirement programs and pension plans, and repayments of salary advances or other loans.

EMPLOYER'S RESPONSIBILITY FOR AMOUNTS WITHHELD When employers withhold a portion of employees' earnings for any reason, they must maintain accounting records which will enable them to file required reports and make designated payments of the amounts withheld. From the employers' viewpoint, most amounts withheld from employees' earnings represent current liabilities. In other words, the employers must pay to the government or some other agency the amounts which they withhold from employees' earnings.

Payroll records and procedures

Although payroll records and procedures vary greatly according to the number of employees and the extent of automation in processing payroll data, there are fundamental steps common to payroll work in most organizations. One of these steps taken at the end of each pay period is the preparation of a *payroll sheet* showing the names, earnings, and the net amount payable to each employee. When the computation of the payroll sheet has been completed, the next step is to distribute the payroll costs to various expense accounts and to record the expenses and the related liabilities in the ledger. A general journal entry, such as shown below, may be made to bring into the accounts the data summarized on the payroll sheet.

Recording periodic payroll Sales Salaries Expense	*4,800*	
Office Salaries Expense	*3,200*	
FICA Tax Payable (6% of $8,000)		*480*
Liability for Income Tax Withheld		*1,280*
Liability for Group Insurance Withheld		*150*
Accrued Payroll		*6,090*
To record the payroll for the period Jan. 1–Jan. 15.		

The two debits to expense accounts indicate that the business has incurred a total salary expense of $8,000; however, only $6,090 of this amount will be paid to the employees on payday. The payment will be recorded by a debit to Accrued Payroll and a credit to Cash. The remaining $1,910 (consisting of deductions for taxes and insurance premiums withheld) is lodged in liability accounts. Payment of these liabilities will be made at various later dates.

An earnings record must be maintained for each employee showing gross earnings, withholdings, and other information required by government agencies and by management.

WITHHOLDING STATEMENT By January 31 each year, employers are required to furnish every employee with a *withholding statement (Form W-2).* This form shows the gross earnings for the preceding calendar year and the amounts withheld for FICA tax and income tax. The employer sends one copy of this form to the Director of Internal Revenue (possibly one copy to the state) and also gives two copies to the employee. When the employee files his federal income tax return, he must attach a copy of the withholding statement.

Payroll taxes on the employer

The discussion of payroll taxes up to this point has dealt with taxes levied on employees and withheld from their pay. From the viewpoint of the employing company, such taxes are significant because it must account for and remit the amounts withheld to the appropriate government agencies. Payroll taxes are also levied on the *employer;* these taxes are expenses of the business and are recorded by debits to expense accounts, just as in the case of property taxes or license fees for doing business.

SOCIAL SECURITY (FICA) TAX The employer is taxed to help finance the social security program. The tax is figured at the same rate and on the same amount of earnings used to compute FICA tax on employees. (In all problems and illustrations in this book, the tax is assumed to be 6% on the first $24,000 of gross earnings by each employee in each calendar year.)

FEDERAL UNEMPLOYMENT INSURANCE TAX Unemployment insurance is another part of the national social security program designed to offer temporary relief to unemployed persons. The FUTA tax (Federal Unemployment Tax Act) is levied on *employers only* and is not deducted from the wages of employees. The FUTA tax (also known as "unemployment compensation" or UC) applies to approximately the same classes of employment as the FICA tax. The rates of tax and the wage base subject to the tax are changed from time to time. For purposes of illustration in this book, we shall assume that employers are subject to federal unemployment tax at the rate of 3.4% on the first $6,000 of *each employee's earnings* in each calendar year. However, the employer may take a credit against this tax (not in excess of 2.7% of the first $6,000 of each employee's wages) for amounts that are paid into state unemployment funds. As a result, an employer may be subject to a *federal* tax of only 0.7% on wages up to $6,000 per employee.

STATE UNEMPLOYMENT COMPENSATION TAX All the states participate in the federal-state unemployment insurance program. Although the state laws vary somewhat as to types of covered employment, the usual rate of tax is 2.7% of the first $6,000 of earnings by each employee during a calendar year. Most states have a *merit-rating plan* which causes changes in the tax rate for employers reflecting their record of stability of employment.

ACCOUNTING ENTRY FOR EMPLOYER'S PAYROLL TAXES The entry to record the employer's payroll taxes is usually made at the same time the payroll is recorded. For the payroll illustrated on page 540, the entry for all three of the payroll taxes on the employer is as follows. (None of the employees has earned over $6,000 in the current year.)

Payroll taxes on employer

Payroll Taxes Expense 752	
FICA Tax Payable (6% of $8,000)	480
State Unemployment Tax Payable (2.7% of $8,000)	216
Federal Unemployment Tax Payable (0.7% of $8,000)	56
To record payroll taxes on employer for period ended Jan. 15.	

Thus the total payroll expense for the employer is $8,752, which consists of wages of $8,000 and payroll taxes of $752.

ACCRUAL OF PAYROLL TAXES AT YEAR-END The payroll taxes levied against an employer become a legal liability when wages are actually paid, rather than at the time the services by employees are rendered. If the wages earned in a given accounting period are paid in the same period, the payroll tax expense is clearly applicable to that period. However, at year-end, most businesses make an adjusting entry to accrue wages earned by employees but not payable until the following period. Should the related payroll taxes on the employer also be accrued? Logically, both wages and taxes on such wages are an expense of the period in which the wages are earned and should therefore be accrued. However, as a practical matter, many businesses do not accrue payroll taxes because legally the liability does not come into being until the following year when the wages are paid. In determining income subject to federal income tax, the legal concept prevails, and payroll taxes cannot be deducted until the period in which paid.

PRESENTATION OF PAYROLL TAXES IN THE FINANCIAL STATEMENTS The payroll taxes levied on the employer and the taxes withheld from employees are current liabilities of the business until payment to the government is made. The following accounts are, therefore, classified in the balance sheet as current liabilities: FICA Tax Payable, Federal Unemployment Tax Payable, State Unemployment Tax Payable, and Liability for Income Tax Withheld. In many localities, additional liabilities may exist because of state and city income taxes.

Payroll Taxes Expense appears in the income statement and is apportioned between selling expenses and general expenses on the basis of the amount of payroll originating in each functional division. Thus, payroll taxes on salaries of salespeople are classified as a selling expense, and payroll taxes on office salaries are classified as a general expense.

PAYMENT OF PAYROLL TAXES A business must use the calendar year in accounting for payroll taxes, even though it uses a fiscal year for its financial statements and its income tax returns. Four times a year, the employer is required to report to the government the amounts withheld from employees' pay for income tax and FICA tax. The FICA tax on the employer is also reported on the same tax form. These reports are made during the month following the close of each quarter of the year. If the amounts withheld from employees plus payroll taxes on the employer are significant in amount, they must be deposited at frequent intervals with a Federal Reserve bank or a designated commercial bank.

The employer must file a federal unemployment tax return by January 31 of each year for the preceding calendar year. Most states require employers to file tax returns and to make payment of the state unemployment compensation tax on a quarterly basis.

Other current liabilities

In addition to the current liabilities discussed in this chapter, a wide variety of short-term obligations may be found in the balance sheet of a typical business unit. Most of these, such as accounts payable, dividends payable, deferred revenue, and corporate income taxes payable, were discussed in earlier chapters. Other examples of current liabilities include advances from customers, liabilities for services received by the business before the end of the period but not billed until the following period, and *estimated liabilities.*

An estimated liability is one known to exist, but for which the dollar amount is uncertain. A common example is the liability of a manufacturer to honor any warranty on products sold. For example, assume that a company manufactures and sells television sets which carry a two-year warranty. To achieve the objective of offsetting current revenue with all related expenses, the liability for future warranty repairs on television sets sold during the current period must be estimated at the balance sheet date. This estimate will be based upon the company's past experience.

Loss contingencies

In Chapter 10, we discussed the *contingent liability* which arises when notes receivable are discounted at a bank. A contingent liability may be regarded as a *possible* liability, which may develop into a full-fledged liability or may be eliminated entirely by a future event. Contingent liabilities are also called *loss contingencies.* "Loss contingencies," however, is a broader term, encompassing the possible impairment of assets as well as the possible existence of liabilities.

A common loss contingency is the possibility of loss which exists when a lawsuit is filed against a company. Until the lawsuit is resolved, however, uncertainty exists as to the amount, if any, of the company's liability. Central to the definition of a loss contingency is the presence of *uncertainty*—uncertainty as to both the amount of loss and whether, in fact, a loss has actually occurred.

Loss contingencies are recorded in the accounting records at estimated amounts only when both of the following criteria are met: (1) it is *probable* that a loss has been incurred, and (2) the amount of loss can be *reasonably estimated.*[9] An example of a loss contingency which meets these criteria and is recorded in the accounts is the estimated loss from doubtful accounts receivable. Loss contingencies which do not meet both of these criteria should still be *disclosed in footnotes* to the financial statements whenever there is at least a *reasonable possibility* that a loss has been incurred. Pending lawsuits, for example, almost always are disclosed in footnotes, and the loss, if any, is not recorded in the accounting records until the lawsuit is settled.

When loss contingencies are disclosed in footnotes to the financial statements, the footnote should describe the nature of the contingency and, if possible, provide an estimate of the amount of possible loss. If a reasonable estimate of the amount of possible loss cannot be made, the footnote should include the range of possible loss or a statement that an estimate cannot be made. The following footnote is typical of the disclosure of the loss contingency arising from pending litigation:

Footnote disclosure of a loss contingency Note 8: Contingencies

In October of the current year, the Company was named as defendant in a lawsuit alleging patent infringement and claiming damages of $408 million. The Company denies all charges in this case and is preparing its defenses against them. The Company is advised by legal counsel that it is not possible at this time to determine the ultimate legal and financial responsibility with respect to this litigation.

Users of financial statements should pay close attention to the footnote disclosure of loss contingencies. Even though no loss has yet been recorded in the accounting records, some loss contingencies may be so material in amount as to threaten the continued existence of the company.

KEY TERMS INTRODUCED OR EMPHASIZED IN CHAPTER 13

Amortization of discount or premium on bonds payable The process of systematically writing off a portion of bond discount to increase interest expense or writing off a portion of bond premium to decrease interest expense each period the bonds are outstanding.

Bond sinking fund Cash set aside by the corporation at regular intervals (usually with a trustee) to be used to pay the bonds at maturity.

Capital lease A lease contract which, in essence, finances the eventual purchase by the lessee of leased property. The lessor accounts for a capital lease as a sale of property; the lessee records an asset and a liability equal to the present value of the future lease payments. Also called a *financing lease.*

Carrying value of bonds The face amount of the bonds plus any unamortized premium or minus any unamortized discount.

Convertible bonds Bonds which can be exchanged for a specified amount of common stock of the issuing corporation at the option of the bondholder.

[9]*FASB Statement No. 5,* "Accounting for Contingencies," FASB (Stamford, Conn: 1975).

Coupon bonds Semiannual interest coupons are attached to the bonds, each coupon bearing a different date. Coupons can be detached as they come due and collected through a bank. Also called *bearer bonds* because they are transferred by delivery. The holder of the bond is assumed to be the owner.

Debenture bond An unsecured bond, the value of which rests on the general credit of the corporation. Not secured by pledge of specific assets.

Discount on bonds payable Amount by which the face amount of the bond exceeds the price received by the corporation at the date of issuance. Indicates that the contractual rate of interest is lower than the market rate of interest.

Effective interest method of amortization Discount or premium on bonds is amortized by the difference between the contractual cash interest payment each period and the amount of interest computed by applying the effective interest rate to the carrying value of the bonds at the beginning of the current interest period. Causes bond interest expense to be a constant percentage of the carrying value of the liability.

Effective interest rate The actual rate of interest expense to the borrowing corporation, taking into account the contractual cash interest payments and the discount or premium to be amortized.

Federal unemployment compensation tax (FUTA) A tax imposed on the employer by the Federal Unemployment Tax Act based on amount of payrolls. Designed to provide temporary payments to unemployed persons.

FICA tax A tax imposed by the Federal Insurance Contribution Act on both employer and employees. Used to finance the social security program.

Lessee The tenant, user, or renter of leased property.

Lessor The owner of property leased to a lessee.

Loss contingency A situation involving uncertainty as to whether or not a loss has occurred. The uncertainty will be resolved by a future event. An example of a loss contingency is the possible loss related to a lawsuit pending against a company. Although loss contingencies are sometimes recorded in the accounts, they are more frequently disclosed only in footnotes in the financial statements.

Nominal interest rate The contractual rate of interest printed on bonds. The nominal interest rate, applied to the face value of the bonds, determines the amount of the annual cash interest payments to bondholders. Also called the *contract interest rate.*

Off-balance-sheet financing An arrangement in which the use of resources is financed without the obligation for future payments appearing as a liability in the balance sheet. An operating lease is the most common example of off-balance-sheet financing.

Operating lease A lease contract which is in essence a rental agreement. The lessee has the use of the leased property, but the lessor retains the usual risks and rewards of ownership. The periodic lease payments are accounted for as rent expense by the lessee and as rental revenue by the lessor.

Premium on bonds payable Amount by which the issuance price of a bond exceeds the face value. Indicates that the contractual rate of interest is higher than the market rate.

Present value of a future amount The amount of money that an informed investor would pay today for the right to receive the future amount, based upon a specific rate of return required by the investor. Bond prices are the present value to investors of the future principal and interest payments. Capital leases are recorded as an asset and a related liability in the accounting records of the lessee at the present value of the future lease payments.

State unemployment compensation tax A tax levied on employers only and based on payrolls. A part of the joint federal-state program to provide payments to unemployed persons.

DEMONSTRATION PROBLEM FOR YOUR REVIEW

The balance sheet for the Colorado Corporation on December 31, Year 6, included the following liabilities:

Current liabilities:

Notes payable, due June 30, Year 7	$ 100,000	
Less: Discount on notes payable	3,750	$ 96,250
Accounts payable		141,000
Income taxes payable, due Mar. 15, Year 7		85,000
Accrued liabilities relating to payroll:		
FICA tax payable	$ 1,500	
Liability for income tax withheld	4,200	
State unemployment tax payable	360	
Federal unemployment tax payable	1,400	7,460
Total current liabilities		$ 329,710

Long-term liabilities:

8¾% bonds payable, due Jan. 1, Year 15	$5,000,000	
Less: Discount on bonds payable	72,000	4,928,000
Total liabilities		**$5,257,710**

During January of Year 7, the corporation completed the following transactions relating to liabilities:

(*1*) Borrowed $50,000 from City Bank on January 7, Year 7, and issued a 9%, six-month promissory note for $50,000 to the bank.

(*2*) Cash disbursements during January included payments to merchandise creditors, $128,000, and to liquidate the accrued liabilities relating to payroll, $7,460.

(*3*) Purchases of merchandise on account during January amounted to $112,500. The company uses a periodic inventory system.

(*4*) The payroll for January is summarized below:

Wages Expense	FICA Tax Withheld	Income Tax Withheld	Take-Home Pay	Payroll Taxes on Employer
$65,000	$3,900	$5,050	$56,050	$5,980

Payroll taxes on the employer consist of FICA tax, 6%; state unemployment tax, 2.7%; federal unemployment tax, 0.7%. Employees were paid on January 31; however, none of the taxes relating to the January payroll has been remitted to governmental agencies.

(*5*) On January 1, Year 7, the 8¾% bonds were called at a price of 102 and new 7½%, 20-year bonds were issued on January 10 as follows:

7½% bonds—$10,000,000 @ 101½	$10,150,000
Add: Interest from Jan. 1 to Jan. 10 (nine days)	18,750
Proceeds on issuance of bonds	$10,168,750

The face value of the 7½% bonds ($10,000,000), the premium on bonds payable ($150,000), and the bond interest payable ($18,750) should be recorded in three separate liability accounts. The 7½% bonds mature on January 1, Year 27, and call for the payment of interest at January 1 and July 1 of each year.

(*6*) The corporation has 250,000 shares of $10 par value capital stock outstanding. On January 5, Year 7, a cash dividend of 30 cents a share was declared, payable on February 10, Year 7, to holders of record on January 28, Year 7.

Instructions

a Prepare the journal entries to record the foregoing transactions.

b Prepare the adjusting entries required to bring the accounts up to date at January 31, Year 7. All discounts and premiums should be amortized through January 31 by the straight-line method.

c Prepare the liabilities section of the balance sheet at January 31, Year 7.

SOLUTION TO DEMONSTRATION PROBLEM

a *(1) Cash* 50,000

      Notes Payable   50,000

      Borrowed $50,000 from City Bank on Jan. 7,

      Year 7. Issued a six-month, 9% note payable.

(2) Accounts Payable 128,000

      FICA Tax Payable 1,500

      Liability for Income Tax Withheld 4,200

      State Unemployment Tax Payable 360

      Federal Unemployment Tax Payable 1,400

      Cash   135,460

      To record cash disbursements during January in

      payment for current liabilities.

(3) Purchases 112,500

      Accounts Payable   112,500

      To record purchase of merchandise on account

      during January.

(4) Wages Expense 65,000

      FICA Tax Payable   3,900

      Liability for Income Tax Withheld   5,050

      Accrued Payroll   56,050

      To record payroll for January.

      Accrued Payroll 56,050

      Cash   56,050

      To record payment of wages for January.

      Payroll Taxes Expense 6,110

      FICA Tax Payable   3,900

      State Unemployment Tax Payable   1,755

      Federal Unemployment Tax Payable   455

      To record payroll taxes on employer for January.

(5) 8¾% Bonds Payable 5,000,000

      Loss on Retirement of Bonds 172,000

      Discount on Bonds Payable   72,000

      Cash   5,100,000

      To record retirement of bonds at 102 on Jan. 1,

      Year 7.

Cash	10,168,750	
$7\frac{1}{2}$% Bonds Payable		10,000,000
Premium on Bonds Payable		150,000
Bond Interest Payable		18,750

To record issuance of bonds on Jan. 10, Year 7,
at $101\frac{1}{2}$ plus accrued interest for nine days.

(6) Dividends	75,000	
Dividends Payable		75,000

To record declaration of a cash dividend of 30
cents a share on 250,000 shares of capital stock.
The dividend is payable on Feb. 10, Year 7, to
holders of record on Jan. 28, Year 7.

b Adjusting entries:

Interest Expense	625	
Discount on Notes Payable		625

To record January interest on $100,000 note payable
maturing June 30, Year 7: $3,750 \times \frac{1}{6} = 625.

Interest Expense	300	
Interest Payable		300

To record accrued interest on $50,000, 9% note from Jan. 7
to Jan. 31: $50,000 \times \frac{24}{360} \times 9\% = 300.

Bond Interest Expense	43,125	
Premium on Bonds Payable ($150,000 \times \frac{1}{240}$)	625	
Bond Interest Payable		43,750

To record accrued interest and amortization of premium on
bonds payable for January ($10,000,000 \times 7\frac{1}{2}\% \times \frac{1}{12} =$
$62,500, less $18,750 recorded on Jan. 10 when bonds were
issued = $43,750).

c Liabilities section of the balance sheet at Jan. 31, Year 7:

Current liabilities:

Notes payable	$	150,000	
Less: Discount on notes payable		3,125	$ 146,875
Accounts payable			125,500
Income taxes payable, due March 15, Year 7			85,000
Dividends payable			75,000

Accrued liabilities:

Liability for income and FICA taxes withheld and payroll taxes (1)	$	15,060	
Interest on notes and bonds payable (2)		62,800	77,860
Total current liabilities			$ 510,235

Long-term liabilities:

$7\frac{1}{2}$% bonds payable, due Jan. 1, Year 27	$10,000,000	
Add: Premium on bonds payable	149,375	10,149,375
Total liabilities		$10,659,610

(1) $5,050 + $3,900 + $6,110 = $15,060
(2) $300 + $18,750 + $43,750 = $62,800

REVIEW QUESTIONS

1 Distinguish between the two terms in each of the following pairs:
 a Mortgage bond; debenture bond
 b Nominal (or contract) interest rate; effective interest rate
 c Fixed-maturity bond; serial bond
 d Coupon bond; registered bond
 e Operating lease; capital lease
 f Estimated liability; contingent liability

2 Discuss the advantages and disadvantages of a *call provision* in a bond contract from the viewpoint of (*a*) the bondholder and (*b*) the issuing corporation.

3 What is a *convertible bond?* Discuss the advantages and disadvantages of convertible bonds from the standpoint of the investor and the issuing corporation.

4 The Computer Sharing Co. has paid-in capital of $10 million and retained earnings of $3 million. The company has just issued $1 million in 20-year, 8% bonds. It is proposed that a policy be established of appropriating $50,000 of retained earnings each year to enable the company to retire the bonds at maturity. Evaluate the merits of this proposal in accomplishing the desired result.

5 The following excerpt is taken from an article in a leading business periodical: "In the bond market high interest rates mean low prices. Bonds pay out a fixed percentage of their face value, usually $1,000; a 5% bond, for instance, will pay $50 a year. In order for its yield to rise to $6\frac{1}{4}$%, its price would have to drop to $800." Give a critical evaluation of this quotation.

6 A recent annual report of Lear Siegler, Inc., contained the following note accompanying the financial statements: "The loan agreements . . . contain provisions as to working capital requirements and payment of cash dividends. At June 30, retained earnings of approximately $13,400,000 were available for payment of cash dividends." What is the meaning of this note and why is it considered necessary to attach such a note to financial statements? (The total retained earnings of Lear Siegler, Inc., at this date amounted to $77.5 million; working capital amounted to $100 million; and total liabilities amounted to $142 million.)

7 Explain why the effective rate of interest differs from the contract rate when bonds are issued (*a*) at a discount and (*b*) at a premium.

8 When the effective interest method is used to amortize bond discount or premium, the amount of bond interest expense will differ in each period from that of the preceding period. Explain how the amount of bond interest expense changes from one period to another when the bonds are issued (*a*) at a discount and (*b*) at a premium.

9 Explain why the effective interest method of amortizing bond discount or premium is considered to be theoretically preferable to the straight-line method.

10 An investor buys a $1,000, 9%, 10-year bond at 110 and a $1,000, 7%, 10-year bond at 90, both on the date of issue. Compute the average annual interest income that will be earned on these bonds if they are held to maturity.

11 John Lee buys a $1,000, 8% bond for 106, five years from the maturity date. After holding the bond for four years, he sells it for 102. Lee claims that he has a loss of $40 on the sale. A friend argues that Lee has made a gain on the sale. Explain the difference in viewpoint. With whom do you agree? Why?

12 Explain how the lessee accounts for an operating lease and a capital lease. Why is an operating lease sometimes called *off-balance-sheet financing?*

13 Name the federal taxes that most employers are required to withhold from employees. What account or accounts would be credited with the amounts withheld?

14 Distinguish between an *employee* and an *independent contractor.* Why is this distinction important with respect to payroll accounting?

15 Explain which of the following taxes relating to an employee's wages are borne by the employee and which by the employer:
a FICA tax
b Federal unemployment tax
c State unemployment tax
d Federal income tax

16 What purposes are served by maintaining a detailed earnings record for each employee?

17 Are the payroll taxes levied against employers considered a legal liability and a deductible expense for income tax purposes in the period the wages are earned by the employees or in the period the wages are paid?

18 Under what conditions are *loss contingencies* recorded at estimated amounts in the accounting records?

19 A lawsuit has been filed against Telmar Corporation alleging violations of federal antitrust laws and claiming damages which, when trebled, total $1.2 billion. Telmar Corporation denies the charges and intends to contest the suit vigorously. Legal counsel advises the company that the litigation will last for several years and that a reasonable estimate of the final outcome cannot be made at this time.

Should Telmar Corporation include in its current balance sheet a liability for the damages claimed in this lawsuit? Explain fully.

20 With reference to question **19** above, illustrate the disclosure of the pending lawsuit which should be included in the current financial statements of Telmar Corporation.

EXERCISES

Ex. 13-1 Birch Corporation obtained all necessary approvals to issue $10,000,000 face value of 9%, 10-year bonds, dated December 31, Year 4. Interest payment dates were June 30 and December 31. The bonds were not issued, however, until four months later, May 1, Year 5. On this date the entire issue was sold at a price of 100 plus accrued interest. Prepare the journal entries required on:
a May 1, Year 5, to record the issuance of the bonds
b June 30, Year 5, to record the first semiannual interest payment on the bond issue
c December 31, Year 5, to record the semiannual bond interest payment and to close the Bond Interest expense account at year-end

Ex. 13-2 Companies A and B have the same amount of operating income, but different capital structures. Determine the amount earned per share of common stock for each of the two companies and explain the source of any difference.

	Company A	Company B
5% debenture bonds payable	$500,000	$ 200,000
6% cumulative preferred stock, $100 par	500,000	300,000
Common stock, $50 par value	500,000	1,000,000
Retained earnings	250,000	250,000
Operating income, before interest and income taxes		
(assume a 40% tax rate)	300,000	300,000

Ex. 13-3 Crest Company issued $100,000 par value 6% bonds on July 1, Year 5, at 97½. Interest is due on June 30 and December 31 of each year, and the bonds mature on June 30, Year 15. The fiscal year ends on December 31; bond discount is amortized by the straight-line method. Prepare the following journal entries:

a July 1, Year 5, to record the issuance of the bonds
b December 31, Year 5, to pay interest and amortize the bond discount
c June 30, Year 15, to pay interest, amortize the bond discount, and retire the bonds at maturity

Ex. 13-4 North Company issued $10 million of 7%, 10-year bonds on January 1, Year 1. Interest is payable semiannually on June 30 and December 31. The bonds were sold to an underwriting group at 105.

South Company issued $10 million of 6%, 10-year bonds on January 1, Year 1. Interest is payable semiannually on June 30 and December 31. The bonds were sold to an underwriting group at 95.

Prepare journal entries to record all transactions during Year 1 for (a) the North Company bond issue and (b) the South Company bond issue. Assume that both companies amortize bond discount or premium by the straight-line method at each interest payment date.

Ex. 13-5 The following liability appears on the balance sheet of the Sunrise Company on December 31, Year 1:

Long-term liabilities:
Bonds payable, 6%, due December 31, Year 15 . . . . . . $1,000,000
Premium on bonds payable 42,000 $1,042,000

On January 1, Year 2, 20% of the bonds are retired at 98. Interest was paid on December 31, Year 1.

a Record the retirement of $200,000 of bonds on January 1, Year 2.
b Record the interest payment for the six months ending December 31, Year 2, and the amortization of the premium on December 31, Year 2, assuming that amortization is recorded by the straight-line method only at the end of each year.

Ex. 13-6 Basin Corporation has issued $1,000,000 of 10-year, 7% bonds payable on the date printed on the bonds and has received proceeds of $932,050, resulting in an effective annual interest rate of 8%. Interest is payable semiannually. The effective interest method is to be used to amortize the bond discount.

Instructions
a Prepare a journal entry to record the issuance of the bonds.
b Prepare a journal entry to record the payment of interest and amortization of discount at the first semiannual interest payment date. (See the amortization table for bonds sold at a discount on page 528.) Round the interest expense for the period to the nearest $10.
c Prepare a journal entry to record the payment of interest and amortization of discount at the end of the fifth six-month interest period. (See table as in b.) Round interest expense for the period to the nearest $10.

Ex. 13-7 Crown Point Corporation issued on the authorization date $1,000,000 of 10-year, 7% bonds payable and received proceeds of $1,074,430, resulting in an effective interest rate of 6%. The premium is to be amortized by the effective interest method. Interest is payable semiannually.

Instructions
a Show how the liability for the bonds would appear on a balance sheet prepared immediately after issuance of the bonds.
b Show how the liability for the bonds would appear on a balance sheet prepared after 16 semiannual interest periods (two years prior to maturity). Refer to the amortization table for bonds sold at a premium on page 530. Round unamortized premium to the nearest $10.
c If these 7% bonds were sold by Crown Point Corporation to yield 6% and interest is paid semiannually, show the necessary *calculations* to determine: interest expense by the effective interest method for the first six-month period, the premium amortized at the end of that first period, and the cash interest payment. Your calculations should include use of the effective interest rate and also the contractual rate.

Ex. 13-8 Brand Corporation issued $1,000,000 of 7%, 10-year convertible bonds dated December 31, Year 8, at a price of 98. Semiannual interest payment dates were June 30 and December 31. The conversion rate was 20 shares of $10 par common stock for each $1,000 bond. Four years later on December 31, Year 12, bondholders converted $250,000 face value of bonds into common stock. Assume that unamortized discount on this date amounted to $12,000 for the entire bond issue. Prepare a journal entry to record the conversion on the bonds.

Ex. 13-9 Martin earns a salary of $18,000 a year from Rand Corporation. FICA taxes are 6% of wages up to $24,000. Federal unemployment taxes are 3.4% of wages up to $6,000 a year, but a credit against this FUTA tax is permitted for payment to the state of 2.7% of wages up to $6,000 a year. Federal income tax of $3,600 was withheld from Martin's paychecks during the year.
a Prepare in general journal form a compound entry summarizing the payroll transactions for employee Martin for the full year. (In drafting this entry, ignore any payments of tax during the year and let the liability accounts show the totals for the year. Credit Cash for the amount paid to Martin.)
b What is the total yearly cost (including taxes) to Rand Corporation of having Martin on the payroll at an annual salary of $18,000?

Ex. 13-10 The payroll record of Miller Company for the week ended January 7 showed the following amounts for total earnings: sales employees $8,800; office employees $7,200. Amounts withheld consisted of FICA taxes at a 6% rate on all earnings for this period, federal income taxes $1,920, and medical insurance $600.
a After computing the amount of FICA taxes withheld, prepare a general journal entry to record the payroll. Do not include taxes on the employer.
b Prepare a general journal entry to record the payroll taxes expense to Miller Company relating to this payroll. Assume that the federal unemployment tax rate is 3.4% of the first $6,000 paid each employee, and that 2.7% of this tax is payable to the state. No employee received more than $6,000 in this first pay period of the year.

PROBLEMS

13-1 On September 1, Year 1, American Farm Equipment issued $3 million in 9% debenture bonds. Interest is payable semiannually on March 1 and September 1, and the bonds mature on September 1, Year 11. Company policy is to amortize bond discount or premium by the straight-line method at each interest payment date; the company's fiscal year ends at December 31.

Instructions Make the necessary adjusting entries at December 31, Year 1, and the journal entry to record the payment of bond interest on March 1, Year 2, under each of the following assumptions:
a The bonds were issued at 96.
b The bonds were issued at 102.
c Compute the net bond liability at December 31, Year 1, under assumptions in *a* and *b* above.

13-2 The items shown below appear in the balance sheet of Pilsner Breweries at December 31, Year 6:

Current liabilities:

Bond interest payable (for three months from Oct. 1
to Dec. 31) . . . . $ 200,000
Long-term debt:

Bonds payable, 8%, due Apr. 1, Year 17 . . . . $10,000,000
Less: Discount on bonds payable   196,800   9,803,200

The bonds are callable on any interest date. On October 1, Year 7, Pilsner Breweries called $2 million of the bonds at 103.

Instructions
a Prepare journal entries to record the semiannual interest payment on April 1, Year 7. Discount is amortized by the straight-line method at each interest payment date and was amortized to December 31, Year 6. Base the amortization on the 123-month period from December 31, Year 6 to April 1, Year 17.
b Prepare journal entries to record the amortization of bond discount and payment of bond interest at October 1, Year 7, and also to record the calling of $2 million of the bonds at this date.
c Prepare a journal entry to record the accrual of interest at December 31, Year 7. Include the amortization of bond discount to the year-end.

13-3 Kentucky Coal Mines obtained authorization to issue $800,000 of 9%, 10-year bonds, dated May 1, Year 1. Interest payment dates were May 1 and November 1. Issuance of the bonds did not take place until July 1, Year 1. On this date, the entire bond issue was sold to a private pension fund at a price which included the two months' accrued interest. Kentucky Coal Mines follows the policy of amortizing bond discount or premium by the straight-line method at each interest date as well as for year-end adjusting entries at December 31.

Instructions
a Prepare all journal entries necessary to record the issuance of the bonds and bond interest expense during Year 1, assuming that the sales price of the bonds on July 1 was $841,500 (including accrued interest).
b Assume that the sales price of the bonds on July 1 had been $790,760 (including accrued interest). Prepare journal entries for Year 1 parallel to those in part *a* above.
c Show the proper balance sheet presentation of the liability for bonds payable (including accrued interest) in the balance sheet prepared at December 31, *Year 6,* assuming that the original sales price of the bonds (including accrued interest) had been:
(1) $841,500, as described in part *a*
(2) $790,760, as described in part *b*

13-4 Red Sky Shipping maintains its accounts on a calendar-year basis. On June 30, Year 4, the company issued $6,000,000 face value of 7.6% bonds at a price of 97$\frac{1}{4}$, resulting in an effective rate of interest of 8%. Semiannual interest payment dates are June 30 and December 31. The bonds mature on June 30, Year 14.

Instructions

a Prepare the required journal entries on:

(1) June 30, Year 4 to record the sale of the bonds.

(2) December 31, Year 4, to pay interest and amortize the discount using the effective interest method.

(3) June 30, Year 14, to pay interest, amortize the discount, and retire the bonds. As of the beginning of this last interest period, the carrying value of the bonds is $5,988,461. (Use a separate journal entry to show the retirement of the bonds.)

b Show how the accounts, Bonds Payable and Discount on Bonds Payable, should appear on the balance sheet at December 31, Year 4.

13-5 On December 31, Year 4, Napa Vineyards sold an $8,000,000, $9\frac{1}{2}$%, 12-year bond issue to an underwriter at a price of $103\frac{1}{2}$. This price results in an effective annual interest rate of 9%. The bonds were dated December 31, Year 4, and the interest payment dates were June 30 and December 31. Napa Vineyards follows a policy of amortizing the bond premium by the effective interest method at each semiannual payment date.

Instructions

a Prepare an amortization table for the first two years (four interest periods) of the life of this bond issue. Round all amounts to the nearest dollar and use the following column headings:

(A) Six-Month Interest Period	(B) Interest Paid Semi- annually ($8,000,000 × $4\frac{3}{4}$%)	(C) Effective Semi- annual Interest Expense (Carrying Value × $4\frac{1}{2}$%)	(D) Premium Amortization (A − B)	(E) Bond Premium Balance	(E) Carrying Value of Bonds, End of Period ($8,000,000 + D)

b Using the information in your amortization table, prepare all journal entries necessary to record the bond issue and the bond interest expense during Year 5.

c Show the proper balance sheet presentation of the liability for bonds payable at December 31, Year 6.

13-6 Roan Antelope, Inc., on September 1, Year 1, issued $9,000,000 par value, $8\frac{1}{2}$%, 10-year bonds payable with interest dates of March 1 and September 1. The company maintains its accounts on a calendar-year basis and follows the policy of amortizing bond discount and bond premium by the effective interest method at the semiannual interest payment dates as well as at the year-end adjusting of the accounts.

Instructions

a Prepare the necessary journal entries to record the following transactions, assuming that the bonds were sold for $8,700,000, a price resulting in an effective annual interest rate of 9%.

(1) Sale of the bonds on September 1, Year 1

(2) Adjustment of the accounts at December 31, Year 1, for accrued interest and amortization of discount

(3) Payment of bond interest and amortization of discount on March 1, Year 2

b Assume that the sales price of the bonds on September 1, Year 1, had been $9,300,000, resulting in an effective annual interest rate of 8%. Prepare journal entries parallel to those called for in **a** above at the dates of September 1, Year 1; December 31, Year 1; and March 1, Year 2.

c State the amounts of bond interest expense for Year 1 and the **net** amount of the liability for the bonds payable at December 31, Year 1, under the independent assumptions set forth in both **a** and **b** above. Show your computations.

13-7 The following information is taken from the trial balances for Nakazawa imports, Inc.

	Adjusted December 31		Unadjusted December 31
	Year 1	Year 2	Year 3
6% bonds payable, due Oct. 1, Year 11	$1,000,000	$1,000,000	$800,000
Discount on bonds payable	23,400	21,000	19,200
Bond interest expense (including amortization of discount)	10,400	62,400	46,800
Bond interest payable	15,000	15,000	
Gain on retirement of bonds			10,000

The bonds were issued on November 1, Year 1, with one month's accrued interest. On October 1 of Year 3, $200,000 of bonds were retired at a price of 95. No discount on bonds payable was written off at the time of the retirement, thus resulting in a recorded gain of $10,000 on the retirement.

The company follows the policy of amortizing bond discount by the straight-line method at the semiannual interest payment dates as well as at the year-end adjusting of the accounts.

Instructions

a Prepare the entry that was made to record the issuance of the bonds on November 1, Year 1. (First, compute the discount at the date of issuance; note the $2,400 decrease in Discount on Bonds Payable during the 12 months between the first two trial balances.)

b Prepare a *correcting entry* required to measure properly the gain on retirement of bonds. (Compute the carrying value of the bonds retired.)

c Prepare the adjusting entry required at the end of Year 3 to record the accrued interest and to amortize the discount for the period October 1 to December 31.

d What will be the adjusted bond interest expense for Year 4 if $800,000 of bonds remain outstanding? Why does it differ from the bond interest expense in Year 2 and Year 3?

13-8 Beach Equipment Co. frequently uses long-term lease contracts as a means of financing the sale of its products. On November 1, Year 1, Beach Equipment Co. leased to Star Industries a machine carried in inventory at a cost of $18,120. The terms of the lease called for 48 monthly payments of $650 each, beginning November 30, Year 1. The present value of these payments, discounted at an implied interest rate of 1% per month, is equal to $24,680, the regular sales price of the machine. At the end of the lease, title to the machine will transfer to Star Industries.

Instructions

a Prepare journal entries in the accounts of Beach Equipment Co. on:
   (1) November 1 to record the sale financed by the lease and the related cost of goods sold. (Debit Lease Payments Receivable for the present value of the future lease payments.)
   (2) November 30, to record receipt of the first $650 monthly payment. (Prepare a compound journal entry which allocates the cash receipt between interest revenue and reduction of Lease Payments Receivable. The portion of each monthly payment recognized as interest revenue is equal to 1% of the balance of the account Lease Payment Receivable, at the beginning of that month. Round all interest computations to the nearest dollar.)
   (3) December 31, to record receipt of the second monthly payment.

b Prepare journal entries in the accounts of Star Industries on:
   (1) November 1, to record acquisition of the leased machine.
   (2) November 30, to record the first monthly lease payment. (Determine the portion of the payment representing interest expense in a manner parallel to that described in part a.)

(3) December 31, to record the second monthly lease payment.

(4) December 31, to recognize depreciation on the leased machine through year-end. Compute depreciation expense by the straight-line method, using a 10-year service life and an estimated salvage value of $6,680.

c Compute the net carrying value of the leased machine in the balance sheet of Star Industries at December 31, Year 1.

d Compute the amount of Star Industries' lease payment obligation at December 31, Year 1.

13-9 Maria Mandella invested in $420,000 face value of 9%, 10-year bonds at a price of 95. The investment was made at the date of original issuance of the bonds and consequently neither accrued interest nor involved a broker's commission. Shortly after this transaction, the market price of the bonds dropped to 90. After holding the bonds exactly six years, Mandella sold them at a price of 102. The broker's commission charged was $1,500. There was no accrued interest at the date of sale because the sale occurred immediately after receipt of the semiannual interest payment.

Instructions

a Assume that Mandella at the date of purchase had no intention of holding the bonds to maturity and did not amortize the discount. Determine the total interest earned during the six-year period and the gain or loss on disposal.

b Assume that Mandella did intend to hold the bonds until maturity and did amortize the discount. When Mandella sold the bonds six years later, her carrying value for the investment was $411,600. Determine the total interest earned during the six-year period and the gain or loss on disposal.

c What is the most probable reason for the price of the bonds being above their face value at the date Mandella disposed of them? Would amortization of discount on the bonds have produced a more realistic measurement of yearly income in this case? Explain.

13-10 During January, Beverly Corporation incurred salaries expense of $11,200, classified as follows: $8,000 of salaries expense for the sales force and $3,200 salaries expense for office personnel.

FICA taxes were withheld from employees' earnings at an assumed rate of 6%. Other amounts withheld were $1,500 for federal income taxes and $180 for group insurance premiums.

Instructions

a Prepare a general journal entry to record the payroll and the deductions from employees' earnings. Do not include payroll taxes on the employer in this journal entry.

b Prepare a general journal entry to record the payroll taxes on the *employer* as a result of the above payroll. Assume an FICA tax of 6%, a state unemployment tax of 2.7%, and a federal unemployment tax of $<.7\%$ on the entire payroll.

c Prepare a combined general journal entry which will record the total payroll and all taxes and deductions applicable to both the employer and employees. This combined entry could be used instead of the entries called for in a and b above.

d What is the total payroll expense of Beverly Corporation for January? Show computations.

13-11 Two of the employees of Window Craft receive monthly salaries; the remaining three employees are paid an hourly rate with provision for time and one-half for overtime. The basic data for the May 31 payroll are given below:

Employee	Hours		Pay Rate	Com- pensation to April 30	Gross Pay Due for May	Federal Income Tax Withheld
	Reg	OT				
Allen	160	15	$ 8.00/hr	$ 6,000	$1,460	$ 275
Benson	160		7.00/hr	4,000	1,120	230
Cramer	160	12	5.00/hr	3,560	890	125
Dodson	Salary		1,440.00/mo	5,760	1,440	300
Eller	Salary		3,000.00/mo	12,000	3,000	505
Total					$7,910	$1,435

Other data Compensation of Dodson and Eller is considered an administrative expense; the balance of the earnings is chargeable to Shop Wages. Payroll taxes apply as follows: FICA, 6% up to maximum of $24,000; state unemployment, 2.7% up to maximum of $6,000; federal unemployment, <.7% up to maximum of $6,000. Window Craft has group insurance and a retirement plan under which all employees contribute 5% of their gross pay and the company matches this contribution. Both employees' and employer's contributions are deposited with the Reliable Insurance Company at the end of each month.

Instructions
a Prepare a payroll record for May using the following columns:

Employee	Gross Pay	Amount Subject to		Federal Income Tax Withheld	FICA Tax Withheld	Retire- ment Deduc- tion	Net Pay Due
		Unemploy- ment Taxes	FICA Taxes				

b Explain how the gross pay for Cramer was computed for the month of May.
c Explain why the federal income taxes withheld for Allen are less than those withheld for Dodson despite the fact that Allen received a higher gross compensation.
d Prepare in general journal form the entry to record the payroll for the month of May and the amounts withheld from employees.
e Prepare in general journal form the entry to record the employer's payroll taxes and insurance plan contributions for the month of May.

BUSINESS DECISION PROBLEM 13

Yellow Bus Company reported the balances given below at the end of the current year:

Total assets	$14,800,000
Current liabilities	3,600,000
Long-term liabilities	400,000
Stockholders' equity:	
Capital stock, $10 par value	$ 4,000,000
Paid-in capital in excess of par	3,000,000
Retained earnings	3,800,000

The company is planning an expansion of its plant facilities, and a study shows that $12 million of new funds will be required to finance the expansion. Two proposals are under consideration:

Stock Financing   Issue 200,000 shares of capital stock at a price of $60 per share.

Bond Financing   Borrow $12 million on a 20-year bond issue, with interest at 7%.

The assets and liabilities of Yellow Bus Company have remained relatively constant over the past five years, and during this period the earnings **after** income taxes have averaged 10% of the stockholders' equity as reported at the end of the current year. The company expects that its earnings **before** income taxes will increase by an amount equal to 12% of the new investment in plant facilities.

Past and future income taxes for the company may be estimated at 40% of income before income taxes.

Instructions

a Prove that the company's average income **before** income taxes during the past five years was $1,800,000.

b Prepare a schedule showing the expected earnings per share of capital stock during the first year of operations following the completion of the $12 million expansion, under each of the two proposed means of financing.

c Evaluate the two proposed means of financing from the viewpoint of a major stockholder of Yellow Bus Company.

14 Accounting Principles and Concepts; Current-Value Accounting

Throughout this book we try to explain the theoretical roots of each new accounting principle or standard as it comes under consideration. When you travel through new territory, however, you may find it useful to pause at some intermediate stage in your trip to consider what you have seen and to sort out your observations into some meaningful overall impression. This seems an appropriate point in our discussion of accounting for such a pause. You now have an overview of the accounting process and should be better prepared to understand how accounting procedures are shaped by theoretical concepts.

A basic objective of accounting

A basic objective of accounting is to provide useful information for making economic decisions. Investors, managers, economists, bankers, labor leaders, and government administrators all rely upon financial statements and other accounting reports in making the decisions which shape our economy. In determining the proper content of financial statements and other accounting reports, it is necessary to consider the *information needs* of the users of these statements and reports.

THE NEEDS OF MANAGEMENT Managers are interested in receiving information that will aid them in making operating decisions. The area of accounting designed to meet this need is primarily concerned with producing reports and summaries for internal use by management and is known as *management accounting.*

In management accounting, theory is not a major issue, because any information that aids in making rational choices among alternative courses of action is relevant and useful. One measurement method may be used for one managerial purpose and another measurement method for a different purpose. For example, in setting the selling price of some merchandise, management may be less interested in the actual recorded cost of goods on hand than in the estimated cost of replacing these articles as they are sold. Accounting measurements of past operating results and current financial position are useful to management, but it is not necessary that all internal information be developed in accordance with any particular set of accounting principles.

THE NEEDS OF STOCKHOLDERS AND CREDITORS While management accounting provides information for use within the business, *financial accounting* deals primarily with reporting of financial information to outsiders. Measurement of periodic net income and financial position and the reporting of the results to stockholders and creditors are the key objectives of financial accounting.

In reporting to stockholders and creditors, different considerations come into play. Corporate managers, even in small companies, have always been accountable to the owners who employ them. But the responsibility for managing a large corporation carries with it a great deal of economic and social power and requires a more extensive accountability. In most large corporations, stock ownership is widely scattered. The owner of even several thousand of the nearly 300 million shares of General Motors common stock can scarcely expect to exert much influence on managerial policy. As stockholder power has diminished, managerial power and responsibility have broadened.

Modern corporate managers are accountable not only to stockholders and creditors but also to employees, customers, potential investors, and the public at large. Financial statements are the primary means by which management reports on its accountability. Such statements are used to evaluate management's performance, to measure borrowing power, to guide investment decisions, and to support arguments on taxes, development of energy sources, and other public policy issues.

In this book we are primarily concerned with the *reporting of financial information to outsiders.* We shall therefore concentrate on the accounting principles and reporting standards relating to general-purpose financial statements, rather than special-purpose accounting reports to management.

THE NEED FOR ACCOUNTING PRINCIPLES It is vital to the functioning of our economy that financial statements be widely used and clearly understood. Users of these statements must have confidence in the reliability of the accounting information. Also, it is important for financial statements to be prepared in a manner which permits them to be compared fairly with prior years' statements and with financial statements of other companies. In short, we need a well-defined body of accounting principles or standards to guide corporate managers in preparing financial statements which will achieve the objectives of *understandability, reliability,* and *comparability.*

Generally accepted accounting principles

The principles which constitute the "ground rules" for financial reporting are termed *generally accepted accounting principles.* The financial statements of all publicly owned corporations should be prepared in conformity with generally accepted accounting principles. To assure outsiders that financial statements have been prepared in accordance with these principles, the financial statements of publicly owned corporations are audited by independent certified public accountants.

Accounting principles are also referred to as *standards, assumptions, postulates, and concepts.* The various terms used to describe accounting principles indicate the many efforts which have been made to develop a satisfactory framework of accounting theory.[1] For example, the word *standards* was chosen rather than *principles* when the Financial Accounting Standards Board replaced the Accounting Principles Board as the top rule-making body of the accounting profession. The efforts to construct a satisfactory body of accounting theory are still in process, because accounting theory must continually change with changes in the business environment and changes in the needs of financial statement users. Accounting principles are not rooted in laws of nature, as are the laws of the physical sciences. *Accounting principles or standards are developed in relation to what we consider to be the most important objectives of financial reporting.*

For example, in recent years accountants as well as business executives have recognized that the cost to society of maintaining an economic activity, such as a manufacturing plant, includes the pollution of air and water and other damage to the environment. Research is currently being undertaken to develop accounting principles for the identification and measurement of these "social costs," and also for methods of measuring and reporting the human resources that are so important to the successful operation of a business.

The conceptual framework project

The most recent effort to develop a comprehensive framework for financial accounting and reporting is the conceptual framework project currently being undertaken by the Financial Accounting Standards Board. The FASB has described the framework which it hopes to develop as

---

[1] See, for example, *Accounting Research Study No. 1,* "The Basic Postulates of Accounting," AICPA (New York: 1961); *Accounting Research Study No. 3,* "A Tentative Set of Broad Accounting Principles for Business Enterprises," AICPA (New York: 1962); and *Objectives of Financial Statements,* AICPA (New York: 1973).

". . . a *constitution,* a coherent system of interrelated objectives and fundamentals that can lead to consistent standards and that prescribe the nature, function, and limits of financial accounting and financial statements." [2]

To assist in the development of such a framework, the FASB has issued a *Discussion Memorandum* describing the objectives of financial statements and several alternative theories of income measurement and asset valuation. This FASB Discussion Memorandum has been sent to accountants, business executives, government officials, educators, and others interested in the development of accounting theory and standards. These persons are encouraged to send their comments and suggestions to the FASB for consideration in developing the conceptual framework.

It is difficult to predict the extent to which the conceptual framework project may affect the basic concepts and principles currently used in developing accounting information. Perhaps the changes will be few; on the other hand, the proposed changes could be as major as a departure from historical cost as the basis for asset valuation and income determination. In any case, the conceptual framework project is indicative of the continuing effort within the accounting profession to improve the relevance and reliability of accounting information.

Authoritative support for accounting principles

To qualify as "generally accepted," an accounting principle must usually receive "substantial authoritative support." The most influential authoritative groups in this country include (*1*) the American Institute of Certified Public Accountants (AICPA), the professional association of licensed CPAs; (*2*) the Financial Accounting Standards Board which includes representatives from public accounting, industry, education, and government; and (*3*) the Securities and Exchange Commission (SEC), an agency of the federal government established to administer laws and regulations relating to the publication of financial information by corporations whose stock is publicly owned.[3] Also important in the development of accounting theory has been the American Accounting Association, an organization of accounting educators.

AMERICAN INSTITUTE OF CERTIFIED PUBLIC ACCOUNTANTS (AICPA) The AICPA has long been concerned with stating and defining accounting principles because its members daily face the problem of making decisions about generally accepted principles as they perform audits and other professional work. Some years ago, the AICPA established an Ac-

---

[2] *FASB Discussion Memorandum,* "Conceptual Framework for Financial Accounting and Reporting: Elements of Financial Statements and Their Measurement," FASB (Stamford, Conn: 1976).

[3] Other professional organizations which have influenced the development of accounting principles are the National Association of Accountants and the Financial Executives Institute. In addition to the SEC, the following government regulatory agencies influence financial reporting of business units falling under their jurisdiction: Federal Power Commission, Interstate Commerce Commission, Civil Aeronautics Board, and Federal Communications Commission.

counting Principles Board, composed of practitioners, educators, and industry representatives. This Board was authorized to issue *Opinions* which would improve financial reporting and narrow areas of differences and inconsistencies in accounting practices. These *Opinions* are regarded as expressions of generally accepted accounting principles. At the same time, the AICPA expanded its research efforts and sponsored a series of Accounting Research Studies to aid the APB in its work. The Accounting Principles Board issued 31 formal *Opinions* on specific accounting problems, and also issued broad *Statements* designed to improve the quality of financial reporting. For example, *Statement No. 4,* "Basic Concepts and Accounting Principles Underlying Financial Statements of Business Enterprises," was issued with the objective of advancing the written expression of financial accounting principles.

In 1973, the Accounting Principles Board was replaced by the Financial Accounting Standards Board. However, the *Opinions* and *Statements* of the APB remain in effect.

FINANCIAL ACCOUNTING STANDARDS BOARD (FASB) The FASB was established by the AICPA as an independent body to assume the responsibilities of the former Accounting Principles Board. The FASB consists of seven full-time members, including representatives from public accounting, industry, government, and accounting education.

Lending support to the FASB are an advisory council and a large research staff. The FASB is authorized to issue *Statements of Financial Accounting Standards,* which represent expressions of generally accepted accounting principles. As discussed earlier in this chapter, the FASB is also attempting to develop a broad conceptual framework for financial accounting and reporting.

SECURITIES AND EXCHANGE COMMISSION (SEC) The SEC has considerable opportunity to exercise its authority since it may reject corporate financial statements that do not, in the opinion of the Commission, meet acceptable standards. The views of the Commission on various accounting issues are published in the SEC's *Accounting Series Releases,* or *ASRs.* Recently in *ASR 190,* the SEC gave powerful support to the disclosure of replacement costs for certain elements of corporate financial statements.

AMERICAN ACCOUNTING ASSOCIATION (AAA) The AAA has sponsored a number of research studies and monographs in which individual authors and Association committees attempt to summarize accounting principles. These statements have no doubt had considerable influence on the thinking of accounting theorists and practitioners. However, the AAA lacks the power of the AICPA to impose its collective view on accounting practice; it therefore exercises its influence through the prestige of its authors and the persuasiveness of their views.

In addition to the above sources, "substantial authoritative support" may include accounting practices commonly found in certain industries and in the literature of accounting, including books, journal articles, and expert testimony offered in court.

The accounting environment

The principles of accounting are shaped by the environment in which the accounting process is employed. Accounting is concerned with economic activity, that is, the ownership and exchange of goods and services. Accounting systems developed in response to the need for information about business activity as an aid to management and to outsiders in making rational economic decisions. Since money is a common denominator in which the value of goods and services is measured, the accounting process is implemented in terms of a monetary unit. Most goods and services produced in our economy are distributed through exchange rather than being directly consumed by producers. It is logical, therefore, to base accounting measurements on exchange (market) prices generated by *past, present,* and *future* transactions and events.

For example, when accountants report the original cost of a plant site acquired some years ago, they are reflecting a past exchange. When they state inventory at market by using the lower-of-cost-or-market rule, they are using a present exchange price (market value) as the basis for their measurement. When they record a liability for income taxes, they are measuring the present effect of a future cash outflow to the government.

Since present decisions can affect only current and future outcomes, current and future exchange prices are in general more relevant for decision making than past exchange prices. We live in a world of uncertainty, however, and estimates of future, and even current, exchange prices are often subject to wide margins of error. Where to draw the line of acceptability in the trade-off between *reliability* and *relevance* is one of the crucial issues in accounting theory. The need for reliable and verifiable data is an important constraint, particularly with respect to information reported to outsiders. This factor has led accountants to rely heavily on past exchange prices as the basis for their measurements.

In the remaining sections of this chapter we shall summarize briefly the major principles that govern the accounting process and comment on some areas of controversy. We have noted the need for accepted principles to foster confidence in the published financial statements of large publicly owned corporations. Accounting principles concerned with the measurement of income and the valuation of assets are equally applicable to profit-making organizations of any size or form. However, the FASB is currently considering whether accounting principles relating to *disclosure* of information (such as earnings per share) should be less rigorous for a small, closely held business than for a publicly owned corporation.

The accounting entity concept

One of the basic principles of accounting is that information is compiled for a clearly defined accounting entity. Most economic activity is carried on through entities. An individual person is an accounting entity. So is a business enterprise, whether conducted as a single proprietorship, partnership, or corporation. The estate of a deceased person is an accounting entity, as are all nonprofit clubs and organizations. The basic accounting equation, Assets = Liabilities + Owners' Equity, reflects the *accounting entity concept* since the elements of the equation relate to the particular entity whose economic activity is being metered in financial statements.

We should distinguish between accounting and legal entities. In some cases the two coincide. For example, corporations, estates, trusts, and governmental agencies are both accounting and legal entities. In other cases, accounting entities differ from legal entities. For example, the *proprietorship* is an *accounting* entity, as indicated by the fact that all the assets and liabilities of the *business unit* are included in its financial statements. The business proprietorship is not a *legal* entity; the *proprietor* is a legal entity. He is legally liable both for his personal obligations and for those incurred in his business. For accounting purposes, the proprietor as an individual and his business enterprise are separate entities. Furthermore, a proprietor may own several businesses, each of which is treated as a separate entity for accounting purposes.

The choice of an accounting entity is somewhat flexible, as in the case of several business activities owned by one person or group of persons. The decision rests in part on the kinds and amount of information desired by management. As a general rule, we can say that any legal or economic unit which controls economic resources and is accountable for those resources is an accounting entity.

CONSOLIDATED ACCOUNTING ENTITIES A single accounting entity may also include more than one legal entity. Several corporations, for example, may be combined to form a single accounting entity. Since corporations are usually granted the power to hold title to any form of property, one corporation may own shares of stock in another. When one corporation controls another corporation through the ownership of a majority of its capital stock, the controlling corporation is called a *parent* company, and the company whose stock is owned is called a *subsidiary* company. Because both the parent and subsidiary companies are legal entities, separate financial statements must be prepared for each company. However, it also may be useful to prepare financial statements which view the *affiliated* companies (the parent company and its subsidiaries) as if they were a single unified business. Such statements are called *consolidated financial statements.*

In a *consolidated balance sheet,* the assets and liabilities of the affiliated companies are combined and reported as though only a single entity existed. Similarly, in a *consolidated income statement,* the revenue and expenses of the affiliated companies are combined, on the assumption that the results of operations for a single economic entity are being measured.

There are a number of economic, financial, legal, and tax advantages which encourage managers to operate through subsidiaries rather than through a single business entity. As a result corporate affiliations are common in the United States. A majority of the companies with shares listed on the New York Stock Exchange have one or more subsidiaries and include consolidated financial statements in their annual reports. (See the titles of the financial statements in the Appendix of this book.) The preparation of consolidated financial statements is a complex topic which is covered in *Modern Advanced Accounting* of this series.

The going-concern assumption

An underlying assumption in accounting is that an accounting entity will continue in operation for a period of time sufficient to carry out its existing commitments. The assumption of continuity, especially in the case of corporations, is in accord with experience in our economic system. This assumption leads to the concept of the *going concern.* In general, the going-concern assumption justifies ignoring immediate liquidating values in presenting assets and liabilities in the balance sheet.

For example, suppose that a company has just purchased a five-year insurance policy for $5,000. If we assume that the business will continue in operation for five years or more, we will consider the $5,000 cost of the insurance as an asset which provides services (freedom from risk) to the business over a five-year period. On the other hand, if we assume that the business is likely to terminate in the near future, the insurance policy should be recorded at its cancellation value—the amount of cash which can be obtained from the insurance company as a refund on immediate cancellation of the policy, which may be, say, $4,500.

In summary, the going-concern assumption is used by nearly all companies but may be dropped when it is not in accord with the facts. Accountants are sometimes asked to prepare a statement of financial position for an enterprise that is about to liquidate. In this case the assumption of continuity is no longer valid and the accountant drops the going-concern assumption and reports assets at their current liquidating value and liabilities at the amount required to settle the debts immediately.

The time period principle

We assume an indefinite life for most accounting entities. But accountants are asked to measure operating progress and changes in economic position at relatively short time intervals during this indefinite life. Users of financial statements want periodic measurements for decision-making purposes.

Dividing the life of an enterprise into time segments, such as a year or a quarter of a year, and measuring changes in financial position for these short periods is a difficult process. A more precise measurement of net income and financial position can be made when a business has been liquidated and its resources have been fully converted into cash. At any time prior to liquidation, the worth of some assets and the amount of some liabilities are matters of speculation. Thus periodic measures of net income and financial position are at best only informed estimates.

The tentative nature of periodic measurements of net income should be understood by those who rely on periodic accounting information. The need for frequent measurements creates many of accounting's most serious problems. For example, the attempt to measure net income over short time periods requires the selection of inventory flow assumptions and depreciation methods. The end-of-period adjustments discussed in Chapter 4 stem directly from the need to update accounting information to a particular point in time.

The monetary principle

The monetary principle means that money is used as the basic measuring unit for financial reporting. Money is the common denominator in which accounting measurements are made and summarized. The dollar, or any other monetary unit, represents a unit of value; that is, it reflects ability to command goods and services. Implicit in the use of money as a measuring unit is the *assumption that the dollar is a stable unit of value,* just as the mile is a stable unit of distance and an acre is a stable unit of area.

Having accepted money as a measuring unit, accountants freely combine dollar measures of economic transactions that occur at various times during the life of an accounting entity. They combine, for example, a $20,000 cost of equipment purchased in 1970 and the $40,000 cost of similar equipment purchased in 1980 and report the total as a $60,000 investment in equipment.

Unlike the mile and the acre, which are stable units of distance and area, the dollar *is not a stable unit of value.* The prices of goods and services in our economy change over time. When the *general price level* (a phrase used to describe the average of all prices) increases, the value of money (that is, its ability to command goods and services) decreases.

Despite the steady erosion in the purchasing power of the dollar in the United States during the last 40 years, accountants have continued to prepare financial statements in which the value of the dollar is assumed to be stable. This somewhat unrealistic assumption is one of the reasons why financial statements are viewed by some users as misleading. Restatement of accounting information for the changing value of the dollar and the preparation of supplementary statements in terms of replacement costs have received much attention in recent years. Such approaches to new financial reporting practices will be discussed in a subsequent section of this chapter.

The objectivity principle

The term *objective* refers to measurements that are unbiased and subject to verification by independent experts. For example, the price established in an arm's-length transaction is an objective measure of exchange value at the time of the transaction. It is not surprising, therefore, that exchange prices established in business transactions constitute much of the raw material from which accounting information is generated.

If a measurement is objective, 10 competent investigators who make the same measurement will come up with substantially identical results. However, 10 competent accountants who set out independently to measure the net income of a given business would not arrive at an identical result. Variations would arise because of the existence of alternative accounting methods. For example, in measuring inventory and cost of goods sold, one accountant might use the lifo method, and another the weighted-average method. These choices could produce significant variations in net income.

Accountants rely on various kinds of evidence to support their financial measurements, but they seek always the most objective evidence available. Invoices, contracts, paid checks, and physical counts of inventory are examples of objective evidence.

Despite the goal of objectivity, it is not possible to insulate accounting information from opinion and personal judgment. The cost of a depreciable asset can be determined objectively but not the periodic depreciation expense. To measure the cost of the asset services that have been used up during a given period requires estimates of the residual value and service life of the asset and judgment as to the depreciation method that should be used.

Objectivity in accounting has its roots in the quest for reliability. Accountants want to make their economic measurements reliable and, at the same time, as relevant to decision makers as possible. The accountant is constantly faced with the necessity of compromising between what users of financial information would like to know and what it is possible to measure with a reasonable degree of reliability.

Asset valuation: the cost principle

Both the balance sheet and the income statement are extensively affected by the cost principle. Assets are initially recorded in the accounts at cost, and no adjustment is made to this valuation in later periods, except to allocate a portion of the original cost to expense as the assets expire. At the time an asset is originally acquired, cost represents the "fair market value" of the goods or services exchanged, as evidenced by an arm's-length transaction. With the passage of time, however, the fair market value of such assets as land and buildings may change greatly from their historical cost. These later changes in fair market value generally have been ignored in the accounts, and the assets have continued to be valued in the balance sheet at historical cost (less the portion of that cost which has been allocated to expense).

Increasing numbers of professional accountants believe that current market values should be used as the basis for asset valuation rather than historical cost. These accountants argue that current values would result in a more meaningful balance sheet. Also, they claim that current values should be allocated to expense to represent fairly the cost to the entity of the goods or services consumed in the effort to generate revenue.

The cost principle is derived from the principle of **objectivity.** Those who support the cost principle argue that it is important that users have confidence in financial statements, and this confidence can best be maintained if accountants recognize changes in assets and liabilities only on the basis of completed transactions. Objective evidence generally exists to support cost, but evidence supporting current values may be less readily available.

Measuring revenue: the realization principle

When should revenue be recognized? Under the assumptions of accrual accounting, revenue should be recognized "when it is earned." However, the "earning" of revenue usually is an extended **economic process** and does not actually take place at a single point in time.

Some revenue, such as interest earned, is directly related to time periods. For this type of revenue, it is easy to determine how much revenue has been earned by computing how much of the earning process is complete. However, the earning process for sales revenue relates to **economic activity** rather than to a specific period of time. In a manufacturing business, for example, the earning process involves (1) acquisition of raw materials, (2) production of finished goods, (3) sale of the finished goods, and (4) collection of cash from credit customers.

In the manufacturing example, there is little objective evidence to indicate how much revenue has been earned during the first two stages of the earning process. Accountants therefore usually do not recognize revenue until the revenue has been **realized.** Revenue is realized when both of the following conditions are met: (1) the earning process is essentially complete and (2) objective evidence exists as to the amount of revenue earned.

In most cases, the realization principle indicates that revenue should be recognized *at the time of the sale of goods or the rendering of services.* Recognizing revenue at this point is logical because the firm has essentially completed the earning process and the realized value of the goods or services sold can be measured objectively in terms of the price billed to customers. At any time prior to sale, the ultimate realizable value of the goods or services sold can only be estimated. After the sale, the only step that remains is to collect from the customer, and this is usually a relatively certain event.

Under certain special circumstances, accountants may deviate from the realization principle. In Chapter 3, we described a complete *cash basis* of income measurement whereby revenue is considered realized only when cash is collected from customers and expenses are recorded only when cash is actually paid out. Lawyers, accountants, and doctors, for example, generally use the cash basis of accounting in computing their taxable income. In computing realized revenue on the cash basis, receivables from clients or customers are ignored; only the actual cash collections are recorded as revenue.

THE INSTALLMENT METHOD Companies selling goods on the installment plan sometimes use the *installment method* of accounting. This method may be considered appropriate when collections extend over relatively long periods of time and there is a strong possibility that full collection will not be made. As customers make installment payments, the seller recognizes the gross profit on sales in proportion to the cash collected. If the gross profit on installment sales is 30%, then out of every dollar collected on installment accounts receivable, the sum of 30 cents represents *realized gross profit.* For example, assume that in Year 1 a retailer sells for $400 a television set which cost $280, or 70% of sales price. The collections and the profit earned would be recognized over a three-year period as follows:

	Year	Cash Collected	−	Cost Recovery, 70%	=	Profit Earned, 30%
Installment method illustrated	1	$150		$105		$ 45
	2	200		140		60
	3	50		35		15
	Totals	$400		$280		$120

This method of profit recognition exists largely because it is allowed for income tax purposes; it postpones the payment of income taxes until cash is collected from customers. From an accounting viewpoint, there is little theoretical justification for delaying the recognition of profit beyond the point of sale. Few if any cases exist in which the realizable value of accounts receivable cannot be measured in the period of sale through the establishment of an adequate allowance for doubtful accounts.

LONG-TERM CONSTRUCTION CONTRACTS There are some circumstances in which the accountant finds it appropriate to recognize revenue as realized *during production* or when production is completed. An example arises in the case of *long-term construction contracts,* such as the building of a dam over a three-year period. In this case the revenue (contract price) is known when the construction job is begun, and it would be unreasonable to assume that the entire revenue is realized in the accounting period in which the project is completed. The accountant therefore estimates the portion of the dam completed during each accounting period, and recognizes revenue and profits in proportion to the work completed. This is known as the *percentage-of-completion method* of accounting for long-term contracts.

Assume, for example, that the costs to be incurred over a three-year period on a $5,000,000 contract are estimated at $4,000,000. Using the percentage-of-completion method of accounting, the profits on the contract would be recognized over the three-year period as follows:

	Year	Actual Cost Incurred	Actual Cost as Percentage of Estimated Total Cost	Portion of Contract Price Realized	Profit Considered Realized
Profit recognized as work progresses	1	$ 600,000	15	$ 750,000	$150,000
	2	2,000,000	50	2,500,000	500,000
	3	1,452,000	*	1,750,000 *balance*	298,000 *balance*
	Totals	$4,052,000		$5,000,000	$948,000

* Balance required to complete the contract.

The portion of the contract price realized in Years 1 and 2 is determined by taking the percentage of estimated total cost incurred in each year and applying it to the contract price of $5,000,000. Because 15% ($600,000/$4,000,000) of the total estimated cost was incurred in Year 1, 15% of the total estimated profit of $1,000,000 ($5,000,000 − $4,000,000) was considered realized; in Year 2, 50% ($2,000,000/$4,000,000) of the cost was incurred, and therefore 50% of the estimated profit was considered realized. In Year 3, however, the total actual cost is known and the profit on the contract is determined to be $948,000 ($5,000,000 − $4,052,000). Since profits of $650,000 ($150,000 + $500,000) were previously recognized in Years 1 and 2, the rest of the profit, $298,000, must be recognized in Year 3. If at the end of any accounting period it appears that a loss will be incurred on a contract in progress, *the loss should be recognized at once.*

If it is difficult to estimate the degree of contract completion or if there are extreme uncertainties involved in measuring the ultimate profit on a contract in progress, profit may be recognized when the *production is completed.* This approach is often referred to as the *completed-contract method* and is supported by many accountants because it is conservative, requires little subjective judgment, and is advantageous for income tax purposes. The income tax advantage lies in delaying the recognition of taxable income and thus postponing the payment of income taxes. If the completed-contract method of accounting for long-term construction contracts had been used in the preceding example, no profit would have been recognized in Years 1 and 2; the entire profit of $948,000 would be recorded in Year 3 when the contract was completed and actual costs known.

Measuring expenses: the matching principle

Revenue, the gross increase in net assets resulting from the production or sale of goods and services, is offset by expenses incurred in bringing the firm's output to the point of sale. Examples of expenses relating to revenue are the cost of merchandise sold, the expiration of asset services, and out-of-pocket expenditures for operating costs. The measurement of expenses occurs in two stages: (*1*) measuring the *cost* of goods and services that will be consumed or expire in generating revenue and (*2*) determining *when* the goods and services acquired have contributed to revenue and their cost thus *becomes an expense.* The second aspect of the measurement process is often referred to as *matching costs and revenue* and is fundamental to the *accrual basis* of accounting.

   Costs are matched with revenue in two major ways:

1 IN RELATION TO THE PRODUCT SOLD OR SERVICE RENDERED If goods or services can be related to the product or service which constitutes the output of the enterprise, its cost becomes an expense when the product is sold or the service rendered to customers. The cost of goods sold in a merchandising firm is a good example of this type of expense. Similarly, a commission paid to a real estate salesperson by a real estate brokerage office is an expense directly related to the revenue generated by the salesperson.

2 IN RELATION TO THE TIME PERIOD DURING WHICH REVENUE IS EARNED Some costs incurred by businesses cannot be directly related to the product or service output of the firm. Expired fire insurance, property taxes, depreciation on a building, the salary of the president of the company—all are examples of costs incurred in generating revenue which cannot be related to specific transactions. The accountant refers to this class of costs as *period costs,* and charges them to expense by associating them with the period of time during which they are incurred and presumably contribute to revenue, rather than by associating them with specific revenue-producing transactions.

Recognition of gains and losses

The same principles applied in recognizing revenue are applicable to the measurement of gains and losses on assets other than inventories. In general, an increase in the market value of a productive asset, such as land or a building, is not recognized until the asset in question is sold, in which case the amount of the gain is objectively determinable.

If a productive asset increases in value while it is in service, the accountant ordinarily does not record this gain because it has not been realized. "Not realized" means that the gain in value has not been substantiated by a transaction in which an exchange price has been established.

Accountants are not so insistent on following the rules of *realization* in measuring losses. We have seen in Chapter 11, for example, that the lower-of-cost-or-market valuation of inventories results in the recognition of losses in inventory investment prior to the sale of the goods in question. Recognizing losses when inventories appear to be worth less than their cost but refusing to recognize gains when inventories appear to be worth more than their cost is logically inconsistent. This inconsistency is justified by an accounting presumption that assets should not be reported in the balance sheet in excess of the amount which can be expected to be recovered through revenue.

The consistency principle

The principle of *consistency* implies that a particular accounting method, once adopted, will not be changed from period to period. This assumption is important because it assists users of financial statements in interpreting changes in financial position and changes in net income.

As a practical matter, management can change an accounting method when in its judgment a different method would better serve the needs of users of financial statements. It would hardly be a virtue to employ an improper accounting method consistently year after year. When a significant change in accounting occurs, however, the independent public accountant must report both the fact that a change in method has been made and the dollar effect of the change. In published financial statements, this disclosure is incorporated in the CPA's opinion. A typical disclosure might be as follows: "During the current year the company changed from the declining-balance method of computing depreciation to the straight-line method. This change in method had the effect of increasing net income by $210,000."

If income statements for previous years are included alongside the current statement for comparison purposes, the statements for the preceding years should be presented as previously reported. The cumulative effect of retroactive application of the new accounting principle on the owners' equity at the beginning of the period in which the change is made should be included in the net income of the current period.[4]

Consistency applies to a single accounting entity and increases the comparability of financial statements from period to period. Different companies, even those in the same industry, may follow different accounting methods. For this reason, it is important to determine the accounting methods used by companies whose financial statements are being compared.

The disclosure principle

Adequate disclosure means that all *material* and *relevant facts* concerning financial position and the results of operations *are communicated to users.* This can be accomplished either in the financial statements or in the notes accompanying the statements. Such disclosure should make the financial statements more useful and less subject to misinterpretation.

Adequate disclosure does not require that information be presented in great detail; it does require, however, that no important facts be withheld. For example, if a company has been named as defendant in a large lawsuit, this information must be disclosed. If accounts receivable have been pledged as collateral in obtaining a loan, the financial statements would be incomplete without disclosure of this fact. Naturally, there are practical limits to the amount of disclosure that can be made in financial statements or the accompanying notes. As a minimum, the following information generally should be disclosed:

1 Terms of major borrowing arrangements and existence of large contingent liabilities

2 Contractual provisions relating to leasing arrangements, employee pension and bonus plans, and major proposed asset acquisitions

3 Accounting methods used in preparing the financial statements

4 Changes in accounting methods made during the latest period

5 Other significant events affecting financial position, including major new contracts for sale of goods or services, labor strikes, shortages of raw materials, and pending legislation which may significantly affect operations

6 For large corporations, the estimated replacement cost of (*1*) inventories, (*2*) cost of goods sold, (*3*) plant and equipment, and (*4*) depreciation, in accordance with *ASR 190* issued by the SEC

Supplementary disclosure through footnotes, however, should not take the place of sound accounting practices in preparing financial statements. The primary information made available to readers of financial statements is derived from the accounting records, but it is not necessarily limited to such information. The key point to keep in mind is that the supplementary information should be *relevant to the user.* Even significant events which occur *after* the end of the accounting period but before the financial statements are released may be disclosed.

[4] For a full discussion of this subject, see *APB Opinion No. 20,* "Accounting Changes," AICPA (New York: 1971).

Materiality

The term *materiality* refers to the *relative importance* of an item or event. Disclosure of relevant information is closely related to the concept of materiality; what is material is likely to be relevant. Accountants are primarily concerned with significant information and are not overly concerned with those items which have little effect on financial statements. For example, should the cost of a pencil sharpener, a wastepaper basket, or a stapler be recorded in asset accounts and depreciated over their useful lives? Even though more than one period will benefit from the use of these assets, the concept of materiality permits the immediate recognition of the cost of these items as an expense on grounds that it would be too expensive to undertake depreciation accounting for such low-cost assets and that the results would not differ significantly.

We must recognize that the materiality of an item is a relative matter; what is material for one business unit may not be material for another. Materiality of an item may depend not only on its *amount* but also on its *nature.* In summary, we can state the following rule: *An item is material if there is a reasonable expectation that knowledge of it would influence the decisions of prudent users of financial statements.*

Conservatism as a guide in resolving uncertainties

We have previously referred to the use of *conservatism* in connection with the measurement of net income and the reporting of accounts receivable and inventories in the balance sheet. Although the concept of conservatism may not qualify as an accounting principle, it has long been a powerful influence upon asset valuation and income determination. Conservatism is most useful when matters of judgment or estimates are involved. Ideally, accountants should base their estimates on sound logic and select those accounting methods which neither overstate nor understate the facts. When some doubt exists about the valuation of an asset or the realization of a gain, however, the accountant traditionally leans in the direction of caution and selects the accounting option which produces a lower net income for the current period and a less favorable financial position. Conservatism, however, may be viewed as a double-edged sword. If an asset is prematurely recognized as an expense in Year 1, for example, the balance sheet and net income for Year 1 will be conservatively stated but the net income for Year 2 will be overstated.

An example of conservatism is the traditional practice of pricing inventory at the lower of cost or market (replacement cost). Decreases in the market value of the inventory are recognized as a part of the cost of goods sold in the current period, but increases in market value of inventory are ignored. A judicious application of conservatism to the accounting process should produce more useful information; in contrast, the excessive use of conservatism or failure to apply conservatism may produce misleading information and result in losses to creditors and stockholders.

Opinion on financial statements rendered by independent CPAs

After independent certified public accountants have audited the financial statements and accounting records of a business, they attest to the reasonableness of the financial statements by issuing an *audit opinion* (sometimes called *auditors' report*). This opinion is published as part of the company's annual report to stockholders. Because of its importance, the wording of the audit opinion has been carefully considered and a standard form has been developed. Considering the extensive investigation that precedes it, the audit opinion is surprisingly short. It usually consists of two brief paragraphs, unless the CPAs comment on unusual features of the financial picture. The first paragraph describes the *scope* of the auditors' examination; the second states their *opinion* of the financial statements. A report by a CPA firm might read as follows:

Typical audit opinion

We have examined the balance sheet of American Oil Corporation as of September 30, 19____, and the related statements of income, retained earnings, and changes in financial position for the year then ended. Our examination was made in accordance with generally accepted auditing standards, and accordingly included such tests of the accounting records and such other auditing procedures as we considered necessary in the circumstances.

In our opinion, the financial statements referred to above present fairly the financial position of American Oil Corporation at September 30, 19____, and the results of its operations and the changes in its financial position for the year then ended, in conformity with generally accepted accounting principles applied on a basis consistent with that of the preceding year.

Observe that CPAs *do not guarantee* the accuracy of the financial statements. The financial statements are issued by management of the business: the CPAs render a professional opinion as to the "fairness" of the presentation. The important point to keep in mind is that the *primary responsibility for the reliability of the financial statements rests with the management* of the business entity issuing the financial statements.

The phrase "in conformity with generally accepted accounting principles" in the second paragraph of the audit opinion is particularly relevant to our discussion in this chapter. *A complete authoritative list of generally accepted accounting principles does not exist.* Yet the widespread reliance upon this phrase implies that there is general consensus as to what these accounting principles are.

THE SEARCH FOR BETTER FINANCIAL REPORTING

Accounting is a man-made information system. It is an imperfect system, and constant efforts are being made to improve the precision and relevance of accounting measurements and the usefulness of the end products of the accounting process—financial statements. Because economic conditions are full of uncertainty and business transactions are often complex, the end products of the accounting process must be accepted for what they are—tentative in nature and subject to certain limitations. Accordingly, we should not expect financial statements to attain a higher level of certainty than the business transactions which they summarize.

Although accounting may never become a precise science, it is apparent that further improvements are possible in measuring and communicating financial information. Should accountants, for example, continue to adhere to the assumption that the monetary unit is stable and that historical costs are the most relevant measures of "value" for financial reporting purposes? In the remaining pages of this chapter, we shall examine the implications of this important question.

Inflation—the greatest challenge to accounting

Inflation may be defined as either an increase in the general price level or a decrease in the purchasing power of the dollar. The *general price level* is the weighted average of the prices of all goods and services in the economy. It is measured by a *general price index* with a base year assigned a value of 100. The index compares the level of current prices with that of the base year. Assume, for example, that Year 1 is the base year. If prices rise by 10% during Year 2, the price index at the end of Year 2 will be 110. At the end of Year 9 the price index might be 200, indicating that the general price level had doubled since Year 1. The most common measures of the general price level are the consumer price index, the wholesale price index, and the Gross National Product Implicit Price Deflator. The GNP Deflator is the most comprehensive index and is widely accepted as the best measure of the general price level.

The reciprocal of the price index (100 divided by the current price index) represents the *purchasing power of the dollar* in the current year relative to that in the base year. Thus, if the price index in Year 1 = 100 and in Year 5 = 125, the purchasing power of the Year 5 dollar is only 80% (100 ÷ 125) of that of the Year 1 dollar. In other words, prices have increased by 25% and the value of the dollar (in terms of purchasing power) has decreased by 20%.

We have experienced persistent inflation in the United States for almost 40 years; more importantly, the forces which have been built into our economic and political institutions almost guarantee that inflation will continue. The only question is how severe the inflationary trend will be. Our traditional accounting process is based upon the assumption of a stable dollar. This cost-based system works extremely well in periods of stable prices; it works reasonably well during prolonged but mild inflation; but it loses virtually all meaning if inflation becomes extreme. The greatest single challenge to the accounting profession today is to develop new accounting methods that will bring financial statements into accord with the economic reality of an inflationary environment.

Profits—fact or illusion?

Corporate profits are watched closely by business managers, investors, and government officials. The trend of these profits plays a significant role in the allocation of the nation's investment resources, in levels of employment, and in national economic policy. As a result of the **stable monetary assumption,** however, a strong argument may be made that much of the corporate profit reported today is an illusion.

In the measurement of business income, a distinction must be drawn between profit and the recovery of costs. A business earns a profit only when the value of goods sold and services rendered (revenue) **exceeds** the value of resources consumed in the earning process (costs and expenses). Accountants have traditionally assigned "values" to resources consumed in the earning process by using historical dollar amounts. Depreciation expense, for example, may be based upon prices paid to acquire assets 10 or 20 years ago.

When the general price level is rising rapidly, such historical costs may significantly understate the current economic value of the resources being consumed. If costs and expenses are understated, it follows that reported profits are overstated. In other words, the stable monetary assumption may lead to reporting **illusory** profits; much of the net income reported by corporations actually may be a return of costs.

When reported profit is actually a return of costs, what we label as income taxes is in reality a tax upon invested capital. Moreover, dividends labeled as distributions of earnings are in fact being paid from capital. The reporting of large, but fictitious, profits also leads to demands for higher wages consistent with the reported profits.

In summary, the real world is one of inflation. If we continue to measure profits on the assumption that price levels do not change, financial statements will be misleading and out of touch with reality. Several broad social consequences appear to follow. For one, corporate liquidity (debt-paying ability) may fall so low as to bring an economic crisis. Secondly, since we allocate economic resources in large part on the basis of financial statements, poor allocation of resources may be the end consequence of ignoring inflation in our financial reporting. Finally, the overstatement of profits may lead to an unrecognized failure to maintain reasonable rates of capital formation. A nation with a declining rate of capital formation will find it difficult to hold its relative position in a competitive world economy or to achieve a rising standard of living.

Two approaches to "inflation accounting"

Two alternative approaches to modifying our accounting process to cope with inflation have received much attention. These two approaches are:

1 The adjustment of historical cost financial statements for changes in general purchasing power.
2 Current-value accounting. This approach envisions a series of transitional steps away from historical cost accounting, the first of which would be limited to requiring footnote disclosure of the current values for inventories, cost of goods sold, plant and equipment, and depreciation. A second step would involve preparing supplementary financial statements expressed in current values for most items, and a final step would call for a set of current-value financial statements to become the *primary* financial statements of a company.

To illustrate these approaches to "inflation accounting," assume that in Year 1 you purchased 500 pounds of sugar for $100 when the general price index was at 100. Early in Year 2, you sold the sugar for $108 when the general price index was at 110 and the replacement cost of 500 pounds of sugar was $104. What is the amount of your profit or loss on this transaction? The amount of profit or loss determined under current accounting standards (unadjusted historical cost) and the two "inflation accounting" alternatives is shown below.

	Unadjusted Historical Cost	Historical Cost Adjusted for Changes in the General Price Level	Current-Value Accounting
Which Revenue	$108	$108	$108
"cost" of Cost of goods sold	100	110	104
goods sold **is most** Profit (loss)	$ 8	$ (2)	$ 4
realistic?			

Under each method, an amount is deducted from revenue to provide for recovery of cost. However, the value assigned to the "cost" of goods sold differs under each of the three approaches.

UNADJUSTED HISTORICAL COST This method is used in current accounting practice. The use of unadjusted historical cost is based upon the assumption that the dollar is a stable unit of measure. Profit is determined by comparing sales revenue with the *historical cost* of the asset sold. In using this approach to income determination, accountants assume that a business is as well off when it has recovered its *original dollar investment,* and that it is better off whenever it recovers more than the original number of dollars invested in any given asset.

In our example of buying and selling sugar, the profit figure of $8 shows *how many dollars* you came out ahead. However, this approach ignores the fact that Year 1 dollars and Year 2 dollars are *not equivalent in terms of purchasing power.* It also ignores the fact that the $100 deduction intended to provide for the recovery of cost is not sufficient to allow you to *replace* the 500 pounds of sugar.

HISTORICAL COST ADJUSTED FOR CHANGES IN THE GENERAL PRICE LEVEL When financial statements are adjusted for changes in the general price level, historical amounts are restated as the number of current dollars *equivalent in purchasing power* to the historical cost. Profit is determined by comparing revenue with the *amount of purchasing power* (stated in current dollars) originally invested.

The general price index tells us that $110 in Year 2 is equivalent in purchasing power to the $100 invested in sugar in Year 1. But you do not have $110 in Year 2; you received only $108 dollars from the sale of the sugar. Thus, you have sustained a *$2 loss in purchasing power.*

CURRENT-VALUE ACCOUNTING In current-value accounting, profit is measured by comparing revenue with the *current replacement cost* of the assets consumed in the earning process. The logic of this approach lies in the concept of the going concern. What will you do with the $108 received from the sale of the sugar? If you are going to continue in the sugar business, you will have to buy more sugar. At current market prices, it will cost you $104 to replace 500 pounds of sugar; the remaining $4, therefore, is designated as profit.

Current-value accounting recognizes in the income statement the costs which a going concern actually has to pay to replace its expiring assets. The resulting profit figure, therefore, closely parallels the maximum amount which a business could distribute as dividends and still be able to maintain the present size and scale of its operations.

WHICH APPROACH MEASURES INCOME? Which of these three approaches correctly measures income? The answer is that all three methods provide a correct measurement, but that each approach utilizes a different definition of "cost" and of "income." The real question confronting the accounting profession is which of these alternative measures of income is the *most useful to decision makers?* This question is being considered very carefully by the FASB, the SEC, and other interested parties. However, there is not yet widespread agreement as to the answer.

Financial statements adjusted for changes in the general price level

As previously emphasized, dollars of the current year and dollars of past years are not equivalent in terms of purchasing power. The historical dollar amounts appearing in financial statements, however, may be restated as the number of current dollars representing an equivalent amount of purchasing power. Since current dollars command less purchasing power than did the dollars of past years, a *larger* number of current dollars is always necessary to represent the purchasing power of a historical dollar amount. Financial statements in which all amounts have been restated in current dollars are called **common dollar financial statements,** or **general price level financial statements.**

Both the FASB and the APB have recommended, but not required, that companies include in their annual reports **supplemental** common dollar financial statements.[5] The common dollar financial statements were not intended to replace conventional statements but to supplement them. Most companies have not prepared these supplemental statements, however, because of the uncertainty as to whether price level accounting or current-value accounting will prevail as the generally accepted method of reporting the effects of inflation. Although the number of companies that prepare common dollar statements is not large, a study of the principles involved in the preparation of common dollar statements is helpful in understanding the effects of inflation upon a business entity and the limitations of historical cost financial statements.

An extended discussion of the procedures used to prepare common dollar statements is beyond the scope of this book, but the process may be visualized through a brief discussion of a simplified example.

Illustration of common dollar financial statements

Assume that Flation Company began business on January 1, Year 1, when the general price level index stood at 100. During the year, the price level rose at a uniform rate. The average price level during the year was 125, and at December 31 the price level was 150. Comparative historical dollar balance sheets at the beginning and end of the year are shown below:

FLATION COMPANY
Comparative Balance Sheets
At Beginning and End of Year 1

	December 31	January 1
Assets:		
Cash	$50,000	$ 20,000
Inventory	15,000	40,000
Equipment (net of accumulated depreciation)	30,000	40,000
Total assets	$95,000	$100,000
Liabilities & stockholders' equity:		
Current liabilities	$10,000	$ 30,000
Capital stock	70,000	70,000
Retained earnings	15,000	–0–
Total liabilities & stockholders' equity	$95,000	$100,000

---

[5] See *APB Statement No. 3,* "Financial Statements Restated for General Price Level Changes," AICPA (New York: 1969) and *FASB Exposure Draft,* "Financial Reporting in Units of General Purchasing Power," FASB (Stamford, Conn.: 1974).

During the year, Flation Company sold $25,000 of its beginning inventory for $50,000 cash and paid $20,000 of its current liabilities. We shall assume that the sales and debt repayment were Flation Company's only transactions during the year, and that these transactions occurred uniformly throughout the year. Flation Company's equipment is being depreciated over four years.

Preparing a common dollar balance sheet

The basic feature of a common dollar balance sheet is that all amounts are stated in terms of current dollars. The conversion of Flation Company's December 31 balance sheet from historical dollars to common dollars is illustrated below:

FLATION COMPANY
Conversion to Common Dollar Balance Sheet
December 31, Year 1

	Historical Dollars	Conversion Ratio	Common Dollars
Assets:			
Cash	$50,000		$ 50,000
Inventory	15,000	× 150/100	22,500
Equipment (net of accumulated depreciation)	30,000	× 150/100	45,000
Total assets	$95,000		$117,500
Liabilities & stockholders' equity:			
Current liabilities	$10,000		$ 10,000
Capital stock	70,000	× 150/100	105,000
Retained earnings	15,000	*	2,500
Total liabilities & stockholders' equity	$95,000		$117,500

* See common dollar income statement on p. 584.

In a common dollar balance sheet, the assets, liabilities, and stockholders' equity are *restated in the number of current dollars equivalent in purchasing power to the historical dollar amounts.* To restate a historical dollar amount in terms of current dollars, we multiply the historical amount by the *ratio of the current price level to the historical price level.* For example, assume land was purchased for $10,000 when the price level stood at 100. If the price level is now 170, we may find the number of current dollars equivalent to the purchasing power originally invested in the land by multiplying the $10,000 historical cost by *170/100*. The result, $17,000, represents the number of current dollars equivalent in purchasing power to the 10,000 historical dollars.

An explanation of the differences between the historical dollar balances and the common dollar balances will make clear the nature of the conversion process.

MONETARY ITEMS First note that the balances of two items, cash and current liabilities, are exactly the same in both the historical dollar and common dollar balance sheets. The reason for this is that cash, claims to cash, and obligations to pay cash represent monetary resources and obligations which are *fixed in dollar amount.* If we have $50,000 cash and the price level rises, we still have $50,000 even though these dollars will now buy fewer goods and services. Similarly, if we owe $10,000 and the price level rises, we still owe $10,000 even though the debt may be paid using less valuable dollars.

Assets representing claims to a fixed number of dollars and liabilities to pay a fixed number of dollars are called *monetary items.* The dollar amounts of monetary items should *not be restated* in preparing a common dollar balance sheet.

NONMONETARY ITEMS Nonmonetary items include all items in the balance sheet which *are not* claims or obligations of fixed-dollar amount. The historical dollar amount of nonmonetary items *must be restated in terms of current dollars.*

In our example, the inventory and equipment were acquired when the general price level was 100. Since the general price level is now 150, the cost of these assets would be restated in current dollars by multiplying the historical cost by the conversion ratio *150/100*. Capital stock is also a nonmonetary item. To determine the number of current dollars equivalent in purchasing power to the original investment made by stockholders when the general price level was 100, we would again multiply by the conversion ratio of *150/100*.

The restated balance of the retained earnings will be derived from the common dollar income statement.

Preparing a common dollar income statement

The conversion of Flation Company's conventional income statement to common dollars is illustrated on page 584.

FLATION COMPANY
Conversion to Common Dollar Income Statement
For the Year Ended December 31, Year 1

	Historical Dollars	Conversion Ratio	Common Dollars
Sales	$50,000	× 150/125	$60,000
Cost of goods sold	25,000	× 150/100	37,500
Gross profit on sales	$25,000		$22,500
Depreciation expense	10,000	× 150/100	15,000
Net income (in historical dollars)	$15,000		
Operating income (in purchasing power)			$ 7,500
Less: Loss in purchasing power from holding monetary assets during rising price levels (Schedule A)*			(16,000)
Add: Gain in purchasing power from owing money during rising price levels (Schedule A)*			11,000
Net income (in purchasing power)			$ 2,500

*See p. 585.

RESTATING SALES Notice that the conversion ratio used to restate sales revenue in current dollars is *150/125* rather than 150/100. The reason for this is that the dollars representing the sales revenue were received uniformly throughout the year. Thus, *on the average,* these dollars were received when the price level was 125 (average price level during the year).

RESTATING THE COST OF GOODS SOLD The cost of goods sold in our example came entirely from the beginning inventory, which had been acquired when the price level was 100. To determine the number of current dollars equivalent to the historical cost of goods sold, we must multiply the historical amount by the conversion ratio of *150/100*. If the cost of goods sold had not come entirely from beginning inventory, the restatement of the cost of goods sold would be more complex.

RESTATING DEPRECIATION EXPENSE Depreciation expense represents the allocation of the historical cost of the equipment against revenue. Since the equipment was acquired when the price level stood at 100, the conversion ratio of *150/100* should be used to restate the depreciation expense in terms of current dollars. Since depreciable assets are long-lived, the price level prevailing when the assets were acquired may be substantially different from the current price level. In such cases, the amount of depreciation expense recognized becomes one of the most significant differences between historical dollar and common dollar financial statements.

Gains and losses in purchasing power

The common dollar income statement introduces a new consideration in the determination of net income: gains and losses in purchasing power from holding monetary items. Holding monetary assets during a period of rising prices results in a loss of purchasing power because the value of money is falling. In contrast, owing money during a period of rising prices gives rise to a gain in purchasing power because debts may be repaid using dollars of less purchasing power than those originally borrowed. Purchasing power gains and losses may be computed by the following type of analysis.

FLATION COMPANY   *Schedule A*

Analysis of Cash Transactions for Year 1

	Historical Dollars	Conversion Ratio	Common Dollars
Beginning cash balance, Jan. 1	$20,000	× 150/100*	$30,000
Cash received from sales	50,000	× 150/125†	60,000
Cash payments on liabilities	(20,000)	× 150/125†	(24,000)
Ending cash balance, Dec. 31	$50,000		

Implied purchasing power on hand, in current dollars	$66,000
Less: Actual cash on hand, Dec. 31	50,000
Loss in purchasing power from holding cash during rising price levels	$16,000

Analysis of Current Liability Transactions for Year 1

	Historical Dollars	Conversion Ratio	Common Dollars
Beginning balance of current liabilities, Jan. 1 .	$30,000	× 150/100*	$45,000
Payments made on liabilities	(20,000)	× 150/125†	(24,000)
Ending balance of current liabilities, Dec. 31 . .	$10,000		

Implied purchasing power owed, in current dollars	$21,000
Less: Actual amount owed, Dec. 31	10,000
Gain in purchasing power from owing money during rising price levels	$11,000

* Historical amount recorded when price level was 100.
† Historical amount recorded at average price level of 125.

    The analysis of cash transactions is begun by restating the beginning cash balance, the cash receipts throughout the year, and the cash payments throughout the year in terms of current dollars. From this analysis, we see that Flation Company started with $30,000 of purchasing power (stated in current dollars), received another $60,000 of purchasing power, and paid out $24,000 of purchasing power. This implies that $66,000 of purchasing power should still be on hand, if there had been no loss. However, the actual cash on hand amounts to only $50,000. Thus,

Flation company has lost $16,000 in **purchasing power** by holding cash while the value of money declined. Flation Company **has not actually lost any cash;** the cash on hand has lost $16,000 of its purchasing power.

Similar reasoning is used in the analysis of current liabilities. Flation Company started out owing $45,000 in terms of the purchasing power of current dollars. The company repaid $24,000 of purchasing power during the year, implying that it still owed $21,000 if the original purchasing power were to be repaid. However, current liabilities are a monetary item, and Flation Company must pay only the fixed dollar amount of $10,000 to eliminate the debts. Thus, Flation Company will have to repay $11,000 less **purchasing power** than it originally borrowed, resulting in a gain in purchasing power.

Interpreting the common dollar income statement

The basic difference between historical dollar and common dollar financial statements is the unit of measure. Historical dollar statements use the dollar as a basic unit of measure. The unit of measure in common dollar financial statements is the **purchasing power of the current dollar.**

A conventional income statement shows how many dollars were added to stockholders' equity from the operation of the business. Identifying a dollar increase in stockholders' equity as "income" implies that the stockholders are better off when they recover more than the original number of dollars they invested. No attention is given to the fact that a greater number of dollars may still have less purchasing power than was originally invested.

A common dollar income statement measures changes in the purchasing power represented by stockholders' equity. An increase in the purchasing power of stockholders' equity means that the amount currently invested in the business commands more goods and services than the amount originally invested. Our conventional income statement shows us that Flation Company increased stockholders' equity by $15,000 during the year, but our common dollar income statement shows us that the purchasing power of stockholders' equity increased by only $2,500.

Current-value accounting distinguished from general price level accounting

We have used the expression **general price level accounting** to describe financial statements in which historical costs were adjusted to reflect changes in the general price level. General price level accounting does not abandon historical cost as the basis of measurement but simply expresses cost in terms of the current value of money. Also, general purchasing power accounting does not mean that **replacement costs** (which may be assumed to approximate fair market value) are used in the preparation of financial statements. For example, a tract of land which cost $100,000 many years ago would be stated at $150,000 in common dollars if the general price level had risen by 50%. However, the replacement cost of the land might be $400,000 because land prices might have risen much more than the general price level.

Current-value accounting, on the other hand, does represent a departure from the historical cost concept. It requires that accountants develop new techniques for measuring the current cost of replacing various types of assets and for converting historical operating costs into current replacement costs as of the dates that sales were made. These new techniques have not yet been agreed upon. The accounting profession is now in the process of experimenting with various valuation methods and considering possible related changes in the format of financial statements.

Current-value accounting—objectives and problems

The term *current value* is used in this discussion to mean replacement cost. In *Accounting Series Release No. 190* the SEC required disclosure of certain replacement cost information for large corporations. Replacement cost means the lowest amount that would have to be paid in the normal course of business to obtain a new asset of equivalent operating or productive capability.

The purpose of disclosing replacement cost is to help investors obtain an understanding of the current costs of operating the business. For example, depreciation expense computed on the basis of replacement cost of the assets in use will usually be much greater than depreciation expense computed on the basis of historical costs. In addition, the required disclosure of replacement cost may help investors determine the current value of inventories and of plant facilities, thus acquiring a new perspective on the economic value of these elements in the balance sheet.

The present SEC rule requires that the disclosure of replacement costs be included in a note to the financial statements, or in separate schedules. Keep in mind that at present the complete primary set of financial statements continues to be based on historical cost. The information on replacement costs is supplementary to the conventional financial statements and is not a substitute for them.

The specific information to be disclosed on replacement costs may be summed up under five headings:

1 *Inventories.* Each annual balance sheet must disclose the current replacement cost of inventories at the year-end.

2 *Plant and equipment.* The estimated current cost of replacing new the productive facilities of the company and also the depreciated cost of such facilities.

3 *Cost of goods sold.* The cost of goods sold for the current and the preceding year must be computed as the replacement cost of the goods and services sold at the dates sales were made.

4 *Depreciation, depletion, and amortization.* Straight-line depreciation, depletion, and amortization must be computed on the basis of the current replacement cost of plant and equipment.

5 Description of the methods followed in developing the above estimates.

Disclosure of this information on replacement costs is required only at the end of the fiscal year, and not in connection with interim financial statements.

A principal problem to be solved if current-value accounting is to succeed is the development of uniform standards for measuring the current value of various types of assets and operating expenses. Consideration also must be given to the most effective methods of presenting this information. It appears likely that *specific* price index numbers will be the most objective and satisfactory means of developing much replacement cost data. However, these will be specialized indexes measuring changes in the prices of *specific groups of commodities and services* rather than a single index of the general price level.

What direction will inflation accounting take?

The techniques for restating financial statements for changes in the general price level have been known for many years. Yet despite support from both the FASB and the APB, the preparation of common dollar financial statements has not become a widespread practice.

Current-value accounting is a much newer idea and appears to be gaining acceptance in many countries. The British government has given approval to a System of Current Cost Accounting and has arranged for development of methods to implement it. In the Netherlands, large corporations are basing depreciation on replacement cost and determining cost of goods sold in terms of replacement values. In Australia, the Institute of Chartered Accountants has gone on record as favoring the valuation of assets at current cost and the measurement of profit by stating both revenue and expenses at current values. In the United States, the Securities and Exchange Commission, by requiring disclosure of replacement cost for large corporations, appears to have taken a first step toward general adoption of current-value accounting.

One factor contributing to support for current-value accounting is that common dollar financial statements are based upon the *general* price level and not upon the prices of *specific* goods and services. Any given company has inventories of specific commodities for which prices may be changing in quite a different manner from the general price level.

ILLUSTRATIVE CASE. In a recent year the wholesale price of sugar declined from over 60 cents a pound to approximately 12 cents a pound although the general price level was rising strongly. A company in the sugar industry would have presented much more realistic financial statements by using current-value accounting than by adjusting its historical costs by the upward change in the general price level.

It is important to recognize, however, that the use of current-value accounting does not mean that changes in the general price level should be ignored. General price level accounting and current-value accounting each convey different types of useful information. The two approaches are not mutually exclusive; that is, the use of one does not preclude use of the other. Both approaches may be used within a single set of financial statements. In all probability, the gradual modification of the accounting process to disclose more clearly the effects of inflation will involve experimentation with both general price level and current-value accounting.

KEY TERMS INTRODUCED OR EMPHASIZED IN CHAPTER 14

Audit opinion The report issued by a firm of certified public accountants after auditing the financial statements of a business. Expresses an opinion on the fairness of the financial statements and indicates the nature and limits of the responsibility being assumed by the independent auditors.

Common dollar financial statements A much-discussed proposal to prepare financial statements in which historical costs are adjusted for changes in the general price level. Designed to offset the distortion of financial statements caused by inflation. Also known as *general price level financial statements.*

Conservatism A traditional practice of resolving uncertainties by choosing asset valuation at the lower point of the range of reasonableness. Also refers to the policy of postponing recognition of revenue to a later date when a range of reasonable choice exists. Designed to avoid overstatement of financial strength and earnings.

Consistency An assumption that once a particular accounting method is adopted, it will not be changed from period to period. Intended to make financial statements of a given company comparable from year to year.

Consolidated financial statements Financial statements which present the financial position and operating results of a group of affiliated corporations as though the group represented a single unified business.

Cost principle The traditional, widely used policy of accounting for assets at their historical cost determined through arm's-length bargaining. Justified by the need for objective evidence to support the valuation of assets.

Current-value accounting The valuation of assets and measurement of income in terms of current values rather than historical cost. An approach designed to avoid the distortion of financial statements by inflation.

Disclosure principle Financial statements should disclose all material and relevant information about the financial position and operating results of a business. The notes accompanying financial statements are an important means of disclosure.

Entity concept Any legal or economic unit which controls economic resources and is accountable for these resources may be considered an accounting entity. The resources and the transactions of the entity are not to be intermingled with those of its owner or owners.

General price level The weighted-average price of all goods and services in the economy. Inflation may be defined as an increase in the general price level.

Generally accepted accounting principles Those accounting principles which have received substantial authoritative support, such as the approval of the FASB, the AICPA, or the SEC. Often referred to by the acronym GAAP.

Going-concern assumption An assumption that a business entity will continue in operation indefinitely and thus will carry out its existing commitments. If evidence to the contrary exists, then the assumption of liquidation would prevail and assets would be valued at their estimated liquidation values.

Installment method An accounting method used principally in the determination of taxable income. It provides for recognition of realized profit on installment contracts in proportion to cash collected.

Matching principle The revenue earned during an accounting period is compared or matched with the expenses incurred in generating this revenue in order to measure income. Fundamental to the accrual basis of accounting.

Materiality The relative importance of an amount or item. An item which is not important or significant enough to influence the decisions of prudent users of financial statements is considered as *not* material. The accounting treatment of immaterial items may be guided by convenience rather than by theoretical principles. For example, purchase of 10 gallons of gasoline is treated as the incurring of an expense rather than the acquisition of an asset.

Monetary items With respect to changes in price levels, monetary items include assets representing claims to a fixed number of dollars (such as cash and receivables) and all liabilities. Monetary items are not restated when preparing general purchasing power financial statements.

Monetary (stable-dollar) assumption In using money as a measuring unit and preparing financial statements expressed in dollars, accountants make the assumption that the dollar is a stable unit of measurement. This assumption is obviously faulty as a result of continued inflation, and strenuous efforts are being made to change to current-value accounting or general price-level-adjusted measurements.

Objectivity (objective evidence) The valuation of assets and the measurement of income are to be based as much as possible on objective evidence, such as exchange prices in arm's-length transactions. Objective evidence is subject to verification by independent experts.

Percentage-of-completion method A method of accounting for long-term construction projects which recognizes revenue and profits in proportion to the work completed, based on an estimate of the portion of the project completed each accounting period.

Purchasing power The ability of money to buy goods and services. As the general price level rises, the purchasing power of the dollar declines. Thus, in periods of inflation, an ever-increasing number of dollars is necessary to represent a given amount of purchasing power.

Realization principle The principle of recognizing revenue in the accounts only when earned. Revenue is realized when the earning process is virtually complete, which is usually at the time of sale of goods or rendering service to customers.

DEMONSTRATION PROBLEM FOR YOUR REVIEW

The information below relates to the operations of The Hobby Shop, Inc., during the current year:

Sales (net of returns and allowances)	*$400,000*
Cost of goods purchased for resale (net)	*270,000*
Inventory at Jan. 1 (at sales price)	*50,000*
Inventory at Dec. 31 (at sales price), replacement cost $58,000	*100,000*
Cash payments for operating expenses, including prepayments	*80,000*
Estimated profit on sales orders for goods not yet delivered to customers	*12,100*
Depreciation expense based on actual cost	*10,000*
Depreciation expense based on current fair value	*15,000*
Increase in short-term prepayments during the year	*300*
Estimated uncollectible accounts receivable at end of year	*1,100*
Increase in accrued liabilities during the year	*1,500*
Increase in goodwill (value of the business) during the year	*25,000*
Net purchasing power gain resulting from increase in general price level during the year	*4,200*

The gross profit on sales is constant on all items normally included in inventory.

Instructions
a Prepare a schedule computing the relationship between the sales value and the cost of the merchandise handled by The Hobby Shop, Inc., during the current year.

b Prepare an income statement for the current year in accordance with generally accepted accounting principles. Ending inventory is to be valued at the lower of cost or market. Indicate the proper disposition of any item not used in preparing the income statement. Ignore income taxes.

SOLUTION TO DEMONSTRATION PROBLEM

a   *Computation of Cost Percentage*

Sales, net	*$400,000*
Add: Ending inventory, at sales price	*100,000*
Goods available for sale, at sales price	*$500,000*
Less: Beginning inventory, at sales price	*50,000*
Purchases, at sales price	*$450,000*
Cost percentage ($270,000 ÷ $450,000)	*60%*

b

THE HOBBY SHOP, INC.

Income Statement

For the Current Year

Sales, net		$400,000
Cost of goods sold:		
Inventory, Jan. 1 (60% × $50,000)	$ 30,000	
Purchases, net	270,000	
Cost of goods available for sale	$300,000	
Less: Inventory at Dec. 31, at lower of cost or market		
(cost = 60% × $100,000, or $60,000)	58,000	
Cost of goods sold		242,000
Gross profit on sales		$158,000
Operating expenses (see below)		92,300
Net income		$ 65,700
Operating expenses:		
Cash payments	$ 80,000	
Depreciation (on actual cost)	10,000	
Increase in accrued liabilities during the year	1,500	
Uncollectible accounts expense	1,100	
Subtotal	$ 92,600	
Less: Increase in short-term prepayments during the year	300	
Operating expenses on accrual basis	$ 92,300	

The estimated profit on sales orders for goods not yet delivered to customers, $12,100, is not realized and should not appear in the income statement. The sales have not been completed.

Depreciation expense based on current fair value, $15,000, does not appear in the conventional income statement prepared on the basis of historical costs.

The increase in the value of goodwill, $25,000, is not realized and therefore does not appear in the income statement.

The net purchasing power gain resulting from increase in the general price level during the year, $4,200, would appear in common dollar statements but not in historical cost financial statements prepared in accordance with generally accepted accounting principles.

REVIEW QUESTIONS

1 What is a basic objective of accounting?

2 What is the primary informational need of managers? How do the needs of creditors and owners differ from those of management?

3 To qualify as "generally accepted," accounting principles must receive substantial authoritative support. Name three groups or organizations in the United States which have been most influential in giving substantial authoritative support to accounting principles.

4 Accounting measurements are based on past, present, and future exchange transactions. Give an example of accounting measurement based on each kind of transaction.

5 Explain what is meant by the expression "trade-off between *reliability* and *relevance*" in connection with the preparation of financial statements.

6 Barker Company has at the end of the current period an inventory of merchandise which cost $500,000. It would cost $600,000 to replace this inventory, and it is estimated that the goods will probably be sold for a total of $700,000. If the firm were to terminate operations immediately, the inventory could probably be sold for $480,000. Discuss the relative reliability and relevance of each of these dollar measurements of the ending inventory.

7 Why is it necessary for accountants to assume the existence of a clearly defined accounting entity?

8 What are *consolidated financial statements?*

9 If the going-concern assumption were dropped, there would be no point in having current asset and current liability classifications in the balance sheet. Explain.

10 "The matching of costs and revenue is the natural extension of the time period principle." Evaluate this statement.

11 Define *objectivity, consistency, materiality,* and *conservatism.*

12 Is the assumption that the dollar is a stable unit of measure realistic? What alternative procedures would you suggest?

13 *a* Why is it important that any change in accounting methods from one period to the next be disclosed?
b Does the concept of consistency mean that all companies in a given industry follow similar accounting methods?

14 Briefly define the principle of *disclosure.* List five examples of information that should be disclosed in financial statements or in notes accompanying the statements.

15 List four stages of the productive process which might become the accountant's basis for recognizing changes in the value of a firm's output. Which stage is most commonly used as a basis for revenue recognition? Why?

16 A CPA firm's standard audit opinion consists of two major paragraphs. Describe the essential content of each paragraph.

17 Define *monetary assets* and indicate whether a gain or loss results from the holding of such assets during a period of rising prices.

18 Why is it advantageous to be in debt during an inflationary period?

19 Evaluate the following statement: "During a period of rising prices, the conventional income statement overstates net income because the amount of depreciation recorded is less than the value of the service potential of assets consumed."

20 In presenting financial information to their stockholders and the public, corporations do not report in units of general purchasing power or in *common dollar* terms, although such statements are occasionally presented in addition to regular financial statements as supplementary information. Why has the use of common dollars in financial reporting not gained general acceptance?

21 Publicly owned corporations are required to include in their annual reports a description of the accounting principles followed in the preparation of their financial statements. What advantages do you see in this practice?

22 What efforts, if any, are being made in countries other than the United States to supplement or replace historical cost in financial statements in reaction to continued inflation?

23 How does general purchasing power accounting differ from current-value accounting? For which one would the Gross National Product Implicit Price Deflator be used?

EXERCISES

Ex. 14-1 For each situation described below, indicate the concept (or concepts) of accounting that is violated, if any. You may choose among the following concepts: Conservatism, consistency, disclosure, entity, going concern, matching, materiality, objectivity.

Situations
a A pencil sharpener acquired by a small business at a cost of $5 is estimated to have a useful life of 10 years and is recorded by a debit to the Office Equipment account.
b The machinery used by a car wash business was shown in the balance sheet at its estimated scrap value which was far below the book value.
c The assets of a partnership are combined with the separate assets of the partners in preparing a balance sheet.
d The cost of merchandise purchased is recognized as expense before it is sold in order to report a less favorable financial position.
e Plans to dispose of a major segment of the business are not communicated to readers of the balance sheet.
f A portion of the cost of a major television promotional campaign in the month of May is deferred and arbitrarily allocated to revenue over a five-year period.
g The method of depreciation is changed every two years and the change is disclosed in financial statements.

Ex. 14-2 The Clinton Corporation recognizes the profit on a long-term construction project as work progresses. From the information given below, compute the profit that should be recognized each year, assuming that the original cost estimate on the contract was $6,000,000 and that the contract price is $7,500,000:

Year	Costs Incurred	Profit Considered Realized
1	$1,200,000	$?
2	3,000,000	?
3	1,762,000	?
Total	$5,962,000	$1,538,000

Ex. 14-3 The following information relating to the latest fiscal year is available for Bartel's Hardware Store, Inc.

	Balance, Jan. 1	Cash Receipts or (Payments)	Balance, Dec. 31
Accounts receivable—sale of merchandise . .	$17,000	$380,000	$25,500
Accounts payable	19,750	(238,200)	21,200
Prepaid supplies	1,360	(4,900)	750
Merchandise inventories	41,000		43,600
Accrued operating expenses payable	5,500	(79,000)	9,000
Accrued income taxes payable	3,200	(13,100)	2,800

Compute the net income for the year:
a On a *cash basis,* showing only cash receipts and disbursements.
b On an *accrual basis,* as required by generally accepted accounting principles.

Ex. 14-4 On September 15, Year 1, Susan Moore sold a piece of property which cost her $48,000 for $80,000, net of commissions and other selling expenses. The terms of sale were as follows: down payment, $8,000; balance, $3,000 on the fifteenth day of each month for 24 months, starting October 15, Year 1. Compute the gross profit to be recognized by Moore in Year 1, Year 2, and Year 3 *(a)* on the *accrual basis* of accounting and *(b)* on the *installment basis* of accounting.

Ex. 14-5 This exercise emphasizes the significance of accrued and deferred revenue and expenses in applying the matching principle. Naylor Company reported net income for the period of $72,000, but failed to make adjusting entries for the following items:

(1) Included in the revenue account was the amount of $8,400 which should be considered as deferred revenue, as the services for which the customer had paid would not be rendered by Naylor Company until the following year.

(2) Accrued expense relating to unpaid salaries, $5,200.

(3) Accrued revenue for services rendered, $4,100.

(4) Included in the Rent Expense account was the amount of $3,800 of rent paid applicable to the following year.

(5) A payment of $4,100 for ordinary repairs to driveways and fences had been charged to the Land account.

Compute the corrected net income. Your answer should begin with "Net income as reported . . . $72,000," and show on a separate line the increase or decrease caused by each of the five items.

Ex. 14-6 Three companies started business with $500,000 at the beginning of the current year when the general price index stood at 125. The First Company invested the money in a note receivable due in four years; the Second Company invested its cash in land; and the Third Company purchased a building for $2,000,000, assuming a liability for the unpaid balance of $1,500,000. The price level stood at 140 at the end of the year. Compute the purchasing power gain or loss for each company during the year.

Ex. 14-7 Samson Corporation was organized in Year 1 with total invested capital of $3 million for the purpose of acquiring land for long-term investment. At this time, the general price index was 100. In Year 5, the general price index stands at 140 but the price of all land in the area in which the Samson Corporation invested has doubled in value. Rental receipts for grazing and farming during the five-year period were sufficient to pay all carrying charges on the land.

a Does the company hold any monetary items? What is the purchasing power gain or loss, if any, for the Samson Corporation during the five-year period?

b After giving consideration to the change in the general price level, what is the "economic" gain or loss from holding the land during this period?

PROBLEMS

14-1 Nantucket Boat Works builds custom sailboats. During the first year of operations, the company built four boats for Island Charter Company. The four boats had a total cost of $252,000 and were sold for a total price of $360,000, due on an installment basis. Island Charter Company paid $120,000 of this sales price during the first year, plus an additional amount for interest charges.

At year-end, work is in progress on two other boats which are 60% complete. The contract price for these two boats totals $220,000 and costs incurred on these boats during the year total $96,000 (60% of estimated total costs of $160,000).

Instructions Compute the gross profit for Nantucket Boat Works during its first year of operations under each of the following assumptions. (Interest earned from Island Charter Company does not enter into the computation of gross profit.)

a The entire profit is recognized on the four boats completed and profit on the two boats under construction is recognized on a percentage-of-completion basis.

b Profit on the four boats completed is recognized on the installment basis and no portion of the profit on the two boats under construction will be recognized until the boats are completed, delivered to customers, and cash is collected.

14-2 In each of the situations described below, the question is whether generally accepted accounting principles have been properly observed. In each case state the accounting principle or concept, if any, that has been violated and explain briefly the nature of the violation. If you believe the treatment *is in accord with generally accepted accounting principles,* state this as your position and defend it.

   a For a number of years the Waterman Company used the declining-balance method of depreciation both on its financial accounting records and in its income tax returns. During the current year the company decided to employ the straight-line method of depreciation in its accounting records but to continue to use the declining-balance method for income tax purposes.

   b During the current year the Louis Company adopted a policy of charging purchases of small tools (unit cost less than $100) to expense as soon as they were acquired. In prior years the company had carried an asset account Small Tools which it had depreciated at the rate of 10% of the book value at the beginning of each year. The balance in the Small Tools account represented about 1% of the company's total plant and equipment, and depreciation on small tools was 0.4% of sales revenue. It is expected that purchases of small tools each year will run about the same as the depreciation that would be taken on these small tools.

   c Ace Company printed a large mail-order catalog in July of each year, at a cost of $1.8 million. Customers ordered from this catalog throughout the year and the company agreed to maintain the catalog prices for 12 months after the date of issue. The controller charged the entire cost of the catalog to Advertising Expense in August when it was issued. The Ace Company's fiscal year ends on January 31 of each year. In defending this policy, the controller stated, "Once those catalogs are mailed they are gone. We could never get a nickel out of them."

14-3 All sales by Fire Equipment are made on credit, with terms calling for payment 90 days after the date of sale. The company pays a commission of 10% of selling price to its sales staff as soon as the customers pay their accounts.

   During the first three years of operations, the company reported sales on a cash basis; that is, it did not record the sale until the cash was collected. Commissions to the sales staff were recorded only when cash was collected from customers. Net income figures computed on this basis were:

Year 1	$ 60,000
Year 2	90,000
Year 3	135,000

   An accountant, called in at the end of Year 3 to review the store's accounting system, suggested that a better picture of earnings would be obtained if both sales and commissions were recorded on the accrual basis. After analyzing the company's records, the accountant reported that accounts receivable at the end of each year were as follows:

Year 1	$62,000
Year 2	81,000
Year 3	44,200

   Sales commissions should be accrued at the rate of 10% of accounts receivable.

Instructions

   a On the basis of this information, prepare a schedule showing the amount of net income Fire Equipment would have reported in each of the three years if it had followed accrual accounting for its sales and sales commissions. (Ignore income taxes.)

   b Comment on the differences in net income under the two methods and the significance of the trend in the net income figures as revised.

14-4 In each of the situations described below, the question is whether generally accepted accounting principles have been violated. In each case state the accounting principle or concept, if any, that has been violated and explain briefly the nature of the violation. If you believe the treatment *is in accord with generally accepted accounting principles,* state this as your position and briefly defend it.
   a The Lynn Company has purchased a computer for $1.5 million. The company expects to use the computer for five years, at which time it will acquire a larger and faster computer. The new computer is expected to cost $3.5 million. During the current year the company debited $700,000 to the Depreciation Expense account to "provide for one-fifth of the estimated cost of the new computer."
   b Bob Standish is president of Dutchman Mines. During the current year, geologists and engineers revised upward the estimated value of ore deposits on the company's property. Standish instructed the accountant for Dutchman Mines to record goodwill of $2 million, the estimated value of unmined ore in excess of previous estimates. The offsetting credit was made to revenue.
   c Merchandise inventory which cost $2 million is reported in the balance sheet at $3 million, the expected sales price less estimated direct selling expenses.
   d Jefferson Company reports net income for the current year of $1,300,010. In the audit report the auditors stated: "We certify that the results of operations shown in the income statement are a true and accurate portrayal of the company's operations for the current year."
   e The Lee Oil Company reported on its balance sheet as an intangible asset the total of all wages, supplies, depreciation on equipment, and other costs related to the drilling of a producing oil well and then amortized this asset as oil was produced from the well.

14-5 Galleon Corporation invested $150,000 cash, which was not needed for current operations, in a time deposit at the beginning of Year 1. The cash remained in the time deposit throughout the year; and since the company has ample cash on hand to meet future requirements, the board of directors is considering leaving the $150,000 invested in the time deposit (with extension of the maturity date, as appropriate) for an indefinite period of time.
   An index of the general price level stood at 150 at the beginning of Year 1 and at 200 at the end of Year 1. In a presentation to the board of directors, Linda St. John, the controller of the company, wishes to demonstate the loss of purchasing power that has resulted from holding this investment during a period of inflation. She is uncertain whether to measure the purchasing power loss in terms of end-of-year dollars, beginning-of-year dollars, or base-year dollars. St. John's assistant has made the following comparative calculations:

	End-of-Year Dollars (Index = 200)	Beginning-of-Year Dollars (Index = 150)	Base-Year Dollars (Index = 100)
Balance of time deposit at beginning of Year 1	$200,000 (A)	$150,000	$100,000 (C)
Balance of time deposit at the end of Year 1	150,000	112,500 (B)	75,000 (D)
Loss of purchasing power	$ 50,000	$ 37,500	$ 25,000

Instructions
   a Explain how the figures labeled *(A)*, *(B)*, *(C)*, *(D)* in the assistant's schedule were computed, and why.
   b Which measuring unit would you suggest that St. John use in making her presentation to the board of directors? Explain your reasoning.
   c On a common dollar balance sheet prepared at the end of Year 1, at what figure would the time deposit be reported? Why? What would be the amount of purchasing power loss reported on common dollar financial statements, relating to the ownership of this time deposit?

d If, instead of a time deposit, the $150,000 were a note payable by the Galleon Corporation, due two years after the beginning of Year 1, how would this affect the assistant's analysis of the effect of the decline in the purchasing power of money during the period?

14-6 Edward Lopez received large amounts of income from investments in mining properties and consequently was subject to a very high income tax rate. At the beginning of the current year he organized Lopez Engineering Company, a single proprietorship which carried on construction work and also engaged in the purchase and sale of building materials.

Because Lopez was concerned about the large amount of income taxes he expected to pay on income from mining investments, he gave the following instructions to the accountant: "In preparing the income statement for the first year of operations of Lopez Engineering Company, I want you to be as conservative as possible. Wherever alternative methods are available, you should choose the method which will lead to the minimum income tax this year."

The accountant followed these instructions and prepared the following income statement:

LOPEZ ENGINEERING COMPANY

Income Statement

First Year of Operations

Revenue:		
Sales—regular		$137,000
Collections on installment sales		180,000
Construction work completed		53,000
Total revenue		$370,000
Costs and expenses:		
Cost of goods sold—regular	$ 95,800	
Cost of goods sold—installment basis, 70% of collections	126,000	
Cost of construction work completed	43,800	
Operating expenses	110,000	
Interest expense	29,400	
Total costs and expenses		405,000
Loss for first year of operations		$(35,000)

Lopez was pleased to know that he will be able to reduce his other taxable income as a result of the loss from his business. He was, however, concerned because his banker refused to lend him $60,000 for use in his business because, as the banker put it, "You've lost too much money in your first year of operations and I have a policy against lending money to unprofitable businesses." At this point, Lopez comes to you for advice and gives you additional information relating to the items appearing in the income statement. After reviewing this information, you suggest that the following changes be made:

(*1*) Installment sales amounted to $390,000, the cost of the goods was $273,000, or 70% of sales. The accountant reported only the cash collections as revenue and deducted a proportional amount as the cost of the goods sold on the installment basis. You recommend that the entire income on installment sales be included in the income statement.

(2) The revenue and cost of construction work include three contracts started and completed in the first year. In addition, the following data relate to the six contracts started in the first year which will be completed in the following year.

Total contract price	$645,000
Total estimated cost of contracts	540,000
Actual costs incurred in first year	180,000

You suggest that profit on these contracts be recognized on the percent-age-of-completion basis.

(3) The ending inventory of goods to be sold on the regular basis was valued on the lifo basis at $30,600; this inventory on a fifo basis would have been $33,600. You propose that the first-in, first-out method be used in preparing the income statement to be resubmitted to the banker.

(4) Included in operating expense is depreciation of $9,600, computed by using an accelerated method. You recommend the use of the straight-line depreciation method, which would result in depreciation of only $7,200.

(5) Also included in operating expenses is $9,000 of expenditures which are applicable to future periods. You suggest that these items be deferred and reported in the balance sheet as assets.

Instructions

a Prepare a revised income statement for Lopez Engineering Company, giving effect to the changes in accounting you suggested to Lopez. (Ignore income taxes.) Certain key figures to appear in the revised income statement should be computed in supporting schedules. Reference to these supporting schedules should appear in the revised income statement. The appropriate supporting schedules are indicated in *b* below. (The first item of revenue, Sales—regular, means sales made on 30-day open account as opposed to sales on the installment plan.)

b Prepare the following separate schedules to support the revised income statement:

(1) A schedule showing the revenue from construction work measured on the percentage-of-completion basis

(2) A schedule showing the cost of goods sold—regular (30-day open account sales)

(3) A schedule showing the cost of construction work

(4) A schedule showing operating expenses

14-7 Sweeney Corporation was organized at the beginning of Year 1. The opening balance sheet is shown below:

SWEENEY CORPORATION

Balance Sheet

Beginning of Year 1

Cash	$100,000	Accounts payable	$150,000
Inventories	300,000	Capital stock	250,000
		Total liabilities &	
Total assets	$400,000	stockholders' equity	$400,000

At the beginning of Year 1, the general price index stood at 100; during Year 1 the average price level was 120, and at year-end the price level was 140. During Year 1, Sweeney Corporation sold $200,000 of its inventory for $300,000 cash, paid $120,000 cash on accounts payable, and paid cash operating expenses of $78,000. These transactions occurred at a uniform rate throughout the year. The company was involved in no other transactions during Year 1.

Instructions

a Prepare an analysis of cash transactions in terms of historical dollars and common (end-of-year) dollars.

b Prepare an analysis of accounts payable transactions in terms of historical dollars and common (end-of-year) dollars.

c Prepare a comparative income statement for Year 1 in historical and common (end-of-year) dollars.

d Prepare a comparative balance sheet as of the end of Year 1 in historical and common (end-of-year) dollars.

e Write a brief statement comparing the results as shown in the financial statements prepared in historical and common (end-of-year) dollars.

14-8 After reading an article concerning the SEC's rule on the disclosure of replacement cost in financial statements, Dave Burton, sole proprietor of Burton Company, instructed his newly employed accountant to utilize replacement costs in the preparation of the year-end balance sheet and to provide footnotes disclosing all needed supplementary information. The accountant (whose experience and study of accounting had been quite limited) complied with Burton's instructions to the best of his ability and produced the following balance sheet.

BURTON COMPANY

Balance Sheet

December 31, 19___

Assets

Cash		*$ 24,000*
Accounts receivable (Note #1)		*84,320*
Inventory, at replacement cost (Note #2)		*142,600*
Land, buildings, and equipment (Note #3)	*$190,000*	
Less: Accumulated depreciation (Note #4)	*80,000*	*110,000*
Office supplies (Note #5)		*1*
		$360,921

Liabilities & Owner's Equity

Notes payable to bank	*$120,000*
Interest payable (Note #6)	*10,000*
Accounts payable (Note #7)	*104,000*
Mortgage payable (Note #8)	*40,000*
Dave Burton, capital	*86,921*
	$360,921

Note 1. Accounts receivable include a receivable for $24,000 withdrawn in cash by Dave Burton during the current year at the rate of $2,000 per month. Burton has indicated that he may in the future pay this amount back to the company.

Accounts receivable have been reduced by the amount of $8,000 due from Murray Company because that company is both a customer and a supplier.

Burton Company owes Murray Company $9,000 in purchase invoices and has accounts receivable from Murray Company of $8,000. In preparing the balance sheet, a net figure of $1,000 owing to Murray Company was computed by offsetting the account receivable against the account payable.

Note 2. The cost of the inventory to Burton Company was $131,000, but inquiries of suppliers at year-end indicated the goods in stock have a current replacement cost of $142,600. The company has been using the fifo method.

Note 3. The land cost $20,000 but is shown at its current value of $100,000, as estimated by a local realtor. The building, which cost $60,000, is estimated to have a replacement cost of $80,000. The furniture in use in the business is not owned but rented; however $10,000 of furniture in Burton's home is included in the company's assets because it was paid for with company funds and a monthly staff meeting of all employees is held at Burton's home. No depreciation has been recorded on the furniture.

Note 4. The accumulated depreciation was increased from the $40,000 balance in the accounts to $80,000 because of the estimated increased replacement cost of the building.

Note 5. Office supplies all bear the company name and would produce nothing if offered for sale. The cost of $2,400 has therefore been reduced to the nominal amount of $1 in accordance with the accounting principle of conservatism.

Note 6. A bank loan of $100,000 has been restated on the balance sheet as $120,000 to reflect the change in the price level. Also, interest payable of $8,000 per the accounting records has been increased to $10,000 to reflect the increase in the general level of interest rates since the loan was obtained from the bank.

Note 7. Accounts payable were reduced $8,000 by offsetting a receivable from Murray Company, as explained in Note #1.

Note 8. The mortgage, payable in 10 years, has been increased from the ledger figure of $30,000 to reflect the rise in the price level since it was incurred.

Instructions

a Burton and the accountant appear to misunderstand the SEC position on disclosure of replacement costs. Explain the basic error or errors in their efforts to follow the SEC's official views on replacement cost.

b For each footnote and related balance sheet item which you believe represents a violation of generally accepted accounting principles, write a sentence or two stating your criticism.

c Prepare a corrected balance sheet in accordance with generally accepted accounting principles. Include footnotes only if you believe the needed information cannot be satisfactorily presented in the body of the balance sheet.

BUSINESS DECISION PROBLEM 14

For many years, Festival Films used the lifo method of inventory valuation and the declining-balance method of depreciation in measuring the net income of its mail-order business. In addition, the company charged off all costs of catalogs as incurred. In Year 10, the company changed its inventory pricing method to fifo, adopted the straight-line method of depreciation, and decided to charge off catalog costs only as catalogs are distributed to potential customers.

The following information for the last three years is taken from the company's accounting records:

	Year 10	Year 9	Year 8
Sales (net)	$500,000	$400,000	$350,000
Purchases (net)	300,000	220,000	200,000
Ending inventory—fifo	50,000	45,000	40,000
Ending inventory—lifo	30,000	28,000	25,000
Depreciation—declining-balance method	27,500	30,000	35,000
Depreciation—straight-line method	20,000	20,000	20,000
Operating expenses other than depreciation	120,500	93,000	80,000
Catalog costs included in operating expenses but considered applicable to future revenue	18,500	8,000	5,000
Net income as computed by Festival Films	100,000	60,000	37,000

At the end of Year 10, Festival Films prepared the following comparative income statement and presented it to a banker in connection with an application for a substantial long-term loan:

FESTIVAL FILMS
Comparative Income Statement
For Years Ended December 31

	Year 10	Year 9
Sales (net)	$500,000	$400,000
Cost of goods sold*	278,000	217,000
Gross profit on sales	$222,000	$183,000
Operating expenses	122,000	123,000
Net income	$100,000	$ 60,000

*Based on lifo inventory method in Year 9; inventory at end of Year 10 was valued on fifo basis.

The loan officer for the Pacific National Bank, where Festival Films has applied for the loan, asks you to help decide whether to lend the money to Festival Films.

Instructions
a Prepare a detailed explanation of the way Festival Films computed the income statement for Year 10, and briefly evaluate its approach.
b Determine whether Festival Films' net income has, in fact, increased in Year 10, and recommend whether the comparative income statement for Years 9 and 10 should be prepared (1) on the same accounting basis as in prior years or (2) on the revised accounting basis. You should prepare a comparative income statement both ways and indicate which approach is more appropriate.

15

Statement of Changes in Financial Position: Cash Flows

The heartbeat of any profit-making enterprise is reflected in the pulsing rhythm of its operating cycle. The business obtains cash from various sources and invests it in inventories. These inventories are in turn sold to customers, often on credit. When customers pay their accounts, the company again has cash to apply against its debts and begin the operating cycle anew.

The balance sheet portrays the overall financial position of the business at a specific date during this recurring cycle of investment, recovery of investment, and reinvestment. The income statement shows the growth in the amount of resources as a result of operations. In a sense, the fate of any given business enterprise is read in the income statement, since it tells whether revenue is larger or smaller during any period than the cost of the resources used up in generating this revenue. In this chapter we introduce a third major financial statement, the *statement of changes in financial position*[1] and a related summary of cash movements, the *cash flow statement.*

[1] In *Opinion No. 19,* "Reporting Changes in Financial Position," the Accounting Principles Board of the AICPA concluded (p. 373) that "information concerning the financing and investing activities of a business enterprise and the changes in its financial position for a period is essential for financial statement users, particularly owners and creditors, in making economic decisions. When financial statements purporting to present both financial position (balance sheet) and results of operations (statement of income and retained earnings) are issued, a statement summarizing changes in financial position should also be presented as a basic financial statement for each period for which an income statement is presented."

STATEMENT OF CHANGES IN FINANCIAL POSITION

A statement of changes in financial position helps us to understand how and why the financial position of a business has changed during the period. This statement summarizes the long-term *financing and investing activities* of the business; it shows where the financial resources (funds) have come from and where they have gone. With this understanding of how funds have flowed into the business and how these funds have been used, we can begin to answer such important questions as: Do the normal operations of the business generate sufficient funds to enable the company to continue paying dividends? Did the company have to borrow to finance the acquisition of new plant assets, or was it able to generate the funds from current operations? Is the business becoming more or less solvent? And perhaps the most puzzling question: How can a profitable business be running low on cash and working capital? Even though a business operates profitably, its working capital may decline and the business may even become insolvent. If this situation occurs, many people will demand an explanation.

The statement of changes in financial position give us answers to these questions, because it shows in detail the amount of funds received from each source and the amount of funds used for each purpose throughout the year. In fact, this financial statement used to be called a *Statement of Sources and Applications of Funds.* Many people still call it simply a *Funds Statement.* However, the name officially recommended by the FASB is the *Statement of Changes in Financial Position.*

"Funds" defined as working capital

In ordinary usage, the term *funds* usually means cash. Accountants and financial executives, however, think of "funds" in a broader sense. They view the funds available to a company as its *working capital*—the difference between current assets and current liabilities.

Short-term credit is often used as a substitute for cash; notes and accounts payable as well as various accrued liabilities are used to meet the short-term financing needs of a business. Current assets are constantly being converted into cash, which is then used to pay current liabilities. The net amount of short-term liquid resources available to a business firm at any given time, therefore, is represented by its working capital—the difference between current assets and current liabilities. This explains why it is natural to think of working capital as a "fund" of liquid resources on hand at any given time.

If the amount of working capital increased during a given fiscal period, this means that more working capital was generated than was used for various business purposes; if a decrease in working capital occurred, the reverse is true. One of the key purposes of the statement of changes in financial position is to explain fully the increase or decrease in working capital during a fiscal period. This is done by showing where working capital originated and how it was used.

Sources and uses of working capital

Any transaction that increases the amount of working capital is a *source of working capital.* For example, the sale of merchandise at a price greater than its cost is a source of working capital, because the increase in cash or receivables from the sale is greater than the decrease in inventories.

Any transaction that decreases working capital is a *use of working capital.* For example, either incurring a current liability to acquire a non-current asset or using cash to pay expenses represents a decrease in working capital.

On the other hand, some transactions affect current assets or current liabilities but do not change the amount of working capital. For example, the collection of an account receivable (which increases cash and decreases an account receivable by an equal amount) is not a source of working capital. Similarly, the payment of an account payable (which decreases cash and decreases an account payable by an equal amount) does not change the amount of working capital.

The principal sources and uses of working capital are listed below:

Sources of working capital:

1 *Current operations.* If the inflow of funds from sales exceeds the outflow of funds to cover the cost of merchandise purchases and expenses of doing business, current operations will provide a net source of funds. If the inflow of funds from sales is less than these outflows, operations will result in a net use of funds. Not all expenses require the use of funds in the current period; therefore, the amount of funds provided by operations is *not* the same as the amount of net income earned during the period. Differences between the amount of working capital provided by operations and the amount of net income will be discussed later in the chapter.

In the long run, operations must result in a net source of funds if the business is to survive. A business cannot obtain funds through other sources indefinitely if those funds will only be consumed by business operations.

2 *Sale of noncurrent assets.* A business may obtain working capital by selling noncurrent assets, such as plant and equipment or long-term investments, in exchange for current assets. As long as current assets are received, the sale is a source of funds *regardless of whether the noncurrent assets are sold at a gain or a loss.* For example, assume that a company sells land which cost $40,000 for $30,000 in cash. Although the land was sold at a loss, the company has increased its current assets by $30,000. Thus, the transaction is a source of working capital.

3 *Long-term borrowing.* Long-term borrowing, such as issuing bonds payable, results in an increase in current assets, thereby increasing working capital. *Short-term borrowing,* however, does *not* increase working capital. When a company borrows cash by signing a short-term note payable, working capital is unchanged because the increase in current assets is offset by an increase in current liabilities of the same amount.

4 *Sale of additional shares of stock.* The sale of capital stock results in an inflow of current assets, thereby increasing working capital. In a similar manner, additional investments of current assets by owners represent sources of funds

to single proprietorships and partnerships. The issuance of capital stock in conjunction with a stock dividend or a stock split, however, does not bring any new resources into the company and is not a source of funds.

Uses of working capital:

1 **Declaration of cash dividends.** The declaration of cash dividend results in a current liability (dividend payable) and is therefore a use of funds. Note that it is the *declaration* of the dividend, rather than the payment of the dividend, which is the use of funds. Actual payment of the dividend reduces current assets and current liabilities by the same amount and thus has no effect upon the amount of working capital. Stock dividends do not involve any distribution of assets and, therefore, are not a use of funds.

2 **Purchase of noncurrent assets.** The purchase of noncurrent assets, such as plant and equipment, usually reduces current assets or increases current liabilities. In either case, working capital is reduced. Special situations in which noncurrent assets are acquired in exchange for other noncurrent assets or long-term liabilities are discussed later in this chapter.

3 **Repayment of long-term debt.** Working capital is decreased when current assets are used to repay long-term debt. However, repayment of short-term debt is not a use of funds, since current assets and current liabilities decrease by the same amount.

4 **Repurchase of outstanding stock.** When cash is paid out to repurchase outstanding shares of stock, working capital is reduced.

Simple illustration

Suppose that John Claire started a business, Claire Company, as a single proprietorship on April 30 by investing $30,000 cash; the company rented a building on May 1 and completed the transactions shown below during the month of May.

(*1*) Claire invested an additional $10,000 cash in the business.

(*2*) Purchased merchandise costing $40,000 on credit and sold three-fourths of this, also on credit, for $58,000.

(*3*) Collected $45,000 on receivables; paid $32,000 on accounts payable.

(*4*) Paid $15,500 cash for operating expenses.

(*5*) Purchased land for the construction of a store. Gave $15,000 cash and a six-month note for $12,000 in payment for the land.

(*6*) Withdrew $2,000 from the business for personal use.

The financial statements at the end of May are shown below.

CLAIRE COMPANY
Income Statement
For Month of May

Sales		$58,000
Cost of goods sold:		
Purchases	$40,000	
Less: Ending inventory (one-fourth of purchases)	10,000	30,000
Gross profit on sales		$28,000
Operating expenses		15,500
Net income for month of May		$12,500

Statements covering one month's operations of single proprietorship

CLAIRE COMPANY
Comparative Balance Sheet

Assets	May 31	May 1
Cash	$20,500	$30,000
Accounts receivable	13,000	
Inventory	10,000	
Land	27,000	
Total assets	$70,500	$30,000

Liabilities & Owner's Equity		
Note payable	$12,000	
Accounts payable	8,000	
John Claire, capital	50,500	$30,000
Total liabilities & owner's equity	$70,500	$30,000

The working capital amounted to $30,000 (consisting entirely of cash) on May 1 but was only $23,500 ($43,500 − $20,000) on May 31, a decrease of $6,500. In analyzing the six transactions completed during the month of May, we see that working capital was increased and decreased as follows:

CLAIRE COMPANY
Effect of Transactions on Working Capital
For Month of May

Land and the owner's capital accounts were increased as a result of these transactions

Increases:		
Additional investment by owner		$10,000
Sale of merchandise for more than cost ($58,000 − $30,000)		28,000
Total increases in working capital		$38,000
Decreases:		
Payment of operating expenses	$15,500	
Payment of cash for purchase of land	15,000	
Issuance of current note payable for purchase of land	12,000	
Withdrawal by owner	2,000	44,500
Decrease in working capital during May		$ 6,500

A complete list of transactions for a fiscal period may not be readily available, and even if it were, analysis of such a list would be a laborious process. In practice, a statement of changes in financial position is prepared by analyzing the **changes that occurred in the noncurrent accounts** during the fiscal period. An analysis of the comparative balance sheet for Claire Company indicates that the Land account increased by $27,000. This increase indicates that land, a noncurrent asset was purchased during the period. Purchase of a noncurrent asset is a use of funds. Claire's capital account increased by $20,500 as a result of (1) additional investment of $10,000 (a source of funds), (2) net income of $12,500 (a source of funds), and (3) a withdrawal of $2,000 (a use of funds). We can therefore prepare the following statement of changes in financial position, including the composition of working capital, for the month of May:

CLAIRE COMPANY
Statement of Changes in Financial Position
For Month of May

A simple statement of changes in financial position

Sources of working capital:		
Operations (net income)		$12,500
Additional investment by owner		10,000
Total sources of working capital		$22,500
Uses of working capital:		
Purchase of land	$27,000	
Withdrawal by owner	2,000	
Total uses of working capital		29,000
Decrease in working capital		$ 6,500

	End of May	Beginning of May	Increase or (Decrease) in Working Capital
Composition of working capital:			
Current assets:			
Cash	$20,500	$30,000	$ (9,500)
Accounts receivable	13,000	–0–	13,000
Inventory	10,000	–0–	10,000
Total current assets	$43,500	$30,000	
Current liabilities:			
Note payable	$12,000	$ –0–	(12,000)
Accounts payable	8,000	–0–	(8,000)
Total current liabilities	$20,000	$ –0–	
Working capital	$23,500	$30,000	
Decrease in working capital			$ (6,500)

The differences between net income, net cash flow, and the change in working capital should be carefully noted in the foregoing example. Although Claire Company's net income for May was $12,500, its cash account *decreased* by $9,500 and its working capital *decreased* by $6,500.

Effect of transactions on working capital

In preparing a statement of changes in financial position, it is convenient to view all business transactions as falling into three categories:

1 Transactions which affect **only current asset or current liability accounts.** These transactions produce changes in working capital accounts but do not change the amount of working capital. For example, the purchase of merchandise increases inventory and accounts payable but has no effect on working capital; it may therefore be ignored in preparing a statement of changes in financial position.

2 Transactions which affect a **current asset or current liability account and a nonworking capital account.** These transactions bring about either an increase or a decrease in the amount of working capital. The issuance of long-term bonds, for example, increases current assets and increases bonds payable, a nonworking capital account; therefore, the issuance of bonds payable is a source of working capital. Similarly, when the bonds approach maturity they are transferred to the current liability classification in the balance sheet. This causes a reduction (a use) of working capital. If changes in non-working capital accounts are analyzed, these events are brought to light, and their effect on working capital will be reported in the statement of changes in financial position.

3 Transactions which affect **only noncurrent accounts** and therefore have no direct effect on the amount of working capital. The entry to record depreciation is an example of such a transaction. Other transactions in this category, such as the issuance of capital stock in exchange for plant assets, are called **exchange transactions** and are viewed as **both a source and use of working capital,** but do not change the amount of working capital.

EXCHANGE TRANSACTIONS Suppose that a building worth $105,000 is acquired in exchange for 10,000 shares of $5 par value capital stock. The entry to record this purchase would be:

An	*Building* 105,000	
exchange	*Capital Stock*	*50,000*
transaction	*Paid-in Capital in Excess of Par*	*55,000*

Exchange of 10,000 shares of $5 par value capital stock for building worth $105,000.

This exchange transaction does not involve any current asset or current liability accounts and therefore has no **direct** effect upon working capital. However, the transaction may be viewed as consisting of two parts: (*1*) the sale of capital stock for $105,000 and (*2*) the use of this $105,000 to purchase a building. Instead of being omitted from the statement of changes in financial position, an exchange transaction of this type is shown as **both a source of funds** (sale of capital stock) **and a use of funds** (purchase of building). This treatment is consistent with the objective of explaining in the statement of changes in financial position all the long-term financing activities of the business.

The acquisition of plant assets by issuing long-term debt and the conversion of bonds payable or preferred stock into common stock are other examples of exchange transactions which have no direct effect upon working capital. In the statement of changes in financial position, however, these transactions are shown as both a source and a use of working capital.

Most transactions affecting only long-term accounts are exchange transactions. Two exceptions, however, are stock splits and stock dividends. Stock splits and stock dividends do not involve an exchange and *do not* affect the financial position of the business. For this reason, stock splits and stock dividends *are not shown* in a statement of changes in financial position.

Working capital provided by operations

Working capital provided by operations is the net increase or decrease in working capital resulting from the normal business activities of earning revenue and paying expenses. There are many similarities between working capital provided by operations and net income. For example, earning revenue increases net income and the related inflow of cash and receivables increases working capital. However, there also are significant differences between net income and the amount of working capital provided by operations.

SOME EXPENSES DO NOT REDUCE WORKING CAPITAL Some expenses, such as depreciation, amortization of intangible assets, and amortization of discount on bonds payable, reduce net income but have no immediate effect on the amount of working capital provided by normal operations.

To illustrate, assume that on December 31, Year 1, City Delivery Service buys three trucks at a cost of $30,000. As of January 1, Year 2, the company has no assets other than the trucks and has no liabilities. During Year 2 the company does business on a cash basis, collecting revenue of $40,000 and paying expenses of $22,000, thus showing an $18,000 increase in cash, which is its only working capital account. The company then records depreciation expense of $6,000 on its trucks, resulting in a $12,000 net income for Year 2. What is the amount of working capital provided by operations in Year 2? The recording of depreciation expense reduced net income, *but it did not reduce working capital;* working capital provided by operations remains at $18,000. The $12,000 net income figure therefore *understates* the amount of working capital provided by operations by the amount of depreciation expense recorded during the period.

One objective of the statement of changes in financial position is to explain any differences between net income and the amount of working capital provided by operations. If we are to convert the $12,000 net income of City Delivery Service to the amount of working capital provided by operations, we must *add back* the depreciation expense of $6,000. The computation of working capital provided by operations in the statement of changes in financial position of City Delivery Service for Year 2 is shown below:

Sources of working capital:
  Operations:
    Net income $12,000
    Add: Depreciation expense 6,000
    Working capital provided by operations $18,000

DEPRECIATION IS NOT A SOURCE OF FUNDS The addition of depreciation expense to the net income figure has led some people to view depreciation expense as a source of funds. It is important for the user of financial statements to understand that depreciation is neither a source nor a use of working capital. *No funds flow into a business as a result of recording depreciation expense.* It is shown in the statement of changes in financial position merely to explain one of the differences between the concept of net income and the concept of working capital provided by operations.

SOME ITEMS WHICH INCREASE INCOME DO NOT INCREASE WORKING CAPITAL We have seen that some expenses do not reduce working capital. Similarly, some items in the income statement increase net income without increasing working capital; such items must be *deducted* from net income in arriving at working capital provided by operations. An example of such an item is the amortization of premium on bonds payable, which causes annual interest expense to be less than the cash payments of interest to bondholders.[2]

NONOPERATING GAINS AND LOSSES Extraordinary and nonoperating gains and losses, if material in amount, should be eliminated from net income in order to show the working capital provided by "normal" operations. For example, assume that land costing $100,000 is sold at a net gain of $50,000. In the statement of changes in financial position, the entire $150,000 in proceeds from the sale should be reported as "working capital provided by the sale of land." The $50,000 nonoperating gain, however, is included in the net income for the period. In determining the amount of working capital provided by operations, this $50,000 nonoperating gain must be *deducted* from the net income figure because the entire proceeds from the sale of the land are reported elsewhere in the statement of changes in financial position.

As a separate example, assume that the same land is sold for $70,000; then the nonoperating loss of $30,000 should be *added* to net income in

---

[2] The treatment of this item in the working paper and in the statement of changes in financial position is illustrated in the Demonstration Problem on pages 624–627.

arriving at the income from operations, and the working capital provided through sale of land should be reported at $70,000.

COMPUTATION OF WORKING CAPITAL PROVIDED BY OPERATIONS: A SUMMARY The foregoing discussion relating to the measurement of working capital provided by operations can be summarized as follows:

Computation of Working Capital Provided by Operations

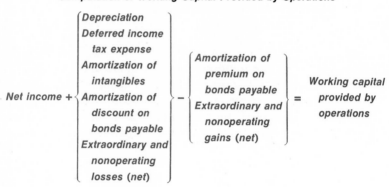

Impact of operations on working capital

Preparation of more complex statement of changes in financial position

To illustrate the points just discussed, we shall prepare a statement of changes in financial position for the Allison Corporation from the comparative balance sheet and the condensed income statement shown below and on page 613. Note that the balance sheet is not classified, except for current assets and current liabilities.

ALLISON CORPORATION
Comparative Balance Sheet
At December 31

Assets	Year 4	Year 3
Current assets:		
Cash	$ 15,000	$ 35,000
Accounts receivable (net)	105,000	85,000
Inventory	200,000	120,000
Short-term prepayments	25,000	12,000
Total current assets	$345,000	$252,000
Land	140,000	50,000
Equipment	290,000	230,000
Less: Accumulated depreciation	(107,500)	(80,000)
Total assets	$667,500	$452,000

Can you give the reasons for the increase of $57,500 in working capital?

Liabilities & Stockholders' Equity

Current liabilities:		
Notes payable to merchandise creditors	$ 60,000	$ 40,000
Accounts payable	85,000	50,000
Accrued liabilities	22,500	42,000
Total current liabilities	$167,500	$132,000
Notes payable, due Jan. 1, Year 17	15,000	10,000
Bonds payable, due June 30, Year 20	160,000	100,000
Capital stock, $5 par	215,000	110,000
Paid-in capital in excess of par	50,000	30,000
Retained earnings	60,000	70,000
Total liabilities & stockholders' equity	$667,500	$452,000

ALLISON CORPORATION
Condensed Income Statement
For Year Ended December 31, Year 4

Sales (net)		$900,000
Cost of goods sold		585,000
Gross profit on sales		$315,000
Operating expenses and income taxes	$255,000	
Gain on sale of land	(20,000)	235,000
Net income		$ 80,000

A summary of the transactions completed by Allison Corporation which resulted in changes in *noncurrent accounts* during Year 4 follows:

1 Changes in noncurrent assets:
 a Land costing $10,000 was sold for $30,000. Another parcel of land was acquired in exchange for bonds payable of $100,000.
 b Equipment was purchased for $60,000; the invoice was paid within ten days.
 c Depreciation of $27,500 was recorded.

2 Changes in noncurrent liabilities:
 a An additional $5,000 was borrowed on long-term notes due in Year 17.
 b Bonds payable of $40,000 were retired at a price equal to par value and additional bonds of $100,000 were issued in exchange for land.

3 Changes in stockholders' equity accounts:
 a A 50% stock dividend was declared in January, requiring a transfer of $55,000 from the Retained Earnings account to the Capital Stock account.
 b In February, 10,000 shares of $5 par value stock were sold at $7 per share, thus increasing Capital Stock by $50,000 and Paid-in Capital in Excess of Par by $20,000.
 c In addition to the $55,000 reduction in retained earnings as a result of the 50% stock dividend, cash dividends of $35,000 were declared.
 d The net income for the year, $80,000 (including the nonoperating gain of $20,000), was transferred to the Retained Earnings account.

From the comparative balance sheets, the income statement, and the summary of the transactions during the year which changed noncurrent accounts, we can prepare a statement of changes in financial position by completing the following three steps:

1 Compute the change in working capital during the period.
2 Prepare a working paper for analysis of changes in noncurrent accounts.
3 Prepare the statement of changes in financial position.

COMPUTATION OF INCREASE IN WORKING CAPITAL DURING THE PERIOD
The first step in preparing a statement of changes in financial position is to determine the net increase or decrease in working capital during the period covered by the statement.

The working capital of the Allison Corporation increased by $57,500 during Year 4, determined as follows:

ALLISON CORPORATION
Computation of Increase in Working Capital during Year 4

	Dec. 31, Year 4	Dec. 31, Year 3
Current assets	$345,000	$252,000
Less: Current liabilities	167,500	132,000
Working capital	$177,500	$120,000
Increase in working capital during Year 4 ($177,500 − $120,000)		57,500
	$177,500	$177,500

Sources of working capital exceed uses by $57,500

The purpose of the statement of changes in financial position is to explain the reasons for the change in working capital. This is accomplished by listing the specific sources and uses of working capital during the period. Since the working capital for the Allison Corporation increased by $57,500, the sources of working capital during Year 4 exceeded the uses by this amount. But before a statement of changes in financial position can be prepared, we must analyze the changes which took place during the year in the noncurrent accounts.

PREPARATION OF WORKING PAPER FOR ANALYSIS OF CHANGES IN NON-CURRENT ACCOUNTS A working paper showing the analysis of changes in noncurrent accounts for the Allison Corporation is illustrated on page 615. The amount of working capital and the balances in noncurrent accounts at the beginning of the period are listed in the first column of the working paper; balances at the end of the year are listed in the last (right-hand) column. The two middle columns are used to *explain the changes* in each *noncurrent* account during the year and to indicate whether each change corresponds to a source or a use of funds. Trans-

Debits	Account Balances, Jan. 1, Year 4	Analysis of Transactions for Year 4 Debit	Analysis of Transactions for Year 4 Credit	Account Balances, Dec. 31, Year 4
Working capital	120,000	(x) 57,500		177,500
Land	50,000	(4) 100,000	(3) 10,000	140,000
Equipment	230,000	(7) 60,000		290,000
Total	400,000			607,500

Credits				
Accumulated depreciation	80,000		(2) 27,500	107,500
Notes payable, due Jan. 1, Year 17	10,000		(6) 5,000	15,000
Bonds payable, due June 30, Year 20 . . .	100,000	(8) 40,000	(4) 100,000	160,000
Capital stock, $5 par	110,000		(5) 50,000⎫ (10) 55,000⎭	215,000
Paid-in capital in excess of par	30,000		(5) 20,000	50,000
Retained earnings	70,000	(9) 35,000 (10) 55,000	(1) 80,000⎫ ⎭	60,000
Total	400,000	347,500	347,500	607,500

Sources of working capital:		Sources	Uses	
Operations—net income		(1) 80,000		(From
Add: Depreciation		(2) 27,500		operations,
Less: Gain on sale of land			(3) 20,000	$87,500)
Sale of land		(3) 30,000		
Issuance of bonds payable		(4) 100,000		
Sale of capital stock		(5) 70,000		
Borrowed on notes payable,				
due Jan. 1, Year 17		(6) 5,000		
Uses of working capital:				
Purchase of land in exchange				
for bonds payable			(4) 100,000	
Purchase of equipment			(7) 60,000	
Retirement of bonds payable			(8) 40,000	
Cash dividends declared			(9) 35,000	
Total sources and uses of				
working capital		312,500	255,000	
Increase in working capital dur. Year 4 . .			(x) 57,500	
		312,500	312,500	

Explanation of transactions for Year 4:

(1) Net income $80,000 (including a gain of $20,000 on sale of land) is transferred to Retained Earnings. This is a tentative source of working capital to be adjusted in (2) and (3) below.

(2) Depreciation for the year, $27,500, is added to net income in arriving at the working capital provided by operations because it did not reduce a current asset or increase a current liability.

(3) Sale of land for $30,000; the gain of $20,000 is deducted from net income in order that entire proceeds can be reported separately as a source of working capital.

(4) Issuance of $100,000 of bonds payable in exchange for land.

(5) Sale of capital stock, providing working capital of $70,000.

(6) Working capital was provided by borrowing $5,000 on long-term notes.

(7) Working capital was reduced through purchase of equipment, $60,000.

(8) Working capital of $40,000 was used to retire bonds payable.

(9) Cash dividends declared, $35,000; this is a use of working capital.

(10) Board of directors declared a 50% stock dividend; this transaction had no effect on working capital.

(x) Balancing figure—increase in working capital during Year 4.

actions for the year (in summary form) are recorded in these middle columns and an offsetting entry is made in the lower section of the working papers indicating the effect of each transaction upon working capital.

Explanation of transactions in working paper By studying the changes in the noncurrent accounts during Year 4, we are able to find the specific reasons for the $57,500 increase in working capital. As previously stated, only changes in the noncurrent accounts represent sources and uses of working capital. The analyses of the transactions completed by the Allison Corporation during Year 4 are explained below:

(*1*) The net income of $80,000 is credited to the Retained Earnings account and is shown under "sources of working capital: operations." Net income represents an increase in stockholders' equity and is one of the major sources of working capital for most businesses. Net income, however, is only a tentative measure of the increase in working capital from operations because not all revenue and expense items represent sources and uses of working capital (depreciation, for example). Furthermore, any extraordinary and nonoperating items are eliminated from net income because the transactions giving rise to such items are reported separately if they generate or use working capital.

(*2*) Since depreciation expense does not reduce a current asset or increase a current liability, it has no effect on working capital. Therefore, the depreciation expense of $27,500 for the year is shown as an addition to net income in the working paper and is credited to Accumulated Depreciation. The net income, $80,000, plus depreciation expense, $27,500, or a total of $107,500, represents a *tentative* increase in working capital as a result of profitable operations. This $107,500 figure is viewed as tentative because it will be reduced in adjustment (*3*) by the amount of the gain on the sale of land ($20,000) which was included in the net income of $80,000; this gain will be included in the $30,000 source of working capital on the sale of land.

(*3*) The sale of land is recorded as a source of working capital of $30,000 because cash was generated when the land was sold. The cost of the land, $10,000, is credited to the Land account and the gain, $20,000, is shown as a reduction to the net income in order that the net proceeds on the sale of the land ($30,000) can be listed as a source of working capital. This adjustment gives us net "working capital provided by operations," $87,500, consisting of income *before the gain on the sale of land,* $60,000, plus depreciation, $27,500.

(*4*) The issuance of $100,000 par value bonds in exchange for land is an exchange transaction, representing both a source and a use of funds. First, an entry is made in the top portion of the working papers explaining the $100,000 increase in the Bonds Payable account and an offsetting entry is made below showing a $100,000 source of funds. Next, a debit entry is made in the upper portion of the working papers explaining the $100,000 increase in the Land account and an offsetting entry is made below showing the $100,000 use of funds.

(*5*) The sale of capital stock in February for $70,000 is recorded in the upper portion of the working papers by credits to Capital Stock, $50,000 (10,000 shares with a $5 par value), and to Paid-in Capital in Excess of Par, $20,000. The issuance of capital stock is a source of funds; therefore, the offsetting entry in the lower section of the working papers is entered in the Sources column.

(6) An increase in long-term debt is a source of funds. Therefore, the borrowing of $5,000 on long-term notes payable is recorded in the working paper as a credit to Notes Payable and a source of working capital.

(7) Equipment was purchased for $60,000, causing a reduction in working capital. This is recorded in the working paper by a debit to Equipment and an offsetting entry describing the use of funds.

(8) During Year 4, Allison Corporation retired $40,000 of bonds payable at par. A reduction in long-term debt represents a use of working capital. The transaction is recorded in the working paper by a debit to Bonds Payable and an offsetting entry describing the use of funds. If a retirement of bonds payable results in a material loss or gain, the loss or gain would be reported in the income statement and would be eliminated from net income in the same manner as the gain on sale of land in transaction (3) above.

(9) Cash dividends declared on capital stock outstanding reduce both working capital and stockholders' equity and should be listed on a statement of changes in financial position as a use of working capital. The required working paper entry is a debit to Retained Earnings and an offsetting entry showing the use of funds. A cash dividend need not be paid in order to represent a reduction in working capital. The *declaration* of the cash dividend establishes a current liability and thus reduces working capital. The actual payment of the cash dividend has no effect on working capital because the payment merely reduces a current liability (Dividends Payable) and a current asset (Cash) by the same amount; *a transaction which changes only current accounts cannot be a source or use of working capital.*

(10) The declaration of a stock dividend is merely a transfer from retained earnings to paid-in capital; a stock dividend has no effect on working capital because no working capital account is changed. The working paper entry to recognize the 50% stock dividend distributed by the Allison Corporation in January is a debit to Retained Earnings for $55,000 and a credit to Capital Stock for the same amount.

(x) After all changes in noncurrent accounts are analyzed in the working paper, the gross sources, $312,500, and uses, $255,000, of working capital are totaled. At this point, the increase in working capital during the year, $57,500, should be entered as a debit to Working Capital on the first line of the second column in the working paper and also as a balancing figure on the next to the last line of the third column in the working paper. The account balances at December 31, Year 4, can now be determined and totals obtained for the debits and credits in the top portion of the working paper. If the totals agree, we know that our analysis is correct, at least so far as the mechanics are concerned.

PREPARATION OF STATEMENT OF CHANGES IN FINANCIAL POSITION The foregoing working paper analysis explained all changes in noncurrent accounts that took place during Year 4. In making this analysis, we listed the sources and uses of working capital in the lower section of the working paper on page 615. The increase of $57,500 in working capital has been confirmed and a statement of changes in financial position, including changes in the composition of working capital, can now be prepared as follows:

Statement
of changes
in financial
position
shows
sources and
uses of
working
capital

ALLISON CORPORATION
Statement of Changes in Financial Position
For Year Ended December 31, Year 4

Sources of working capital:

Operations:

Income before gain on sale of land		$ 60,000
Add: Expense not requiring the use of current funds—depreciation		27,500
Total working capital provided by operations		$ 87,500
Sales of land		30,000
Issuance of bonds payable		100,000
Sale of capital stock		70,000
Borrowed on long-term notes payable, due Jan. 1, Year 17		5,000
Total sources of working capital		$292,500

Uses of working capital:

Purchase of land in exchange for bonds payable	$100,000	
Purchase of equipment	60,000	
Retirement of bonds payable	40,000	
Declaration of cash dividends	35,000	
Total uses of working capital		235,000
Increase in working capital		$ 57,500

Changes in Composition of Working Capital

	End of Year 4	End of Year 3	Increases or (Decreases) in Working Capital
Composition of working capital:			
Current assets:			
Cash	$ 15,000	$ 35,000	$(20,000)
Accounts receivable (net)	105,000	85,000	20,000
Inventory	200,000	120,000	80,000
Short-term prepayments	25,000	12,000	13,000
Total current assets	$345,000	$252,000	
Current liabilities:			
Notes payable to merchandise creditors	$ 60,000	$ 40,000	(20,000)
Accounts payable	85,000	50,000	(35,000)
Accrued liabilities	22,500	42,000	19,500
Total current liabilities	$167,500	$132,000	
Working capital	$177,500	$120,000	
Increase in working capital			$ 57,500

We can see that working capital provided by operations amounted to $87,500, and another $205,000 of working capital came from nonoperating sources (sale of land, sale of additional capital stock, and long-term borrowing). Working capital totaling $235,000 was used to purchase land

and equipment, retire bonds payable, and declare cash dividends. These sources and uses resulted in a net increase of $57,500 in working capital. The statement of changes in financial position thus provides a concise view of the way in which the Allison Corporation generated and used its working capital during the year.

Investors and creditors find the statement of changes in financial position helpful not only in evaluating the past performance of a company but also in projecting its future movements of working capital and in evaluating probable *liquidity* (the ability to pay debts as they become payable).

A statement of changes in financial position for a large listed corporation appears in the Appendix of this book.

CASH FLOW ANALYSIS

While the statement of changes in financial position reports the inflow and outflow of working capital during an accounting period, management is often more concerned with having enough cash to meet its operating needs and to pay maturing liabilities. Cash is the most liquid asset, and the efficient use of cash is one of the most important tasks of management. A *cash flow statement* is often prepared in order to give a full and complete picture of cash receipts and disbursements for an accounting period. Such a cash flow statement may also be useful in preparing a cash budget.

A cash flow statement is definitely not a substitute for an income statement. Income statements, as we have shown in prior chapters, are prepared on an accrual basis. Accrual accounting was developed to overcome the limitations of cash movements as indicators of business performance. Cash outlays simply represent investments which may or may not prove sound. Cash receipts represent disinvestment and, taken by themselves, tell nothing about whether the inflow is beneficial or not. The accountant's measurement of net income is designed to tell something about the fate of a company's overall investment and disinvestment activities during a given period of time. Despite its imperfections, the income statement is still the best means we have for reporting operating performance of business enterprises.

However, there are occasions when one may wish to reverse the accrual process and determine the amount of cash generated by operations. Reports of past cash flow may reveal a good deal about the financial problems and policies of a company. Forecasts of cash flows and cash budgets are useful managerial planning tools. The measurement of past and future cash flows from all sources, including operations, provides valuable information.

Cash flow from operations

Suppose we wish to convert a company's income statement into a report of its cash flow from operations. How should we go about adjusting the data on the income statement to convert it into cash flow information?

To answer this question, we must consider the relationship between accrual basis income statement amounts and cash movements within the firm. For illustrative purposes, consider the income statement of the Allison Corporation for Year 4, which was presented earlier in this chapter.

ALLISON CORPORATION

Condensed Income Statement

For Year Ended December 31, Year 4

Condensed	Sales (net)		$900,000
income *statement:*	Cost of goods sold		585,000
accrual	Gross profit on sales		$315,000
basis	Operating expenses and income taxes	$255,000	
	Gain on sale of land	(20,000)	235,000
	Net income		$ 80,000

From our preceding discussion of Allison Corporation's transactions in Year 4, we already know that cash was received from the sale of land ($30,000), from the sale of capital stock ($70,000), and from borrowing on long-term notes ($5,000). We also know that cash was paid to acquire equipment ($60,000), to retire bonds payable ($40,000), and to pay cash dividends ($35,000). The remaining cash movements must consist of cash receipts from customers and cash payments for purchases and expenses, including income taxes.

CASH RECEIPTS FROM CUSTOMERS Sales on account are an important factor in most companies. The relationship between the amount of cash collected from customers and the net sales reported in the income statement depends on the change in accounts receivable between the beginning and end of any period. The relationship may be stated as follows:

Converting sales to cash basis

$$\text{Net sales} \begin{cases} - \text{ increase in accounts receivable} \\ \qquad\qquad\qquad \text{or} \\ + \text{ decrease in accounts receivable} \end{cases} = \begin{array}{l} \text{cash receipts from} \\ \text{customers} \end{array}$$

In the Allison Corporation example, a glance at the comparative balance sheet on pages 612–613 tells us that net accounts receivable increased from $85,000 to $105,000 during Year 4, an increase of $20,000.

Therefore, the cash receipts from customers during Year 4 can be determined as follows:

Net sales on cash basis

Net sales	*$900,000*
Less: Increase in net accounts receivable during the year	*20,000*
Cash receipts from customers	*$880,000*

CASH PAYMENTS FOR PURCHASES The relationship between the cost of goods sold for a period and the cash payments for the purchase of merchandise depends both on the change in inventory and the change in notes and accounts payable to merchandise creditors during the period. The relationship may be stated, in two stages, as follows:

Converting cost of goods sold to cash basis

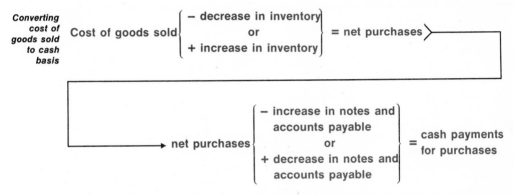

Again referring to the Allison Corporation example, we can see that the company increased its inventory by $80,000 and that notes and accounts payable to merchandise creditors increased by $55,000 during the year. The cash payments for purchases during Year 4 would be computed as follows:

Cost of goods sold on cash basis

Cost of goods sold	*$585,000*
Add: Increase in inventory	*80,000*
Net purchases (accrual basis)	*$665,000*
Less: Increase in notes and accounts payable to creditors	*55,000*
Cash payments for purchases.	*$610,000*

The result of this computation makes sense. If a company is increasing its inventory, it will be buying more merchandise than it sells during the period; furthermore, if the company is increasing its notes and accounts payable to merchandise creditors, it is not paying for all its current purchases.

CASH PAYMENTS FOR EXPENSES Expenses in the income statement arise from three major sources: cash expenditures, the write-off of prepayments, and incurring obligations for accrued expenses. The relationship between operating expenses and cash payments, therefore, depends on changes in asset accounts representing the prepayment of expenses, and on changes in accrued liability accounts. These relationships may be stated as follows:

Converting an expense on accrual basis to cash basis

Expense $\left\{ \begin{array}{l} \text{– increase in related accrued liability} \\ \text{or} \\ \text{+ decrease in related accrued liability} \\ \text{– decrease in related prepayment} \\ \text{or} \\ \text{+ increase in related prepayment} \end{array} \right\}$ = cash payments for expense

In the case of a noncash expense such as depreciation, the decrease in the book value of a depreciable asset is exactly equal to the expense recorded, and the resultant cash payment is zero.

Using the information for the Allison Corporation, we can summarize the relationship between the operating expenses and income taxes reported in the income statement and cash payments for these expenses during Year 4 as follows:

Expenses on cash basis

Total operating expenses and income taxes in the income statement	$255,000
Add: Decrease in accrued liabilities	19,500
Increase in short-term prepayments	13,000
Less: Depreciation, a noncash expense	(27,500)
Cash payments for operating expenses and income taxes	$260,000

CONVERSION OF AN INCOME STATEMENT TO CASH BASIS The conversion of the income statement of the Allison Corporation from an accrual to a cash basis is shown on page 623. Note that this schedule incorporates the adjustments discussed in the preceding paragraphs.

The cash flow from operations for the Allison Corporation, $10,000, is lower than the amount of income before the gain on the sale of land, $60,000, during Year 4. This difference is caused by a series of variations between revenue and expense transactions on the accrual basis and the related cash inflows and outflows during the year.

ALLISON CORPORATION
Conversion of Income Statement from Accrual to Cash Basis
For Year Ended December 31, Year 4

	Income Statement (Accrual Basis)	Add (Deduct)	Cash Basis
Net sales.	$900,000		
Less: Increase in accounts receivable . .		$(20,000)	$880,000
Cost of goods sold	585,000		
Add: Increase in inventory		80,000	
Less: Increase in notes and accounts			
payable to merchandise creditors		(55,000)	610,000
Gross profit on sales	$315,000		$270,000
Operating expenses and income taxes . .	255,000		
Add: Decrease in accrued liabilities		19,500	
Increase in short-term prepayments .		13,000	
Less: Depreciation expense		(27,500)	260,000
Income before gain on sale of land			
(accrual basis)	$ 60,000		
Cash flow from operations			$ 10,000

How much is "cash flow" for Year 4?

CASH FLOW STATEMENT The cash flow from operations computed above for the Allison Corporation does not tell the complete story of cash movements during the period. Let us now combine the $10,000 cash flow from operations with the information relating to cash receipts and payments obtained from the comparative balance sheet by way of the statement of changes in financial position. The result will be a statement that explains in full the $20,000 decrease in the cash balance during Year 4. Such a cash flow statement for the Allison Corporation is shown below:

ALLISON CORPORATION
Cash Flow Statement
For Year Ended December 31, Year 4

Complete summary of cash movements for Year 4

Purchase of equipment		$ 60,000
Retirement of bonds payable		40,000
Payment of cash dividends		35,000
Total cash payments		$135,000
Cash receipts:		
Cash generated from operations (see schedule above).	$10,000	
Sale of land.	30,000	
Sale of capital stock	70,000	
Borrowing on long-term notes	5,000	
Total cash receipts		115,000
Decrease in cash during the year		$ 20,000

The Allison Corporation example was sufficiently simple that we could develop cash flow information from a direct inspection of the income statement and comparative balance sheets. In more complex situations, the accountant will usually use a working paper to convert the income statement from an accrual to a cash basis and to develop cash flow information in a systematic fashion. Familiarity with these working paper procedures is not necessary in order to be able to understand and interpret cash flow information; therefore, discussion of this process is reserved for the *Intermediate Accounting* volume in this series.

KEY TERMS INTRODUCED OR EMPHASIZED IN CHAPTER 15

Cash basis A method of measuring operating results in terms of cash receipts and cash payments rather than revenue earned and expenses incurred.

Cash flow statement A statement showing the sources of cash receipts and purpose of cash payments during an accounting period. This statement is useful for explaining changes in the balance of the Cash account, but it is not a substitute for an income statement.

Exchange transaction In the context of a statement of changes in financial position, exchange transactions are financing or investing activities which do not directly affect working capital accounts. An example of such a transaction is the purchase of plant assets by issuing common stock. Such transactions should be shown in a funds statement as both a source and a use of working capital.

Funds In the context of a statement of changes in financial position, "funds" are usually defined as working capital.

Noncurrent account Any balance sheet account *other than* a current asset or a current liability. Noncurrent accounts include long-term investments, plant assets, intangible assets, long-term liabilities, and stockholders' equity accounts.

Statement of changes in financial position A financial statement showing the sources and uses of working capital during the accounting period. In addition, this statement shows financing and investing activities, such as exchange transactions, which do not directly affect working capital.

Working capital Current assets minus current liabilities. Working capital represents the net amount of liquid resources available to a business.

DEMONSTRATION PROBLEM FOR YOUR REVIEW

The comparative financial data for Liquid Gas Company for the last two years are shown below and on page 625:

		December 31	
Debits		*Year 2*	*Year 1*
Cash		$ 39,220	$ 15,800
Receivables (net of allowance for doubtful accounts)		41,400	24,000
Inventories, lower of cost or market		27,600	36,800
Short-term prepayments		4,180	4,400
Land		9,000	19,000
Buildings		270,000	250,000
Equipment		478,600	450,000
Total debits		$870,000	$800,000

Credits	Year 2	Year 1
Accumulated depreciation: buildings	$ 95,000	$ 77,000
Accumulated depreciation: equipment	153,000	120,000
Accounts payable	59,200	30,000
Accrued liabilities	20,000	10,000
Bonds payable	90,000	90,000
Premium on bonds payable	2,800	3,000
Preferred stock ($100 par)	70,000	100,000
Common stock ($25 par)	260,000	250,000
Paid-in capital in excess of par	45,000	40,000
Retained earnings	75,000	80,000
Total credits	$870,000	$800,000

Other data
(1) During Year 2, the board of directors of the company authorized a transfer of $15,000 from retained earnings to reflect a 4% stock dividend on the common stock.
(2) Cash dividends of $6,000 were paid on the preferred stock, and cash dividends of $50,000 were paid on the common stock.
(3) During Year 2, 300 shares of preferred stock were retired at par value.
(4) The only entries recorded in the Retained Earnings account were for dividends and to close the Income Summary account, which had a credit balance of $66,000 after the loss on the sale of the land.
(5) There were no sales or retirements of buildings and equipment during the year; land was sold for $8,000, resulting in a loss of $2,000.

Instructions
a Compute the change in working capital during Year 2. You may use totals for current assets and current liabilities.
b Prepare a working paper for a statement of changes in financial position for Year 2.
c Prepare a statement of changes in financial position for Year 2, without showing the composition of working capital.
d Prepare a cash flow statement, with a supporting schedule converting the net income from the accrual basis to the cash basis.

SOLUTION TO DEMONSTRATION PROBLEM

a Computation of decrease in working capital:

	As of December 31	
	Year 2	Year 1
Current assets	$112,400	$81,000
Less: Current liabilities	79,200	40,000
Working capital	$ 33,200	$41,000
Decrease in working capital during Year 2	7,800	
	$ 41,000	$41,000

LIQUID GAS COMPANY
Working Paper for Statement of Changes in Financial Position
For Year 2

Debits	Account Balances Dec. 31, Year 1	Analysis of Transactions for Year 2 Debit	Analysis of Transactions for Year 2 Credit		Account Balances Dec. 31, Year 2
Working capital	41,000		(x)	7,800	33,200
Land	19,000		(5)	10,000	9,000
Buildings	250,000	(6) 20,000			270,000
Equipment	450,000	(7) 28,600			478,600
Total	760,000				790,800

Credits					
Accumulated depreciation: buildings	77,000		(2)	18,000	95,000
Accumulated depreciation: equipment	120,000		(2)	33,000	153,000
Bonds payable	90,000				90,000
Premium on bonds payable	3,000	(8) 200			2,800
Preferred stock, $100 par	100,000	(9) 30,000			70,000
Common stock, $25 par	250,000		(3)	10,000	260,000
Paid-in capital in excess of par	40,000		(3)	5,000	45,000
Retained earnings	80,000	(3) 15,000 (4) 56,000	(1)	66,000	75,000
Total	760,000	149,800		149,800	790,800

		Sources	Uses	
Sources of working capital:				
Operations—net income		(1) 66,000		
Add: Depreciation		(2) 51,000		(From
Loss on sale of land		(5) 2,000		operations,
Less: Amortization of premium				$118,800)
on bonds payable			(8) 200	
Sale of land		(5) 8,000		
Uses of working capital:				
Payment of cash dividends			(4) 56,000	
Purchase of buildings			(6) 20,000	
Purchase of equipment			(7) 28,600	
Retirement of preferred stock			(9) 30,000	
Total sources and uses of				
working capital		127,000	134,800	
Decrease in working capital		(x) 7,800		
		134,800	134,800	

Explanation of transactions for Year 2:
(1) Net income, $66,000, including a loss of $2,000 on sale of land, transferred to Retained Earnings.
(2) Depreciation for the year, $51,000 (buildings, $18,000, and equipment, $33,000) is added to net income because it is an expense which did not reduce working capital.
(3) Entry to record 4% stock dividend; no effect on working capital.
(4) Cash dividends declared, $56,000 (preferred stock, $6,000, and common, $50,000).
(5) To record sale of land for $8,000; the loss of $2,000 is added to net income because the loss reduced net income but had no effect on working capital.
(6) To record working capital used for purchase of buildings.
(7) To record working capital used for purchase of equipment.
(8) To record amortization of premium on bonds payable; the amortization increased net income but had no effect on working capital.
(9) To record working capital applied to retirement of preferred stock.
(x) Balancing figure—decrease in working capital during Year 2.

c

LIQUID GAS COMPANY
Statement of Changes in Financial Position
For Year 2

Sources of working capital:

  Operations:

Income before loss on sale of land		$ 68,000
Add: Expense not requiring the use of working capital—		
depreciation	$51,000	
Less: Increase in net income which did not provide		
working capital—amortization of premium on bonds		
payable	200	50,800
Total working capital provided by operations		$118,800
Sale of land		8,000
Total sources of working capital		$126,800

Uses of working capital:

Declaration of cash dividends	$56,000	
Purchase of buildings	20,000	
Purchase of equipment	28,600	
Retirement of preferred stock	30,000	
Total uses of working capital		134,600
Decrease in working capital		$ 7,800

d

LIQUID GAS COMPANY
Cash Flow Statement
For Year 2

Cash receipts:

Cash generated from operations (see Schedule A below)		$150,020
Sale of land		8,000
Total cash receipts		$158,020

Cash payments:

Payment of cash dividends	$56,000	
Purchase of buildings	20,000	
Purchase of equipment	28,600	
Retirement of preferred stock	30,000	
Total cash payments		134,600
Increase in cash during the year		$ 23,420

Schedule A—Cash generated from operations:

Working capital provided by operations—part c		$118,800
Add: Decrease in inventories	$ 9,200	
Decrease in short-term prepayments	220	
Increase in accounts payable	29,200	
Increase in accrued liabilities	10,000	48,620
Less: Increase in receivables		(17,400)
Cash generated from operations		$150,020

REVIEW QUESTIONS

1 Why is working capital viewed as a "fund of liquid resources"?

2 What are the primary ways in which a firm generates working capital and the primary ways in which a firm uses working capital?

3 List four transactions which are neither a source nor a use of working capital and which are not disclosed in a statement of changes in financial position.

4 Sources of funds include borrowing, sale of noncurrent assets, operations, and sale of capital stock. Which of these possible sources of funds do you consider to be most important to the long-run survival of a business?

5 What information can a reader gain from a statement of changes in financial position that is not apparent from reading an income statement?

6 In preparing a statement of changes in financial position, business transactions may be classified into three categories. List these categories and indicate which category results in changes in working capital.

7 Give examples of expenses, other than depreciation expense, which reduce net income but which do not result in the use of working capital during the period.

8 Give an example of an increase in net income which does not result in an increase in working capital during the period.

9 The following quotation appeared in the annual report of a large corporation: "Depreciation, depletion, and amortization charges provide funds which cause our working capital provided by operations to consistently exceed our net income." Evaluate this quotation.

10 Although extraordinary and nonoperating gains and losses may be included in net income, what reason can you give for excluding such gains and losses in computing the working capital provided by operations? Use the following facts to illustrate your point: Net income including gain on sale of land, $100,000; sale of land, with a book value of $70,000, for $150,000.

11 Miller Corporation acquired a building for $300,000, paying $60,000 cash and issuing a long-term note payable for the balance. What is the effect of this transaction upon the working capital of Miller Corporation? How should the transaction be shown in a statement of changes in financial position?

12 During the year, holders of $4 million of Dallas Company convertible bonds converted their bonds into shares of Dallas company common stock. The president of Dallas Company made the following statement: "By issuing common stock to retire these bonds, the company has saved $4 million in cash. Our statement of changes in financial position will not have to show the retirement of the bonds among the uses of working capital." Do you agree with this statement? Explain.

13 What is the major difference between the statement of changes in financial position and a cash flow statement?

14 Give several examples of transactions which can reduce the amount of cash generated by operations, as shown in a cash flow statement, without reducing working capital.

15 The president of Dexter Corporation was puzzled by the following statement made by the accountant: "Our working capital provided by operations amounted to $85,000 last year but our cash generated from operations was only $10,000 because of the increases in our inventory and receivables and the decrease in our accounts payable." Explain what the accountant meant.

16 An outside member of the board of directors of a small corporation made the following comment after studying the comparative financial statements for the past two years: "I have trouble understanding why our cash has increased steadily during the past two years, yet our profits have been negligible; we have paid no dividends; and inventories, receivables, payables, cost of plant and equipment, long-term debt, and capital stock have remained essentially unchanged." Write a brief statement explaining how this situation might occur.

EXERCISES

Ex. 15-1 Indicate the amount of the increase or decrease (if any) in working capital as a result of each of the following events:

a Purchase and retirement of bonds payable, $1,000,000, at 96. The unamortized premium on bonds payable at the time of the retirement was $50,000.

b Declaration of a 25% stock dividend on $600,000 of par value capital stock outstanding.

c Purchase of equipment costing $400,000 for $100,000 cash and $75,000 (plus interest) payable every six months over the next two years.

d A $40,000 write-down of inventory to a market value below cost.

Ex. 15-2 Briefly explain how each of the following situations should be reported in the statement of changes in financial position.

a Depreciation of $100,000 was recorded in Year 1; however, $25,000 of this amount is included in the ending inventory of finished goods.

b In July of Year 1, the 10,000 shares of $50 par value capital stock were split 3 for 1 and in November of Year 1, a 10% stock dividend was distributed.

c Cash of $10,000 was paid and capital stock with a market value of $90,000 was issued to acquire land worth $100,000.

Ex. 15-3 The Ridgeway Corporation reports a net loss of $20,000 on its income statement. In arriving at this figure, the following items among others were included:

Amortization of patents	$ 4,000
Amortization of premium on bonds payable	2,500
Gain on sale of land	10,000
Depreciation expense	12,500
Uninsured fire damage to building	22,100

What was the working capital increase or decrease as a result of **operations?**

Ex. 15-4 A summary of the comparative financial position for the Barber Corporation for the current year appears below:

	End of Current Year	Beginning of Current Year
Working capital	$160,000	$165,000
Land	80,000	50,000
Buildings	120,000	100,000
Less: Accumulated depreciation	(50,000)	(45,000)
	$310,000	$270,000
Notes payable, due in 5 years	$ 30,000	$ -0-
Capital stock, no-par value	200,000	200,000
Retained earnings	80,000	70,000
	$310,000	$270,000

The net income was $22,000 and included no nonoperating gains or losses. Depreciation expense for the current year was $5,000. A cash dividend was declared at the end of the current year.

Prepare a statement of changes in financial position for the current year without using a working paper.

Ex. 15-5 The data below are taken from the records of the Ferraro Company:

	End of Year	Beginning of Year
Accounts receivable	$ 20,200	$10,200
Inventories	32,000	40,000
Short-term prepayments	2,300	1,500
Accounts payable (merchandise creditors)	28,000	25,000
Accrued expenses payable	1,000	1,200
Net sales	300,000	
Cost of goods sold	180,000	
Operating expenses (includes depreciation of $10,000)	80,000	

From the foregoing information, compute the following:
a Cash collected from customers during the year
b Cash paid to merchandise creditors during the year
c Cash paid for operating expenses during the year

Ex. 15-6 The information below is taken from comparative financial statements for the Mulvey Corporation:

	Year 10	Year 9
Net income (there were no extraordinary items)	$60,000	$37,000
Depreciation expense	42,500	31,800
Inventory at end of year	15,000	28,000
Accounts receivable at end of year	9,000	12,000
Accounts payable at end of year	8,000	6,000
Cash dividends declared in December of each year, payable Jan. 15 of following year	22,500	15,000

From the data above, determine the following:
a The **working capital** provided by operations in Year 10
b The **cash** generated by operations in Year 10
c **Working capital** used for dividends in Year 10

PROBLEMS

15-1 Below is given a list of business transactions and adjustments. For each item you are to indicate the effect first on working capital, and second on cash. In each case the possible effects are an increase, a decrease, or no change.
(1) Machinery sold for cash in excess of its carrying value
(2) Empty warehouse destroyed by fire; one-half of its carrying value covered by insurance and recorded as a receivable from the insurance company
(3) Amortization of discount on bonds payable
(4) Premium paid for a three-year insurance policy
(5) Declaration of a cash dividend

(6) Payment of previously declared cash dividend on common stock
(7) Payment of an account payable
(8) Depreciation recorded for the period
(9) Sale of long-term investment at a loss
(10) Payment of the current year's income tax liability, which was previously recorded in the accounting records
(11) Exchange of convertible bonds for the company's common stock
(12) An uncollectible account receivable written off against the Allowance for Doubtful Accounts

Instructions
a List the numbers 1 to 12 on your answer sheet, and set up two columns headed "working capital effect" and "cash effect." For each transaction, write the words *increase, decrease,* or *no change* in the appropriate column to indicate the effect of the transaction on working capital and cash.
b Are any of the transactions listed above considered "exchange transactions" which would be listed as both a source and use of working capital in a statement of changes in financial position? Explain.

15-2 The following information is taken from the annual report of El Toro Corporation:

	Year 2	Year 1
Current assets	$240,000	$162,000
Equipment	360,000	252,000
Less: Accumulated depreciation	(120,000)	(72,000)
Long-term investments	48,000	60,000
Current liabilities	138,000	48,000
Capital stock	120,000	120,000
Retained earnings	270,000	234,000

Cash dividends declared amounted to $42,000; no equipment items were sold; investments were sold at a gain of $6,000; and net income (including the $6,000 nonoperating gain) for Year 2 was $78,000.

Instructions From the information given, prepare a statement of changes in financial position for Year 2, without using working papers.

15-3 During Year 6 Wildcat Tractor Company showed the following *changes* in amount for the groups of accounts listed below. For example, current assets increased by $80,000 during Year 6, and this amount therefore appears in the "Debit" change column.

	Changes during Year 6	
	Debit	Credit
Current assets	$ 80,000	
Plant and equipment	160,000	
Accumulated depreciation		$ 40,000
Current liabilities	48,000	
Capital stock, $10 par		128,000
Paid-in capital in excess of par		32,000
Retained earnings		88,000
	$288,000	$288,000

During Year 6 the company issued 12,800 shares of capital stock and applied the proceeds to the purchase of equipment. There were no retirements of plant and equipment items in Year 6. Dividends of $64,000 were declared and paid during Year 6.

Instructions Prepare a statement of changes in financial position for Year 6, without using working papers.

15-4 The following balance sheet data for Year 5 were obtained from the records of Augusta National Corporation:

	Dec. 31	Jan. 1
Current assets	$298,700	$202,500
Plant and equipment (net)	334,000	319,000
Goodwill (amortized over 10 years)	8,500	10,000
Current liabilities	150,000	81,500
Bonds payable, 7%	200,000	–0–
Discount on bonds payable	3,800	–0–
Preferred stock, $100 par	–0–	200,000
Common stock, no par	150,000	150,000
Retained earnings	145,000	100,000

Additional data

(1) The statement of retained earnings for Year 5 follows:

Beginning balance		$100,000
Add: Net income, including gain on disposal of land		80,000
Subtotal		$180,000
Less: Amount paid to retire preferred stock in excess of		
carrying (book) value	$10,000	
Cash dividends declared	25,000	35,000
Ending balance		$145,000

(2) Ten-year bonds of $200,000 face value were issued on July 1 at 98; the proceeds and some additional cash were used to retire the entire issue of preferred stock at its call price of $105 per share.

(3) Land having a cost of $60,000 was exchanged at its fair value of $100,000 for equipment with a value of $120,000; the balance of $20,000 was paid in cash. A $40,000 gain was recognized on the exchange.

(4) Depreciation for the year was $45,000, amortization of goodwill was $1,500, and amortization of discount on bonds payable was $200.

Instructions

a Prepare a working paper for a statement of changes in financial position.

b Prepare a statement of changes in financial position. Report working capital provided from operations in a single amount as determined in the working paper.

15-5 Comparative account balances for Long Island Corporation at the end of Years 9 and 10 are listed below:

	Year 10	Year 9
Cash	$ 60,000	$ 100,000
Accounts receivable (net)	150,000	175,000
Merchandise inventory	325,000	250,000
Land for future expansion	75,000	
Plant and equipment (see accumulated depreciation below)	800,000	625,000
Patents (net of amortization)	90,000	100,000
	$1,500,000	$1,250,000
Accumulated depreciation	$ 262,500	$ 200,000
Accounts payable	152,500	75,000
Dividends payable	10,000	
Notes payable due in Year 14	25,000	
Capital stock, $10 par	1,000,000	875,000
Retained earnings	50,000	100,000
	$1,500,000	$1,250,000

The following additional information is available for your consideration:
(1) The net loss for Year 10 amounted to $40,000.
(2) Cash dividends of $10,000 were declared.
(3) Land for future expansion was acquired.
(4) Equipment costing $175,000 was purchased for cash; $25,000 was borrowed for three years in order to pay for this equipment.
(5) Additional shares of capital stock were sold at par value.
(6) Other changes in noncurrent accounts resulted from the usual transactions recorded in such accounts.

Instructions
a Prepare a schedule computing the change in working capital during Year 10.
b Prepare working papers for a statement of changes in financial position for Year 10.
c Prepare a formal statement of changes in financial position for Year 10.

15-6 The accounting records of Earth Movers, Inc. showed the following balances at the end of Year 4 and Year 5:

Debits	Year 5	Year 4
Cash	$ 93,000	$ 120,000
Accounts receivable	165,000	105,000
Merchandise inventory	285,000	450,000
Long-term investments	45,000	
Equipment	1,170,000	675,000
Accumulated depreciation	(240,000)	(180,000)
Land	240,000	105,000
	$1,758,000	$1,275,000

Credits	Year 5	Year 4
Accounts payable	$ 135,000	$ 60,000
Notes payable (current).	15,000	90,000
Bonds payable, due in Year 10	300,000	240,000
Unamortized premium on bonds payable	5,400	5,700
Capital stock, $10 par	600,000	450,000
Paid-in capital in excess of par	240,000	150,000
Retained earnings	462,600	279,300
	$1,758,000	$1,275,000

Net income for Year 5 amounted to $258,000. Cash dividends of $74,700 were declared and paid during Year 5. Additional purchases of investments, equipment, and land were completed during Year 5, financed in part through the sale of bonds at par and 15,000 shares of capital stock. Equipment costing $75,000 was sold at a price equal to its book value of $30,000.

Instructions
a Prepare a schedule of changes in working capital during Year 5.
b Prepare working papers for a statement of changes in financial position for Year 5. See the solution to the demonstration problem in this chapter for proper handling of the premium on bonds payable.
c Prepare a formal statement of changes in financial position for Year 5.

15-7 A condensed balance sheet at January 1, Year 10, and the statement of changes in financial position for Year 10 for Intruder Alert, Inc., are shown below and on page 635.

INTRUDER ALERT, INC.
Balance Sheet
January 1, Year 10

Assets

Current assets	$ 86,000
Land	40,000
Equipment	96,000
Less: Accumulated depreciation	(30,000)
Patents (net of accumulated amortization)	10,000
Total assets	$202,000

Liabilities & Stockholders' Equity

Current liabilities	$ 36,000
Capital stock, no-par value	94,000
Retained earnings	72,000
Total liabilities & stockholders' equity	$202,000

INTRUDER ALERT, INC.
Statement of Changes in Financial Position
For Year 10

Working capital, Jan. 1, Year 10		$ 50,000
Sources of working capital:		
Operations:		
Net income	$48,000	
Add: Depreciation expense	20,000	
Amortization of patents	2,000	
Less: Gain on disposal of equipment	(8,000)	
Working capital provided by operations		62,000
Issuance of capital stock		22,000
Disposal of equipment		14,000
Subtotal		$148,000
Uses of working capital:		
Dividends declared	$16,000	
Purchase of land	28,000	
Purchase of equipment	62,000	106,000
Working capital, Dec. 31, Year 10		$ 42,000

Equipment costing $18,000, with accumulated depreciation of $12,000, was sold in Year 10. Total assets at December 31, Year 10, were $278,000.

Instructions Using the information above, prepare a condensed balance sheet at December 31, Year 10. Supporting schedules should be in good form.

15-8 The following information is presented to you by Linda Kahn, owner of Linda's Fashion Boutique:

Balance Sheet

Assets	Year 2	Year 1
Cash	$ 10,000	$ 40,000
Marketable securities	15,000	20,000
Accounts receivable (net)	100,000	35,000
Inventory	80,000	60,000
Equipment (net of accumulated depreciation)	35,000	45,000
Total assets	$240,000	$200,000

Liabilities & Owner's Capital

	Year 2	Year 1
Accounts payable	$ 37,000	$ 40,000
Accrued liabilities	8,000	2,500
Note payable to bank (due early in Year 2)		12,500
Linda Kahn, capital	195,000	145,000
Total liabilities & owner's capital	$240,000	$200,000

Income Statement for Year 2

Sales (net)		$400,000
Cost of goods sold		300,000
Gross profit on sales		$100,000
Operating expenses (including $10,000 depreciation)	$60,000	
Loss on sale of marketable securities.	500	60,500
Net income		$ 39,500
Drawings by owner		22,500
Increase in owner's capital as a result of operations		$ 17,000

Kahn is concerned over the decrease in her cash position during Year 2, particularly in view of the fact that she invested an additional $33,000 in the business and had a net income of $39,500 during the year. She asks you to prepare a statement which will explain the decrease in the Cash account. You point out that while cash decreased by $30,000, the working capital increased by $60,000. You conclude that a statement of cash receipts and cash disbursements, showing cash collected from customers, cash paid to merchandise creditors, cash paid for operating expenses, etc., would give her the information she needs.

Instructions
a Prepare a schedule showing the conversion of the income statement from an accrual to a cash basis, thus determining the net cash outflow from operations.
b Prepare a cash flow statement which explains the decrease of $30,000 in cash during Year 2.
c Prepare a statement of changes in financial position without using a working paper.

15-9 When the controller of Trans-Alaska Corporation presented the following condensed comparative financial statements to the board of directors at the close of Year 2, the reaction of the board members was very favorable.

TRANS-ALASKA CORPORATION
Comparative Income Statements
(in thousands of dollars)

	Year 2	Year 1
Net sales.	$970	$680
Cost of goods sold	590	480
Gross profit on sales	$380	$200
Operating expenses, including depreciation	(180)	(140)
Income taxes	(90)	(25)
Net income	$110	$ 35

TRANS-ALASKA CORPORATION
Comparative Financial Position
As of December 31
(in thousands of dollars)

Current assets	$ 410	$395
Less: Current liabilities	200	225
Working capital	$ 210	$170
Plant and equipment (net)	970	650
Total assets minus current liabilities	$1,180	$820
Financed by following sources of long-term capital:		
Long-term liabilities	$ 250	
Capital stock ($50 par value)	500	$500
Retained earnings	430	320
Total sources of long-term capital	$1,180	$820

Noting that net income rose from $3.50 per share of capital stock to $11 per share, one member of the board proposed that a substantial cash dividend be paid. "Our working capital is up by $40,000; we should be able to make a distribution to stockholders," he commented. To which the controller replied that the company's cash position was precarious and pointed out that at the end of Year 2, a cash balance of only $15,000 was on hand, a decline from $145,000 at the end of Year 1. The controller also reminded the board that the company bought $400,000 of new equipment during Year 2. When a board member asked for an explanation of the increase of $40,000 in working capital, the controller presented the following schedule (in thousands of dollars):

		Effect on *Working Capital*
Increase in working capital:		
Accounts receivable increased by		$ 83
Inventories increased by		45
Prepaid expenses increased by		17
Accounts payable were reduced by		62
Accrued expenses payable were reduced by		28
Total increases in working capital		$235
Decreases in working capital:		
Cash decreased by	$130	
Income tax liability increased by	65	195
Increase in working capital during Year 2		$ 40

After examining this schedule, the board member shook his head and said, "I still don't understand how our cash position can be so tight in the face of a tripling of net income and a substantial increase in working capital!"

Instructions
a Prepare a statement converting Trans-Alaska Corporation's income statement to a cash basis, determining the cash generated by operations during Year 2.
b From the information in *a* and an inspection of the comparative statement of

financial position, prepare a cash flow statement for Year 2, explaining the $130,000 decrease in the cash balance.

c Prepare a statement accounting for the increase in working capital (statement of changes in financial position) for Trans-Alaska Corporation in a more acceptable form.

d Write a brief note of explanation to the board member.

BUSINESS DECISION PROBLEM 15

Maverick Corporation has working capital of $6,150,000 at the beginning of Year 5. Restrictions contained in bank loans require that working capital not fall below $6,000,000. The following projected information is available for Year 5:

(1) Budgeted net income (including nonoperating items) is $7,500,000. The following items were included in estimating net income: depreciation, $2,100,000; amortization of premium on bonds payable, $150,000; uncollectible accounts expense, $180,000; and income taxes, $6,300,000. The estimate of net income also included the nonoperating items described below.

(2) Sale of plant assets with a carrying value of $1,200,000 is expected to bring $1,500,000 net of income taxes.

(3) Additional plant assets costing $15,000,000 will be acquired. Payment will be as follows: 20% cash, 20% short-term note, and 60% through issuance of capital stock.

(4) Long-term investment will be sold at cost, $300,000.

(5) Bonds payable in the amount of $1,500,000, bearing interest at 11%, will be redeemed at 105 approximately 10 years prior to maturity in order to eliminate the high interest expense of $165,000 per year. The elimination of this interest and the gain or loss on the retirement of bonds payable were taken into account in estimating net income for Year 5. These bonds had been issued at par.

(6) Tentative planned cash dividend, $4,500,000.

Instructions

a Consider all the information given above and prepare a projected statement of changes in financial position (without showing the composition of working capital) in order to determine the estimated increase or decrease in working capital for Year 5. Some of the information given may be irrelevant.

b The planned cash dividend of $4,500,000 represents the same dividend per share as paid last year. The company would like to maintain dividends at this level. Does it appear likely that the past dividend policy can be maintained in Year 5? What factors other than working capital position should be considered in determining the level of cash dividends declared by the board of directors?

16 Analysis and Interpretation of Financial Statements

Financial statements are the instrument panel of a business enterprise. They constitute a report on managerial performance, attesting to managerial success or failure and flashing warning signals of impending difficulties. To read a complex instrument panel, one must understand the gauges and their calibration to make sense out of the array of data they convey. Similarly, one must understand the inner workings of the accounting system and the significance of various financial relationships to interpret the data appearing in financial statements. To a reader with a knowledge of accounting, a set of financial statements tells a great deal about a business enterprise.

The financial affairs of a business may be of interest to a number of different groups; management, creditors, investors, politicians, union officials, and government agencies. Each of these groups has somewhat different needs, and accordingly each tends to concentrate on particular aspects of a company's financial picture.

What is your opinion of the level of corporate profits?

As a college student who has completed (or almost completed) a course in accounting, you have a much better understanding of corporate profits than do people who have never studied accounting. The level of earnings of large corporations is a controversial topic, a favorite topic in many political speeches and at many cocktail parties. Many of the statements one reads or hears from these sources are emotional rather than rational, and fiction rather than fact. Public opinion polls show that the public believes the average manufacturing company has an after-tax profit of about 30% of sales, when in fact such profit has been about 5% of sales in recent years. A widespread public belief that profits are six times the actual rate may lead to some unwise legislation.

An in-depth knowledge of accounting does not enable you to say at what level corporate earnings *should be;* however, a knowledge of accounting does enable you to read audited financial statements that show what the level of corporate earnings *actually is.* Moreover, you are aware that the information in published financial statements of corporations has been audited by CPA firms and has been reviewed in detail by government agencies, such as the Securities and Exchange Commission and the IRS. Consequently, you know that the profits reported in these published financial statements are reasonably reliable; they have been determined in accordance with generally accepted accounting principles and verified by independent experts.

When such troublesome problems as severe unemployment and rising prices for consumer goods and services affect so many people, it is not surprising that some political leaders look for a scapegoat to hold responsible. Often, the blame has been laid on corporate profits, which sometimes have been labeled as "outrageous," "scandalous," and even "obscene." Usually the speaker who uses these emotional adjectives cites an absolute dollar amount of profits without relating it in any way to the volume of sales or the amount of assets necessary to produce the quoted profit figure.

As a specific example, let us look at the profits of one of the world's largest and most successful corporations, Exxon. The oil industry has been particularly subject to criticism for so-called "excessive" profits, and Exxon is the world's largest oil company. A recent annual report of Exxon Corporation (audited by Price Waterhouse & Co.) shows that profits amounted to about $2\frac{1}{2}$ billion dollars. Standing alone, that figure seems enormous, but we need to look a little further. Total revenue was a little under 50 billion dollars, so net income amounted to approximately *5% of sales.* Let us assume that Exxon's profits on gasoline are in line with its overall 5% profit rate and that gasoline is selling for, say, 60 cents a gallon. Even if our assumption that profit on gasoline is about the same as on fuel oil and other products is not entirely true, we could still safely say that the elimination of all profits by Exxon would not cause the price of gasoline to drop significantly.

The audited income statement of Exxon also shows that *income taxes and other taxes* were over $15 billion, or about six times as much as the company's profits. (A major portion of these taxes was paid to foreign governments.) Would you say that it is corporate profits or taxation which contributed significantly to high gasoline prices?

Another favorite tactic in attacking profits of corporations is to use percentages in a misleading manner. For example, assume that a corporation has net income in Year 1 of $1,000,000; that in Year 2 net income drops to $100,000; and that in Year 3 net income rises to $1,000,000. Clearly, Year 3 is no more profitable than Year 1, but a critic of corporate profits might say: "This company's profits in Year 3 rose by 900%, an unbelievable and unjustifiable increase." What needs to be added is that the 900% increase in Year 3 exactly offset the 90% decline in Year 2. Few people seem to realize that a 90% decline in earnings must be followed by a 900% increase just to get back to the starting point.

There are many ways of appraising the adequacy of corporate earnings; certainly, earnings should be compared with total assets and with invested capital as well as with sales. In this chapter we shall look at a number of ways of evaluating corporate profits and solvency.

Sources of financial information

For the most part, this discussion will be limited to the kind of analysis that can be made by "outsiders" who do not have access to internal accounting records. Investors must rely to a considerable extent on financial statements in published annual and quarterly reports. In the case of large publicly owned corporations, additional information that must be filed with the Securities and Exchange Commission is available. Financial information for most corporations is also published by Moody's Investors Service, Standard & Poor's Corporation, and stock brokerage firms.

Bankers are usually able to secure more detailed information by requesting it as a condition for granting a loan. Trade creditors may obtain financial information for businesses of almost any size from credit-rating agencies such as Dun & Bradstreet, Inc.

COMPARATIVE FINANCIAL STATEMENTS The change in financial data over time is best exhibited in statements showing data for two or more years placed side by side in adjacent columns. Such statements are called *comparative financial statements.*

The usefulness of comparative financial statements covering two or more years is well recognized. Published annual reports often contain comparative financial statements covering a period as long as 10 years. By observing the change in various items period by period, the analyst may gain valuable clues as to growth and other important trends affecting the business. A highly condensed comparative balance sheet is shown on page 642.

BENSON CORPORATION
Comparative Balance Sheet
As of December 31
(in thousands of dollars)

	Year 3	Year 2	Year 1
Assets:			
Current assets	$180	$150	$120
Plant and equipment (net)	450	300	345
Total assets	$630	$450	$465
Liabilities & Stockholders' Equity:			
Current liabilities	$ 60	$ 80	$120
Long-term liabilities	200	100	–0–
Capital stock	300	300	300
Retained earnings (deficit)	70	(30)	45
Total liabilities & stockholders' equity	$630	$450	$465

Condensed three-year balance sheet

Tools of analysis

Few figures in a financial statement are highly significant in and of themselves. It is their relationship to other quantities, or the amount and direction of change since a previous date, that is important. Analysis is largely a matter of establishing significant relationships and pointing up changes and trends. Three widely used analytical techniques are (*1*) dollar and percentage changes, (*2*) component percentages, and (*3*) ratios.

DOLLAR AND PERCENTAGE CHANGES The dollar amount of change from year to year is significant, but expressing the change in percentage terms adds perspective. For example, if sales this year have increased by $100,000, the fact that this is an increase of 10% over last year's sales of $1 million puts it in a different perspective that if it represented a 1% increase over sales of $10 million for the prior year.

The dollar amount of any change is the difference between the amount for a *comparison* year and for a *base* year. The percentage change is computed by dividing the amount of the change between years by the amount for the base year. This is illustrated in the tabulation below, using data from the comparative balance sheet above.

	In Thousands			Increase or (Decrease)			
				Year 3 over Year 2		Year 2 over Year 1	
	Year 3	Year 2	Year 1	Amount	%	Amount	%
Current assets	$180	$150	$120	$30	20%	$30	25%
Current liabilities	$ 60	$ 80	$120	($20)	(25%)	($40)	(33.3%)

Dollar and percentage changes

Although current assets increased $30,000 in both Year 2 and Year 3, the percentage of change differs because of the shift in the base year from Year 1 to Year 2. These calculations present no problems when the figures for the base year are positive amounts. If a negative amount or a zero amount appears in the base year, a percentage change cannot be computed. For example, in the comparative balance sheet on page 642, there were no long-term liabilities in Year 1; therefore the percentage change to Year 2 for this liability cannot be calculated.

COMPONENT PERCENTAGES   The phrase "a piece of pie" is subject to varying interpretations until it is known whether the piece represents one-sixth or one-half of the total pie. The percentage relationship between any particular financial item and a significant total that includes this item is known as a *component percentage;* this is often a useful means of showing relationships or the relative importance of the item in question. Thus if inventories are 50% of total current assets, they are a far more significant factor in the current position of a company than if they are only 10% of total current assets.

One application of component percentages is to express each item on the balance sheet as a percentage of total assets. This shows quickly the relative importance of current and noncurrent assets, and the relative amount of financing obtained from current creditors, long-term creditors, and stockholders.

COMPARATIVE INCOME STATEMENT   Another application of component percentages is to express all items on an income statement as a percentage of net sales. Such a statement is sometimes called a *common size* income statement. A highly condensed income statement in dollars and in common size form is illustrated below.

Income Statement

	Dollars		Component Percentages	
	Year 2	Year 1	Year 2	Year 1
Net sales	$500,000	$200,000	100.0%	100.0%
Cost of goods sold	350,000	120,000	70.0	60.0
Gross profit on sales	$150,000	$ 80,000	30.0%	40.0%
Expenses (including income taxes)	100,000	50,000	20.0	25.0
Net income	$ 50,000	$ 30,000	10.0%	15.0%

How successful was Year 2?

Looking only at the component percentages, we see that the decline in the gross profit rate from 40 to 30% was only partially offset by the decrease in expenses as a percentage of net sales, causing net income to decrease from 15 to 10% of net sales. The dollar amounts in the first pair of columns, however, present an entirely different picture. It is true that net sales increased faster than net income, but net income improved significantly in Year 2, a fact not apparent from a review of component percentages alone. This points out an important limitation in the use of component percentages. Changes in the component percentage may result from a change in the component, in the total, or in both. Reverting to our previous analogy, it is important to know not only the relative size of a piece of pie, but also the size of the pie; 10% of a large pie may be a bigger piece than 15% of a smaller pie.

RATIOS A ratio is a simple mathematical expression of the relationship of one item to another. Ratios may be expressed in a number of ways. For example, if we wish to clarify the relationship between sales of $800,000 and net income of $40,000, we may state: (*1*) The ratio of net income to sales is 1 to 20 (or $1:20$); (*2*) for every $1 of sales, the company has an average net income of 5 cents; (*3*) net income is $\frac{1}{20}$ of sales. In each case the ratio is merely a means of describing the relationship between sales and net income in a simple form.

In order to compute a meaningful ratio, there must be a significant relationship between the two figures. A ratio focuses attention on a relationship which is significant, but a full interpretation of the ratio usually requires further investigation of the underlying data. Ratios are an aid to analysis and interpretation; they are not a substitute for sound thinking.

Standards of comparison

In using dollar and percentage changes, component percentages, and ratios, financial analysts constantly search for some standard of comparison against which to judge whether the relationships that they have found are favorable or unfavorable. Two such standards are (*1*) the past performance of the company and (2) the performance of other companies in the same industry.

PAST PERFORMANCE OF THE COMPANY Comparing analytical data for a current period with similar computations for prior years affords some basis for judging whether the position of the business is improving or worsening. This comparison of data over time is sometimes called *horizontal* or *dynamic* analysis, to express the idea of reviewing data for a number of periods. It is distinguished from *vertical* or *static* analysis, which refers to the review of the financial information for only one accounting period.

In addition to determining whether the situation is improving or becoming worse, horizontal analysis may aid in making estimates of future prospects. Since changes may reverse their direction at any time, however, projecting past trends into the future is always a somewhat risky statistical pastime.

A weakness of horizontal analysis is that comparison with the past does not afford any basis for evaluation in absolute terms. The fact that net income was 2% of sales last year and is 3% of sales this year indicates improvement, but if there is evidence that net income *should be* 5% of sales, the record for both years is unfavorable.

INDUSTRY STANDARDS The limitations of horizontal analysis may be overcome to some extent by finding some other standard of performance as a yardstick against which to measure the record of any particular firm.[1] The yardstick may be a comparable company, the average record of several companies in the same industry, or some predetermined standard.

Suppose that Y Company suffers a 5% drop in its sales during the current year. The discovery that the sales of all companies in the same industry fell an average of 20% would indicate that this was a favorable rather than an unfavorable performance. Assume further that Y Company's net income is 2% of net sales. Based on comparison with other companies in the industry, this would be substandard performance if Y Company were an automobile manufacturer; but it would be a satisfactory record if Y Company were a grocery chain.

When we compare a given company with its competitors or with industry averages, our conclusions will be valid only if the companies in question are reasonably comparable. Because of the large number of diversified companies formed in recent years, the term *industry* is difficult to define, and companies that fall roughly within the same industry may not be comparable in many respects. One company may engage only in the marketing of oil products; another may be a fully integrated producer from the well to the gas pump, yet both are said to be in the "oil industry."

Differences in accounting methods may lessen the comparability of financial data for two companies. For example, companies may employ different depreciation methods or estimates of the useful life of substantially similar assets; inventories may be valued by different methods; and the timing of revenue recognition may differ significantly among companies engaged in certain industries. Despite these limitations, studying comparative performances is a useful method of analysis if carefully and intelligently done.

---

[1] For example, the Robert Morris Associates publishes *Annual Statement Studies* which contains detailed data obtained from 27,000 annual reports grouped in 223 industry classifications. Assets, liabilities, and stockholders' equity are presented as a percentage of total assets; income statement amounts are expressed as a percentage of net sales; and key ratios are given (expressed as the median for each industry, the upper quartile, and the lower quartile). Measurements, within each of the 223 industry groups, are grouped according to the size of the firm. Similarly, Dun & Bradstreet, Inc., annually publishes *Key Business Ratios* in 125 lines of business divided by retailing, wholesaling, manufacturing, and construction. A total of 14 ratios are presented for each of the 125 industry groups.

Objectives of financial analysis

Business decisions are made on the basis of the best available estimates of the outcome of such decisions. The purpose of financial analysis is to provide information about a business unit for decision-making purposes, and such information need not be limited to accounting data. While ratios and other relationships based on *past performance* may be helpful in predicting the future earnings performance and financial health of a company, we must be aware of the inherent limitations of such data. Financial statements are essentially summary records of the past, and we must go beyond the financial statements and look into the nature of the company, its competitive position within the industry, its product lines, its research expenditures, and, above all, the quality of its management.

The key objectives of financial analysis are to determine the company's earnings performance and the soundness and liquidity of its financial position. We are essentially interested in financial analysis as a predictive tool; accordingly, we want to examine both quantitative and qualitative data in order to ascertain the *quality of earnings* and the *quality and protection of assets.* In periods of recession when business failures are common, the balance sheet takes on increased importance because the question of liquidity is uppermost in the minds of many in the business community. When business conditions are good, the income statement receives more attention as people become absorbed in profit possibilities.

QUALITY OF EARNINGS Profits are the lifeblood of a business entity. No entity can survive for long and accomplish its other goals unless it is profitable. Continuous losses drain assets from the business, consume owners' equity, and leave the company at the mercy of creditors. For this reason, we are interested not only in the total *amount* of earnings but also in the *rate* of earnings on sales, on total assets, and on owners' equity. In addition, we must look to the *stability* and *source* of earnings. An erratic earnings performance over a period of years, for example, is less desirable than a steady level of earnings. A history of increasing earnings is preferable to a "flat" earnings record.

A breakdown of sales and earnings by *major product lines* is useful in evaluating the future performance of a company. In recent years many publicly owned companies have broadened their reporting to include sales and profits by product lines, and the Securities and Exchange Commission now requires such reporting from most companies.

Financial analysts often express the opinion that the earnings of one company are of higher quality than earnings of other similar companies. This concept of *quality of earnings* arises because each company management can choose from a wide variety of accounting principles and methods, all of which are considered generally acceptable. The financial analyst should ascertain whether the accounting principles and methods selected by management lead to a conservative measurement of earnings or tend to inflate current reported earnings by deferring certain costs and anticipating certain revenue. A company's management is often under heavy pressure to report rising earnings, and accounting policies may be tailored toward this objective. We have already pointed out the impact on current reported earnings of the choice between the lifo and fifo methods of inventory valuation and the choice of depreciation policies. In judging the quality of earnings, other appropriate questions are: What has been the effect on earnings of any accounting changes? How much of the net income is attributable to nonrecurring or nonoperating items? The very existence of a concept of *quality of earnings* is evidence that accountants still have some distance to travel in developing a body of accounting standards which will ensure a reasonable comparability of earnings reported by different companies.

QUALITY OF ASSETS AND THE RELATIVE AMOUNT OF DEBT Although a satisfactory level of earnings may be a good indication of the company's long-run ability to pay its debts and dividends, we must also look at the composition of assets, their condition and liquidity, the relationship between current assets and current liabilities, and the total amount of debt outstanding. A company may be profitable and yet be unable to pay its liabilities on time; sales and earnings may be satisfactory but plant and equipment may be deteriorating because of poor maintenance policies; valuable patents may be expiring; substantial losses may be in prospect from slow-moving inventories and past-due receivables. Extensive use of credit and a liberal dividend policy may result in a low owners' equity and thus expose stockholders to substantial risks in case of a downturn in business.

IMPACT OF INFLATION

During a period of inflation, financial statements which are prepared in terms of historical costs do not reflect fully the economic resources or the *real income* (in terms of purchasing power) of a business enterprise. We have already noted that the SEC requires that large corporations disclose in footnotes the replacement cost of inventories, cost of goods sold, plant and equipment, and depreciation. Financial analysts should therefore attempt to evaluate the impact of inflation on the financial position and results of operations of the company being studied. They should raise such questions as: How much of the net income can be attributed to the increase in the general price level? Is depreciation expense understated in terms of current price levels? Are profits exaggerated because the replacement cost of inventories is higher than the cost of units charged to cost of goods sold? Is the company gaining or losing from inflation because of the composition of its assets and because its liabilities will be liquidated with "cheaper" dollars? Will the company be able to keep its "physical capital" intact by paying the higher prices necessary to replace plant assets as they wear out? The fundamental issues of modifying accounting information to cope with the impact of inflation were discussed in Chapter 14.

Illustrative analysis for Seacliff Company

Keep in mind the above discussion of analytical principles as you study the illustrative financial analysis which follows. The basic information for our discussion is contained in a set of condensed two-year comparative financial statements for Seacliff Company shown on the following pages. Summarized statement data, together with computations of dollar increases and decreases, and component percentages where applicable, have been compiled.

Using the information in these statements, let us consider the kind of analysis that might be of particular interest to (*1*) common stockholders, (*2*) long-term creditors, (*3*) preferred stockholders, and (*4*) short-term creditors. Organizing our discussion in this way emphasizes the differences in the viewpoint of these groups; all of them have, of course, a considerable common interest in the performance of the company as a whole. This approach should be viewed as only one of many that may be used in analyzing financial statements. Furthermore, the ratios and other measurements illustrated here are not exhaustive; the number of measurements that may be developed for various analytical purposes is almost without limit.

SEACLIFF COMPANY
Condensed Comparative Balance Sheet*
December 31

			Increase or (Decrease)		Percentage of Total Assets	
Assets	*Year 2*	*Year 1*	*Dollars*	*%*	*Year 2*	*Year 1*
Current assets	*$390,000*	*$288,000*	*$102,000*	*35.4*	*41.1*	*33.5*
Plant and equipment (net)	*500,000*	*467,000*	*33,000*	*7.1*	*52.6*	*54.3*
Other assets (loans to officers)	*60,000*	*105,000*	*(45,000)*	*(42.9)*	*6.3*	*12.2*
Total assets	*$950,000*	*$860,000*	*$ 90,000*	*10.5*	*100.0*	*100.0*

Liabilities & Stock-holders' Equity	Year 2	Year 1	Increase or (Decrease) Dollars	%	Percentage of Total Assets Year 2	Year 1
Liabilities:						
Current liabilities	$147,400	$ 94,000	$ 53,400	56.8	15.5	10.9
Long-term liabilities	200,000	250,000	(50,000)	(20.0)	21.1	29.1
Total liabilities	$347,400	$344,000	$ 3,400	1.0	36.6	40.0
Stockholders' equity:						
6% preferred stock, $100 par, callable at $105	$100,000	$100,000			10.5	11.6
Common stock, $50 par	250,000	200,000	$ 50,000	25.0	26.3	23.2
Paid-in capital in excess of par . .	70,000	40,000	30,000	75.0	7.4	4.7
Retained earnings	182,600	176,000	6,600	3.8	19.2	20.5
Total stockholders' equity	$602,600	$516,000	$ 86,600	16.8	63.4	60.0
Total liabilities & stockholders' equity	$950,000	$860,000	$ 90,000	10.5	100.0	100.0

* In order to focus attention on important subtotals, this statement is highly condensed and does not show individual asset and liability items. These details will be introduced as needed in the text discussion. For example, a list of Seacliff Company's current assets and current liabilities appears on page 659.

SEACLIFF COMPANY
Comparative Income Statement
Years Ended December 31

	Year 2	Year 1	Increase or (Decrease) Dollars	%	Percentage of Net Sales Year 2	Year 1
Net sales	$900,000	$750,000	$150,000	20.0	100.0	100.0
Cost of goods sold	585,000	468,800	116,200	24.8	65.0	62.5
Gross profit on sales	$315,000	$281,200	$ 33,800	12.0	35.0	37.5
Operating expenses:						
Selling expenses	$117,000	$ 75,000	$ 42,000	56.0	13.0	10.0
Administrative expenses	126,000	94,500	31,500	33.3	14.0	12.6
Total operating expenses	$243,000	$169,500	$ 73,500	43.4	27.0	22.6
Operating income	$ 72,000	$111,700	$(39,700)	(35.5)	8.0	14.9
Interest expense	12,000	15,000	(3,000)	(20.0)	1.3	2.0
Income before income taxes	$ 60,000	$ 96,700	$(36,700)	(38.0)	6.7	12.9
Income taxes	23,400	44,200	(20,800)	(47.1)	2.6	5.9
Net income	$ 36,600	$ 52,500	$(15,900)	(30.3)	4.1	7.0
Earnings per share of common stock	$6.12	$11.63	$(5.51)	(47.4)		

SEACLIFF COMPANY
Statement of Retained Earnings
Years Ended December 31

	Year 2	Year 1	Increase or (Decrease) Dollars	%
Balance, beginning of year	$176,000	$149,500	$26,500	17.7
Net income	36,600	52,500	(15,900)	(30.3)
	$212,600	$202,000	$10,600	5.2
Less: Dividends on common stock	$ 24,000	$ 20,000	$ 4,000	20.0
Dividends on preferred stock	6,000	6,000		
	$ 30,000	$ 26,000	$ 4,000	15.4
Balance, end of year	$182,600	$176,000	$ 6,600	3.8

Analysis by common stockholders

Common stockholders and potential investors in common stock look first at a company's earnings record. Their investment is in shares of stock, so *earnings per share and dividends per share* are of particular interest.

EARNINGS PER SHARE OF COMMON STOCK As indicated in Chapter 8, earnings per share of common stock are computed by dividing the income available to common stockholders by the number of shares of common stock outstanding. Any preferred dividend requirements must be subtracted from net income to determine income available for common stock, as shown in the following computations for Seacliff Company:

Earnings per Share of Common Stock

		Year 2	Year 1
Earnings related to number of common shares outstanding	Net income	$36,600	$52,500
	Less: Preferred dividend requirements	6,000	6,000
	Income available for common stock . . . .(a)	$30,600	$46,500
	Shares of common outstanding, during the year . . . .(b)	5,000	4,000
	Earnings per share of common stock (a ÷ b)	$6.12	$11.63

Earnings per share of common stock are shown in the income statement below the net income figure. When the income statement includes operations discontinued during the period, the earnings per share of common stock may be reported in the income statement in three amounts as follows: (*1*) income from continuing operations, (*2*) income (or loss) from discontinued operations, and (*3*) net income. Similar treatment may be appropriate for extraordinary items. Seacliff Company had no discontinued operations or extraordinary items and therefore the amount earned per share is computed by dividing the net income available for the common stock by the number of common shares outstanding during the year. The computation of earnings per share in more complicated situations was illustrated in Chapter 8.

DIVIDEND YIELD AND PRICE-EARNINGS RATIO The importance of dividends varies among stockholders. Earnings reinvested in the business should produce an increase in the net income of the firm and thus tend to make each share of stock more valuable. Because the federal income tax rates applicable to dividend income are much higher than the rate of tax on capital gains from the sale of shares of stock, some stockholders may prefer that the company reinvest most of its earnings. Others may be more interested in dividend income despite the tax disadvantage.

In comparing the merits of alternative investment opportunities, we should relate earnings and dividends per share to the market value of the stock. Dividends per share divided by market price per share determines the *yield* rate of a company's stock. Dividend yield is especially important to those investors whose objective is to maximize the dividend revenue from their investments.

Earnings performance of common stock is often expressed as a *price-earnings ratio* by dividing the market price per share by the earnings per share. Thus, a stock selling for $60 per share and earning $3 per share may be said to have a price-earnings ratio of 20 times earnings ($60 ÷ $3). The price-earnings ratio of the 30 stocks included in the Dow-Jones Industrial Average has varied widely in recent years, ranging from a low of about 6 for the group to a high of about 20.

Assume that the 1,000 additional shares of common stock issued by Seacliff on January 1, Year 2, received the full dividend of $4.80 paid in Year 2. When these new shares were issued, Seacliff Company announced that it planned to continue indefinitely the $4.80 dividend per common share currently being paid. With this assumption and the use of assumed market prices of the common stock at December 31, Year 1 and Year 2, the earnings per share and dividend yield may be summarized as follows:

		Earnings and Dividends per Share of Common Stock				
Earnings and dividends related to market price of common stock	*Date*	*Assumed Market Value per Share*	*Earnings per Share*	*Price-Earnings Ratio*	*Dividends per Share*	*Dividend Yield, %*
	Dec. 31, Year 1	$125	$11.63	11	$5.00	4.0
	Dec. 31, Year 2	$100	$ 6.12	16	$4.80	4.8

The decline in market value during Year 2 presumably reflects the decrease in earnings per share. Investors appraising this stock at December 31, Year 2, would consider whether a price-earnings ratio of 16 and a dividend yield of 4.8% represented a satisfactory situation in the light of alternative investment opportunities. They would also place considerable weight on estimates of the company's prospective future earnings and the probable effect of such estimated earnings on the market price of the stock and on dividend payments.

BOOK VALUE PER SHARE OF COMMON STOCK The procedure for computing book value per share were fully described in Chapter 8 and will not be repeated here. We will, however, determine the book value per share of common stock for the Seacliff Company:

Book Value per Share of Common Stock

		Year 2	Year 1
Total stockholders' equity		*$602,600*	*$516,000*
Less: Equity of preferred stockholders (1,000 shares at call price of $105)		*105,000*	*105,000*
Equity of common stockholders	*(a)*	*$497,600*	*$411,000*
Shares of common stock outstanding	*(b)*	*5,000*	*4,000*
Book value per share of common stock (a ÷ b)		*$99.52*	*$102.75*

Why did book value per share decrease?

Book value per share was reduced by $9.35 in Year 2 as a result of dividend payments and the issuance of 1,000 additional shares of common stock at $80 per share, a figure significantly below the book value of $102.75 per share at the end of Year 1; book value was increased by earnings of $6.12 per share in Year 2, thus causing a net decrease of $3.23 in the book value per share.

REVENUE AND EXPENSE ANALYSIS The trend of earnings of Seacliff Company is unfavorable and stockholders will want to know the reasons for the decline in net income. The comparative income statement on page 649 shows that despite a 20% increase in net sales, net income fell from $52,500 in Year 1 to $36,600 in Year 2, a decline of 30.3%. The *net income as a percentage of net sales* went from 7.0 to only 4.1%. The primary causes of this decline were the increases in selling expenses (56.0%), in general and administrative expenses (33.3%), and in the cost of goods sold (24.8%), all exceeding the 20% increase in net sales.

These observations suggest the need for further investigation. Suppose we find that Seacliff Company cut its selling prices in Year 2. This fact would explain the decrease in *gross profit rate* from 37.5 to 35% and would also show that sales volume in physical units rose more than 20%, since it takes proportionally more sales at lower prices to produce a given increase in dollar sales. Since the dollar amount of gross profit increased $33,800 in Year 2, the strategy of reducing sales prices to increase volume would have been successful if there had been little change in operating expenses. Operating expenses, however, rose by $73,500, resulting in a $39,700 decrease in operating income.

The next step would be to find which expenses increased and why. An investor may be handicapped here, because detailed operating expenses are not usually shown in published statements. Some conclusions, however, can be reached on the basis of even the condensed information available in the comparative income statement for Seacliff Company shown on page 649.

The substantial increase in selling expenses presumably reflects greater selling effort during Year 2 in an attempt to improve sales volume. However, the fact that selling expenses increased $42,000 while gross profit increased only $33,800 indicates that the cost of this increased sales effort was not justified in terms of results. Even more disturbing is the increase in general and administrative expenses. Some growth in administrative expenses might be expected to accompany increased sales volume, but because some of the expenses are fixed, the growth generally should be **less than proportional** to any increase in sales. The increase in general and administrative expenses from 12.6 to 14% of sales would be of serious concern to informed investors.

Management generally has greater control over operating expenses than over revenue. The **operating expense ratio** is often used as a measure of management's ability to control its operating expenses. The unfavorable trend in this ratio for Seacliff Company is shown below:

Operating Expense Ratio

		Year 2	Year 1
Operating expenses	(a)	$243,000	$169,500
Net sales	(b)	$900,000	$750,000
Operating expense ratio (a ÷ b)		27.0%	22.6%

Does a higher operating expense ratio indicate higher net income?

If management were able to increase the sales volume while at the same time increasing the gross profit rate and decreasing the operating expense ratio, the effect on net income could be quite dramatic. For example, if Seacliff Company increased its sales in Year 3 by 11% to $1,000,000, increased its gross profit rate from 35 to 38%, and reduced the operating expense ratio from 27 to 24%, its operating income would increase from $72,000 to $140,000 ($1,000,000 − $620,000 − $240,000), an increase of over 94%.

Return on investment (ROI)

The rate of return on investment (often called ROI) is a test of management's efficiency in using available resources. Regardless of the size of the organization, capital is a scarce resource and must be used efficiently. In other words, management has a limited amount of dollars to work with, and a good manager is the one who can get the most out of the resources which are available. In judging the performance of branch managers or of company-wide management, it is reasonable to raise the question: What rate of return have you earned on the resources under your control? The concept of return on investment can be applied to a number of situations: for example, evaluating a branch, a total business, a product line, or an individual investment. A number of different ratios have been developed for the ROI concept, each well suited to a particular situation. We shall consider the return on total assets and the return on common stockholders' equity as examples of the return on investment concept.

RETURN ON TOTAL ASSETS An important test of management's ability to earn a return on funds supplied from all sources is the rate of return on total assets.

The income figure used in computing this ratio should be *income before deducting interest expense,* since interest is a payment to creditors for money used to *acquire assets.* Income before interest reflects earnings throughout the year and therefore should be related to the *average* investment in assets during the year. The computation of this ratio for Seacliff Company is shown below:

Percentage Return on Total Assets

			Year 2	Year 1
Earnings related to investment in assets	Net income		$ 36,600	$ 52,500
	Add back: Interest expense		12,000	15,000
	Income before interest expense	(a)	$ 48,600	$ 67,500
	Total assets, beginning of year		$860,000	$820,000
	Total assets, end of year		950,000	860,000
	Average investment in assets	(b)	$905,000	$840,000
	Return on total assets (a ÷ b)		5.4%	8.0%

This ratio shows that earnings per dollar of assets invested have fallen off in Year 2. If the same ratios were available for other companies of similar kind and size, the significance of this decline could be better appraised.

Management's effectiveness in employing assets can be measured by dividing sales for the year by the average assets used in producing these sales. In computing this *asset turnover* rate, those assets not contributing directly to sales (such as long-term investments and loans to officers) should be excluded. A higher asset turnover suggests that management is making better use of assets, and if the ratio of income (before interest expense) to sales remains relatively constant, a higher rate of return on total assets will result.[2]

RETURN ON COMMON STOCKHOLDERS' EQUITY Because interest and dividends paid to creditors and preferred stockholders are fixed in amount, a company may earn a greater or smaller return on the common stockholders' equity than on its total assets. The computation of return on stockholders' equity for Seacliff Company is shown below:

Return on Common Stockholders' Equity

		Year 2	Year 1
Net income		$ 36,600	$ 52,500
Less: Preferred dividend requirements		6,000	6,000
Net income available for common stock	(a)	$ 30,600	$ 46,500
Common stockholders' equity, beginning of year		$416,000	$389,500
Common stockholders' equity, end of year		502,600	416,000
Average common stockholders' equity	(b)	$459,300	$402,750
Return on common stockholders' equity (a ÷ b)		6.7%	11.5%

Does the use of leverage benefit common stockholders?

In both years the rate of return to common stockholders was higher than the return on total assets, because the average combined rate of interest paid to creditors and dividends to preferred stockholders was less than the rate earned on each dollar of assets used in the business.

Leverage

When the return on total assets is greater than the average cost of borrowed capital, as was the case in Seacliff Company, the common stockholders may benefit from the use of leverage. *Leverage* (or *trading on the equity*) refers to financing assets with capital raised by borrowing or by issuing preferred stock. If the borrowed capital can be invested to earn a

---

[2] In order to show that the return on total assets is dependent on both the asset turnover rate and the earnings rate on sales, we can develop the following formula:

$$\frac{Sales}{Assets} \times \frac{Income\ before\ interest\ expense}{Sales} = Return\ on\ assets$$

If we assume sales of $100, assets of $50, and net income of $10, the formula yields the following result:

$$\frac{\$100}{\$50} \times \frac{\$10}{\$100} = 20\%$$

The asset turnover (2 times) multiplied by earnings rate on sales (10%) results in a 20% return on assets. Assume that management is able to improve the asset turnover by increasing sales to $200 without increasing total assets and that the earnings rate on sales actually declines to 8%. Then the formula yields:

$$\frac{\$200}{\$50} \times \frac{\$16}{\$200} = 32\%$$

Despite a lower earnings rate on sales (8%), the return on total assets increased dramatically because assets were more effectively utilized, as indicated by the higher asset turnover rate of 4 times ($200 ÷ $50).

return **greater** than the cost of borrowing, net income and the return on common stockholders' equity will **increase.** However, leverage can act as a "double-edged sword"; the effects may be favorable or unfavorable to the holders of common stock. If the return on total assets should fall **below** the average cost of borrowed capital, leverage will **reduce** net income and the return on common stockholders' equity. When this unfavorable situation occurs, the problem is often compounded by the fact that most companies do not have sufficient amounts of cash to retire long-term debt or preferred stock on short notice. Therefore, the common stockholders may become "locked in" for a long period of time to the unfavorable effects of leverage.

When the return on assets exceeds the cost of borrowed capital, the extensive use of leverage can increase dramatically the return on common stockholders' equity. However, extensive leverage also increases the **risk** to common stockholders that their return may be reduced dramatically in future years. Furthermore, if a business incurs so much debt that it becomes unable to meet the required interest and principal payments, creditors may force liquidation or reorganization of the business, to the detriment of stockholders.

In deciding how much leverage is appropriate, the common stockholders should consider the **stability** of the company's return on assets, as well as the relationship of this return to the average cost of borrowed capital. Also, they should consider the amount of risk that they are willing to accept in the effort to increase the return on their investment.

Leverage most frequently is achieved through debt financing, including both current and long-term liabilities. One advantage of debt financing is that interest payments are deductible in determining taxable income. Leverage can also be achieved through the issuance of preferred stock. Since preferred stock dividends are **not** deductible for income tax purposes, however, the advantage gained in this respect will be much smaller than in the case of debt financing.

EQUITY RATIO One indicator of the amount of leverage used by a business is the equity ratio. This ratio measures the proportion of the total assets financed by stockholders, as distinguished from creditors. It is computed by dividing total stockholders' equity by total assets. A **low** equity ratio indicates an extensive use of leverage, that is, a large proportion of financing provided by creditors. A high equity ratio, on the other hand, indicates that the business is making little use of leverage.

The equity ratio at year-end for Seacliff is determined as follows:

Equity Ratio

		Year 2	Year 1
Proportion of assets financed by stockholders	Total stockholders' equity ....(a)	$602,600	$516,000
	Total assets (or total liabilities & stockholders' equity) ....(b)	$950,000	$860,000
	Equity ratio (a ÷ b)	63.4%	60.0%

Seacliff Company has a higher equity ratio in Year 2 than in Year 1. Is this favorable or unfavorable?

From the viewpoint of the common stockholder, a low equity ratio will produce maximum benefits if management is able to earn a rate of return on assets greater than the rate of interest paid to creditors. However, a low equity ratio can be very unfavorable if the return on assets falls below the rate of interest paid to creditors. Since the return on total assets earned by Seacliff Company has declined from 8% in Year 1 to a relatively low 5.4% in Year 2, the common stockholders should *not* favor a low equity ratio. The action by management in Year 2 of retiring $50,000 in long-term liabilities will help to protect the common stockholders from the unfavorable effects of leverage should the return on assets continue to decline.

Analysis by long-term creditors

Bondholders and other long-term creditors are primarily interested in three factors: (*1*) the rate of return on their investment, (*2*) the firm's ability to meet its interest requirements, and (*3*) the firm's ability to repay the principal of the debt when it falls due.

YIELD RATE ON BONDS The yield rate on bonds or other long-term indebtedness cannot be computed in the same manner as the yield rate on shares of stock, because bonds, unlike stocks, have a definite maturity date and amount. The ownership of a 6%, 10-year bond represents the right to receive $1,000 at the end of 10 years and the right to receive $60 per year during each of the next 10 years. If the market price of this bond is $950, the yield rate on an investment in the bond is the rate of interest that will make the present value of these two contractual rights equal to $950. *The yield rate varies inversely with changes in the market price of the bond.* If the price of a bond is above maturity value, the yield rate is less than the bond interest rate; if the price of a bond is below maturity value, the yield rate is higher than the bond interest rate.

NUMBER OF TIMES INTEREST EARNED Long-term creditors have learned from experience that one of the best indications of the safety of their investment is the fact that, over the life of the debt, the company has sufficient income to cover its interest requirements by a wide margin. A failure to cover interest requirements may have serious repercussions on the stability and solvency of the firm.

A common measure of debt safety is the ratio of income available for the payment of interest to the annual interest expense, called *times interest earned.* This computation for Seacliff Company would be:

Number of Times Interest Earned

		Year 2	Year 1
Long-term	*Operating income (before interest and income taxes)* . . . . . .*(a)*	*$72,000*	*$111,700*
creditors *watch this*	*Annual interest expense* . . . .*(b)*	*$12,000*	*$ 15,000*
ratio	*Times interest earned (a ÷ b)*	*6.0*	*7.4*

The decline in the ratio during Year 2 is unfavorable, but a ratio of 6.0 times interest earned for that year would still be considered quite strong in many industries. In the electric utilities industry, for example, the interest coverage ratio for the leading companies presently averages about 3, with the ratio of individual companies varying from 2 to 6.

DEBT RATIO Long-term creditors are interested in the amount of debt outstanding in relation to the amount of capital contributed by stockholders. The **debt ratio** is computed by dividing total liabilities by total assets, shown below for Seacliff Company.

Debt Ratio

		Year 2	Year 1
What por-	*Total liabilities* . . . .*(a)*	*$347,400*	*$344,000*
tion of total *assets is*	*Total assets (or total liabilities & stockholders' equity)* . . . .*(b)*	*$950,000*	*$860,000*
financed by *debt?*	*Debt ratio (a ÷ b)*	*36.6%*	*40.0%*

From a creditor's viewpoint, the lower the debt ratio (or the higher the equity ratio) the better, since this means that stockholders have contributed the bulk of the funds to the business, and therefore the margin of protection to creditors against a shrinkage of the assets is high.

Analysis by preferred stockholders

If preferred stock is convertible, the interests of preferred stockholders are similar to those of common stockholders. If preferred stock is not convertible, the interests of preferred stockholders are more closely comparable to those of long-term creditors.

Preferred stockholders are interested in the yield on their investment. The yield is computed by dividing the dividend per share by the market value per share. The dividend per share of Seacliff Company preferred stock is $6. If we assume that the market value at December 31, Year 2, is $80 per share, the yield rate at that time would be 7.5% ($6 ÷ $80).

The primary measurement of the safety of an investment in preferred stock is the ability of the firm to meet its preferred dividend requirements. The best test of this ability is the ratio of the net income available to pay the preferred dividend to the amount of the annual dividend, as follows:

Times Preferred Dividends Earned

		Year 2	Year 1
Is the Net income available to pay preferred dividends ....(a)		$36,600	$52,500
preferred Annual preferred dividend requirements ....(b)		$ 6,000	$ 6,000
dividend *safe?* Times dividends earned (a ÷ b)		6.1	8.8

Although the margin of protection declined in Year 2, the annual preferred dividend requirement still appears well protected.

Analysis by short-term creditors

Bankers and other short-term creditors share the interest of stockholders and bondholders in the profitablility and long-run stability of a business. Their primary interest, however, is in the current position of the firm—its ability to generate sufficient funds (working capital) to meet current operating needs and to pay current debts promptly. Thus the analysis of financial statements by a banker considering a short-term loan, or by a trade creditor investigating the credit status of a customer, is likely to center on the working capital position of the prospective debtor.

AMOUNT OF WORKING CAPITAL The details of the working capital of Seacliff Company are shown below:

SEACLIFF COMPANY
Comparative Schedule of Working Capital
As of December 31

	Year 2	Year 1	Increase or (Decrease) Dollars	%	Percentage of Total Current Items Year 2	Year 1
Current assets:						
Cash	$ 38,000	$ 40,000	$ (2,000)	(5.0)	9.7	13.9
Receivables (net)	117,000	86,000	31,000	36.0	30.0	29.9
Inventories	180,000	120,000	60,000	50.0	46.2	41.6
Prepaid expenses	55,000	42,000	13,000	31.0	14.1	14.6
Total current assets	$390,000	$288,000	$102,000	35.4	100.0	100.0
Current liabilities:						
Notes payable to creditors	$ 50,000	$ 10,000	$ 40,000	400.0	33.9	10.7
Accounts payable	66,000	30,000	36,000	120.0	44.8	31.9
Accrued liabilities	31,400	54,000	(22,600)	(41.9)	21.3	57.4
Total current liabilities.......	$147,400	$ 94,000	$ 53,400	56.8	100.0	100.0
Working capital..............	$242,600	$194,000	$ 48,600	25.0		

The amount of working capital is measured by the **excess of current assets over current liabilities.** Thus, working capital represents the amount of cash, near-cash items, and cash substitutes (prepayments) on hand after providing for payment of all current liabilities.

This schedule shows that current assets increased $102,000, while current liabilities rose by only $53,400, with the result that working capital increased $48,600. There was a shift in the composition of the current assets and current liabilities; cash decreased from 13.9 to 9.8% of current assets, and inventory rose from 41.6 to 46.1%. Inventory is a less liquid resource than cash. Therefore, although the amount of working capital increased in Year 2, the quality of working capital is not as liquid as in Year 1. Although creditors want to see large amounts of high-quality working capital, management must consider that excess amounts of cash are not productive and do not generate a high return.

THE CURRENT RATIO   One means of further evaluating these changes in working capital is to observe the relationship between current assets and current liabilities, a test known as the **current ratio.** The current ratio for the Seacliff Company is computed below:

Current Ratio

		Year 2	Year 1
Does this indicate satisfactory debt-paying ability?	Total current assets . . . .(a)	$390,000	$288,000
	Total current liabilities . . . .(b)	$147,400	$ 94,000
	Current ratio (a ÷ b).	2.6	

Despite the increase of $48,600 in the amount of working capital in Year 2, current assets per dollar of current liabilities declined. The margin of safety (current ratio), however, still appears satisfactory.

In interpreting the current ratio, a number of factors should be kept in mind:

1 Creditors tend to feel that the larger the current ratio the better; however, from a managerial view there is an upper limit. Too high a current ratio may indicate that capital is not being used productively in the business.

2 Because creditors tend to stress the current ratio as an indication of short-term solvency, some firms may take conscious steps to improve this ratio just before statements are prepared at the end of a fiscal period for submission to bankers or other creditors. This may be done by postponing purchases, pressing collections on accounts receivable, and using the cash collected to pay off current liabilities.

3 The current ratio computed at the end of a fiscal year may not be representative of the current position of the company throughout the year. Since many firms

arrange their fiscal year to end during a low point in the seasonal swing of business activity, the current ratio at year-end is likely to be more favorable than at any other time during the year.

Use of both the current ratio and the amount of working capital helps to place debt-paying ability in its proper perspective. For example, if Company X has current assets of $200,000 and current liabilities of $100,000 and Company Y has current assets of $2,000,000 and current liabilities of $1,900,000, each company has $100,000 of working capital, but the current position of Company X is clearly superior to that of Company Y. The current ratio for Company X is quite satisfactory at 2 to 1, but Company Y's current ratio is very low—only slightly above 1 to 1. As another example, assume that Company A and Company B both have current ratios of 3 to 1. However, Company A has working capital of $20,000 and Company B has working capital of $200,000. Although both companies appear to be good credit risks, Company B would no doubt be able to qualify for a much *larger* bank loan than would Company A.

A widely used rule of thumb is that a current ratio of 2 to 1 or better is satisfactory. As with all rules of thumb this is an arbitrary standard, subject to numerous exceptions and qualifications.

ADJUSTMENT FOR UNDERSTATED INVENTORIES The cost of inventory is a major factor in the computation of the current ratio or the amount of working capital. If a company uses the *lifo* inventory method, the cost of inventory appearing in the balance sheet may be unrealistically low in terms of current replacement costs. In such cases, many financial analysts substitute the *current replacement cost* of inventories for the historical cost figure in computing the current ratio or amount of working capital. Many large corporations disclose the current replacement cost of their inventories in a footnote to their financial statements.

QUICK RATIO Because inventories and prepaid expenses are further removed from conversion into cash than other current assets, a ratio known as the *quick ratio* or *acid-test ratio* is sometimes computed as a supplement to the current ratio. This ratio compares the highly liquid current assets (cash, marketable securities, and receivables) with current liabilities. Seacliff Company has no marketable securities; its quick ratio is computed as follows:

Quick Ratio

			Year 2	Year 1
A measure of liquidity	Quick assets (cash and receivables)	(a)	$155,000	$126,000
	Current liabilities	(b)	$147,400	$ 94,000
	Quick ratio (a ÷ b)		1.1	1.3

Here again the analysis reveals an unfavorable trend. Whether the quick ratio is adequate depends on the amount of receivables included among quick assets and the average time required to collect receivables as compared to the credit period extended by suppliers. If the credit periods extended to customers and granted by creditors are roughly equal, a quick ratio of 1.0 or better would be considered satisfactory.

Some financial analysts compute a *liquidity ratio* as a measure of immediate ability to pay short-term debts. This ratio is computed by dividing the total of cash and marketable securities owned by the total current liabilities outstanding.

INVENTORY TURNOVER   The cost of goods sold figure on the income statement represents the total cost of all goods that have been transferred out of inventories during any given period. Therefore the relationship between cost of goods sold and the average balance of inventories maintained throughout the year indicates the number of times that inventories "turn over" and are replaced each year.

Ideally we should total the inventories at the end of each month and divide by 12 to obtain an average inventory. This information is not always available, however, and the nearest substitute is a simple average of the inventory at the beginning and at the end of the year. This tends to overstate the turnover rate, since many companies choose an accounting year that ends when inventories are at a minimum.

Assuming that only beginning and ending inventories are available, the computation of inventory turnover for Seacliff Company may be illustrated as follows:

Inventory Turnover

			Year 2	Year 1
What does	Cost of goods sold . . . .(a)		$585,000	$468,800
inventory				
turnover	Inventory, beginning of year		$120,000	$100,000
mean?	Inventory, end of year		180,000	120,000
	Average inventory . . . .(b)		$150,000	$110,000
	Average inventory turnover per year (a ÷ b)		3.9 times	4.3 times
	Average days to turn over (*divide 365 days by inventory*			
	turnover)		94 days	85 days

The trend indicated by this analysis is unfavorable, since the average investment in inventories in relation to the cost of goods sold is rising. Stating this another way, the company required on the average 9 days more during Year 2 to turn over its inventories than during Year 1. Furthermore, the inventory status *at the end of the year* has changed even more: At the end of Year 1 there were 94 days' sales represented in the ending inventory ($120,000/$468,800 × 365 days) compared with 112 days' sales contained in the ending inventory at the end of Year 2 ($180,000/$585,000 × 365 days).

The relation between inventory turnover and gross profit per dollar of sales may be significant. A high inventory turnover and a low gross profit rate frequently go hand in hand. This, however, is merely another way of saying that if the gross profit rate is low, a high volume of business is necessary to produce a satisfactory return on total assets. Although a high inventory turnover is usually regarded as a good sign, a rate that is high in relation to that of similar firms may indicate that the company is losing sales by a failure to maintain an adequate stock of goods to serve its customers promptly.

ACCOUNTS RECEIVABLE TURNOVER The turnover of accounts receivable is computed in a manner comparable to that just described for inventories. The ratio between the net sales for the period and the average balance in accounts receivable is a rough indication of the average time required to convert receivables into cash. Ideally, a monthly average of receivables should be used, and only *sales on credit* should be included in the sales figure. For illustrative purposes, we shall assume that Seacliff Company sells entirely on credit and that only the beginning and ending balances of receivables are available:

Accounts Receivable Turnover

		Year 2	Year 1
Are Net sales on credit . . . .(a)		$900,000	$750,000
customers **paying** Receivables, beginning of year		$ 86,000	$ 80,000
promptly? Receivables, end of year		117,000	86,000
Average receivables . . . .(b)		$101,500	$ 83,000
Receivable turnover per year (a ÷ b)		8.9 times	9.0 times
Average age of receivables (divide 365 days by receivable turnover)		41 days	41 days

There has been no significant change in the average time required to collect receivables. The interpretation of the average age of receivables would depend upon the company's credit terms and the seasonal activity immediately before year-end. If the company grants 30-day credit terms to its customers, for example, the above analysis indicates that accounts receivable collections are lagging. If the terms were for 60 days, however, there is evidence that collections are being made ahead of schedule. On the other hand, if the sales in the last month of the year were unusually large, the average age of receivables as computed above can be misleading.

The *operating cycle* in Year 2 was approximately 135 days (computed by adding the 94 days required to turn over inventory and the average 41 days required to collect receivables). This compares to an operating cycle of only 126 days in Year 1, computed as 85 days to dispose of the inventory plus 41 days to collect the resulting receivables. The operating cycle measures the time interval required to convert inventory into accounts receivable and then accounts receivable into cash. A trend toward a longer operating cycle suggests that inventory and receivables are increasing relative to sales and that profits may be hurt because of lower sales volume and an increasing investment in current assets.

Summary of analytical measurements

The basic ratios and other measurements discussed in this chapter and their significance are summarized below and on page 665.

Ratio or Other Measurement	Method of Computation	Significance
1 Earnings per share on common stock	$\dfrac{\text{Net income} - \text{preferred dividends}}{\text{Shares of common outstanding}}$	Gives the amount of earnings applicable to a share of common stock.
2 Dividend yield	$\dfrac{\text{Dividend per share}}{\text{Market price per share}}$	Shows the rate earned by stockholders based on current price for a share of stock.
3 Price-earnings ratio	$\dfrac{\text{Market price per share}}{\text{Earnings per share}}$	Indicates whether price of stock is in line with earnings.
4 Book value per share of common stock	$\dfrac{\text{Common stockholders' equity}}{\text{Shares of common outstanding}}$	Measures the recorded value of net assets behind each share of common stock.
5 Operating expense ratio	$\dfrac{\text{Operating expenses}}{\text{Net sales}}$	Indicates management's ability to control expenses.
6 Return on total assets	$\dfrac{\text{Net income} + \text{interest expense}}{\text{Average investment in assets}}$	Measures the productivity of assets regardless of capital structures.
7 Return on common stockholders' equity	$\dfrac{\text{Net income} - \text{preferred dividends}}{\text{Average common stockholders' equity}}$	Indicates the earning power of common stockholders' equity.
8 Equity ratio	$\dfrac{\text{Total stockholders' equity}}{\text{Total assets}}$	Shows the protection to creditors and the extent of leverage being used.
9 Number of times interest earned	$\dfrac{\text{Operating income}}{\text{Annual interest expense}}$	Measures the coverage of interest requirements, particularly on long-term debt.
10 Debt ratio	$\dfrac{\text{Total liabilities}}{\text{Total assets}}$	Indicates the percentage of assets financed through borrowing; it shows the extent of leverage being used.
11 Times preferred dividends earned	$\dfrac{\text{Net income}}{\text{Annual preferred dividends}}$	Shows the adequacy of current earnings to pay dividends on preferred stock.

12 Current ratio	$\dfrac{\textit{Current assets}}{\textit{Current liabilities}}$	*Measures short-run debt-paying ability.*
13 Quick (acid-test) ratio	$\dfrac{\textit{Quick assets}}{\textit{Current liabilities}}$	*Measures the short-term liquidity of a firm.*
14 Inventory turnover	$\dfrac{\textit{Cost of goods sold}}{\textit{Average inventory}}$	*Indicates management's ability to control the investment in inventory.*
15 Accounts receivable turnover	$\dfrac{\textit{Net sales on credit}}{\textit{Average receivables}}$	*Indicates reasonableness of accounts receivable balance and effectiveness of collections.*

The student should keep in mind the fact that the full significance of any of the foregoing ratios or other measurements depends on the *direction of its trend* and on its *relationship to some predetermined standard* or industry average.

KEY TERMS INTRODUCED OR EMPHASIZED IN CHAPTER 16

Common size financial statement All items are stated in percentages rather than dollar amounts. In the balance sheet each item is expressed as a percentage of total assets; in the income statement each item is expressed as a percentage of net sales.

Comparative financial statements Financial statement data for two or more successive years placed side by side in adjacent columns to facilitate study of changes.

Component percentage The percentage relationship of any financial statement item to a total including that item. For example, each type of asset as a percentage of total assets.

Horizontal analysis Comparison of the change in a financial statement item such as inventories during two or more accounting periods.

Leverage Refers to the practice of financing assets with borrowed capital. Extensive leverage creates the possibility for the rate of return on common stockholders' equity to be substantially above or below the rate of return on total assets. When the rate of return on total assets exceeds the average cost of borrowed capital, leverage increases net income and the return on common stockholders' equity. However, when the return on total assets is less than the average cost of borrowed capital, leverage reduces net income and the return on common stockholders' equity. Leverage is also called *trading on the equity.*

Quality of assets The concept that some companies have assets of better quality than others, such as well-balanced composition of assets, well-maintained plant and equipment, and receivables that are all current. A lower quality of assets might be indicated by poor maintenance of plant and equipment, slow-moving inventories with high danger of obsolescence, past-due receivables, and patents approaching an expiration date.

Quality of earnings Earnings are said to be of high quality if they are stable, the source seems assured, and the methods used in measuring income are conservative. The existence of this concept suggests that the range of alternative but acceptable accounting principles may still be too wide to produce financial statements that are comparable.

Rate of return on investment (ROI) The overall test of management's ability to earn a satisfactory return on the assets under its control. Numerous variations of the ROI concept are used such as return on total assets, return on total equities, etc.

Ratios See pages 664–665 for list of ratios, methods of computation, and significance.

Vertical analysis Comparison of a particular financial statement item to a total including that item, such as inventories as a percentage of current assets, or operating expenses in relation to net sales.

DEMONSTRATION PROBLEM FOR YOUR REVIEW

The accounting records of King Corporation showed the following balances at the end of Years 1 and 2:

	Year 2	Year 1
Cash	$ 35,000	$ 25,000
Accounts receivable (net)	91,000	90,000
Inventory	160,000	140,000
Short-term prepayments	4,000	5,000
Investment in land	90,000	100,000
Equipment	880,000	640,000
Less: Accumulated depreciation	(260,000)	(200,000)
	$1,000,000	$ 800,000
Accounts payable	$ 105,000	$ 46,000
Income taxes payable and other accrued liabilities	40,000	25,000
Bonds payable—8%	280,000	280,000
Premium on bonds payable	3,600	4,000
Capital stock, $5 par	165,000	110,000
Retained earnings	406,400	335,000
	$1,000,000	$ 800,000
Sales (net of discounts and allowances)	$2,200,000	$1,600,000
Cost of goods sold	1,606,000	1,120,000
Gross profit on sales	$ 594,000	$ 480,000
Expenses (including $22,400 interest expense)	(330,000)	(352,000)
Income taxes	(91,000)	(48,000)
Extraordinary loss	(6,600)	–0–
Net income	$ 166,400	$ 80,000

Cash dividends of $40,000 were paid and a 50% stock dividend was distributed early in Year 2. All sales were made on credit at a relatively uniform rate during the year. Inventory and receivables did not fluctuate materially. The market price of the company's stock on December 31, Year 2, was $86 per share; on December 31, Year 1, it was $43.50 (before the 50% stock dividend distributed in Year 2).

Instructions Compute the following for Year 2 and Year 1:
(1) Quick ratio
(2) Current ratio
(3) Equity ratio

(4) Debt ratio
(5) Book value per share of capital stock (based on shares outstanding after 50% stock dividend in Year 2)
(6) Earnings per share of capital stock (including extraordinary loss)
(7) Price-earnings ratio
(8) Gross profit percentage
(9) Operating expense ratio
(10) Income before extraordinary loss as a percentage of net sales
(11) Inventory turnover (Assume an average inventory of $150,000 for both years.)
(12) Accounts receivable turnover (Assume average accounts receivable of $90,000 for Year 1.)
(13) Times bond interest earned (before interest expense and income taxes)

SOLUTION TO DEMONSTRATION PROBLEM

	Year 2	Year 1
(1) Quick ratio:		
$126,000 ÷ $145,000	*.9 to 1*	
$115,000 ÷ $71,000		*1.6 to 1*
(2) Current ratio:		
$290,000 ÷ $145,000	*2 to 1*	
$260,000 ÷ $71,000		*3.7 to 1*
(3) Equity ratio:		
$571,400 ÷ $1,000,000	*57%*	
$445,000 ÷ $800,000		*56%*
(4) Debt ratio:		
$428,600 ÷ $1,000,000	*43%*	
$355,000 ÷ $800,000		*44%*
(5) Book value per share of capital stock:		
$571,400 ÷ 33,000 shares	*$17.32*	
$445,000 ÷ 33,000* shares		*$13.48*
(6) Earnings per share of capital stock (including extraordinary loss of $0.20 per share in Year 2):		
$166,400 ÷ 33,000 shares	*$5.04*	
$80,000 ÷ 33,000* shares		*$2.42*
(7) Price-earnings ratio:		
$86 ÷ $5.04	*17 times*	
$43.50 ÷ 1.5* = $29, adjusted market price; $29 ÷ $2.42		*12 times*
(8) Gross profit percentage:		
$594,000 ÷ $2,200,000	*27%*	
$480,000 ÷ $1,600,000		*30%*
(9) Operating expense ratio:		
($330,000 − $22,400) ÷ $2,200,000	*14%*	
($352,000 − $22,400) ÷ $1,600,000		*20.6%*

* Adjusted retroactively for 50% stock dividend.

(10) *Income before extraordinary loss as a percentage of*
    net sales:
    $173,000 ÷ $2,200,000 . . . .   *7.9%*
    $80,000 ÷ $1,600,000 . . . .   *5%*

(11) *Inventory turnover:*
    $1,606,000 ÷ $150,000 . . . .   *10.7 times*
    $1,120,000 ÷ $150,000 . . . .   *7.5 times*

(12) *Accounts receivable turnover:*
    $2,200,000 ÷ $90,500 . . . .   *24.3 times*
    $1,600,000 ÷ $90,000 . . . .   *17.8 times*

(13) *Times bond interest earned:*
    ($166,400 + $22,400 + $91,000) ÷ $22,400 . . . .   *12.5 times*
    ($80,000 + $22,400 + $48,000) ÷ $22,400 . . . .   *6.7 times*

REVIEW QUESTIONS

1 ***a*** What groups are interested in the financial affairs of publicly owned corporations?
   b List some of the more important sources of financial information for investors.

2 In financial statement analysis, what is the basic objective of observing trends in data and ratios? What is an alternative standard of comparison?

3 In financial analysis, what information is produced by computing a ratio that is not available in a simple observation of the underlying data?

4 Explain the distinction between *percentage change* and *component percentages.*

5 "Although net income declined this year as compared with last year, it increased from 3% to 5% of net sales." Are sales increasing or decreasing?

6 Differentiate between *horizontal* and *vertical* analysis.

7 Assume that the Chemco Corporation is engaged in the manufacture and distribution of a variety of chemicals. In analyzing the financial statements of this corporation, why would you want to refer to the ratios and other measurements of companies in the chemical industry? In comparing the financial results of the Chemco Corporation with another chemical company, why would you be interested in the accounting procedures used by the two companies?

8 What is the objective of financial analysis? What types of information may be relevant in evaluating the future profitability of a company?

9 What single ratio do you think should be of greatest interest to:
   a a banker considering a short-term loan?
   b a common stockholder?
   c an insurance company considering a long-term mortgage loan?

10 Modern Company earned an 8% return on its total assets. Current liabilities are 10% of total assets. Long-term bonds carrying a $6\frac{1}{2}$% coupon rate are equal to 30% of total assets. There is no preferred stock. Would you expect the rate of return on stockholders' equity to be greater or less than 8%? Explain.

11 In deciding whether a company's equity ratio is favorable or unfavorable, creditors and stockholders may have different views. Why?

12 Company A has a current ratio of 3 to 1. Company B has a current ratio of 2 to 1. Does this mean that A's operating cycle is longer than B's? Why?

13 An investor states, "I bought this stock for $50 several years ago and it now sells for $100. It paid $5 per share in dividends last year so I'm earning 10% on my investment." Criticize this statement.

14 Company C experiences a considerable seasonal variation in its business. The high point in the year's activities comes in November, the low point in July. During which month would you expect the company's current ratio to be higher? If the company were choosing a fiscal year for accounting purposes, how would you advise them?

15 Both the inventory turnover and accounts receivable turnover increased from 10 times to 15 times from Year 1 to Year 2, but net income decreased. Can you offer some possible reasons for this?

16 Is the rate of return on investment (ROI) intended primarily to measure liquidity, solvency, or some other aspect of business operations? Explain.

17 Mention three financial amounts to which corporate profits can logically be compared in judging their adequacy or reasonableness.

18 Under what circumstances would you consider a corporate net income of $1,000,000 for the year as being unreasonably low? Under what circumstances would you consider a corporate profit of $1,000,000 as being unreasonably high?

EXERCISES

Ex. 16-1 Selected information taken from the balance sheets of Young Company for two successive years is shown below. Compute the percentage change from the base year to the following year whenever possible.

	Year 2	Year 1
a Cash	$ 36,000	$ 30,000
b Sales	325,000	250,000
c Retained earnings (deficit)	20,000	(10,000)
d Current liabilities	120,000	80,000
e Notes payable	60,000	–0–
f Accounts receivable	80,000	50,000
g Marketable securities	20,000	25,000

Ex. 16-2 Prepare **common size** income statements for Hart Company, a single proprietorship, for the two years shown below by converting the dollar amounts into percentages. In each year, sales will appear as 100%, and other items will be expressed as a percentage of sales. Round the figures to the nearest tenth of one percent. (Income taxes are not involved since the business is not incorporated.)

HART COMPANY
Comparative Income Statements
For the Year Ended December 31, Years 1 and 2

	Year 2	Year 1
Sales	$500,000	$400,000
Cost of goods sold	330,000	256,000
Gross profit	$170,000	$144,000
Operating expenses	139,500	128,000
Net income	$ 30,500	$ 16,000

Ex. 16-3 The information below relates to the activities of a retail store:

	Year 2	Year 1
Sales (terms 2/10, n/30).	$480,000	$360,000
Cost of goods sold	312,000	252,000
Inventory at end of year	57,000	63,000
Accounts receivable at end of year	70,000	58,000

Compute the following for Year 2:
a Gross profit percentage
b Inventory turnover
c Accounts receivable turnover

Ex. 16-4 Given below is a condensed balance sheet for the Walnut Company:

Assets		Liabilities & Stockholders' Equity	
Cash	$ 30,000	Current liabilities.	$ 75,000
Accounts receivable	60,000	Long-term liabilities	150,000
Inventory	135,000	Capital stock, $10 par	300,000
Prepaid expenses	45,000	Retained earnings	75,000
Plant assets (net)	300,000		
Other assets	30,000	Total liabilities &	
Total assets	$600,000	stockholders' equity. . . .	$600,000

During the latest year, the company earned a gross profit of $480,000 on sales of $1,200,000. Accounts receivable, inventory, and plant assets remained rela- tively constant during the year. From this information, compute the following:
a Current ratio
b Acid-test ratio
c Equity ratio
d Asset turnover
e Accounts receivable turnover (all sales are on credit)
f Inventory turnover
g Book value per share of capital stock

Ex. 16-5 The following information is available for the Otis Corporation:

	Year 2	Year 1
Total assets (40% of which are current)	$400,000	$325,000
Current liabilities.	$ 80,000	$100,000
Bonds payable, 7%	100,000	50,000
Capital stock, $10 stated value	150,000	150,000
Retained earnings	70,000	25,000
Total liabilities & stockholders' equity.	$400,000	$325,000

The income tax rate is 50% and dividends of $6,000 were declared and paid in Year 2. Compute the following:
a Current ratio for Year 2 and Year 1
b Debt ratio for Year 2 and Year 1
c Earnings per share for Year 2

Ex. 16-6 The following information relates to the operations of the Lava Corporation:

Sales (60% on credit)	$2,500,000
Beginning inventory, Year 1	350,000
Purchases	2,100,000
Ending inventory, Year 1	?
Ending accounts receivable, Year 1	150,000

Sales are made at 25% above cost. Compute:
a The inventory turnover for Year 1.
b The number of days credit sales in accounts receivable at the end of Year 1. A year equals 365 days.

Ex. 16-7 Figures for two companies engaged in the same line of business are presented below for the latest year:

	A Company	B Company
Sales (all on credit)	$1,600,000	$1,200,000
Total assets	800,000	400,000
Total liabilities	200,000	100,000
Average receivables	200,000	100,000
Average inventory	240,000	140,000
Gross profit as a percentage of sales	40%	30%
Operating expenses as a percentage of sales	37%	25%
Net income as a percentage of sales	3%	5%

Compute the following for each company:
a Net income
b Net income as a percentage of total assets
c Net income as a percentage of stockholders' equity
d Accounts receivable turnover
e Inventory turnover

PROBLEMS

16-1 The following information was developed from the financial statements of Quarry Tile, Inc.

	Year 11	Year 10
Net income	$ 46,000	$ 38,000
Net income as a percentage of sales	5%	4%
Gross profit on sales	$322,000	$342,000
Income taxes as a percentage of income before income taxes	20%	20%

Instructions
a Compute the net sales for each year.
b Compute the cost of goods sold in dollars and as a percentage of sales for each year.
c Compute the federal income taxes for each year.
d Prepare a comparative income statement for Years 10 and 11. Show the following items: Net sales, cost of goods sold, gross profit on sales, operating expenses, income before income taxes, income taxes, and net income.
e What favorable trends and unfavorable trends do you see in this year-to-year comparison of the income statement data of Quarry Tile, Inc.?

16-2 Harvest King manufactures and distributes a full line of farm machinery. Given below for Year 1 is the income statement for the company and a common size summary for the industry in which the company operates:

	Harvest King	Industry Average
Sales (net)	$2,000,000	100%
Cost of goods sold	1,440,000	68
Gross profit on sales	$ 560,000	32%
Operating expenses:		
Selling	$ 160,000	7%
General and administrative	180,000	10
Total operating expenses	$ 340,000	17%
Operating income	$ 220,000	15%
Income taxes	100,000	6
Net income	$ 120,000	9%

Instructions
a Prepare a common size income statement comparing the operating results of Harvest King for Year 1 with the average for the farm machinery industry.
b Explain the significance of the results obtained in the comparative common size income statement prepared in part **a**.

16-3 Listed below is the working capital information for the Washington Corporation at the end of Year 1:

Cash	$225,000
Temporary investments in marketable securities	120,000
Notes receivable—current	180,000
Accounts receivable	300,000
Allowance for doubtful accounts	15,000
Inventory	240,000
Prepaid expenses	30,000
Notes payable within one year	90,000
Accounts payable	247,500
Accrued liabilities	22,500

The following transactions are completed early in Year 2:
(0) Sold inventory costing $36,000 for $30,000.
(1) Declared a cash dividend, $120,000.
(2) Declared a 10% stock dividend.
(3) Paid accounts payable, $60,000.
(4) Purchased goods on account, $45,000.
(5) Collected cash on accounts receivable, $90,000.
(6) Borrowed cash on short-term note, $150,000.
(7) Issued additional shares of capital stock for cash, $450,000.
(8) Sold temporary investments costing $30,000 for $27,000 cash.
(9) Acquired temporary investments, $52,500. Paid cash.
(10) Wrote off uncollectible accounts, $9,000.
(11) Sold inventory costing $37,500 for $48,000.
(12) Acquired plant and equipment for cash, $240,000.

Instructions
a Compute the following at the end of **Year 1:** (1) Current ratio, (2) acid-test ratio, and (3) working capital.
b Indicate the effect (increase, decrease, none) of each transaction listed above for **Year 2** on the current ratio, acid-test ratio, and working capital. Use the following four-column format (item *0* is given as an example):

Effect on

Item	Current Ratio	Acid-Test Ratio	Working Capital
0	Decrease	Increase	Decrease

16-4 Listed in the left-hand column below is a series of business transactions and events relating to the activities of Potomac Mills. Opposite each transaction is listed a particular ratio used in financial analysis:

Transaction	Ratio
(1) Purchased inventory on open account.	Quick ratio
(2) A larger physical volume of goods was sold at smaller unit prices.	Gross profit percentage
(3) Corporation declared a cash dividend.	Current ratio
(4) An uncollectible account receivable was written off against the allowance account.	Current ratio
(5) Issued additional shares of common stock and used proceeds to retire long-term debt.	Debt ratio
(6) Paid stock dividend on common stock, in common stock.	Earnings per share
(7) Conversion of bonds payable into common stock.	Times interest charges earned
(8) Appropriated retained earnings.	Rate of return on stockholders' equity
(9) During period of rising prices, company changed from fifo to lifo method of inventory pricing.	Inventory turnover
(10) Paid previously declared cash dividend.	Debt ratio
(11) Purchased factory supplies on open account.	Current ratio (assume that ratio is greater than 1:1)
(12) Issued shares of capital stock in exchange for patents.	Equity ratio

Instructions What effect would each transaction or event have on the ratio listed opposite to it; that is, as a result of this event would the ratio increase, decrease, or remain unchanged? Why?

16-5 The following information is taken from the records of Craftsman Clocks at the end of Year 1:

Sales (all on credit)	$600,000
Cost of goods sold	360,000
Average inventory (fifo method)	60,000
Average accounts receivable	100,000
Interest expense	10,000
Net income for Year 1	42,000
Total assets	400,000
Total liabilities	169,000

The corporation did not declare dividends during the year and capital stock was neither issued nor retired.

Instructions From the information given, compute the following for Year 1:
a Inventory turnover
b Accounts receivable turnover
c Total operating expenses, assuming that income taxes amounted to $12,000 (Interest expense is a nonoperating expense.)
d Gross profit percentage
e Rate earned on average stockholders' equity
f Rate earned on total assets (Use end-of-year total.)
g Craftsman Clocks has an opportunity to obtain a long-term loan at an annual interest rate of 8% and could use this additional capital at the same rate of profitability as indicated above. Would obtaining the loan be desirable from the viewpoint of the stockholders? Explain.

16-6 Given below are selected balance sheet items and ratios for the Metro Corporation at June 30, Year 8:

Total stockholders' equity (includes 100,000 shares of no-par value capital stock issued at $6 per share)	$1,000,000
Plant and equipment (net)	470,000
Asset turnover rate per year (sales ÷ total assets)	3 times
Inventory turnover rate per year	6 times
Average accounts receivable collection period (assuming a 360-day year)	30 days
Gross profit percentage	30%
Ratio of current liabilities to stockholders' equity (there is no long-term debt)	1.2 to 1
Acid-test ratio (quick ratio)	0.8 to 1

Assume that balance sheet figures represent average amounts and that all sales are made on account.

Instructions From the foregoing information, construct a balance sheet for the Metro Corporation as of June 30, Year 8, in as much detail as the data permit.

16-7 The financial information given below for Continental Transfer Co. and American Van Lines (except market price per share of stock) is stated in thousands of dollars. The figures are as of the end of the current year. The two companies are in the same industry and are quite similar as to operations, facilities, and accounting methods. Both companies pay income taxes equal to 50% of income before income taxes.

Assets	Continental Transfer Co.	American Van Lines
Current assets	$ 97,450	$132,320
Plant and equipment	397,550	495,680
Less: Accumulated depreciation	(55,000)	(78,000)
Total assets	$440,000	$550,000

Liabilities & Stockholders' Equity		
Current liabilities	$ 34,000	$ 65,000
Bonds payable, 8%, due in 15 years	120,000	100,000
Capital stock, no par*	150,000	200,000
Retained earnings	136,000	185,000
Total liabilities & stockholders' equity	$440,000	$550,000

Analysis of retained earnings:		
Balance, beginning of year	$125,200	$167,200
Net income for the year	19,800	37,400
Dividends	(9,000)	(19,600)
Balance, end of year	$136,000	$185,000
Market price of capital stock, per share	$30	$61
*Number of shares of capital stock outstanding	6 million	8 million

Instructions
a Although market prices for the bonds are not stated, which company's bonds do you think will sell at the higher price per $1,000 bond? Which company's bonds will probably yield the higher rate of return? (You may assume that the safer the bonds, according to your analysis, the lower the yield rate.)
b What are the dividend yield, the price-earnings ratio, and the book value per share for the stock of each company? Which company's stock is a better investment?

16-8 John Gale, the accountant for Southbay Corporation, prepared the financial statements for Year 1, including all ratios, and agreed to bring them along on a hunting trip with the executives of the corporation. To his embarrassment, he found that only certain fragmentary information had been placed in his briefcase and the completed statements had been left in his office. One hour before Gale was to present the financial statements to the executives, he was able to come up with the following information:

SOUTHBAY CORPORATION
Balance Sheet
End of Year 1
(in thousands of dollars)

Assets			Liabilities & Stockholders' Equity		
Current assets:			Current liabilities	$	?
Cash	$	?	Long-term debt, 8% interest		?
Accounts receivable (net)		?	Total liabilities	$	?
Inventory		?	Stockholders' equity:		
Total current assets	$	?	Capital stock, $5 par . . . $300		
Plant assets:			Retained earnings 100		
Machinery and equipment $580			Total stockholders' equity . .		400
Less: Accumulated					
depreciation 80		500	Total liabilities &		
Total assets	$	?	stockholders' equity	$	?

SOUTHBAY CORPORATION
Income Statement
For Year 1
(in thousands of dollars)

Net sales.	$	?
Cost of goods sold		?
Gross profit on sales (25% of net sales)	$	?
Operating expenses		?
Operating income (10% of net sales)	$	?
Interest expense		28
Income before income taxes	$	?
Income taxes—40% of income before income taxes		?
Net income		$60

Additional information
(1) The equity ratio was 40%; the debt ratio was 60%.
(2) The only interest expense paid was on the long-term debt.
(3) The beginning inventory was $150,000; the inventory turnover was 4.8 times. (Inventory turnover = cost of goods sold ÷ average inventory.)
(4) The current ratio was 2 to 1; the acid-test ratio was 1 to 1.
(5) The beginning balance in accounts receivable was $80,000; the accounts receivable turnover for Year 1 was 12.8 times. All sales were made on account. (Accounts receivable turnover = net sales ÷ average accounts receivable.)

Instructions Using only the information available, the accountant asks you to help complete the financial statements for the Southbay Corporation. Present supporting computations and explanations for all amounts appearing in the

balance sheet and the income statement. *Hint:* In completing the income statement, start with the net income figure (60% of income before income taxes) and
work up.

16-9 Certain financial information relating to two companies, London Conspiracy and
Coventry Clothiers, as of the end of the current year, is shown below. All figures
(except market price per share of stock) are in thousands of dollars.

Assets	*London Conspiracy*	*Coventry Clothiers*
Cash	$ 126.0	$ 180.0
Marketable securities, at cost	129.0	453.0
Accounts receivable, net	145.0	167.0
Inventories.............................	755.6	384.3
Prepaid expenses	24.4	15.7
Plant and equipment, net.................	1,680.0	1,570.0
Intangibles and other assets	140.0	30.0
Total assets	$3,000.0	$2,800.0

Liabilities & Stockholders' Equity		
Accounts payable	$ 344.6	$ 304.1
Accrued liabilities, including income taxes........	155.4	95.9
Bonds payable, 7%, due in 10 years	200.0	500.0
Capital stock ($10 par)...................	1,000.0	600.0
Capital in excess of par	450.0	750.0
Retained earnings	910.0	550.0
Treasury stock (1,000 shares, at cost)	(60.0)	–0–
Total liabilities & stockholders' equity	$3,000.0	$2,800.0

Analysis of retained earnings:		
Balance, beginning of year	$ 712.0	$ 430.0
Add: Net income.........................	297.0	240.0
Less: Dividends	(99.0)	(120.0)
Balance, end of year	$ 910.0	$ 550.0
Market price per share of stock, end of year	$50	$40

Instructions London Conspiracy and Coventry Clothiers are generally comparable in the nature of their operations, products, and accounting procedures
used. Write a short answer to each of the following questions, using whatever
analytical computations you feel will best support your answer. Show the amounts
used in calculating all ratios and percentages. Carry per-share computations to
the nearest cent and percentages one place beyond the decimal point, for
example, 9.8%.
a What is the book value per share of stock for each company?
b From the viewpoint of creditors, which company has a more conservative
capital structure? Determine the percentage of total assets financed by each
group.
c What is the price-earnings ratio and the dividend yield on the stock of each
company?
d Which company has a more liquid financial position?

BUSINESS DECISION PROBLEM 16

Condensed comparative financial statements for Pacific Corporation appear below:

PACIFIC CORPORATION
Comparative Balance Sheets
As of May 31
(in thousands of dollars)

Assets	Year 3	Year 2	Year 1
Current assets	$ 3,960	$ 2,610	$ 3,600
Plant and equipment (net of depreciation)	21,240	19,890	14,400
Total assets	$25,200	$22,500	$18,000

Liabilities & Stockholders' Equity	Year 3	Year 2	Year 1
Current liabilities	$ 2,214	$ 2,052	$ 1,800
Long-term liabilities	4,716	3,708	3,600
Capital stock ($10 par)	12,600	12,600	8,100
Retained earnings	5,670	4,140	4,500
Total liabilities & stockholders' equity	$25,200	$22,500	$18,000

PACIFIC CORPORATION
Comparative Income Statements
For Years Ended May 31
(in thousands of dollars)

	Year 3	Year 2	Year 1
Net sales.	$90,000	$75,000	$60,000
Cost of goods sold	58,500	46,500	36,000
Gross profit on sales	$31,500	$28,500	$24,000
Operating expenses	28,170	25,275	21,240
Income before income taxes	$ 3,330	$ 3,225	$ 2,760
Income taxes	1,530	1,500	1,260
Net income	$ 1,800	$ 1,725	$ 1,500
Cash dividends paid (plus 20% in stock in Year 2) . .	$270	$465	$405
Cash dividends per share	$0.63	$1.11	$1.50

Instructions
a Prepare a three-year comparative balance sheet in percentages rather than dollars, using Year 1 as the base year.
b Prepare common size comparative income statements for the three-year period, expressing all items as percentage components of net sales for each year.

c Comment on the significant trends and relationships revealed by the analytical computations in *a* and *b.* These comments should cover current assets and current liabilities, plant and equipment, capital stock, retained earnings, and dividends.

d If the capital stock of this company were selling at $11.50 per share, would you consider it to be overpriced, underpriced, or fairly priced? Consider such factors as book value per share, earnings per share, dividend yield, trend of sales, and trend of the gross profit percentage. Also consider the types of investors to whom the stock would be attractive or unattractive.

Income Taxes and Business Decisions

"A penny saved is a penny earned" according to an old saying credited to Benjamin Franklin. However, now that corporations (as well as some individuals) are subject to approximately a 50% income tax rate, we can modify this bit of folklore to read: "A dollar of income tax saved is worth two dollars of income earned."

In other words, about half of what a corporation earns, and half of what some individuals earn, must be paid to the federal government as income taxes. If advance tax planning will enable a corporation or an individual to save a dollar of income taxes, that dollar saved may be the equivalent of two dollars of before-tax earnings. Furthermore, there are a good many perfectly legal actions which can be taken to save or at least to postpone income taxes.

The critical importance of income taxes

Taxes levied by federal, state, and local governments are a significant part of the cost of operating a typical household, as well as a business enterprise. The knowledge required to be expert in taxation has made it a field of specialization among professional accountants. However, every manager who makes business decisions, and every individual who makes personal investments, urgently needs some knowledge of income taxes to be aware of the tax implications of these decisions. A general knowledge of income taxes will help any business manager or owner to benefit more fully from the advice of the professional tax accountant.

Some understanding of income taxes will also aid the individual citizen in voting intelligently, because a great many of the issues decided in every election have tax implications. Such issues as pollution, inflation, foreign policy, and employment are quite closely linked with income taxes. For example, the offering of special tax incentives to encourage businesses to launch massive programs to reduce pollution is one approach to protection of the environment.

In terms of revenue generated, the four most important kinds of taxes in the United States are *income taxes, sales taxes, property taxes,* and *excise taxes.* Income taxes probably exceed all others in terms of the amounts involved, and they also exert a pervasive influence on all types of business decisions. For this reason we shall limit our discussion to the basic federal income tax rules applicable to individuals, partnerships, and corporations.

Income taxes are usually determined from information contained in accounting records. The amount of income tax is computed by applying the appropriate tax rates (as set by federal, state, and some local governments) to *taxable income.* As explained more fully later in this chapter, *taxable income* is not necessarily the same as *accounting income* even though both are derived from the accounting records. Although taxes are involuntary and often unrelated to benefits received, some degree of control over the amount of tax is usually attainable. Business managers may legally alter the amount of taxes they pay by their choice of form of business organization, methods of financing, and alternative accounting methods. Thus income taxes are inevitably an important factor in arriving at business decisions.

The federal income tax: history and objectives

The present federal income tax dates from the passage of the Sixteenth Amendment to the Constitution in 1913.[1] This amendment, only 30 words in length,[2] removed all questions of the constitutionality of income taxes and paved the way for the more than 50 revenue acts passed by Congress since that date. In 1939 these tax laws were first combined into what is known as the Internal Revenue Code. The administration and enforcement of the tax laws are duties of the Treasury Department, operating through a division known as the Internal Revenue Service (IRS). The Treasury Department publishes its interpretation of the tax laws in Treasury regulations; the final word in interpretation lies with the federal courts.

Originally the purpose of the federal income tax was simply to obtain revenue for the government. And at first, the tax rates were quite low—by today's standards. In 1913 a married person with taxable income of $15,000 would have been subject to a tax rate of 1%, resulting in a tax liability of $150. Today, a married person with a $15,000 taxable income

---

[1] A federal income tax was proposed as early as 1815, and an income tax law was actually passed and income taxes collected during the Civil War. This law was upheld by the Supreme Court, but it was repealed when the need for revenue subsided after the war. In 1894 a new income tax law was passed, but the Supreme Court declared this law invalid on constitutional grounds.

[2] It reads: "The Congress shall have power to lay and collect taxes on incomes, from whatever source derived, without apportionment among the several States, and without regard to any census or enumeration."

(worth far less in purchasing power) would pay over $3,000 in federal income tax. The maximum federal income tax rate in 1913 was 7%. Today it is 70%.

The purpose of federal income tax today includes a number of goals in addition to raising revenue. Among these other goals are to combat inflation or deflation, to influence the rate of economic growth, to encourage full employment, to favor small businesses, and to redistribute national income on a more equal basis.

The effect of income taxes on business decisions

To minimize and to postpone income taxes are the goals of tax planning. Almost every business decision is a choice among alternative courses of action. For example, should we lease or buy business automobiles; should we obtain needed capital by issuing bonds or preferred stock; should we use straight-line depreciation or an accelerated method? Some of these alternatives will lead to much lower income taxes than others. Tax planning, therefore, means *determining in advance the income tax effect* of every proposed business action and then making business decisions which will lead to the smallest tax liability. Tax practice is an important element of the services furnished to clients by CPA firms. This service includes not only the computing of taxes and preparing of tax returns, but also tax planning.

Classes of taxpayers

In the eyes of the income tax law, there are four major classes of taxpayers: *individuals, corporations, estates,* and *trusts.* Proprietorships and partnerships are not taxed as business units; their income is taxed directly to the individual proprietor or partners, *whether or not actually withdrawn from the business.* A single proprietor reports his or her business income on an individual tax return; the members of a partnership include on their individual tax returns their respective shares of the partnership net income. An individual taxpayer's income tax return must include not only any business income from a proprietorship or partnership, but also any salary or other income and any deductions affecting the tax liability. A partnership must file an *information return* showing the computation of total partnership net income and the allocation of this income to each partner.

A corporation is a separate taxable entity; it must file an income tax return and pay a tax on its annual taxable income. In addition, individual stockholders must report dividends received as part of their personal taxable income. The taxing of corporate dividends has led to the charge that there is "double taxation" of corporate income—once to the corporation and again when it is distributed to stockholders.

The *income before taxes* earned by a corporation may be subject to a federal corporate income tax rate of 48%. If the 52 cents remaining after taxes is distributed as dividends to individual stockholders, it is taxed to them personally at rates varying from 14 to 70%, depending on their individual tax brackets. Thus, the 52 cents of after-tax income to the corporation could be reduced by 70%, or 36 cents of individual income tax, leaving 16 cents of the original dollar for the shareholder. In summary, *federal income taxes can take as much as 84 cents out of a dollar earned by a corporation and distributed as a dividend to a shareholder.* The remaining 16 cents could be further reduced by state income taxes.

Special and complex rules apply to the determination of taxable income for estates and trusts. These rules will not be discussed in this chapter.

Cash basis of accounting for individual tax returns

Almost all individual tax returns are prepared on the cash basis of measuring income. Revenue is recognized when collected; expenses are recognized when paid. The cash basis is advantageous for the individual taxpayer for several reasons. The income of most individuals comes in the form of salaries, interest, and dividends. At the end of each year, employers are required to inform each employee and the IRS of the salary earned and the income tax withheld during the year. This report (a W-2 form) must be prepared on the cash basis without any accrual of unpaid wages. Companies paying interest and dividends also are required to use the cash basis in reporting the amounts paid during the year. Thus, most individuals are provided with reports prepared on a cash basis for use in preparing their individual tax returns.

The cash basis has other advantages for the individual taxpayer and for many professional firms and service-type businesses. It is simple, requires a minimum of record keeping, and often permits tax saving by shifting the timing of revenue and expense transactions from one year to another. For example, a dentist whose taxable income is higher than usual in the current year may decide in December to delay billing patients until January 1, and thus postpone the receipt of gross income to the next year. The timing of expense payments near the year-end is also controllable by a taxpayer using the cash basis. A taxpayer who has received a bill for a deductible expense item in December may choose to pay it before or after December 31 and thereby influence the amount of taxable income in each year. Further comparison of the cash basis with the accrual basis of income measurement is presented later in this chapter.

Tax rates

All taxes may be characterized as progressive, proportional, or regressive with respect to any given base. A *progressive* tax becomes a larger portion of the base as that base increases. Federal income taxes are *progressive* with respect to income, since a higher tax *rate* applies as the amount of taxable income increases. A *proportional* tax remains a constant percentage of the base no matter how that base changes. For example, a 6% sales tax remains a constant percentage of sales regardless of changes in the dollar amount of sales. A *regressive* tax becomes a smaller percentage of the base as the base increases. Regressive taxes, however, are extremely rare.

Tax rate schedules

Tax rates for individuals at present vary from 14 to 70%, depending on the amount of income. Persons with very low incomes pay no income tax. Different tax rate schedules apply to (1) single taxpayers, (2) married

Single Taxpayers			
Taxable Income		**Tax**	
Not over $2,200		-0-	
Over—	**But not over—**		**of the amount over—**
$2,200	$2,700	14%	$2,200
$2,700	$3,200	$70+15%	$2,700
$3,200	$3,700	$145+16%	$3,200
$3,700	$4,200	$225+17%	$3,700
$4,200	$6,200	$310+19%	$4,200
$6,200	$8,200	$690+21%	$6,200
$8,200	$10,200	$1,110+24%	$8,200
$10,200	$12,200	$1,590+25%	$10,200
$12,200	$14,200	$2,090+27%	$12,200
$14,200	$16,200	$2,630+29%	$14,200
$16,200	$18,200	$3,210+31%	$16,200
$18,200	$20,200	$3,830+34%	$18,200
$20,200	$22,200	$4,510+36%	$20,200
$22,200	$24,200	$5,230+38%	$22,200
$24,200	$28,200	$5,990+40%	$24,200
$28,200	$34,200	$7,590+45%	$28,200
$34,200	$40,200	$10,290+50%	$34,200
$40,200	$46,200	$13,290+55%	$40,200
$46,200	$52,200	$16,590+60%	$46,200
$52,200	$62,200	$20,190+62%	$52,200
$62,200	$72,200	$26,390+64%	$62,200
$72,200	$82,200	$32,790+66%	$72,200
$82,200	$92,200	$39,390+68%	$82,200
$92,200	$102,200	$46,190+69%	$92,200
$102,200	. . . . . .	$53,090+70%	$102,200

Example: Find the tax for a single person having taxable income of $21,000.

Answer: Tax on $20,200 as shown on tax rate schedule $4,510

Tax on $800 excess at 36% 288

Tax on $21,000 for a single person $4,798

taxpayers filing joint returns, (*3*) married taxpayers filing separate returns, and (*4*) single taxpayers who qualify as the head of a household. In computing the amount of the tax, the tax rates are applied to **taxable income,** a term which means gross income less certain exclusions and deductions specified in the tax law. The rate schedules on page 684 and below show the personal income tax rates for single taxpayers and for married taxpayers filing joint returns. These rates are subject to frequent revision by Congress; in fact, a revision was under consideration by Congress at the time this was written.

Married Taxpayers Filing Joint Returns			
Taxable Income		*Tax*	
Not over $3,200		*–0–*	
Over—	*But not over—*		*of the amount over—*
$3,200	*$4,200*	*14%*	*$3,200*
$4,200	*$5,200*	*$140+15%*	*$4,200*
$5,200	*$6,200*	*$290+16%*	*$5,200*
$6,200	*$7,200*	*$450+17%*	*$6,200*
$7,200	*$11,200*	*$620+19%*	*$7,200*
$11,200	*$15,200*	*$1,380+22%*	*$11,200*
$15,200	*$19,200*	*$2,260+25%*	*$15,200*
$19,200	*$23,200*	*$3,260+28%*	*$19,200*
$23,200	*$27,200*	*$4,380+32%*	*$23,200*
$27,200	*$31,200*	*$5,660+36%*	*$27,200*
$31,200	*$35,200*	*$7,100+39%*	*$31,200*
$35,200	*$39,200*	*$8,660+42%*	*$35,200*
$39,200	*$43,200*	*$10,340+45%*	*$39,200*
$43,200	*$47,200*	*$12,140+48%*	*$43,200*
$47,200	*$55,200*	*$14,060+50%*	*$47,200*
$55,200	*$67,200*	*$18,060+53%*	*$55,200*
$67,200	*$79,200*	*$24,420+55%*	*$67,200*
$79,200	*$91,200*	*$31,020+58%*	*$79,200*
$91,200	*$103,200*	*$37,980+60%*	*$91,200*
$103,200	*$123,200*	*$45,180+62%*	*$103,200*
$123,200	*$143,200*	*$57,580+64%*	*$123,200*
$143,200	*$163,200*	*$70,380+66%*	*$143,200*
$163,200	*$183,200*	*$83,580+68%*	*$163,200*
$183,200	*$203,200*	*$97,180+69%*	*$183,200*
$203,200	. . . . . .	*$110,980+70%*	*$203,200*

Example: Find the tax for a married couple filing a joint return and having a taxable income of $45,000.

Answer: Tax on $43,200 as shown on tax rate schedule $12,140

Tax on $1,800 excess at 48% 864

Tax on $45,000 for a married couple filing a joint return $13,004

The steeply progressive nature of income taxes

To illustrate the steeply progressive nature of income taxes, let us compare two single taxpayers, one of whom has a relatively low income and the other a relatively high income. Assume that Tom Jones has taxable income of $4,000 a year and Mary Smith has taxable income of $40,000 a year. According to the tax rate schedules, Jones would owe tax of $276 and Smith would owe tax of $13,190. The tax owed by Jones is 7% of his total taxable income of $4,000; the tax owed by Smith is 33% of her total taxable income of $40,000.

Next, let us consider how much additional income tax each of these two individuals would have to pay on any additional income. According to the Tax Rate Schedules, an increase of $100 in income for Jones would be taxed at 17%. However, an increase of $100 in income for Smith would be taxed at 50%. (For the sake of simplicity in this example, we have assumed that both taxpayers use the tax rate schedule. In practice, Jones would use the tax table discussed later in this chapter.)

Notice that different and lower tax rates are applicable to the taxable income of married taxpayers who combine their income and deductions on a *joint return.* The schedules for married taxpayers filing separate returns and for heads of households are not shown in this chapter.

Marginal tax rates compared with average tax rates

In any analysis of income taxes, it is important to distinguish the *marginal* rate of tax from the *average* rate. If a single person has a taxable income of $28,200, his or her income tax will be $7,590, an average tax rate of about 27% of taxable income. On the next dollar of income, however, the tax is 45 cents because the individual is subject to a marginal tax rate of 45% on income over $28,200.

Assume that you are an unmarried executive with a taxable income of $28,200 and are considering a change to a new job that pays $6,000 more per year in salary. Using the tax rate schedules illustrated, your present tax is $7,590, but your marginal tax rate on the proposed $6,000 increase is 45%. Your decision with respect to the new job may well be affected by the fact that you would be able to keep only slightly more than half ($3,300) of the $6,000 increase in salary. Assume further that you live in a state with a relatively high state income tax. California, for example, has an income tax rate of 11% on income above $15,500 earned by a single person. Thus, you would be able to keep less than half of the proposed salary increase of $6,000.

Another way of looking at the impact of income taxes is from the viewpoint of the employer. A company that wants to increase the salary of an executive must pay about $2 for every $1 to be received by the executive in take-home pay.

Maximum tax on personal service income (earned income)

The maximum federal tax on *personal service income (earned income)* is limited to 50%. Wages, salaries, and other compensation for personal services are defined as earned income. For example, a single person with an earned income of $102,200 is subject to a marginal tax rate of 50%. However, an individual who received this same amount of income from dividends or interest on investments would be subject to a marginal tax rate of 70%.

Income taxes and inflation

As salaries and prices in general have risen sharply in recent years, people find themselves in higher income tax brackets even though their higher salaries represent no increase in purchasing power. Because income tax rates are steeply progressive, this means that many people must pay a *higher percentage* of their earnings as income taxes merely as a result of inflation. Thus, income taxes are actually being increased in each year of inflation even though the schedule of tax rates remains unchanged. A $20,000 salary may buy no more today than a $10,000 salary some years ago, but a $20,000 salary is taxed at a much higher rate.

Income tax formula for individuals

The federal government supplies standard income tax forms on which taxpayers are guided to a proper computation of their taxable income and the amount of the tax. It is helpful to visualize the computation in terms of an income tax formula. The general formula for the determination of taxable income for all taxpayers (other than corporations, estates, and trusts) is outlined on page 689.

The actual sequence and presentation of material on income tax forms differs somewhat from the arrangement in this formula. However, it is easier to understand the structure and logic of the federal income tax and to analyze tax rules and their effect by referring to the tax formula.

Total income and gross income

Total income is an accounting concept; gross income is a tax concept. *Total income* includes, in the words of the law, "all income from whatever source derived." To determine whether an amount received by an individual taxpayer should be included in total income, one need only ask, "Is it income or is it a return of capital?"

Gross income for tax purposes is all income not excluded by law. To determine whether any given income item is included in taxable gross income, one must ask, "Is there a provision in the tax law excluding this item of income from gross income?" Among the items of miscellaneous income which must be included in gross income are prizes and awards won, tips received, and gains from sale of personal property. The fact that income arises from an illegal transaction does not keep it from being taxable. To identify exclusions from gross income, it is necessary to refer to the tax law and sometimes to Treasury regulations and court decisions.

Among the items presently *excluded from gross income* by statute are interest on state and municipal bonds, gifts and inheritances, life insurance proceeds, workmen's compensation and sick pay, social security benefits and the portion of receipts from annuities that represents return of cost, pensions to veterans, compensation for damages, and the first $100 of dividends from corporations ($200 on a joint tax return).

Deductions to arrive at adjusted gross income

The deductions from *gross income* allowed in computing *adjusted gross income* are discussed below:

1 *Business expenses of a single proprietorship.* These include all ordinary and necessary expenses of carrying on a trade, business, or profession (other than as an employee). For the actual tax computation, business expenses are deducted from business revenue, and net business income is then included in adjusted gross income.

2 *Business expenses of an employee.* Some expenses incurred by employees in connection with their employment are allowed as a deduction if the employees are not reimbursed by the employer. These include, for example, travel and transportation as part of employees' duties, expenses of "outside salespersons," and certain moving expenses. The costs of commuting from home to work are not deductible.

3 *Expenses attributable to rental properties.* The owner of rental property, such as an apartment building, incurs a variety of operating expenses. Depreciation, property taxes, repairs, maintenance, interest on indebtedness related to property, and any other expense incurred in connection with the earning of rental income are allowed as a deduction. This means that only the *net income* derived from rental property is included in adjusted gross income.

4 *Losses from the sale of property used in business.* The loss resulting from the sale of property used in a trade or business may be deducted against other items of gross income.[3]

5 *Net capital losses.* Up to $3,000 of net capital losses may be deducted to arrive at adjusted gross income. Capital gains and losses are discussed on pages 692 to 694.

6 *Long-term capital gain deduction.* One-half of the excess of net long-term capital gains over net short-term capital losses is a deduction to arrive at adjusted gross income. In other words, only one-half of a long-term capital gain is taxable.

7 *Net operating loss carry-over.* Taxable income may be either positive or negative. If positive income were taxed and no allowance made for operating losses, a taxpayer whose business income fluctuated between income and loss would pay a relatively higher tax than one having a steady income averaging the same amount. Therefore, the tax law allows the carry-back and carry-over

---

[3] Losses arising from the sale of personal property, such as a home or personal automobile, are not deductible. On the other hand, gains from the sale of personal property are taxable. This appears inconsistent, until one realizes that a loss on the sale of personal property usually reflects depreciation through use, which is a personal expense.

General Federal Income Tax Formula for Individuals

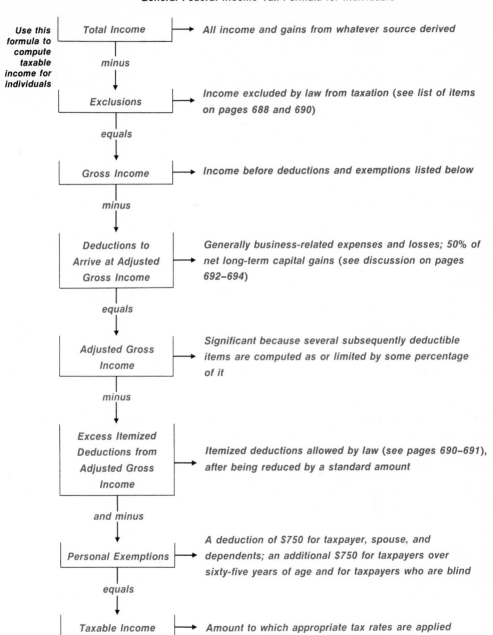

Use this formula to compute taxable income for individuals

Total Income	All income and gains from whatever source derived
minus	
Exclusions	Income excluded by law from taxation (*see list of items on pages 688 and 690*)
equals	
Gross Income	Income before deductions and exemptions listed below
minus	
Deductions to Arrive at Adjusted Gross Income	Generally business-related expenses and losses; 50% of net long-term capital gains (*see discussion on pages 692–694*)
equals	
Adjusted Gross Income	Significant because several subsequently deductible items are computed as or limited by some percentage of it
minus	
Excess Itemized Deductions from Adjusted Gross Income	Itemized deductions allowed by law (*see pages 690–691*), after being reduced by a standard amount
and minus	
Personal Exemptions	A deduction of $750 for taxpayer, spouse, and dependents; an additional $750 for taxpayers over sixty-five years of age and for taxpayers who are blind
equals	
Taxable Income	Amount to which appropriate tax rates are applied

of net operating losses as an offset against the income of other years. At the present time a loss may be carried back against the income of the three preceding years, and then forward against the income of the next seven years.

8 Contributions to retirement plans. Individuals who are self-employed are permitted to deduct from gross income the amounts they contribute to a retirement plan. The present limit on such contributions is the lower of $7,500 or 15% of the self-employed person's annual earnings. By taking a deduction for this contribution, a self-employed person earning $50,000 or more can reduce adjusted gross income by as much as $7,500 each year. The amounts contributed plus earnings on the fund are taxable when the taxpayer retires and begins making withdrawals from the fund. This type of retirement plan (often referred to as a *Keogh H.R.10 plan*) is intended to provide self-employed persons with opportunities similar to those of persons employed by organizations with well-defined pension or retirement plans.

Another type of retirement plan (distinct from the Keogh H.R.10 plan) is designed for employees who are not covered by a pension plan by the employing organization. This plan, called an *individual retirement arrangement (IRA)* permits an employee to contribute to the plan and to deduct from gross income 15% of compensation received, but not more than $1,500 a year.

Deductions from adjusted gross income (itemized deductions)

Remember that there are two basic groups of deductions for individuals: (1) items deductible from gross income to arrive at adjusted gross income and (2) items deductible from adjusted gross income to arrive at taxable income. We are now considering the second group of items (such as charitable contributions, interest on home mortgage, and personal taxes) which an individual may deduct *from* adjusted gross income. These items are referred to as *itemized deductions.*

The importance of itemizing deductions lies in the fact that every deduction reduces the income subject to tax. The taxpayer should retain documentary evidence supporting the deductions claimed.

ZERO BRACKET AMOUNT Prior to 1977, taxpayers were entitled to take a standard deduction computed as a percentage of adjusted gross income. As an alternative, taxpayers could itemize their deductions. Effective in 1977, however, the tax laws provided a new *zero bracket amount,* which replaced the standard deduction. This zero bracket amount was built into the tax tables in order to simplify the computation of tax liability. The result is to assure a given amount of tax-free income to all taxpayers. Presently, the zero bracket amount is $3,200 for married taxpayers filing a joint return, and $2,200 for single taxpayers.

EXCESS ITEMIZED DEDUCTIONS We have seen that the zero bracket amount is the equivalent of a standard deduction from adjusted gross income. The amount of income subject to tax can be reduced further by single taxpayers who itemize deductions in excess of $2,200 and by married taxpayers filing a joint return who itemize deductions in excess of

$3,200. In other words, a reduction in tax is possible if a taxpayer has relatively large amounts of such items as contributions, interest, and property taxes, and the combined amount of these itemized deductions is in excess of the zero bracket amount. The term *excess itemized deductions* means the excess of itemized deductions over the zero bracket amount.

The major categories of itemized deductions allowable under the law are described below:

1 *Interest.*   Interest on any indebtedness, within certain limits.

2 *Taxes.*   State and local real and personal property taxes; state income taxes, all sales taxes, and state and local gasoline taxes are deductible by the person on whom they are imposed. No federal taxes qualify as itemized deductions.

3 *Contributions.*   Contributions by individuals to charitable, religious, educational, and certain other nonprofit organizations are deductible, within certain limits. Gifts to friends, relatives, or other persons are not deductible.

4 *Medical expenses.*   Medical and dental expenses of the taxpayer and his or her family are deductible to the extent that they exceed 3% of adjusted gross income, subject to certain maximum limits, and limits on the deductibility of drugs and medicines. A taxpayer may deduct one-half of medical insurance costs up to $150 without regard to the 3% exclusion.

5 *Casualty losses.*   Losses in excess of $100 from any fire, storm, earthquake, shipwreck, theft, or other sudden, unexpected, or unusual causes are deductible.

6 *Expenses related to the production of income.*   In this category are included any necessary expenses in producing income or for the management of income-producing property, other than those deductible to arrive at adjusted gross income. Some examples of *miscellaneous deductible expenses* are union dues, work clothes, professional dues, subscriptions to professional periodicals, investment advisers' fees, legal fees relating to investments, fees paid to employment agencies to get a job, and fees for income tax advice and for preparation of tax returns. Examples of *miscellaneous nondeductible expenses* are the cost of going to and from work, gifts to needy friends, most living expenses, baby-sitting expenses, the cost of school tuition, and gambling losses in excess of gambling winnings.

Personal exemptions

In addition to itemized deductions, a deduction from adjusted gross income is allowed for *personal exemptions.* One exemption each is allowed for the taxpayer, his spouse, and each person who qualifies as a dependent of the taxpayer. Recently the amount of each personal exemption has been $750. The amount of the personal exemption may be changed by Congress at any time. Proposals for an increase to $1,000 or more have been much discussed in recent years.

The term *dependent* has a particular meaning under law. Briefly but incompletely stated, a dependent is a person who (*1*) receives over one-half of his or her support from the taxpayer, (*2*) is either closely related to the taxpayer or lives in the taxpayer's home, and (*3*) has gross income during the year of less than the current exemption amount unless he or she is a child of the taxpayer and is under nineteen years of age or is a full-time student.[4] A taxpayer and spouse may each claim an additional personal exemption if sixty-five years of age or over, and another exemption if blind. These additional exemptions do not apply to dependents.

Taxpayers who use the tax tables must determine the **number** of personal exemptions to which they are entitled in order to select the appropriate column in the tax tables. However they do not use the $750 deduction **amount,** because these amounts have been taken into account in constructing the tax tables. The personal exemption, unlike itemized deductions, does not require any record keeping as supporting evidence.

Taxable income

We have now traced the steps required to determine the taxable income of an individual. In brief, this process includes (*1*) computation of total income, (*2*) exclusion of certain items specified by law to determine gross income, (*3*) deduction of business-related expenses to arrive at adjusted gross income, and (*4*) deduction of excess itemized deductions and personal exemptions to arrive at the key figure of taxable income. The concept of taxable income is most important because it is the amount to which the appropriate tax rate is applied to determine the tax liability.

Capital gains and losses

Certain kinds of property are defined under the tax law as capital assets.[5] The most common types of capital assets owned by individuals are securities and real estate. Gains and losses from the sale of such assets are granted special treatment for income tax purposes. Because long-term capital gains generally are taxed at **less** than the rates applicable to **ordinary income,** there is a strong incentive for taxpayers to invest in equities that offer possible capital gains.

The rationale underlying special treatment of capital gains is to strengthen the economy by encouraging investment in equities by individuals and by business concerns. If our future economy is to be strong and healthy, investment capital must flow into new growth industries. New growth industries do not offer investors assured low-risk income, but do offer the possibility of capital appreciation. Our tax laws can provide an incentive for risk-taking by investors, if capital gains are taxed at much lower rates than low-risk income such as interest on bonds and insured bank deposits.

[4] A child under nineteen or a full-time student who qualifies as a dependent in all other respects but who earns over the current exemption amount in any one year has, in effect, two personal exemptions. One may be taken by the taxpayer who claims him or her as a dependent; the other he will claim for himself on his own personal income tax return.

[5] Capital assets are defined by exclusion. The Internal Revenue Code states that capital assets include all items of property *except* (a) trade accounts and notes receivable; (b) inventories in a trade or business; (c) real or depreciable property in a trade or business; (d) copyrights, literary, musical, or artistic compositions in the hands of their creator; (e) letters or similar property in the hands of original recipient; (f) government obligations issued on a discount basis and due within one year without interest.

AMOUNT OF GAIN OR LOSS The tax gain (or loss) from the sale or exchange of capital assets is the difference between the selling price and the *basis* of property sold. Basis rules are complicated; tax basis depends, among other things, on how the property was acquired (purchase, gift, or inheritance), whether it is personal or business property, and in some cases whether it is sold at a gain or at a loss. In general, the basis of purchased property is its cost, reduced by any depreciation that has been allowed in computing taxable income.

LONG TERM VERSUS SHORT TERM Long and short are relative terms: in income taxation the dividing line was traditionally six months but was changed to nine months for the year 1977 and to one year in 1978 and thereafter. Long-term capital gains or losses result from the sale or exchange of capital assets held *for more than* one year; short-term capital gains and losses result from those held one year or less.

The term *net short-term gain* means short-term gains in excess of short-term losses. Net short-term gains must be reported in full and are taxed as ordinary income. Only one-half of long-term gains, reduced by any net short-term losses, are included in adjusted gross income, and the maximum rate of tax on the *total* gain is generally 25% of gains up to $50,000.[6] For example, suppose that Bob Savage, a taxpayer subject to a marginal tax rate of 30%, has a $1,000 net long-term capital gain and no net short-term capital loss. Savage would include only $500 in adjusted gross income and pay a $150 (30% of $500) tax on the gain. The tax rate applicable to the $1,000 long-term gain is 15%, one-half of Savage's marginal rate.

On the other hand, suppose that the same taxpayer has a marginal tax rate of 70%. If he were to include $500 (one-half of the $1,000 net long-term gain) in adjusted gross income and apply the 70% marginal rate, the tax would be $350, or 35% of the total $1,000 net long-term gain. Instead, he would be entitled to compute the tax on the long-term capital gain at $250 (25% of $1,000). In this case the rate of tax applicable to the long-term capital gain would be *less* than one-half of the taxpayer's marginal rate of tax on other income.

LIMITED DEDUCTIBILITY OF CAPITAL LOSSES In general, capital *losses,* either long-term or short-term, are deductible only against capital gains. If total capital losses exceed gains, however, individual taxpayers (but not corporations) may deduct capital losses against other gross income up to a maximum of $3,000 a year. For example, if an individual incurred a capital loss of $100,000 but also had a salary of $50,000, he or she would have gross income subject to taxation of $47,000. The unused capital loss could be carried forward and offset against capital gains, if any, in future years, or against other income at the rate of $3,000 a year. Thus, a great

---

[6] The effective maximum tax on net long-term gains in excess of $50,000 may be 35% or more for taxpayers in the highest tax bracket.

many years would be required to offset the $100,000 capital loss against other income.

Critics of our present tax laws point out that persons who save and invest are taxed in a similar manner to those who gamble on horse races. (Gambling gains are taxable; gambling losses cannot be offset against other income.) Similarly, gains from investment are taxed heavily and losses from investments are generally not permitted as deductions if they exceed gains. This policy may be inconsistent with the national goal of encouraging investment. Although the United States formerly had world-wide recognition for its high productivity, the ratio of capital investment to gross national product has now fallen far below many other nations. The tax laws of some other countries are more conducive to investment, for example, no tax on capital gains.

Only 50% of a net long-term capital loss can be used in arriving at the maximum which can be offset against other income in a single year. In other words, a net long-term capital loss of $4,000 would be required to entitle the taxpayer to take a $2,000 deduction. Although capital losses not deductible in any given year may be carried forward to future tax years, it is apparent that a large capital loss as in the preceding example probably will not be utilized fully in future years unless the taxpayer is fortunate enough to have a large capital gain.

BUSINESS PLANT AND EQUIPMENT Buildings, machinery, and other depreciable property used in a trade or business are not capital assets under the tax law. This means that a net loss realized on the sale or disposal of such business property is fully deductible. However, gains on such property held more than one year may be granted capital gains treatment under certain complex conditions. That portion of any gain resulting from reduction of an asset's basis through depreciation is taxable as ordinary income. This rule (called "recapture of depreciation") stems from the fact that depreciation offsets income taxed at ordinary rates. If the provision for recapture of depreciation did not exist, taxpayers would have a motivation to reduce ordinary income by depreciating assets as rapidly as possible and selling them at a gain taxable at less than the rates applicable to ordinary income. Gains on the sale of assets used in business and held one year or less are taxable as ordinary income.

Tax tables

Beginning in 1977 the *tax rate schedules* shown on pages 684–685 were used by all single taxpayers with incomes in excess of $20,000 and all married taxpayers with income in excess of $40,000. Most taxpayers with incomes below these levels were required to compute their taxes by using the *tax tables* shown on page 695. Our interest is in the basic concepts of the income tax structure rather than in the mechanics of filling out tax returns; consequently, only small portions of these very lengthy tax tables are illustrated.

Tax Table for Single Persons

(The $2,200 zero bracket amount for single persons and the personal exemptions have been built into these tables. Consequently, a separate deduction is not to be taken for them.)

If line 34, Form 1040 is—		And the total number of exemptions claimed on line 7 is—		
Over	But not over	1	2	3
		Your tax is—		
If $3,200 or less your tax is 0				
3,200	3,250	4	0	0
3,250	3,300	11	0	0
3,300	3,350	18	0	0
3,350	3,400	25	0	0
10,000	10,050	1,227	1,062	909
10,050	10,100	1,238	1,073	919
10,100	10,150	1,249	1,084	928
10,150	10,200	1,260	1,095	938
19,800	19,850	3,948	3,693	3,456
19,850	19,900	3,965	3,710	3,472
19,900	19,950	3,982	3,727	3,487
19,950	20,000	3,999	3,744	3,503

Tax Tables for Married Persons Filing Jointly

(The $3,200 zero bracket amount for married persons filing joint returns and the personal exemptions have been built into these tables. Consequently, a separate deduction is not to be taken for them.)

If line 34, Form 1040 is—		And the total number of exemptions claimed on line 7 is							
Over	But not over	2	3	4	5	6	7	8	9
		Your tax is—							
If $5,200 or less your tax is 0									
5,200	5,250	4	0	0	0	0	0	0	0
5,250	5,300	11	0	0	0	0	0	0	0
5,300	5,350	18	0	0	0	0	0	0	0
5,350	5,400	25	0	0	0	0	0	0	0
10,000	10,050	765	624	450	288	132	0	0	0
10,050	10,100	774	634	459	296	140	0	0	0
10,100	10,150	782	643	467	305	148	0	0	0
10,150	10,200	791	653	476	313	156	4	0	0
39,800	39,850	9,793	9,478	9,163	8,848	8,503	8,171	7,844	7,516
39,850	39,900	9,814	9,499	9,184	8,869	8,524	8,191	7,863	7,536
39,900	39,950	9,835	9,520	9,205	8,890	8,545	8,210	7,883	7,555
39,950	40,000	9,856	9,541	9,226	8,911	8,566	8,230	7,902	7,575

Tax credits

Tax credits differ from deductions. As previously explained, a deduction (such as charitable contributions) reduces the tax liability indirectly because it is subtracted from adjusted gross income and thus leads to a smaller amount of taxable income. A tax credit, however, is **subtracted directly from the tax owed.** Applying tax credits against the tax due is one of the concluding steps in preparation of the tax return.

One of the most important tax credits is the **investment credit** arising from purchase of certain depreciable business property. The investment credit is an example of efforts to provide tax incentives as a means of stimulating business investment and thus increasing the level of economic activity. When a business buys certain types of new long-lived equipment, such as office equipment or machinery, it can take a credit of 10% of the cost of the property as a deduction from the income tax for the year. The use of an investment credit does not affect the depreciation of the asset.

Among other types of tax credits currently available are the new jobs credit, the credit for wages paid in work incentive programs, foreign tax credit, credit for the elderly, credit for political contributions, and credit for child and dependent care expenses. Many restrictions limit the use of these credits to reduce income taxes.

Quarterly payments of estimated tax

For self-employed persons such as doctors, dentists, and owners of small businesses, there is of course no salary and no withholding. Other examples of income on which no withholding occurs are rental income, dividends, and interest received. To equalize the treatment of employees and self-employed persons, the tax law requires persons who have taxable income in excess of a given amount, from which no withholding has been made, to file a **declaration of estimated tax** and to pay estimated income taxes in quarterly installments. Any underpayment or overpayment is adjusted when the tax return is filed.

A declaration of estimated tax is a statement which a taxpayer having income not subject to withholding must file with the IRS by April 15 each year. The declaration shows the taxable income expected for the current year and the quarterly payments of estimated tax to be made. The first of the quarterly payments must accompany the declaration.

Although salaried employees are subject to withholding, many have other income such as dividends which are not subject to withholding. These persons must therefore file a declaration of estimated tax and make quarterly payments if the income not subject to withholding is substantial.

Tax returns, tax refunds, and payment of the tax

Whether you must file a tax return depends upon the amount of your income and your filing status. At present, a single person with income of

$2,950 or more (the personal exemption plus the zero bracket amount) must file a return. A married couple filing jointly and having income of $4,700 or more must file. However, for a self-employed person, net earnings from self-employment of as little as $400 impose a requirement to file a return. These dollar limits, along with tax rates, are likely to be changed from year to year. The return must be filed within $3\frac{1}{2}$ months after the close of the taxable year. Most taxpayers are on a calendar-year basis; therefore, the deadline for filing is April 15.

WITHHOLDING MAKES THE SYSTEM WORK The payment of federal income taxes is on a "pay as you go" basis. The procedure by which employers withhold income taxes from the salaries of employees has been discussed previously in Chapter 13. Without the withholding feature, the present income tax system would probably be unworkable. The high rate of income taxes would pose an impossible collection problem if employees received their total earnings in cash and were later called upon at the end of the year to pay the government a major portion of a year's salary.

The amounts withheld from an employee's salary for income tax can be considered as payments on account. If the amount of income tax as computed by preparing a tax return at the end of the year is less than the amount withheld during the year, the taxpayer is entitled to a refund. On the other hand, if the tax as computed at year-end is more than the amount withheld, the balance must be paid with the tax return. Persons who are entitled to a refund because withholdings or payments of estimated tax exceed the tax liability as computed at year-end will of course file a tax return to obtain a refund, even though they might not have sufficient income to make the filing of a tax return compulsory.

Computation of individual income tax illustrated

The computation of the federal income tax for Mary and John Reed is illustrated on page 698.

In this example it is assumed that the Reeds provide over one-half the support of their two children. John Reed is a practicing attorney who received $59,000 in gross fees from his law practice and incurred $30,000 of business expenses. Mary Reed earned $24,400 during the year as a CPA working for a national firm of accountants. During the year, $4,000 was withheld from her salary for federal income taxes. Just before the end of the year, John Reed contributed $3,000 to a Keogh H.R.10 retirement plan. The Reeds received $700 interest on municipal bonds, and $320 on savings accounts. Dividends received on stock jointly owned amounted to $25,800. During the year stock purchased several years ago by John Reed for $1,600 was sold for $2,400, net of brokerage fees, thus producing an $800 long-term capital gain.

The Reeds have total itemized deductions (contributions, interest expense, taxes, medical costs, etc.) of $11,920. They paid a total of $16,000 on their declaration of estimated tax during the year. John Reed is entitled to an investment credit of $1,000 on $10,000 worth of office equipment purchased during the year.

On the basis of these facts, the taxable income for the Reeds is shown to be $65,000. Since they file a joint return, the tax on this amount of taxable income may be computed from the tax rate schedules for married couples filing jointly and is $23,254. This tax is reduced by the $1,000 investment credit, producing a tax liability of $22,254. Taking withholdings and payments on declared estimated tax into account, the Reeds have already paid income taxes of $20,000 and thus owe $2,254 at the time of filing their tax return.

MARY AND JOHN REED

Illustrative Federal Income Tax Computation

For the Year 19___

Gross income (excluding $700 interest on municipal bonds):			
Gross fees from John Reed's law practice	$59,000		
Less: Expenses incurred in law practice	30,000	$29,000	
Salary received by Mary Reed		24,400	
Dividends ($25,800 less $200 exclusion)		25,600	
Interest earned on savings account		320	
Long-term capital gain on stock held over one year		800	$80,120
Deductions to arrive at adjusted gross income:			
Long-term capital gain deduction (50% of $800)		$ 400	
Deduction for John Reed's contribution to a (Keogh H.R.10)			
retirement plan		3,000	3,400
Adjusted gross income			$76,720
Deductions from adjusted gross income:			
Excess itemized deductions (itemized deductions			
minus $3,200)		$ 8,720	
Personal exemptions (4 × $750)		3,000	11,720
Taxable income			$65,000
Computation of tax (using tax rate schedule on page 685)			
Tax on $55,200 (joint return)		$18,060	
Tax on $9,800 at 53%		5,194	$23,254
Less: Investment tax credit (10% of $10,000)			1,000
Total tax			$22,254
Less: Advance payments and amounts withheld:			
Payments by Reeds on declaration of estimated tax		$16,000	
Tax withheld from Mary Reed's salary		4,000	20,000
Amount of tax remaining to be paid with return			$ 2,254

Partnerships

A partnership was defined in Chapter 7 as an association of two or more persons to carry on as co-owners a business for profit. This concept of a partnership is also applicable for tax purposes. A partner's contribution to the firm may consist of cash or other assets, personal services, or both. Partnerships are not considered taxable entities by income tax statutes. Under the federal income tax law, partnerships are treated as a conduit through which taxable income flows to the partners. Although a partnership pays no income tax, it must file an *information return* showing the computation of net income or loss and the share of net income or loss allocable to each partner. The partners must include on their personal tax returns their respective shares of the net income or loss of the partnership.

Certain items of partnership income and deductions are segregated, and all partners are required to treat their respective shares of these items as if they had received or paid them personally. In general, these segregated items are those granted special tax treatment; they include tax-exempt interest, capital gains and losses, charitable contributions, and cash dividends received.

In certain types of business (motion pictures, oil and gas exploration, leasing, and farming), special rules apply when a partnership operates at a loss. The amount of the partnership loss which partners can deduct on their personal returns cannot exceed the amount which partners have placed *at risk* by investment in the partnership business. These "at risk" rules are intended to prevent partnerships from being used as tax-avoidance devices.

Taxation of corporations

A corporation is a separate taxable entity. Our discussion is focused on the general business corporation and does not cover certain other types of corporations for which special tax treatment applies. Every corporation, unless specifically exempt from taxation, must file an income tax return whether or not it has taxable income or owes any tax.

The earning of taxable income inevitably creates a liability to pay income taxes. This liability and the related charge to expense must be entered in the accounting records before financial statements are prepared. The following journal entry is typical.

Income Taxes Expense *60,000*
    Income Taxes Payable *60,000*
To record income taxes for the current period.

Corporation tax rates

The corporation tax rate schedule is much simpler than the schedule for individuals. Corporations are subject to a *normal* tax on all their taxable income and a *surtax* on taxable income above $50,000. The rates in effect at the time this was written are shown below. These rates are subject to frequent change by Congress.

Normal tax on first $25,000 of taxable income	*20%*
Normal tax on taxable income in excess of $25,000	*22%*
Surtax on taxable income in excess of $50,000	*26%*

As indicated by the above table, a corporation with taxable income of $25,000 or less would be subject to tax of 20%. A corporation with taxable income above $25,000 but less than $50,000 would be subject to tax of 20% on the first $25,000 and to a tax rate of 22% on the amount above $25,000. Finally, a corporation with taxable income of more than $50,000 would use three rates in calculating its tax: 20% on the first $25,000; 22% on the second $25,000; and 48% on all additional taxable income. The 48% rate is the total of the normal tax of 22% and the surtax of 26%. Note that above $50,000 the income tax on corporations is not progressive. No matter how large taxable income may be, the rate remains the same for amounts above $50,000.

Computation of taxable income of corporations

The taxable income of corporations is computed in much the same way as for individuals: that is, by deducting ordinary business expenses from gross income. However, the following major differences from taxation of individuals must be considered:

1 *Dividends received.* The dividends received by a corporation on its investments in stocks of other corporations are included in gross income but 85% of such dividends can be deducted from gross income. The net result is that only 15% of dividend income is taxable to the receiving corporation. Corporations are not entitled to the dividend exclusion of $100 allowed to individual taxpayers.

2 *Capital gains and losses.* Net long-term capital gains of corporations are subject to a maximum tax of 30%. A corporation is not entitled to the 50% long-term capital gain deduction as is an individual. If a corporation's taxable income (including any long-term capital gain) is below $50,000, the corporation pays only the normal tax on the long-term capital gain rather than the 30% maximum capital gain tax rate.

The dividing line between long-term and short-term capital gains and losses is one year—the same as for individuals. Corporations may deduct capital losses only to the extent of capital gains. However, if capital losses exceed capital gains, the net loss may be offset against any capital gains of the three preceding years (carry-back) or the following five years (carry-forward).

3 *Contributions.* Corporations may deduct charitable contributions only to the extent of 5% of taxable income, computed before the deduction of any contributions or the deduction applicable to dividend income. Contributions in

excess of the limit may be carried forward for five succeeding years if contributions (including those carried forward) are within the 5% limit.

4 Other variations from taxation of individuals. The concept of adjusted gross income is not applicable to a corporation because there is no deduction for personal exemptions and no zero bracket amount. *Gross income* minus the deductions allowed to corporations equals *taxable income.*

Illustrative tax computation for corporation

To illustrate some of the features of the income tax law as it applies to corporations, a *tax computation* for Stone Corporation is shown below. Remember that this illustration is not an income statement and does not show items in the sequence of an income statement.

STONE CORPORATION
Illustrative Tax Computation

	Revenue:		
difference between income per accounting records ($84,000) and taxable income ($80,000)	Sales		$400,000
	Dividends received from domestic corporations		20,000
	Total revenue		$420,000
	Expenses:		
	Cost of goods sold	$236,000	
	Other expenses (includes capital loss of $12,000)	100,000	336,000
	Income per accounting records		$ 84,000
	Add back (items not deductible for tax purposes):		
	Capital loss deducted as part of operating expenses*		12,000
	Charitable contributions in excess of 5% limit		1,000
			$ 97,000
	Special deductions:		
	Dividends received credit (85% of $20,000)		17,000
	Taxable income		$ 80,000
	Tax computation:		
	Normal tax: 20% of $25,000	$ 5,000	
	22% of ($80,000 − $25,000)	12,100	$ 17,100
	Surtax: 26% of ($80,000 − $50,000)		7,800
	Total income tax		$ 24,900†
	Deduct: Quarterly payments of estimated tax		24,000
	Balance of tax payable with tax return		$ 900

*The capital loss can be carried back three years and offset against capital gains if any.

†Alternative computation: $80,000 × 48%, or $38,400 less $13,500 = $24,900.

In computing tax for a corporation, it is often convenient to multiply the entire taxable income by 48% and then deduct $13,500. This $13,500 figure represents the "saving" of 28% on the first $25,000 of taxable income or $7,000, plus the "saving" of 26% of the second $25,000 of taxable income or $6,500. In other words, a corporation's taxable income is taxed at the combined rate of 48% except for the first $50,000 on which the tax is always $13,500 less than it would be if taxed at 48%. The actual tax on the first $50,000 of taxable income is $10,500. This is $13,500 less than the $24,000 which would result from applying a 48% rate to $50,000. For example, the tax on $1,000,000 of taxable income may be computed by either of the two methods shown below:

		Method 1	Method 2
Normal tax:			
20% of $25,000		$ 5,000	
22% of ($1,000,000 – $25,000)		214,500	
Surtax:			
26% of ($1,000,000 – $50,000)		247,000	
Combined tax on entire taxable income of $1,000,000 at 48% .			$480,000
Less: 28% of first $25,000 which is taxed at			
only 20%	$7,000		
26% of second $25,000 which is taxed at			
only 22%	6,500		13,500
Total income tax		$466,500	$466,500

The fact that tax rates on corporations are not as high as the top tax rates on individuals has caused some taxpayers to consider creating corporations as a means of avoiding taxes. In response, Congress has established two additional taxes to limit the use of closely held corporations as a device for holding property and avoiding individual income taxes. These two taxes are the ***accumulated earnings tax*** and the ***personal holding company tax.***

Accumulated earnings tax

The stockholders of a closely held corporation may be tempted to avoid personal tax on dividends by retaining earnings in the corporation rather than distributing these earnings as dividends. To prevent such actions, a penalty surtax called the ***accumulated earnings tax*** is imposed on the income of a corporation in any year it accumulates earnings as a means of avoiding tax on its shareholders. The rate of the penalty surtax is $27\frac{1}{2}$% on the first $100,000 and $38\frac{1}{2}$% on additional amounts. The tax is not imposed on a corporation that does not accumulate earnings beyond $150,000. Remember that the accumulated earnings tax can be avoided by declaring dividends or by proving that the earnings have been accumulated to meet reasonable needs of the business.

Personal holding company tax

A corporation with only a few stockholders and ***deriving its income mostly from investments*** may be classified as a personal holding company and subjected to a special tax of 70% of its undistributed income. This tax is in addition to the normal tax and surtax on taxable income of corporations. The purpose of this tax is to discourage individuals from transferring income-producing property to corporations in order to avoid tax by reason of the difference between the rates of tax on individuals and corporations.

Accounting income versus taxable income

In the determination of *accounting income,* the objective is to measure business operating results as accurately as possible in accordance with the generally accepted accounting principles summarized in Chapter 14. *Taxable income,* on the other hand, is a legal concept governed by statute and subject to sudden and frequent change by Congress. In setting the rules for determining taxable income, Congress is interested not only in meeting the revenue needs of government but in achieving certain public policy objectives. For example, the exclusion of interest on municipal bonds from taxable income is intended to make these bonds more attractive to investors and thus make it easier for the cities to borrow money. Since accounting income and taxable income are determined with different purposes in mind, it is not surprising that they often differ by material amounts. This distinction between accounting income and taxable income is important to every business, regardless of whether it is organized as a single proprietorship, a partnership, or a corporation.

Cash basis versus accrual basis of accounting

The accrual basis of measuring business income has been discussed throughout the preceding chapters of this book, because it is the method used by most business enterprises in their accounting records and financial statements. Revenue is recognized when it is realized, and expenses are recorded when they are incurred, without regard to the timing of receipt or payment. Any taxpayer who maintains a set of accounting records may elect to use the accrual basis for tax purposes. When the production, purchase, or sale of merchandise is a significant factor in a business, the accrual method of accounting for these items is mandatory for income tax purposes as well.

The *cash basis* of accounting does not measure income in the accounting sense but has much merit in the area of tax accounting. Revenue is recognized when cash is received, and expenses are recorded when they are paid. This method is widely used for tax purposes because it is simple, requires a minimum of records, and provides reasonably satisfactory results for individuals not engaged in business and for businesses in which receivables, payables, and inventories are not a major factor. From the government's viewpoint, the logical time to collect tax on income is when the taxpayer receives the income in cash. At any earlier date the taxpayer may not have the cash to pay income taxes; at any later date the cash may have been used for other purposes.

The cash basis of accounting allowed for income tax purposes and used by individuals, most professional firms, and many service-type companies varies in two important ways from a simple offsetting of cash receipts and disbursements.

1 On the revenue side, a cash basis taxpayer must report revenue when it has been *constructively received,* even though the cash is not yet in his or her possession. Constructive receipt means that the revenue is so much within the control of the taxpayer as to be equivalent to receipt. For example, if a taxpayer has a savings account, the interest on that account is considered to be constructively received for income tax purposes even though the taxpayer does not draw it out.

2 On the expenditure side, the cost of acquiring depreciable property having a service life of more than one year is not deductible in the year of purchase. The taxpayer must treat such a purchase as the acquisition of an asset and deduct depreciation in appropriate years. A similar treatment must be given to major prepayments, such as rent paid in advance or insurance premiums which cover more than one year.

The superiority of the accrual basis in measuring the operating results and financial position of a business does not mean that the accrual basis is preferable for income tax purposes. Taxpayers may benefit by electing the cash basis, when allowed, because it often permits postponing the recognition of taxable income and the payment of the related tax. Such postponement means that taxpayers using the cash basis have the *interest-free use of funds* that otherwise would be paid in taxes.

A small corporation with annual income of about $50,000 (the level at which the 26% surtax is imposed) may find the cash basis of accounting quite helpful in avoiding the surtax. The objective is to keep taxable income close to but just below the level at which the surtax is incurred. Near the close of a given year if it appears that taxable income will exceed $50,000, the company may shift income to the following year by delaying billings and collections and by paying expenses earlier than usual. The timing of expenditures for repairs may be speeded up.

On the other hand, if near the end of the year it appears that taxable income will be significantly below $50,000, reverse procedures may be used to shift a part of next year's income into the current year to come as close as possible to the surtax level.

Special tax treatment of revenue and expense

Even when the accrual method is used for tax purposes, differences between taxable and accounting income may occur. Some differences result from special tax rules which are unrelated to accounting principles.

1 Some items included in accounting income are not taxable. For example, interest on state or municipal bonds is excluded from taxable income.

2 Some business expenses are not deductible. For example, goodwill is amortized in determining accounting income, but for income tax purposes goodwill is considered a permanent asset and amortization is not a deductible expense.

3 Special deductions in excess of actual business expenses are allowed some taxpayers. For example, depletion deductions in excess of actual cost are allowed taxpayers in some mining industries. However, the *statutory depletion* (or *percentage depletion*) allowance which formerly existed for income derived from oil and gas operations has been eliminated.

In addition, the *timing* of the recognition of certain revenue and expenses under tax rules differs from that under accounting principles. Some items of income received in advance may be taxed in the year of receipt while certain accrued expenses may not be deductible for income tax purposes until they are actually paid in cash.

Alternative accounting methods offering possible tax advantages

You are already aware from your study of various methods of depreciation and various methods of inventory valuation that the choice of accounting methods can have considerable effect on the net income a company reports for a given year. The tax law permits taxpayers to follow certain accounting methods in the computation of taxable income which differ from the methods used in the accounting records and financial statements. Business executives therefore are faced with the problem of choosing accounting methods for income tax purposes that will result in minimizing their tax burdens—usually by postponing the tax to later years.

For example, a company which uses straight-line depreciation for accounting purposes may choose to use the double-declining-balance method of depreciation in its income tax return. Taxpayers generally choose for income tax purposes those accounting methods which cause expenses to be recognized as soon as possible and revenue to be recognized as late as possible. However, the tax laws require that a business electing the lifo method of inventory valuation must also use this method for financial reporting.

There are many other examples of elective methods which postpone income taxes. Companies which sell merchandise on the installment basis may elect to report income on their tax returns in proportion to the cash received on the installment contracts rather that at the time of the sale of the merchandise. Taxpayers engaged in exploration for oil may charge the cost of drilling oil wells to expense as incurred rather than capitalizing these costs for later depreciation. Ranchers may treat the cost of cattle feed as expense in the year of purchase rather than in the year the feed is consumed.

Interperiod income tax allocation

We have seen that differences between generally accepted accounting principles and income tax rules can be material. Some businesses might consider it more convenient to maintain their accounting records in conformity with the tax rules, but the result would be to distort financial statements. It is clearly preferable to maintain accounting records by the principles that produce relevant information about business operations. The data contained in the records can then be adjusted by use of work sheets to arrive at taxable income.

When a corporation follows one method in its accounting records and financial statements and a different method for its income tax return, a financial reporting problem arises. The difference in method will usually have the effect of postponing the recognition of income on the tax return (either because an expense deduction is accelerated or because revenue recognition is postponed). The question is whether the income tax expense should be accrued when the income is recognized in the accounting records, or when it is actually subject to taxation.

To illustrate the problem, let us consider a very simple case. Suppose the Pryor Company has before-tax accounting income of $200,000 in each of two years. However, the company takes as a tax deduction in Year 1 an expense of $80,000 which is reported for accounting purposes in Year 2. The company's accounting and taxable income, and the actual income taxes due (assuming an average tax rate of 40%) are shown below:

	Year 1	Year 2
Accounting income (before income taxes)	*$200,000*	*$200,000*
Taxable income	*120,000*	*280,000*
Actual income taxes due each year, at assumed rate of 40% of		
taxable income	*48,000*	*112,000*

Let us assume the Pryor Company reports in its income statement in each year the amount of income taxes due for that year as computed on the company's income tax returns. The effect on reported net income as shown in the company's financial statements would be as follows:

	Year 1	Year 2
Accounting income (before income taxes)	*$200,000*	*$200,000*
Income taxes expense (amount actually due)	*48,000*	*112,000*
Net income	*$152,000*	*$ 88,000*

Company reports actual taxes

The readers of Pryor Company's income statement might well wonder why the same $200,000 accounting income before income taxes in the two years produced such widely varying amounts of tax expense and net income.

To deal with this distortion between pretax income and after-tax income, an accounting policy known as *interperiod income tax allocation* is required for financial reporting purposes.[7] Briefly, the objective of income tax allocation is to accrue income taxes in relation to accounting income, whenever differences between accounting and taxable income are caused by differences in the *timing* of revenue or expenses. In the Pryor Company example, this means we would report in the Year 1 income statement a tax expense based on $200,000 of accounting income even though a portion of this income ($80,000) will not be subject to income tax until Year 2. The effect of this accounting procedure is demonstrated by the following journal entries to record the income tax expense in each of the two years:

Entries to record income tax allocation	*Year 1 Income Taxes Expense*	*80,000*	
	Current Income Tax Liability		*48,000*
	Deferred Income Tax Liability		*32,000*
	To record current and deferred income taxes at 40% of accounting income of $200,000.		
	Year 2 Income Taxes Expense	*80,000*	
	Deferred Income Tax Liability	*32,000*	
	Current Income Tax Liability		*112,000*
	To record income taxes of 40% of accounting income of $200,000 and to record actual income taxes due.		

Using tax allocation procedures, Pryor Company's financial statements would report net income during the two-year period as follows:

Company uses tax allocation procedure *Income before income taxes*	*$200,000*	*$200,000*
Income taxes expense (tax allocation basis)	*80,000*	*80,000*
Net income	*$120,000*	*$120,000*

In this example, the difference between taxable income and accounting income (caused by the accelerated deduction of an expense) was fully offset in a period of two years. In practice, differences between accounting and taxable income may persist over extended time periods and deferred tax liabilities may accumulate to significant amounts. For example, in a recent balance sheet of Sears, Roebuck and Co., deferred taxes of $690 million were reported as a result of the use of the installment sales method for income tax purposes while reporting net income in financial statements on the usual accrual method.

In contrast to the example for the Pryor Company in which income taxes were deferred, income taxes *may be prepaid* when taxable income exceeds accounting income because of timing differences. The portion of taxes paid on income deferred for accounting purposes would be re-

---

[7] For a more complete discussion of tax allocation procedures, see *APB Opinion No. 11,* "Accounting for Income Taxes," AICPA (New York: 1967).

ported as prepaid taxes in the balance sheet. When the income is reported as earned for accounting purposes in a later period, the *prepaid taxes are recognized as tax expense* applicable to the income currently reported but *taxed in an earlier period.*[8]

TAX PLANNING

Federal income tax laws have become so complex that detailed tax planning has become a way of life for most business firms. Almost all companies today engage professional tax specialists to review the tax aspects of major business decisions and to develop plans for legally minimizing income taxes.

Tax avoidance and tax evasion

Newspaper stories tell us each year of some taxpayers who have deliberately understated their taxable income by failing to report a portion of income received or by claiming fictitious deductions such as an excess number of personal exemptions. Such purposeful understatement of taxable income is called *tax evasion* and is, of course, illegal. On the other hand, *tax avoidance* (the arranging of business and financial affairs in a manner that will minimize tax liability) is entirely legal. Because it is important for everyone to recognize areas in which tax savings may be substantial, a few of the major opportunities for tax planning are discussed in the following sections of this chapter.

Form of business organization

Tax factors should be carefully considered at the time a business is organized. As a single proprietor or partner, a business owner will pay taxes at individual rates, ranging currently from 14 to 70%, on the business income earned in any year *whether or not it is withdrawn from the business.* Corporations, on the other hand, are taxed on earnings at rates varying from 20 to 48%. In determining taxable income, corporations deduct salaries paid to owners for services but cannot deduct dividends paid to stockholders. Both salaries and dividends are taxed to their recipients.

These factors must be weighed in deciding in any given situation whether the corporate or noncorporate form of business organization is preferable. There is no simple rule of thumb, even considering only these basic differences. To illustrate, suppose that Able, a married man, starts a

---

[8] A good example of this treatment is found in the annual report of the Ford Motor Company. A recent balance sheet showed "Income Taxes Allocable to the Following Year," $206.5 million, as a current asset. This large prepaid tax came about as a result of estimated car warranty expense being deducted from revenue in the period in which cars were sold; for income tax purposes, this expense is deductible only when it is actually incurred.

business which he expects will produce, before any compensation to himself and before income taxes, an average annual income of $80,000. Able plans to withdraw $20,000 yearly from the business. The combined corporate and individual taxes under the corporate and single proprietorship form of business organization are summarized below.

At first glance this comparison suggests that the corporate form of organization is favorable from an income tax viewpoint. It must be noted, however, that the $44,700 ($60,000 − $15,300) of earnings retained in the corporation will be taxed to Able as ordinary income when and if distributed as dividends. On the other hand, if Able later sells his business and realizes these earnings in the form of the increased value of the capital stock, any gain may be taxed at a maximum of, say, 25%. In either case Able can postpone the payment of tax as long as these earnings remain invested in the business. However, if earnings are allowed to accumulate in the corporation beyond the $150,000 limit and beyond the reasonable needs of the business, the penalty of the undistributed earnings tax might be imposed.

Form of Business Organization

			Corporate	Single Proprietorship
Which form of business organization produces a lower tax?	Business income		$80,000	$80,000
	Salary to Able		20,000	
	Taxable income		$60,000	$80,000
	Corporate tax:			
	20% of first $25,000	$5,000		
	22% of next $25,000	5,500		
	48% on excess of $10,000	4,800	15,300	
	Net income		$44,700	$80,000
	Combined corporate and individual tax:			
	Corporate tax on $60,000 income (above)		$15,300	
	Individual tax—joint return:*			
	On Able's $20,000 salary		3,484	
	On Able's $80,000 share of business income			$31,484
	Total tax on business income		$18,784	$31,484

*Able's personal exemptions and deductions have been ignored, on the assumption that his other income equals personal exemptions and deductions.

If Able decided to withdraw all net income from the business each year, the tax on corporate net income plus the personal tax on his $20,000 salary and the $44,700 that he would receive in dividends would amount to $38,395, compared to only $31,484 tax paid on the $80,000 of earnings from the single proprietorship. The amount of $38,395 consists of $15,300 corporate tax plus $23,095 tax on personal income of $64,700.

Under this assumption the income tax results under the single proprietorship form of organization are preferable. It is clear that both the marginal rate of tax to which individual business owners are subject and the extent to which profits are to be withdrawn from the business must be considered in assessing the relative advantages of one form of business organization over another.

Under certain conditions, small, closely held corporations may elect to be Subchapter S corporations, in which case the corporation pays no tax but the individual shareholders are taxed directly on the corporation's earnings.

Planning business transactions to minimize income taxes

Business transactions may often be arranged in such a way as to produce favorable tax treatment. For example, when real estate is sold under an installment contract, the taxable gain may be prorated over the period during which installment payments are received by the seller. To qualify for this treatment, payments received during the first year must not exceed 30% of the selling price. By arranging the transaction to meet these conditions, a substantial postponement of tax payments may be secured. For this reason farms, apartment buildings, and some other types of real estate are often offered for sale with a down payment of 29%.

Sometimes sellers try to arrange a transaction one way to their tax benefit and the buyers try to shape it another way to produce tax savings for them. Income tax effects thus become a part of price negotiations. For example, in buying improved real estate, the purchasers will try to allocate as much of the cost of the property to the building and as little to the land as possible, since building costs can be depreciated for tax purposes. Similarly, in buying a going business, the buyers will want as much as possible of the total purchase price to be attributed to inventories or to depreciable assets rather than to goodwill. The cost of goods sold and depreciation are deductible against ordinary income, whereas goodwill cannot be amortized for tax purposes. The point is, *any failure to consider the tax consequences of major business transactions can be costly.*

Some examples of provisions of the federal tax laws clearly designed to affect business decisions include (*1*) accelerated depreciation, (*2*) additional first-year depreciation of 20% on assets of tangible personal property costing up to $10,000, (*3*) rapid depreciation on assets "critical to the public interest" such as pollution-control facilities and coal-mine safety equipment, (*4*) tax-free exchanges of certain types of assets or securities pursuant to a corporate merger, and (*5*) *investment tax credits* when certain types of depreciable assets are acquired.

Tax planning in the choice of financial structure

In deciding upon the best means of raising capital to start or expand a business, consideration should be given to income taxes. Different forms of business financing produce different amounts of tax expense. Interest on debt, for example, is *fully deductible,* but dividends on preferred or common stock are not. This factor operates as a strong incentive to finance expansion by borrowing.

Let us suppose that a company subject to a 48% marginal tax rate needs $100,000 to invest in productive assets on which it can earn a 12% annual return. If the company obtains the needed money by issuing $100,000 in 8% preferred stock, it will earn *after taxes* only $6,240, which is not even enough to cover the $8,000 preferred dividend. (This after-tax amount is computed as $12,000 income less taxes at 48% of $12,000.)

Now let us assume on the other hand that the company borrowed $100,000 at 8% interest. The additional gross income would be $12,000 but interest expense of $8,000 would be deducted, leaving taxable income of $4,000. The tax on the $4,000 at 48% would be $1,920, leaving after-tax income of $2,080. Analysis along these lines is also needed in choosing between debt financing and financing by issuing common stock.

The choice of financial structure should also be considered from the viewpoint of investors, especially in the case of a small, closely held corporation:

ILLUSTRATIVE CASE Assume that the owners of a small incorporated business decide to invest an additional $50,000 in the business to finance expanded operations. Should the owners make a $50,000 loan to the corporation or purchase $50,000 worth of additional capital stock? The loan may be advantageous because the $50,000 cash invested will be returned by the corporation at the maturity date of the loan without imposing any individual income tax on the owners. The loan may be designated to mature in installments or at a single fixed date. Renewal of the note is easily arranged if desired.

If the $50,000 investment were made by purchase of additional shares of capital stock, the return of these funds to the owners would be more difficult. If the $50,000 came back to the owners in the form of dividends, a considerable portion would be consumed by individual income taxes. If the corporation repurchased $50,000 worth of its own capital stock, the retained earnings account would become restricted by this amount. In summary, it is easier for persons in control of a small corporation to get their money back if the investment takes the form of a loan to the corporation rather than the purchase of additional capital stock.

Income taxes as a factor in preparing cash budgets

Taxable income computed on the accrual basis is not necessarily matched by an inflow of cash. A healthy profit picture accompanied by a tight cash position is not unusual for a rapidly growing company. Income taxes are a substantial cash drain and an important factor in preparing cash budgets. In other words, a profitable growing business may find itself without the cash needed to pay its tax liability.

Tax shelters

A tax shelter is an investment which produces a loss for tax purposes in the near term but hopefully proves profitable in the long run. Near the close of each year, many newspaper advertisements offer an opportunity to invest in a program which promises to reduce the investor's present tax liability yet produce future profits. These programs have a particular appeal to persons in very high tax brackets who face the prospect of paying most of a year's net income as taxes.

A limited partnership organization is often used, so that each investor may claim his or her share of the immediate losses. Typical of the types of ventures are oil and gas drilling programs and real estate investments offering high leverage and accelerated depreciation. Unfortunately, many so-called tax shelters have proved to be merely unprofitable investments, in which the investors saved taxes but lost larger amounts of capital. A sound approach to tax shelters should probably be based on the premise that if an investment does not appear *worthwhile without the promised tax benefits, it should be avoided.*

Some tax shelters, on the other hand, are not of a high-risk nature. State and municipal bonds offer a modest rate of interest which is tax-exempt. Investment in real property with deductions for mortgage interest, property taxes, and depreciation will often show losses which offset other taxable income, yet eventually prove profitable because of rising market value, especially in periods of inflation.

KEY TERMS INTRODUCED OR EMPHASIZED IN CHAPTER 17

Accumulated earnings tax A penalty surtax designed to prevent corporations from retaining earnings beyond reasonable business needs so that shareholders could avoid individual income tax that would result from distribution of the earnings as dividends.

Adjusted gross income A subtotal in an individual's tax return computed by deducting from gross income any business-related expenses and other deductions authorized by law. A key figure to which many measurements are linked.

Capital asset Stocks, bonds, and rental property not used in a trade or business.

Capital gain or loss The difference between the cost basis of a capital asset and the amount received from its sale.

Cash basis of accounting Revenue is recorded when received in cash and expenses are recorded in the period in which payment is made. Widely used for individual tax returns and for tax returns of professional firms and service-type businesses. Gives taxpayers a degree of control over taxable income by deliberate timing of collections and payments. Not used in most financial statements because it fails to match revenue with related expenses.

Declaration of estimated tax Self-employed persons and others with income not subject to withholding must file by April 15 each year a declaration of estimated tax for the current year and must make quarterly payments of such tax.

Excess itemized deductions The excess of itemized deductions over the zero bracket amount.

Gross income All income and gains from whatever source derived unless specifically excluded by law, such as interest on state and municipal bonds.

Interperiod tax allocation Allocation of income tax expense among accounting periods because of timing differences between accounting income and taxable income. Causes income tax expense reported in financial statements to be in logical relation to accounting income.

Itemized deductions Personal expenses deductible from adjusted gross income, such as interest, taxes, contributions, medical expenses, casualty losses, and expenses incurred in production of income.

Long-term capital gains and losses Gains and losses resulting from sale of capital assets owned for more than a specified period (one year). A net long-term capital gain qualifies for a special tax rate.

Marginal tax rate The rate to which a taxpayer is subject on the top dollar of income earned.

Maximum tax on personal service income (earned income) Under present law the maximum rate on earned income is 50%, whereas income from investments or other sources may be taxed at rates up to 70%.

Personal exemption A deduction (presently $750) from adjusted gross income for the taxpayer, the taxpayer's spouse, and each dependent.

Tax credit An amount to be subtracted from the tax itself. Examples are investment credit, new jobs credit, and credit for wages paid in work incentive programs.

Tax planning A systematic process of minimizing income taxes by considering in advance the tax consequences of alternative business or investment actions. A major factor in choosing the form of business organization and capital structure, in lease-or-buy decisions, and in timing of transactions.

Tax shelters Investment programs designed to show losses in the short term to be offset against other taxable income, but offering the hope of long-run profits.

Taxable income The computed amount to which the appropriate tax rate is to be applied to arrive at the tax liability.

Zero bracket amount A specified amount of income not subject to individual income tax. Presently $2,200 for single taxpayers and $3,200 for married taxpayers filing jointly. Replaced the standard deduction.

DEMONSTRATION PROBLEM FOR YOUR REVIEW

Robert Sandison has been engaged in various businesses for many years and has always prepared his own income tax return. In Year 11 Sandison decided to ask a certified public accountant to prepare his income tax returns.

Early in Year 12, Sandison presented the following tax information for Year 11 to the CPA:

Personal revenue:

Salary from Sandi Construction Company, after withholding of $3,168 federal income taxes and social security taxes of $1,140	$ 14,692
Dividends from Sandi Construction Company (jointly owned)	16,875
Drawings from Northwest Lumber Company	6,000
Drawings from S & S Business Advisers	9,600
Interest income—City of Norwalk bonds	800
Interest income—savings account	950
Proceeds on sale of stock:	
Sale of stock acquired two years ago for $6,200	14,200
Sale of stock held for three months, cost $4,100	3,400
Sale of stock held for over six years, cost $3,500	1,800

Personal expenses:

Contribution to St. Jerome's Church	$ 610
Interest on mortgage, $3,820; on personal note, $400	4,220
Property taxes, including $400 on vacant land in Arizona and a special assessment of $500 on residence for street widening	3,980
Sales taxes, including $580 paid on purchase of new automobile for personal use	850
Income taxes paid to state	1,900
Medical expenses	1,100
Subscription to investment advisory service	385

Single proprietorship—wholesale lumber, doing business as Northwest Lumber Company:

Sales	118,000
Cost of goods sold	82,000
Operating expenses	38,800
Drawings by Sandison	6,000

Partnership—engaged in business consulting under the name of S & S Business Advisers:

Fees earned	76,300
Gain on sale of vacant lot acquired four years ago	4,400
Salaries paid to employees	32,400
Supplies expense	3,500
Contributions to charity	1,000
Rent expense	4,800
Miscellaneous business expenses	7,100
Drawings (Sandison, $9,600 and Sims, $6,400)	16,000

Corporation—engaged in construction under the name of Sandi Construction Company:

Customer billings	230,000
Materials used	70,000
Construction labor	60,000
Officers' salaries expense	25,000
Legal and professional expense	3,500
Advertising expense	2,000
Other business expenses	19,800
Loss on sale of equipment	4,200
Cash dividends paid	22,500

Sandison has a 60% share in the profits of S & S Business Advisers and John Sims has a 40% share. Sandison owns 75% of the stock of Sandi Construction Company. Because of this controlling interest, he has assumed responsibility for the preparation of the income tax returns for these organizations.

Sandison is married, has five children, and supports his seventy-nine-year-old mother. He is fifty-five years old and his wife is younger but will not give her date of birth. The oldest child, Bill, is twenty years old and attends school full time. Sandison provides all of his son's support, even though Bill earns approximately $1,400 per year from odd jobs and from investments inherited from his grandfather.

In April of Year 11, Sandison paid $3,100 balance due on his federal income tax return for Year 10. In addition to the income taxes withheld by the Sandi

Construction Company, Sandison made four quarterly payments of $2,000 each on his estimated tax for Year 11.

Instructions Using the income tax table on page 685, prepare the joint return for Mr. and Mrs. Sandison for last year, showing the amount of tax due (or refund coming). You should also prepare in summary form the information on the partnership tax return for S & S Business Advisers and the corporation income tax return for the Sandi Construction Company. Assume that a personal exemption is $750, that the corporate tax rate is 20% on the first $25,000 of taxable income, 22% on the next $25,000, and 48% on any income in excess of $50,000, and that Sandi Construction Company has not paid any part of its income tax for Year 11.

SOLUTION TO DEMONSTRATION PROBLEM

S & S BUSINESS ADVISERS (a partnership)
Computation of Ordinary Income
For Year Ended December 31, Year 11

Fees earned		$76,300
Operating expenses:		
Salaries paid to employees	$32,400	
Supplies expense	3,500	
Rent expense	4,800	
Miscellaneous business expenses	7,100	47,800
Ordinary income		$28,500

Ordinary income and other items are to be included in partners' individual tax returns as follows:

	Sandison (60%)	Sims (40%)
Ordinary income, $28,500	$17,100	$11,400
Gain on sale of vacant lot, long-term capital gain, $4,400	2,640	1,760
Contributions to charity, $1,000	600	400

SANDI CONSTRUCTION COMPANY
Income Tax Return
For Year Ended December 31, Year 11

Customer billings		$230,000
Operating expenses:		
Materials used	$70,000	
Construction labor	60,000	
Officers' salaries expense	25,000	
Legal and professional expenses	3,500	
Advertising expense	2,000	
Other business expenses	19,800	
Loss on sale of equipment	4,200	184,500
Taxable income		$ 45,500
Total income tax: 20% of $25,000	$5,000	
22% of $20,500	4,510	$ 9,510

MR. AND MRS. SANDISON
Joint Income Tax Return
For Year 11

Gross income:

Salary from Sandi Construction Company ($14,692 + $3,168 + $1,140)		$19,000	
Dividends from Sandi Construction Company ($16,875, less $200 exclusion)		16,675	
Interest on savings account		950	
Income from S & S Business Advisers, a partnership		17,100	
Net long-term capital gain:			
Stock acquired two years ago	$8,000		
Stock held over six years	(1,700)		
Gain on sale of vacant lot—from partnership return	2,640		
Total long-term capital gain	$8,940		
Less: Short-term loss on stock held for three months	700	8,240	$61,965

Deductions to arrive at adjusted gross income:

Loss incurred by Northwest Lumber Company, a single proprietorship ($118,000 − $82,000 − $38,800)	$ 2,800	
Long-term capital gain deduction (50% of $8,240)	4,120	6,920
Adjusted gross income		$55,045

Deductions from adjusted gross income:

Itemized deductions:

Contributions ($600 from partnership return and $610 to St. Jerome's Church)	$ 1,210		
Interest paid	4,220		
Property taxes ($3,980 − $500)	3,480		
Sales taxes	850		
Income taxes paid to state	1,900		
Subscription to investment advisory service	385		
Total itemized deductions	$12,045		
Less: Zero bracket amount	3,200		
Excess itemized deductions	$ 8,845		
Personal exemptions (8 × $750)	6,000	14,845	
Taxable income for Year 11		$40,200	

Computation of tax for Year 11:

Tax on $39,200 on joint return (see page 685)	$10,340	
Tax on $1,000 excess at 45%	450	$10,790

Deduct:

Withheld from Mr. Sandison's salary	$ 3,168	
Payments on declaration of estimated tax ($2,000 × 4)	8,000	11,168
Overpayment of tax for Year 11		$ 378

Notes:
(1) The loss from single proprietorship is properly deducted in arriving at adjusted gross income despite the fact that Sandison withdrew $6,000 from the business.
(2) Sandison's share of ordinary income from the partnership (S & S Business Advisers), $17,100, is fully taxable despite the fact that Sandison withdrew only $9,600 from the partnership.
(3) Sandison's salary from the Sandi Construction Company is included in gross income as $19,000, the gross salary before any deductions.
(4) The ordinary income for the partnership is determined without taking into account the contribution to charity of $1,000 or the long-term capital gain of $4,400. These items are reported by the partners on their personal income tax return on the basis of the profit-and-loss-sharing ratio agreed upon by the partners.
(5) The special assessment on residence for street widening, $500, is not deductible in arriving at taxable income.
(6) Medical expenses are less than 3% of adjusted gross income, and therefore none is deductible.
(7) Sandison's son, Bill, qualifies as a dependent even though he earned $1,400 because he is a full-time student.
(8) Interest on City of Norwalk bonds, $800, is not taxable.

REVIEW QUESTIONS

1 List several ways in which business owners may legally alter the amount of taxes they pay.

2 What is meant by the expression "tax planning"?

3 What are the four major classes of taxpayers under the federal income tax law?

4 It has been claimed that corporate income is subject to "double taxation." Explain the meaning of this expression.

5 Taxes are characterized as *progressive, proportional,* or *regressive* with respect to any given base. Describe an income tax rate structure that would fit each of these characterizations.

6 During the current year, John Davis, a bachelor, expects a taxable income of $45,000. Using the schedules on pages 684–685, determine how much federal income tax Davis would save were he to get married before the end of the year, assuming that his bride had no taxable income or itemized deductions and that the personal exemption is $750.

7 State in equation form the federal income tax formula for individuals, beginning with total income and ending with taxable income.

8 Avery and Baker are both high-income single taxpayers who have exactly the same amount of taxable income. However, Avery is subject to a marginal tax rate far lower than the marginal rate for Baker. Neither of them has any capital gains or losses. What is the most probable explanation of the large difference in marginal tax rates for these two individuals?

9 List some differences in the tax rules for corporations in contrast to those for individuals.

10 Helen Bame, M.D., files her income tax return on a cash basis. During the current year she collected $12,600 from patients for medical services rendered in prior years, and billed patients $77,000 for services rendered this year. She has accounts receivable of $16,400 relating to this year's billings at the end of the year. What amount of gross income from her practice should Bame report on her tax return?

11 Joe Gilmore files his income tax return on a cash basis. During the current year $300 of interest was credited to him on his savings account; he withdrew this interest on January 18 of the following year. Gilmore purchased a piece of business equipment having an estimated service life of five years in December of the current year. He also paid a year's rent in advance on certain business property on December 29 of the current year. Explain how these items would be treated on Gilmore's current year's income tax return.

12 From an individual taxpayer's viewpoint, it is better to have a $10,000 net long-term capital gain than $10,000 of ordinary income; however, ordinary losses are usually more advantageous than net capital losses. Explain.

13 Even when a taxpayer uses the accrual method of accounting, taxable income may differ from accounting income. Give four examples of differences between the tax treatment and accounting treatment of items that are included in the determination of income.

14 Under what circumstances is the accounting procedure known as *income tax allocation* appropriate? Explain the purpose of this procedure.

15 List some tax factors to be considered in deciding whether to organize a new business as a corporation or as a partnership.

16 Explain how the corporate income tax makes debt financing in general more attractive than financing through the issuance of preferred stock.

EXERCISES

Ex. 17-1 From the tax rate schedules on pages 684–685, compute the tax for each of the following. (Assume that the 50% limitation on earned income does not apply.)

	Taxable Income
a Single taxpayer	$ 16,000
b Single taxpayer	125,000
c Married couple filing joint return	16,000
d Married couple filing joint return	125,000

Ex. 17-2 From the following information for William and Susan Jones, a married couple filing a joint tax return, compute the taxable income.

Total income, including gifts, inheritances, interest on municipal bonds, etc.	$49,200
Exclusions (gifts, inheritances, interest on municipal bonds, etc.)	17,520
Deductions to arrive at adjusted gross income	1,680
Itemized deductions (assume zero bracket amount of $3,200)	6,690
Personal exemptions ($750 each)	5,250
Income taxes withheld from salary	4,320

Ex. 17-3 Some of the following items should be included in gross income; others on the list should be excluded. For each item listed, write the identifying letter and the word *included* or *excluded* to show whether the item belongs in gross income on the federal income tax return of an individual.

a Kickbacks received by automobile salespersons from insurance brokers to whom they referred customers

b Prize money received by participating in television quiz show

c Social security benefits

d Tips received by waiter

e Money inherited from estate of relative

f Interest received on investment in municipal bonds

g Profit on sale of sailboat purchased and renovated before being sold *h* Gift from relative

    i Dividends of $75 received from investment in General Motors stock (no other dividends received during year)

    j Interest of $90 received from investment in American Airlines bonds (no other bond interest during year)

    k Vacation trip received as prize in lottery

    l Compensation received for damages suffered in automobile accident

Ex. 17-4 Shirley Jones is single, employed as an engineer, and has an adjusted gross income of $22,000. She is in the process of determining whether to itemize deductions on her federal tax return and has prepared a preliminary list of transactions from her checkbook and other records. For each item listed, write the identifying letter and the word **deductible** or **nondeductible.** Finally, state whether it will be advantageous for Jones to itemize deductions on her tax return. Assume a zero bracket amount of $2,200.

a *Interest paid on installment contract on automobile*	$ 180
b *Gift to an unemployed relative*	300
c *Professional dues*	60
d *Contribution to Red Cross*	25
e *Cost of commuting between home and work*	800
f *Property taxes*	1,200
g *Contributions to college fund drive*	100
h *State income taxes paid*	1,300
i *Medical expenses (not covered by insurance)*	500
j *Gasoline taxes*	50
k *Subscriptions to professional journals*	40
l *Cash stolen in a burglary*	80

Ex. 17-5 Malibu Corporation reports the following income during Year 1:

Operating income (income before extraordinary items and income taxes)	$550,000
Long-term capital gain	250,000
Extraordinary item:	
Loss (fully deductible)	50,000

Assume that corporate tax rates are as follows:

On first $25,000 of taxable income	20%
On next $25,000 of taxable income	22%
On taxable income over $50,000	48%
On long-term capital gains	30%

Compute the total tax liability for Malibu Corporation for Year 1.

Ex. 17-6 Howard and Sara Wilson, a married couple, file a joint return and claim one exemption each plus two exemptions for dependents. They have gathered the following information in getting ready to prepare their tax return.

Federal income taxes withheld from salaries	$ 9,400
Payments of estimated tax	5,400
Itemized deductions (remember zero bracket amount)	3,480
Total income (including $800 interest on municipal bonds)	60,000
Business-related expenses	5,200

Compute (a) gross income, (b) adjusted gross income, (c) taxable income, and (d) amount of tax remaining to be paid. (Use the Tax Rate Schedule for married individuals filing joint returns, page 685, and assume a zero bracket amount of $3,200.)

Ex. 17-7 Mission Bay Corporation deducted on its tax return for Year 5 an expense of $100,000 which was not recognized as an expense for accounting purposes until Year 6. The corporation's accounting income before income taxes in each of the two years was $425,000. The company uses tax allocation procedures.

a Prepare the journal entries required at the end of Year 5 and Year 6 to record income tax expense. Use corporate tax rates of 20% for the first $25,000 of taxable income, 22% for the next $25,000, and 48% for taxable income over $50,000.

b Prepare a two-column schedule showing the net income to appear on the financial statements for Years 5 and 6, assuming tax allocation procedures are used. Also prepare a similar schedule on the assumption that tax allocation procedures are not used.

PROBLEMS

17-1 a You are to consider the income tax status of each of the items listed below. List the numbers 1 to 15 on your answer sheet. For each item state whether it is *included in gross income* or *excluded from gross income* for federal income tax on individuals.

(1) Cash dividends received on stock of General Motors Corporation.
(2) Value of a color TV set won as a prize in a quiz contest.
(3) Gain on the sale of an original painting.
(4) Inheritance received on death of a rich uncle.
(5) Interest received on Kansas City municipal bonds.
(6) Proceeds of life insurance policy received on death of husband.
(7) Tips received by a waitress.
(8) Value of U.S. Treasury bonds received as a gift from aunt.
(9) Rent received on personal residence while on extended vacation trip.
(10) Share of income from partnership in excess of drawings.
(11) Amount received as damages for injury in automobile accident.
(12) Salary received from a corporation by a stockholder who owns directly or indirectly all the shares of the company's outstanding stock.
(13) Gain on sale of Signal Company's capital stock.
(14) Taxpayer owed $1,000 on a note payable. During the current year the taxpayer painted a building owned by the creditor, and in return the creditor canceled the note.
(15) Las Vegas vacation given by employer as reward for outstanding service.

b Consider the deductibility status of each of the items listed below for the purpose of preparing an individual's income tax return. List the numbers 1 to 11 on your answer sheet. For each item state whether the item is *deducted to arrive at adjusted gross income; deducted from adjusted gross income;* or *not deductible.*

(1) Dave Carter uses his vacation to paint a house (not his residence) which he owns and rents to others. A professional painter had bid $1,200 to do the job.
(2) Cost of commuting between home and place of employment.
(3) State sales tax paid on purchase of sailboat.
(4) Uninsured damage to roof of house caused by tornado.
(5) Interest paid on gambling debts.
(6) Capital loss on sale of investment in securities sold three months after purchase.
(7) Gambling losses. No gambling gains during the year.
(8) Expenses incurred in moving across country to accept position with different employer. Not reimbursed.

(9) Travel expense incurred by sales personnel in calling on various customers. Not reimbursed.

(10) Fee paid to CPA for services in contesting assessment of additional income taxes by IRS.

(11) Net operating loss carry-over by single proprietor.

17-2 Ryan Corporation is completing its first year of operation. The company has been successful and a tentative estimate by the controller indicated an income before taxes of $250,000 for the year. Among the items entering into the calculation of the taxable income were the following:

(1) Inventories were reported on a first-in, first-out basis and amounted to $132,500 at year-end.

(2) Accounts receivable of $3,250 were written off and recorded as uncollectible accounts expense.

(3) Depreciation of $15,000 was recorded using the straight-line method.

Officers of the corporation are concerned over the large amount of income taxes to be paid and decide to change accounting methods for both financial reporting and tax purposes as follows:

(1) Inventories on a last-in, first-out basis would amount to $100,000.

(2) An acceptable allowance for uncollectible accounts, after the write-off of $3,250, would be $10,000.

(3) Use of accelerated methods of depreciation would increase depreciation expense from $15,000 to $28,750.

Instructions

a Determine the taxable income of Ryan Corporation on the revised basis.

b If the tax rates for corporations are 20% on the first $25,000 of taxable income, 22% on the next $25,000, and 48% on any taxable income in excess of $50,000, compute the reduction in the current year's income tax liability for Ryan Corporation resulting from the accounting changes.

17-3 The following two cases are independent of each other. See the instructions following the second case.

Case A The following information relates to the income tax situation of Rick Jones for the current year.

Total income	$96,000
Personal exemptions	6,000
Deductions to arrive at adjusted gross income	7,680
Itemized deductions	12,040
Exclusions from gross income	1,920

Case B Jill Friday, a psychiatrist, uses the accrual basis of accounting in maintaining accounting records for her business and in preparing financial statements, but uses cash basis accounting in determining her income subject to federal income tax. For the current year, her business net income (computed on an accrual basis) was $90,480. A comparison of the current balance sheet for the business with a balance sheet prepared a year earlier showed an increase of $14,400 in accounts receivable from clients during the current year. Current liabilities for rent, salaries owed to employees, and other operating expenses were $8,160 less at year-end than they were one year ago. The business income of $90,480 included $1,440 of interest received on municipal bonds.

Apart from the business, Friday has a personal savings account to which $864 was credited during the year, none of which was withdrawn. In addition to business expenses taken into account in computing net income of her business, Friday has $1,632 in deductions to arrive at adjusted gross income. Her personal exemptions amount to $4,500, and her itemized deductions are $5,000.

Instructions For each of the situations described above, determine the amount of the taxpayer's adjusted gross income and the taxable income for the year. Assume a zero bracket amount of $2,200 in each case.

17-4 In preliminary calculations the chief accountant of Dale Corporation computed income before income taxes to be $350,000 for the first year of operations. Some of the steps included in arriving at this figure are listed below.

(1) Depreciation of $21,000 was recognized under the straight-line method.

(2) The direct charge-off method of measuring uncollectible accounts expense was followed. Accounts receivable of $4,550 were identified as uncollectible and were written off.

(3) The cost of ending inventories was determined on a first-in, first-out basis and amounted to $185,500.

The accountant pointed out to the president of the company that alternative accounting methods could be selected which would result in a smaller amount of taxable income. After some discussion it was agreed to make the following changes in accounting methods for both accounting and tax purposes:

(1) Accelerated depreciation was adopted and the revised figure for depreciation expense was $40,250.

(2) The allowance method of estimating uncollectible accounts expense was adopted. An aging of accounts receivable led to the conclusion that an allowance for uncollectible accounts of $14,000 was required with respect to customers' accounts other than the $4,550 of receivables which had already been written off as worthless.

(3) The last-in, first-out method of measuring inventory cost was adopted. Ending inventories amounted to $140,000 under this method.

Instructions

a Compute the taxable income of Dale Corporation after giving effect to the above changes.

b Assume the tax rates for corporations are 20% on the first $25,000 of taxable income, 22% on the next $25,000, and 48% on any taxable income in excess of $50,000. Determine the tax reduction resulting from the accounting changes.

17-5 Bill and Hannah Bailey own a successful small company, Bailey Corporation. The outstanding capital stock consists of 1,000 shares of $100 par value, of which 400 shares are owned by Bill and 600 by Hannah. In order to finance a new branch operation, the corporation needs an additional $100,000 in cash. Bill and Hannah have this amount on deposit with a savings and loan association and intend to put these personal funds into the corporation in order to establish the new branch. They will either arrange for the corporation to issue to them at par an additional 1,000 shares of stock, or they will make a loan to the corporation at an interest rate of 9%.

Income before taxes of the corporation has been consistently averaging $150,000 a year, and annual dividends of $64,000 have been paid regularly. It is expected that the new branch will cause *income before taxes* to increase by $30,000. If new common stock is issued to finance the expansion, the total annual dividend of $64,000 will be continued unchanged. If a loan of $100,000 is arranged, the dividend will be reduced by $9,000, the amount of annual interest on the loan.

Instructions

a From the standpoint of the individual income tax return which Bill and Hannah file jointly, would there be any saving as between the stock issuance and the loan? Explain.

b From the standpoint of getting their money out of the corporation (assuming that the new branch is profitable), should Bill and Hannah choose capital stock or a loan for the infusion of new funds to the corporation?

c Prepare a two-column schedule, with one column headed If New Stock Is Used and the other headed If Loan Is Used. For each of these proposed methods of financing, show (*1*) the present corporate income *before taxes;* (*2*) the corporate income *before taxes* after the expansion; (*3*) the corporate income taxes after the expansion; and (*4*) the corporate net income after the expansion.

17-6 Bill and Shirley Grey own a hardware business and an apartment building. They file a joint federal income tax return. The Greys furnish over one-half the support of their son who attends college and who earned $2,560 in part-time jobs and summer employment. They also support Mr. Grey's father, who is seventy-two years old and has no taxable income of his own.

The depreciation basis of the apartment building is $160,000; depreciation is recorded at the rate of 4% per year on a straight-line basis. During the current year, the Greys had the following cash receipts and expenditures applicable to the hardware business, the apartment building, other investments, and personal activities.

Cash receipts:

Cash withdrawn from hardware business (sales, $384,800; cost of goods sold, $284,800; operating expenses, $52,000)	*$36,000*
Gross rentals from apartment building	*28,800*
Cash dividends on stock owned jointly	*2,960*
Interest on River City bonds	*976*
Received from sale of stock purchased two years ago for $9,792	*13,472*
Received from sale of stock purchased four months previously for $6,656	*4,832*
Received from sale of motorboat purchased three years ago for $4,792 and used entirely for pleasure	*2,712*

Cash expenditures:

Expenditures relating to apartment building:

Interest on mortgage	*7,200*
Property taxes	*4,720*
Insurance (one year)	*560*
Utilities	*2,368*
Repairs and maintenance	*3,872*
Gardening	*640*

Other cash expenditures:

Mortgage interest on residence	*1,827*
Property taxes on residence	*4,773*
Insurance on residence	*224*
State income tax paid	*1,728*
State sales and gasoline taxes	*656*
Charitable contributions	*2,264*
Medical expenses	*1,376*
Payments on declaration of estimated tax for current year	*8,672*

Instructions

a Determine the amount of taxable income Bill and Shirley Grey would report on their federal income tax return for the current year. In your computation of taxable income, first list the revenue and expenses of the hardware business and show the net income from that business. Second, show the revenue and expenses of the apartment building and the amount of net income from this source. Third, show the data for dividends and capital gains. After combining the above amounts to determine adjusted gross income, list the itemized deductions and personal exemptions to arrive at taxable income. Assume that the zero bracket amount is $3,200 and that the personal exemption is $750 each.

b Compute the income tax liability for Bill and Shirley Grey using the tax rate schedule on page 685. Indicate the amount of tax due (or refund to be received).

17-7 The following information appears in the accounting records of the Valley Corporation for the current year:

Net sales	$978,000
Cost of goods sold	697,200
Dividend revenue (on stock of domestic subsidiary corporation)	20,000
Dividends declared on common stock	50,000
Selling expenses	98,900
Administrative expenses	86,250
Gain on sale of capital asset acquired five years ago	8,800

During the current year the Valley Corporation incurred $30,000 of sales promotion expenses which may be deducted in computing taxable income, but which the company has chosen to defer on its accounting records and charge against revenue during the two subsequent years when the benefits of the sales promotion are reflected in revenue. The controller will follow tax allocation procedures in reporting the income taxes expense on the income statement during the current year.

Instructions

a Prepare an income statement for Valley Corporation for the current year. In a separate supporting schedule show your computation of the provision for federal income taxes for the year, using the corporation rate schedule on page 700. (Remember the capital gain is taxed at 30%.)

b Prepare the journal entry which should be made to record the company's current income taxes expense, income tax liability, and deferred income tax liability as of the end of the year.

17-8 The accounting records of Springfield Corporation included the following information for the current year:

Net sales	$7,500,000
Cost of goods sold	5,400,000
Dividends received from a domestic corporation	300,000
Dividends declared by board of directors on common stock of Springfield Corporation	600,000
Selling expenses	720,000
Administrative expenses	780,000
Earthquake loss (fully deductible for income tax purposes)	150,000

In December of the current year, Springfield Corporation spent $225,000 to move its corporate headquarters from one city to another. This expenditure was deducted in computing taxable income, but the company chose to defer it in the accounting records and charge it against revenue of the two subsequent years. The deferral was considered to achieve a better matching of costs with the increased revenue arising from the move. The company will follow income tax allocation procedures in reporting income taxes on the income statement during the current year.

Instructions

a Prepare an income statement for Springfield Corporation for the current year. At the bottom of the income statement show earnings per share data, including the effect of the extraordinary item (earthquake loss). The company has 300,000 shares of capital stock outstanding. In a separate schedule show your computation of federal income taxes for the year, using the following rate schedule:

First $25,000 of taxable income *20%*

Next $25,000 of taxable income *22%*

On excess over $50,000 . . . . *48%*

b Prepare the journal entry which should be made to record the income taxes expense and income tax liability (both current and deferred) at the end of the current year. Any tax effect resulting from the full deductibility of the earthquake loss should be offset against the Earthquake Loss account.

BUSINESS DECISION PROBLEM 17

Gary Allen is in the process of organizing a business which is expected to produce, before any compensation to Allen and before income taxes, an income of $72,000 per year. In deciding whether to operate as a single proprietorship or as a corporation, Allen is willing to make the choice on the basis of the relative income tax advantage under either form of organization.

Allen is married, files a joint return with his wife, has no other dependents, and has itemized deductions that average around $11,000 per year.

If the business is operated as a single proprietorship, the Allens expect to withdraw the entire income of $72,000 each year.

If the business is operated as a corporation, the Allens will own all the shares; they will pay themselves salaries totaling $42,000 and will withdraw as dividends the entire amount of the corporation's net income after income taxes.

It may be assumed that the accounting income and the taxable income for the corporation would be the same and that the personal exemption is $750. Mr. and Mrs. Allen have only minor amounts of nonbusiness income, which may be ignored. The maximum tax rate on earned income of individuals is also to be ignored in working this problem.

Instructions

a Determine the relative income tax advantage to the Allens of operating either as a single proprietorship or as a corporation, and make a recommendation as to the form of organization they should adopt. Use the individual (joint return) and corporate tax rate schedules given on pages 685 and 700.

b Suppose that the Allens planned to withdraw only $42,000 per year from the business, as drawings from a single proprietorship or as salaries from a corporation. Would this affect your recommendation? Explain.

Appendix

Financial Statements of a Publicly Owned Company

The financial statements of Johnson & Johnson, a company listed on the New York Stock Exchange, are presented on the following pages. These financial statements have been audited by Coopers & Lybrand, an international firm of certified public accountants. The audit report is attached. This particular company was selected because its financial statements provide realistic illustrations of many of the financial reporting issues discussed in this book.

Notice that several pages of explanatory notes are included with the basic financial statements. These explanatory notes supplement the condensed information in the financial statements and are designed to carry out the disclosure principle discussed in Chapter 14 of this book. As indicated in Chapter 14, the disclosure principle means that all material and relevant facts should be communicated to the users of financial statements.

Johnson & Johnson and Subsidiaries

Consolidated Balance Sheet at January 1, 1978 and January 2, 1977
(Dollars in Thousands Except Per Share Figures)

ASSETS

	1977	1976
Current Assets		
Cash and certificates of deposit	$ 66,335	47,509
Marketable securities, at cost, which approximates market value	301,529	230,591
Accounts receivable, less allowances $13,740 (1976 $11,182)	385,585	315,179
Inventories (Notes 1 and 3)	502,540	456,170
Expenses applicable to future operations	23,789	17,883
Total current assets	1,279,778	1,067,332
Marketable Securities, Non-Current, at cost, which approximates market value	45,964	59,612
Property, Plant and Equipment, at cost, less accumulated depreciation and amortization $409,353 (1976 $357,923) (Notes 1 and 4)	652,371	568,456
Other Assets	41,679	35,319
Total assets	$2,019,792	1,730,719

LIABILITIES AND STOCKHOLDERS' EQUITY

	1977	1976
Current Liabilities		
Loans and notes payable (Note 6)	$ 34,410	26,290
Accounts payable	150,597	125,023
Taxes on income	71,782	56,304
Other accrued liabilities	126,709	94,223
Total current liabilities	383,498	301,840
Long-Term Debt (Note 6)	37,109	26,708
Certificates of Extra Compensation (Note 9)	29,560	29,001
Deferred Investment Tax Credit	15,843	13,793
Other Liabilities and Deferrals	68,043	51,292
Minority Interests in International Subsidiaries	6,664	6,146
Stockholders' Equity		
Preferred Stock—without par value (authorized and unissued 2,000,000 shares)	—	—
Common Stock—par value $2.50 per share		
(authorized 70,000,000 shares; issued 58,584,517 and 58,353,499 shares) (Note 7)	146,461	145,884
Additional capital	85,469	74,738
Retained earnings	1,248,096	1,082,548
	1,480,026	1,303,170
Less common stock held in treasury, at cost (78,733 and 101,883 shares)	951	1,231
Total stockholders' equity	1,479,075	1,301,939
Total liabilities and stockholders' equity	$2,019,792	1,730,719

See Notes to Consolidated Financial Statements

Johnson & Johnson and Subsidiaries

Consolidated Statement of Earnings and Retained Earnings

For the 52 Weeks Ended January 1, 1978 and the 53 Weeks Ended January 2, 1977
(Dollars in Thousands Except Per Share Figures)

	1977	1976*
Revenues		
Sales to customers	$2,914,081	2,522,510
Other revenues		
Interest income	18,976	19,274
Royalties and miscellaneous	16,776	16,737
	35,752	36,011
Total revenues	2,949,833	2,558,521
Costs and Expenses		
Cost of products sold (Note 12)	1,499,750	1,335,409
Selling, distribution and administrative expenses	1,002,344	847,923
Currency losses (gains) (Note 12)	(604)	3,664
Other expenses	16,148	9,981
Total costs and expenses	2,517,638	2,196,977
Earnings before provision for taxes on income	432,195	361,544
Provision for taxes on income (Note 5)	184,877	156,168
Net Earnings	247,318	205,376
Retained earnings at beginning of period	1,082,548	938,181
Cash dividends paid (per share: 1977, $1.40; 1976, $1.05)	(81,770)	(61,009)
Retained earnings at end of period	$1,248,096	1,082,548
Net Earnings Per Share (Note 1)	$4.23	3.53

Consolidated Statement of Common Stock, Additional Capital and Treasury Stock

For the 52 Weeks Ended January 1, 1978 and the 53 Weeks Ended January 2, 1977
(Dollars in Thousands)

	Common Stock Issued		Additional Capital	Treasury Stock	
	No. Shares	Amount	Amount	No. Shares	Amount
Balance, December 28, 1975	58,136,616	$145,342	$68,545	101,883	$1,231
Stock issued to employees under options exercised, stock compensation agreements, and awards	82,435	206	6,106	—	—
Pooling of interests	134,448	336	87	—	—
Balance, January 2, 1977	58,353,499	145,884	74,738	101,883	1,231
Stock issued to employees under stock compensation agreements, and awards	84,146	210	6,012	—	—
Pooling of interests	146,872	367	4,354	(16,000)	(193)
Other changes	—	—	365	(7,150)	(87)
Balance, January 1, 1978	58,584,517	$146,461	$85,469	78,733	$ 951

*Reclassified to conform to 1977 presentation. See Note 12.
See Notes to Consolidated Financial Statements

Johnson & Johnson and Subsidiaries

Consolidated Statement of Changes in Financial Position

For the 52 Weeks Ended January 1, 1978 and the 53 Weeks Ended January 2, 1977
(Dollars in Thousands)

	1977	1976
Resources Provided		
Net Earnings	$247,318	205,376
Expenses not requiring the outlay of working capital:		
Depreciation and amortization	86,496	77,542
Other	22,342	29,758
Working capital provided from operations	356,156	312,676
Decrease (increase) in marketable securities, non-current	13,648	(25,465)
Increase (decrease) in long-term debt	10,401	(12,694)
Proceeds from the sales of property, plant and equipment	9,145	1,357
	389,350	275,874
Resources Used		
Additions to property, plant and equipment	171,718	119,207
Cash dividends paid	81,770	61,009
Other items	5,074	8,449
	258,562	188,665
Increase in Working Capital	$130,788	87,209
Increases (Decreases) in Components of Working Capital:		
Current Assets		
Cash and marketable securities	$ 89,764	39,879
Accounts receivable	70,406	26,714
Inventories	46,370	59,230
Expenses applicable to future operations	5,906	(3,398)
	212,446	122,425
Current Liabilities		
Loans and notes payable	8,120	(1,285)
Accounts payable	25,574	25,599
Taxes on income	15,478	26,377
Other accrued liabilities	32,486	(15,475)
	81,658	35,216
Increase in Working Capital	$130,788	87,209

See Notes to Consolidated Financial Statements

Johnson & Johnson and Subsidiaries

Notes to Consolidated Financial Statements

Note 1 **Summary of Significant Accounting Policies**

Principles of Consolidation The consolidated statements include the accounts of Johnson & Johnson and subsidiaries. All material intercompany accounts are eliminated.

Inventories Inventories are valued at the lower of cost or market. While cost is determined principally by the first-in, first-out (FIFO) method, the majority of domestic inventories are valued using the last-in, first-out (LIFO) method.

Depreciation and Amortization Charges to earnings for depreciation and amortization of property, plant and equipment are generally determined using an accelerated method over the estimated useful lives of domestic assets and the straight-line method over the estimated useful lives of international assets. Usually the same methods are used for both financial reporting and tax return purposes.

Research Research costs are charged directly against earnings in the year in which incurred and amounted to $131,811,000 and $112,537,000 for years 1977 and 1976 respectively.

Income Taxes Domestic investment tax credits and certain international tax incentives are deferred. The deferred amount is amortized as a reduction of the provision for taxes on income over the estimated lives of the related assets.

The Company intends to continue to reinvest its undistributed international earnings to expand its international operations. Therefore no tax has been provided to cover the repatriation of such undistributed earnings. At January 1, 1978, the cumulative amount of undistributed international earnings for which the Company has not provided United States income taxes was approximately $231,000,000.

Earnings per Share Earnings per share are calculated using the average number of shares outstanding during each year. Shares issuable under stock option and compensation plans would not materially reduce earnings per share.

Annual Closing Date The Company has followed the concept of a fiscal year which ends on the Sunday nearest to the end of the calendar month of December. For the year 1977, the Sunday closest to the end of December was January 1, 1978, and Johnson & Johnson's 1977 fiscal year ended on that date. Normally, each fiscal year consists of 52 weeks, but every five or six years, as was the case in 1976, the fiscal year consists of 53 weeks.

Note 2 International Subsidiaries

The following amounts are included in the consolidated financial statements for international subsidiaries located outside of the United States:

	1977	1976
Current assets	$ 533,843,000	467,559,000
Current liabilities	228,580,000	187,513,000
Net property, plant and equipment	292,072,000	229,504,000
Parent company equity in net assets	492,135,000	429,123,000
Excess of parent company equity over investment	413,221,000	351,105,000
Sales to customers	1,200,498,000	1,029,338,000
Net earnings (after elimination of minority interests)	117,966,000	97,884,000

Note 3 Inventories

	1977	1976
Raw materials and supplies	$ 157,973,000	142,817,000
Goods in process	94,736,000	88,078,000
Finished goods	249,831,000	225,275,000
	$ 502,540,000	456,170,000

The following inventory amounts have been valued using the methods noted:

	1977	1976
LIFO method	$ 169,008,000	137,299,000
FIFO method	333,532,000	318,871,000
Total	$ 502,540,000	456,170,000

If all inventories were valued on the FIFO basis, total inventories would have been $568,909,000 and $506,945,000 at January 1, 1978 and January 2, 1977, respectively.

Note 4 Property, Plant and Equipment

	1977	1976
Land and land improvements	$ 67,935,000	62,718,000
Building and building equipment	405,159,000	365,240,000
Machinery and equipment	529,655,000	449,000,000
Construction in process	58,975,000	49,421,000
	1,061,724,000	926,379,000
Less accumulated depreciation and amortization	409,353,000	357,923,000
	$ 652,371,000	568,456,000

Note 5   Income Taxes

Income tax expense consists of:
(Dollars in Thousands)

Year 1977	U.S.	International	Total Provision For Taxes on Income
Federal and international			
Currently payable	$76,095	96,055	172,150
Net tax effect—			
timing differences	(7,560)	7,436	(124)
Net deferred			
investment tax credit	2,050	—	2,050
Domestic state and local	10,801	—	10,801
	$81,386	103,491	184,877
Effective tax rate	38.6%	46.7%	42.8%

Year 1976			
Federal and international			
Currently payable	$63,728	78,902	142,630
Net tax effect—			
timing differences	(2,356)	4,079	1,723
Net deferred			
investment tax credit	2,139	—	2,139
Domestic state and local	9,676	—	9,676
	$73,187	82,981	156,168
Effective tax rate	40.5%	45.9%	43.2%

A comparison of the federal statutory rate of 48% to the Company's effective tax rate is as follows:

	% of Pre-Tax Income	
	1977	1976
Statutory tax rate	48.0%	48.0%
Tax exempt Puerto Rico operations	(4.9)	(3.5)
Difference in effective tax rate		
of international subsidiaries	(.7)	(1.0)
Domestic state and local income taxes	1.3	1.4
Tax exempt income on marketable securities	(.7)	(.7)
Amortization of deferred investment tax credit	(.6)	(.6)
All other	.4	(.4)
Effective tax rate	42.8%	43.2%

The Company has domestic subsidiaries operating in Puerto Rico under tax exemption grants expiring at various dates between 1985 and 1992. The estimated tax savings of these subsidiaries compared to the federal statutory rate of 48% was $21,089,000 in 1977 compared to $12,481,000 in 1976.

Note 6 Borrowings

Loans and notes payable generally result from bank borrowings of international subsidiaries. The interest rates on such loans and notes vary from 5% to 19% according to local conditions. The maximum aggregate and average short-term debt outstanding during the year were $27,470,000 and $23,088,000 respectively. Aggregate maturities of long-term debt obligations for each of the next five years are $6,940,000, $8,603,000, $6,228,000, $4,189,000 and $3,142,000.

Note 7 Stock Option and Stock Compensation Plans

The Company has stock option plans which provide for the granting of options to certain officers and employees to purchase shares of its common stock within prescribed periods at prices equal to the fair market value on the date of grant.

Activity during 1977 and 1976 under the Company's stock option plans is summarized below in shares:

	1977	**1976**
Held at beginning of year by 1,620 (1976—1,504) employees	1,805,480	1,485,367
Granted to 637 (1976—641) employees	529,500	472,850
	2,334,980	1,958,217
Exercised	—	(11,837)
Cancelled or expired	(205,570)	(140,900)
Held at end of year by 1,791 (1976—1,620) employees	2,129,410	1,805,480

There were no options exercised during 1977. The price range of options exercised during 1976 was $57.19 to $89.38. The price range of options held at the end of the year was $63.00 to $125.88 (1976—$72.69 to $127.63). The number of shares exercisable at year-end was 494,576 (1976—373,608).

At year-end, the Company was obligated to deliver, over a period of not more than two years, 87,850 (1976—72,018) shares of common stock in performance of outstanding stock compensation agreements with 3,482 (1976—3,075) employees.

There were 4,533,319 shares of common stock reserved for issuance under all stock option and compensation plans at January 1, 1978.

Note 8 Retirement and Pension Plans

The Company has various retirement and pension plans which cover substantially all employees of its domestic operations. Certain international subsidiaries also have retirement plans. Pension expense is primarily determined by the aggregate level funding method which allocates costs related to both prior and future service on a level basis over the remaining future service lives of plan members. In general, the amounts are paid into trusts and approximate the annual pension expense. Total pension expense related to these plans amounted to $33,350,000 in 1977 and $28,888,000 in 1976.

As of the last valuations, the aggregate value of the assets of the various domestic plans exceeds the actuarially computed amount of the vested benefits.

Note 9   Certificates of Extra Compensation

The Company has a deferred compensation program for senior management and other key personnel. The value of units awarded under the program is related to the asset value and historical earning power of the Company's common stock. Amounts earned under the program are payable only after employment with the Company has ended.

Note 10   Rental Expense and Lease Commitments

Rentals of space, vehicles, and office and data processing equipment under operating leases amounted to approximately $42,588,000 in 1977 and $36,121,000 in 1976. The approximate minimum rental payments required under operating leases that have initial or remaining noncancellable lease terms in excess of one year at January 1, 1978 are as follows:

1978	—	$14,696,000
1979	—	12,452,000
1980	—	8,814,000
1981	—	4,809,000
1982	—	3,174,000
After 1982	—	29,442,000

Total minimum payments $73,387,000

Commitments under capital leases are not significant.

Note 11   Pending Legal Proceedings

The Company is involved in numerous product liability cases in the United States, a large majority of which concern contraceptive products. The Company cannot predict what liability may be imposed on it in connection with such suits. It believes the liability, if any, resulting from such suits will be substantially covered by insurance and that any uninsured liability resulting from such cases will not have a materially adverse effect on its operations or financial position.

In March, 1976, the Federal Trade Commission served a comprehensive subpoena on the Company in connection with an investigation by the Commission into the Company's surgical dressings, sutures and first-aid products businesses. It is not possible at this time to predict the eventual outcome of this investigation. However, the Company is confident of the propriety of the conduct of its business.

Ethicon, Inc., a subsidiary of Johnson & Johnson, is involved in a series of related patent suits brought in the United States, Canada, the United Kingdom, Germany and France, charging infringement by Ethicon of patents covering a synthetic absorbable suture. These proceedings are still in progress and the Company cannot, as yet, assess their probable outcome. However, the Company believes that the suits will not have a materially adverse effect on its operations or financial position.

In addition, the Company is involved in a number of patent, trademark, private antitrust and other lawsuits incidental to its business. The Company believes that such proceedings in the aggregate will not have a materially adverse effect on its operations or financial position.

Note 12   Statement of Earnings Reclassification

Prior to 1977, the Company included the effect of certain currency fluctuations relating to international inventories as part of the net currency losses on translation of assets and liabilities. In 1977, such costs are included in Cost of Products Sold rather than Currency Losses (Gains). This change in classification is in accordance with Interpretation No. 17 of SFAS No. 8 and has no effect on net earnings. 1976 results have been reclassified to conform to this treatment.

Note 13   Segments of Business

See pages 38 and 39 for segments of business information.

Note 14   Selected Quarterly Financial Data (Unaudited)

Selected unaudited quarterly financial data for the years 1977 and 1976 were:
(Dollars in Thousands Except Per Share Figures)

Year 1977	1st Quarter	2nd Quarter	3rd Quarter	4th Quarter	Total Year
Sales to customers..	$717,488	739,454	744,844	712,295	2,914,081
Cost of products sold	372,732	378,836	385,422	362,760	1,499,750
Earnings before provision for taxes on income.......	112,613	115,552	109,405	94,625	432,195
Net earnings	$ 61,689	66,618	62,121	56,890	247,318
Net earnings per share	$1.06	1.14	1.06	.97	4.23

Year 1976	1st Quarter	2nd Quarter	3rd Quarter	4th Quarter	Total Year
Sales to customers..	$602,326	644,143	636,916	639,125	2,522,510
Cost of products sold	319,913	338,506	336,219	340,771	1,335,409
Earnings before provision for taxes on income.......	89,692	101,034	93,992	76,826	361,544
Net earnings.......	$ 50,091	57,376	53,429	44,480	205,376
Net earnings per share........	$.86	.99	.92	.76	3.53

Note 15   Replacement Cost Information (Unaudited)

Current replacement cost information for certain assets and expenses will be disclosed in the Company's Annual Report Form 10-K filed with the Securities and Exchange Commission.

Due to the cumulative effect of inflation over the period of years in which plant and equipment are in use, the replacement cost generally exceeds historical cost. Inventories valued under the LIFO method are reflected at amounts less than current price levels. Such replacement costs, however, are not necessarily indicative of either the amounts for which the assets could be sold or management's intentions for replacement of such assets; nor are they necessarily representative of costs that might be incurred in a future period.

Report of Certified Public Accountants

To the Stockholders and Board of Directors of Johnson & Johnson

We have examined the consolidated balance sheet of Johnson & Johnson and subsidiaries as of January 1, 1978 and January 2, 1977, and the related consolidated statements of earnings and retained earnings, common stock, additional capital and treasury stock, and changes in financial position for the years then ended. Our examinations were made in accordance with generally accepted auditing standards and, accordingly, included such tests of the accounting records and such other auditing procedures as we considered necessary in the circumstances.

In our opinion, the financial statements referred to above present fairly the financial position of Johnson & Johnson and subsidiaries at January 1, 1978 and January 2, 1977 and the results of their operations and the changes in their financial position for the years then ended, in conformity with generally accepted accounting principles applied on a consistent basis.

New York, New York
February 22, 1978

Coopers & Lybrand

Common Stock:	Listed New York and Toronto Stock Exchanges Stock Symbol JNJ
Transfer Agents:	Morgan Guaranty Trust Company of New York 30 West Broadway, New York, New York 10015
	Canada Permanent Trust Company Canada Permanent Tower 20 Eglinton Avenue West Yonge Eglinton Center, Toronto, Ontario, Canada
Registrars:	Morgan Guaranty Trust Company of New York 30 West Broadway, New York, New York 10015
	Bank of Montreal, Toronto Branch 50 King Street West, Toronto, Ontario, Canada

Index

Index